FROMMER'S
DOLLARWISE GUIDE TO
FLORIDA

by Marylyn Springer

1986-87 Edition

Published by Frommer/Pasmantier Publishers
A Division of Simon & Schuster, Inc.
1230 Avenue of the Americas
New York, NY 10020

ISBN 0-671-55596-0

Manufactured in the United States of America

CONTENTS

MAPS

To MCS, in gratitude for the most enduring of many gifts to me, a fascination with language, and in salute to her unflagging enthusiasm for her chosen place in the sun.

DOLLARWISE GUIDE TO FLORIDA

A ROYAL BRITISH LANDLORD, so the story goes, owns land under the U.S. Embassy in London that no amount of American entreaty can convince him to sell. Ambassador after ambassador has been dispatched to offer million-dollar deals, but to no avail. Frustrated by that famed British resistance, one U.S. ambassador finally felt compelled to ask the titled gentleman just what on earth he *would* take for the land. He frowned. He pondered. At last he replied—he would consider Florida.

He'll have to get in line.

1. The Reason Why

In the drizzling days of spring and the chilly, cheerless nights of February, 42 million people "consider" Florida, and every last one of them sets off by plane, train, bus, or car to get a two-week piece of this sand-trimmed rock on the southernmost tip of the nation.

They arrive tense and racing, jumpy and crisis-weary. Slowly, in long, lazy days on silver beaches and in jasmine-scented velvet nights, Florida works its magic as inexorably as the diamond-tipped tides that lap endlessly over these shores. Warm in body and soothed in spirit, they whiz away, willing victims to the seductive snare of the nation's last resort.

It's a magic place, this Florida, a place that stuns you with the exotic, that sharpens your senses and lulls your fears. It assails you with pastel colors never dimmed by industrial grime, delights you with air clear as a teardrop and waters as infallibly warm in January as they are in June.

Scoff as you will, but you'll waken some miserable March morning when the Christmas snow has become a dirty-gray blanket that dampens your toes and chills your soul, when sleet seems a way of life and spring light-years away. Then *you* too will "consider" Florida—and hours later, on sand soft as talcum, in warm opalescent waters, you too, for all your cosmopolitan sophistication, will find yourself bewitched, dazzled, convinced you've stumbled into some exotic foreign land.

You *have*. This is America's tropics, the southernmost place in the U.S., a state like no other in the continental 48. When you cross the border, you are already 120 miles south of any beach California can boast and more than 1000 miles south of the fabled French Riviera!

Thanks to the Gulf Stream, you can come here on the coldest days and find the nation's warmest winds, or arrive in summer to find tropical breezes cooling the land.

It is, of course, those incredibly cooperative temperatures that have lured people for thousands of years to this U-shaped limestone peninsula, jettisoned by ancient upheavals and bathed by warm waters. Beneath the sand you stand upon is a land half a billion years old. Over it roamed camels and rhinoceros, whose bones merged into deep deposits of phosphate, a mineral vital to those who live here now. Beneath your feet, cold springs are rushing through porous limestone to emerge in streams of water that support the 11,000,000 people who inhabit this land.

It's a place like no other, a place where everything is different, unexpected. Strange sweet-scented blossoms, instead of surviving on the land like any normal flower, lure living creatures into their lovely lethal blooms. Weird reptiles with long snouts, short legs, and a hide created by committee lurk in dark ancient waters. Even birds don't come in basic brown but in the exotic colors of sunset, dwelling in deep-green forests like brushstrokes on a pointillist canvas, their spectacular plumage camouflaged by brilliant scarlet hibiscus, flaming poinciana trees, burgundy bougainvillea.

It is a land of contrasts, from a delicate strip of sandy coral islands strung out like a trailing ribbon on a gift package to vast fields of Florida "prairie" grass.

Its climate is strange. No falling leaves, no drifts of snow, and only two temperatures: warm and warmer.

It doesn't even rain the same here. There are no long gloomy days of dreary gray chill. Instead suddenly, in an ear-splitting, cracking thunderclap, lashing torrents pour from a great impenetrable gray curtain hung from scudding black clouds. Rain falls not gently, not softly, but with ripping intensity, with roars and cracks of thunder that send the timid cowering. Then, flash. Gone. Nothing left but trailing white wisps racing across the skies as rays of sun as sharp as rapiers shatter droplets into a cataclysm of rainbows and spread nature's art gallery across the sky.

Weird things grow here: the traveler palm, a jungle St. Bernard whose leaves point north and whose base carries a quart of life-saving water; spiky aloe, whose jellied inner core soothes sunburn; gangly mangroves, whose roots forsake the ground to live on air but dip into water, catching flotsam that will someday become an island.

Its creatures are oddballs: manatees, those round, plump, whiskered throwbacks to antiquity, the cows of the sea; frolicking porpoises, whose squeaks and squeals may someday tell us of underwater mysteries; gray/white cattle with camel humps, floppy ears, and flapping chin wattles; tiny deer no bigger than collie dogs.

Those who live here are as exotic as the land around them. They're isolationists by geographical accident, iconoclasts by choice and experience, neither overcome nor unimpressed by the trappings of success.

Conditioned by generations of alteration, by great tidal sweeps of change across their land, they can take the measure of a man with unerring accuracy. Once strangers themselves in a strange land, they are quick to forgive fear and eccentricity but will never forget a slight to their chosen place in the sun.

For generations "conch" fishermen in the south and whip-snapping "crackers" in the north have fought to tame this unyielding land. They share it now with those who came here only yesterday, searching for the brass ring of prosperity or a peaceful place to wind down their lives. They share it willingly, recognizing that daring and courage similar to their own has helped these newcomers forsake less adventurous but more predictable lives to stake their futures on Florida.

It is perhaps their admiration for the offbeat that makes Floridians the most cussed individualists you'll ever meet. Not one tree changes in Florida without argument: cut it down, leave it standing, transplant it, or build a treehouse and rent it. They've been at it for generations. In fact, when Massachusetts Revolutionaries harried the British with midnight rides, Floridians hung Sam Adams and John Hancock in effigy in St. Augustine's public square, then toasted King George III!

A CAPSULE HISTORY: Two hundred years earlier Ponce de Léon arrived here on Easter morning in 1513 to name the new land after Spain's *pascua florida* Easter celebration, only to start the state's first argument over who should own this land. Florida's Indians had the last word: they shot an arrow into his armor and sent him back to Puerto Rico to die without gold, without his mysterious fountain of youth, and without Florida.

Three other Spaniards didn't do much better. Hernando de Soto marched through Florida with 700 troops, hassled all the way by Florida Indians, and never found the gold he sought before he died on the banks of the Mississippi. Panfilo de Narvaez, who gets credit for discovering Tampa Bay, found a gold piece but no welcome among the Apalachee Indians, who killed most of his men. Up in Pensacola, conquistador Don Tristan de Luna tried futilely to organize a Pensacola colony, but all he did was start a longevity argument with St. Augustine that continues to this day.

Even those 100,000 original Floridians, the Indians who were here when Columbus discovered the New World, were a nonconformist lot. Seven-foot-tall Calusas on the west coast and Tequestas on the southern tip refused to work the land, choosing instead to hunt and fish and fight. Over on Tampa Bay, in the forests of Ocala and up in Tallahassee, the Tocobaga, Timucuan, and Apalachee Indians argued that farming was survival. None lived long enough to win the dispute. By 1765 all were dead, victims of disease, warfare, and enslavement by the Spanish, leaving as a memorial only great mounds of shells and skeletons 6000 years old.

Their successors, immigrant Creek Indians, were no conformists either— they split from their tribe in the 1700s and moved to Florida to become, in Spanish, *cimarrones,* wild ones, runaways—Seminoles.

Legion are the characters who have populated this land. Spain's king plucked smuggler Pedro Menéndez de Avilés from a Spanish jail and set him off to start the nation's first colony in St. Augustine in 1545. Stationed here to protect Spanish galleons from treasure-seeking pirates who already called Florida home, Menéndez arrived to find a small French colony of Protestant Huguenots huddled in Fort Caroline, 50 miles away. That sparked another of the many Florida arguments over possession. Menéndez attacked the French, finally winning by default when a ship carrying his Huguenot opponents was wrecked on the shores of a bay that was later to be called Matanzas ("slaughter") in memory of Menéndez's hasty dispatch of the wreck's survivors.

Spaniards and Englishmen, whose blood runs thick in Floridian veins, never did get along too well, and whatever dispute they were having always seemed to involve Florida. When British seaman Sir Francis Drake did in the

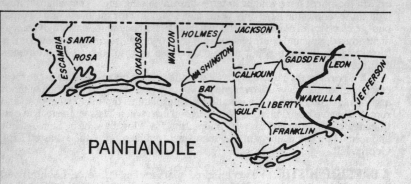

PANHANDLE

GULF OF MEXICO

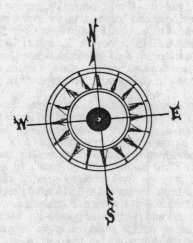

FLORIDA COUNTIES AND REGIONS

NORTH FLORIDA

ATLANTIC OCEAN

CENTRAL FLORIDA

SOUTH FLORIDA

GULF COAST

FLORIDA KEYS

Spanish Armada in 1588, Britain acquired high seas sovereignty. As it turned out, she also acquired Florida in a historic swap with Spain, which settled for Cuba, perhaps with relief.

In the Revolutionary War, Florida, untouched by curbs on trade and freedom, bet its future on the British, a bad gamble. When Britain lost the American colonies, Florida became a military and economic liability to the motherland, which promptly tossed it back to the Spanish.

By now the state reached all the way from the Atlantic to the Mississippi, and was divided into English East and Spanish West Florida. Spain decided not to disturb the status quo and let the ragtag lot left behind by the British stay on in Spanish Florida. That was a mistake.

Before long, typically Floridian machinations hatched every sort of bizarre plot to wrest Florida from Spain, although the plotters were characteristically divided on what to do with the state once it was freed.

Into the fray came Pres. Thomas Jefferson, who wanted to annex Florida (perhaps he needed a vacation), and was forever scheming with Florida adventurers or sending Gen. Andrew Jackson down to harass the Spanish. Spain finally tossed in the towel and sold Florida to the United States for $5 million. But in canny cracker style, the $5 million was never paid: Floridians claimed it all as payment for damages incurred during the Spanish occupation!

Florida, free at last to go its independent way, was by now a land of huge plantations that needed growing space. Fertile farmlands controlled by the peaceful Seminoles ranged from Tallahassee to Lake Okeechobee and seemed a good place to start expansion. To get those lands, General Jackson, who caused more trouble in Florida than the British and Spanish put together, moved in to push the tribe southward. He set off a bloody and altogether justifiable Seminole rebellion known as the First Seminole War. In 1823 the Seminoles ended that war by agreeing to settle in Central Florida on a reservation extending from Ocala to Lake Okeechobee. But peace was not to last. Soon someone had dreamed up a "compromise" plan to ship the Indians off to a reservation in Oklahoma, then called the "Indian Territory." That idea was answered by a great debater indeed, the tribal leader and fierce warrior Osceola, whose response was wordless—he just tossed his long knife into the white man's treaty, so the tribe remains today technically at war with the United States.

Blood ran over the land for seven years, beginning with a Christmas Day ambush of Maj. Francis Dade and 100 of his men near Tampa. Plantations burned and guns roared as 1500 Indians used guerrilla tactics to hold out against 9000 soldiers, who won finally but dishonorably by capturing Osceola under a flag of truce. Imprisoned in the Castillo de San Marcos in St. Augustine, the Seminole warrior was later shipped off to die in a South Carolina prison. Seminole resistance died with him. Most of the tribe was exiled to Oklahoma with just 300 remaining behind, hiding in the impenetrable Everglades, where their descendants still dwell.

Those bitter clashes behind them, Floridians argued once again, this time over the wisdom of joining the United States. In 1845 they finally agreed to do so, wearily choosing a flag emblazoned: "Let Us Alone."

Florida wasn't exactly booming in those days. Just 60,000 people lived here in 1850, scattered about in small settlements and traveling on river steamers, rough roads, and small railroads. Most were farmers, many earning their cracker appellation tending herds of cattle with long snapping whips. Stability proved fertile breeding ground for some of that individualism to surface. Fierce debates arose between small businessmen and plantation owners, first over state economics, then over participation in a great storm brewing a few miles north—the War Between the States. Secession prevailed, but Floridians argued so bitterly over the nature and extent of the state's participation in the Confederacy that at the close of the war the harassed governor committed suicide.

What many had warned would happen to plantations without slave labor did happen. After Reconstruction, Florida was, in a word, broke. Its railroads were bankrupt and its land was tied up as security for the railroads. Wily crackers made a deal: to millionaire Hamilton Disston, a Philadelphia manufacturer, went four million acres of land right smack across the state; to Florida went $1 million of Disston's money. Poor Disston should have gotten the better part of the deal, but various reverses and a major national economic slump made him the first of many land developers to bite Florida dust.

Meanwhile, Florida wasn't doing too badly. Henry Flagler, another millionaire, who'd made a fortune helping John D. Rockefeller get Standard Oil on its feet, was searching, they say, for a divorce from a deranged second wife. New York wouldn't change its no-divorce laws so Flagler looked south. With a wisdom both farsighted and myopic, Florida changed its no-divorce law long enough for Henry to take a third bride, then changed it right back again!

Flagler became the pied piper of the peninsula, laying his railroad tracks down the sunny east coast, luring frozen northerners farther and farther south. He spent tens of millions of dollars in the state, climaxing his efforts with the "Railroad That Went to Sea," a $27-million link between Key West and the mainland. On the west coast, still another millionaire, Henry Plant, did likewise and the boom was on. On the heels of Plant and Flagler came a wild-eyed, frenzied gaggle of land developers, their sights firmly fixed on a rainbow that ended in the Sunshine State.

Florida's land boom in the 1920s was a Marx Brothers comedy. Salesmen larded beaches with doubloons and promised instant millionairedom. They stood in the streets of Miami, Palm Beach, and Tampa and sold scraps of paper promises. They collected millions of dollars in downpayments, stuffing greenbacks casually into shoes and shoeboxes. They attracted throngs of hopeful, about-to-be-millionaires—one million in one year, two million the next. So helter-skelter and hysterical was the rush to get south that once the trains pulled into the station they couldn't get back out again because so many were backed up behind them! Some developers made a killing in real estate, some just killed themselves when weather once again intervened in the state's history: in 1935 a wicked hurricane finished off what a national depression had started.

In the aftermath of promotion, the state went wild with development. Nothing stood in the way of those who would tear down, but in recent years conservation has once again given Floridians something to argue about, and it's had its successes too: once-threatened alligators have increased to such numbers they now appear legally on some of the more bizarre menus; manatees hunted out of the big springs of the central peninsula are back again, along with otter, beaver, heron, great white egrets, and roseate spoonbills once nearly decimated for the fancy hat plumes of the early 1900s.

Just as they have for centuries, clear springs bubble in deep-emerald forests. Warm turquoise seas border strips of silver sand. The Garden of Eden's Torreya tree grows here and, mysteriously, nowhere else in the world.

All of this is why so many tourists come to Florida, and why so many never leave.

THE CLIMATE: If there's one thing that separates Florida from the rest of its continental buddies, it's sunshine: when you need it bad, they've got it good.

Temperatures

It has that warming sun for reasons of latitude and longitude, Gulf Stream currents, and to hear some people talk, the uplifted voices of hundreds of hoteliers and restaurateurs beseeching Mother Nature not to fail them this season.

She rarely does. From December to April you can count on average winter temperatures of at least 60 to 70 degrees south of Orlando, 10 to 15 degrees lower north of that city. Even if, as sometimes happens, there's a freak cold spell (in Florida all cold spells are by definition freaks—ask any chamber of commerce), it's still warmer here than back home in Hoboken (or anyplace else north of the state line).

In summer, temperatures from Orlando south reach into the 80s but rarely touch 90, and offshore breezes cool coastal areas. Summer, it must be admitted, is definitely warm (no Floridian uses the word "hot" between May and November), particularly inland in cities like Orlando where you should plan summer activities for morning and late afternoon, leaving the middle of the day for a poolside snooze or a long lunch in the confines of a cool, quiet restaurant. Everything but *everything* is air-conditioned in Florida, however, so you can always find a comfortable place to cool off.

There's no doubt it is humid in spring when tropical showers sometimes dampen the land briefly several times a day. There's also no doubt that spring is one of the prettiest times of year to visit the state. Popular resorts are quieter, peak summer temperatures are nowhere in sight, and you can see the state in spring glory. Flaming poincianas turn streets into blazing bonfires of color and orchid trees drop a plush purple carpet. Bougainvillea break into a downright lyrical display of color with harmony sung by azaleas, trumpet vines, tiger lilies, and geraniums.

Fall is quieter yet, and while you may not notice a nip, really hot days are gone. In fall Floridians take a breather between visitor onslaughts, which means some restaurants may be closed, although nearly everything else remains open all year.

North of Orlando, everything's just the opposite. In winter it gets cool ("cold" is a four-letter word in Florida) and in the deepest winter months temperatures sometimes drop into the 50s, only very occasionally lower. A few snowflakes have been known to fall, although that really *is* rare. The average winter temperature in the Panhandle is about 64 degrees. In summer the Panhandle and northern Crown region are quite comfortable, with weather much like the rest of the nation and crowds of Southerners on the beaches enjoying it. A pleasant corollary to the Panhandle's lower winter temperatures is correspondingly lower prices. You can stay in some very plush quarters, a fully equipped seaside condominium, for instance, for as little as $300 . . . a month!

Christmas is a special time of year in Florida, just as it is everywhere. Without snow for natural glitter, Floridians go hog wild, trimming lawn and lane with colored spotlights and silvery tinsel. Palm trees are bedecked with flashy ornaments and glistening lights and some homeowners spend thousands on Christmas decor to win prizes in annual competitions.

In waterside communities, boating fans sponsor Christmas boat-a-cades through the waterways. Fort Lauderdale has an especially spectacular one with more than 200 yachts, decorated mast to gunwale, winding through the waterways. This one comes complete with Santa Claus ho-ho-ing through loudspeakers and celebrities manning a lead boat accompanied by bands and choruses. Something similar goes on along Madeira/St. Petersburg Beach. Best of all, prices at Christmas have not yet reached the heights they will reach by February 1, so you can expect to pay about 20% less than in peak season.

Hurricanes and Tropical Storms

Tumultuous times are rarely fun, whether by human or natural disorders. But they do occur, demanding considerable and immediate attention. I am referring, of course, to hurricanes. They are a little frightening, but—and this is the important part for visitors—they are *never* a surprise.

Thanks to a very hard-working weather service and some pilots with stomachs as iron as their nerve, Floridians now know far in advance when a storm is brewing. Pilots fly into the eye of the storm and keep tabs on it, reporting to Floridians who plot it on weather charts the way other Americans do crossword puzzles. Everyone begins to batten down long before a storm nears land.

Killer hurricanes that wreaked havoc 50 years or more ago taught Floridians some somber lessons. Now very strict building codes have been designed to keep buildings as impervious as possible to a storm. What you need to know as a visitor is that you will have plenty of time to leave the area, or the state, if a big wind is about to blow. But even if you stay, you are likely to weather the storm safely, thanks to emergency crews with lots of practice. Officially, the storm season runs from June to November, but storms in summer are rare—most occur between August and November.

Suntans and Sunburns

On to something considerably more pleasant: sun. That's what you want, that's what you came here to get, and that's what Florida is going to give you.

What Florida cannot yet give you is a cure for sunburn. Hoteliers and doctors, if need be, will hold your hand, bring you an aspirin, smear some aloe plant on your back, and commiserate, but that's cold comfort when your back is on fire. I know *you* wouldn't do anything silly like staying out in the sun for four hours the first day you arrive, but perhaps you can pass this advice on to someone else:

No matter how innocent those little rays of sunshine look, no matter how many clouds are blocking the sun, no matter how overcast the day, Ole Sol is burning your epidermis. It won't help to hide in the ocean or the pool—that sun will find you wherever you are. Skin that has spent the last few months swaddled in clothes is no match for the Florida sun. Suntan oils can help, but they can also hurt. If you recall what happens when you apply heat to a frying pan full of oil, you'll get some idea how your unsuspecting cells are being sauteed.

Sunscreens are very effective products, and combined with a sensible sunning schedule can give you a nice tan instead of a blotchy mess that flakes off behind you in little trails of peeling skin. As for that tanning schedule, it goes something like this: stay out of the sun between 11 a.m. and 2 p.m., at least for the first few days. During other hours, get only 10 minutes of sun the first day, 15 the second, then 25, 35, 50, 75, and on the seventh day, 105 minutes.

2. Visitor Information

Florida has been opening its hotels, homes, and hearts to new arrivals for generations so it's had plenty of time to compile answers to your many questions and find ways to make your visit a happy and carefree trip.

TOURIST INFORMATION: If you drop a line to the **Florida Department of Commerce, Tourism Division,** Visitor Inquiry Section, 126 Van Buren St., Tallahassee, FL 32301 (tel. 904/487-1462), explain just what cities you're interested in visiting, and mention any specific interests you might have, they'll respond with all you ever wanted to know, and more. Ask for the state's fine publication *Florida Vacation Guide,* which costs $2.50 and is crammed with information on Florida and its facilities. . . . Florida's Department of Commerce, Tourism

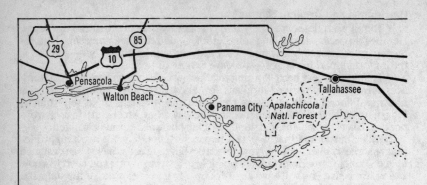

GULF OF MEXICO

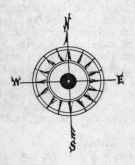

FLORIDA

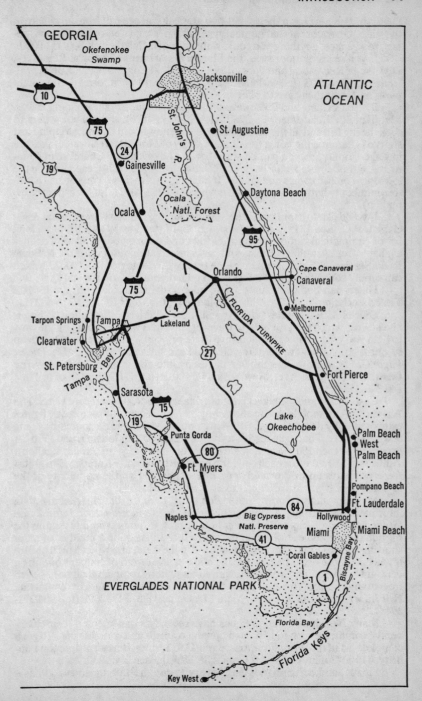

Division, also now has a special **toll-free number** you can call from anywhere in the state. Operators at that number have all the latest word on attractions, hotels, roads, most anything you could want to know. Call them at 800/432-0700.

If you're an outdoor type, the **Florida Department of Natural Resources,** Division of Recreation and Parks, Room 613, 3900 Commonwealth Blvd., Tallahassee, FL 32303 (tel. 904/488-7326), has a wealth of information on state parks and what they have to offer.

Florida's **Game and Freshwater Fish Commission,** Bryant Building, 620 S. Meridian St., Tallahassee, FL 32301 (tel. 904/488-4676), can tell you where to seek the big fish and all the details you need to know about fishing, stopping just short of guaranteeing you a fish dinner. Many of Florida's freshwater lakes are in Lake County, so you can be sure that the **Lake County Chamber of Commerce,** 601 N. Shore Dr., Eustis, FL 32726 (tel. 904/357-3434), can give you the low-down on fish camps and guides. If hunting is your game, you can call a toll-free number to find out what season is when: 800/282-8002 (also for fishing information).

If you'd like to camp out in this sunny state, the **Florida Campground Association,** P.O. Box 13355, Tallahassee, FL 32317 (tel. 904/893-4690), has a long list of commercial campgrounds in Florida and descriptions of camp facilities available free. Another camping and parks information resource is the **National Parks Service,** U.S. Department of the Interior, Washington, DC 20025, which can supply you with general information on national parks in the state.

Hikers can find out what trails to hike through Florida from the **Florida Trail Association,** P.O. Box 13708, Gainesville, FL 32604 (tel. 904/378-8823).

Official Airline Guides (OAG) publishes a wealth of information on hotels and airlines which is distributed to travel agents, who will be happy, by the way, to help you plan a trip *to* the Sunshine State or *from* it on cruises or Caribbean sojourns. If you're a frequent traveler, you can subscribe to the OAG's *Pocket Flight Guide,* which tells you what planes fly into and around the state. Write them at 888 Seventh Ave., New York, NY 10019 (tel. 212/977-8300, or toll free 800/323-3537).

Costs of **automobile travel** have not changed radically in recent years. The American Automobile Association, which keeps records of such costs, figures estimated daily driving costs in 1984 at about $136 daily for a couple traveling 500 miles a day. That includes $50 a day for meals, $51 for lodging, and $7 in car expenses for each 100 miles traveled (based on an average of 22 miles a gallon). Add about $10 a day for each child traveling with you and be prepared to adjust these estimates up or down 25% to 75% depending on the popularity of the region in which you are driving, the association says.

My next suggestion is more along the lines of bargain-seeking than information-gathering. A new publication called *Florida Exit Information Guide* is being distributed at many hotels, motels, and restaurants along the Florida border and elsewhere in the state. It contains quite a number of maps showing various exits from major highways in the state, and where you'll end up if you take those exits. Included in the booklet are dozens of coupons offering a discount on everything from ice-cream cones to hotel rooms and dinners—even free orange juice. You can get a free copy of the brochure by contacting **Exit Information Guide,** 618 S. Main St., Gainesville, FL 32601 (tel. 904/371-3948).

Many Florida cities and regions have recently supplemented their chambers of commerce with tourist development councils and commissions. To get a complete list of those organizations, write **TDC Listing, Bureau of Tourism Publicity,** 410-D Collins Bldg., 107 Gaines St., Tallahassee, FL 32301.

Finally, and certainly not least, every town (and I do mean *every)* has a

chamber of commerce and/or a **visitor information bureau** waiting to answer your questions. Some of the state's most dedicated boosters work for the chambers of commerce, and are wonderful people to know when you need help with anything. If you're looking for a room, write to any chamber of commerce and ask to have your name circulated among members. You'll soon hear from everyone in town. Wherever you go in Florida, if you need help with anything, from a city map to a dentist, go to the chamber of commerce. Helpful, friendly, knowledgeable people will help you out of a jam—and sometimes even take you home with them. They're wonderful and can't be praised highly enough for the long hours they give to the state and its visitors.

To get all the numbers and addresses of every chamber of commerce in the state, write to the **Florida Chamber of Commerce,** Box 11309, 136 S. Bronough St., Tallahassee, FL 32303 (tel. 904/222-2831). Two lists are available: one for $2.12, another for $7.88, the latter offering more detailed information than the former, but both contain all the names and addresses of the many chambers of commerce and tourism-related organizations.

BOOKS TO READ: Florida has proven itself many things to many people, some of whom have recorded their admiration in fascinating volumes about the state. I'm not offering any comprehensive bibliography here, just some of my favorites—books I think will give you an intriguing look at Florida to help you see behind the surface and into the heart of this lovely land.

If you ever pick up just one shell, Anne Morrow Lindbergh's *Gift from the Sea* will enchant you. Ms. Lindbergh and her aviator husband were Sanibel vacationers, and it was there she was inspired to pen some touching observations on the ties that bind us to the sea and to each other.

Robert Wilder left behind a New York advertising career to take a shot at novels. He managed to turn the story of early Tory immigration to the Bahamas (much of it from Florida) into a beautiful saga of life in the islands, *Wind from the Carolinas.* He wrote a similar recreation of life in early Florida called *Bright Feather,* a touching story of Osceola's hopeless struggle to save himself and his people from destruction by the same inexorable forces that were at work on other Indian tribes around the nation. Wilder's masterful work offers a fascinating look at the St. Augustine and Apalachicola River Valley in the early 1800s, and is a gripping novel besides.

Florida's favorite daughter is Marjorie Kinnan Rawlings, and she's most deserving of the honor. Not only did she write a Pulitzer Prize–winning novel, *The Yearling,* about country life in Florida, but she wrote *Cross Creek,* a haunting story about her part in that life. *Cross Creek* didn't please everyone in the tiny enclave she inhabited, but it has been enchanting readers outside that community for decades. She added to that autobiographical novel with a *Cross Creek Cookbook,* containing recipes still used today by a nearby restaurant.

No one has written more beautifully about the canny, charming, and sometimes cantankerous inhabitants of northern Florida than Gloria Jahoda, in a book called *The Other Florida.* Ms. Jahoda moved to Tallahassee from New York, much to the dismay of her friends who were convinced she was dropping off the face of the earth. In *The Other Florida* Jahoda shows them that heart is where the home is.

If you like mysteries, John MacDonald's novels are a look at the Gold Coast through the eyes of yacht-dwelling detective Travis McGee, who lives in Fort Lauderdale's Bahia Mar yacht basin aboard a boat invariably draped with long-legged women with problems. Naturally, McGee helps.

Harriet Beecher Stowe, of *Uncle Tom's Cabin* fame, moved to Mandarin near Jacksonville and wrote a little tome called *Palmetto Leaves,* which offers an intriguing look at Florida life. Poet Sidney Lanier wrote beautifully about the state in a book called *Florida, Its Scenery, Climate and History.*

Finally, in 1791 William Bartram, son of the internationally recognized botanist John Bartram, published a book about travels with his father, including some fascinating experiences in Florida. It's called *Travels Through North and South Carolina, Georgia and East and West Florida.* His book met with acclaim in England and was given to Samuel Taylor Coleridge, who is said to have been reading it when he fell asleep to dream his famous tale of "Xanadu . . . where blossomed many an incense-bearing tree/ And here were forests ancient as the hills/ Enfolding sunny spots of greenery. . . ."

What I'm about to mention is not a book, but it is something to read. It's a **calendar** published by the Environmental Information Center of the Florida Conservation Foundation. You'll find some entertaining cartoons in it (a recent calendar cartoon showed a group of bulldozers and construction equipment behind a huge billboard reading "Scenic View Under Construction"). In line with the interests of its publishers, the calendar also features an often-amusing record of the history of environmental issues in Florida. You can get a copy by writing the organization at 935 Orange Ave., Winter Park, FL 32789 (tel. 305/ 644-5377). A "minimum donation" of $5 is requested for each calendar.

READERS' RECOMMENDATIONS: "A fine 140-page publication available on Florida and packed with tourist information can be obtained from the **Florida Tourist Information Center,** 3811 N. Andrews Ave., Fort Lauderdale, FL 33309 (tel. 305/566-0700)" (Barry Ferguson, Bremen, Ky.).[*Author's note:* The Information Center is a private organization, originally organized as a hotel-booking center, and it still serves in that capacity. It also distributes, free, the booklet this reader recommends.] . . . "**Betty Brothers,** a real estate agent in the Florida Keys, has written several books, among them *Trigger Fish: Tales of the Florida Keys,* which is geared to the younger set" (Linda Sambel, Pittsfield, Mass.).

Florida? Why not?

3. Tips on Food and Lodging

HOTELS AND MOTELS: I cannot stress too often that in and around peak seasons (December to May in central and southern Florida; May to September in the Panhandle), it is just short of insanity to travel to Florida without a reservation. Many are the tales of woe from visitors who spent all those beautiful beach hours (sometimes days!) pounding the pavement in search of a room. It isn't worth it—and it isn't necessary. A telephone call or a note can save you much grief, and perhaps even a miserable night in the car.

If you persist in unplanned forays and can stand the suspense, here's a searcher's tip: you'll often have most success from 4 to 6 p.m. when reservations that haven't been claimed are cancelled and given away on a first-come basis.

In Florida you need never fear being stranded so far out in the boondocks that you can't find a hotel. In the backwoods you may be, but without a hotel or motel somewhere near? Never. Moderately priced chain motels like Howard Johnson's, Holiday Inn, Days Inn, and Motel 6 (a really low-budget stop) have representatives everywhere in Florida. When one of those operations was something extra-special, I've noted that for you. Otherwise, here's a list of toll-free numbers for the major chain operations in moderate price brackets. (Note: **Motel 6** toll-free numbers vary by state. Check with toll-free information—800/ 555-1212—for the area in which you'd like to stay.)

Best Western (tel. 800/334-7234); **Days Inn** (tel. 800/325-2525); **Econo-lodge** (tel. 800/446-6900), in Virginia (tel. 800/582-5882); **Holiday Inn** (tel. 800/

465-4239); **Howard Johnson's** (tel. 800/654-2000); **Quality Inns** (tel. 800/228-5151); **Ramada Inns** (tel. 800/228-2828); **Red Carpet Inns** (tel. 800/323-4444); **Rodeway Inns** (tel. 800/228-2000); **Scottish Inns** (tel. 800/643-8960); **TraveLodge** and **Viscount** (tel. 800/255-3050).

Now, some final words about saving money on Florida hotel rooms: small motels a block or two from the sand are cheaper (sometimes 50% cheaper) than larger oceanside resorts; in beachfront hotels, rooms not facing the ocean are often cheaper than those overlooking the water; the fewer a resort's amenities (like telephones, restaurants, lobbies, etc.), the lower the price; and, of course, the less popular the season and the farther outside large resort cities you go, the less you'll pay (although massive sports resorts are exceptions to that).

Miami is the most expensive city in the state (though much more moderately priced than many American and European cities of a similar size), so prices go down as you radiate outward. Orlando, thanks to the popularity of Walt Disney World, is something of an aberration as prices there tend to stay about the same year round and are on the high side of moderate, offset a bit by many moderately priced restaurants. You'll find the cheapest beach vacations in Florida north of a line that runs from about Daytona on the east coast to Tampa on the west. When you get a bill in the Panhandle, you're likely to think they've made a mistake—in your favor!

As for that little matter of price. All the prices I've mentioned here, except in one or two cases specifically noted, are for a *room for two*. When you inquire about prices in Florida, you will always be given the price of a double room. "Always" is, of course, a big promise, so let me add that occasionally in summer some Miami Beach hotels do advertise a price per person, but in general you need not fear that a quoted price is per person. Prices hop around like a Mexican jumping bean in Florida, so be prepared for a few dollars higher than what I've quoted and do expect higher prices during any special event like football games, Speed Weeks in Daytona, etc.

Prices for a third or fourth person sharing a room are usually very low, perhaps $5 or less, and children sharing a room with their parents are free in most large motels and many smaller ones too.

Florida even has its own language: hotel-speak. When you ask a hotel for its rate, they'll start reeling off words like efficiencies, hotel rooms, villas, apartments, and Bahama beds. Here's what they mean:

Hotel rooms—the typical room with one or two beds, sometimes king- or queen-size beds.

Twins—two single beds in the room.

A double—one double bed in the room in small hotels, usually two double beds in large hotels.

An efficiency—an especially large room with an area set aside for cooking and usually equipped with stove, oven, small refrigerator, dishes, pots, etc.

One-bedroom apartments—usually two rooms, but sometimes three, one for sleeping plus a kitchen and sometimes a small living room.

Bahama or Hollywood beds—Usually found in an efficiency, Bahama beds are twin beds, usually with back bolster cushions and no headboard. Covers go on the beds during the day so they look just like couches. Hollywood beds are just another word for the same thing. Both are also sometimes called studio beds or couches, but they differ from a "roll-out" or convertible couch in that they have box springs as well as mattresses and are generally more comfortable than convertible couches.

Condominium resort—Somewhere along the way someone decided a good way to sell condominium apartments was to operate a number of the apartments as a hotel, thus making them a dandy write-off and an income-provider

GULF OF MEXICO

FLORIDA
ATTRACTIONS

GEORGIA

Okefenokee
Swamp

Stephen Foster
Center

U.S. 10

U.S. 75

U.S. 19

24

Gainesville

St. John's R.

Fort Clinch
Jacksonville

ATLANTIC
OCEAN

Alligator Farm
Sightseeing Train
St. Augustine
Wax Museum
Oldest Store Museum
Oldest House
Castillo de San Marcos

Ocala
Natl. Forest

Ocala
Silver Springs

Daytona Beach

Homosassa Springs
Weeki Wachee

Citrus Tower

U.S. 75

Busch Gardens

Tarpon Springs
Tiki Gardens
Clearwater

Sunken Gardens
St. Petersburg

Tampa Bay

MGM's Bounty Exhibit

Sarasota

U.S. 75

19

Punta Gorda

Aquarama Waltzing Waters
Edison Winter Home

Everglades Wonder Gardens

African Safari at Caribbean Gardens

Walt Disney
World

4

Tampa

Lakeland
Cypress
Gardens

27

U.S. 95

Kennedy Space Center
Tours

Cape Canaveral
Canaveral

Sea World
Orlando

Circus
World

Melbourne

FLORIDA TURNPIKE

Fort Pierce

Lake
Okeechobee

Lion Country
Safari

80

Ft. Myers

84

Big Cypress
Natl. Preserve

Naples

41

Palm Beach
West
Palm Beach

Pompano Beach

Ft. Lauderdale
Vizcaya
Hollywood
Planet Ocean
Miami
Monkey Jungle
Coral Gables
Miami Beach

Seaquarium
Parrot Jungle
Fairchild
Tropical
Gardens

1

Biscayne Bay

EVERGLADES NATIONAL PARK

Florida Bay

Florida Keys

Key West Conch Tour Train
Key West

for owners. As people began to demand better and fancier accommodations with golf courses, restaurants, pools, and entertainment, condominiums became the perfect solution to both the needs of the owner and the needs of the traveler.

Villas—A term often encountered at condominium resorts and usually referring to a complete apartment with one or two separate bedrooms, large living room, kitchen. The term also is now sometimes used by large hotels to indicate an especially plush room, a large suite, or perhaps a cottage set off by itself.

CONDOMINIUMS: If you're staying a while, you might like a real home away from home in a condominium apartment. Thousands of condo owners in Florida rent their apartments seasonally, and sometimes by the week during slow seasons. Condominiums are a bargain since you have all the amenities of a hotel (except perhaps restaurants, and sometimes even those) and a great deal more space for the dollar. A note to the chamber of commerce in any city will elicit response from condominium owners. If you want still more choice, here's a list of a few (by no means all) condominium rental agents in some of the popular condo areas:

Fort Lauderdale Area

Cleo de Mott Associates, 1700 NE 26th St., Fort Lauderdale, FL 33305 (tel. 305/565-4831).

The Keys

Sylvia M. Mead, Mile Marker 82, Islamorada, FL 33036 (tel. 305/664-4446); **Marathon Realty,** 10800 Overseas Hwy., Marathon, FL 33050 (tel. 305/743-4500); **Casa Solana,** 3312 Northside Dr., Key West, FL 33040 (tel. 305/294-6262).

Palm Beach

Carter Realty, 449 Blue Heron Blvd., Riviera Beach, FL 33404 (tel. 305/844-6334); **Century 21,** 119 E. Ocean Ave., Lantana, FL 33460 (tel. 305/588-6267).

The Panhandle

Metro America Realty, 5900 Ninth Ave., Pensacola, FL 32501 (tel. 904/244-2121); **John W. Brooks Realty, Inc.,** 106 Miracle Strip Pkwy., Fort Walton Beach, FL 32548 (tel. 904/244-2121).

Miami/Miami Beach

Century 21, 2665 Collins Ave., Miami Beach, FL 33139 (tel. 305/672-3131); **Condo Resales & Rental,** 1801 S. Ocean Dr., Hollywood, FL 33020 (tel. 305/945-6579); **Keyes,** 100 Biscayne Blvd., Miami, FL 33152 (tel. 305/371-3592).

Sanibel/Captiva Islands

Executive Service, Inc., 455 Periwinkle Way, Sanibel, FL 33957 (tel. 813/472-4195); **Priscilla Murphy Realty,** 9067 Causeway Rd., Sanibel, FL 33957 (tel. 813/472-4113).

TIME-SHARING: Interval ownership, also called time-sharing, has gone slightly crazy in Florida, with even the tiniest motels offering the vacationer the chance to "buy" ownership of accommodations for several thousand dollars (although you do not *own* the property). Since the time-sharing dust has not yet settled to my satisfaction, I have generally avoided properties that are converting to time-sharing operations or are already heavily involved. There are two major reasons for that: (1) a resort's prices seem to me not to be stable during a conversion, and (2) if they're running a boiler-room operation, as some most definitely are, you're likely to be subjected to a sales pitch, like it or not, a practice I find abhorrent at best. If you want to know more about time-sharing, you won't have any difficulty finding out: newspapers will tell you who's selling and sellers will offer you everything from silver dollars to instant cameras to listen to their sales spiels.

RESTAURANTS: Nothing changes faster in Florida than restaurants, and the bigger the city, the faster the change. I've tried to stick to restaurants that have emerged victors in the war of the whisks, but I'm offering no guarantees on either continued existence or price. As for those prices, I've tried to indicate about what I think you'll pay for a *basic* meal. If you love soups before, desserts after, and a bottle of wine or a martini or two in between, your bill will rise accordingly and rapidly. In general, dinner entree prices in Florida include salad, vegetable, meat, bread, butter, and often coffee.

Florida restaurants are much more casual than their counterparts in other sections of the nation. For men, a jacket in hand (not necessarily on shoulders) will do just fine, even in peak winter season in southern Florida when things are at their most formal. Palm Beach and Miami Beach are perhaps the most formal cities in Florida, so at top restaurants and hotels there the absence of a tie and jacket may be at best frowned upon, at worst cause for dismissal.

Elsewhere, and in all moderately priced restaurants, you won't feel out of place without a tie in winter, and certainly not in summer, when Miami and every other city in Florida slips into as little as possible.

For women, dresses or attractive pants outfits go anywhere; designer jeans, almost anywhere. At beachside restaurants and some of the more rustic seafood spots, shorts and shirts are acceptable; bathing suits, only if covered. Must you wear shoes? Yes.

Local Foods

Even food is different in Florida. Next to their Persian lime brothers, for instance, key limes look like little yellow jokes, but the pie that comes from them (it must be yellow to be authentic) is a symphony of Graham cracker crust and whipped cream or meringue. You can only get the authentic version of this creation in Florida.

Further, and lest you still think Florida purveys only sunshine, listen to these statistics. Florida produces more than $12 billion in agricultural products each year, including more than 50% of the world's grapefruit, 25% of the world's oranges, and 90% of the nation's limes. It is the world's largest citrus-producing region.

Tomatoes you buy in the dead of winter have probably come from Florida —that's the state's largest winter crop, much of it grown south of Miami in Homestead, a major tomato-farming community in the state. Up in Zellwood in central Florida and around Belle Glade, the rich mucklands produce peppers, eggplants, sugarcane, pecans, kumquats, and some strange tropical fruits called carambola, mangoes, and papayas.

As you drive through the state you'll also see hundreds of little rectangular boxes sitting in the fields. These are occupied by thousands of bees, which produce more honey each year than is produced in any other state in the nation.

Chicago may be the world's butcher but Florida ranks second in the nation in beef production, right after Texas. Cowboys still ride the range here and there. In fact, there are more cows in Florida than in any other state east of the

Mississippi. Florida has more than 21,000 cattle ranches! You'll see many of these vast ranches in central Florida, and you can even visit one—and attend a cattle auction—in Kissimmee, near Orlando. Florida cattle farms are now experimenting with a new cattle breed said to produce meat with fewer calories and less cholesterol.

Finally, Florida is one of the nation's most prolific producers of seafood. Fishermen here pull more than a billion pounds of fin and claw from the sea each year.

Stone crabs are a special Florida treat, and it's nice to know no one has to kill anything to get them. Stone crab fishermen near Naples, on the west coast of the state, capture the crabs, break off one large claw, then throw the crabs back into the deep, where they grow another claw to replace the missing one. Stone crabs are best during their harvest season (mid-October to mid-May). Many restaurants can produce them later in the year, but they'll probably have been frozen.

So much seafood comes from these waters it's hard to know where to start, so I'll just mention some with which you may not be familiar. Pompano is a very light and delicate fish much loved by gourmets. Scamp is not misspelled scampi, but a flaky white fish found on the state's west coast. It's rarely seen on menus since fishermen usually keep it for themselves! North Florida's mullet lives in clear, sandy water, and has a light, much-loved flavor different from and better than mullet found elsewhere in the nation.

Florida lobsters aren't like Maine lobsters. They're much smaller and usually much cheaper. Apalachicola oysters are a Florida specialty, and are as different from their Bon Secour Alabama brothers as they are from any other oysters. Rock shrimp, sometimes called *langostinos,* are something like shrimp-size lobsters. Clams and scallops are abundant here. You'll find two kinds of scallops, bay and deep sea, the former much tinier and sweeter.

Fresh hearts of palm (try Cap's Place, in Lighthouse Point near Fort Lauderdale) are a delicacy far superior to the canned variety. They're cut from the heart of the cabbage palm with a technique learned from the Seminoles. Once you try them, you'll be forever spoiled for the canned version.

From the many nationalities that have merged on this land (Bahamians, Cubans, Indians, Spanish, English, French) Floridians have acquired a taste for crusty Cuban bread and steaming thick black coffee in thimble-size cups; for conch chowder made from ground conch (pronounced "konk," it's the creature that lives inside the pink shells you "listen" to), tomatoes, and plenty of hot spices, topped by a dollop of sherry; for spicy conch salad marinated in fermented lime juice; for paella, a rice and seafood and vegetable combination; for piccadillo, a mix of ground meat, olives, and raisins in a spicy sauce; for pilau, a spicy stew found in the St. Augustine area; for Creole foods like muffeleta sandwiches and gumbo served in the Panhandle.

Citrus

Breathtakingly beautiful citrus groves cover the rolling hills of central Florida from horizon to horizon. In cold snaps those old tires you'll see piled in fields are burned to heat the air and keep frost from nipping tender trees. At groves throughout Florida you can pick your own oranges, send oranges to friends here or abroad, ship fruit home, and usually get all the orange juice you can drink free! If you're taking some citrus home on a plane, be sure to put your name or some identifying ribbon on it since everyone else on the plane is likely to have some too. If you'd like to see frozen orange juice in the making, visit the Minute Maid plant at Auburndale, 11 miles east of Lakeland on US 92, from November through mid-April for free tours.

Here's a look at some of the citrus you'll find here:

Navel oranges—best from November to January and recognizable from tiny "navels" and smooth skin, usually almost seedless and easily peeled.

Valencia oranges—March to July, juicy and aromatic.

Temple oranges—January to March, a favorite eating orange with a lightly pitted skin.

Murcott oranges—February to April, and almost red inside.

Hamlin oranges—October to December, seedless, thin-skinned, a juice orange.

Pineapple oranges—December to February, very juicy and very sweet.

Tangelos—December to March, a cross between tangerines and oranges, with an easy-peel skin.

Tangerines—December to February, the zipper-skin fruit.

Duncan grapefruit—October to May, a thin, pale-yellow skin, very juicy and seedy.

Seedless grapefruit—November to June, smooth yellow skin, few seeds.

Pink seedless—October to May, rose-colored interior.

Other interesting ones are tiny pucker-maker **kumquats** often used in jellies, Persian **limes** (the big green ones), and Ponderosa **lemons,** often nearly as big as a large orange.

Many of the exotic fruits of the tropics grow here: mangoes, papayas, carambolas, Surinam cherries, and dozens more. You can learn about them at Redlands Fruit and Spice Park or Fairchild Gardens in Miami.

You can even try citrus wine! It's made at Florida Vineyard and Fruit Gardens at Orange Lake between Gainesville and Ocala, and sold in most liquor and some grocery stores, and at roadside Stuckey's stores along the Florida Turnpike.

Citrus candies and jellies, goat's milk fudge, and coconut patties are favorites in Florida too. You can buy coconuts (which are brown and slosh when you shake them if they're ripe) already hulled in grocery stores.

Food festivals are favorite entertainment in Florida. Among the most popular are the corn festival in Zellwood (near Orlando) each May, the Strawberry Festival in Plant City in February, and the Watermelon Festival each June in Monticello. There are dozens of seafood festivals too.

4. Final Thoughts

ABOUT THIS BOOK: No restaurant, hotel, or other establishment has paid to be included in this book. What you read are personal recommendations, carefully checked out and judged by the strict yardstick of value. If they measured up—gave good value for your money—they were included, regardless of price range.

Because, however, most of today's travelers are in the medium-income group, you'll find that the majority of listings are geared to neither the super-rich nor the best-things-in-life-are-free contingent. Rather, the book is aimed at the dollarwise, middle-income traveler who wants occasionally to splurge and occasionally to save, but always to get maximum value for his or her dollar. The evaluations in this book were made with an eye on cost, but primarily with an eye on quality.

A WORD ABOUT PRICES QUOTED: Inflation, it seems, is here to stay as a part of the American scene. Thus the prices shown here are *only those in effect at the time of writing*. Even if there is a variation in price by the time you reach a particular destination, however, the price *range* is likely to be the same—that is, a medium-range hotel today will probably still be medium-priced for the area even with a hike in charges, although "medium" may be somewhat higher than at the time of this writing. In this sense, this is a *guide* as the name says, to finding low-, medium-, and top-priced facilities.

AN INVITATION TO READERS: Like all Dollarwise Guides, the *Dollarwise Guide to Florida* is our best effort to clue you in on how to get the most for your money. If, as a dollarwise traveler, you find I've missed an establishment that you find to be a particularly good value (or even one that's just fun and other readers ought to know about), I'd like to hear about it. I invite you to write so it may be included in the next edition of this book. If, on the other hand, by the time you get to a particular destination you find a restaurant or hotel is *not* up to my description (chefs *do* change and hotels *do* deteriorate!), please write me about that as well—the last thing I want in this book is misleading or untimely information. Any additional travel tips you may come up with (off days to visit attractions when they're less crowded, etc.) will also be appreciated. And, oh, yes, if you find this guide to be especially helpful, do drop me a line about *that*. You have my word that each and every letter will be read by me personally, although I find it well-nigh impossible to *answer* each and every one. Be assured, however: I'm listening. Send whatever you have to say to Marylyn Springer, c/o Frommer/Pasmantier Publishing Corp., 1230 Avenue of the Americas, New York, NY 10020.

5. The $25-a-Day Travel Club—How to Save Money on All Your Travels

In this book we'll be looking at how to get your money's worth in Florida, but there is a "device" for saving money and determining value on *all* your trips. It's the popular, international $25-a-Day Travel Club, now in its 23rd successful year of operation. The Club was formed at the urging of numerous readers of the $$$-a-Day and Dollarwise Guides, who felt that such an organization could provide continuing travel information and a sense of community to value-minded travelers in all parts of the world. And so it does!

In keeping with the budget concept, the annual membership fee is low and is immediately exceeded by the value of your benefits. Upon receipt of $18 (U.S. residents), or $20 U.S. by check drawn on a U.S. bank or via international postal money order in U.S. funds (Canadian, Mexican, and other foreign residents) to cover one year's membership, we will send all new members the following items.

(1) *Any two* of the following books

Please designate in your letter which two you wish to receive:

Europe on $25 a Day
Australia on $25 a Day
England on $35 a Day
Greece including Istanbul and Turkey's Aegean Coast on $25 a Day
Hawaii on $35 a Day
Ireland on $25 a Day
India on $15 & $25 a Day
Israel on $30 & $35 a Day
Mexico on $20 a Day
New York on $35 a Day
New Zealand on $20 & $25 a Day

Scandinavia on $35 a Day
Scotland and Wales on $35 a Day
South America on $25 a Day
Spain and Morocco (plus the Canary Is.) on $35 a Day
Washington, D.C. on $40 a Day

Dollarwise Guide to Austria and Hungary
Dollarwise Guide to Bermuda and The Bahamas
Dollarwise Guide to Canada
Dollarwise Guide to the Caribbean
Dollarwise Guide to Egypt
Dollarwise Guide to England and Scotland
Dollarwise Guide to France
Dollarwise Guide to Germany
Dollarwise Guide to Italy
Dollarwise Guide to Japan and Hong Kong
Dollarwise Guide to Portugal (plus Madeira and the Azores)
Dollarwise Guide to Switzerland and Liechtenstein
Dollarwise Guide to California and Las Vegas
Dollarwise Guide to Florida
Dollarwise Guide to New England
Dollarwise Guide to the Northwest
Dollarwise Guide to the Southeast and New Orleans
Dollarwise Guide to the Southwest
(Dollarwise Guides discuss accommodations and facilities in all price ranges, with emphasis on the medium-priced.)

A Guide for the Disabled Traveler
(A guide to the best destinations for wheelchair travelers and other disabled vacationers in Europe, the United States, and Canada by an experienced wheelchair traveler. Includes detailed information about accommodations, restaurants, sights, transportation, and their accessibility.)

A Shopper's Guide to the Best Bargains in England, Scotland, and Wales
(Describes in detail hundreds of places to shop—department stores, factory outlets, street markets, and craft centers—for great quality British bargains.)

Bed & Breakfast—North America
(This guide contains a directory of over 150 organizations that offer bed & breakfast referrals and reservations throughout North America. The scenic attractions, businesses, and major schools and universities near the homes of each are also listed.)

Dollarwise Guide to Cruises
(This complete guide covers all the basics of cruising—ports of call, costs, fly-cruise package bargains, cabin selection booking, embarkation and debarkation and describes in detail over 60 or so ships cruising in Alaska, the Caribbean, Mexico, Hawaii, Panama, Canada, and the United States.)

Dollarwise Guide to Skiing USA—East
(Rates and describes the many resorts in Massachusetts, Vermont, New Hampshire, Connecticut, Maine, Quebec, New York, Pennsylvania, plus new areas in North Carolina, the Virginias, and Maryland. Includes detailed information about lodging, dining, and non-skier activities.)

Dollarwise Guide to Skiing USA—West
(All the diverse ski resorts of the West—in California, Colorado, Idaho, New Mexico, Montana, Oregon, and Wyoming—are fully described and rated. Lodging, dining, and non-skier activities are also included.)

Frommer's Travel Diary and Record Book
(A 72-page diary for personal travel notes plus a section for such vital data as passport and traveler's check numbers, itinerary, postcard list, special people and places to visit, and a reference section with temperature and conversion charts, and world maps with distance zones.)

How to Beat the High Cost of Travel
(This practical guide details how to save money on absolutely all travel items—accommodations, transportation, dining, sightseeing, shopping, taxes, and more. Includes special budget information for seniors, students, singles, and families.)

Marilyn Wood's Wonderful Weekends
(This very selective guide covers the best mini-vacation destinations within a 175-mile radius of New York City. It describes special country inns and other accommodations, restaurants, picnic spots, sights, and activities—all the information needed for a two- or three-day stay.)

Museums in New York
(A complete guide to all the museums, historic houses, gardens, zoos, and more in the five boroughs. Illustrated with over 200 photographs.)

Swap and Go—Home Exchanging Made Easy
(Two veteran home exchangers explain in detail all the money-saving benefits of a home exchange, and then describe precisely how to do it. Also includes information on home rentals and many tips on low-cost travel.)

The Fast 'n' Easy Phrase Book
(The four most useful languages—French, German, Spanish, and Italian—all in one convenient, easy-to-use phrase guide.)

The New York Urban Athlete
(The ultimate guide to all the sports facilities in New York City for jocks and novices.)

Where to Stay USA
(By the Council on International Educational Exchange, this extraordinary guide is the first to list accommodations in all 50 states that cost anywhere from $3 to $25 per night.)

(2) A one-year subscription to *The Wonderful World of Budget Travel*

This quarterly eight-page tabloid newspaper keeps you up to date on fast-breaking developments in low-cost travel in all parts of the world bringing you the latest money-saving information—the kind of information you'd have to pay $25 a year to obtain elsewhere. This consumer-conscious publication also features columns of special interest to readers: **Hospitality Exchange** (members all over the world who are willing to provide hospitality to other members as they pass through their home cities); **Share-a-Trip** (offers and requests from members for travel companions who can share costs and help avoid the burdensome single supplement); and **Readers Ask . . . Readers Reply** (travel questions from members to which other members reply with authentic firsthand information).

(3) A copy of *Arthur Frommer's Guide to New York*

This is a pocket-size guide to hotels, restaurants, nightspots, and sightseeing attractions in all price ranges throughout the New York area.

(4) Your personal membership card

Membership entitles you to purchase through the Club all Arthur Frommer publications for a third to a half off their regular retail prices during the term of your membership.

So why not join this hardy band of international budgeteers and participate in its exchange of travel information and hospitality? Simply send your name and address, together with your annual membership fee of $18 (U.S. residents) or $20 U.S. (Canadian, Mexican, and other foreign residents), by check drawn on a U.S. bank or via international postal money order in U.S. funds to: $25-a-Day Travel Club, Inc., Frommer/Pasmantier Publishers, 1230 Avenue of the Americas, New York, NY 10020. And please remember to specify which *two* of the books in section (1) above you wish to receive in your initial package of members' benefits. Or, if you prefer, use the last page of this book, simply checking off the two books you select and enclosing $18 or $20 in U.S. currency.

Once you are a member, there is no obligation to buy additional books. No books will be mailed to you without your specific order.

Chapter I

GETTING TO AND AROUND FLORIDA

1. Getting There
2. Getting Around

NOT LONG AGO I VISITED a fabled group of islands across the Atlantic, finally setting trembling foot ashore after a long, wet, bouncing journey across an open sea, a crashing arrival at a clump of limestone rock, and a terrifying leap from heaving craft to slippery pitted rock.

It is my very great pleasure to tell you that getting to Florida is fraught with none of those terrors. Getting there, in fact, could hardly be easier—and in these days of rip-roaring airline competition, could hardly be cheaper.

This sunny peninsula is prime time in the travel business, a place so many people want to visit that airlines, trains, buses, and car-rental companies are locked in cut-throat competition for a place in the sun. Fortune thus smiles upon the south-bound traveler: competition translates to low prices and to so many money-saving deals that it hardly pays to stay home.

Finding your way to those deals through the maze of fares, tours, packages, and optional extras, however, is like touring the Everglades without a compass: you may succeed, but you'll spend weeks wandering in the wilderness.

There is an easy way: visit a travel agent. It won't cost you a cent to pick the willing brains of these walking computers who spend all their time studying tariffs, hotels, and tour packages. A travel agent's only business is travel, and survival in that business depends on knowing how to satisfy travelers on every economic level. Agents' help is free since their income comes solely from commissions paid by travel entities like airlines, car-rental companies, and hotels. You'll still have to make the big decisions on how much time and money you want to spend in the Sunshine State, but with an agent's help the planning can be easy.

1. Getting There

To give you an idea how you can escape to the tropics—and how much that escape will cost—here's a look at air, train, and bus fares, and even a glance at what you can expect to spend traveling by automobile. Now here comes the disclaimer: I wouldn't guarantee the cost of toothpaste tomorrow much less air fares a month or two from now, so please don't blame me if the prices you're quoted on transportation costs differ from what you read here. If there's one thing I *can* guarantee it's that those prices will be different—but, glorious day, they may even be *lower!*

BY AIR: You can slosh through the slush of Manhattan or Düsseldorf, St. Louis or London, some March morning, then enter the miraculous silver bird and emerge a few hours later to dip a very grateful toe into Florida's warm turquoise waters. Such is the glory of the Wright brothers' invention.

Such is the glory of airline competition that air fares may be one of the only things left in the world whose cost actually goes down! In the wake of deregulation, competition has led to so many different kinds of fares—APEX, Super-APEX, chicken-feed, peanut, no-frills, excursion, half fares, discounted fares—that I'm fully expecting to see a no-fare fare any day now.

While we're all waiting for that glorious moment, you should be aware that (1) the farther ahead you can plan your trip, the more air fare money you're likely to save; (2) the more unpopular the hour and day you travel (like wee a.m. hours and nonweekend or holiday days), the better deal you'll find; and (3) the more you tell airline reservationists or travel agents about your age, your travel companions, your destination, and/or your budget, the better equipped they are to find you a bargain.

To give you an idea—and I want to stress that this is *only an indication*—of what you'll pay to get to Florida by air, here's a look at economy-class (coach) round-trip tickets in effect on several airlines when this book went to press. (If anything's certain about Florida air service, it's change, but for the moment this is how it looks.)

To	From New York	From Chicago	From Los Angeles	From Houston
Miami	$200	$300	$500	$200
Tampa	$200	$300	$500	$200
Orlando	$200	$300	$500	$200

Every airline serving the state has at least one (and usually many) package plans which help you save money on rental cars and hotel rooms in the state, and often throw in a number of attraction admissions and discounts as well. Any airline or travel agent will be happy to tell you about these budget-wise Florida travel packages.

Many small airlines have joined the crowded skies in recent years. They remain in business by offering inexpensive flights they hope will make up in volume what they lose in mark-up. Arrow and People Express are good examples of these. Often you can save a bundle by flying one of these carriers, although you do have to consider the cost of transportation to departure and arrival points, for instance: Buffalo, Sarasota, or West Palm Beach.

BY TRAIN: As a train-lover, I couldn't be happier about what's happening to the silver streakers on the Florida run. A few years ago trains were costing about as much as planes and sometimes more, and they weren't getting much good press on the quality of their service.

Those things, happily, are changing now: Amtrak's prices are quite competitive; its service has improved both in quality and quantity; and there are new or refurbished cars on the route. All these things are making it more comfortable than ever to travel by train.

If you have the time to spend, trains offer a lovely, leisurely way to see the beauties of this sunny peninsula.

At the moment two trains travel to Florida along the northeast coastal corridor from New York to Miami and Tampa/St. Petersburg. The *Silver Meteor* is the more direct of the two, leaving New York's Penn Station about 4:15 p.m. and arriving in Miami about 6:17 p.m. the following day. The *Silver Star* leaves the same station at 11:05 a.m. and arrives in St. Petersburg about 12:17 p.m. the following day.

At Jacksonville the *Silver Star* splits, so part of the train can travel to Tampa, part to Miami. The *Silver Meteor* splits just south of Kissimmee for the same two destinations, so it's wise to note carefully which cars are going where. Major stops on the New York–Miami run include Newark, Trenton, Philadelphia, Wilmington, Baltimore, Washington, Richmond, Raleigh, Columbia, Charleston, Savannah, and Jacksonville. In 1983 Amtrak inaugurated direct service between Miami and Tampa. Called the *Silver Palm* (isn't that a lovely name?), the train zips between the two cities each day leaving Miami at 8 a.m. and arriving in Tampa at 1:15 p.m. The *Silver Palm* streaks southeast from Tampa to Miami at 4:30 p.m., arriving at 9:30 p.m. The fare is just $39.50 one way, $56 round trip, about a third of the air fare between those cities! This new train stops in Hollywood, Fort Lauderdale, Deerfield Beach, Delray Beach, West Palm Beach, Sebring, Winter Haven, and Lakeland. From Miami and Miami Beach hotels, and from Winter Haven and Tampa, Amtrak offers what it calls "dedicated" bus service. That translates roughly to bus service from hotels in Miami to the train station in Hollywood; from Winter Haven to Walt Disney World and Orlando hotels; and from Tampa to St. Petersburg and Clearwater areas. Very convenient.

To get to the state by train from the Midwest, you may now ride a through-coach via Washington, D.C. To get to Florida by train from the western reaches of the U.S. you go via New Orleans or Atlanta, where you can catch a bus to Jacksonville and reboard the train for the rest of the journey.

You can save a bundle on round-trip "excursion" fares—$150 round trip!—or the railroad's Family Plan (which charges the head of the household full fare; a spouse and/or accompanying child 12 through 21, half fare, and children 2 through 11, one-quarter fare; under 2, free). If you're handicapped or a senior citizen (65 or over), you get a 25% discount on Amtrak.

Amtrak also now has a regional rail travel arrangement that offers money-saving rail travel within and between various regions of the U.S. Ask the line for details of the program, then figure out how you can use it to best advantage.

Since the journey will take 24 hours or more, you might consider a **slumber coach,** which is the railroad's economy sleeper for one or two and includes private toilet facilities. Amtrak's single **roomettes** are a cut above the slumber coach and offer slightly classier and roomier travel. As this guide went to press, slumber coach accommodations cost an additional $49.50 single, $85 double, and a roomette ran $138 single. Amtrak also has a bedroom for two which offers still more space and can accommodate up to four people. The rate for two is $248. Roomettes and bedroom facilities include all meals too.

Food service on trains has changed from the old cooked-aboard style to something approximating airline food service to the current system somewhere between the two. Many meals are prepackaged and heated on the trains, but some are now cooked aboard—including a steak with all the trimmings for just $10! While it may not be the finest of gourmet fare, train chow is easily as good as what you'll eat on an airplane and very reasonably priced in the $7 to $8 range for dinner.

Amtrak has also revived the flagging fortunes of the **Florida Auto Train,** which carries passengers and their cars from Lorton, Virginia (just south of Washington, D.C.), to Sanford, Florida, near Orlando. The Auto Train has domed cars for a good view of passing scenery, and includes a buffet dinner and breakfast in the ticket price. Movies are shown after dinner. Sounds to me like the perfect way to "drive" to Florida. Southbound fares are $130 for adults, $98 for children 2 to 11, and $200 for your car. Northbound fares are the same in the busiest seasons of the year from January to April, but special incentive fares as low as $79 for adults, $59 for children, and $124 for cars are often available when the predominant traffic is southbound. That special northbound offer often occurs from mid-October to mid-January, so be sure to ask, particularly if your plans are flexible. Sleeping accommodations—recommended—in either direction are $225 for a bedroom and $100 for a roomette.

If you're coming to Florida from Europe, you can buy a **USA Railpass** (available only to overseas visitors) at $110 for 7 days, $125 to $375 for 14 days, $450 for 21 days, and $525 for a month of unlimited train travel. Top travel agents like Thomas Cook in England and Cuoni on the continent, plus some airlines, sell the passes.

For information on tour packages and timetables, write to Amtrak Distribution Center, P.O. Box 311, Addison, IL 60101, or call the railroad toll free in any of the continental states. The toll-free number is 800/872-7245.

Amtrak Fares
From (one-way/round-trip)

To	New York	Chicago	Washington
Miami	$168/$336	$175/$239	$151/$302
Orlando	$159/$318	$175/$239	$134/$268
St. Petersburg	$166/$332	$175/$239	$142/$284
Jacksonville	$122/$244	$175/$239	$122/$244

BY BUS: If you like the idea of leaving the driving to them, you might consider traveling to Florida by bus. **Greyhound** and **Trailways** can bring you here from anywhere. What's more, with Trailways' Eagle Pass or Greyhound's Ameripass, you can travel anywhere for a flat fee of about $189 for 7 days, $249 for 15 days, and $349 for 30 days, with extensions available for about $10 a day. Children under 11 pay half fare.

Express buses have cut the time you'll spend getting here, but you still should plan at least 36 hours from Chicago to Miami, about 28 hours from New York, 24 hours from Washington, and about three days from Los Angeles.

Buses offer quite good prices on round-trip excursion tickets.

From (one-way/round-trip)

To	New York	Chicago	Los Angeles	Washington
Miami	$109/$218	$129/$245	$129/$245	$108/$205
Orlando	$109/$218	$120/$228	$99/$245	$96/$182
Jacksonville	$109/$218	$108/$205	$99/$245	$90/$171
St. Petersburg	$109/$218	$120/$229	$99/$245	$108/$205

BY CAR: Hundreds of thousands of Florida travelers get to the Sunshine State by car, arriving after two or three days of leisurely travel through the deep pine forests of Georgia, the tobacco fields of Virginia, the breathtaking mountain vistas of Appalachia, or the serene coastal highways of the Deep South.

Those blessed with stamina, determination, hampers full of road food, and a compulsion not to miss a minute of sunshine, sometimes alternate drivers to arrive from the Northeast or Midwest in 24 to 26 hours. Good roads and plenty of rapid expressways make that possible. Certainly it is less expensive to travel by car despite increasing fuel prices. According to recent figures compiled by the American Automobile Association, you can figure on paying about $136 a couple a day for food, lodging, and car expenses.

If you do drive to Florida, you'll be welcomed with plenty of sunny smiles at the state's **Welcome Centers,** on major arterial roads along Florida's borders. Stations are at major state-line crossing points, including Yulee (I-95), Hillyard (US 1 and US 301), Campbellton (US 231), Jennings (I-75), Pensacola (I-10), and in Tallahassee in the new Capitol Building.

2. Getting Around

BY AIR: Right in there pitching for business in Florida are **Eastern, Republic, Delta, Pan Am** and **People Express.**

Here's a look at what airlines were charging for intrastate one-way travel when this guide went to press: Miami–Jacksonville, $135; Miami–Tampa, $91; Miami–Orlando, $87; Miami–Pensacola, $175; Miami–Tallahassee, $151; Miami–Key West, $40; Jacksonville–Tampa, $102; Orlando–Tallahassee, $110; and Orlando–Tampa, $77.

BY TRAIN: Amtrak trains serve 22 cities in the state with the *Silver Meteor* traveling from Jacksonville to St. Petersburg via Palatka, Deland (for Daytona), Sanford, Winter Park, Orlando, Kissimmee, Lakeland, Tampa, Clearwater, and St. Petersburg. Meanwhile, the *Silver Star* travels from Jacksonville to Miami with stops at Waldo (for Gainesville), Ocala, Wildwood, Kissimmee, Winter Haven, Sebring, West Palm Beach, Delray Beach, Deerfield Beach, Fort Lauderdale, Hollywood, and Miami.

Some sample one-way/round-trip fares are: Jacksonville–St. Petersburg, $33.50/$46.50; Jacksonville–Miami, $52/$72; Jacksonville–Orlando, $20.50/$28.50; Orlando (Kissimmee)—Miami, $38.50/$53; Miami–West Palm Beach, $9.85/$13.80; and Jacksonville–West Palm Beach, $42/$58.

BY BUS: **Greyhound, Trailways,** and local bus lines are listed in each chapter. They make it comparatively easy to get around, particularly in the larger cities, although you will not find in Florida any mass transportation system approximating those in the large cities of the Midwest, Northeast, or Europe.

One-way intrastate fares run from about $5 to about $605, depending on how far you're traveling.

Greyhound offers you a big, free map of its route system in the U.S. too. It's got lots of bus-trip-planning tips and is a great way for the kids to learn geography. You can get one by writing the company at Station 1810, Greyhound Tower, Phoenix, AZ 85077. The company also has several package tours from Miami to Orlando and to various tourist attractions in Orlando.

BY CAR: Florida's emphasis on its two shining lights, the Gold Coast and Orlando's Walt Disney World, has left much of the rest of the state in shadow. If there's one single misconception about the Sunshine State, it is distance.

Distance

You cannot bunk down in Miami Beach, run up to Walt Disney World for the afternoon, and be back in time for the 11 p.m. news. From the southern tip of Florida to the northern border is 500 miles. You'll drive 400 miles to get from Jacksonville on the east coast to Pensacola at the Alabama border, and the rest of this water-fringed peninsula is 100 to 200 miles across.

Florida stretches across two time zones, Eastern in most of the state, Cen-

GETTING AROUND FLORIDA
(Driving Times and Distances)

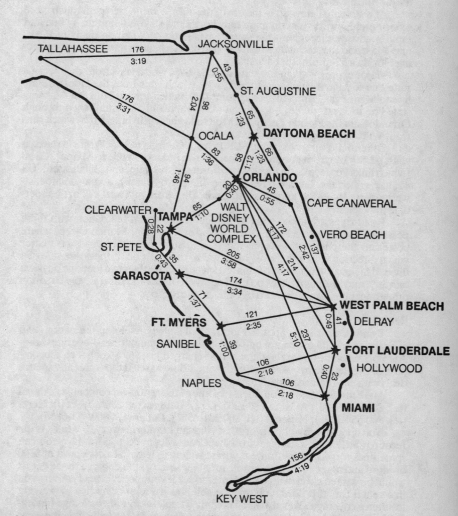

Map courtesy of Alamo Rent A Car

tral in much of the Panhandle. On its limestone surface are 10,000 lakes, more than 166 rivers, and dozens of springs, one so deep nobody has yet found the bottom. Florida is huge and it's . . . flat. Up in the Panhandle near the Georgia border you'll find the state's highest point, all of 345 feet above sea level!

Because it is so flat and so large, Florida has become a driver's state. Miami workers think nothing of driving 25 to 50 miles home each night, and on the state's west coast it can take nearly an hour to get from a hotel on the beach to dinner on the mainland.

Major Routes and Rules

As a state that grew up in the era of the auto, Florida has spent much more money on highways than on mass transportation, so you'll find many fine and rapid roadways throughout the state. Fast as you *could* go on many of them, may I just add that the state's highway patrol seems quite serious about enforcing Florida's 55-m.p.h. speed limit.

Major expressways in the state include **I-95,** which runs from the Georgia state line to Miami via the east coast; **I-75,** which goes from the Georgia state line to Miami via Tampa/St. Petersburg; **I-10,** which travels from the Alabama state line to Jacksonville; **I-4,** which links Tampa and Daytona Beach through Orlando; and the **Florida Turnpike,** a toll road varying in price to $5, which runs from Wildwood in central Florida to Miami.

Other major arteries include **US 1** (from Georgia to Key West via the east coast), **US A1A** (from Fernandina Beach north of Jacksonville to Miami), **US 98** (which links Pensacola, on the western border of the state, and Tallahassee), **US 41,** also called the **Tamiami Trail** (from Tampa to Miami), and a similar east-west artery, **Route 84,** known as **Alligator Alley** from just west of Fort Lauderdale to Naples.

Road rules are about what you'd find anywhere in the nation with these possible exceptions: you can turn right on red lights in Florida except where posted to the contrary; you are required to stop for school buses no matter which direction you or they are going (unless the bus is on the opposite side of a divided highway which has an unpaved space of more than five feet or a physical barrier); and headlights must be used between sunset and sunrise, low beams in other hours if vision is reduced by rain, smoke, or fog.

Rental Cars

Renting a car is cheaper in Florida than anywhere else in the nation, and every major rental-car company—and hundreds of minor ones—operates here. Alamo, one of the budget leaders, in 1985 charged just $69 a week for a subcompact Chevrolet. Be sure to check with your airline to see if they offer any special deals with car-rental companies.

Here are the toll-free numbers of some of the rental-car companies: **Alamo** (tel. 800/327-9633); **Avis** (tel. 800/331-1212); **Budget** (tel. 800/228-9650); **Hertz** (tel. 800/654-3131); **National** (tel. 800/331-4567); **Dollar** (tel. 800/421-6868).

You should know, however, that companies offering very low rates often recoup a little with insurance, for which you will pay $5 to $7 a day. You can sometimes forgo that insurance if you're willing to leave a cash deposit of $300 or more and agree to be responsible for all or some of the damage to the car. It would be wise to check with your insurer to see if your policy already covers you in a rental car. If it does, you may be able to save a lot of money by waiving insurance coverage. You also need not buy complete collision coverage (another $3 or so a day) if you're willing to absorb a $500 to $1000 deductible if the car is damaged.

In Florida, by the way, most rental-car companies set the minimum rental age at 21 for men, 18 for women, when reserving through an airline or travel agent, 25 years old when booking directly. A few have even set a maximum age.

Some of the accoutrements of car touring that make life on the road easier are maps with city insets (and/or city maps purchased as soon as you roll into town), a Styrofoam cooler with ice and some sustenance (in case your hunger and a good restaurant don't occur simultaneously), a plug-in hot pot (or one of those coils that boil water) and instant tea or coffee for morning gratification. (Don't forget that many Florida hotels and motels offer free continental breakfasts that are real time- and money-savers when you're traveling.) Finally, ziplock plastic bags are worth their weight as litter bags, wet laundry holders, and heaven knows how many other uses; foil-wrapped towelettes are great for everything from cleaning windows to cooling a sun-warmed brow.

Chapter II

MIAMI AND
MIAMI BEACH

ACROSS AN ARROW-STRAIGHT CAUSEWAY, over a little rise, and suddenly you drop unceremoniously into a watery wonderland. All around you are waters streaked with turquoise and jade, sandy beaches fringed in palms, a pastel fantasyland so dazzling, so breathtakingly beautiful that you understand in seconds why these twin cities are the most famous resort in the world.

For 50 years Miami Beach has been synonymous with silvery sands, shining waters, breeze-kissed palms, sun-filled days, the good life, the ultimate resort. You've scoffed and jeered at the adjectives only to arrive here one day and discover that absolutely every one of them is true!

Try as they will to build separate identities, these two cities are irrevocably linked by climate and focus, by past and future. Surrounded by two dozen communities, Miami and Miami Beach are now physically joined into one giant metropolis that encompasses much of the southern tip of the state. Each year they lure here nearly 14 million travelers in search of sun, sand, sea, and the resort life that taught the world the meaning of glamorous.

So famous are the duo that they seem always to have been here, the brevity of their history eclipsed by the magnitude of their fame. Yet not much more than half a century ago, "binder boys" stood on the sidewalks of Miami hawking real estate that turned paupers into millionaires and back again in months. That those hucksters were able to sell a piece of mangrove swamp and mosquito-infested jungle is thanks, they say, to a miracle wrought by one Julia Tuttle, a shrewd and feisty lady who knew how to say plenty without talking much. If the legends are true, Ms. Tuttle very much wanted railroad magnate Henry Flagler to toot his little train to Miami. Flagler didn't think much of the idea and made no move southward until the day a freak freeze created frozen orange juice as far south as Palm Beach. When Julia heard about the citrus damage, she sent Flagler a blooming branch of orange blossoms from toasty Miami. He extended his railroad and the boom was on.

Ten years earlier a wooden bridge was all that connected Miami to Miami Beach. Avocado farmer John Collins, whose name now graces the main boulevard of Miami Beach, used it to get his crop to market until he dumped that career and sold 1600 acres of unprofitable avocado farm to Carl Fisher. Fisher, who had made a fortune in automobile headlights and built the Indianapolis Speedway, could afford the gamble. His money and a pump soon dredged sand from the bay bottom and wrought a man-made island called Miami Beach. Miracle that it was, Fisher's efforts were not heard round the world. At one point the despairing millionaire offered to *give* a solid block of oceanfront land to anyone who would build a hotel on it. Alas, there were no takers. When Florida's real estate boom swung into high gear in the 1920s, Fisher was said to have acquired a worth of $100 million. When everything bottomed in 1929, he lost almost as much.

But in the years that followed, Miami Beach, the starlet, got itself discovered. Up went hotel after endless hotel, each more amazing than the last, each trying to grab the traveler's attention with facades that have to be seen to be believed. On one, a giant sea maiden, plaster hair streaming out over the driveway, holds aloft what is either a trident or the biggest rat-tailed comb in town. Collins Avenue's hotel row is a sight like no other in the world, one no Florida traveler should miss. It's a drive that will amaze you and amuse you, and, finally, help you to understand this bizarre and sometimes slightly berserk city that's the epitome of blatant, blaring resortomania, an island at once garish and childishly touching, sophisticated and naïve, the never-say-die grande dame of resorts.

Meanwhile, across the causeways, miles from the island of Miami Beach, an already-big city is bursting at the seams. Discovered by international visitors, this young city of Miami is on the grow again. In five years it has added the world's largest Holiday Inn, posh marble-clad hotels operated by Italian, Spanish, and British chains, a plush new Hyatt hotel, and a huge new conference center. Real estate is once again selling with a vigor the binder boys would have loved. These days Miami is a major international banking center and home to so many South American corporations that most of the city's population can now manage an occasional *gracias*.

In this burgeoning metropolis you can revel in posh and plush hotels or sneak off to shady suburbs like Coral Gables, Key Biscayne, and Coconut Grove; drink thick, black coffee amid the chatter of Little Havana; and explore beaches and neighborhoods that easily rival Miami Beach's glamor. You can be entertained in glitzy showrooms, dine in some of the nation's best restaurants, chortle at the antics of parrots and porpoises, and see one of the nation's great cities in the throes of yet another metamorphosis.

1. Getting There and Getting Around

GETTING THERE: No fewer than 78 airlines fly into **Miami International Airport,** so you shouldn't have any trouble getting here. Domestic carriers include American, Continental, Delta, Eastern, Northwest Orient, Ozark, People Express, Piedmont, Republic, TWA, United, and USAir. Air Canada brings thousands of Canadians south, Lufthansa comes in from Germany, and British

Airways flies directly here from the British Isles. Every South and Latin American nation and every Caribbean country with a flag carrier flies it into Miamai. The few European flag carriers that do not fly directly here have connections from other cities. You'll land in the western section of the city at Lejeune Road and NW 36th Street.

Miami's International Airport has in recent years become a thoroughly modern Millie. International travelers zip out to awaiting aircraft on a whooshing monorail. Concourses are lined with smart and fascinating boutiques featuring an array of products as international as the passengers who arrive here. So sophisticated has this airport become, in fact, that you can do your banking here, exchange currency, buy American Indian—or Asian Indian—creations, seek information in several languages (most prominent of which is Spanish), even play electronic games!

If you want to do some shopping while you wait for a plane, stow your gear in a locker and trot off. Lockers are located near exit doors and baggage storage facilities that will take care of your treasures for days are located at Concourse B on the upper level, Concourse F on the lower level. Lockers are 50¢ or less for 24 hours; storage is several dollars a day depending on how much you're storing.

If you need help with anything ranging from directions to a hotel room, a multilingual staff is on duty in person from 7 a.m. to 11 p.m. At other hours you can still get your questions answered: a telephone at the Information Desk (tel. 871-7515) is manned around the clock. In peak season—winter, of course—the Information Desk staff has an up-to-date list of hotel vacancies to help you find a room. At any time of year the staff can supply you with a list of area hotels arranged by price. The desk is on the second level of the airport at Concourse E. Paging is also done from this desk.

The airport has a raft of fast-food eateries and a quite elegant dining room, Top of the Port Restaurant, that's become a popular spot. Prices are on the high side of moderate, but this is definitely the most tranquil spot in the airport.

Dade County's Metropolitan Transit Authority has four **bus** routes that pass through thcan supply you with a list of area hotels arranged by price. The desk is on the second level of the airport at Concourse E. Paging is also done from this desk.

Red Top Airport Limousines (tel. 526-5764) will take you to downtown and Miami Beach hotels for about $7, and also go to cities along the Gold Coast as far north as Fort Lauderdale. The fare is $10 per person to Fort Lauderdale, where you can board another limo that will take you to cities farther north.

Like many big cities, Miami got many complaints about rude cabbies who loathed the idea of losing their place in the airport taxi line-up to take some unsuspecting arrival on a short hop to local airport-area hotels. Miami solved that problem by creating a fleet of "blue cabs" (they're all painted a bright blue) officially known as **Airport Area Taxi Service.** So if you're staying in a hotel near the airport, save yourself a lot of grief by looking for the blue cabs. Rates are the same.

Be warned, too, that some less-than-scrupulous folks who happen to own big black limousines often pull up at arrival gates and offer to drive you to hotels. If you've got a big family or are traveling with several other people, you may be able to strike a good deal. Otherwise, forget it and stick with the taxis and the official limousine service (which uses medium-size white vans).

If you're renting a car, don't forget that rental-car companies provide free transportation to their airport-area rental offices.

And don't forget that many large hotels near the airport and even downtown may provide free transportation.

Miami's airport, by the way, is just eight miles from downtown, about $10 by **cab.**

Amtrak trains roll in here too, twice a day, making their most southerly stop at 8303 NW 37th Ave. (tel. 638-7300).

Greyhound and **Trailways** buses come from all over the nation and the state to terminals downtown. Greyhound is at 950 NE 2nd Ave. (tel. 374-7222) and Trailways is at 99 NE 4th St. (tel. 373-6561).

GETTING AROUND: Dozens of **rental-car companies** operate in the city at rates that change frequently but average about $80 to $100 a week. **Alamo,** at 1490 NW Lejeune Rd. (tel. 526-6510), is a strong budget contender and can always be counted on for competitive rates. **Greyhound** has an office in the terminal and at other locations, and also offers budget rates. All except the smallest local companies (and even many of those) will pick you up at the airport, take you to your car, then deliver you when you leave town, all at no charge. **Avis,** 255 NE 1st St. (tel. 377-2531), **Hertz,** 666 Biscayne Blvd. (tel. 377-4601), and **National** (tel. 526-6200) all have in-airport rental desks at Miami International.

Yellow Cab (tel. 444-4444) operates many, many taxis in town. That cab company, and all others, charge $1 at the drop, $1.20 a mile. **Metro Cab** (tel. 888-8888) is another large city cab company.

Buses operated by the Metropolitan Dade County Transit Authority (tel. 638-6700) take you anywhere in the county for 75¢, and workers will be happy to give you information on routes. The service operates from about dawn to dusk. In downtown Miami there is a **shuttle bus,** the Round Towner, which plies Biscayne Boulevard. It costs 35¢.

Miami's proudest new acquisition is its sleek **MetroRail,** a whizzing aboveground rapid transit system that at the moment transports passengers between downtown Miami and South Miami. Within the next couple of years the line will extend north to Hialeah and west to Miami International Airport. Rides are $1. You can find out the exact schedule for the train by calling 638-6700.

From south to north, the stations by name and address are: Dadeland South (9150 Dadeland Blvd.), Dadeland North (8300 S. Dixie Hwy.), South Miami (5949 Sunset Dr. at SW 7th St.), University (5500 Ponce de Leon Blvd.), Douglas Road (3100 SW 37th Ave. at Douglas Road), Coconut Grove (2780 SW 27th Ave.), Vizcaya (3201 SW First Ave.), Brickell (101 SW First Ave.), Government Center (101 NW 1st St.), Overtown (100 NW 6th St.), Culmer (701 NW 11th St.), Civic Center (1501 NW 12th Ave.), Santa Clara (2050 NW 12th Ave.), Allapattah (3501 NW 12th Ave.), Earlington Heights (2100 NW 41st. St.), Brownsville (5200 NW 27th Ave.), Martin Luther King, Jr. (6205 NW 27th Ave.), Northside (3150 NW 79th St.), Hialeah (115 E. 21st St.), and Okeechobee (205 W. Okeechobee Rd.).

I wouldn't recommend **bicycles** for much downtown travel, but if you're staying in the suburbs or over on Miami Beach (and can keep a sharp eye out for gawking drivers), you can enjoy a bicycle here. That's particularly true in Coral Gables and Coconut Grove, where you'll find bicycle trails. The Metro-Dade Department of Tourism (tel. 305/375-4694) can supply you with a brochure, *Miami on Two Wheels,* which maps out some pretty trips around town. On Miami Beach, try the **Miami Beach Bicycle Center,** 923 W. 39th St. (tel. 531-4161), and in Coconut Grove, **Dade Cycle Shops,** 3043 Grand Ave. (tel. 443-6075). Key Biscayne is a bicyclist's heaven—**Key Biscayne Mangrove Bicycle Rentals** at 260 Crandon Blvd.(tel. 361-7284) can supply you with two wheels. Rates are $7.50 a day.

2. Orientation

Despite their best efforts to build separate identities, Miami and Miami Beach are to most people the same place, with surrounding communities tossed casually into the amalgam. Boundary lines in this huge metropolis have long been fuzzed by border-to-border expansion, but part of the fun of visiting the area is discovering these cities within cities. Here's a look at some of them.

MIAMI BEACH: In the 1930s the southern tip of the beach, now known as **South Beach,** *was* Miami Beach. With the current revival of interest in the 1930s and in art deco, this end of the beach is getting more attention than ever. It is now listed on the National Register of historic places for its more than 100 unique art deco buildings. Two amazing renovations here, the Victor and Cardozo Hotels, are so beautifully done that you'll step right into a time machine and back to the days of F. Scott Fitzgerald.

Speaking of the old, that's something you see a lot of on South Beach in winter, for this is the gathering place of elderly visitors who have been coming for decades to the same room in the same hotel to sit in the same porch chair and talk to the same friends. It's a sociological study that's excited many a budding anthropologist and is indeed something to see: mah-jong on the sand, day-long gossips, and impromptu vaudeville performances by talent that is rusty but lusty.

In the middle of the beach is Hotel Row, and in the middle of that is the only hotel in the world that's always been a tourist attraction, the fabled Fontainebleau. Thousands stream, gawking, through this hotel each year, and enough hotel stationery disappears for each guest to write 35 letters!

A little farther north are the handsome cities of **Surfside** and **Bal Harbour,** the latter the site of posh Bal Harbour Shops where at Gucci's enclave a dignified gentleman at the door ushers you into hushed recesses.

These days Miami Beach is crowing over its "new" beach, a $65-million strip of silica widened by a dredging operation that pumped enough offshore sand onto the beach to create a 300-foot-wide strip. There's a mile-long beach boardwalk too.

MIAMI: **Coral Gables,** just south of Miami, was the creation of a dreamer named George Merrick, who in the early 1900s built a charming city of stone archways, an imposing city hall, and a swimming pool that's often called one of the world's most beautiful swimming holes. The Biltmore Hotel, a city landmark and a lovely old-world creation with frescoed ceilings, is now the Metropolitan Museum and Art Center. In Coral Gables is the University of Miami's 260-acre campus and 20,000 students.

Coconut Grove is past and present linked. In its shady streets "old" Miami lives on, attracting artists, crafts workers, wealthy escapists, international boutiques. Bohemians and billionaires mix with ease here, and once a year at the February Art Festival all the rest of the city drops in to stir the batter. Antique Coconut Grove Theater presents outstanding plays and Dinner Key Marina is stem to stern in sailing craft. Coconut Grove has the oldest streets in the county and more 19th-century buildings than any other area of South Florida.

Key Biscayne is "the beach" to much of Miami, so on weekends a nightmarish line of traffic forms at the causeway entrance to the key. Once past the 50¢ tollbooth, you'll discover why everyone streams here for sunshine. Beautiful strips of sand line both sides of the causeway and shallow waters lap at the shore. On the key, jungly Crandon Park offers more than two miles of sand.

In downtown Miami on SW 8th Street you'll find Miami's **Little Havana,** an area revitalized by Castro-fleeing Cubans in the early 1960s. Today it's a lilting, laughing melange of Latin nightclubs, inexpensive restaurants, strolling *tunas* (singers), a touch of Old Spain.

Downtown along Biscayne Boulevard is Bayfront Park, 62 acres of tropical blooms, pools, shady walkways, with a bandshell where open-air concerts are performed free and the Torch of Friendship burns, honoring Miami's ties with Latin American neighbors. A few blocks north, massive cruise ships line up at **Dodge Island** like fat ducks as they drop off and pick up passengers headed for Caribbean isles and ports around the globe. It's now the busiest cruise port in the world, with more than a million passengers each year.

A LITTLE GEOGRAPHY: Getting around these cities can be an exasperating business if you try to travel during the rush hours (from 7 to 9 a.m. and from 4 to 6 p.m.) and if you don't buy a map and get your bearings. Here's a cartographer's look at what you'll find here.

Miami is divided into quadrants by **Flagler Street** and **Miami Avenue.** Courts, avenues, and places run north-south, streets and terraces east-west, with numbers starting downtown and going up in outlying areas. Note the NW, SW, etc., in addresses or you're lost. **Biscayne Boulevard** is also US 1, and runs north-south through downtown.

On Miami Beach, **Collins Avenue** is the number one thoroughfare, running north-south all the way up the seven-mile island. East-west streets are numbered from one on the south. Six causeways link Miami and Miami Beach. From south to north they are at 5th Street (McArthur Causeway); just north of 17th Street at Dade Boulevard (Venetian Causeway), connecting to downtown Miami; at 41st Street (Julia Tuttle Causeway), connecting to the airport; at 71st Street (North Bay Causeway); at 96th Street (Broad Causeway), for Miami addresses above 79th Street; and at 163rd Street on Miami Beach connecting to 167th Street on the Mainland (163rd Street or Sunny Isles Causeway).

I-95 is the quick route north from Miami, and is also the closest expressway to downtown Miami and the beaches. Farther west, the **Palmetto Expressway** and the **Florida Turnpike** both head north and south.

Traffic is hideous at rush hours and parking is a real problem. Garages downtown and on Miami Beach will save your nerves even if they do cost a few dollars.

To get to the suburbs from downtown Miami, first take US 1 south. Then turn left at Rickenbacker Causeway for Key Biscayne. At the next traffic light on US 1 (South Bayshore Drive), bear left for Coconut Grove. Turn right off US 1 at Coral Way (SW 22nd Avenue) to get to Coral Gables.

USEFUL INFORMATION: For **police or medical emergency,** call 911 anywhere in the county. . . . For **doctor or dental referrals,** call the Dade County Medical or Dental Association (tel. 326-1177 for a doctor, 667-3647 for a dentist). . . . For quick cleaning, call **Parisian Cleaners** (tel. 576-2450) and ask for the location nearest you. . . . **Eckerd Drugs** at 4878 Biscayne Blvd. (tel. 576-4374) and several other locations can fill prescriptions 24 hours a day. . . . **Pantry Pride** grocery stores are all over the county and open around the clock.

TOURIST INFORMATION: The **Miami Beach Visitor and Convention Authority,** 555 17th St., Miami Beach, FL 33139 (tel. 305/673-7070), has lots of brochures and information on current and future events, and employees who keep up with *every* detail. . . . The **Miami Beach Chamber of Commerce,** 1920 Meridien Ave., Miami Beach, FL 33139 (tel. 305/672-1270), will be happy to help you too. . . . The **Southern Florida Resort Hotel Association,** 6801 Collins

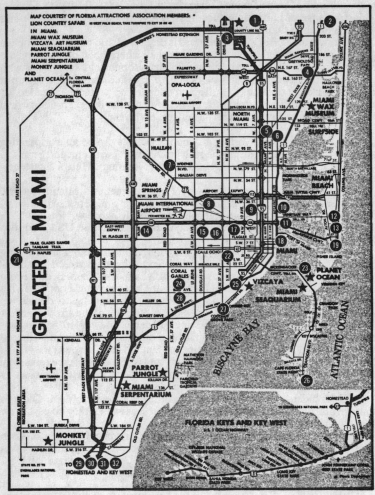

Copyright © Pierre Dupeyroux

Ave., Miami Beach, FL 33139 (tel. toll free 800/531-3553, or 305/864-2288), will ask its members to send you hotel information. The friendly folks at the **Coral Gables Chamber of Commerce** will see that you get a self-guided tour map so you can investigate this lovely city. They're at 50 Aragon Ave., Coral Gables, FL 33134 (tel. 305/446-1657). . . . The **Coconut Grove Chamber of Commerce** has all the answers about its arty community and will help you if you'll stop by 3437B Main Hwy., Coconut Grove, FL 33133 or call them at 305/444-7270. . . . The same applies to the **Key Biscayne Chamber of Commerce**, at 95 W. McIntier St., Key Biscayne, FL 33149 (tel. 305/361-5207). . . . In Miami, the **City of Miami Office of Public Information,** at 174 E. Flagler St. (tel. 305/579-6327), has information on the city, but for the big picture call the **Metro Dade Department of Tourism,** 234 W. Flagler St., Miami, FL 33130 (tel. 305/375-4694), where very well-informed folks seem to know everything about everything in Greater Miami and the beaches.

KEY TO THE NUMBERED POINTS OF INTEREST ON THE GREATER MIAMI MAP: 1. Lion Country Safari; 2. Seminole Okalee Indian Village (4 mi. north on U.S. 441); 3. Gulfstream Park Race Track; 4. Calder Race Course; 5. 163rd St. Shopping Center; 6. Monastery of St. Bernard; 7. Florida International Univ.; 8. Miami Wax Museum; 9. Bal Harbour Shops; 10. Biscayne Kennel Club; 11. Barry College; 12. Westland Mall; 13. Hialeah Race Track; 14. Decorator's Row; 15. Miami Jai-Alai Fronton; 16. Fashion District; 17. Miami Stadium; 18. Omni Mall; 19. Watson Park; 20. Miami Beach Theater of Performing Arts; 21. Lincoln Road Mall; 22. Midway Mall; 23. Expo Center; 24. Flagler Kennel Club; 25. Dade County Auditorium; 26. Orange Bowl; 28. Flagler Street; 29. Bayfront Park; 30. On Tamiami Trail; 31. Florida International Univ.; 32. "Little Havana"; 33. Miracle Mile; 34. Marine Stadium; 35. Planet Ocean; 36. Metropolitan Museum & Art Center; 37. Museum of Science, Planetarium, Historical Museum; 38. Vizcaya Art Museum; 39. Miami Seaquarium; 40. Mayfair Mall; 41. Coconut Grove Expo Center; 42. Univ. of Miami, Lowe Art Museum; 43. Dadeland Mall; 44. Parrot Jungle; 45. Fairchild Tropical Garden; 46. Historical Lighthouse & Museum; 47. The Falls; 48. Metro-Zoo; 49. Monkey Jungle; 50. Cutter Ridge Mall; 51. Orchid Jungle; 52. Coral Castle; 53. Key West Conch Tour Train

3. Where to Stay

How much you pay for a hotel room hereabouts depends on where it is, when it is, and how much ocean you can see from the window.

On Miami Beach, the luxury strip known as Hotel Row extends from Lincoln Road to Surfside and Bal Harbour, where it gives way to more moderately priced accommodations on Motel Row. On South Beach—with two notable exceptions—hotels are old and look it, frequently offering very basic accommodations that are little more than roof and bed. Prices are lower, but I don't think they're low enough to compensate.

When you go can make as much as a 50% difference in the bottom line of your motel bill. Traditionally, rates drop just after Easter and stay very low until about Thanksgiving, although these days international summer travelers are blurring those traditional seasonal dips a bit. On the other side of the coin, you can now find more services and entertainment in summer as the area reaches for year-round-destination status.

In downtown Miami prices are high all the time (as they are in most cities), but you'll find some very luxurious hotels for your money.

Miami and Miami Beach have been resorts for a long, long time, so you can be sure all but the very smallest motels have color televisions, phones, and swimming pool (although sometimes they're saltwater), so except where those things are missing I haven't mentioned what most travelers take for granted these days. I've also divided hotels first by location and then in descending order by price.

BED AND BREAKFAST: An interesting way to see it like a native in Miami is via the B&B home-away-from-home. Here the **Tropical Isles Bed and Breakfast** is operated by Ursula Mucci, P.O. Box 490382, Key Biscayne, FL 33149 (tel. 305/361-2937). (Ursula can lead you to a lagoon where you can swim with tame fish.) Another similar operation, **Bed & Breakfast Company**, is headed by Marcella Schaible, P.O. Box 262, South Miami, FL 33243 (tel. 305/661-3270).

HOTELS IN MIAMI BEACH: Hotels on the beach are naturally more expensive, but when they're beautiful, they're *very* beautiful. Prices change rapidly and seasonally here too, so anticipate slightly higher figures to give your budget some breathing space. You'll always save money by forgoing ocean-front or ocean-view rooms, which can be 50% higher than less desirable views.

The Luxury Leaders

The flagship, landmark, and number one pride and joy of Miami Beach is the **Fontainebleau Hilton**, 4441 Collins Ave., Miami Beach, FL 33140 (tel. 305/538-2000; there are toll-free numbers in every state), a 14-story tower-ing mass of concrete that curves its elegant way around nearly half a mile of oceanfront. So famous was this strip of real estate that until the Hilton moved in a few years back, the hotel felt it unnecessary to put its name out front—if you didn't know this was the Fontainebleau you didn't deserve to know!

Owner Stephen Muss put $43 million into a massive renovation of the Fon-tainebleau Hilton's fading elegance and began with a quite incredible rock grot-to swimming pool. In the middle of this 140- by 140-foot creation, water cascades down a five-story half-acre man-made mountain containing a Lagoon Saloon. Around the pool are three whirlpools, a beachfront bar, and masses of tropical foliage that creates a jungly waterside hideaway between hotel and beach. On the walkway to the pool is an open-air café under the trees, where a calypso band plays. Inside the sweeping lobby, a tall ficus tree reaches up from the center of a huge round bar to an overhead skylight. Nothing is small here. You can get lost in the lobby. You will certainly get scrambled in the maze of corridors and shops.

When Hilton renovated "the Font," all the furniture was refinished and double and king-size beds were built especially for the hotel. Color schemes differ—peach, lime green, sky blue, golden yellow—so at least you have a chance of finding the right room! All of them have big closets and separate dressing rooms, loads and loads of room to walk around in, and balconies if you want one.

On 16 acres here you'll find 1224 rooms, including 60 suites, two outdoor pools, 30 cabanas, windsurfing and other water sports, a two-level tennis com-plex, shuttle service to a nearby golf course, 11 different spots for dining and drinking, including the sophisticated Poodle Lounge and Steak House with black walls, shining crystal, mirrors, art deco decor, and an eye-popping black lounge with dramatic lighting focusing on pale-pink female manne-quins surrounded by huge transparent bubbles. The Dining Galleries are a cluster of restaurants filled with antiques and art treasures, and feature four different dazzlingly contemporary dining spots. The service is wonder-ful.

To read the figures on numbers of employees here (144 maids, 275 food workers) or the quantities consumed (4000 fresh oranges squeezed every day) is to gain just the slightest idea how huge, how slick this great hotel is. One owner humbly termed it the "eighth wonder of the world."

To stay in the Fontainebleau Hilton is to hobnob with moviemakers and stars, national leaders, kings, shahs. Television shows and movies have been filmed here (*Tony Rome, Goldfinger,* "Surfside 6," Ed Sullivan's "Toast of the Town"). Stars have stopped here: Frank Sinatra, Gary Cooper, Joe DiMaggio, Lana Turner, and Joan Crawford (who got a standing ovation as she strolled through the lobby). The famous and the infamous have called it home. Today the Fontainebleau Hilton lives on, a shining star that's found a fountain of youth. You'll pay $125 to $180 double daily from December to May, $275 to $550 for suites (there's even one for $1200). In summer, prices certainly don't crash, but they do drop: to $95 to $150 daily for two, $220 to $425 for larger quarters.

Up the street a bit, the **Doral-on-the-Ocean,** 4833 Collins Ave., Miami Beach, FL 33140 (tel. 305/532-3600, or toll free 800/327-6334), would be enough all by itself, but when you team it with its western sister, the posh **Doral Country Club,** you've got it all. When you stay at either of these two quite beautiful hotels you can use all the facilities at the other, and there are even daytime shuttles to get you back and forth. At the oceanfront property, an impressive baroque decor greets you, and equally impressive rooms offer refrigerators, separate dressing rooms, even bathroom phones. Doral's Starlight supper club is an enchanting place, with tiny lights sparkling in the ceiling. Doubles in season range from $124 to $136, and in other months are $90 to $120 (about $20 higher at the Country Club).

Eden Roc Americana, 4525 Collins Ave., Miami Beach, FL 33140 (tel. 305/531-0000), has for more than 30 years been one of the stars of Miami Beach hotels. Now operated by Americana Hotels, this show spot is looking showier than ever these days thanks to yet another renovation, a project the hotel likes to call not a renovation but a rehabilitation. "When you've got a wonderful hotel like this one filled with huge crystal chandeliers and marble and brass, you don't just tear it out and start over, you rehabilitate it and bring it back to its original beauty," the hotel's director of sales reports proudly. Well, rehabilitate they have.

You'll still find the same spacious rooms, but now they're dolled up with what seems to be acres of marble in the bathrooms and walls-full of mirrors in the rooms. Deep jewel tones appear in some rooms while others are outfitted in muted earthy shades. A brand-new fixture in the hotel: Sadie's, a New York deli complete with bunches of sausages hanging on the walls, big bowls of green tomatoes and pickles on the tables, and Israeli music for entertainment. Still there but prettier than ever is the resort's Porch Restaurant and its ocean-view lounge, which also offers you an underwater look at what's going on in the swimming pool. Summer rates at the Americana are $65 to $125, and winter rates about twice that.

A recent renovation at the **Sheraton Bal Harbour,** 9701 Collins Ave., Miami Beach, FL 33154 (tel. 305/865-7511, or toll free 800/325-3535), turned this hotel into an even showier showplace than it already was. First they redecorated the Bal Masque supper club, famed for its Las Vegas showgirl revues; then they redesigned the lobby to create Caribbean color schemes of green and blue with jade marble floors. A two-story atrium enclosed in glass has a cascading fountain and a lobby bar features exotic seashells encased in resins. Twin pools were connected by a landscaped waterway, and an original Lalique mask of an elegant sea lady sets the tone for a coral and gray dining room punctuated by polished steel. Rooms here are very large with contemporary decor. Some have balconies overlooking the sea, some are penthouse suites, and some are lanais by the pool. Rates for two are $135 to $180 in peak season, $80 to $115 in other months (oceanfront terrace suites and lanais are higher). Children under 18 are free.

Konover Hotel, 5445 Collins Ave., Miami Beach, FL 33140 (tel. 305/865-1500, or toll free 800/327-0535), used to be a Playboy hotel and still has that plush dramatic look you find at Playboy operations: sweeps of thick carpets, vivid colors, attractive paintings, contemporary decor, even a black-glass facade that once sported the rabbit. Now it's a newly refurbished property sporting **a**

Las Vegas–type revue, a big swimming pool and wading pool, sauna, exercise rooms and solarium, a lounge with dance music, a coffeeshop, and a handsome dining room. Nicest of all is a hard-working staff that really seems to go out of its way to make you happy. Two people pay $89 to $115 in winter, $69 to $89 in other seasons.

The **Deauville Hotel** lobby is a knockout and the rest of this stunning 550-room hotel matches. Right on the ocean at 6701 Collins Ave., Miami Beach, FL 33141 (tel. 305/865-8511, or toll free 800/327-6656), the Deauville glitters with chandeliers and glows with contemporary furniture scattered about a massive lobby where the sun gleams through two-story windows. Upstairs in your room you'll find oversize beds, walk-in closets, mirrored walls, and lovely ocean views through a wall of glass. Outside is all that beach, plus three tennis courts, a glamorous saltwater swimming pool surrounded by lounge chairs for sunning, a whirlpool, sauna, and an exercise room. Inside are a dramatic black lounge with a piano bar, a top nightclub, and an elegant candlelit dining room where chefs present outstanding cuisine amid glittering crystal chandeliers, silver, and fresh flowers. From mid-December to May, two people pay $85 to $115, $55 to $75 in other months.

Giant crystal chandeliers glitter in the enormous lobby of the **Carillon Beach Hotel,** 6801 Collins Ave., Miami Beach, FL 33140 (tel. 305/861-4242, or toll free 800/327-7729), another of Miami Beach's glamorous Hotel Row resorts. At the Carillon you're right in the middle of Miami Beach, but if you want some wide open spaces you can get them at Doral Country Club, where you can play golf or tennis free as a Carillon guest. Very pretty rooms, with lots of glass so you can look out over the Atlantic, are decorated in light, bright colors. There's always dancing and entertainment in the Silver Screen lounge and haute cuisine in the Delmonico Room. Rates for double rooms in season run from $69 to $89, dropping to $59 to $79 in other months.

You get two hotels for the price of one at the **Sans Souci,** 3101 Collins Ave. (tel. 305/531-8261), and the **Versailles,** 3425 Collins Ave. (tel. 305/531-6092, or toll free 800/327-3144), both Miami Beach, FL 33140. Such a buddy system do these two beachfront hotels have that when you stay at one you can use all the facilities of the other as well. Between them there isn't much missing.

The Sans Souci is the smaller of the two, although not by much, with 258 rooms overlooking the ocean and a big, big swimming pool capped by a high diving board. Earthy colors and contrasting deep navies and beiges give the San Souci's rooms a contemporary look. There's a *très chic* lobby where you can watch the passing parade in the comfort of puffy couches and an up-to-the-minute decor. Rooms have big picture windows, and on the upper stories you can get a pelican's-eye view of the action on the beach from a private balcony. There is stereo music, as well as a color television and refrigerator in all rooms. For evening entertainment there's a lounge and lobby bar, the Electric Island disco and Terrace dining room.

Atop the Versailles Hotel is a gold-domed architectural furbelow that's a landmark on Miami Beach. Beneath that dome are 275 smartly decorated rooms full of bright colors and capped by big picture windows overlooking all that blue ocean outside. Also an oceanside property, the Versailles has lots of entertainment: a poolside bar, a Hide-Away lounge, a nightclub with razzle-dazzle entertainment, a pizza pub, a lobby bar, and eating places green with plants and gardeny with lattice trim. You can find something to eat here from morning to midnight. Any time of year there's a steady round of activities at these two hotels, where rates range from $60 to $90 from mid-December to late April (higher prices at the Sans Souci for oceanfront rooms), $39 to $52 in other months.

If the reflection in your mirror some morning is more appalling than appealing, rush right to the phone and call **Harbor Island Spa,** 7900 Harbor Island, Miami Beach, FL 33141 (tel. 305/751-7561, or toll free 800/327-7510), where they'll calm you down and invite you for a renovation. It's all here: yoga, free massages, steamroom, sauna, whirlpool, mineral-water swimming pool, health bar, diet-controlled chowline, golf, tennis, lanais, and lots of evening entertainment so you can dance off a few calories. Rooms are attractively furnished and have the basic amenities, plus you'll be treated to facials, herbal wraps, evening movies, vitamin pills, and Roman pools. In summer there's an "11 nights for the price of 7" deal at $82 to $145 *per person.* In winter, prices began at about $80 to $110 per day *per person.*

Harbour House, 102nd Street at the ocean, 10275 Collins Ave., Miami Beach, FL 33154 (tel. 305/864-2251), has thought of everything: not only does every one of the very attractive rooms have a kitchen, but there's even a gourmet grocery in the building. You're greeted by an elegant marble lobby and treated to a formal dining room, an inviting lounge, tennis, a putting green, a full mile of beach, a solarium, and two swimming pools. The spacious rooms have pretty touches like Victorian wicker chairs, bright floral prints, a couch for lazy-day reclining, and dazzling views of the ocean from private balconies. Outside, the beautifully landscaped grounds are a tranquil spot to stroll past bubbling fountains and swaying palms. Harbour House rises 14 stories into the sky, and goes on and on with extras: art galleries and classes, beauty and barber shops, a health club, boutiques, even a doctor and dentist in the building. A very big and lovely spot, in summer Harbour House charges $46 to $73, depending on the view, and $74 to $114 in winter.

There's an air of subdued elegance at the **Sea View Hotel,** 9909 Collins Ave., Miami Beach, FL 33154 (tel. 305/866-4441), where you'll find tasteful furnishings in jewel-like colors. The renovated lobby, terrace room, and a cocktail lounge lend a European elegance. Rooms here are very large, with lots of closet space and pretty dark-wood furniture, arched headboards, and contemporary touches. (Refrigerators are available if you ask.) Outside this posh and pleasant address is a full mile of private sand, a huge pool, cabanas, shuffleboard courts, a solarium. They're happy to point out that servants' and chauffeurs' quarters are also available. Poolside, there's a snack counter and bar, and for other meals there's a formal dining room with dinner dances and a very handsome paneled lounge for sundown celebrating. For a quiet and elegant stay here you'll pay $77 to $130 from mid-December to mid-April, $44 to $70 in other months.

First-Class Hotels

A clever designer at **Palms on the Ocean,** 9449 Collins Ave., Surfside, FL 33154 (tel. 305/865-3551, or toll free 800/327-6644), made a couch out of a bed and created a room divider at the same time, so rooms here are now larger than ever. A renovation program equipped rooms with new dark carpets offset by bedspreads in bright earth tones. In the resort's Coconut Lounge the beat goes on nightly, and an outdoor terrace is a serene spot for dining. Winter rates, from

December through April, are $69 to $90 double. In other months, rates drop to $35 to $64 for two.

I could sit forever on a balcony at the **Thunderbird,** 18401 Collins Ave., Miami Beach, FL 33160 (tel. 305/931-7700, or toll free 800/327-2044), and when you see what a tranquil spot this is, you may do likewise. You'll get into the tropical ambience when you step into the lobby where palms grow up to the ceiling in a lush garden. You'll really ease into things when you see big bright rooms with two double beds (or a king-size bed) in a trim contemporary setting with white furniture. You'll be immersed when you see the view over the pool and ocean from your balcony or terrace. The Thunderbird is home to Christine Lee's Gaslight Restaurant, one of the city's best loved Chinese restaurants. If you're a tennis player, you can lob free here, and if you'd like to learn to waterski, they'll give you a lesson free. Windsurfing's a new sport here too. In winter season, two people pay $70 to $96 and in summer, $40 to $52, with higher prices for an oceanfront or poolside lanai.

Beacharbour, 189th Street and Collins Avenue, Sunny Isles, FL 33160 (tel. 305/931-8900, or toll free 800/327-2042), is a slick harbor for visitors to drop anchor. Big, big picture windows overlook manicured grounds; carpeted terraces view sweeping vistas of white sands and blue Atlantic. You can watch the waves from the hotel's dining room too, or sneak off to a patio bar to listen to musical entertainment. Lots of entertainment here from a nifty revue to a piano lounge and poolside warblers. In-room movies are a special feature, and all rooms have refrigerators to store your afternoon snacks. There's a private beach, Olympic-size pool, another heated pool, and a kiddie splasher. A double room costs $40 to $80 (view is everything) from mid-December to May, $30 to $40 in other months.

If you like apartment living, **Beekman Towers,** 9499 Collins Ave., Miami Beach, FL 33154 (tel. 305/861-5313), is a plush central address featuring luxurious one- or two-bedroom apartments with all the conveniences of home (maybe more). You'll have lots and lots of space here, where living rooms are 15 by 29 feet, for instance, and open onto private terraces overlooking lovely sea or city views. Some smaller studio apartments are tucked away too, and also have pretty private terraces. Walk-in closets are a welcome extra if you're staying, and lively citrus colors add a welcome tropical air. In peak season, you'll pay $57 to $75 a day for studio apartments, $81 to $130 for larger quarters accommodating four. In other months, prices drop to $39 to $95. Ask about money-saving weekly and monthly rates. Beekman Towers is quite a quiet place; it has a pool, patio, and pretty beach, and is near shopping and restaurants.

Step out onto a terrace overlooking ocean liners cruising past the golden sands of Miami Beach at the **Singapore Resort Motel,** 9601 Collins Ave., Miami Beach, FL 33154 (tel. 305/865-9931, or toll free 800/327-4911). A block-long hotel stretching out alongside those famous sands, the Singapore tries to think of everything: there's even a 20-station physical-fitness course right on the sand. A little city of its own, the Singapore has two pools and a patio bar, sundeck, private beach, coffeeshop, and dining room, free tennis nearby, a beauty salon, boutiques, free parking, a lounge that rocks to the wee hours, plus attractive rooms with two double beds and bright tropical colors. Some rooms have kitchenettes, and two-room suites are available. Two people pay $66 to $85 in winter, $36 to $48 in summer and fall.

Marco Polo, 19200 Collins Ave., Miami Beach, FL 33160 (tel. 305/932-

2233, or toll free 800/327-6363), is a fanciful place with faintly Moorish touches and lots of bright colors. These days, the hotel is often home to standing-room-only musical shows, and at any time this resort is a swinging place much loved by the younger set who frequent its lively lounges. Vivid colors are a highlight of the rooms, many of which have balconies overlooking the city and the ocean. There's lots and lots of space in quarters here, with his-and-hers walk-in closets, separate dressing rooms with two vanities, even refrigerators. Other goodies include a pool, shopping arcade, bars that rock until 5 a.m., a rib room and Polynesian restaurant, tennis, games, and an outdoor bar. A very lively place, the Marco Polo charges $65 to $95 double for a room or efficiency to May, when prices drop to $32 to $56. Extra guests sharing your room are $8.

Nights are active at the **Newport,** 16701 Collins Ave., Miami Beach, FL 33160 (tel. 305/949-1300, or toll free 800/327-5476), where one of the city's most popular nightclubs holds forth in rocking splendor with SRO crowds to 5 a.m. A massive hotel stretching out along two full blocks of sand, the Newport is strong on bright, bright colors, and features lots of lively colors in the rooms as well. Extra-length beds are a special feature, and big walls of glass open onto wide balconies with spectacular ocean views. The Newport is very close to a big shopping center and there are lots of restaurants nearby, although the restaurant here does wonders with thick steaks. If you want rip-roaring action and very good shows, make a beeline to the Seven Seas Lounge, where things don't quiet down until the sun rises. You'll pay $39 to $53 in summer and fall, $52 to $79 for suites; prices are $75 to $98 in winter.

If ever there were a nostalgic example of fanciful Miami Beach–chic architecture, it's the **Castaways,** 163rd Street at the ocean, Miami Beach, FL 33160 (tel. 305/945-3461, or toll free 800/327-8782). Rising alongside the ocean like an Oriental hallucination with flairing orange roof, Japanese lanterns, pagoda, and shoji screen, the Castaways is the epitome of Miami Beach fantasy. Here you'll find large, comfortable rooms in bright colors, some with kitchenettes and some with private terraces. Amenities include four swimming pools, tennis courts, restaurants, and bars. There's lots of ocean and water sports here, dozens of shops and restaurants nearby—everything you need for a South Seas island adventure on Miami Beach. Prices in high season are $46 to $68, dropping in summer to $32 to $46.

Moderately Priced Hotels

Hawaiian Isle, 17601 Collins Ave., Miami Beach, FL 33160 (tel. 305/932-2121, or toll free 800/327-5275), brings a touch of the exotic to Miami Beach. Bamboo and straw matting decorate a dining room and bar; there's an Outrigger oceanfront lounge, and bright tropical colors in average-size rooms with refrigerators. Beach umbrellas line 400 feet of private sand and you can roam about on five acres of grounds. For entertainment there are poolside songsters, water sports, Bingo, Ping-Pong, volleyball, tennis, and basketball. You can join in lots of planned activities from egg-tossing contests to Everglades trips, and fraternize at complimentary cocktail parties. A lively disco rocks until the wee hours, and there's plenty to keep the children busy. In winter, you'll pay $51 to $64 for rooms or kitchenettes; in summer, $30 to $40.

Another attractive, moderately priced Miami Beach motel is the **Dunes,** 7001 Collins Ave., Miami Beach, FL 33160 (tel. 305/947-7511). A tropical atmosphere prevails in rooms where big picture windows offer pretty views and shed a bright glow over orange or blue and green decor. The Dunes is close to shopping and restaurants, but I don't know when you'll find time to leave this resort's bar, restaurant, beach, pool, or sport and game tournaments. (If you do, they'll find you a babysitter.) The Dunes is a nice casual spot where people mingle at the patio bar and joke with the friendly, efficient workers. You'll pay $51 to $71 for a double room here in peak season, $18 to $38 in summer.

You can have a room with a balcony overlooking pretty lawns and bright blossoms at **Château by the Sea,** 19115 Collins Ave., Miami Beach, FL 33160 (tel. 305/931-8800). A rustic exterior prevails here, but inside there's a very contemporary look, from the glittering lounge (where there's nightly entertainment in season) to the cheery rooms sparked with lively colors. All the resort amenities are here, from a good restaurant specializing in seafood and steaks to a big swimming pool, shuffleboard, shops, and a patio bar. You can have a refrigerator in your room if you ask, too. Room rates in winter are $54 to $76, (location is everything), dropping in summer to $28 to $53. Two children or adults can bunk in with you at no extra charge.

A small and simple spot in the middle of quiet Bal Harbour is the **Coronado Motel,** 9501 Collins Ave., Miami Beach, FL 33154 (tel. 305/866-1625). The friendly staff prides itself on cleanliness, so you'll find everything spic and span. The pretty lobby is crowned by a dazzling crystal chandelier, and is a nice place to meet for shopping expeditions to nearby Bal Harbour Shopping Center. You could easily do without a car here since so many restaurants are right nearby, and the beach is just outside your private balcony. Nice-size rooms are decorated in bright colors and have refrigerators, and for an extra $1 a day, hotplates. Every morning you can have coffee and pastry on the house, then wander out for a swim in the heated pool or a sunning session on the beach. In this location you can hardly beat the prices: $52 to $65 in peak season through mid-March, $40 to $50 to May, and $28 to $40 in summer, $3 more for efficiencies.

Waikiki, 18801 Collins Ave., Miami Beach, FL 33160 (tel. 305/931-8600, or toll free 800/327-6363), is under the same management as the Marco Polo Hotel, a few blocks up the road. There are 350 rooms here, with two double beds in each, and all are decorated in lively tropical colors. Three swimming pools are scattered about the grounds, and there's a cocktail lounge and restaurant. They show movies or have Bingo games every night. Two people pay $42 to $64 for hotel rooms, $5 more with kitchenettes. Children stay in their parents' room for free, except during holidays and February, when there's a $4-per-person charge. In summer, rates drop to $20 to $36.

The **Pan American Resort Hotel,** 17875 Collins Ave., Miami Beach, FL 33160 (tel. 305/932-1100), is a quiet spot along the ocean in Sunny Isles with a putting green to play on and a pool to swim in, plus an attractive beamed dining room and lounge, a pretty patio dining area, a poolside bar, coffeeshop, and beauty and barber shops. There are refrigerators in the comfortable rooms, and balconies with beautiful views of the sea. The Pan American is spiffy, with a bright up-to-date decor, and the pool bar's a lively spot to while away an afternoon. Rooms here go for $108 to $128 January through March, $58 to $78 in other months.

Lobbies are important things on Miami Beach, and at the **Desert Inn,** 17201 Collins Ave., Miami Beach, FL 33160 (tel. 305/947-0621, or toll free 800/ 327-6362), the lobby is cavernous. You shouldn't have any trouble finding this desert-theme resort—just look for the covered wagon and horses outside the entrance. Spread out over two blocks, the Desert Inn has handsome paneled rooms with big picture windows and bright floral prints, and all have refrigerators too. A laundromat on the grounds is helpful, and while that's whirring you can spend your time on the tennis court or in the pool. There's dining inside or out, dancing every night in the lounge, and a steady round of entertainment for both adults and children. Prices in winter range from $49 to $72; in summer, from $29 to $39 ($6 a day more for efficiencies). Meal plans can save you money here, too.

Very Special Hotels

Art deco architecture reached its zenith in Miami, and Miami Beach has retained more art deco structures than any other city in the country. Now you can see what life was like in the 1920s when this art style was born via a visit to one of four "new" art deco hotels. A large hotel development company bought six of the hotels and was hard at work in 1985 to bring them back to their former glory. First to open was the Carlyle, a study in fascinating terrazzo floors, lots of curving lines, and typical art deco features, right down to deco furnishings salvaged from rooms in the hotels.

Next comes the **Cardozo Hotel,** 1144 Ocean Dr., Miami Beach, FL 33139 (tel. 305/534-2135). If you think things were beautiful in art deco days, you'll adore the Cardozo, which, with its sister hotel, the Victor, is the shining star of Miami Beach's art deco renovation. What they've done with this old beauty is nothing short of a miracle. All the modern comforts have been added without destroying the classic old 1930s architectural furbelows like pale pastels, puffy furniture, round mirrors, and oval shapes. One pretty corner room overlooking the beach curves at the edges to follow the building's lines, and has been carpeted in pale aqua accented by a peach bedspread and drapes that tie the two colors together. Painted furniture that could easily sell for thousands in a New York antique store was left in the hotel and it was refurbished and covered in the pastels so popular in that period. Downstairs in the lobby are puffy art deco couches, a multicolored terrazzo floor in an intricate design, a reception desk made of pink marble dust, an etched-glass elevator door, a fireplace trimmed with mirrors. You can have one of the Cardozo's rooms for $60 to $100 in high season, $40 to $60 in summer. (Ask for one of the renovated rooms since not all rooms are quite so glamorous.) Those prices, on Miami Beach just across from a long, long strip of public sand, are a bargain indeed.

Included among the six deco hotels being restored are the **Leslie, Cavalier, Victor,** and **Senator.** For the moment all are listed at 1250 Ocean Dr., Miami Beach, FL 33139 (tel. 305/531-1235), and all are located on the south end of Miami in about the 1000 to 1200 block of Collins Avenue, which some claim is the loveliest strip of beach on Miami Beach. What's more, many rooms face right onto the beach across the street. Rates are in the $50 to $100 bracket year round at these hotels, which provide a fascinating journey back in time to days of F. Scott Fitzgerald and the like.

Budget Hotels

A few blocks up the street at 1565 Collins Ave., Miami Beach, FL 33139 (tel. 305/538-3711), the **St. Moritz** is another art deco design hotel, but the deco's mostly on the outside these days. There are full-size refrigerators in these basic medium-size rooms, and some have a nice view of the beach and the resort's huge pool, right on the sand. For a room for two you'll pay $45 to $51 in the winter months, $26 to $36 in other seasons.

Rooms are not gilt trimmed at the **Ankara,** 2360 Collins Ave., Miami Beach, FL 33139 (tel. 305/538-6666, or toll free 800/538-8424), but then neither are the prices. You'll pay just $35 for an average-size hotel room, a little more for a spacious efficiency in high season. In other months prices drop a few dollars, and at anytime you'll find bright colors here, a nice pool, and lots of beach to play on.

A likely budget selection is the **Beach Motel,** 8601 Harding Ave., Miami Beach, FL 33141 (tel. 305/861-2001, or 305/866-1180), which isn't right on the sand but isn't far away either. All rooms have kitchenettes and shower, and there's a heated pool in the center of the grounds. In winter, rates range from $38 a day for an efficiency, from $42 for larger quarters. In summer, prices drop to $20 to $25 a day, and there are money-saving weekly and monthly rates.

Ocean Roc, 19505 Collins Ave., Miami Beach, FL 33160 (tel. 305/931-7600, or toll free 800/327-0553), used to be a Holiday Inn so the rooms are especially spacious and decorated in lively colors. Two double beds don't begin to fill up the space, and big private balconies give you even more breathing room. Tennis is free, plus there's a little pool for children, a big one for adults, an oceanfront restaurant, and an attractive bar. The Ocean Roc is one of the northernmost of the motel row resorts, so it's quite a relaxing location that seems far from everything—but isn't. Winter rates are just $44 to $58, dropping in summer to $20 to $36 (lower for long stays).

HOTELS IN MIAMI: You'll find most of Miami's hotels downtown, at the airport, in Coral Gables, or in Coconut Grove, so I've picked out a few of the best representatives in those neighborhoods.

Downtown

As in any big city, Miami's downtown hotels are expensive, but quality is high. Poshest of the downtown hotels is the magnificent **Omni International,** at 1601 Biscayne Blvd., Miami, FL 33132 (tel. 305/374-0000, or toll free 800/228-2121), a spectacularly contemporary spot with waterfalls gurgling from level to level in a dramatic lobby lounge. The casually elegant Fish Market Restaurant serves fish and seafood in the $10 to $26 range. You can zip right from your spacious ultramodern room, decorated with lots of shiny glass, chrome, and soft contemporary hues, to the massive Omni shopping center, where 165 of the city's most elegant boutiques and department stores offer up treasures from many lands. Easily the city's most elegant hostelry, the Omni charges $75 to $125 year round.

The **Hotel at Plaza Venetia,** 555 NE 15th St., Miami, FL 33100 (tel. 305/374-2900), is a new hotel occupying three floors of a 25-story apartment tower on Biscayne Bay. Right next door to the Omni, the Hotel at Plaza Venetia has 50 handsomely decorated rooms with very contemporary decor, and balconies overlooking the marina and bay. There are plush suites, a health spa, two dining rooms, tennis courts, racquetball courts, and a pool. Rates for two are $75, extra guests pay $25 each, and suites run $175 to $250.

A $12-million renovation metamorphosed the **Everglades Hotel,** 244 Biscayne Blvd., Miami, FL 33132 (tel. 305/379-5461, or toll free 800/327-5700), into a shining contemporary hostelry. Deep carpets in glowing colors set the tone for sparklingly contemporary rooms in earth tones. The lobby is lovely again, and the Brasserie restaurant, decorated in rosewood and brass, has taken the city by storm, thanks to a talented French chef who's producing outstanding cuisine at quite reasonable prices (in the $10 to $15 range). In winter months, a double room here is $65, and larger quarters run $85.

Another beautifully revamped downtown hotel is the **Best Western PLM Marina Park,** 340 Biscayne Blvd., Miami, FL 33132 (tel. 305/371-4400), which bears no resemblance whatsoever to the old hotel that once inhabited this spot. Now there are plush rooms decorated in airy wicker or rattan, with fascinating ornate headboards and colors that shine like jewels. From many windows there's a serene view of the city and the marina across the street. Downstairs is a riveting lounge with brick walls and a huge tented ceiling. The hotel's quite convenient to the port if you're off on a cruise. The Best Western PLM Marina Park has an appealing European inn coziness about it, and when its long-range plans are complete, it will have a raft of interesting boutiques too. Two people pay $60 to $80 in season and $54 to $74 in other months, with higher prices for suites.

El Plaza Hotel, 100 NE 10th St., Miami, FL 33132 (tel. 305/371-6420, or toll free 800/528-1234), is a Best Western hotel with a courtesy shuttle service to the Port of Miami if you're leaving on a cruise. Just a few blocks north of the downtown shopping area, El Plaza has attractive rooms with modern furnishings and a lively decor. There are also a dining room and lounge in this newly revamped hotel. Rates are $45 double in winter, $40 in summer.

Key Biscayne

Far from the crowds of bustling Miami—but not very far—and close to the sea are several resorts popular all year with visitors in winter and with Miamians escaping to the beach in summer.

Top of the pack is the **Sonesta Beach Hotel and Tennis Club,** 6350 Ocean Dr., Key Biscayne, FL 33149 (tel. 305/361-2021, or toll free 800/343-7170), a massive hotel with every possible sport from swimming to tennis, sailing, and golf. For dining there are five restaurants, including the Rib Room and the outstanding Japanese-Chinese Two Dragons restaurant. For entertainment, will four lounges do? On a street behind the hotel, the Sonesta has bought up every house that came on the market, redecorated them, and now rents them as luxurious villas (some have as many as five bedrooms!). All the 293 rooms here have private balconies, two double or king-size beds, and contemporary furnishings. It's a lovely waterside hideaway that in summer has "Just Us Kids" programs that are so jam-packed with activities it's a wonder adults don't picket to join them. You'll pay $170 to $190 in winter months, $105 to $135 in summer, for two. Villas range from $375 to $525 in peak season, about 25% less in summer.

Key Biscayne Hotel and Villas, 701 Ocean Dr., Key Biscayne, FL 33149 (tel. 305/361-5431), is an elegant older hotel, its 100 cheerful rooms with refrigerators and picture windows overlooking the ocean or the island. One-, two-, and three-bedroom villas have high beamed ceilings and second-story bedrooms. There's a pool, handsome dining rooms and lounges, tennis courts, and a par-three golf course right beside the sea. On Sunday an international buffet is a sumptuous feast, and there are lots of other social events plus a children's program. Genteel elegance is the word here. Winter rates are $145 to $160 double; summer rates, $75 to $85. Villas begin at $200 in winter, $105 in summer.

Sheraton Royal Biscayne, 555 Ocean Dr., Key Biscayne, FL 33149 (tel. 305/361-5775, or toll free 800/325-3535), is a serene hideaway with a 1200-foot strip of sand, two pools, sailing, fishing, tennis courts, golf nearby, and spacious, pretty rooms decorated in tropical colors. You can sit on your screened porch and listen to the sound of the waves breaking over the sand in the evening. Royal Biscayne likes to call itself a Caribbean island in Florida, and with its sleepy serenity and all that beach I think they're pretty close to right. In winter, rates are $125 to $135; in summer and fall, $70 to $90.

Even a small motel can command top prices on Key Biscayne, and that's why the **Silver Sands Oceanfront Motel,** 301 Ocean Dr., Key Biscayne, FL 33149 (tel. 305/361-5441), can price its efficiency apartments at $89 to $169 for two in winter months, $58 to $119 in summer. One of the most popular spots in town is the motel's Sand Bar, where you can while away an afternoon staring out across the sea through walls of glass. Outside on the wooded grounds there's always a laughing crowd at the pool. Inside, there's a comfortable restaurant serving good beef and seafood at moderate prices. Oceanfront patio apartments at Silver Sands are $169 in winter, $119 in summer.

At the Airport

Not far from the airport is the very plush and comfortable **Doral Country Club and Resort,** 4400 NW 87th Ave., Miami, FL 33148 (tel. 305/592-2000), sister to the Doral-on-the-Ocean. Set down in the middle of one of the nation's most famous golf complexes and home of the Doral Open, the resort has regular shuttle transportation to the beach so you won't feel deprived of sand. How you could feel deprived of anything here I can't imagine, since there are lovely spacious rooms decorated in lively colors, 19 tennis courts, *four* golf courses, lakes, bicycles, a spa, pool, clubhouse, restaurants, and lounges. There's a serene air about the place too, that may, now that I think of it, be the result of many a subdued golfer's umpteen-over-par score on the "Blue Monster" course. Two people pay $72 to $88 in summer, $145 to $167 in peak season.

The **Marriott Hotel–Airport** is an attractive 788-room hotel quite near the airport at 1201 NW LeJeune Rd. (tel. 305/649-5000, or toll free 800/228-9290), where you can look out over the lights of Miami and a nearby lake through big picture windows. Nice extra touches are electric alarm clocks, in-room movies, and automated wake-up service. You'll find lots of tennis courts and a full program of instruction and clinics. The newly renovated Porter's restaurant has a spectacular view over the city, and two lounges offer spirited entertainment. A room for two is $85.

Radisson Mart Plaza, 711 NW 72nd Ave., Miami, FL 33126 (tel. 305/261-3800, or toll free 800/228-9822), is another of Miami's newest arrivals. Opened in 1984, the hotel offers 334 quite luxurious rooms, all with plenty of extra amentities like special soaps and shampoos. Health fans can work up a sweat at the fitness center, on the racquetball or tennis courts, or in the resort's pool, sauna, and whirlpool, then destroy their efforts in the plush continental dining room here. Located five minutes from the airport, the hotel is a favorite stopping spot for those attending trade shows and meetings at nearby Miami International Merchandise Mart and Expo Center. Rates at the Radisson are $65 to $95 single. The highest prices are paid for rooms on a special floor called the Plaza Club, which offers complimentary breakfast in the morning and an open bar each evening. Double rates are $75 to $105.

The **Sheraton River House,** 3900 NW 21st St. (tel. 305/871-3800, or toll free 800/325-3535), has spacious, comfortable rooms with sweeping wicker headboards, airy tropical furniture and colors, and big picture windows overlooking the tranquil Miami River. There are tennis courts, a pool, a sauna. If you want to go really first class, the Sheraton has rooms in the Continental Tower with brass beds, vivid colors, plush carpets, phones at bed and bath, chocolates on your pillow, and a newspaper at your door. The Sheraton is home to Daphne's, the hotel's sophisticated restaurant where waitresses wear chic outfits and smart hats, and are sometimes difficult to distinguish from diners in same. Thick steaks, hefty slabs of prime rib, interesting salads, and a devastating chocolate mousse pie are on the menu here, where you dine for $15 to $20 amid stained glass, leather chairs, and original artwork. A lively disco makes this a Miami gathering spot too. Rooms run $85 to $95, single or double, in season, and suites begin at $95 and rise to $280. Other months, prices range from $75 to $95.

If you're flying in and right back out again, the **Airport International Hotel,** P.O. Box 5920, Miami, FL 33159, in the terminal (tel. 305/871-4100, or toll free

800/327-1276), has double soundproofing to silence jet roar and comfortable, colorful rooms with king-size or extra-long double beds. They're used to harried travelers here, so check-in and check-out is fast, and there's a multilingual staff and 24-hour wake-up service. They'll arrange babysitters and welcome your pet, then send you up to a handsome rooftop restaurant and cocktail lounge where you can watch those mechanized birds zoom off into the sunset. Double rates are $79 to $84, singles cost $69 to $74, and the friendly management will give you half-price rates if you need the room just for the day.

Restaurant chains dreamed up cafeterias so there doesn't seem to be any reason why **Serv-Ur-Self Miami Airways Motor Lodge,** 5001 NW 36th St., Miami Springs, FL 33166 (tel. 305/883-4700), shouldn't run a cafeteria-like motel. Here you get your towels, soap, and glasses when you arrive and return them when you leave (exchanging them in between for new ones), thus eliminating the cost of a maid. Rooms are budget-basic, but there's a pretty pool outside and family suites are available. The rates are the best part of this operation: $33—plus discounts of 3% to 30% for stays of 2 to 11 days. Self Service Inns also operates the **Airliner Hotel,** 4155 NW 24th St., Miami, FL 33148 (tel. 305/871-2611). Rates are $44 double.

READER'S TIP: "You should mention that if one plans on staying at the **Doral Country Club,** one should have a car. The shuttle from the Doral Country Club to Doral-on-the-Ocean operates daytime only. In the evening if you want to return to the country club, you must spend at least $15 in taxi fares" (Diane Miyazaki, New York, N.Y.).

Coral Gables

Miracles will happen, even in a big city certainly not known in recent years for the production of miracles. However, this miracle actually occurred in the lovely suburb of Coral Gables where the main street is called Miracle Mile, so perhaps that explains it.

All this is by way of introduction to a delightful little hotel called **Hotel Place St. Michel,** 162 Alcazar, Coral Gables, FL 33134 (tel. 305/444-1666). Once a derelict old wreck of a building whose really lovely underpinnings had been hidden by 1950s "modernization," Place St. Michel is once again in its glory. Little by little some hard-working historians took down the false ceilings and plastic excesses to reveal beautiful woodwork, high ceilings, and then they stocked the rooms here with English and French antiques and opened up to the loud huzzahs of all the community.

This lush old Spanish city that's home to the University of Miami also has a few small motels along US 1 near the campus, and one large hotel downtown.

Poshest and plushest of the lot is the **David William Hotel,** 700 Biltmore Way, Coral Gables, FL 33134 (tel. 305/445-7821, or toll free 800/327-8770). It's the city's number one hostelry address, and here you'll find everything from a marble and crystal lobby to a rooftop half-acre pool, gymnasium, sauna, masseurs, and attractive, spacious rooms and efficiencies, some with private terraces. Perhaps more famous than the hotel itself is its Chez Vendôme restaurant, where you dine in a fin-de-siècle setting on some of the city's most outstanding cooking, much of it flambé tableside preparations. Another dining room, the 700 Club, is high atop the building, dramatically decorated in leather and velvet, a spot for fine wines and outstanding culinary accomplishments. Prices at both restaurants are in the $25 range. Rates at the hotel are $90 to $100 in peak season, $70 to $90 in summer, with suites beginning at $125 in winter.

The **University Inn,** 1390 S. Dixie Hwy., Coral Gables, FL 33146 (tel. 305/667-2554), is a place I've spent many tranquil hours dining at the small waterside restaurant. Beautiful lawns slope down to the edge of a waterway, and the spacious, well-kept rooms are a good value. There's a tranquil, unhurried, friendly air about this inn just across the street from the University of Miami campus. Two people pay $45 to $50 in winter, about $10 less in summer.

Coconut Grove

In such a lovely community you'd expect to find a lovely hotel or two, and you will.

You'll never see anything quite like the drama of the **Coconut Grove Mutiny in Sailboat Bay,** 2951 S. Bayshore Dr., Coconut Grove, FL 33133 (tel. 305/442-2400, or toll free 800/327-0372). Some of the rooms here are not just harmonious, they're symphonies. How about Roman tubs, a bed on a lighted chrome platform, or a room done all in black and gray with silver geometric metal sculpture and track lighting? Or an African room with walls covered with straw matting, bed splashed with animal-hide print, chairs covered with zebra stripes? Corners hold dramatic moon-shot sculptures or puffy corner seats, colors glow like jewels, canopies and mirrors surround beds—and wonder of wonders, it's all tastefully done! Outside, the pool is surrounded by a jungle of tropical plants, with wooden platforms here and there for serene al fresco dining. Everywhere you look is the glow of polished mahogany or the charm of dramatic flower arrangements. Some rooms have big clam shells filled with scented soap, marble sinks, huge round tubs. Across the street is a beautiful view of a bay full of sailboats. A hotel like this you don't see every day, so if you're in the mood for a damn-the-expense-I'm-entitled visit, Mutiny! Rates, which include croissants, fresh orange juice, fresh fruit bowl, coffee, and the *Miami Herald* every morning, are $125 for a hotel room, $185 for Roman tub rooms, and $155 for suites.

When the **Grand Bay Hotel,** 2669 S. Bayshore Dr., Coconut Grove, FL 33133 (tel. 305/858-9600, or toll free 800/327-2788), opened in late 1983, invitations to the opening of this posh new hotel were such hot items one expected scalpers to be standing at the entrance. With French nightclub entrepreneur Régine in attendance at her plush top-floor nightspot and every socialite in town glittering, this hotel was the place to be seen. It still is.

A very beautiful hotel indeed, Grand Bay has something more important than mere physical beauty—panache. Here you sip tea from silver pots each afternoon, dine in an elegant French nouveau atmosphere, and sleep in rooms of subtle elegance.

No check-in counter here. Instead you're greeted by a concierge at a goldleaf-trimmed antique desk. Huge bowls of fresh flowers (often orchids) are carefully placed to attract, without overwhelming, the eye. A comfortable lobby is skillfully divided to offer intimate little groupings of handsome furnishings, cozy retreats in which a quiet conversation with friends is possible.

Outside, a towering red metal sculpture is a fitting frontal piece for the unusual stepped architecture of this hotel. Beautiful landscaping at the pool and on every level of the hotel just adds one more touch to the elegance of the place. Rates at the Grand Bay are $155 to $175 double from mid-December through mid-May, and suites run $225 to $600; in summer, double rates are $135 to $155 for rooms. Grand Bay is operated by the posh CIGA Hotels chain of Italy.

Over at the **Coconut Grove Hotel,** 2649 S. Bayshore Dr., Coconut Grove, FL 33133 (tel. 305/858-2500, or toll free 800/327-8771), a mini-swinger room has a queen-size bed covered in fur, several levels, and a mirror over the bed. If you're not quite that much of a swinger, there are also rooms with contemporary chrome canopy frames and deep colors, as well as attractive suites with living rooms. Two restaurants, Top of the Grove and Café Brasserie, are outstanding dining spots (see my dining recommendations), and the hotel has tennis courts, sauna, swimming pool, boutiques, and water sports. Rooms are $120 double, year round.

Grove Isle, 4 Grove Isle Dr., Coconut Grove, FL 33133 (tel. 305/858-8300), is one of Miami's newest and poshest hotels, an enclave that shares an island with a private club of the same name. It is elegant, it is expensive, and it is exclusive. Contemporary sculpture by some of the world's finest modern sculptors—Lieberman, Calder, Miró, Dubuffet—greet arrivals, dot the lobby, and rise beside the swimming pool. Two formal sculpture gardens make for a fascinating stroll. Now about five years old, the hotel has just four floors and 50 rooms, each with a tasteful Oriental theme. Black lacquer furniture is set against matching walls that contrast with cream bedspreads and rust-colored accents. Each room has a built-in safe.

For playtime, there's a large swimming pool, 12 lighted tennis courts, bike and jogging paths, and an exercise room with saunas, steamroom, and whirlpool baths. In the dining room, haute cuisine is matched by haute couture and haute prices (à la carte dinners are about $25). Rates at Grove Isle are $140 to $175 from mid-December to mid-April.

4. Where to Dine

Miamians work, but only between meals. Business starts over breakfast, moves on to lunch, and gets really serious over five-course dinners. While Miami is a city bustling with international commerce and some very high finance, it differs greatly in pace from its big-city counterparts, thanks to a liberal sprinkling of Latin Americans and Europeans to whom a two-hour lunch falls about an hour short of civilized. In southern Florida you'll find restaurants on every corner, in every office building, every hotel, and many a condominium. You'll find every price bracket, every theme, and every culinary specialty from haute to Hungarian, gefilte fish to gnocchi. Locating "this great little restaurant just in back of the . . ." is half the fun of a Miami vacation. To get you started on your search, I've divided the area up by cities and by types of cuisine offered. And remember that the prices I've cited are for entrees, although that usually includes salad, one or two vegetables, and often coffee as well.

RESTAURANTS IN MIAMI BEACH: Many many hotels on Miami Beach have fine restaurants, and you'll find a wide range of cuisine and prices.

Continental

Dining Galleries, at the Fontainebleau Hilton, 4441 Collins Ave. (tel. 538-2000), are simply gorgeous—chic, elegant, très posh. You can dine here on things like terrine de foie gras Strasbourg and pompano with crab Savarin for about $35. Lunch begins at 11:30 a.m. weekdays; dinner is from 6 p.m. to 1 a.m. daily.

Baroque decor (Miami Beach interpretation), opulence, drama, stained-glass skylights, Viennese crystal chandeliers, art nouveau touches, antiques from every era—that's the **Forge,** 432 Arthur Godfrey Rd. (tel. 538-8533). In a huge wine cellar lie treasures of the collector's world, from rare classical wines to something one dares to drink. From the kitchen come award-winning preparations of steaks, chops, prime rib, seafood, some nouvelle cuisine specialties. Try the cream of escargots soup. The Forge is open from 6 p.m. to 2:30 a.m. daily, with an adjoining lounge open until 5 a.m. Reservations are necessary, especially in winter. Prices begin at $9.95, but are far more likely to reach about $20 to $25 a person.

Dominique's, in the Alexander Hotel, 5225 Collins Ave. (tel. 865-6500), rose to fame in Washington, D.C., where it is the place to be seen now as always. Miamians were, of course, thrilled when chef Dominique D'Ermo was lured to Miami, specifically to very posh quarters in a very posh hotel called the Alexander. Dominique's has not failed Miami. While the hype surrounding the restaurant's opening was so great as to make you wonder if they were trying to cover minimum with maximum, Dominique's has turned out to be one of the city's finest.

You will be impressed by the setting: you enter by glass-enclosed walkways bounded by gardens and dine amid the poshest of accoutrements, from Oriental rugs to glowing antique French furnishings, in a delicate pink-and-green color scheme. Service is positively impeccable, yet not stuffy or overbearing, and the food is wonderful, laden with classically rich sauces, delicately applied herbs, and the best of meats and seafood. You may let your taste buds roam through such treats as pasta stuffed with salmon and topped with lobster sauce, veal scallops daubed with goose liver and served atop fettuccine in a cream and peppercorn sauce, or quail with tiny fried quail eggs with a raspberry vinegar and honey sauce. Prices are high but entrees are accompanied by five vegetables that create a colorful display. Top it all with huge and sinfully rich desserts, dark chocolate truffles perhaps. Entrees fall in the $20 to $30 price range, appetizers in the $10 bracket, and desserts run $4 to $6, so figure $40 to $50 a person for dinner, more with wine. Hours are 7:30 a.m. to 2:30 p.m. for breakfast and lunch, and 6 to 11:30 p.m. for dinner.

Steaks

You'll know you're at **Embers,** 245 22nd St. (tel. 538-4345), when you sniff the irresistible perfume of hickory smoke wafting through the air. Inside you'll see open brick ovens and spits turning ribs, duck, and chicken over an open fire, and grills sizzling prime steaks. Seafood fans can get a two-pound Maine lobster, fresh red snapper, and stone crabs here too. You'll pay $12 to $17 for dinner at Embers, which opens at 4 p.m. for early-bird specials and closes at 11 p.m. daily.

Two good steak houses on Miami Beach were, the last I heard, under the same ownership: **Nick and Arthur's,** 1601 79th St. Causeway (tel. 864-2200), and **Place for Steak,** 1335 79th St. Causeway (tel. 758-5581). Both are landmarks with good continental cuisine and excellent steaks in the $15 to $20 bracket. Nick and Arthur's overlooks Biscayne Bay and is open from 5:30 to 10 p.m. daily. Place for Steak hours are 6 p.m. to 4 a.m., with light suppers served after 11 p.m. and entertainment to the wee hours.

Danish

For years **Prince Hamlet** was one of the most famous restaurants in Miami and one of the best loved of the city's dining spots. Then the neighborhood in which the restaurant was located suffered some setbacks and to everyone's amazement Prince Hamlet closed its doors. In 1984 to the good wishes of herring-starved Miami diners, Prince Hamlet's Danish founder got it all going again and reopened his landmark restaurant at a new location—on the north end of Miami Beach at 19115 Collins Ave. (tel. 932-8488), in a section known as Sunny Isles.

Much to everyone's relief, Prince Hamlet still features a groaning Danish cold table, but now it's even larger than it used to be, laden with all kinds of seafood, fresh vegetables, cheese, salads, and cold pasta creations. A wondrous spot for the true trencherman, Prince Hamlet offers 22 entrees ranging from rack of lamb to roast duck, chicken, snapper, salmon, scampi, and steaks, all of them including a visit to that cold table. Prices are quite reasonable too, considering that you could live for a week on what you can consume here: the range is $15 to $20 for dinner, which is served daily from 5:30 to 11 p.m. On Sunday the Prince closes at 10 p.m.

French

A number of years ago, talented restauranteur Roger Chauveron moved to Miami but fortunately he didn't retire, just brought his successful **Café Chauveron,** 9561 E. Bay Harbour Dr. (tel. 866-8779), with him and created a legendary restaurant that's been winning top culinary awards since the day it opened. Subtle decor, a tranquil waterside setting, and talented, subtle service are all guaranteed at Café Chauveron, as is some of the most exquisitely prepared food outside Paris. Try salmon mousse with lobster sauce, chateaubriand bouquetière, a Grand Marnier soufflé or chocolate mousse for which any gourmand would sacrifice his Dieter's Anonymous membership. At least five specialties are prepared daily, so be sure to ask what's cooking. My life's goal is to savor my way through each item on the menu (I'm a long way from completing that task). You can't go wrong, but you could perhaps go broke. Entrees on this à la carte menu run $18 to $25, but it's a memorable experience. The café's open from 6 to 11 p.m. daily (closed June through mid-October).

Another Grand Marnier soufflé maker is **Ma Folie Restaurant,** 1045 95th St., Bay Harbor Island (tel. 865-6011), where the house specialty is made with chopped chestnuts and walnuts. Duck, veal, and pistachio go into a delectable terrine here, and many items on the menu are prepared en croûte. You'll pay $20 to $25 for an excellent dinner here from 5:30 to 11 p.m. daily. Jackets are required.

Italian

Gatti, 1427 West Ave. (tel. 673-1717), serves top-notch northern Italian cuisine in a formal ristorante that's been a culinary landmark for 60 years. Pastas made right here are so light you should keep a fork on them to hold them down, and seafood gets very special treatment at Gatti. Fresh vegetables and bread baked in their own kitchens are two of the treats in store, but for quality like this you pay $20 or more for a complete dinner. Gatti is open from 5:30 to 10:30 p.m. daily (except Monday) in winter, but closes in mid-May, reopening in early November.

Ristorante Tiberio, 9700 Collins Ave. (tel. 861-6161; outside Florida, toll free 800/TIBERIO), is as fashionable and chic as the buyers who waft around the Bal Harbour Shopping Center, home to this elegant and expensive dining spot. Waiters are formally attired and efficient, the pastas memorable and light. Try veal Amerigo Vespucci (topped with mushrooms and truffles in brandy cream) or sole in a wine-laced sauce. Expect to pay $30 or so for dinner. Tiberio is open noon to 2:30 p.m. and 6 to 11 p.m. every day but Sunday, later on weekends.

Oriental

A highlight of an evening at **Christine Lee's Gaslight,** 18406 Collins Ave., in the Thunderbird Motel (tel. 931-7700), is a tableside visit with Ms. Lee herself, who strolls around her tasteful Oriental empire to be sure all is going well. The decor is as chic as the owner, and the cuisine is Cantonese, Mandarin, and Szechuan, things like coconut shrimp or braised duckling (fried golden and sprinkled with toasted almonds and nesting on a bed of bean sprouts). If there are four or more of you, try a Mandarin or Szechuan feast. Entrees are in the $10 to $15 range, $24 each for the "feasts." The restaurant's open from 5 p.m. to 1 a.m. daily. There's lots of entertainment in the adjacent bar too.

Seafood

Joe's Stone Crabs, 227 Biscayne St. (tel. 673-0365), is down on the very tip of South Beach still dispensing heaping platters of stone crabs as it has for 70 years. The atmosphere is basic subdued nautical with cypress walls and nothing much you can damage as you dig through those succulent claws. There's lots of other good seafood on the menu, but when stone crabs are on it, don't miss this grown-in-Florida treat. For these treasures from the sea you'll pay about $16 a person. The restaurant is open from 11:30 a.m. to 2 p.m. Tuesday through Saturday for lunch and from 5 to 10 p.m. daily for dinner (closed mid-May to October), but get there early or be prepared for a long, long wait.

Budget Stops

You can only stuff yourself on mousse au saumon and canard bigarade for just so long and then you've got to have . . . a pizza. Chicagoans should love—and others try—the Chicago-style deep-dish, thick-crust pizza at **My Pi,** 239 Sunny Isles Blvd. (tel. 945-1387). The hamburgers are good here too: they're on black bread and topped with mozzarella. It's open from 11:30 a.m. to 11 p.m. Monday to Thursday, to 1 a.m. on Friday and Saturday, and 1 to 11 p.m. on Sunday. Pizza prices begin at about $4 to $8. There are two other locations in the South Miami area, at 9541 S. Dixie Hwy. and 13856 N. Kendall Dr.

To pass by **Pumpernik's,** 12599 Biscayne Blvd. (tel. 891-1225), is to miss seeing the great mainstream of Miami Beach life streaming through these portals for a go at bowls of kosher dills and coleslaw, pickled tomatoes, matzoh-ball soup, enormous sandwiches, and dinners for one that could feed three or four. Low prices in the $10 or less range for dinner, $3 to $5 for lunch, make this a belt-bustin', budget-wise stop. The colorful crowd that pops in here makes meals a sociological study as well. Open 7 a.m. to 1 a.m. daily, later on Saturday.

Wolfie Cohen's Rascal House, 17190 Collins Ave. (tel. 947-4581), is carved from the same inimitable mold as Pumpernik's and has long lines from about 6 p.m. every night, so go early. Copious quantities make this a mecca for stuffees and for anyone who likes good cooking, potato pancakes with sour cream, sensational onion rolls, mile-high sandwiches. Open from 7 a.m. to 1:30 a.m. daily.

After a long hard day with Gucci and Neiman-Marcus, slip off to the cool confines of **Miss Grimble's,** 9700 Collins Ave., in the Bal Harbour Shops (tel. 861-4544). Sit out at tiny tables under the trees or inside in a little café/teashop where you can rest your eyes on fluffy quiches, fresh spinach salads, croissants, and pastries that may change what you say when the next boutique asks you your size. It's open from 11 a.m. to 9:30 p.m. daily in the winter months, but closes earlier in summer. Prices are in the $6 to $8 range.

RESTAURANTS IN MIAMI: Miami has a raft of award-winning restaurants and more opening every day.

American/Continental

If you've been roaming Omni for hours and could use a place to sit and sip, head for **Arthur's Eating House,** 1444 Biscayne Blvd. (tel. 371-4444), a downtown sanctum where you can dine on fat sandwiches for lunch and a wide range of steaks, veal, and seafood for dinner. Desserts and breads are made right here, and served in a contemporary atmosphere of mirrors, plants, and dramatic graphics. Nightly entertainment features top names in jazz. Prices are in the $11 to $16 range for dinner, and Arthur's is open from 11:30 a.m. to midnight daily (except Sunday, when 5 p.m. is the opening hour).

Sink into velvet and snappy chrome surroundings at **Tuttle's,** 600 NE 36th

St., in the Charter Club (tel. 576-7676), named for pioneer Julia Tuttle, who would be stunned to see what glitter Miami attracts these days. There's a wide range of continental cuisine on the menu, with some Greek touches like phyllo-encased feta and mushroom triangles or rack of lamb. People-watching is fun here, but doesn't come cheap. Figure to spend $20 or more for dinner. Hours begin at noon and end when the last boom of the restaurant's nifty disco is silenced. There's Sunday brunch there too ($13), from 11:30 a.m. to 2:30 p.m. Reservations are wise.

Reflections on the Bay, Miamarina, NE 5th Street (tel. 371-6433), occupies quarters high up on the second level of a building at Miami's downtown yacht marina. From that lofty perch you can get a look at some spectacular sunsets followed by lots of glitter as the lights of this growing city brighten up the night. A posh spot, Reflections is a popular place for business lunches and after-work sipping that often moves right on into dinner. You dine on delicacies like lobster mousse, gingered clams, and pompano, served in this glass-enclosed salon overlooking sleek sailing craft. You also pay for the privilege, to the tune of about $18 to $25 for dinner, served from 6 to 11 p.m. daily, 5 to 10 p.m. on Sunday. A set-price dinner, complete from soup to dessert and coffee, is $29. Lunch occurs on weekdays only, from noon to 3 p.m., and Sunday brunch is served from 11 a.m. to 3 p.m.

Tucked away on the first floor of an office building downtown is **Cye's Rivergate,** 444 Brickell Ave. (tel. 358-9100). It's one of the top spots for lunch, and has very good evening musical entertainment and dancing. You'll find steaks, chops, kebabs, and straightforward cooking here, with entree prices in the $15 range. Cye's opens at 11:30 a.m. and closes at midnight (1 a.m. on Saturday), with abbreviated post-11 p.m. dinners available for late-night revelers.

David Harrison's Secret Garden, 411 NE Second Ave. (tel. 573-3331), is a magical place put together by a truly creative Miami restaurateur who once ran Food Among the Flowers. A study in mirrors, marble, white-trimmed French windows, skylights, and, of course, Harrison's signature flowers, this new two-story restaurant is a wonderful place to abandon the hustle for an hour or two of serenity in both atmosphere and food. On the menu here are such innovative treats as roast chicken with fresh raspberries, escargots in walnut butter, crunchy conch fritters served on a conch shell, and snapper teamed with papaya, banana, and grapefruit. Complete a sense-satisfying evening with chocolate mousse thick as cake or a kiwi tart. Dinner entrees are in the $12 to $17 range. Lunch is every bit as stunningly creative and is served from 11:30 a.m. to 3 p.m. weekdays. Dinner is from 6:30 to 11 p.m. daily except Sunday (Secret Garden closes at midnight on Saturday).

French

It's hard to imagine any nicer combination than food and flowers, and harder yet to imagine any lovelier combination of the two than **David Harrison's Food Among the Flowers,** 21 NE 36th St. (tel. 576-0028). Harrison is also one of the city's best known floral designers, so at his restaurant you'll see banks of blooms in a dramatic black setting punctuated by white arched lattices and tiny pinpoints of light. Even the food is likely to show up wearing flowers here. Menus change with the season, but you can always count on outstanding culinary creations like poached sole topped with mussels, rack of lamb, and lavosh crackers, with entree prices in the $13 to $20 range. It's open from 11:30 a.m. to 3 p.m. on weekdays and 6:30 to 10 p.m. for dinner daily, later on weekends.

Omni Hotel, at 1601 Biscayne Blvd. (tel. 374-0000), has two outstanding restaurants: the **Terrace Café,** overlooking a plush and lush tropical garden, and the **Fish Market,** a *très chic* spot with stunning furnishings. Prices at the Terrace

Café, which is open daily from 7 a.m. to 11 p.m., range from $4.95 to $18. The Fish Market is open 6:30 to 11 p.m. (closed Sunday), with entree prices in the $11 to $26 range.

Truffles, 1060 NE 79th St. (tel. 754-6683), has quickly achieved considerable fame in Miami and its beaches, and for good reason: the food is terrific and the staff is very pleasant. Truffles do crop up on the menu here, but the cooking is quite eclectic, ranging from calf liver sauteed with apples and capers to an Austrian schnitzel dinner for two. The chef here specializes in pastas and makes some fabulous ones, including tortellini teamed with sweetbreads, thin slices of tomatoes, and peaches, and tossed with cream and mint leaves, or combined with poached mussels, shallots, cream, cauliflower, leeks, and chives. Spinach linguine joins julienne strips of duck and fresh corn, and angel-hair pasta is united with scallops, shrimp, clams, and crab in a velouté sauce. In between are a couple of dozen taste treats like roast duck, steak tartare, and some interesting veal creations, all served with a salad, fresh vegetables, and potatoes. Prices are as reasonable as the cooking is good: $10 to $15 buys quite a complete dinner. You'll find this dark-brown wood-sided restaurant just past Tenth Avenue on the 79th Street Causeway, but the entrance and the parking lot are at the back so keep your eyes open as you pass Tenth Avenue. Truffles is open from 11:30 a.m. to 3 p.m. daily for lunch and 5 to 11 p.m. for dinner.

Seafood

You'll probably have to wait at **Mike Gordon's,** 1201 NE 79th St. (tel. 751-4429), but since 1946 legions of Miamians have considered it a worthwhile wait. You can watch the yachts buzz by while they're finding you a place. Once you've got one, you'll dine on extraordinarily good cooking—red snapper chowder or black grouper, plus oysters and clams shucked before your eyes. It's open from noon to 10 p.m. Tuesday through Sunday, with prices in the $10 to $15 range.

Joe's Seafood Market and Restaurant, 400 NW North River Dr. (tel. 374-5637), is one of those places you thought you could never find in a big, bustling city like Miami. It's rustic, simple, right on a wharf overlooking the Miami River, and reasonably priced. Expect nothing fancy, no toney sauces or fine china—just very fresh seafood served by people who know what fresh seafood should be (the place began as a seafood-processing plant). Little by little Joe's responded to demand and now features snapper filets, black grouper steaks, sea trout, fried shrimp, deviled crab, squid, and conch for prices that hover between $6 and $8. You can spend more if you're after swordfish, shrimp in a green sauce, Florida lobster, or stone crabs (say, $10 to $15), but you don't have to—and that's a miracle in Miami. You can dine indoors in air conditioning or outdoors watching yachts rumble by. Hours are 11 a.m. to 9 p.m. daily, closing an hour later on Tuesday, Friday, and Saturday.

Budget Bets

Once upon a time a famed Havana bartender named Constante created a drink that was to become an international favorite, the frozen daiquiri. That drink drew droves (including Hemingway) to a restaurant called **El Floridita** that has now been cloned in downtown Miami at 145 E. Flagler St. (tel. 358-1556). Cuban daiquiri connoisseurs assure me that Miami's Floridita comes very close in excellence to the Havana creation. Even if you don't want a daiquiri you'll like the romantic setting, down in what comes as close as Miami can come to a basement. You won't pay more than $10 to $15 for good seafood and Cuban fare, and there's entertainment too. Open from 11:30 a.m. to 10 p.m. daily.

Seafood comes right out of the depths of fishing boats that dock at **East**

Coast Fisheries, 360 W. Flagler St. (tel. 373-5516), which is first a wholesale fish house and second a restaurant. The setting couldn't be simpler, but the seafood couldn't be fresher either. Everything's sea-fresh, simply cooked and simply sensational. The chowder is made from grouper here, the shrimp is to die for, and prices are in the $10 to $15 (or less) range. Open 10 a.m. to 10 p.m. daily.

Tony Roma's, 15700 Biscayne Blvd. (tel. 949-2214), is a clone of the phenomenally successful Fort Lauderdale operation with those same spicy, crunchy barbecued ribs and loaves of crispy onion rings for prices that hover at $10 or less. There's another Tony's at 6601 S. Dixie Hwy. (tel. 667-4806), and they're both open from 11 a.m. to 5 a.m. daily, from 5 p.m. on Sunday.

I couldn't decide whether to list **Lila's** (pronounced *Lee*-la) under Little Havana or under "Budget," and finally decided that prices like these just had to be front and center. At Lila's, 2290 SW 8th St. (tel. 643-3345), you can stock up on steaks that lop over the plate and are buried under a mountain of french fries for, get this, $4.10! Lila's done so well with her Cuban steaks and fries (the steaks are the thin ones popular in Cuban restaurants) that she's now opened three other restaurants, in Westchester Mall on Coral Way, in Hallandale, and in Hialeah. You can't beat the original though, for color or for culinary outpourings. Open 11 a.m. to 10 p.m.

Want to see the home of the Whopper? Well, it's right here in Miami at **Brickell Bridge Restaurant,** 550 Brickell Ave. (tel. 347-4213), once owned by Jim McLamore who went on to create Burger King and a burger that was to rise to fame. Opened 30 years ago, this simple, unpretentious restaurant has retained many of the employees who were here when the place opened—and many of the customers have been coming here that long too! Burgers are, of course, one of the restaurant's top creations, but they do very good work here with daily specials like pork roast with apple and prune stuffing, manicotti, vegetable soup, London broil, sandwiches, salads, and big breakfasts. Brickell Bridge has some of the most reasonable prices in Miami, so you can gorge here, complete with free macaroni salad on the table, for less than $7 or $8, lots less if you're careful. The atmosphere is simple with orange booths and some potted plants, but the crowd is loyal and chummy so you'll feel comfortable—and well fed. Hours are 6 a.m. to 7 p.m. weekdays, closing at 2 p.m. on Saturday; closed Sunday.

Ribit, ribit—what's this huge green lily pad doing here in Coconut Grove? Why, it's the home of Señor Frog, what else? Funky, frog-green, and fun begin to describe a zany spot called **Señor Frog's,** 3008 Grand Ave., Coconut Grove (tel. 448-0999). Sepia photos of Mexican revolutionary heroes adorn the walls, and outdoors there's a shady patio where you can imbibe a couple of Dos Equis beers and munch on free baskets of tortilla chips and zippy tomato-jalapeña sauce. Later you can chow down on Talk-to-Me-Sideways brochette, moo flute or peep flute (those are beef or chicken flutas tortillas), taupeño soup (in which is buried a huge thing that looks like a mushroom but turns out to be an eye-watering chili pepper), or yummy enchiladas in a green sauce made with tomato-like vegetables called tomatillos or stuffed with roast pork. You'll pay less than $5 to $10 for anything on the menu here. Señor Frog welcomes you to his pad from 11:30 a.m. to midnight daily, until 2 a.m. on Friday and Saturday nights.

Vegetarian

Granny Feelgood's Restaurant, 555 NE 15th St., Miami (tel. 371-2085), is a wealth of natural foods: tofu, soy pancakes, omelets, carrot juice, vegetarian cheeseburgers, and the like. If you're not quite ready to go, um, cold turkey vegetarian, you can ease into this with lobster salad platters, pasta, eggs, or chicken parmesan. Granny produces quite an extensive menu, ranging from a platter of fresh fruit to stir-fried chicken, nachos, and guacamole. Prices are right too—well under $10 for most selections. Granny is open from 11 a.m. to 9 p.m. weekdays, closing at 3 p.m. on Saturday and closed altogether on Sunday. A second location, albeit a very crowded one at lunch hour, is at 190 SE First Ave.

RESTAURANTS IN LITTLE HAVANA: For my money there are no better or tastier bargains in Miami than Little Havana's raft of inexpensive and colorful restaurants. You can eat like the proverbial king (or a Hawaiian queen) here for much more reasonable prices than you'll find in many area restaurants—and feel as if you've just landed in Cuba at the same time. Fun and food are an unbeatable combination, and you'll find them in Little Havana, which is Miami's SW 8th Street.

The Food

Menus in Little Havana explain things in English to accommodate hordes of Norteamericano diners who have come to know and love Cuban food. But just to be sure you understand, here's a list and a brief explanation of some of the most popular Cuban dishes:

Arroz con pollo (pronounced ah-*rose* cone poyo) is roast chicken and yellow rice dotted with red pimiento.

Picadillo (pronounced peek-ah-*dee*-yo), one of my favorites, is a combination of ground meat, a rich brown gravy, peas, pimiento, olives, and raisins.

Platanos (pronounced *plot*-a-nose) or **plantains,** a mildly flavored fruit used to make **tostones** (pronounced toast-*tone*-ace)—which are round slices of fried green plantains—or to create platanos—which are ripe fried plantains. Tostones are crunchy, very bland, and usually have a slightly salty flavor, while platanos are sweet and soft.

Pan Cubano (pronounced pawn *Kew*-bawn-oh) is a long white loaf of bread with a crumbly, crusty exterior.

Ropa vieja (pronounced rope-ah vee-*ay*-ha) literally means old clothes, named for its stringy resemblance to rags, but it is a rich beef stew.

Cafe Cubano (pronounced caw-*fay* Kew-bawn-oh) is very strong, black coffee thickened with lots of sugar and served in tiny cups holding only a couple of tablespoons, just enough to open your eyes for a week. If you want the kind of coffee you usually drink, ask for **cafe regular** (pronounced caw-*fay* ray-goo-*lar).*

Palomilla (pronounced paul-oh-*me*-ya), is a thin sliced steak, similar to what English speakers call minute steak, usually served with onions, parsley, and a towering pile of thick french fries.

Camarones (pronounced caw-mar-*own*-ace) is shrimp.

Paella (pronounced paw-*eh*-ya) is a combination of chicken and often Spanish sausage, seafood, and pork, mixed with yellow rice and peas.

Fabada Asturiana and **caldo gallego** (pronounced faw-*baw*-dah Astew-ee-*awna* and call-dough gall-*yeggo)* are thick Basque soups made with beans and sausage.

The Restaurants

A note here on dining at Cuban restaurants: Cubans rarely begin even *thinking* of dinner before 8 or 9 p.m. So if you find a dining room practically empty at normal American dining hours from 6 to 8 p.m., don't assume the place isn't popular. Stay, and you'll discover that about the time you are finishing dinner at 10 or 11 p.m. the crowds are just arriving!

Juanito's Centro Vasco, 2235 SW 8th St. (tel. 643-9606), is the epitome of

Miami's Cuban restaurants, the one almost everyone will send you to and one of the forerunners of dozens of successful Cuban restaurants. Juanito's was a popular place in Havana; it's every bit as popular here, and has been since 1965 when Juanito Saizarbitoria opened this emporium. Try some unusual specialties like oxtail or just stick to more familiar fare like snapper fingers in a delicate wine sauce, steaks with interesting Spanish touches, fried garbanzos, gazpacho, sangría. You'll pay about $10 to $15 for dinner. Centro Vasco is open, with entertainment and a lounge, from noon to midnight daily.

Congratulations to Juan Delgado for creating a dining room that's tasteful in both decor and cuisine. At Delgado's simple and comfortable **Casa Juan,** 3800 SW 8th St. (tel. 442-2449), you dine on Castillian garlic soup, lobster and chicken Costa Brava, veal, seafood salads topped with clams, and an excellent filet that's a house specialty—great food and prices that rarely go beyond $12 to $15. Open from noon to 3 p.m. for lunch Tuesday through Friday, from 6:30 to 10:30 p.m. for dinner every day but Monday. Doors open at 2 p.m. on Sunday and close later on weekends.

Colorful sashes of jai-alai players gird the waists of waiters at **Bilbao,** 5910 SW 8th St. (tel. 266-2010), and wall murals show you how things were back in Spain's Basque country. Friendly service that's perfectly bilingual and happy chattering Cuban families out for celebrations are trademarks of Bilbao. Gorge on picadillo, black beans, plaintains, and all the standard favorites, or try the exotic flavors of baby eel, sopa de ajo (that's garlic soup, and much more delicate than you'd expect), seafood in a cream sauce, or seafood à la Bilbaine. For a fine dinner in an atmosphere that's foreign but not intimidating, you'll pay about $15 to $20, although many items are much lower than that. A lunch special on weekdays is an economical way to sample the specialties here. Bilbao is open from noon to 11 p.m. daily, a little later on weekends. There's a lively lounge here with Latin bands for dancing into the wee hours.

Budgeteers should head for **La Tasca,** 2741 W. Flagler St. (tel. 642-3762), where you can eat enough for an army and still spend less than $10. Arroz con pollo, paella, ropa vieja, pork, chicken, seafood, and a long list of inexpensive items make this a money-saving choice. Open noon to 11:30 p.m. daily, La Tasca is quite close to the Dade County Auditorium if you're planning an evening of the opera, concerts, or dance programs there.

Everyone who's anyone in Little Havana passes through the doors of **Versailles,** 3555 SW 8th St. (tel. 445-7614), a pretty little place lined with mirrors in the back room and with a lunch counter in front. Order your coffee Americano here or you'll get the super-thick teensy little cups of rich Cuban coffee (which, by the way, is wonderful). Politicians flock here in campaign times and even Florida's governor worked a day here once when he was campaigning. Good media noche sandwiches (grilled ham and cheese) and all the usual Cuban flavors are here, from yellow rice to batida milkshakes in exotic flavors like mango. Prices are very low, in the $5 range or less for many things. Versailles is open from 8 a.m. to 2 a.m. weekdays, later on Friday and Saturday, and from 9 a.m. on Sunday.

La Carretera, 3632 SW 8th St. (tel. 444-7501), shows nostalgic slides of Old Havana during dinner while preparing excellent seafood and beef at prices in the $6 to $8 range, a full lunch for $4 (and in Little Havana, that's *really* full). It's open 24 hours.

Miami's only Venezuelan restaurant, **El Chipi,** 2982 SW 22nd St. (tel. 442-1882), produces arequipas with cream, a cornbread specialty of that nation, and intriguing seafood fare for prices in the $10 range. Open 11 a.m. to 11 p.m. daily.

La Esquina de Teja, 101 SW 12th Ave. (tel. 545-5341), is named after a famous corner in Havana and produces typical Cuban fare for prices well under $10. It's open daily from 7 a.m. to midnight. Even Ronald Reagan has dined here!

El Meson Castellano, 2395 NW 7th St. (tel. 642-4087), serves one of the traditional appetizers of Cuba—a fruit cocktail of apple, papaya, mango, orange, melon, and whatever else they can find in the market sweetened by a light honey sauce. Specialties include chicken broiled with a crispy skin, cocido madrileño (a soup of chick peas, Spanish sausage, ham, chicken, beef, and cabbage), lamb roast in the Galician style, and white beans refried with pieces of Spanish sausage. Your finale should be brazo gitano, a cake stuffed with egg custard. You won't pay more than $6 or $8 for dinner entrees at this lively restaurant open from 10 a.m. to 10 p.m. every day.

Malaga, 740 SW 8th St. (tel. 858-4224), has as many—maybe more— American customers as it does Hispanic diners. Hundreds of pounds of arroz con pollo a la chorrera (chicken and rice) are created in this kitchen, along with an excellent paella laden with pork, fish, and chicken, as well as seafood and rice; pork chops; boliche mechadeo, created from eye of the round roast stuffed with rice and beans; and fabada Asturiana, a Basque soup of white beans with sausage. If you like fish, waiters will bring out trays of red snapper so you can see how fresh and how big they are. Prices here are in the $7 to $10 range for sumptuous dinners, and hours are 11 a.m. to 11 p.m. daily.

Latin Quarters, 3472 SW 8th St. (tel. 443-7647), is run by a chef with experience—he's been cooking for more than 50 years! He's also been learning about wine all that time and now boasts a huge wine cellar to go with the varied offerings available here. There's no telling what will be on the menu, as things change every day here, but you'll probably find big bowls of steaming caldo gallego, a thick white bean soup; chilindron de cordero, a lamb stew; costilla de res asada, which translates loosely as beef chops; and the house specialty, fricandó, beef stuffed with sausage and roasted. Certainly you'll never walk out of here hungry: dinners, which rarely top $6, are accompanied by rice, black beans, and fried plantains or a potato-like vegetable called yuca. Latin Quarters is open from 11:30 a.m. to 1 a.m. daily.

CORAL GABLES: Restaurants in this old and wealthy city fall in all price brackets and are often tucked away in romantic settings.

Continental

The Studio, 2340 SW 32nd Ave. (tel. 445-5371), has had some very high heights and some bottoming-out lows, but is back up there again as one of the city's favorite spots. I'd go for the garlic bread alone, but fortunately they also toss in an appetizer tray, Caesar house salad (tossed tableside), super onion soup, and a variety of well-loved dishes Americans have adopted as their own: beef Stroganoff, coq au vin, veal Cordon Bleu. You'll pay only about $15 here, perhaps less. Open 5 to 11 p.m. Tuesday through Sunday.

There's a pillow for the dainty feet of mademoiselle and a rose for the delicate hand at **Vinton's,** 116 Alhambra Circle in La Palma Hotel (tel. 445-2511). There's a very special atmosphere here. You can sit out under the stars in a pretty courtyard or inside in eclectic but charmingly romantic surroundings. On Monday there are fixed-price dinners with many a gourmet touch; other nights there is a list of French-inspired creations that will send you away richer in spirit and calories. Vinton's is open from 11:30 a.m. to 2:30 p.m. weekdays and 6 to 11 p.m. daily, except Sunday. Average entree prices are about $15 to $20. Pretheater dinners from 6:30 p.m., too.

The **Painted Bird,** 65 Merrick Way (tel. 445-1200), rose from obscurity to become one of Coral Gables' most discussed restaurants. No wonder either, for there is some very good cooking going on at this attractive restaurant outfitted in dark woods and shades of peach and plum. Cooking here falls into what one might call American contemporary, with new and unusual blendings of flavors: filet of beef topped with brie and figs or with artichoke sauce or chervil butter; duckling combined with apples and cashews; veal with prosciutto and kiwi; rack of lamb with guava and garlic. So many surprises are there, that you'll want to keep going back to try yet another of the restaurant's triumphs. Prices don't preclude those return visits either, ranging from about $11 to $15, including salad. You should probably figure on spending a little more than that, however, for the temptations—an appetizer of Greek feta cheese and spinach fritters topped with walnuts and wrapped in flaky pastry, for instance—are many. Hours are 11:30 a.m. to 2:30 p.m. weekdays, 6 to 10 p.m. daily, closing an hour later on weekends.

French

A charming decor of etched glass and mirrors makes the **French Connection,** 219 Palermo Ave. (tel. 442-8587), a pretty place to sample delicious creamy concoctions en croûte, escargots au roquefort, and there's even an ice cream en croûte. You'll pay $10 to $15 for a full dinner here. Make your own French connection for lunch from 11:30 a.m. to 2:30 p.m. weekdays, for dinner from 6 to 11:30 p.m. every day.

In the David William Hotel, 700 Biltmore Way (tel. 445-7821), are two upper-crust and upper-price spots, **Chez Vendôme** and the **700 Club.** Chez Vendôme is *très élégante,* a formal dining room with many continental selections and dinner prices in the $20 to $25 range. The 700 Club is smaller, more intimate, with a smashing view of the shady streets of Coral Gables. Beef and seafood selections here are in the same general $20 to $25 bracket. Both are open for lunch from 11:30 a.m. to 3 p.m. daily except Sunday, and for dinner from 5:30 to 11:30 p.m. every day of the week.

Mustachioed Maurice charms you with his bubbling personality, then bewitches you with his pâtés and seafood, his veal and Calvados chicken, his vacherin and puffy pastries at **Chez Maurice,** 382 Miracle Mile (tel. 448-8984). So dazzled are you in this cozy atmosphere of wood beams and half-timbered walls that you don't even mind the check, which is likely to fall in the $10 to $15 range for entrees. Lunch is served from 11 a.m. to 3 p.m. Monday through Friday, dinner from 6 to 11 p.m. every day but Sunday.

Charade, at 2900 Ponce de Leon Blvd. (tel. 448-6077), is tucked away on this busy boulevard in one of the loveliest buildings in this lovely town. In the center of things outside is a charming Spanish-inspired courtyard, but the focus inside is on outstanding Swiss/French cooking that has inspired such delicacies as veal geschnetzeltes (veal and mushrooms bathed in a wine and cream sauce), pan-fried rainbow trout stuffed with prosciutto, bouillabaisse, and shrimp sauteed with onions and spiced with curry and brandy. Prices are in the $10 to $15 range, and the restaurant's open for lunch from 11 a.m. to 3 p.m. weekdays and for dinner from 6:30 to 11 p.m. every day. Reservations are wise.

Good value and good food are the trademarks of **Madrid,** 2475 Douglas Rd. (tel. 446-2250), which has been a landmark in Miami since the 1950s. To really keep the check down, try their gazpacho-to-flan nightly specials. Lobster, roast suckling pig, white or black bean soup, pork chops fried in garlic sauce, snapper in green sauce, and paella are all on the menu here, where you'll pay $10 to $15 for dinner. It's open from 11:30 a.m. to 11 p.m. daily, later on weekends (closed Sunday).

Café de Artistas, 2312 Ponce de Leon Blvd. (tel. 444-8770), has taken

Miami diners by storm, becoming hysterically popular in practically no time at all. No wonder—the decor is beautiful and the food is outstanding. You dine here in a high-beamed dining room featuring black lacquered furnishings and black-cushioned chairs that contrast with white and forest-green table linens.

Technically the food here is not pure French, but Spanish with French overtones. Whatever the technicalities, you'll love the bean soup flavored with sherry, gorge on the homard à la Parisienne and poached lobster salad à la Russe, and feast on such treats as mariscos Don Diego (shrimp, scallops, crab, and lobster flavored with tomato mayonnaise, caviar, and brandy), roast duck (topped with sauteed bananas, peaches, oranges, and almonds), snapper steeped in garlic and tomato sauce, steak tartare, zarzuela (a Spanish bouillabaisse), and porc à l'orange. For dessert, try sin with pajamas, a combination of flan, several scoops of ice cream, profiteroles, fruit, dark chocolate sauce, and billows of whipped cream. Join me at Dieters Anonymous—tomorrow. Menus are à la carte, with entree prices in the $12 to $17 range, but figure about $20 or more per person for dinner—you won't be able to resist. Hours are 11:30 a.m. to 11 p.m. weekdays, 6 p.m. to midnight on Saturday, and 1 to 10 p.m. on Sunday.

To see the chocolatey glory of the chocolate mousse cake topped with sabayon at **Le Festival,** 2121 Salzedo (tel. 442-8545), is to abandon without regret those New Year's resolutions. After you've dined on chicken doused with champagne cream sauce, tournedos, soufflés or delicate pâtés, what difference can a little chocolate mousse cake make? You'll pay $10 to $15 for this temporary breakdown, and it's worth every calorie. Le Festival is open for lunch from 11:45 a.m. to 2:30 p.m. on weekdays, for dinner from 6 to 10 p.m. every day but Sunday. On winter weekends there are seatings at 7 and 9:15 p.m. only, and reservations are mandatory.

Papery crêpes, hearty onion soup and lobster bisque, quiches, and croque monsieur are the openers at **La Crêpe St. Michel,** 2315 Ponce de Leon Blvd., in the King Richard Hotel (tel. 446-6572). Then they toss in art deco chandeliers rescued from the old Mayfair Theater, background music from the 1930s, and a cozy, friendly ambience. Finis, monsieur—I give up. It's open from 11 a.m. to 11 p.m. daily (from 5 p.m. on Sunday) and stays open later on weekends. You'll pay $10 or less for most things.

Indian/Thai

Indian food may *sound* strange, but once you try these exotic flavors, you'll be hooked forever. You might as well begin trying them at **House of India,** 22 Merrick Way (tel. 444-2348), which has been holding forth since 1975 and now welcomes a loyal crowd of devotees who flock here to try flaky pastry vegetable samosas, fiery curries, mild and intriguingly spiced chicken tandoori. They stop here to take advantage of very reasonable prices too: the luncheon buffet, weekdays and Saturday from 11:30 a.m. to 3 p.m., is just $5 to $6; dinner, daily from 5 to 10 p.m. (an hour later on weekends), is likely to be less than $10.

House of Siam, 380 Andalusia Ave. (tel. 446-2360), ranks among the best of the many Thai restaurants that have been opening in South Florida in recent years. The atmosphere is simple and straightforward here, but the food is quite good and quite inexpensive. If you've never sampled Thai food, this may be the time to Thai on some tom yum goong, a light broth tangy with lime juice and lemon grass, a touch of hot pepper, a float of scallions, and shrimp. Fire-lovers should adore jumping shrimp, charcoal-grilled then blended with lemon grass and chili peppers. Samplers will delight in more than 60 entree items, and whoever is paying the bill will delight in a check that is unlikely to top $10 to $15 *for two.* Hours here are 11:30 a.m. to 10:30 p.m. daily, 5:30 to 10:30 p.m. on Sunday.

Italian

Raimondo's, 4612 LeJeune Rd. (tel. 666-9919), has long been lauded as one of the best Italian restaurants in the city and seems even more appetizing now that it's moved to this new location. There's a fabulous antipasto display at the door and beautiful dessert selections as well. Northern Italian cuisine is the specialty here, which means lots of creamy sauces and delicate touches. Waiters are often privy to information about other good things cooking in the kitchen, so ask. Saltimbocca, osso buco, zuppa de pesce, and chicken Luigi are good choices. Entree prices are in the $15 to $20 range, and Raimondo's is open from 6 to 11 p.m. daily.

Budget

In days gone by I spent many a joyous gorged-out hour at **Shorty's Barbecue,** 9200 S. Dixie Hwy., South Miami (tel. 665-5732), which had all the prerequisites I required in those days: cheap and spicy food, and lots of it. Shorty's burned down once in the interim, but the charcoal pits have been fired up again and are still going strong, producing great barbecued ribs and chicken. The coleslaw here is the best anywhere in the world and not at all like that ordinary grated stuff—it's little squares of cabbage and lots of celery seed with mystery ingredients. Finish it all off with corn on the cob and something bubbly and you'll see why I bargained many an hour's help with term papers for a ride to Shorty's. Prices still are less than $7 for a platter of ribs. Shorty's is open from 11 a.m. to 10 p.m. daily, opening half an hour later on weekends. There's always a crowd at the dinner hour, but it's worth the wait.

Vegetarian

Seeking vegetables? **The Spiral,** 1630 Ponce de Leon Blvd. (tel. 447-0646), is the place. Casual, and open from 11:30 a.m. to 10 p.m. daily (for dinner only on Saturday and Sunday), the Spiral feeds you fresh fish, homemade soups, pita sandwiches, homemade desserts and (naturally) yogurt, at prices in the $6 to $8 range.

RESTAURANTS IN COCONUT GROVE: Just locating restaurants in Coconut Grove can be a challenge. Many are tucked away on tiny streets, but all of them are as pretty as the small community around them.

Continental

Hotel restaurants are all too often as overpriced as they are undertalented in the kitchen. Not so with the **Grand Bay Hotel,** 2669 S. Bayshore Dr. (tel. 858-9600), which welcomes you to a tasteful French nouveau dining room that's a study in mauve, pink, fabulous floral creations, and candlelight glittering on brass and crystal. Lovely as it is, Grand Bay's dining room is not outrageously expensive—unless you cannot live without beluga caviar or the rarest of champagnes. Instead, you dine on such things as crabmeat wrapped in pasta and tied with a strip of celery, an unusual salad of arugula and endive, entrecôte dijonnaise, perhaps stuffed quail with a bordelaise sauce and quail eggs, pretty pastry desserts. Yet entree prices fall in a comfortable $16 to $20 range for most selections. Grand Bay's dining room is open from 7 to 11 a.m., 11:30 a.m. to 3 p.m., and 6 to 11:30 p.m. daily.

You'll see the real thing, that moon over Miami, at the **Top of the Grove,** 2649 S. Bayshore Dr. (tel. 858-2500), high atop the Coconut Grove Hotel. It changes its menu every three months, but can always be counted on to provide innovative treasures like smoked trout or scallops ceviche, quail, poached salmon wrapped in lettuce leaves, desserts that are sugary hallucinations. Entree prices are in the $15 to $20 bracket, and the dining room is open from 6 p.m. every day but Sunday, with dancing from 9 p.m. Tuesday through Saturday, and light suppers to 1 a.m. weekdays (until 3 a.m. on Friday and Saturday).

Café Europa, 3159 Commodore Plaza (tel. 448-5723), is an elegant café with indoor or outdoor dining in the $15 to $20 range for dinner. So popular has the salad dressing proven that it's now bottled and sold to diners, who also seek the chef's recipes for escargots au roquefort or artichoke hearts Mornay. Open from noon to 11 p.m. daily, later on weekends.

Restaurateur Monty Trainor went head-to-head with Miami's SRO Joe's Stone Crabs Restaurant when he opened **Monty's Stone Crabs** at 3390 Mary St. (tel. 448-9919) in Coconut Grove. Monty's also features those delectable South Florida crab claws at this good-looking dining spot replete with lots of oak, marble, and brass. Stone crabs are the star, but other seafood selections play very good supporting roles at this new Grove dining spot which features entree prices in the $10 to $15 range. Hours are 11:30 a.m. to midnight daily.

Kaleidoscope, 3312 Commodore Plaza (tel. 446-5010), is jammed at lunch when the multitudes flock here for crêpes, eggs Benedict, or unusual sandwiches. It's not much less crowded at dinner when intriguing seafood, beef, pork, and duck dishes are on the menu. They know what people want at Kaleidoscope, and deliver it to them with a friendly dispatch that's made this a favorite gathering spot in Coconut Grove. You can dine outside on a terrace or inside in a bistro for prices in the $10 to $15 range. You'd be wise to have reservations. It's open from 11:30 a.m. to 11 p.m. daily (from noon on Sunday), with later closing hours on Saturday and Sunday.

Seafood

Conch is king at **Monty Trainor's Bayshore Restaurant,** 2560 S. Bayshore Dr. (tel. 858-1431). You can have some of that elusive creature that hides inside those big pink-eared shells for prices in the $10 range, or feast on spicy-hot chowders, fritters, shrimp, oysters, perhaps even a grouper or snapper sandwich. Thatched huts are the dining rooms here. It's open from 11 a.m. to 2 a.m. daily. A lounge, open to 3 a.m., booms out jazz or top 40s music every night.

Light Dining

Coco Loco, 3500 Main Hwy. (tel. 446-4652), entertains you with jazz or reggae musicians and feeds you on tacos, refried beans, tostadas, nachos, guacamole, and the like. It's in the Coconut Grove Playhouse and prices are moderate, well under $10. Study loco here between 11 a.m. and midnight weekdays, later on Friday and Saturday. The lounge is open until 3 a.m. or so on weekends, and bands are on hand Thursday through Sunday.

RESTAURANTS IN KEY BISCAYNE: This sandy island is not big enough to have many restaurants, but those it does have are popular with islanders and with those they call "off islanders" (everyone else).

Stefano's, at 24 Crandon Blvd. (tel. 361-7007), is a welcome newcomer that's been getting lots of attention—and with good reason. You can find excellent pastas here, and dine on steaks, veal, chicken, and seafood treats with Italian touches. Stefano's is open from 6 p.m. to midnight daily for dinner; the lounge is open and has entertainment to 5 a.m. Entree prices are in the $10 to $15 range.

The Sonesta Beach Hotel, at 6350 Ocean Dr. on Key Biscayne, has two Oriental restaurants, one Chinese, one Japanese, and both dwell together in a restaurant called the **Two Dragons** (tel. 361-2020). There's a pretty view of garden greenery in the Chinese room's pagodas. Some top creations here are steamed wonton dumplings, roast duck Kowloon, and an intriguing number called Eight Immortals. Try a Japanese beer, Kirin, while you're here. Dinner's from 6 to 11 p.m. daily, later on weekends, and entree prices are in the $15 range.

A former Key Biscayne landmark called the Jamaica Inn has been transformed into a Mexican hacienda complete with pretty inner garden. Called **Dos Amigos Inn and Cantina,** 320 Crandon Blvd. (tel. 361-5481), this revamp of an old spot is specializing in Mexican cookery from tacos to skewered shrimp, and pollo con mole poblano. Dinner prices are in the $8 to $14 range or less, and there's often mariachi entertainment here too. Hours are 5 to 11 p.m. daily, closing an hour later on weekends.

Quite an international spot is this: on the other side of the building the **English Pub** reigns supreme. Filled with a combination of pubby and Key Biscayne historic memorabilia, the pub offers typical pub grub—steak-and-kidney pie, ploughman's cheese sandwiches, steak, chicken, and the like—and plenty of suds. Prices are in the same low range.

5. Culture and Nightlife

Nightlife on Miami Beach and in Miami can be as quiet or as lively as you want it to be. Sparkling sequined beauties strut through Vegas-style dance routines; supper clubs have entertainment and dancing. There's music from jazz band to jukebox, and performers from comedians to dancers, including some of the nation's most famous entertainers.

You can fly to Freeport, the Bahamas (for very low rates and sometimes even for free), if you're willing to stake a few dollars at the gaming tables there.

Here in Miami, as everywhere, lavish entertainment isn't cheap, so be prepared to fork over perhaps $100 for a night of dancing, dining, and entertainment, depending on your proclivity for posh. Drinks are comparatively expensive in top clubs too. Although most smaller lounges don't have cover charges, they frown on one who nurses a solitary drink all evening.

Superstars come to Miami Beach in December and stay through the winter season to provide a continuing round of glittering name entertainment through April. To see the very top stars perform will definitely be expensive—one New Year's Eve recently a top star was pulling $200 a person! You can find out who's where and when in several free magazines distributed in motel and hotel lobbies —*See, Where,* and *This Week in Miami.*

Latin nightclubs are some of the most popular places in town, and not only with the city's large and lively Latin population. Shows at these clubs are every bit the extravaganza you'd see anywhere, with lots of glitter and excitement. It's just the prices that aren't quite so flashy.

If you'd like to see a show or two and leave the driving to them, call **American Sightseeing Tours** at 871-2370 or 871-4992. They'll pick you up at your hotel, give you a choice of nightclubs, and toss in drinks, dinner, tips, and transportation. Tours begin at $28 per person.

First we'll take a look at special events and the culture scene, and then look at Miami and Miami Beach after dark. Also, reread my hotel and restaurant recommendations for additional nightspots and details.

SPECIAL EVENTS: Miami loves a party. At no time of year is that more evident than on New Year's Eve, when the city turns out for its annual **Orange Bowl Parade.** A nationally televised event, the parade features marching bands and floats, high-stepping majorettes, and an Orange Bowl Queen surrounded by her glittering princesses. The parade is the culmination of several weeks of parties, tournaments, and shows of all kinds.

Later in January, the city's Hispanic community celebrates Christmas on Cuban time—three weeks or so after the event! Called the **Festival de los Tres Reyes,** this mid-January celebration honors the Three Kings of biblical fame with a parade and plenty of feasting.

In February the activity moves to Coconut Grove, when artists, sculptors, billionaires, and bohemians gather for the annual **Coconut Grove Art Festival.**

As Miami's Cuban connection has become more familiar to the city's American population, Miamians have begun to capitalize on their city's lusty Latin flavor. Some years ago festival-loving Cubans began a small annual party called **Carnaval Miami.** At first Carnaval looked a little like a party to which no one came, but over the years this fiesta has grown like the proverbial Topsy until today it's a huge ten-day event that lures hundreds of thousands to the merriment, music, and maracas of SW 8th Street. If you're here for this potpourri of Latin music, food, dances, and a wildly colorful parade, you will learn a great deal about the "new" Miami—and perhaps also learn to salsa, drink a coco frio, and pound out a mean beat on the maracas as you dance in the streets. One thing is certain: you won't be bored. Carnaval occurs each March and gets lots of publicity in local newspapers. The **Miami Latin Chamber of Commerce,** 1417 W. Flagler St. (tel. 642-3870), also can fill you in on details of this fun-and-frolic fiesta.

THE CULTURE SCENE: Over the years Miami has taken a lot of flak for its lack of cultural pursuits. That criticism is not really fair, at least not anymore.

The newest star in Miami's cultural life is the **Metro-Dade Cultural Center,** 101 W. Flagler St., which is home to both the Center for the Fine Arts and the Historical Museum of Southern Florida.

Miami's quite proud—and justly so—of its new **Center for the Fine Arts** (tel. 375-1700), which was designed by famed architect Philip Johnson. Top traveling exhibitions are backed by a permanent collection housed in a quite contemporary two-story building. Hours at the downtown museum are 10 a.m. to 5 p.m. Monday to Saturday (closing at 9 p.m. on Thursday), and noon to 5 p.m. on Sunday. Admission is $3.

At the **Historical Museum of Southern Florida** (tel. 375-1492) exhibits chronicle more than 10,000 years of habitation on these sunny shores. Quite an innovative hands-on spot, the museum features a Spanish fort, two Seminole chickees, a sailing ship, a restored trolley car that once clanged its way around the city. Hours and admission fee are the same as the Center for the Fine Arts.

The **Greater Miami Opera Association** (tel. 854-1643) presents grand and light opera in the winter months at the Dade County Auditorium, at 2901 W. Flagler St., Miami, and the **International Cultural Exchange** brings talented international singers, dancers, and musicians to the auditorium all year long.

Producer Zev Bufman must get much of the credit for putting Miami on the theater map: he lures top stars here for a winter-long series of Broadway plays at the **Theater of the Performing Arts** (TOPA), 1700 Washington Ave., Miami Beach (tel. 673-8300). *A Chorus Line, Annie,* and *The Elephant Man* were a few of the many recent shows, and Elizabeth Taylor debuted her popular *Little Foxes* here. Tickets generally cost $25 to $30. The **Miami Beach Symphony** also plays at TOPA, which has recently been renovated, making it better than ever.

In Coconut Grove, **Players State Theater** performs at the lovely old Coconut Grove Playhouse, 3500 Main Hwy. (tel. 442-4000), where tickets to Broadway plays (and sometimes pre-Broadway runs) are $9 to $15.

MIAMI BEACH: Sheraton Bal Harbour Hotel, 9701 Collins Ave. (tel. 865-7511), has won critics' awards for its lavish, sparkling Las Vegas–revue show featuring huge casts of showgirls, spangled and fandangled sets, and costumes glittering with sequins and rhinestones. It's top entertainment, and shows are at 9 and 11 p.m. (it would be wise to check, as times do change). You can have dinner here too. Reserve and bring money.

The **Fontainebleau Hilton**, 4441 Collins Ave. (tel. 538-2000), has not remained one of Miami Beach's flagship hotels all these years by sleeping on the job. They flow with the tides here as you will see if you stop by the hotel's Poodle Lounge, where something is always happening.

For **dinner, dancing,** and **entertainment** in a romantic setting I'm partial to the beautiful Starlight Room at the Doral, where tiny lights that gleam on the ceiling of this rooftop hotel can be seen from down on the street. There's a view from the window that seems to go all the way to Cuba.

Beach hotels (the Konover, Deauville, Eden Roc Americana, Fontainebleau Hilton, Sheraton Bal Harbour, and the Diplomat in nearby Hallandale, to name a few) bring **top-name talent** here during the winter season. It can cost quite a bit to see them, and naturally the bigger the name the bigger the price. Frank Sinatra, Liza Minelli, and Sammy Davis, Jr., have all appeared here and filled huge rooms at prices over $100 a person.

There is no better way to immerse yourself in the city's art deco past while remaining firmly in its deco-rous present than to join the throngs who pack themselves bicep-to-proboscis into **Club Z**, 1235 Washington Ave., Miami Beach (tel. 538-0888). This hysterically popular nightspot began life in 1938 when it was the French Casino, built at a cost of $5 million as sister to a similar showplace of the same name in New York. Over the years it also served as the city's cinema theater and as a vaudeville house.

In 1984 after a $5 million renovation, the building was restored to its former art deco glory. Here you'll find a long, curving bar made of iridescent mother-of-pearl, recessed neon lighting bordered in etched-glass mirrors, chrome-and-glass lighting fixtures rimming a sweeping staircase that rises to a balcony lounge, and spectacular art deco murals. More than 2000 people can see and be seen in here at one time, and on some evenings the place seems stuffed to the max. The cover charge varies according to what's going on, but you can figure to pay $7 to $12 to get in, about $3 for drinks. Club Z is open Friday, Saturday, and Sunday from 10 p.m. to 5 a.m.

Place for Steak, 1335 79th St. Causeway, North Bay Village (tel. 758-5581), features contemporary musical entertainment ranging from a pianist to trios playing nightly from about 8:30 p.m. to 2:30 a.m. No cover.

The 30's Café, 622 Lincoln Rd. (tel. 532-5882), featured jazz, comedy, a pianist and drummer, even a "You Bet Your Life" show, the last time I heard. Entertainment from 8:30 p.m. to 1 a.m. weekends.

Flynn's Ocean 71, 6985 Collins Ave. (tel. 865-4098), specializes in video dance parties with such groups as Forget the Name, NuclearValdes, Trace, and Paragon. Right. Showtime is at 9 p.m.; doors open at 8 p.m. and close at 4 a.m. The cover is $5 to $7.

Bakerstreet, 6890 W. 12th Ave., Miami Lakes (tel. 556-0611), has entertainment or a disk jockey spinning jazz records most evenings from 8 p.m. to 2 a.m. daily.

More jazz/blues spots: **Suzanne's in the Grove,** 2843 S. Bayshore Dr., Coconut Grove (tel. 441-1500), open 9 p.m. to 2 a.m. daily except Sunday; **Tobacco Road,** 626 S. Miami Ave. (tel. 374-1198), with both upstairs and downstairs rooms, open 9 p.m. to 4 a.m. with a $3 to $5 cover charge.

Monty Trainor's Bayshore Inn, 2560 S. Bayshore Dr., Coconut Grove (tel. 858-1431), is another favored jazz-lover's hangout, with performances from 6:30 to 11 p.m. Wednesday through Sunday.

Biscayne Baby, 3336 Virginia St., Coconut Grove (tel. 445-3752), specializes in rock entertainers with shows at 9:30 and 11:30 p.m. and a cover of $3 to $5.

Faces, at 3390 Mary St. in the Mayfair in the Grove shopping mall (tel. 448-9399), abandons its daylight dining face each evening to become a flash-and-glitter disco each evening. Dancing begins about 8 p.m.

A number of top-name performers warm up in winter with performances in Miami. Many of those performances are at **Gusman Cultural Center,** 174 E. Flagler St. in the heart of downtown Miami (tel. 347-3010), or at the **James L. Knight Center,** next door to the Hyatt Hotel at 400 SE 2nd St. (tel. 372-0929). Tickets vary in price.

Cats, 3390 Mary St. (tel. 444-7877), a favorite singles spot at Mayfair in the Grove shopping mall, is a private club, but you can get a guest pass on weekdays and see if this place might be worth the $150 annual membership fee. Cats has recorded music and a disk spinner most nights and a dance show three days a week. It also offers shy and retiring types who don't want to risk face-to-face rejection a chance to pick up a telephone and call across the room and be rejected—perhaps accepted—by telephone. There are even telephones in the rest rooms for the really retiring. Open 11:30 a.m. to 5 a.m. for lunch, dinner, and imbibing.

Copacabana Supper Club, 3600 SW 8th St. (tel. 443-3801), is another Latin spot that has become very popular. It offers good shows with singers, dancers, and an orchestra, and is open from 8 p.m. to 3 p.m. daily except Monday. There's a two-drink minimum and sometimes a small cover charge.

If you're a jazz music fan, you can call a **Jazz Hot Line** (tel. 382-3938) to see what's playing. Blues fans can do the same with the **Blues Hot Line** (tel. 666-6656).

Arthur's, 1444 Biscayne Blvd. (tel. 371-1444), lures some top names in music—pianist George Shearing, for instance—and usually has three shows on weekend evenings. There's no cover charge at this spot, which is open from 8 p.m. to the wee hours with performances Tuesday through Sunday.

Oh dear, what have we here? **Fire and Ice,** 3841 NE Second Ave. (tel. 573-3473), certainly will strike you hot or leave you cold, depending entirely on what you bring here—and I don't mean your companion. Tuesday is a particularly unusual night, a night when this disco sponsors something called Artifacts. Art is feted at this event, and area artists are invited to do their damnedest to turn the evening into an Event that falls somewhere between a happening and a what-happened. Among the memorable Artifacts moments have been the creation of a New York City streetscape, a Dadaist fantasy featuring a Citroen and a coffin filled with colorful bowling pins, and a Suburban Nightmare starring giant boxes of Tide and Kellogg's Corn Flakes. According to reports, a couple of creative types once turned up dressed as a nuclear-powered aircraft intent on getting destroyed here. On really good evenings you may become part of the painting, a little splash here, a couple of daubs there. Fire and Ice flames hot and cold from 8 p.m. to some early a.m. witching hour.

Up on the north end of the beach, the Marco Polo Hotel rocks to the wee hours, as does the Newport. Both draw crowds of young people.

If you like girls wearing as little as possible, **Place Pigalle,** 22nd Street at Collins Avenue (tel. 538-0055), has flocks of exotic dancers performing little or no dancing in little or no clothing from 9 p.m. to 5 a.m. There's a three-drink minimum but this is not a spot for blushers.

Once again, for the most up-to-date information on what's happening each weekend, check the *Miami Herald* or *Miami News* entertainment pages each Friday.

MIAMI: Miami's two jazziest nightclubs are Latin operated, which is not surprising considering the raves one hears about Old Havana's nightclubs. Top spot of the two is **Les Violins,** 1751 Biscayne Blvd. (tel. 371-9910), which produces spectacular shows filled with dancing, singing, strutting showgirls dressed in flashy costumes performing on sets that rise, fall, open up, and practically perform their own show. Shows are usually at 9 and 11 p.m., and there's very good Spanish cuisine here in the $10 to $20 range.

Running a very close second is **Flamenco,** 991 NE 79th St. (tel. 751-8631), which has Flamenco dancers, guitarists, singers, and dinner for prices in the same general range as Les Violins. There are two shows and both are so good you'll feel transported from Miami straight to the Costa del Sol.

Many of Coconut Grove's restaurants have good evening entertainment (see my restaurant recommendations), and you'll spend an amusing evening at **Coco Loco** and hear some good jazz or reggae at **Monty's. Faces,** in the Mayfair Mall (tel. 448-9399), is a sophisticated Coconut Grove spot with a $5 cover charge and frequent ladies' nights.

In July and August stars like Andy Williams, Ray Charles, and Dionne Warwick join the Florida Philharmonic for a series of concerts at **Key Biscayne's Marine Stadium** (tel. 361-6730), an outdoor stadium under the stars on Biscayne Bay. Boaters attend too, with front-row seats right out on the water. You can buy tickets that include dinner at restaurants on the island, and the show, for $25 to $35. Tickets are available through island hotels; the concerts alone cost $5 to $12.

Latin restaurants like **El Floridita, Bilbao, El Baturro,** and **El Cid** in Little Havana have music for dancing and flamenco dancers, guitarists, strolling singers, and lots of fun for nothing more than the price of a drink or two, and those are only $2 to $3.

All over the county **Big Daddy's** and **Flanigan's** have lounges popular with the young set who take advantage of 25¢ or 50¢ drinks and lively entertainment.

Looking for something to do before the 4 a.m. plane? Out near the airport, **Daphne's** in the Sheraton River House is one of the city's hot spots and goes on to the wee hours. **Gambits** in the Marriott Hotel is popular for dancing, and **Scandals Lounge** at Ramada Inn–Airport draws crowds.

On Key Biscayne, **Rogers-on-the-Green,** at the golf course (tel. 361-9460), draws islanders and off-islanders for evening entertainment, and the **Sonesta Beach Hotel** always has something going in its lounges, as does the **Royal Biscayne Hotel.**

For the most up-to-date information on what's happening each weekend, check the *Miami Herald* or *Miami News* entertainment pages on Friday.

6. Seeing the Sights

From the oldest building in the hemisphere to a simulated hurricane, Miami and Miami Beach run the gamut in attractions. Calle Ocho's (Little Havana's 8th Street) infectious gaiety is waiting to entertain you and a performing dolphin would like a moment of your time. Miami beats Miami Beach in manmade attractions, so let's take a look at what to see and do in that city first.

THE SIGHTS OF MIAMI: At the top of my list of things to see in Miami is **Vizcaya,** at 3251 S. Miami Ave. (tel. 579-2708), an enchanting private villa built by James Deering, the International Harvester millionaire, who for $15 million constructed a Renaissance palace and filled it with a fortune in art and treasures he'd collected for more than 20 years. You can tour this 70-room mansion and roam the serene formal gardens put together by 1000 craftsmen who worked on this creation for five years. Those gardens wind around fountains, statuary, and reflecting pools, and range over 10 acres of ground with 20 more acres of untouched jungle. Inside are frescoed ceilings, tapestries, and priceless paintings. Outside, wide steps lead to the sea, where across the water is "moored" a stone barge that serves as a breakwater for the mansion. On some weekends from October to July you can see dramatic sound-and-light shows detailing the huge home's intriguing history. (You can even get married in the romantic stone courtyard—I should know.) Vizcaya is open every day except Christmas from 9:30 a.m. to 5 p.m. Admission is $5 for adults, $3.50 for children 6 to 11.

Right across the street is the **Museum of Science and Space Planetarium** (tel. 854-4247), where you can see some fascinating exhibits of living coral reefs and Mayan artifacts. At the Planetarium you can stargaze with people who know what's up. The museum is open from 10 a.m. to 6 p.m. daily, and admission is $3 for adults and $2.25 for children 3 to 12. For planetarium star, multimedia, and laser showtimes and prices, call 854-2222.

On nearby Virginia Key, **Planet Ocean,** 3979 Rickenbacker Causeway (tel. 361-9455), is where you can see the state's only (I guarantee that) iceberg. You can also climb into a sub, listen in on radio transmissions, and see dozens of exhibits outlining the importance of the ocean to all of us. And here's where that hurricane wind roars. Admission is $5.50 for adults, $2.50 for children 6 to 12. Exhibits are open from 10 a.m. to 6 p.m., but the box office closes at 4:30 p.m.

Here too is one who knows plenty about oceans: Flipper the performing dolphin at **Seaquarium,** Rickenbacker Causeway, Virginia Key (tel. 361-5703). He (or is it she?) and friends do high jumps while laughable sea lions and seals flipper and flutter about. You can see the whole 60 acres on a monorail trip, then visit habitats of sea mammals, birds, and turtles, and sea lion magicians every day from 9 a.m. to 6:30 p.m. with continuous shows. Admission is $8 for adults, $4 for children 6 to 12.

Finally on Key Biscayne is **Bill Baggs State Park,** which isn't exactly an attraction but it's awfully attractive. During some bad days with the Seminole Indians in Miami, the lighthouse keeper here was nearly burned out of his aerie, but he tossed down a keg of gunpowder. It frightened away the survivors and signaled a ship at sea, which came to his rescue.

If you fondly remember that orchid you wore to the prom or got for Mother's Day, you'll adore **Orchid Jungle,** 26715 SW 157th Ave. (tel. 247-4824). It's the world's largest outdoor orchid garden, and has blooms in every color of the rainbow. Admission is $3.50 for adults, $1.25 to $2.80 for children. Hours are 8:30 a.m. to 5:30 p.m.

Two other "jungles," **Monkey Jungle,** 14805 SW 216th St. (tel. 235-1611), and **Parrot Jungle,** 11000 SW 57th Ave. (tel. 666-7834), offer fascinating looks at those creatures. At the latter, parrots and macaws fly free, ham it up for photographers, ride bicycles, and perform in six shows daily from 9:30 a.m. to 5 p.m. at $6.75 for adults, $3.25 for children 6 to 12. At Monkey Jungle, the people are caged and the monkeys roam free. It's open from 9:30 a.m. to 5 p.m., and admission is $5 for adults, $2.50 for children 5 to 12.

Miami has a fascinating new zoo, called **Metro Zoo,** where the animals roam free, separated from visitors by moats and natural barriers. You can get a preview of the zoo (which is nearly complete) on weekends from 10 a.m. to 5:30 p.m. (last entry at 4 p.m.) at $4.50 for adults, $2 for children 3 to 12. Don't miss the big cats slinking around an Angor Wat temple look-alike. The zoo's at 12400 SW 152nd St. (tel. 251-0400).

A vintage steam engine pulling antique railroad cars now chugs along beside Metro Zoo. Called the **Gold Coast Railroad Museum** (tel. 253-0063), the historic railroad cars were once stationed at Fort Lauderdale's airport but were moved here in 1985 to make way for airport expansion. You can ride the cars, which include a 1913 steam locomotive, a Silver Crescent car with observation dome, something called a Ferdinand Magellan, and lots of others, at $7 for adults, $5 for children. If you call in advance, you save $1 on each of the ticket prices. Trains toot off at varying times on Saturday and Sunday mornings and afternoons. To get to the railroad, use the Metro Zoo access road at 12400 SW 152nd St., but turn right at the bridge.

In Coconut Grove, the home of Commodore Ralph Munroe, one of the first Coconut Grove residents, was built at the turn of the century and has been beautifully restored and maintained. Now the **Barnacle State Historic Site,** the home is at 3485 Main Hwy. (tel. 448-9445), and is open from 9 a.m. to 5 p.m., with tours at 9 and 10:30 a.m. and 1 and 2:30 p.m. Wednesday through Sunday. Admission is 50¢ for adults or children.

Publisher William Randolph Hearst dismantled and shipped to Miami the complete Spanish **Monastery of St. Bernard,** built in 1141, the oldest building in this hemisphere. It was to go in his home at San Simeon, but Customs officers, fearing hoof-and-mouth bacteria in the hay the stones were packed in, refused to let it leave Miami. Years later it was rediscovered, but all the stones' code markings were missing—what a jigsaw puzzle! It took five years to solve it, but you can now see the monastery and a collection of priceless medieval art, at 16711 W. Dixie Hwy. (tel. 945-1461). Hours are 10 a.m. to 5 p.m. daily (opening at noon on Sunday); the donation is $3 for adults, 75¢ for children 6 to 12.

A weird sight you might have seen on television's "That's Incredible" is **Coral Castle,** 28655 S. Federal Hwy. (tel. 248-6433), built by a man who hoisted coral rocks weighing as much as 30 tons into place with no modern tools or machinery. No one knows yet quite how he did it, but the woman whose love he sought never saw it—she jilted him on the eve of their wedding. You can see it though, and rock in a stone rocking chair balanced atop a wall or move a three-ton gate with one finger. It's weird and wonderful, this rock castle, and it's open from 9 a.m. to 9 p.m. daily at $5.50 for adults, $4 for children 5 to 10, but two children are admitted for the price of one.

If you're fascinated by exotic tropical plants, you can find out all about them and see 83 acres of tropical greenery at **Fairchild Tropical Garden,** 10910 Old Cutler Rd. (tel. 667-1651). There's a rain forest here, a rare plant house, a sunken garden, and lakes. Motorized tours are available if you don't feel up to 84 acres of hiking. Fairchild is open 9:30 a.m. to 4:30 p.m. daily, and admission is $3 for adults, free for children under 13. Tram rides cost adults $1; children, 50¢.

Redland Fruit and Spice Park, at SW 248th Street and 187th Avenue (tel. 247-5727), has more of the same plus some quite unusual tropical fruits like carambola and Surinam cherry plants. It's free and open from 9 a.m. to 5 p.m. daily. Guided tours are $1 for adults, 50¢ for children.

MIAMI BEACH: Miami Beach has the nation's largest collection of art deco architecture now on the National Register of Historic Places. It's a wonderful place to tour, ogling the soaring lines and funny furbelows of the 1930s. You can get a walking-tour map from the **Miami Design Preservation League** office at 1236 Ocean Dr., Room 11 (tel. 672-1836). Ninety-minute tours of the city's now-famous art deco district begin at 10:30 a.m. every Saturday at the same office and cost $5 a person.

READER'S SIGHTSEEING TIP: "A tour through Miami Beach's historic **art deco district** departs every Saturday morning from Definitely Deco (a 1930s period antique shop), 1001 Washington St., Miami Beach (tel. 253-2522). Tour begins at 10:30 a.m. (but come earlier to browse in the shop and get in the right mood), and usually lasts an hour and a half and costs $4 a person. It's a reasonably easy walking tour and most interesting, especially since a square mile of that area has received Historic Site designation. The tour ends at the Ca :lyle and Cardoza Hotels on Ocean Drive, both recently renovated in the art deco style. Both places serve lunch. Everyone on our tour became fast friends" (Sara Drower, Wilmette, Ill.).

7. Sports
There's practically no end to the sports facilities in Miami, whether you're a participant or a beach warmer.

GOLF: This section could go on forever—there are 42 courses in a 35-mile radius of downtown. There are 34 open to the public, ranging from the city of Miami's **Mel Reese Municipal Course,** at 1802 NW 37th Ave. (tel. 635-6770), to the famous 7000-yard **Blue Course,** nicknamed the "Monster," one of five courses at the Doral Country Club (tel. 592-2000), home of the annual Doral Open. Fees vary from the $6 to $9 charge at Mel Reese to $30 to $50 for winter play at the Doral ($15 to $25 in summer). Carts cost $24.

A sampling of other courses in the area includes the **Key Biscayne Golf Course** on Crandon Boulevard (tel. 361-9129), which charges $22 in winter, $7 in summer, and $17 for carts year round; the **Diplomat,** in Broward County just north of Miami Beach (tel. 949-2442), which charges $15 in winter and gives preference to the hotel's guests; and **Normandy Shores,** an 18-hole municipal course at 2401 Biarritz Dr. on Miami Beach (tel. 673-7775), which charges $12 in winter, $4 in summer. At **Bayshore,** 2301 Alton Rd., Miami Beach (tel. 673-7707), fees are $8 in winter, $4 in summer; and in Coral Gables at the **Biltmore,** 1201 Anastasia Ave. (tel. 442-6485), fees are $9 and carts are optional at $14.

Many hotels and motels can arrange money-saving guest privileges, so be sure to check first with your front desk.

TENNIS: On Miami Beach, **Flamingo Park,** at Michigan Avenue and 12th Street (tel. 673-7761), has 17 public courts, some lighted, and is open from 9 a.m. to 9 p.m. with a fee of $1 per person an hour. The same price prevails at **North Shore Park,** 350 73rd St. (tel. 673-7754), which has 13 courts, and at **Haulover Beach Park,** 10800 Collins Ave. (tel. 940-6719).

On Key Biscayne, **Calusa Park,** Crandon Boulevard (tel. 361-2215), has four public courts.

City recreation departments in Miami Beach (tel. 673-7700), Miami (tel. 579-6916), and the smaller communities will be happy to tell you where courts near you are located.

BEACHES: Beaches are practically everywhere you look in Miami and Miami Beach, but naturally there are a few really pretty ones you'll want to explore. My choice of all of them is Key Biscayne's **Crandon Park Beach** (tel. 361-2869). First, there are four miles of it, lined with palms and sea grapes so you can always find a shady spot. And there are lots of other diversions—windsurfing, picnic tables, beach cabanas ($12.50 a day), and lots of parking. **Bill Baggs State Park** at the tip of the island is pretty too (it's named after a crusading *Miami News* editor), and has lots of shallow water. You can tour the historic lighthouse for 50¢. *(Note to nudists:* On Virginia Key, an island you'll pass on the way to Key Biscayne, there's an all-over tanning spot.)

On Miami Beach, there are nice strips of silica at **Pier Park** (55 Ocean Dr.), where surfers search for waves; at **Lummus Park** (from 6th to 14th Streets); at

21st Street, where young people gather; at 35th Street (for shells). At 46th Street there are rental boats at nearby hotels. Go to 53rd and 64th Streets to avoid crowds, and 74th Street to join crowds. **North Shore Open Space Park,** 79th to 87th Streets, is lined with sea grapes and wooden boardwalks; **Surfside Beach,** at 93rd Street, has pretty white sand, and **Bal Harbour** has an exercise course.

Last, and perhaps best, is **Haulover Beach Park,** which begins at Bal Harbour and continues nearly to 163 Street. Once a narrow strip of land where boats were "hauled over" to the ocean, Haulover offers a mile and a half of sand and sea where you can surf, toss a Frisbee or a fishing line, picnic, barbecue, launch a boat, or roam a paved walkway along the sand. There's a $1 charge for all-day parking.

WATER SPORTS: Water is everywhere, so naturally water sports are not far behind. For instance: **American Sport Diving Schools** (tel. 253-5353) and **New England Divers** (tel. 573-4600) have lessons, equipment, and diving trips from $20. The best diving area is around Fowey Rocks Light just south of Key Biscayne, good for underwater photography (but you must have a diving flag).

You can rent **Hobie Cat sailboats** at the **Eden Roc Americana** (tel. 531-0000), the **Fontainebleau Hilton** (tel. 538-2000), and in Coconut Grove at **Adventurers Yacht and Sailing Club,** 2480 S. Bayshore Dr. (tel. 854-3330), for about $14 to $18 an hour, from $78 to $98 a day. **Windsurfing** boards at the same places go for $10 an hour.

Adventurers Yacht also rents other kinds of sailboats, as does **Castle Harbor Sailboats** at Dinner Key Marina in Coconut Grove (tel. 858-3212).

Surfers shouldn't expect too much (Miami doesn't have really good surfing waves unless there's a storm), but some days the surf is up. When that happens, head to **Haulover Beach Park** or **Pier Park** at South Beach where you'll find areas reserved for surfing.

Coral Gables Venetian Pool, 2701 De Soto Blvd. (tel. 442-6483), is such a treasure you really ought to go over just for a look at this grotto-like creation. It's a wonder of lagoons, porches, and towers of coral rock. Admission is $2.50 for adults, $1 for children.

RUNNING, ROLLING, RIDING, AND GENERAL ROMPING: For **joggers,** there's a Vita course in Coconut Grove's **David Kennedy Park,** and for **bicyclers,** 138 miles of bike paths. **Roller skating** has struck here too, and in Coconut Grove there are several places to rent wheels. One is **Roller Seet,** 3425 Main Hwy. (tel. 446-0665).

South Miami is the center of Miami's equestrian world. Among the ranches offering trail rides, hayrides, and instruction are **Country Gentleman Stables,** 15500 SW 200th St. (tel. 233-6615 or 232-9710); **Golden Eagles Ranch,** 41 SW 122nd Ave. (tel. 221-4312); **Hunting Horn Stable,** 6155 SW 123rd Ave. (tel. 274-3133); and **Quail Roost Ranch,** 15400 Quail Roost Dr. (tel. 253-3308). On the north side of town, **Rockin' N Ranch,** 13501 NE 16th Ave., North Miami (tel. 891-9512), also has trail rides and a pony ring for the youngsters. You'll pay about $5 to $10 a person for an hour's ride.

You can go gliding in Miami too, on thermal drafts that carry you silently atop the world. **Kendall Glider Port,** 16800 SW 237th Ave. (tel. 232-2700), is home base for gliders, which cost $30 for 20 to 30 minutes. Phone ahead or write: Thorpe Aviation, Inc., P.O. Box 970594, Miami, FL 33197.

FISHING: No matter how you like your fish, baked, broiled, or mounted, you can catch one in Miami. **Fish free from bridges** at MacArthur and Rickenbacker

Causeways. For **pier fishing**, head for Haulover Park, Pier Park on South Beach, Sunny Isles, 167th Street and Collins Avenue, or Dinner Key in Coconut Grove.

If you'd like to go after the devils of the deep in the Gulf Stream, seek out a **charter boat** at Dinner Key Marina in Coconut Grove, Haulover Park, Crandon Park Marina on Key Biscayne, Bayfront Miamarina in downtown Miami, or the docks at the Castaways. You'll pay $300 to $500 for six people for a day of fishing.

If you don't think a snapper dinner's worth quite that much, angle aboard a **party boat** which takes out several dozen people. They leave from the same marinas and cost about $20 a person.

PROFESSIONAL SPORTS: Miami is the home of the **Orange Bowl,** 1501 NW 3rd St. (tel. 579-6971), so from August to January you can see plenty of the champion **Miami Dolphins** here (tel. 576-1000), as well as the University of Miami's Hurricanes football team. Ticket prices vary. Don't forget the Orange Bowl parade, the one you see on television every year, takes off down Biscayne Boulevard on New Year's Eve.

At Miami Marine Stadium on Key Biscayne (tel. 361-6730) you can see a nine-hour endurance **speedboat race** in January and top speedboat races all year long. Tickets are about $5.

Miami is the spring training camp for the **Baltimore Orioles,** who practice at the Miami Stadium, 2301 NW Tenth Ave. (tel. 635-5395), from about mid-February.

HORSE RACING: One of the world's most beautiful tracks and now a National Historic Place, is the **Hialeah Race Course,** East Fourth Avenue between 21st and 32nd Streets (tel. 885-8000). Racing fan or not, you shouldn't miss this spectacular track. The grounds ramble on through acres and acres of formal gardens, tropical jungles, and royal palms. The clubhouse and grandstand are in elegant French Mediterranean style with ivy-covered walls and sweeping stone staircases. In the center of it all is a colony of flamingoes that lives on an island in the middle of the track oval. After the seventh race, they fly a circuit around the course in a spectacular display of black-tipped pink plumage.

A shipwreck aquarium houses coral reef fish. There's a French walking ring, and a display of racing silks in the elegant clubhouse. It's open to the public all year long (except the two weeks prior to the racing season), and you can tour it by train.

Some of the nation's finest horses train and run here. Winter racing dates are exchanged with **Gulfstream Park Race Track,** on US 1, Hallandale (tel. 944-1242), but both parks race between January and May. Grandstand admission is $2; clubhouse, $4.

Gulfstream is also a very pretty track, with a long entrance lined with royal palms. On Florida Derby Day, near the end of the season, the track sponsors some amusing races in which jockeys ride all sorts of strange mounts (ostriches, for instance).

Calder Race Course, NW 210th Street and NW 27th Avenue (tel. 625-1311), has summer and fall racing dates from mid-May to mid-January. It's up at the northwest corner of the county and has an attractive Turf Club dining room overlooking the track. Grandstand admission is $2; clubhouse, $4; plus a small additional charge for reserved seats.

American Sightseeing (tel. 871-2370) and **Metro Transit Authority** (tel.

638-6117) run special buses to the tracks, as does **Gray Line** (tel. 633-0375). Fares are about $2.

GREYHOUND RACING: Put a dollar or two on the doggies at the **Biscayne Dog Track,** I-95 at NW 115th Street, Miami (tel. 754-3484), or the **Flagler Dog Track,** 300 NW 37th Ave. (tel. 649-3000). Races are at 8 p.m. daily (except Sunday), with matinees on Tuesday, Thursday, and Saturday. General admission is 50¢; to the clubhouse, $1.

JAI-ALAI: Basques first began this fast handball game in the 1600s and brought it here from Spain. Players wrap a long curved basket *(cesta)* around their wrists and catch a speeding ball *(pelota)* in it, then toss the ball back against a wall for the other player to catch. You bet on individual players, who are as respected in these environs as jockeys are at the racetrack. The ball travels as fast as 100 m.p.h., so the game is dangerous as well as exciting. Miami's **Jai-Alai Fronton** is at NW 36th Street and 36th Avenue (tel. 633-9661), and games start at 7:30 p.m. daily except Sunday (matinees on Monday, Wednesday, and Saturday at noon). The fronton is open from mid-December through late April and from June to September. Admission is $1.

You can learn to play jai-alai if your eye and nerves are good. The nation's only amateur jai-alai fronton is **Miami Amateur Jai-Alai Fronton,** 1935 NE 150th St. (tel. 944-8217), which charges $2 to $3 an hour. A school operates year round. Open 10 a.m. to midnight daily.

8. Shopping

Sometimes Miami seems to be one big shopping center. You can buy everything here from Spanish piñatas to $1000 designer gowns. Wherever you are, you won't be far from a shop. Here are a few places to get you started buying:

Bal Harbour Shops, at Collins Avenue and 97th Street, harbors some very exclusive shops (Gucci, Lapidus, Saks, Neiman-Marcus, for openers) in a beautiful mall filled with flowering orange trees and splashing fountains. Prices are awesome, but so is the style.

Lincoln Road Mall is eight blocks of shops closed to traffic that runs east to west between Collins Avenue and West Avenue at 7th Street. There's a tram that scoots around from one end of the mall to the other, and you're always close to shady benches, fountains, and flowers. It's a nice place for a stroll even when the shops are closed. Lots of boutiques and lots of bargaining here.

In Miami, **Omni,** Biscayne Boulevard at 16th Street, is the crown prince of Miami shopping plazas, a two-level creation filled with 21 restaurants, six movie theaters, shops in every price range, even an Italian carousel. Jordan Marsh department store and a cluster of carpeted, subtly lit, hushed boutiques with names like Bally, Cardin, and Gucci occupy one end of the mall, J. C. Penney the other.

House-proud visitors to Miami might want to have a look in the shops on **Decorator's Row,** at NE 40th Street between North Miami Avenue and NE Second Avenue. All kinds of furniture and accessories for the home are sold here, although if you find something you want to buy, you'll probably have to contact an interior decorator as most of these shops sell to the trade only.

On the north end of town is the Mall at 163rd Street which hypists are now calling **"The Miracle at 163rd Street"**—get it, get it? What they're really talking about is the roofing-over of this mall, which was once a bit seedy but was much improved by the addition of a fiberglass roof. At the 163rd Street Mall you'll find both Burdine's and Jordan Marsh department stores, movie theaters, and quite a number of small shops. It's in North Miami Beach at NE 163rd Street between Biscayne Boulevard and the Golden Glades Interchange on I-95. It's open daily from 10 a.m. to 9:30 p.m. (noon to 5:30 p.m. on Sunday).

A new shopping area on the north end of town is called **Loehmann's Plaza** in honor of the store that is most important here—at least to local socialites, who sneak off, suitably disguised, for a visit to Loehmann's, which sells overruns and extras of designer clothing (labels removed) at discount prices. If you want to know who designed that outfit you can't resist, don't despair. By now everyone has figured out how to read the codes on the price tags, so just ask somebody to decode for you. You'll find Loehmann's and several other discount shops in Marina del Rey at Biscayne Boulevard at 187th Street. Loehmann's is open to 9:30 p.m. Wednesday, normal hours every other day, and noon to 5 p.m. Sunday.

Aventura Mall, 19501 Biscayne Blvd., has four major department stores including Lord & Taylor's, Penney, Sears, and—blare of trumpets—Florida's very first Macy's. More than 200 stores are here selling everything from heels to meals. Open every day from 10 a.m. to 9 p.m., and on Sunday from noon to 5 p.m.

At the south end of the county, **Dadeland Mall,** 7535 N. Kendall Dr., is one of the largest malls in the nation, with five carpeted arcades, fountains, foliage, and dozens of restaurants and shops including representatives of the largest department stores operating in Florida—Burdine's, Jordan Marsh, Sears.

In the middle (in location only, I hasten to add) is Coconut Grove's posh **Mayfair in the Grove,** at 3390 Mary St., where you should bring money not in a wallet but in a shopping bag. Valentino, Ralph Lauren, Pierre Balmain—all the "names" are here.

In Coral Gables, **Miracle Mile** is a four-block-long strip between Douglas and LeJeune Roads filled with shops, restaurants, theaters, and plenty of exclusive names on the front windows.

If you'd like a handcrafted guitar, one of those piñatas for the kids to break open blindfolded on birthdays, bullfight posters, mantillas, oil paintings, furniture, Cuban coffee, or rum-soaked pastries that will knock your socks off, the place to go is **Little Havana,** Miami's SW 8th Street. Prices are lower here than anywhere else in town, and you can have a wonderful time even if you don't buy anything.

Real bargain hunters will want to look at the **Miami Fashion District,** the third-largest garment district in the nation. It's been here, between NW Fifth Avenue and 22nd to 29th Streets, since the early 1930s. You'll find 225 businesses purveying everything from handbags to shoes, home accessories, sporting goods, and electronics. Most of the stores lack fancy fitting rooms and don't offer refunds, but you can find some excellent bargains with a little searching.

A new shopping center in Miami is **The Falls,** just off US 1 and SW 136th Street. Stroll here amid rainforest lagoons, waterfalls, cedar- and glass-trimmed waterside gazebos, and try to remember you're here to look at the stores. The biggest news here is a branch of New York's Bloomingdale's.

9. A Visit to the Everglades

Just a few miles south of Miami on the way to the Florida Keys is a vast primeval prairie that sweeps across 2000 square miles and 1½ million acres of wilderness. Much of this ancient swampland is rarely if ever seen. It harbors a complex biological life chain topped by humans who have sheltered this mysterious swamp from the creeping tide of Florida's commercial development and guarded its fragile population of near-extinct creatures.

Limestone rock underlying the Everglades and, farther north, Big Cypress Swamp, is six million years old. Over it flows fresh water that supports a bustling community of creatures from microscopic algae to the king of Everglades beasts, the alligator.

As you drive through this vast subtropical jungle, you'll see why the Indians who lived in these glades called the waters here Pahayokee (pronounced Pay-*high*-oh-key), the River of Grass. That's all you'll see as you drive into the heart of the Everglades at Flamingo Park, vast sweeps of marshland covered with golden grasses and dotted by islands of trees. These islands, called hammocks (from an Indian word for garden place), shelter live oaks, mahogany, gumbo limbo trees, and a world of creatures from the red-shouldered hawk to tiny tree frogs, nocturnal opossums, great white herons, crocodiles, sea cows, and the nearly extinct Florida panther. All roam these swamps and settle on these islands built up around odd trees called mangroves, which are supported by dense networks of roots reaching into the water. Decaying vegetation that collects around the roots eventually forms islands where wild orchids bloom in desolate stands of gray trees. Spiky-leafed air plants feed on tiny particles of airborne fertilizers. Exotic bromeliads grow here and strangler figs twine around trees finally killing them, then taking their place in the ever-changing forest.

To get there, follow US 1 south through several suburbs of Miami. Just south of Homestead, you'll see a sign directing you to the park entrance and visitor center. At the center (tel. 247-6211), you'll find exhibits, orientation programs, and detail maps of the area. Admission to the park is $2 a car.

FLAMINGO: As you drive the 50 miles to Flamingo, you'll see clearly marked trails and raised boardwalks leading into the swamp. The **Royal Palm Visitor Center** has two very interesting trails, Anhinga (named after a bird that looks unhinged) and the Gumbo Limbo Trail, where the foliage is so thick you can see only a few feet in front of you. At Shark River Basin you can overlook the swamp from an elevated trail, and at Taylor Slough you can spot alligators, water birds, perhaps even otter, deer, black bear, or a bobcat.

Flamingo is a serene little village on Florida Bay where there's an attractive, spacious motel called the **Flamingo Inn**, P.O. Box 428, Flamingo, FL 33030 (tel. 305/253-2241 and 813/695-3101). Rates are $33 double in summer, $55 to $63 in winter.

Flamingo has a popular campground operated by the National Park Service, although the mosquitoes are a little rough in summer. There are no water or electricity hookups, however, just cold showers and space to park your recreation vehicle or pitch a tent. In summer, space is free; in winter, it's $5.

There is a bit of a village here, a very small one, but with all the things you'll need, from groceries to bait and souvenirs.

If you're just driving down for the day, stop in for lunch or dinner at the second-story restaurant where you can dine on excellent fresh seafood and steaks (they'll even cook *your* catch) for $6 to $15 and watch spectacular sunsets through a wall of windows.

If you're looking for something to do here, sail away on **White Water Cruises** ($6.75 for adults, $3.50 for children) that touch down at Cape Sable, the southernmost point in the continental United States. A special sunset cruise is a blazing spectacular—it's $5 for adults, $2.50 for children. Or ride a **Wilderness Tram** (open from November to April; admission is $6 for adults, $3 for children) for a closeup look at the wilderness. You can rent canoes or outboard motorboats, and take off for a day out on your own in this mysterious land. There are marked boat trails so you won't become the Lewis and Clark of the Everglades.

If you'd like to hook your own dinner from the deep, there are charter boats with captains who know where those elusive creatures hide. Make fishing arrangements when you reserve space at the Flamingo Inn or the National Park Service campground since the park is often filled with anglers with similar intentions.

There's a National Park Service Visitor Center and a museum staffed by a naturalist.

Now, there are no guarantees that you're going to see a wild animal, an alligator, or even a bird while you're out here exploring the Everglades. However, there is a place where we can guarantee you a look at some of those shy fellows who inhabit the Glades. It is called, fittingly enough, **Eden of the Everglades.**

Some people are just meant to spend their days in the wilderness, and a fellow named Ervin Stokes is one of those. He worked for it, he earned it, and now he's got it—a little piece of peace he calls **Eden of the Everglades** (tel. 695-2800). Eight acres of swampland along Panther Creek, this Eden offers you a chance to walk on a cypress boardwalk winding through a mangrove forest manned by rainbow-hued macaws, cockatiels, cockatoos, parakeets, lovebirds, toucans, some alligators, tortoises, even a pair of bobcats. Who says this isn't Eden? Eden of the Everglades is on Route 29 about three miles south of US 41 near Everglades City. Admission is $6 for adults, including a boat ride into the backcountry of the Everglades, $4 for children 4 to 11. If you just want to walk through the park, the fee is $4.50 for adults, $2.50 for children. It's open daily from 9 a.m. to 5 p.m.

EVERGLADES CITY: If you're headed to Florida's west coast, you can visit the park from Miami by taking the Tamiami Trail (US 41) west 37 miles to a second park entrance at Everglades City. Along the way you can visit a **Miccosukee Indian Village** on US 41 (look for the signs). The Miccosukees are a branch of the Seminole tribe that settled here 150 years ago, and some still live in the traditional thatched-roof huts called chickees (their sides are open to catch the breeze). At the Indian village you'll see a typical camp with the traditional star-shaped fire, and separate sleeping, working, and cooking quarters. After the tribe moved to the Everglades following the Seminole Wars, they traded animal skins for brightly colored cloth and sewing machines which they still use to create intricate bright patterns from tiny scraps of cloth. Fashioned into dresses, jackets, blouses, and vests, these are colorful souvenirs of the Everglades and a product unique to this tribe. Miccosukees, by the way, may have had the first mother-in-law jokes: their tribes are ruled by women, and grooms have to move into the camp of the bride's mother.

Near Everglades City is **Shark Valley,** where automobiles are forbidden but you can take rubber-tired trams on hour-long journeys into the park to the Shark Valley observation tower. A taped program describes the natural history of the area, and you can ask all your questions of a park ranger. Trams operate at half-hour intervals from 9:30 a.m. to 5 p.m., and the gates are open from 8:30 a.m. to 6 p.m. The cost of the tour is included in the $2 park fee.

If you need help with specific details of a visit to the Everglades, write to the Superintendent, Everglades National Park, P.O. Box 279, Homestead, FL 33030.

While you're here, Everglades City is an interesting spot that's plunked down at the entrance to Florida's Ten Thousand Islands. Land on which the "city" (it's a very tiny settlement) now stands was acquired in the 1920s by advertising executive Baron Collier, who meant to build a metropolis here, and almost succeeded. Between the Depression and a population move northward,

Everglades City never quite made it to fame, but fortunately the **Everglades Rod and Gun Lodge,** Everglades City, FL 33929 (tel. 813/695-2101), was built. For 100 years this lodge has been an exclusive sportsman's hideaway; four presidents (including Truman, Eisenhower, and Nixon), plus Supreme Court Justice Warren Burger and actors Burt Reynolds and David Carradine, have visited here. A huge old banyan tree 15 feet around has stood sentinel over this rambling wood structure for all its years of welcoming fishermen and hunters. Inside the lodge, all that masculine comfort lives on in a high-ceilinged, wood-beamed clubby lobby, plump wing chairs, deep-cushioned couches, a massive hooded fireplace, pool table, and on the wall an eight-foot alligator (with an electric plug in its mouth!). That same atmosphere flows right into the dining room where immense brass chandeliers cast a soft glow over the formal setting, the walls and ceiling paneled in pecky cypress that's now a high-priced rarity (but was once an inexpensive wood). Sea trophies are the only adornment here, and the friendly smiling help will even cook your catch for you for $6. If you somehow are not lucky on the fishing grounds, you can choose from a limited but excellent menu of scallops, stone crabs from fishermen whose traps you'll see nearby, grouper, or any of the 50 varieties of fish that swim in waters a 15-minute boat ride away. Dinner prices are in the $10 range. Everglades Lodge is open all year but is at its best in winter when it lures the famous and fishing fanatics. The Rod and Gun Lodge has 25 rooms, all of them clean and decorated in deep jewel-like colors. Rates are $34 in summer, about $42 in winter.

You'll also find a very nice resort called the **Captain's Table Resort,** Drawer B, Everglades City, FL 33929 (tel. 813/695-4211), with small but very clean and nicely decorated rooms in a two-story building as well as a wide range of other accommodations including villas on stilts and rooms with screened porches. Two people will pay $44 to $96 in the winter season. Next door is the Captain's Table restaurant, a charming place way out here in the wilds with wide glass windows so you can watch the changing moods of the Everglades. Prices are in the $10 to $12 range. It's open for breakfast, lunch, and dinner in winter, less frequently in summer.

Outdoor Resort and Marina, Chokoloskee Island, FL 33929 (tel. 813/695-2881), is a nice place, neat and clean with carefully tended lawns and a trim look from fin to fin. There's nothing pretentious about this simple single-story hideaway, but there's nothing pretentious about the price either: $55 for a kitchenette for four, year round. Motorhome parking is $13 to $16.

If you'd like to tour the park by boat, a park ranger operates a sightseeing boat in the winter months for $7 a person.

Two of the weirdest ways to get around in Florida are contraptions called swamp buggies and airboats. You can ride either or both of them at **Wooten's** (tel. 813/695-2781), just east of the entrance to Everglades City. Swamp buggies are Jeep bodies atop heavy-treaded tractor tires, and they plow through the shallow waters of the swamp for $10. And if you think swamp buggies are a Rube Goldberg creation, wait till you see an airboat! These are flat-bottomed skiffs with airplane propellors, powered by car engines mounted at the rear. They skim across the surface of the swamp, and you can ride on one of the noisy but exciting weirdies for $6 to $10, depending on the length of the trip.

For a pelican's eye view of the Glades, call **Happy Harry Enquist** at 695-4620 or 695-4211 (in Naples, at 394-5700), who will fly you around for about $10 a person.

If you'd like to stay in a very plush resort that is indeed far from the madding crowd, **Port of the Islands** is about 80 miles west of Miami and 20 miles east of Naples (tel. 813/394-3101). This is one gorgeous 200-room place: six tennis courts, a beige stucco building with Mediterranean tiled roofs, arched windows and entrances, double doors with tiny glass panes opening onto balconies, rental boats, trap and skeet shooting, pool, and a private landing strip. One step into the soaring tiled lobby and you know you're somewhere very special. Two stories above you, huge wooden beams stretch across an immense reception area and higher yet is a skylight. Wood-railed loggia hallways rim the second level, and off the halls are elaborately decorated suites and rooms. The focal point of the reception area is a massive fireplace crowned by a starkly dramatic painting of a stately white heron. Beautiful puffy contemporary furniture is everywhere, and there's a pale-peach restaurant and Charley's Bar, a forest-green lounge.

Clustered around the pool are rooms in single-story buildings. They have beamed ceilings, contemporary muted tones, and arched rattan headboards. In winter months, rates are $60 to $80 for most rooms, $115 for suites, $65 and up for efficiencies. In other months, rates drop to $45 and children under 15 are free. The resort was recently listed in the top 20 hunting and fishing lodges in North America.

10. Island Hopping to the Bahamas

Miami is so near the Bahamas that some people have considered swimming it, but if you'd like a little more traditional way to go, try **Bahamasair,** which is that nation's national carrier. For quick trips to the beautiful out island of Eleuthera, also seek out Bahamasair, which flies there and to other Bahamian islands. Both Freeport (on Grand Bahama Island) and Nassau (on New Providence Island) have gambling, and in winter season there are a number of quite inexpensive gambling junkets that go over and return the same day. The price is low, frankly, because the odds favor the house, but at any time you can fly to the islands and back for about $100. (Some junkets may even be free, but require a bankroll and gambling commitment.)

To see things the leisurely way, hop aboard any of the **cruise ships** at Miami's Dodge Island port or Fort Lauderdale's Port Everglades. There are trips of all durations, from a four-day weekend to a year aboard the *Queen Elizabeth II*. To get a peek at the cruise ships, visit the Port of Miami on Dodge Island, where the big white bruisers are lined up like sentinels.

The **Port of Miami** is now the busiest port in the world, welcoming more than two million passengers every year. And many of those decide that a week-long cruise begun and followed by a few days of Miami or Fort Lauderdale sunshine is a very tempting idea.

If you're interested in a cruise or would just like to hear what cruises are all about, I'd (modestly, of course) like to recommend another Frommer book, **Dollarwise Guide to Cruises,** co-authored by (guess who?) Marylyn Springer and Donald A. Schultz. In this book you'll find detailed descriptions of all the ships that sail off into the sunset from Miami and from many other U.S. ports, including Miami's northern neighbor, Fort Lauderdale.

If you'd like to take a look at a cruise ship, find your way to the MacArthur Causeway, which runs along the north side of the port. By the side of the causeway you'll see some trees and some public parking areas where you can stop the car and gaze in awe at these huge ocean ships towering over you like so many fat ducklings in a row.

Most ships depart from the Port of Miami on Saturday in the late afternoon, say, 4 to 5 p.m., so if you stop by on that day, you'll see quite a line of them—and thrill to their booming horns as they announce their departure!

If you'd like to get an even closer look at a ship and what it has to offer, don't hesitate to call any of the cruise lines I'm about to name and ask them for a guest pass. They're anxious to have you for a passenger, so they'll be happy to oblige. Then get on over there and prowl around the ship all you like. You're welcome to have a drink in the open bars and listen to the calypso bands—just be sure to get off when the "all ashore that's going ashore" is sounded.

The cruise companies operating year round from the Port of Miami are Carnival Commodore Cruise Line, Cruise Lines, Dolphin Cruise Line, Eastern Cruises, Norwegian Caribbean Lines, Royal Caribbean Cruise Lines, and Scandinavian World Cruises (which operates one-day, no-overnight cruises).

In the winter months you may also see ships operated by Costa Cruise Line, Fantasy Cruises, and Paquet Cruises.

Chapter III

THE FLORIDA KEYS

1. Upper and Lower Keys
2. Key West

A SILVER RIBBON OF HIGHWAY streaks southward across the merging waters of two great seas. On and on it goes, 113 miles of it slicing through silvery coral islets where palms rustle and sway in unceasing sea breezes. Leapfrogging across 41 bridges, it passes sleepy fishing villages and dazzling strips of sand baking under a relentless tropical sun until at last it reaches bridge 42. Here it flies over seven glorious, spine-tingling miles of diamond-tipped waves and foaming white water lapping gently over bars of golden sand.

It's an incredible feat of engineering, this strip of macadam known as the **Overseas Highway,** a feat begun by none other than that dreamer and empire builder, railroad tycoon and hotelier Henry Flagler. In 1912 aboard his luxurious private car called Rambler, an elderly and nearly blind Flagler rode triumphantly into Key West, $27 million poorer but the proud creator of Flagler's Folly, the "Railroad That Went to Sea" across 29 islands. Time was to prove that Flagler's railroad was more foresight than folly, but his dream died when a vicious hurricane swept across these keys, killing hundreds of people and turning his dream railroad into a mass of twisted metal. Years later Flagler's "folly" formed the bed of the Overseas Highway, which today brings a million sunstruck tourists to these sleepy strips of limestone and coral.

First you'll pass through **Key Largo** (shades of that Bogart-Bacall movie). Today the island's fame is the John Pennekamp Coral Reef State Park, a watery wonderland where you can watch rainbow-hued tropical fish darting about as you swim among them or peer through the hull of a glass-bottomed boat.

Next is **Upper and Lower Matecumbe Keys,** named for the Spanish words *matar* (to kill) and *hombre* (a man), a reference to shipwrecked sailors killed or enslaved by Indians here. Islamorada is the focus here, a purple island named for the color early Spanish explorers saw from the sea. That color was created by purple snail shells covering the beaches.

Then comes **Marathon,** on Vaca Key. Halfway between the mainland and Key West, Marathon was once the site of the supply store for the 3000 railroad workers who said that by the time the tracks reached here, the job had become a marathon, an endurance test.

Bahia Honda (Spanish for deep bay) is the geological transition from Upper to Lower Keys, and is a sandy state park where botanists study rare plants like West Indies satinwood, Jamaica morning glory, and the wild dilly. Here, too, historians can see the remains of Flagler's railroad.

Big Pine Key is a haven for tiny Key deer, some no bigger than collie dogs. Herds of the deer had once dwindled to only a few dozen, but now are protected in a refuge and number about 500, ranging over 18 keys.

Then there's **Sugarloaf Key,** where you'll see one of the weirder sights of these quiet islands—a 30-foot $10,000 bat tower, complete with bat rat protector and bat graveyard, designed to attract migrating bats which scientists hoped would settle in and rid the island of mosquitoes. The project failed—the bats never showed up. There are even some wags who say the mosquitoes ate the bats, but these days islanders have solved the problem with sprays.

Snuggled in between these larger keys are spots with intriguing names like Cudjoe Key (said to be named after someone's Cousin Joe), Lignum Vitae (named for the ironwood trees that grow there), and Duck Key. They're sandy without having many really good beaches; they're neither elegant nor lined with attractions, but they're as hypnotizing as sun and sea can make them, as intriguing today as they were to long-gone pirates.

They're Florida's "out islands," entrancing strips of sand on which you'll discover some of the swashbuckling, rough-and-tumble history of this state, and meet outgoing, eccentric, rock-strong, hospitable, and ever-cheerful islanders who move at a slow pace and can teach you to do likewise.

GETTING THERE: Southern Express flies into Key West and Marathon regularly from Miami and other Florida cities. **Greyhound** buses also travel through all the keys from Miami.

GETTING AROUND: You can rent a bike from **Key Colony Bike Shop** at Mile Marker 53 (tel. 289-1670). Bikes are $7 a day, $35 a week.

Since most people drive here from Miami, rental-car facilities are limited, but **Alamo** has an outlet on the island (tel. 743-5211).

Taxi services operate on all the Keys.

1. Upper and Lower Keys

Here on this string of islands people like to divide the Keys into three sections: upper, middle, and lower. Upper Keys begin at Key Largo and stretch south through Upper and Lower Matecumbe (Islamorada). The Middle Keys run through Marathon, and the Lower Keys are what's left over, including Key West.

Scattered about, and accessible only by boat, are dozens of other keys with fascinating names, my favorite of which is a true conchism: No Name Key.

As you drive through the Keys, you'll see numbered markers along the right-hand side of the road known as Mile Markers. They indicate the distance from Key West and are about the only addresses you'll find in the Keys. The numbers go down as you go south, up as you go north.

READER'S WILDLIFE-VIEWING TIPS: "Travelers are invited at no charge to Betty Brothers Real Estate at the bridge in **Little Torch Key.** Her two pet dolphins are fed and do tricks for anyone who drops by at 10 a.m. and 5 p.m. every day. The dolphins are free to come and go as they please to the open ocean, but always come back every day. On Key Deer Boulevard (1¼ miles north of the Watson Road intersection) is what is known as the **Blue Hole.** This is an old rock quarry filled with fresh water. Several alligators make their home there, as well as other wildlife. Also, drive out onto **No Name Key** after dark, coast slowly down the main road (a dead end), and keep looking into the woods. Your car should soon be surrounded by raccoons begging for food. They eat anything, but Saltines seem to be one of their favorites" (Linda Sambel, Pittsfield, Mass.).

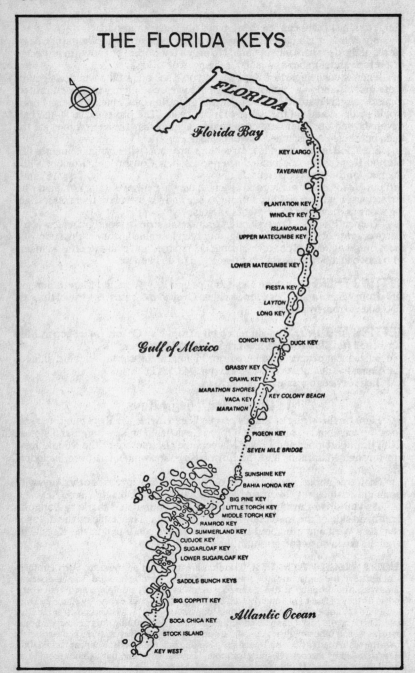

THE FLORIDA KEYS

WHERE TO STAY: Let's take a look at the islands from north to south, starting with Key Largo where you'll find both a **Holiday Inn,** P.O. Box 708, Key Largo, FL 33037 (tel. 305/743-6501), and a **Howard Johnson's,** US 1, Key Largo, FL 33037 (tel. 305/289-1400). Both are spiffy motor lodges that between them can provide tennis courts, swimming pools, glass-bottomed boat tours, fishing, diving, and snorkling, and rates that range from $60 to $70 in peak season, $50 to $60 in summer.

If you'd rather fish than anything, **Gilbert's Motel,** US 1 at Jewfish Creek (tel. 305/451-1133), is right smack on the key, and has radios, TVs, and phones in the motel rooms, as well as a few efficiencies. There's a pool, a ramp for your boat, and a marina, plus a small restaurant that's open from 7 a.m. to 10 p.m. (prices in the $4 to $16 range) and a lounge. Winter room rates are $52 to $76; in summer, $38 to $48.

At Mile Marker 87, you'll find **Plantation Yacht Harbor Resort,** 87000 Overseas Hwy., Islamorada, FL 33036 (tel. 305/852-2381, or in Miami call 305/248-6807), a bright white resort set on acres and acres of grass overlooking the multicolored waters of a yacht harbor. Owned by a Hialeah electronics company which sends its executives here to rest, the resort's an eye-catcher with contemporary colors and decor that differs from room to room but can include sunken sitting rooms, chrome bookcases, color TVs, phones, and private porches (Room 14, all done in light blue, and Room 10 in orange and brown geometrics and chrome, are especially pretty).

Outside, the grounds seem to go on forever, with a pool, tennis courts, private beach, barbecue grills, jet skis, shuffleboard, and basketball. El Capitan dining room, at water's edge, is a lovely place to end the day with some delicacies like cioppino, seafarer's pie, conch fritters, or a steak for prices in the $11 to $15 range. It's open from 7 a.m. to 1 a.m., and the lounge, where you'll find lively entertainment, is open to the wee hours. From mid-November to May and from July through August prices range from $60 to $75; in other months, from $50 to $60; and extra guests cost $8.

Cheeca Lodge, P.O. Box 527, Islamorada, FL 33036, at Mile Marker 82.5 on Upper Matecumbe Key (tel. 305/664-4651, in Miami 305/245-3755, or toll free 800/327-2888), is expensive, but it's worth the money if you're in the mood for a big splurge. Once an exclusive fishing club, the lodge is now open to the public and continues to offer a warm welcome, outstanding service, fine food, and a relaxing hideaway where you can let tomorrow take care of itself.

There's a golf course here (executive, with no hole more than 115 yards), built by the company that puts Jack Nicklaus's courses together, and Nicklaus himself is a frequent guest here. You can play tennis too, swim in a large freshwater pool, fish from a pier, and take your catch inside where an excellent restaurant will apply to it the skills they use on menu items. Spacious rooms are set high over the sea and sport beautiful views of the Atlantic just outside the door. They're tastefully decorated in subtle shades that echo the tones of beach, sky, and sunset outside. Two people pay $150 to $185 a night in winter months, $105 to $115 in other seasons.

Islamorada's a favorite getaway spot for many Miamians who troop off to **Holiday Isle Resort,** US 1, P.O. Box 588, Islamorada, FL 33036 (tel. 305/664-2321), as much to sit in the cool comfortable depths of the Tiki Bar and Restaurant as for the resort's other offerings. There are lots of Polynesian touches here in a maze of beachy-looking apartments, motel rooms, and efficiencies circling a heated pool. There's a strip of beach, a marina and ramp for boaters, and, naturally, fishing. In the Tiki Restaurant you can feast on mango cake, thick and crusty Bimini bread, and fresh seafood for prices in the $10 to $14 range. Evenings, there's entertainment in the lounge. You'll pay $64 to $78 for a double room, $75 to $95 for an efficiency, and $105 to $275 for suites, year round.

Just ten minutes off the shore from **Harbor Lights Resort,** 84951 Overseas Hwy., Islamorada, FL 33036 (tel. 305/664-3611), you can dive among coral gardens and sunken Spanish galleons. In between dives, rest up in this three-story motel where some of the simply decorated rooms have screened porches. Coconut palms shade the pool, and there are various games scattered about the resort's grounds. You'll find an inexpensive harbor here for $41 to $69 in winter, $37 to $61 in summer, less in fall.

Hawk's Cay Resort and Marina, Mile Marker 61, Marathon, FL 33050 (tel. 305/743-7000), used to be called Indies Resort and Marina, but the name is just one of hundreds of things that have changed at this casual and now very comfortable resort on Duck Key. In 1984 the new owners spent $10 million on a top-to-toe revamp of this long-popular getaway, and they have much to show for their money.

A rambling West Indies–style resort on a 60-acre island, Hawk's Cay is now as contemporary as a moon shot, decked out in dusky pinks, greens, and turquoises that somehow seem to reflect these very tropical surroundings. Wicker furnishings are offset by tile floors in those same muted shades, and overhead paddle fans whirr. Here, too, you'll find a lovely sand-ringed saltwater lagoon, freshwater pool, tennis courts, two whirlpool spas, fishing and sailboats, diving and snorkeling equipment, windsurfing boards, bicycles, a fitness trail, and an adult game center with billiards, darts, and bumper pool.

Dining at Hawk's Cay ranges from the poolside Cantina, specializing in piña coladas and conch chowder, to the formal Caribbean Room, where continental cooking is favored, and the dockside Ship's Galley overlooking the marina. Each morning guests are treated to a sumptuous complimentary breakfast buffet in the Palm Terrace dining room.

Rooms are just as lovely as every other part of this spiffy new complex. Large, airy, and tropical, they feature balconies or terraces with wide expanses of glass, walk-in closets, dressing areas, color TV, and telephones. Rates range from $135 to $205 double from January 1 to mid-April, $85 to $300 in other months. Suites also are available and range in price from $220 to $400 in high season.

At Key Vaca (Mile Marker 49) you'll find **Buccaneer Lodge,** 2600 Overseas Hwy., Marathon, FL 33050 (tel. 305/743-9071), a large resort spread out across sandy waterside acreage said still to be haunted by pirates. I didn't see any—just lots of people laughing by the pool and splashing on the inn's sandy beach. There's quite a good dining room, with lots of seafood on the menu for about $10 to $13, and a lounge to while away some cool hours. Summer rates are $35 to $52; in peak season, from December on, $45 to $62.

If you're looking for the true Keys experience, the ultimate rustic off-the-beaten-path hideaway is the **Mariner Resort,** P.O. Box 620, Big Pine Key, FL 33043 (tel. 305/872-2222). At Mile Marker 31, turn west off US 1 and follow the signs. Here you'll find the lazy leisurely atmosphere that is just what the Keys are all about. Rooms are simply but brightly furnished. They aren't huge, but you won't be spending much time in them anyway, with a pool outside, tennis, sailboats, reef-fishing trips, and diving. Best of all is the resort's hideaway restaurant, Peg Leg's, a fascinating place of brass rails, etched glass, and church-pew booths where you'll find easygoing Keys-ites sipping in the Pickled Parrot Lounge, swinging on hanging basket chairs on the porch, or dining on simple seafood fare (in the $10 to $12 range). An 1800-era mahogany bar and massive espresso machine are Peg Leg's pride, and you can see them from 11 a.m. daily.

Rates at the resort are $49 to $59 in winter (and during lobster-spearing season in July), dropping to $39 to $49 in other months.

Few if any of the resorts in Florida can offer you a performing dolphin for entertainment. But Sugar is the star at the **Sugar Loaf Lodge**, Box 148, Mile Marker 17, US 1, Sugar Loaf Key, FL 33044 (tel. 305/745-3211), and performs happily for gawking guests. Paneled rooms are tucked away in one- and two-story buildings overlooking the waters of Sugar Loaf Sound, with bright colors which echo the blue of the waters outside your balcony. There are tennis courts, miniature golf, and a pretty glass-walled restaurant overlooking the water (prices, $10 to $15) so you can watch Sugar. For rooms you'll pay $70 to $80 in peak season (and during late-July lobster-fishing days), $45 to $60 in other months. Children under 12 are free; others are charged $5.

READER'S HOTEL SELECTIONS: "Lou and Ann Minuti own a nice motel on Big Pine Key at Mile Marker 31.5 called the **Big Pine Resort** (tel. 305/872-9090). They have 32 modern rooms and some efficiencies and apartments, all with air conditioning. There is also a swimming pool. Rates at Big Pine Resort are $50 in winter, $55 in summer. I can also recommend the **Royal Palm Recreational Vehicle Park**, US 1, P.O. Box 520, Big Pine Key, FL 33043 (tel. 305/872-9856), at Mile Marker 31.5, which has 37 sites; and **Sunshine Key Camping Resort**, US 1, P.O. Box 790, Sunshine Key, FL 33043 (tel. 305/872-2217), which has 386 sites on a 73-acre island complete with recreational facilities. Rec vehicle parks charge about $15 a day, less by the week" (Linda Sambel, Pittsfield, Mass.).

Camping

At Mile Marker 106, **Happy Vagabond Campground**, P.O. Box 215, Key Largo, FL 33037 (tel. 305/451-1713), has a pool, playground and rec room, grocery, TV room, laundry, and showers at $12 a day for water and an electric hookup, $1 more if you use air conditioning.

Outdoor Resort of America at Long Key, FL 33001 (tel. 305/664-4860), on Islamorada, at Mile Marker 66, has all kinds of amenities: tennis, pool, miniature golf, health club, and sauna. Rates are $20 to $22 for two, $3 per extra person.

State parks in the Upper Keys include **John Pennekamp, Bahia Honda,** and **Long Key.** Camping is $8 a night, but there is a four-day minimum stay and the parks are often very crowded (especially Pennekamp) so it's wise to reserve ahead. Call Pennekamp at 305/451-1202 (or toll free 800/432-2871 in Florida) for reservations.

WHERE TO EAT: Again moving from north to south, let's start with Mile Marker 100 on Key Largo where you'll find **Ganim's Country Kitchen**, 99696 Overseas Hwy. (tel. 451-2895). You can feed a passel of hungry mouths cheap on huge submarines, inexpensive luncheon specials, and family-priced home-style cooking, like breakfast for $1.45. Fresh biscuits, pies, and pastries are made daily. Open 6 a.m. to 2 p.m.

You have to go some to beat **Fudpucker's Ice Cream Parlor,** at Waldorf Plaza, Key Largo (tel. 451-0982). A name like that deserves a look, so while you're looking you might as well indulge in salads, sandwiches, pizza, or 16 flavors of ice cream, even fresh popcorn. Open daily from 11 a.m.

Islamorada is the culinary capital of the Keys and many a Miamian—and even one Fort Lauderdale restaurateur I know—slips off to get in on the goodies. Here you'll find **Ziggie's Conch Restaurant,** at Mile Marker 83 on US 1 (tel. 664-3391), and it's not to be missed. In this unprepossessing little spot, where the decor runs to mounted fish, you'll find simply the best food for many a mile. Most of it's not on the menu though, so be sure to ask what other delectables are being cooked up in the kitchen—fluffy conch fritters, lobster de jonge, oysters Rockefeller, wonderful pastas with unusual sauces. It's sensational. Prices are in the $10 to $15 range, and Ziggie's is open from 5 to 10 p.m., except Thursday (closed from Labor Day to mid-October).

Sid and Roxie's Green Turtle Inn (tel. 664-9031) has been a fixture in the Keys since 1947. From their kitchens at Mile Marker 81.5, Islamorada, come turtle soup and conch chowder so good it's canned and sold through gourmet outlets, and there's plenty of good seafood and steaks in a roadside-tavern atmosphere. Decor in this casual spot is hundreds of business cards stuffed in every empty space. It's open from noon daily, except Monday, and prices are $6.95 to $16.95. You can buy the soups in a six-pack for $9.

A Keys newcomer destined for the heights is Erik Jorgensen, once chef at Miami's posh Chez Vendôme. Now he's bought a houseboat, and clipped miles of red tape to install it as **Erik's** at Mile Marker 85.5 on Windley Key (tel. 664-9141), quite close to Islamorada. Once again he's producing cuisine that draws crowds to his beneath-the-bridge hideaway. Erik is a Viking charmer, and the houseboat is a study in beautiful views inside and out, with lots of crystal, linens, a fireplace, Peruvian llama rugs on the walls, and silk rosebuds on the tables. There's a skylight above and a tiny wine "cellar" with leather high-backed hand-carved chairs and Copenhagen china, silver, and goblets. For the Keys, this is spectacular. For anywhere, this is spectacular! Prices are in the $11 to $15 range, and Erik's labor of love is open from 6 to 11 p.m. Wednesday through Monday, probably also for lunch in winter. Call for reservations.

At Mile Marker 83.5 at the Whale Harbor Docks in Islamorada, you won't have any trouble finding the **Whale Harbor Inn** (tel. 664-4159)—just look for the lighthouse. That lighthouse was high ground during a hurricane that the owners rode out right here, while their chairs floated around in the dining room below. You can see photos of the storm damage at the entrance, and then treat yourself to lunch or dinner inside overlooking a fleet of charter boats. There's a second-story gathering spot called Rott'n Ralph's that probably shouldn't be missed. Downstairs, you dine on lots of fresh seafood in a comfortable casual atmosphere. Prices average $8 to $15, and the restaurant's open from 11 a.m., the lounge to the early a.m., with shows at 10:30 p.m. and 12:30 a.m., Dixieland on Sunday.

If you like quantity as much as quality, don't miss the **Coral Grill** at Mile Marker 83.5, Islamorada (tel. 664-4803), where you can stoke up for a long winter at a belt-busting table guaranteed to send you away in overstuffed joy. More than 40 appetizers, entrees, salads, and desserts, ranging from prime rib to fried shrimp and flaky pies, are featured in the buffet. Meanwhile a downstairs dining room offers menu service which includes a soup and salad bar. Buffet price is $11.95; downstairs dining falls in the $10 to $15 range for dinner. Hours are 4:30 to 9:30 p.m. Tuesday through Saturday, noon to 9 p.m. on Sunday; closed Monday.

You shouldn't have much trouble finding **Marker 88** (tel. 852-9315) since its name is also its location. A bilevel waterfront restaurant with terrific views out over Florida Bay at sunset, Marker 88 is a cheerfully handsome restaurant that is very, very popular hereabouts. Reservations are most wise. Marker 88 deserves its popularity too, for the restaurant serves top-quality food prepared under the supervision of chef/owner André Mueller, who whips up such specialties as baby snapper Rangoon topped with mangoes, papayas, pineapples, and bananas in a lemon-parsley butter; shrimp curry with mango chutney; Florida lobster stuffed with crabmeat; and rack of lamb provençale. Try the lobster bisque and consider one of the restaurant's Caesar, Greek, or German wilted-leaf-lettuce concoctions. Personally I'd never think of resisting the oysters Bienville. The menu is à la carte, and thus can climb pretty high for gorgers like me. Entrees alone are $12 to $20. Despite the fancy food, dress is Keys casual. Hours are 5 to 11 p.m. daily except Monday.

READER'S RESTAURANT SELECTIONS: "On Sugarloaf Key at Mile Marker 20, there is a restaurant called **Mangrove Mama's** (open from January to April; closed Thursday; tel. 745-3030). They use only local seafood, and all their meals, which include home-baked bread, are served in an oldtime Keys atmosphere. The food is excellent and the atmosphere a bit different from most places in the Keys. If you decide to visit the restaurant, try the fish tempura—it's super. The prices are about $7 to $12 per person. [*Author's Note:* Gary Bell, who spends the rest of the year farming in Tennessee, operates this restaurant which is open from 5 to 10 p.m. daily except Thursday, and has had its recipes included in a Florida cookbook called *Cracker Cookin'*.] **Island Jim's,** near Mile Marker 32 on Big Pine Key, serves some of the best steaks and chops I have ever eaten, at prices running approximately $5 to $7. Also on Big Pine Key, near Mile Marker 30, is **Serendipity.** They have great deli sandwiches, grinders (a meal in themselves), and ice-cream sundaes. It's scrupulously clean and the service is excellent" (Linda Sambel, Pittsfield, Mass.).

THE SIGHTS: **John Pennekamp Coral Reef State Park,** Mile Marker 102, Islamorada (tel. 451-1202), is an underwater garden 21 miles long and 4 miles wide, an undersea fairyland of more than 40 species of coral and 650 kinds of colorful tropical fish. Molasses Reef is the focal point of the park, a panorama of unsurpassed beauty in water 25 to 40 feet deep. All kinds and colors of coral and an explosion of fish greet divers, and there's even an underwater statue, *Christ of the Deep.* There's no charge for admission to the visitor center, open 8 a.m. to 5 p.m., but admission to the park (open sunrise to sunset) is 50¢ a person.

Discovery Undersea tours leave at 9 a.m., noon, and 3 p.m. daily, and cost $8.50 for adults, $4 for children under 12. Scuba expeditions are $22.50. Snorkeling trips (at 9:30 a.m. and 1:30 p.m.) are $16 per person. If you throw sailing in with the snorkeling, trips are $40. You can call the Coral Reef Park toll free in Florida at 800/432-2871.

Diver's World, at Mile Marker 99.5 (tel. 451-3200), has daily Pennekamp trips and all the equipment you'll need for $17 to $34.

Theater of the Sea, P.O. Box 407, Islamorada, Mile Marker 83.5 (tel. 664-2431), was featured on NBC's "Today" show and has continuous porpoise and seal shows from 9 a.m. to 4 p.m. daily. You'll see tarpons, bonefish, porcupine fish, colorful parrot fish, angel fish, rays, and five trained dolphins, not to mention some not-very-fun-loving sharks. Admission is $6 for adults, $4 for children 5 to 12 (under 5, free).

If you're wondering about that enormous bubble you see floating in the air around the Seven Mile Bridge, that's **Fat Albert,** a U.S. Air Force thing—but they're not saying just what. Rest secure in the knowledge that Uncle is watching over you aboard this fat little sausage with fins.

Local festivals, art shows, fish fries, and the like are detailed in the **newspaper** of the Upper Keys, *The Keynoter,* published in Marathon.

Another publication, **Florida Keys Magazine,** 6161 Overseas Hwy., Marathon, FL 33050 (tel. 305/743-3721), chronicles some fascinating details of life in the Upper Keys. Stories in the magazine have offered the lowdown on high-flying Fat Albert, an interesting look at Keys birds, the story of Zane Grey's visit to the islands, and a look at an early pioneer woman's struggles as a lime farmer. Lots of news on upcoming activities too.

NIGHTLIFE: Things are pretty quiet evenings in the Upper Keys, but here's a look at a few things you'll find moving after dark. Many of the hotels listed back a few pages have entertainment too.

Key Largo

Gilbert's Motel and Marina (tel. 451-1133) has a trio for listening and dancing on Friday and Saturday nights, and lounges at the **Holiday Inn** (tel. 743-6501) and **Howard Johnson's** (tel. 289-1400) both have entertainment most nights.

The **Unwinder** (tel. 451-0500) at Jewfish Creek has a band every weekend at the outside bar.

Plantation Key/Tavernier

Plantation Yacht Harbor (tel. 852-2381) is the big action in these parts, with dining and dancing nightly except Monday, and piano entertainment Thursday through Monday.

Islamorada

Holiday Isle's **Flying Bridge Lounge** (tel. 644-9290), at Mile Marker 84.5, has entertainment from 9:30 p.m. to 1:30 a.m. Monday through Saturday. At Whale Harbor, **Rott'n Ralph's** (tel. 664-9888) has lounge entertainment every day but Tuesday.

Something's always jumping at **Cheeca Lodge** (tel. 664-4651), where there's entertainment Tuesday through Saturday from 8 p.m.

Marathon

Buccaneer Lodge, at Mile Marker 49 (tel. 743-9071), has entertainment, and the **Brass Monkey Liquor Store and Lounge,** at Mile Marker 50, in the K-Mart Plaza (tel. 743-5737), is open 24 hours.

Smuggler's Cove, Mile Marker 86 (tel. 664-4569), is home to the Matecumbe Minstrels, who perform for listening and dancing nightly under the stars at the Dockside Lounge.

SPORTS: Naturally, fishing and water sports are the big, big thing in the Keys, so you won't have any trouble at all arranging a fishing or diving expedition. Dive shops, charter boats, party boats, boats of all kinds, are scattered everywhere in the Keys. They are especially plentiful at **Gilbert's** on Key Largo and at **Whale Harbor** on Islamorada. You can rent a sailboat or a windsurfer at **Buccaneer Lodge Beach,** at Mile Marker 49 (tel. 743-9071), for prices in the $15 range.

Travel with **Stan Becker** (tel. 872-2620) through the beautiful Key Deer Refuge on Big Pine Key on a seven-hour sojourn including canoes, lunch, and a naturalist's wisdom. The cost is $45 per person, $40 each for four or more.

Key Colony Beach Golf Course, at Mile Marker 53.5 in Marathon (tel. 289-1533), is a par-three course open from 7:30 a.m. to 5 p.m., at $3.50 for nine holes. In Marathon, **Sombrero Country Club,** at Mile Marker 50 (tel. 743-2551), has 18 holes and greens fees of $12; carts cost $12 for two.

2. Key West

It's elegant and antique, contemporary and a little crazy, a world of its own 100 miles—and light-years—away from Miami. It's the farthest you can get from the maddening crowd and is, as a matter of fact, as far as you can get in the United States from anywhere.

As the southernmost city in the nation, Key West has the dubious distinction of being the starting point (or the end) of the Maine-to-Florida seaboard highway known as US 1.

In this tiny town people are short on the frenetic, long on tolerance, and dedicated to the pursuit of self-indulgence, an activity which enjoys a wide variety of interpretations on the island.

People-watchers are likely to suffer from exhaustion quickly here: Key West is home to author Philip Caputo, and has welcomed Gay Talese, Kurt Vonnegut, Jr., Vincent Price, Robert Frost, John Dos Passos, designer Calvin Klein, actor Dustin Hoffman, and was the starting place for singer Jimmy Buffet. It also was home to playwright Tennessee Williams, and of course Papa Hemingway.

What draws the famous, the infamous, and the thousands of the rest of us who are not yet either is a strange, inexplicable magic. You'll feel it as you settle in here and begin to roam among rambling pastel wooden houses that have sheltered generations of lawbreakers and lawmakers. You'll feel it as you stroll beneath huge trees shading sidewalks trod for centuries and peek around corners of towering conch houses, their sprawling verandas trimmed in gingerbread wood cut-outs, their etched glass sparkling, and mahogany glowing.

Just five miles long and three miles wide, the island of Key West was discovered in the 1500s by Spanish explorers who named it Cayo Hueso, "bone island," for the bones of slain settlers they found there. Not much of a start for this island, but a herald of things to come. As Spain took to looting the New World, the Florida Keys became a storm-wracked, nightmare gauntlet for treasure-laden ships to run on their return to Spain. One Friday the 13th in 1733 a fleet of Spanish merchant ships left Cuba bound for Europe carrying what was said to be $68 million in gold and silver. A gale struck off Plantation Key and the fleet floundered. That treasure is still the life's dream of many a diver here.

So shallow are these waters that without lights or maps for guidance, early sailors frequently ran aground. By doing so they created a trade known as wrecking, which involved retrieving valuables from shipwrecks—occasionally even ensuring there would be a shipwreck. At one time nearly everyone in Key West was a wrecker or involved in wrecking operations. A Bahamian named William Curry is said to have built such a financially rewarding career supplying wreckers that he became the first Florida millionaire, wealthy enough to buy a gold Tiffany table service for $100,000.

Wrecking has given rise to many a rollicking tale. Here's one: Since the first wrecker to reach the wreck was dubbed "wrecking master" and entitled to a major share of the loot, the race was on. One wrecker, who worked in his spare time as community pastor, was delivering a solemn sermon when he looked out the church windows and saw a ship foundering on the rocks. With true Keys ingenuity, he launched into a dramatic presentation so gripping that the audience sat riveted as he moved slowly toward the exit. When he knew he was close enough to the door to lead the racing pack, he called out "Wreck ashore!" and tore out the door—first, of course!

They're like that, these people who call themselves "conchs." They're canny, and a little crazy, spirited and loyal, hospitable and happy-go-lucky, sometimes eccentric, always individualistic, rarely surprised, and almost never shocked by the fascinating melange of lifestyles that ebbs and flows across these islands with tidal inevitability. (In addition to its writers, artists, and other "bohemian" types, Key West has joined the ranks of Fire Island, N.Y., and Provincetown, Mass., as a sun-and-fun destination for many gay tourists.)

Only the island-born, by the way, can call themselves "conchs" (pronounced "konks"), but if you manage to stay around seven years you may refer to yourself in polite circles as a "freshwater conch." Tourists, however, must remain tourists until they've visited often or long enough to assume the exalted rank of "Visitor." What better reason to sink in here for a few weeks?

It is perhaps not what these islanders are but what they aren't that makes this place a refuge for the weak and weary, the strong and ambitious, the leftover pieces from the puzzle of life. Forgiving of frailties and immune to differences, Key West manages to contain some of the world's more unusual occupants and suffers little from slavish adoration of tradition. There is, however, one inviolate tradition here, a moment of unspoken homage to nature that unites even this most heterogenous population.

This exercise in Central Park South is known as **Mallory Dock at Sunset,** and consists mainly of showing up on the dock at sunset as the town's *rara avis* congregate to observe the setting sun and each other. Here you'll find jugglers, mimes, blue-grass singers, unskilled-but-willing magicians, anachronistic remnants of the counterculture enveloped in some sweet smoke, the Iguana Man whose best friend is on his shoulder, some socialites, some politicians, who knows? You'll also see a setting sun. That may not sound like much, but way down here in the tropics, Old Sol really does do a rather spectacular job, turning the sky and ocean to molten gold and scarlet before dropping suddenly below the sea in a haze of royal blue.

It's quite a sight, as is most everything in this city that has for three centuries or more rolled with the punches, accepted the inevitability of its invaders, and lured into its seductive web visitors from pirates to Pittsburghers.

ORIENTATION: In Key West, Duval Street is the main drag, running through the middle of town to the edge of Mallory Dock and the Pier House Hotel. US 1 becomes South Roosevelt Boulevard, running past the airport on the Atlantic side of the island, and North Roosevelt Boulevard on the north side of the island. North Roosevelt runs into Truman Avenue (the President once made this city the winter White House), which crosses Duval in the middle of downtown Key West.

GETTING TO AND AROUND THE KEY: You can fly in on **Southern Express** (tel. toll free 800/531-9928) or bus in by **Greyhound,** which has service from Miami and even has a bus directly from Miami International Airport to Key West and back. For schedules, call the company toll free at 800/432-8118 (in Miami, 305/371-2550).

Once here, you can rent cars from **Hertz** (tel. 294-1039), **Avis** (tel. 296-8744), or **Alamo** (tel. 294-6675).

For less expensive transportation that's easier to park, rent a moped from **Moped Hospital,** 601 Truman Ave. (tel. 296-3344), for $3 to $5 an hour, $19 a day. **Lang's** (tel. 296-3287), with five locations on the island, rents bikes and snorkeling gear too. You can also rent a bike for $5 a day, $25 a week, at the **Bike Shop,** 1110 Truman St. (tel. 294-1073).

A taxi company called **Five Six Cab Co.** (tel. 296-6666) operates here for $1.20 a mile plus $2.10 for the first mile, and **Key West Independent Taxi** (tel. 294-7277) has unmetered cabs and will take you from the airport to town for about $5 a person.

VISITOR INFORMATION: They can tell you anything you need to know about this island at **Key West Chamber of Commerce,** 402 Wall St., Key West, FL 33040 (tel. 305/294-2587; toll-free in Florida 800/FLA-KEYS).

Keys dwellers have long been famed for unusual ideas so it comes as no surprise to me that Keysian Susan Mowery has come up with a novel idea called **Island Club International.** Anyone can join this club by paying $36 a year or $6 for a limited-time visitor membership. What you get for your money is a list of dozens of different kinds of businesses that offer special bargain prices and discounts to club members. A list of those wheeling-dealing businesses now fills a 26-page brochure that surely must include nearly every business in the Keys! Cardholders receive everything from half-price dinners or drinks at Keys restaurants and lounges to a discount on jewelry, art, boating, fishing, windsurfing, hotels, rental cars, airline fares, even automotive parts! To make it all even more interesting, this "club" meets once a month for a lively party at which dozens of gifts donated by area businesses are raffled. For the full story, contact Ms. Mowery at Island Club International, P.O. Box 4250, Key West, FL 33041 (tel. 305/296-3280).

Because the island has become popular with gay travelers, there are now some hostelries that cater only to gay men or women or both. Most are quite frank about their target market, however, so don't be shy about asking if you want to find—or avoid—an establishment with such a dedication.

You can also obtain from the **Greater Key West Chamber of Commerce,** 402 Wall St. (tel. 305/294-5959), a copy of a thick brochure called "Key West Visitors Pocket Guide," which lists all the hotels, motels, and guest houses in the city and indicates what "visitor category" each accepts—all male, all female, couples, families, all whatever.

Key West magazine, 1010 Truman Ave., Key West, FL 33040 (tel. 305/294-9922), calls itself the "official magazine of the Conch Republic." Published bimonthly, the magazine details for us outsiders such intrinsically Keysian topics as why Key West people keep parrots as pets—"He's a good companion. He goes out to the bars, the banks, and the post office with me." Frivolity aside, the magazine also includes some interesting articles on Keys highspots (I use that term with some reservations), lists upcoming events, and helps keep you current on what they're thinking—or at least what they say they're thinking—in the Conch Republic these days.

WHERE TO STAY: Key West's hostelries are scattered around a bit, but no matter where you stay you're just a few minutes' drive from those charming old downtown streets you'll want to explore. And when I say downtown, think mite-sized, not Manhattan.

The Luxury Leaders

The **Pier House,** 1 Duval St., Key West, FL 33040 (tel. 305/294-9541), is one of Key West's grandest hotels, refurbished with $3 million and such skill you'd like to keep its decorator on retainer. In Key West you translate "grand" not as multistoried, but as tasteful, pretty, quiet, and fun. At Pier House you'll find a rambling wood-sided oceanfront structure that's long been one of Key West's favorite meeting spots. Rambling over acres of ground and a dazzling strip of private beach, the resort is thoroughly modern from subtle earth colors to wicker furnishings, bold jewel colors, and whirring paddle fans. It has striking geometric lines and 101 rooms, no two alike, tucked into just about every available space.

Worries slip away here as they do everywhere in Key West as you sip a frosty problem-solver at Old Havana Docks lounge, where a parrot perches atop a shoulder and demands to know what you'll have. In the Roof Top bar, where musician Jimmy Buffet began his career, you can watch the sunset and rituals at Mallory Dock through panoramic windows. In the Pier House Restaurant, built out over the sea, you can feast on a gigantic Sunday brunch or an excellent dinner in a greenery-filled, multilevel dining room (prices, $11 to $17) where Tennessee Williams was a frequent guest.

The spacious rooms are comfortable and modern, filled with bright colors. You can have one overlooking the ocean or the plant-bedecked pool area for $110 to $210 in peak season, or a suite for $275 to $350. In other months, rates range from $70 to $140 for rooms, from $100 to $300 for suites. Extra guests pay $20 in winter, $10 in summer.

Marriott's Casa Marina Resort, 1500 Reynolds St., Key West, FL 33040, at the foot of Reynolds Street (tel. 305/296-3535, or toll free 800/228-9290), is as much a landmark on this island as the Hemingway or Audubon Houses, and is just as historic: it was originally built in 1921 by powerhouse Henry Flagler as the pot of gold at the end of his Overseas Railroad rainbow. A Spanish Renaissance-style hotel on 1100 feet of beachfront, Casa Marina was the playground for the likes of the Astors, Robert Frost, Gregory Peck, Guy Lombardo. When a hurricane ruined the railroad, Casa Marina began a downhill slide that lasted until 1978 (for years the hotel was shuttered) when Marriott poured $10 million into restoration of this magnificent memorial to those classically elegant days.

Today you're greeted by attendants in safari suits, and shown to a reception area that's the hotel's showplace. A restored version of Flagler's magnificent entryway, it has a massive fireplace reaching to a beamed ceiling, tall columns, French doors, and serene little groupings of wicker furniture cushioned in deep burgundy tones. Outside on the veranda overlooking the sea, paddle fans whirr and high-backed wicker chairs are inviting. On a lower level, the resort's pool glitters and a 20-foot Jacuzzi whirlpool bubbles and swirls. A long strip of beach is lapped by gentle waves and lined with attractive chaises.

Very large rooms—251 of them, some in a new wing, some in the original hotel—have all the extras you'd expect in a fine hotel: large mirrored dressing areas, attractive tiled bath/shower combinations, two double beds, a glass wall leading to a private balcony. To keep you busy there are tennis courts, a fishing and boating pier, rental sailboats, a game room, exercise room, boutiques, and on Sunday you can lose a whole day at Henry's Restaurant when the hotel presents its massive Sunday brunch that includes, among other things, two steamship rounds of beef, each 70 to 80 pounds, veal, turkey, pork, mutton, grouper, etc. Rates in winter range from $145 to $210 for a lanai room with a balcony; in summer, they're $110 to $145.

On the tiny walkways that meander through the **Key Wester Inn,** Route A1A, on the ocean, Key West, FL 33040 (tel. 305/296-5671, or toll free 800/327-7072; in Florida, 800/432-7413), you'll discover what tropical is all about: firehouse-red ixora, peach hibiscus, pale-blue plumbago twined around cool beige stucco and darkwood railings. The Key Wester's handsome two-story wings and one-story villas overlook the sea across the highway. Inside, rooms and efficiencies are dramatically decorated with deep emerald-green rugs and black and white spreads accented by black easy chairs. Attractively furnished villas have one or two bedrooms, dining room, living room, and private screened porches overlooking the ocean.

The inn has the lively Cocoplum Lounge, plus the Inner Circle nightclub, with top entertainment and dancing beside the largest pool on the island. There's a sauna and health club, gift shop, and beauty salon, and you'll even find a clock set daily to tell you what time sunset occurs so you don't miss Mallory Dock. Key Wester is quite close to the airport, offers guests free tennis and bicycles, and costs $84 to $150 from mid-December to May, $68 to $110 in the summer months.

Best Western Key Ambassador, next door at 1000 S. Roosevelt Blvd., Key West, FL 33040 (tel. 305/296-3500, or toll free 800/528-1234), offers a sumptuous continental breakfast free to guests each morning in a small breakfast room where attendants whip up raisin toast, assorted breads, English muffins, and lots of coffee, tea, and orange juice. In the center of this sprawling resort is a sparkling pool shaded by huge trees that tower over the manicured grounds and multilevel sundeck. Spacious hotel rooms, efficiencies, and studios here have sliding glass doors opening onto balconies from which you'll have a view of the pool or ocean. In winter, you'll pay $84 to $118; in summer, $58 to $84—depending on your view.

Moderately Priced Hotels

Orange and green trim highlights the **Santa Maria**, 1401 Simonton St., Key West, FL 33040 (tel. 305/296-5678), where rooms surround a central courtyard. At the bottom of the pool you'll get another look at Key West's pirate heritage: there's a galleon down there! Balconies overlook the pool, and the medium-size rooms are decorated in more bright shades. Off the eclectically decorated lobby is a small dining room. Rates here are $55 to $85 from December to May 1, $32 to $56 in other months.

Naturally, in this southernmost city there are a number of things that can legitimately call themselves "the southernmost." The **Southernmost Motel**, 1319 Duval St., Key West, FL 33040, at South Street (tel. 305/296-6577), is one of them. A pretty little place just across the street from the huge and colorful "Southernmost House," the motel has a pool lined with yellow polka-dot patio umbrellas. There are lots of colorful blossoms here in shades of pink and yellow, and you'll see those same tropical shades in the rooms, many of which have two double beds and forest-green carpeting set off by yellow accents, plus color TV and phones. There's a rooftop solarium, and the motel's within walking distance of most of Key West. From mid-December to April, rates are $45 to $70, dropping in other months to $35 to $50. The charge for an extra person is $7.

The **South Beach Motel**, 508 South St., Key West, FL 33040 (tel. 305/296-5611), runs from the street to a small fishing pier where a light pole announces "you have now reached the South Pole." There's no refuting that logic, which is indicative of the kind of easy humor you'll find in this small motel that's just across a bay from the Southernmost House. Here you can watch those flaming Keys sunsets in quiet isolation without fighting the traffic at Mallory Dock. A teensy vest-pocket beach dotted with Tiki huts is just next door (it's so small and cute you want to wrap it up and take it home). Rooms are simply furnished but have a nice uncluttered beachside look, and there's a pool where plaster dolphins create mini-waterfalls. An antique Victorian house next door has been restored by the friendly folks who run the South Beach, and is open to guests. Rates are $85 for two in a room with two double beds in peak season, $60 in the summer months.

A sparkling tiled pool surrounded by a jungle of tropical plants is a lovely feature of **Key Lodge,** at Truman Avenue and Duval Street (tel. 305/296-9915 or 296-9750). A tiny motel with just 22 rooms, Key Lodge has a winding driveway out front with the owner's zippy antique convertible parked in it. Inside, you'll find interestingly eclectic rooms (one apartment has a whole wall covered with an antique map); some have paddle fans. They're neat and clean, if a bit on the small side, and rates range from $59 to $68 for motel rooms, $64 to $72 for efficiencies and apartments. An especially large suite is $75 in peak season. In other months, prices drop to $36 to $45.

Key Lodge's owners operate two other motels within three blocks of Key Lodge—**Halfred Motel**, 512 Truman Ave., where prices are about $5 less than those at Key Lodge; and **Red Rooster Inn,** 709 Truman Ave., where prices are $10 less than Key Lodge rates. Neither has a pool or room telephones.

Budget and Very Nice

Key West has a number of guest houses that cater to gay tourists or other guests with very specific interests. You can save money at them, but unless you're as accepting as the locals or know the city well enough to choose the guest house that will best suit you, it may be wise to stick to the following recommendations or to hotels and motor inns.

One very pretty guest house, often recommended by Key West residents, is **Eden House**, 1015 Fleming St., Key West, FL 33040 (tel. 305/296-6868). Two people pay just $40 to $50 in winter months, $25 to $30 in summer. The lower rates are for rooms with a bath down the hall or shared with another room, the higher rates for private baths. Eden House completed a renovation recently and now features cranberry and light-jade shades, all new bedspreads and curtains. Original silkscreen prints in each room are available for sale to guests. Air conditioning is by paddle fans, and there's also a pool to cool you. Guests share a television in the hall and the fun of staying in a 1924 Keys conch house that is now a lovely, inexpensive homestead offering comparatively low rates in an often-pricey town. Double rates are $40 to $55 from December through April, $25 to $35 in other months, with the higher price tags on rooms with private bath.

There's quite a good French restaurant here too, under separate ownership. It's called Rich's and features really sumptuous brunches of such goodies as eggs croustades served in pastry shells with duxelles and béarnaise sauce or a Québécoise tourtière (a rustic pork pie), with a madeira sauce. Prices are $3 to $7 for brunch, $11 to $15 for dinner entrees (veal paillard with artichokes and mushrooms, tournedos of beef Rossini, for instance) which include tomatoes Provençal, rice, and homemade breads.

Key Lime Village Motel, 725 Truman Ave., Key West, FL 33040 (tel. 305/294-6222), is one of the charming finds you can discover in Key West with a little patience and a lot of curiosity. Key Lime is a spot you can trust to be in business tomorrow since it has managed to stay around longer than any motel on the island. I haven't discovered whether the lime came before the cottages or the cottages before the lime, but each of them is painted the color of key limes—yellow. They have wood floors and are decorated in simple, very basic furnishings, some of them wicker or straw. Cottage 7 is especially appealing, with fiber chairs and a bright knock-your-eyes-out orange bedspread. There's a reception cottage with antiques and wicker furnishings, and a game-room cottage with chess, checkers, a library, and the resort's only television. They'll tell you frankly that if you're looking for a big resort with "telephones, televisions, and all that, you're going to be very unhappy here." When you look at the price, however, you're sure to be pleased: $42 to $50 in peak season, $28 to $32 in summer. There's a perfectly lovely pool, surrounded by an explosion of purple bougainvillea and yellow trumpet vines so thick you can hardly find the pool.

Let me say right up front here that the **Southern Cross Hotel**, 326 Duval St., Key West, FL 33040 (tel. 305/294-3200), is not for everyone. In fact it seems safe to say that it is only for those few people willing to sacrifice all fancy amenities for location and an unmistakable, if indescribable, ambience. A paint job a couple of years ago has given this old hotel a much-needed facelift, but it remains kind of cozily shabby, to put the best face on it. Rates are bargain basement in this now-pricey village: $35.50 a night, which buys you clean beds, bathroom, enchantingly high-ceilinged rooms, and a location smack in the middle of town, smack in the middle of Key West's main street. From an advantageous, if somewhat shaky, second-floor balcony here you can look down on the many moods of Duval as it changes from early-morning bustle to afternoon tourist haven to its best face of all in the quiet of early evening. It's a great place in its way, but no Hilton.

Rock bottom in Key West? As I hear it, there's a **Canadian minesweeper** anchored off the Pier House where you can get bunk and breakfast for $10. You'll need to get a ride out there or shout down to someone to come and get you. At those prices, it may be worth the shouting.

READERS' HOTEL SELECTIONS: "We did find a new guest house just opened at the south shore—**La Mer.** This is an absolutely charming guest house. It has been very nicely decorated, and has a private beach that goes with it and a lovely place for breakfast or lunch" (Martin Snyder, Villanova, Penna.). [*Author's Note:* La Mer is at 506 South St., Key West, FL 33040 (tel. 305/294-6691), and charges $60 to $75 from December through April, $45 to $60 in summer.] . . . "I moved into this wonderful guest house, **Wicker Guesthouse,** 913 Duval St., Key West, FL 33040 (tel. 305/296-4275). The owners are very friendly, the complimentary breakfast was plentiful and delightful, and I was able to chat with other vacationers. I strongly recommend it" (Mariette Givoiset, Villeneuve la Garenne, France). [*Author's Note:* Wicker Guesthouse, which occupies a handsome old two-story house rimmed with porches on both floors, also has a whirlpool and includes complimentary breakfast in prices which range from $30 to $40 from mid-April to November, $45 to $55 in winter months. All but one room in the house share a bath; the room with private bath is $10 more. The guest house says it welcomes guests "from all segments of society . . . and we encourage all of our guests to fully and freely express their respective lifestyles." Many guests here are, like Ms. Givoiset, European visitors to the island.]

WHERE TO EAT: Restaurants open and close or are somewhere between the two events with such frequency here that an *old* restaurant is one that's been around more than a year. Casual is the mode here, so for any except the most upper-crust spots you won't need to dress up, particularly in summer when pants longer than your knees are considered formal. In winter things are a bit dressier, but just a bit. This is, after all, the last resort. Remember that the prices I've cited are for entrees, but that these usually include one or two vegetables, salad, and perhaps coffee.

Top of the Line

Claire, 900 Duval St. (tel. 296-5558), draws a very jazzy crowd of glitterati who flock here to drape themselves across a restaurant fashioned with the same drama that designer Robin Wagner applied to the sets of *A Chorus Line.* Claire's Thai chef will prepare a banquet for six with a little advance notice, and there's a wide array of sophisticated selections. You can also down crunchy waffles at a front-porch breakfast from 9 a.m. to 12:30 p.m. Lots of fresh-baked specialties and freshly squeezed orange juice make this spot hog heaven for breakfast gourmands. Claire also has a happy hour and has thought of everything: there are paper tablecloths and you're provided with crayons so you can write all the graffiti you like! Prices are in the $10 to $15 range for dinner. The restaurant is open from 4 p.m. to 2 a.m.

If you share with me a fascination for old houses, book a table at **Pigeon House Patio,** 303 Whitehead St. (tel. 294-1034), a rambling old home built by ships' carpenters in 1886 and moved here during World War I. Pigeon House got its unusual name when an airline without radios used carrier pigeons as messengers and kept the birds here. You can sit outside on a garden patio or inside under a whirring paddle fan to dine on fresh local seafood and continental and American specialties. Prices start at $3.50 for lunch and $8.95 for dinner. The restaurant's open from 11:30 a.m. to 2 a.m. daily.

The Buttery, 1208 Simonton St. (tel. 294-0717), is tucked away in a small shopping area, but once you've discovered this sterling spot you'll find your way back again and again to dine in four candlelit, plant-bedecked rooms, the newest of which is an enclosed garden room. Continental cuisine with French touches and lots of delectable **Key West** seafood is the fare here, where you'll pay $15 to $20 for dinner. It's open nightly from 7 p.m.

Bagatelle's, at 115 Duval St. (tel. 294-7195), is a shining new star in the firmament of restaurants in Key West. Caribbean specials like escargots Martinique and Bahamian cracked conch are the focus here. You dine in the antique atmosphere of an old conch house, upstairs or down on a veranda overlooking Duval Street. You'll pay about $15 to $20 for a full dinner, and the restaurant's open from noon to 1 a.m. daily.

La Terrazza de la Marti, 1125 Duval St. (tel. 294-8435), is known around town as La-Ti-Da and as one of the loveliest spots in the city. La-Ti-Da is indeed a very pretty place with a double-decker porch overlooking a pool. The decor is so perfect that you can hardly find a glass that isn't beautiful. Brunch here ($4 to $13) is a favorite with islanders, who dine on things like brioche stuffed with ham and sausage, and garnished with fruit and vegetables. At 4 p.m. the upstairs bar produces Szechuan specialties in the $11 to $17 range until 11:30 p.m. Fixed-price dinners (7:30 to 10 p.m., with seating on the half hour) are four courses that change each evening, including shrimp or scallops thermidor, for $25. The restaurant's open from 9 a.m. to 11 p.m. daily.

Budget Spots

La Crêperie, 124 Duval St. (tel. 294-7677), is the spot for light lunches or late snacks of quiche, wonderful crêpes, escargots, onion soup, and salads. If you're really starving they can provide steaks, seafood brochette, grouper filet, or bouillabaisse for prices ranging from $10 to $15. You can dine inside or al fresco on the patio from 11:30 a.m. to 2:30 p.m. weekdays and 6 to 11 p.m. daily.

Longtime favorite in the city is the **A & B Lobster House,** 700 Front St. (tel. 294-2536). Atmosphere there isn't—just wood floors, a second-story view over the docks, and basic nautical decor. But great seafood there is: brimming seafood platters plucked right out of the sea and plunked onto your plate with a little talented cookery in between. There are landlubber selections as well, plus a 14-foot salad bar. **A & B** has been at this game for decades so it's safe to assume they're doing something right. This is a jeans and T-shirts place, open from 5 to 10 p.m. daily, except Sunday and the month of September. Dinner prices average about $10 to $15.

El Cacique, 125 Duval St. (tel. 294-4000), is an insignificant little storefront place that turns out some of the best black bean soup and media noche sandwiches, batidas, and Cuban coffee this side of Miami for ridiculously low prices. You can gorge here on all kinds of Cuban treats for $5 or less. The same can be said of **Fourth of July,** 1100 White St. (tel. 294-9131), which will send you out stuffed on black beans and rice, plantains and palomilla, steak, paella Valenciana, or any of 35 other entrees, chased by sangría. El Cacique is open from 11 a.m., the Fourth from 6 a.m., closing at 9 p.m. and 11 p.m., respectively, every day.

Captain Bob's, 908 Caroline St. (tel. 294-9005), is much loved by honeybun fans. Those sweet pastries are the house specialties, but so is seafood straight from the sea. Prices are in the $10 to $15 range for dinner and hours are 6 a.m. to 10:30 p.m. daily.

READER'S RESTAURANT SUGGESTION: "A wonderful Cuban restaurant is **La Lechonera Restaurant,** 900 Catherine St. (tel. 294-3442). The food is excellent and it is more than you can eat at prices of about $4 to $8" (Linda Sambel, Pittsfield, Mass.).

SEEING THE SIGHTS: There's lots to see and do in Key West, from island tours to Hemingway haunts.

Touring the Island

The quickest way to see all of Key West and get your bearings at the same time is to hop aboard the **Conch Tour Train,** which takes you on a 1½-hour narrated tour of the island and tells you some of the greatest anecdotes you'll hear anywhere. You'll even learn the four *natural* ways Key Westers air-conditioned their houses (and we think we've progressed!) and get a good look at the cisterns that were so vital to survival until the water pipe was laid from the mainland and desalinization techniques discovered. More than 60 of this enchanting island's beautiful old conch homes and historical sites are pointed out on this don't-miss tour, which tells you in a nutshell the weird and wonderful history of Key West. Tours leave daily from 9 a.m. to 4 p.m. from depots at 501 Front St., Mallory Square, and 3850 N. Roosevelt Blvd. Fare is $6 for adults, $3 for children over 3. Just show up and hop aboard.

You ride comfortably, if not quite as adventurously, aboard **Old Town Trolley Tours,** Roosevelt Boulevard and Mallory Square (tel. 296-6688). You can board a trolley at Mallory Square or at most major motels in Key West, disembark anywhere you like to shop or look around, then get back on later. Trolleys leave Mallory Square every 30 minutes and give you quite a complete tour of the island with detailed accounts of its wrecking, rollicking history. Tickets are $7 for adults, $3 for children under 12.

Horse-drawn carriage tours of Old Key West begin at Front and Whitehead Streets from 9 a.m. to dark and last 45 minutes. The cost is $5 for adults, $2 for children under 12.

Miss Key West, at the foot of Duval Street (tel. 296-8865), shows you a sunken Spanish galleon and other sunken craft, a naval base, and 45 other sights. There's also a sunset cruise with island music. The fare is $6 for adults, $3 for children 12 to 18. Sailing schedules vary from season to season.

Fireball, a **glass-bottomed boat,** will take you out on a two-hour look at the colorful creatures that adorn a living coral reef just offshore. *Fireball* is docked at the gulf end of Duval Street (tel. 296-6923), and charges $8.50 for adults, $3.50 for children under 12, for the trips, which leave at 9:30 a.m., noon, 2:30 p.m., and at sunset daily from mid-December to mid-April, in summer from mid-June to early September (in other months the noon cruise is dropped). Departure times vary for the sunset cruise, so give them a call to see what time the sun is performing.

Special Events

Key West has become very event-conscious in recent years, partly because there are so many free spirits around ready and willing to throw themselves into any excuse for a party and partly because these conchs are canny enough to know the value of an "Event" in luring visitors.

So you will now find the city celebrating **Hemingway Days,** a week or so of craziness culminating on Papa's birthday, July 21. Events include arm wrestling, beer chugging, a billfish tournament, a Hemingway look-alike contest, and short story competitions, all events in which the master himself is said to have excelled.

From mid-January to March the city celebrates **Old Island Days,** a celebration designed to honor the conchs' cantankerous forefathers, many of whom were Loyalists, remaining perversely loyal to the King of England when the other American colonists were throwing a tea party. Most interesting of the events that occur during these days are the tours of old island homes, most of them private dwellings opened to visitors only for these tours.

Fantasy Fest turns the city into a weird and wild place each October—and significantly enhances what would otherwise be a pretty slim tourist month. Fantasy Fest occurs on the weekend closest to Halloween and comes complete with concerts, street dancing, arts-and-crafts exhibitions, and lots of other exhibitions, including some of the weirdest costumes this side of Fire Island. All I can tell you about this event is that my hairdresser sprayed glow-in-the-dark paint on his hair and perhaps sundry other parts for a recent appearance—and his was among the more conservative costumes.

The Sights

The best known treasure seeker in Florida, maybe the world, is a fellow named Mel Fisher who's successfully sought and found a number of sunken Spanish galleons including the famed *Nuestra Señora de Atocha* and the *Santa Margarita*, both of which went aground on reefs about 40 miles offshore. To get a look at the treasures he's dug up from the briny deep—$60 million worth, they say—hie on over to Mel Fisher's **Treasure Exhibit,** 200 Greene St. (tel. 296-9936). You'll get a closeup look at gorgeous gold and silver jewelry, some precious stones, and lots of coins and artifacts from those galleons that were once the target of folks who lived in these islands. Admission of $5 for adults and $1 for children under 12 includes a look at a National Geographic film on the business of treasure-seeking. Hours are 9 a.m. to 5 p.m. daily.

Key West's oldest house is now a museum. Called the **Wrecker's House,** this 1829 structure is at 322 Duval St. (tel. 294-9502) and was the home of wrecker Capt. Francis B. Watlinton. Here you can learn all about the wrecking game —including the rules! Admission is $1.75 for adults and 50¢ for children under 12; the house is open daily from 10 a.m. to 4 p.m.

Audubon House, 205 Whitehead St., at Green (tel. 294-2116), is named after the famous naturalist and artist who vacationed there. It's one of the island's historic houses, restored and open to the public from 9 a.m. to 5 p.m. daily at $2 for adults, 75¢ for children. Audubon's original life-size etchings of birds and the period furnishings make Key West's past come alive.

The **Ernest Hemingway Museum,** 907 Whitehead St. (tel. 294-1575), is home to more cats than people, just as it was when Hemingway lived here. A Spanish colonial house of 1851 vintage, it was the author's residence from 1931 to 1961, some of his most productive years. Descendants of his six-toed cats still ramble gracefully about, and there's even a special fountain for them created by the author from a Spanish olive jar and plumbing fixtures he lifted from Sloppy Joe's Bar. A pool in the courtyard has a penny imbedded in it—Hemingway said it took his last penny to install the pool! Admission is $2.50 for adults, $1 for children under 12, and the house is open daily from 9 a.m. to 5 p.m.

East Martello Art Gallery and Museum was once part of the fortifications of Key West, and today has displays of the city's successful cigar-making, sponging, and railroad industries. Admission is $2.50, 50¢ for children 7 to 15; under-7s are free. A short distance away, the **West Martello Tower** is now occupied by the Key West Garden Club, which has a lovely display of tropical plants in a garden that's open daily. It's free and both are located on South Roosevelt Boulevard (tel. 296-3913).

At the **Turtle Kraals,** 200 Margaret St. (tel. 296-3060), there's a holding pen full of turtles, sharks, rays, and tropical fish. The Kraals are open from 9 a.m. to 6 p.m., and there's no admission charge.

A historic lighthouse has been made into the **Lighthouse and Military Museum,** 938 Whitehead St. (tel. 294-0012), where you can see one of only two remaining midget subs launched by the Japanese navy during World War II. Admission is $1.50.

Once a year, in February and March, owners of many historic homes open them to the public during the city's **Old Island Days** celebration, when you can also see a conch-blowing contest, attend a wrecker's auction, see the blessing of the shrimp fleet, and try some conch salad, fritters, or chowder.

NIGHTLIFE: Going to Key West without hitting a few of this city's famous and perhaps infamous bars is like going to Florida to sit in the shade. You can meet all kinds of people at these lively, informal, and highly individualistic spots that open about dawn and may never close, for all I know. Things really heat up about cocktail hour, and are in full, high-decibel stride about 10 p.m.

The numero uno don't miss, go-even-if-you-hate-bars, superstar spot is **Sloppy Joe's,** 201 Duval St. It is, of course, true that Hemingway took to Sloppy Joe like a fish to a hook, and it is said that Papa and Sloppy Joe retired on frequent occasions to a locked back room armed with a case of whiskey which they put to good use while Joe told his wildest and wooliest sea stories. Hemingway absorbed those tales, so the story goes, and from them created some of the literary masterpieces he produced while living here. It's even said he did some of his writing in the bar, his manuscript held securely by a beer mug (now that's the way to write a book!). On the wall is a sailfish he's supposed to have caught, and parachute silks adorn the ceiling. It has, shall we say, character—and characters.

Hemingway adored the rustic watering spots of Key West, so it's easy to believe that **Capt. Tony's Saloon,** 428 Green St., is the *real* Sloppy Joe's. That's what they say (whoever *they* are), and it certainly looks plenty like a Sloppy Joe's. There's a fascinating casual-going-on-seedy air about the place that's well nigh irresistible, and besides, everyone in town roams through here at least once an evening. So if you stay put, you'll see most of Key West. Captain Tony himself is a colorful character who's been around Key West a long time, and for what it's worth his bar was *Esquire*-rated as one of the top ten in the country.

You won't have any trouble finding the **Bull and Whistle,** at 224 Duval St., just look for people hanging out of windows and off balconies, and listen for the music. The Bull and Whistle is an incredibly popular spot that's always jammed to the rafters with dancers and general celebrants. Open daily from 9 a.m. to 4 a.m.

More whoop-de-doo at **Lafitte's, The Copa,** and **Delmonico's.**

There is entertainment of a somewhat more subdued nature at **Pier House, Casa Marina,** and the **Key Wester Inn.** (See accommodations listings for addresses).

Turtle Kraals, 2 Lands End Village, at the foot of Margaret St. (tel. 294-2640), is now a cross between an attraction and a lounge/restaurant! There is no admission fee to see the turtle cannery museum and holding tanks full of live sea turtles, sharks, and tropical fish. While you're here, try grouper chowder in the Turtle Kraals Restaurant and sample one of 32 imported beers, a thick piña colada, or a fancy, flavored coffee. Food and drink prices are under $5 and the place is open from noon to 2 a.m. with entertainment.

Plans are under way to restore the city's historic **San Carlos Opera House** for use as a theater. Target date for opening of the theater, backed by a well-known Boca Raton theater operator named Jan McArt, was October 1985. Tourism officials in Key West may have further word on the theater.

Finally, for nighttime activity of a more subdued nature, the **Tennessee Williams Fine Arts Center,** Florida Key Community College in Key West (tel. 294-6232), presents musicals, plays, and dance performances throughout the year.

SPORTS: With all that water around, most sports naturally involve the ocean —so you won't find the hordes of tennis courts and golf courses here that you find elsewhere in the state. (Besides, there's no place to put them on these small islands.)

Golfing

Key West Club, on Stock Island (tel. 294-5232), has an 18-hole, par-72 course open daily. Greens fees are $5 on weekdays, $7.50 on weekends.

Diving and Sailing

When you can't resist the lure of the sea a moment longer, call **Windsurfing Key West**, 700 Waddell St. (tel. 296-8897). They can set you boardsailing and have plenty of other water sports equipment as well.

If you want to see what lives down under the waves, try **Reef Raiders Dive Shop**, on US 1 at Mile Marker 4.5 on Stock Island (tel. 294-0660), which takes groups on diving trips and can set you snorkeling or teach you how to use deep-water diving equipment.

Fishing

Yankee Captain, 33 Boundary Lane (tel. 294-7009), a 100-foot aluminum craft, is docked at Lands End Marina on Carolina Street, and sails to the Dry Tortugas at 11 p.m. Monday and Friday on two-night, one-day trips from December to May for $135.

To find plenty of charter boats, go to **Garrison Bight Marina**, about half-way up the north shore on US 1 at 711 Eisenhower Dr. (tel. 294-3093), where you'll find the city's charter-boat docks. Bay and deep-sea boats are for hire with or without a guide. Drop by about 4 p.m. even if you're not going fishing and pick up some fresh fish for dinner. Charter rates are about $300 a day.

TO SEA TO SEE A NATIONAL MONUMENT: The nation's most inaccessible national monument is **Fort Jefferson**, but it's one that's exciting to visit by boat or plane. You can get there for $85 per person round trip aboard the **Bonefish Seaplane** (tel. 289-0050), which flies from Grassy Key at Mile Marker 59. **Key West Seaplane** (tel. 294-6978) also makes the trip twice a day.

On Dry Tortugas (named by Ponce de Leon for the hundreds of sea turtles he saw sunning there; dry because it has no water) is a massive circular fortress, the largest 19th-century coastal fort built in the United States, with walls 50 feet high and eight feet thick. Work on this massive crumbling structure took 30 years to complete and cost $3.5 million. Although the fort had 140 guns ready and waiting, it never saw a day of battle. Its most noteworthy moment came when it held Dr. Samuel Mudd, who was imprisoned here after he set the broken leg of Abraham Lincoln's assassin, John Wilkes Booth. Mudd spent two years on this desolate island before he was pardoned for his help in a yellow fever epidemic. It's a lovely flight over and you'll pass several sunken ships. Once you get there, a ranger with a very lonely job will be happy to show you around.

SHOPPING: Mallory Square is an enclave of smart shops, and at **Key West Handprint Fabrics** you'll find wildly colorful prints used by dress designer Lilly Pulitzer who created a "look" with them. There's a retail shop with clothing for both men and women.

Key West Fragrances, 524 Front St. (tel. 294-5592), has unusual scents like white ginger and frangipani that make intriguing gifts.

In Pirates Alley, across from Mallory Square, is a little brick courtyard where you can see cigars being rolled by hand, the last example here of that once-vital industry.

Key West's department store has a quite unforgettable name: **Fast Buck Freddie's.** It's at 500 Duval St.

At the southernmost point of the island (you can't miss it) and at several other places around the island, boys dive for **conch** and sell the shells for $2 to $5, sometimes more for the very biggest ones. You can even find one yourself out there in the sea. Just poke an unsuspecting toe around in the sand.

Chapter IV

THE GOLD COAST

1. Palm Beach and Boca Raton
2. Fort Lauderdale

FLORIDA'S GOLD COAST IS PROOF that alchemy exists. Sixty years ago much of what is now glowing beaches, glittering hotels, and condominiums was palmetto scrub and swampland. More mosquitoes lived here than people, and only a barefoot mailman strode the sands between Miami and Palm Beach.

Long, long ago, Abaniki Indians lived here beside the sea. Then came pirates, who lay in wait to scuttle gold-laden Spanish galleons heading home from Central America. What few shoreside pioneers there were in those days picked up some nasty pirate habits and were soon participating in a career known as "wrecking." Adventurers who lived along these sand-trimmed shores didn't shrink at creating their own wrecks, although they rarely had to, since nature usually did it for them. Storms and inadequate navigational aids sent so many ships onto the rocks here that shoreside dwellers held regular meetings to pray for *specific* booty. Divinity answered in considerable style: a great party went on for days in Boca Raton one year in the wake of a wrecked Spanish ship carrying hundreds of barrels of sherry. So well rewarded were wreckers for their unusual trade that by the late 1800s they were complaining about the quality of the products washed ashore and accusing shipowners of scuttling worthless cargoes to turn a profit on insurance money.

Gall like that has long been the byword of this coastline where some flamboyant characters have made miracles and millions turning these sands into a tropical paradise. Perhaps the liveliest of them all was architect Addison Mizner, who came here to die but gave up that dismal project in favor of making himself a millionaire and this bit of Florida the stuff of every northern dream.

As usual, the first empire builder to trek southward was Florida's godfather, Henry Flagler, who brought his railroad tracks to Palm Beach. Mizner rode those tracks for a swim in Florida sunshine, but when he saw these beaches what swam before his eyes were dollar signs.

He started with Palm Beach, whose architecture he considered so unimaginative he is said to have remarked that if he could change the city he'd build something that wasn't made of wood and paint it some color besides yellow. He shortly began to do just that, building first the Everglades Club, an imposing oceanfront stucco edifice that's about the first thing you'll see as you drive northward along the Gold Coast to Palm Beach. With that and subsequent creations, Mizner founded an architectural vogue sometimes known as "Bastard–Spanish–Moorish–Romanesque–Gothic Renaissance–Bull-Market–Damn-the-Expense" style.

His ultimate sights were set, however, on a nearby strip of sand called Boca

Raton. Before long Boca Raton had its first and still most impressive hotel, the Cloister Inn, a $1.25-million creation said to be the most expensive 100-room hotel ever built. Mizner's grand design for an unsurpassed resort (lined with waterways plied by gondolas) centered on the Cloister Inn, but in the land around it was the fortune he sought.

To help sell that land he lured such famous names as Harold Vanderbilt, Marie Dressler, and Irving Berlin to the hotel in a characteristically shrewd bid for attention: "Get the big snobs," Mizner is supposed to have said, "and the little ones will follow." To give that surge of sun-seekers a little impetus, he introduced an advertising campaign that epitomized the style of 1920s Gold Coast land boom: "I Am the Greatest Resort in the World" the ads proclaimed, adding gently in smaller print below, "a few years hence." It worked. Sales at Mizne's development company, which also owned a mile of nearby Boynton Beach, averaged $2 million—a week!

Meanwhile, up in Palm Beach Flagler had already created his Breakers Hotel, a massive wooden edifice that was winter home to an awesome list of monied guests including the Wideners, Wanamakers, and Stotesburys. Nearby, Paris Singer of sewing machine fame was hard at work creating the Addison-designed Singer Island, a resort bent on making "Palm Beach look like a slum."

Little by little the boom spread southward as canny characters up and down the Gold Coast set out to try a little alchemy of their own, turning land into gold. Nothing fazed these slicksters, who didn't blanch at salting beaches with "pirate gold" to stir the pot of already-frenzied buyers. So down and dirty did sales pitches get that at the summit of the plummet Boca Raton was known as Beaucoup Rotten!

Meanwhile, down in Fort Lauderdale general store and ferryboat owner Frank Stranahan was taking in land-buying boarders, and on the streets of Miami binder boys were getting names on the dotted lines of land-sales contracts faster than you can say Boom.

The national economic depression broke the Gold Coast bubble but Mizner went down in characteristic style. When he was sued by a man who claimed he'd been sold his barren plot with false promises, Mizner was asked in court if he really had promised the man he could grow nuts on the land. "Oh, no," Mizner replied, "I said he could *go* nuts on the land."

Some may have gone nuts, and certainly many went broke, but as the years passed the Gold Coast recovered. In succeeding decades a somewhat less spectacular spiral began, including the purchase of Mizner's Cloister Inn by Arthur Vining Davis for $22.5 million, the largest real estate swap in Florida history—and $17 million more than the United States had paid to buy the entire state!

From that boom spiral emerged a golden coastline that has worked its way through gold plate, 18-karat gold, solid gold—and fool's gold—to emerge as a beach-lover's vacation paradise, where gold comes not from nuggets but from nature.

GETTING THERE: **Fort Lauderdale/Hollywood International Airport** has the most service to the area, but you can also fly into Palm Beach International. Fort Lauderdale's airport, which has recently tripled in size, is about 15 minutes from beach hotels. Airlines flying to these cities include Air Canada, Bahamasair, Continental, Delta, Eastern, Northwest, Ozark, Piedmont, People Express, Republic, Southern Express, TWA, United, and Ward Air.

You can get to **Palm Beach International Airport** on Delta, Eastern, Pan Am, People Express, Republic, United, USAir, and TWA.

Amtrak stops twice a day at Fort Lauderdale, arriving at the station near

Broward Boulevard at 200 SW 21st Terrace (tel. 463-8251), just west of the downtown area. Both **Greyhound** and **Trailways** buses connect the city to the state and nation, and have downtown terminals at 515 NE 3rd St. (tel. 764-6551) and 130 NW First Ave. (tel. 463-6327), respectively.

You can also get to Palm Beach by train, arriving at the Amtrak station, 201 S. Tamarind Ave. (tel. 832-6169). Both Trailways and Greyhound have service to the city. Greyhound's terminal is at 100 1st St. (tel. 833-0825) and Trailways is at 501 S. Olive Ave. (tel. 832-1041).

GETTING AROUND: Every national **car-rental company** operates in the two cities. Alamo and Greyhound head the low-price competitors, but Avis, Hertz, National, Budget, Dollar, General, and Econo-Car are among many others competing hard for customers.

From Fort Lauderdale International Airport, **Grey Line Airport Limousines,** 1800 NW 23rd Ave. (tel. 739-1200), will take you to beach hotels in Fort Lauderdale for $5. If you're going farther up the line to Pompano or Boca Raton, the fare rises to $10 to $12. They will also take you to Miami International Airport from Fort Lauderdale hotels or the airport for $12 to $15, but you must call them at a different number for that Miami service: 764-2211.

Broward County, in which Fort Lauderdale is located, has a new fleet of sleek orange-striped white **buses** which zip around the county from dawn to about 9 p.m. daily for 50¢. Friendly folks at the **Broward County Transit Division** (tel. 765-4000) can help you with route information and sell you a $5 weekly pass. There's also a bus called the **Dune Buggy,** which for the same price travels from near the county line on the south at Hallandale through Fort Lauderdale and Hollywood to Pompano. During racing seasons and in winter and spring there are special racetrack buses which stop at major beachfront hotels and can be flagged down at any corner along Route A1A from Pompano to US 1 in Fort Lauderdale. Tickets are $2 round trip, and any beachfront hotel can sell you one or you can pay the driver.

In Palm Beach, the **Palm Beach County Transit system** (Cotran) has service throughout the county, but is not the best way to sightsee since buses are not allowed on the city's main shopping street, Worth Avenue, or on Route A1A, where just about everything else you'll want to see is located. You can call them for route information at 686-4555.

Taxis are, as always, a somewhat expensive way to get around, more so in Fort Lauderdale where things are a bit more spread out than they are on the compact island of Palm Beach. In Broward County, taxi fares are $1.75 for the first mile, $1.20 for each additional mile. Try **Yellow Cab** (tel. 763-8200) or **Broward Checker** (tel. 485-3000).

In Palm Beach, taxis cost $1.50 for the first mile and $1 for each additional mile; **Yellow Cab** operates there (tel. 689-2222).

In Fort Lauderdale you can rent mopeds at **Mr. Moped,** 2925 E. Las Olas Blvd. at the Intracoastal Waterway (tel. 467-3659), for $35 a day. In Palm Beach you can tour on bicycles, which you can rent from **Mark's Bicycles,** 1141 E. Blue Heron Rd., Singer Island (tel. 842-8824), beginning at $10 per day.

A LOOK AT GOLD COAST CITIES: If you're driving, it's interesting to ride up from Miami Beach following Route A1A (or south from any of the northern Gold Coast cities), which runs between the ocean and the Intracoastal Waterway most of the way. To give you an idea what you'll see, here's a look at the Gold Coast, starting at the Dade County border (Golden Beach) and heading north.

First city north of Dade County is **Hallandale,** a strip of sand crowned by dozens of condominiums built along the beaches. If you were here 15 years ago, you'll think you're lost now: many of these towering apartment complexes have risen in the past 10 to 15 years. Flagship of Hallandale is the Diplomat Hotel, and the city is also home to showy Gulfstream Park Race Track.

Hallandale blends right into **Hollywood,** where you'll see a few clusters of very small resorts. A boardwalk along the sand is lined with bars, hot-dog stands, and usually lots of young people out for a day at the beach. If you're a greyhound-racing fan, Hollywood has a dog track open much of the year. Hollywood's a favorite destination for Québec visitors.

Tucked between Hollywood and Fort Lauderdale is the tiny town of **Dania,** once home to many tomato farmers. Today most of the action here is at the Dania Jai-Alai Fronton or huge John Lloyd State Park, where you'll find a lovely wooded strip of beach and plenty of places to picnic on sand less crowded than beaches in neighboring communities. A new beachside complex called Seafare is an interesting array of shops and restaurants.

In Dania, Route A1A turns westward to join US 1, but you can get back on the beach highway again at SW 17th Street in **Fort Lauderdale,** where you cross the Intracoastal Waterway and pass the city's cruise-ship port, Port Everglades. A mile farther north you'll see the city's magnificent beach stretched out in front of you. You can drive right beside it for much of the next three miles to small **Lauderdale-by-the-Sea,** and into **Pompano** where the beach is hidden behind a few resorts and many condominiums. Ocean waters sneak back into view at the city's big fishing pier just north of Atlantic Boulevard.

Next comes **Hillsboro Beach,** one of the most beautiful drives in the area. Here Route A1A scoots between the Intracoastal Waterway and some massive estates built right on the sand. **Hillsboro Inlet** is home to a fishing fleet, and you can always count on finding a fishing trip there, or some fresh fish from someone who's just been lucky at sea.

Continuing northward, you cross the small community of **Deerfield Beach,** where a few small resorts are clustered around the highway, and finally you'll see **Boca Raton,** where the Boca Raton Hotel and Club occupies most of the city's south side.

Delray Beach is home to the horsey set these days, and there's a large breeding farm west of town. Here and in Boca Raton the beach becomes visible again. It's just a few feet from the right side of your car as you drive north along a ridge that runs high above the edge of the sand, so there are some smashing views of turquoise waters that darken as the water deepens. That very dark blue is the Gulf Stream. If you're a diver, you'll find good diving territory off the coast of Boca Raton and Delray. Delray is home to several excellent restaurants and has a sleepy old-town air with many Spanish-style homes lining the streets.

Don't miss the village of **Gulfstream,** which is so tiny you may almost miss it—but many *Fortune 500* types didn't: it's one of the wealthiest villages on the Gold Coast (and the quietest about its net worth).

Farther north on this sand-and-sea boulevard you'll pass **Briny Breezes** (isn't that poetic?), then **Boynton Beach,** which has a very attractive beach high on a dune—it will cost you $10 to sit on it (one of the very few Gold Coast beaches that isn't free).

Drive through **Ocean Ridge, Manalapan, Lake Worth,** and finally you're in **Palm Beach,** where Route A1A takes you right past Mar al Lago, Marjorie Merriweather Post's pink palace, and straight through Palm Beach past the Breakers, to a point about three miles from the tip of the island where you cross the Flagler Bridge to return to US 1 for a few miles. You can pick up Route A1A again at **Singer Island** (you'll see a sign pointing the way) and follow it north to about **Jupiter** where it again joins US 1.

1. Palm Beach and Boca Raton

Town and Country magazine, the news magazine of the very rich, once assessed Florida's Gold Coast by karat. Towns like Fort Lauderdale and Manalapan, John's Island in Vero Beach, and Boca Raton were accorded 18 to 19 karats; Delray Beach, Coral Gables, Coconut Grove, and the village of Gulfstream near Palm Beach, 20 to 23 karats. Palm Beach? Why, you should know without asking. Solid gold, of course.

That's Palm Beach, bastion of those who have no need of upward mobility since there's nowhere higher up. Winter playground of the Rolls-Royce-raffle set, Palm Beach is a place where "divine" has nothing to do with divinity and shopkeepers pay more for a tiny square of Worth Avenue storefront than the average American makes in three years.

Henry Flagler was the man who started all this, and today the wide straight boulevards he created are lined with towering royal palms and gardens perfect to the last petal. Should a blade of grass be out of place, it will, we assure you, be controlled.

Control, after all, is what created Palm Beach—and those who escape here. It's also what has put on the books laws (*laws,* mind you) prohibiting car washes and jogging without a shirt.

Names on guest lists here read like a Guinness Book of Zillionaires—or Ripley's Believe It or Not! Widener, Wanamaker, Vanderbilt, Stotesbury, Dodge, Sanford, Kennedy, Post, Arthur Vining Davis.

If all this sounds a bit intimidating, fear not, for the rich are just like you and me except they drive Rolls-Royces down Worth Avenue and spend the winter in Palm Beach. But even the vanguard of this old guard has loosened up some with the arrival of foreign money and contemporary lifestyles. We won't include Palm Beach's most famous recent visitor, Prince Charles, in those ranks, but Arabs recently bought a $2.2-million piece of property here and an heir to Germany's Krupp empire bought a home sight unseen last year for a price closing rapidly in on $2 million.

In Palm Beach you can move among the royal and the regal, strut your stuff in Gucci and Courrèges, prowl the corridors of the Breakers, and hob with nobs whose average income is precisely twice that of the rest of the nation. It's fun as well as fantasy to roam through streets kept spotless by an army of sanitation workers, past homes so huge an army could perhaps be lost in them, and into stores offering the world's most tempting treasures and highest prices.

To drive through this lovely old town is an adventure all its own, and finding a parking space is even more of an adventure. Surrounding towns are quiet, genteel, antique-lovely villages whose determined residents have successfully warded off the more plastic aspects of modern life.

Boca Raton, whose euphonious name translates somewhat less pleasantly to Rat Bay (a reference, it is said, to sharp rocks at the bay entrance) is lady-in-waiting to Palm Beach. It would have been queen had it not suffered a setback after the scandals of the property boom (during which it was known as Beaucoup Rotten) and the burst with the bubble of the nation's economy in the 1920s. It recovered with alacrity and style, however, and is now said to be the wealthiest community in the nation. Small neighbor Delray Beach was once the toast of the town too, but now is Melba toast, still in the running but not quite the real thing.

North of Palm Beach, the communities of Stuart, Hobe Sound, Jupiter,

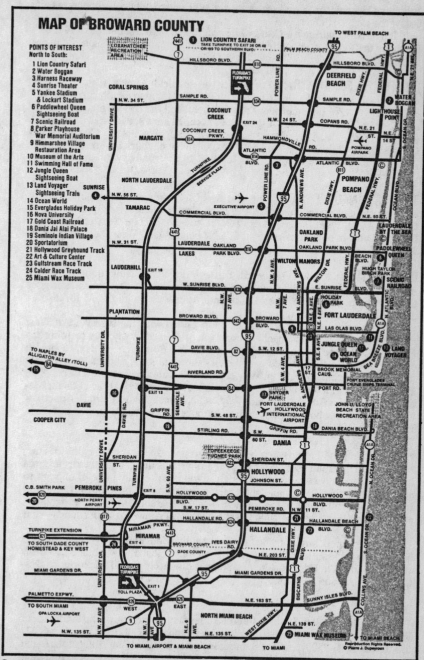

MAP OF BROWARD COUNTY

POINTS OF INTEREST
North to South:

1 Lion Country Safari
2 Water Boggan
3 Harness Raceway
4 Sunrise Theater
5 Yankee Stadium
   & Lockart Stadium
6 Paddlewheel Queen
   Sightseeing Boat
7 Scenic Railroad
8 Parker Playhouse
   War Memorial Auditorium
9 Himmarshee Village
   Restauration Area
10 Museum of the Arts
11 Swimming Hall of Fame
12 Jungle Queen
   Sightseeing Boat
13 Land Voyager
   Sightseeing Train
14 Ocean World
15 Everglades Holiday Park
16 Nova University
17 Gold Coast Railroad
18 Dania Jai Alai Palace
19 Seminole Indian Village
20 Sportatorium
21 Hollywood Greyhound Track
22 Art & Culture Center
23 Gulfstream Race Track
24 Calder Race Track
25 Miami Wax Museum

Juno, and Hutchinson Island are about equally divided between upper crust and below the salt.

It's fun discovering it all, and while you're at it, you'll see some of Florida's (perhaps the nation's) most beautiful communities, and shops. Could you ask for more?

USEFUL INFORMATION: For **police or medical emergencies,** call 655-4000. . . . If you need a **dentist,** the county's dental association can help; call 833-5725. . . . For **nonemergency medical help,** call the county medical society at 582-4116. . . . There's a **24-hour drugstore,** Eckerd's, at 3343 N. Congress (tel. 965-3367). . . . If you bring your dry cleaning in by 9 a.m., **Coconut Palm Cleaners,** 159 Chilean Ave. (tel. 659-7080), can have it back by 4 p.m. that day. . . . For a **24-hour restaurant,** try Clock, at 1420 Broadway in Riviera Beach (tel. 844-9979), or at 1516 N. Dixie Hwy. in Lake Worth (tel. 586-7633).

TOURIST INFORMATION: You can find brochures and information about what to see and do in the city at the **Palm Beach Chamber of Commerce,** 45 Coconut Row, Palm Beach, FL 33480 (tel. 655-3282). The **Greater West Palm Beach Chamber of Commerce** is at 501 N. Flagler Dr., West Palm Beach, FL 33401 (tel. 833-3711).

ORIENTATION: Route A1A wends through the city skirting along the ocean most of the time, and is called North or South County Boulevard as it goes through town. At the north end of town it turns west to join US 1 for a short distance; you can return to it again at Singer Island.

Three bridges link the island of Palm Beach with the mainland of West Palm Beach (when Palm Beachites cross the bridges, they say they're going "to Florida"). On the south end of the island, the Southern Boulevard bridge crosses Lake Worth and goes past the city's international airport. A few miles farther north, the Royal Palm Way crosses the water to become Okeechobee Boulevard. Still farther north your last chance to cross the lake is at Flagler Memorial Bridge on Royal Poinciana Way, which goes to West Palm Beach crossing Olive Street (where you'll find the Chamber of Commerce) and South Dixie Highway, which is US 1.

HOTELS: In posh Palm Beach your quarters are superstar or they are co-star, but they are not road show. Strictly prime time, this upper-crust resort accords high status to only one hotel, although it will occasionally unbend enough to accept two or three other jet-set stops. Those of us who have not yet acquired keys to a Lear must stick to the fringes or sneak off to some very nice and moderately priced resorts nearby (just tell everyone you're staying with friends—and you will be).

I've grouped hotels by location, including Singer Island, downtown, a beach strip just south of the city, and West Palm Beach, then tossed in a posh cluster of hotels in Boca Raton, and some moderately priced selections in Delray Beach for good measure.

Downtown

Queen of the island, world-famous superstar, glamour girl, and landmark of Palm Beach is the massive **Breakers,** Palm Beach, FL 33480 (tel. 305/655-6611, toll free 800/323-7500), a place so fabulously beautiful and carefully crafted that even the doorlocks are tiny brass lion's heads. Only Don Rickles could find fault

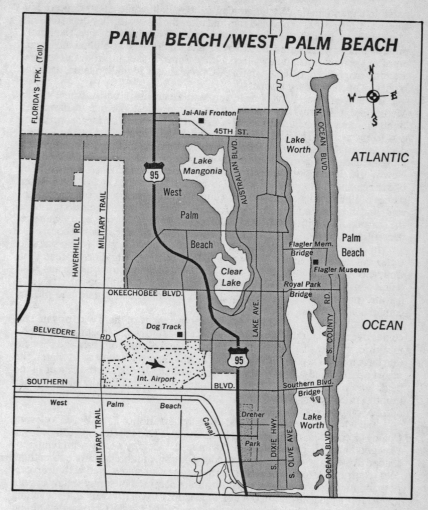

with the Breakers, which you ought to visit even if you don't stay here. It's quite a place—make that palace—a throwback to days when nearly everything was palatial and perfect. It is a wonder indeed, this barrel tile-roofed seaside behemoth. A walk through the Breakers is like strolling through a miniature Versailles. Every one of its public rooms is a glorious anachronistic study in huge glittering crystal chandeliers, tapestries, magnificent ceiling paintings, gilt, massive fireplaces, frescoes, and furbelows. Originally built by railroad magnate Henry Flagler, the Breakers was in those days a vast wooden structure that became winter home to such as the Rockefellers, John Jacob Astor, J. P. Morgan, William Randolph Hearst, Andrew Carnegie, the Duchess of Marlborough, and Pres. Warren Harding. Guests in those days arrived in private railroad cars with servants, and stayed the winter, of course. Their snowbird sojourn culminated in a grand finale, Washington's Birthday Ball: while guests danced, luggage was transported to railroad cars and after the last waltz they departed, still in their finery, to whiz off homeward by track. Twice razed by fire, the hotel's present glamor was created in 1925 by Flagler's heirs, who fashioned the Breakers after the most outstanding villas of Italy. Some 75 artisans from Europe created the magnificent ceiling paintings. One year and $6 million later, the huge hotel was again open for business.

Today you'll see belvedere towers and arches inspired by Rome's Villa Medici and a Florentine fountain at the entrance just like one in Florence's Bobli Gardens. A secluded central courtyard is bordered by loggias streaking east to the ocean. There's a Mediterranean Ballroom inspired by the Palazzo degli Imperial at Genoa, a ceiling in the Gold Room copied from Venice's Doges Palace with portraits of those who participated in the discovery of the New World. In the Florentine Dining Room the beamed ceiling is painted much like the ceiling of Florence's Palazzo Davanzate, and in the Circle Dining Room scenes of Italian cities are lighted by a huge Venetian chandelier of bronze, mirrors, and crystals hanging from a circular skylight. In both, chefs do justice to the surroundings with outstanding cuisine ($20 to $30). Mirrors everywhere reflect solid marble floors and more gold than a Spanish galleon could boast.

In recent years the hotel has added a beach club with an Olympic-size saltwater outdoor pool and a freshwater indoor pool. A palm-lined Ocean Golf Course is now supplemented by Breakers West, which has another course and tennis courts. There's a masseuse and masseur, biking, shuffleboard, croquet, a private (naturally) beach, dancing and entertainment in ornate and plushly comfortable lounges.

If you stay here, you'll find big, big rooms, many of them with private balconies overlooking the sea and all with deep wall-to-wall carpeting, darkwood furniture, vivid colors, big closets and baths, and all the comforts and services that have made this palatial hotel one of Florida's premier resorts. In winter, the resort operates only on a meal plan which includes breakfast and dinner in the peak-season daily rates (October to June) of $175 to $290 double. In other months, prices range from $75 to $130, without meals (for breakfast and dinner, add $27.50 per person).

Tall white pillars trim the lemony-yellow exterior of Palm Beach's elegant **Colony Hotel,** 155 Hammon Ave., Palm Beach, FL 33480 (tel. 305/655-5430), a *very* good address in Palm Beach. Swim in the Colony's long swimming pool shaded by swaying palms, then slip under a poolside umbrella and sip something cool. Retire later to beautifully decorated rooms or suites lined with deep carpets and furnished with light wicker furniture accented by sunny yellow or cool green. Just a block away are the fabulous shops of Worth Avenue. For evening entertainment there's dancing and music every night at the Colony, plus dining in the glow of candlelight at one of the city's most popular gathering spots. "Genteel" is the best word for the Colony, which charges $112 to $165 daily in winter, $50 to $80 in summer.

Another convenient and quite lovely downtown resort is the **Brazilian Court Hotel,** 300 Brazilian Ave., Palm Beach, FL 33480 (tel. 305/655-7740), a small and tranquil hotel with 125 rooms tucked away on pretty grounds just a few blocks from Worth Avenue. Refinement is the key word here: rooms are large and airy, tastefully furnished in light, bright colors, and those who come here are seeking serenity. A heated pool is a gathering spot for guests who have been returning for years and often dine together in the hotel's subtly decorated dining room on well-prepared continental cuisine in the $15 to $20 price range. Open December to May, the hotel charges about $100 to $135, depending on room size and location, and including full breakfast. Suites and the penthouse begin at $180. Subtract about $30 for a room in summer.

A jungle of greenery surrounds the glittering swimming pool at **Heart of Palm Beach Motor Hotel,** 160 Royal Palm Way, Palm Beach, FL 33480 (tel. 305/655-5600), a conveniently located, moderately priced hotel in downtown Palm Beach. Settle into attractive paneled rooms here with big picture windows or sliding glass doors leading to private balconies overlooking this serene city. Bright colors glow against dark wood, and comfortable chairs are a nice place to relax after a long day at the pool. Heart of Palm Beach has some larger accommodations too, if you'd like more space, and the resort's Bird-in-Hand Pub is a cheery place to seek something tall and cool, or to lunch inside, or on the poolside patio. Double rates here are $59 to $89 in summer, rising to $99 to $160 in peak season.

Palm Beach Residence Hotel, at 100 Datura St., West Palm Beach, FL 33401 (tel. 305/655-8800, or toll free 800/238-8000), is a kosher hotel largely for long-term residents. The hotel is set high on the side of a slight rise overlooking the Intracoastal Waterway, and in the distance is the elegance of Palm Beach. Front rooms have balconies overlooking the pool and Lake Worth (which is also the Intracoastal Waterway here). In winter, charges are $45 to $50 double, and in summer drop to $36 to $42.

If you crave that downtown location but don't have the bankbook to finance it in the style of the Breakers or the Colony, here's a real budget find: **Testa's,** 214 Sunset Ave., Palm Beach, FL 33480 (tel. 305/832-2672), famous for its restaurant on Royal Poinciana Way, also has 28 moderately appointed rooms you can rent for $40 double—and you certainly won't have to go far for dinner.

Radisson Hotel Palm Beach, 235 Sunrise Ave., Palm Beach, FL 33480 (tel. 305/659-2255, or toll free 800/228-9822), is conveniently located for theater fans —it's just a few blocks from the city's Royal Poinciana Playhouse. A comparatively small hotel with just 150 rooms, the Radisson is a serene antique spot with beautiful arched façade and red Mediterranean tiled roof, complete with something that looks like a bell tower. Behind that showy entrance is lofty lobby, handsomely decorated rooms and suites, several restaurants and lounges. Although it's quite close to the ocean, it provides plenty of amusements right on its own grounds via a Nautilus health club, a row of posh shops, and both tennis and golf not far away. Its Chercher Lounge often welcomes quite famous faces and its top-flight restaurant, L'Avenue, purveys outstanding continental cuisine. Outside lots of tropical greenery trim the resort's swimming pool and shade the Palm Court where al fresco meals are served at breakfast and lunch. Winter rates at the Radisson, which has quite an enviable location on the north end of the island but quite close to all the best island action, are $115 double for rooms, $135 to $175 for one-bedroom suites, and $235 for two-bedroom suites. From May to mid-December those rates drop to $50, $70, and $85.

South of Downtown on Route A1A

There are some lovely resorts just south of the city and less than a 15-minute drive from Worth Avenue. One of them is the **Palm Beach Hawaiian Inn,** 3550 S. Ocean Blvd.; Palm Beach, FL 33480 (tel. 305/582-5631), about eight miles south of town on Route A1A where it occupies a lovely uncrowded strip of oceanfront sand. The large rooms are nicely decorated in lively colors, and there's a pool and coffeeshop, sundeck and beach cabanas, an oceanfront dining room and patio bar. You can bring your pets along here, and choose your accommodations from a list that includes rooms, efficiencies, one-bedroom apartments, and two-bedroom quarters for four. From mid-January to May two people pay $64 to $66, $90 for suites, and about $38 to $40 in summer, when suites are $65.

The **Palm Beach Ocean Hotel,** 2770 and 2830 S. Ocean Blvd., Palm Beach, FL 33480 (tel. 305/582-5381, or toll free 800/327-9407), used to be a Holiday Inn but you certainly wouldn't recognize that chain here now. Thermasol steambaths and Therms Cuzzi spas spark baths now, and large rooms have been redecorated in lively contemporary colors and furnishings. Some of the 266 rooms are on the oceanfront, some have refrigerators, and no fewer than 83 have those steambaths. For tennis players there are three courts, and for swimmers there are four pools: two heated, one saltwater, and a wading pool. There are two very attractive dining rooms at the resort ($10 to $15 for dinner), one of them a seafood house. You can always find entertainment here, and winter rates are $94 to $122 from January to May, slightly lower in December, and $34 to $70 in summer months.

Another star in the galaxy of Palm Beach resorts is the **Palm Beach Hilton,** 2842 S. Ocean Blvd., Palm Beach, FL 33480 (tel. 305/586-6542, or toll free in Florida 800/432-5141; there are toll-free numbers in every state). Right on the ocean, about ten minutes from Worth Avenue, the Hilton has 134 beautifully decorated rooms with lots of special touches. Of course, there are all the other resort amenities like a big swimming pool, a long strip of private sand, a beauty salon, free valet parking, a cocktail lounge where you can watch the surf rolling in, and a lovely dining room with continental cuisine, entertainment, and dancing every night. There are tennis courts to play on, water sports of all kinds, and beautiful balconies where you can look down on people doing all those things. In winter season, from mid-December to May, rates are $93 to $495 dropping in the summer months to $39 to $230.

On Singer Island

Singer Island is a small key just north of the city where there are several large resorts and some small family operations. One of the larger hotels is the **Hilton Inn of the Palm Beaches,** 3800 N. Ocean Dr., Riviera Beach, FL 33404 (tel. 305/848-5502, and toll-free numbers in most states), which sprawls along a long section of oceanfront sand on Singer Island. Unusual half-circle balconies offer you an ever-changing view of the ocean, and some of the spacious, brightly decorated rooms open right onto the pool, so it's only a few steps between dreams and reality. Bring your tennis racquet and lob a few over the net at the tennis court, night or day, or invest in a snorkel so you can prowl the deep. Some efficiencies are available, and there are suites if you like lots of space. Double rates, determined by view, in winter are $100 to $161; in summer, $61 to $77.

Best Western SeaSpray Inn, 123 Ocean Ave., Palm Beach Shores, FL 33404 (tel. 305/844-0233), is a pretty place where you begin to sink into the tropics the moment you enter the attractive reception area. You know you've arrived as you gaze out over the ocean from your private balcony or sink into the comfort of the SeaSpray's pretty quarters. An unusually shaped motel with lots of jutting angles, the SeaSpray has some rooms that fit into those angles, creating interesting corners and odd nooks. A plant-bedecked rooftop restaurant and cozy lounge, plus tropical furniture and vivid colors, get you into the spirit of this southern resort. There's a pool and sundeck too, and just over there, the golden sands and blue, blue ocean. In peak season, two people pay $73 to $98; in summer, $41 to $63—with ocean views determining prices.

You can go after those really big denizens of the deep—sailfish—at the **Sailfish Marina,** 98 Lake Dr., Palm Beach Shores, FL 33404 (tel. 305/844-1724), where there's a fleet of charter fishing boats right at your door. Just sit by the sparkling aquamarine pool and do nothing at all. Or take a short walk to explore the miles and miles of sand. And inside your room are beamed ceilings, wood paneling, simple contemporary furniture, and bright colors. It's a pretty place for anyone, but nirvana for fishing fans. Rates in summer are $35 to $55 double (for an efficiency for four), $56 to $83 in winter.

West Palm Beach

Flagler built West Palm Beach as a dwelling place for Palm Beach workers, but today it has acquired a personality of its own far removed from the lofty life of Palm Beach. There's no ocean here, but there are some nice resorts convenient to I-95 and one very posh enclave where Prince Charles stayed when he came here for a polo game. When they heard he was coming, the resort spent $80,000 to redecorate his quarters.

One of the most attractive properties in the **Holiday Inn** chain is at 4431 PGA Blvd., Palm Beach, FL 33401 (tel. 305/622-2260, or toll free 800/238-8000), just west of I-95. Set under some tall pines, the resort has won awards for the quality of its 178 spacious, paneled rooms and crisply contemporary decor complete with double or king-size beds and balconies. It could also be cited for its large tiled lobby and handsome candlelit restaurant, its alluring lounge with two-story-tall windows, and its overall efforts to make your stay a pleasant one. If you're a golfer, it's just a few minutes' drive to the PGA championship course. Double rates are $38 to $54 in summer and $64 to $94 in winter.

If you are (or think you'd like to be) a polo groupie, canter on out to **Palm Beach Polo and Country Club,** 13198 Forest Hill Blvd., Palm Beach, FL 33411 (tel. 305/793-1113). You can ride at an equestrian center, play tennis, racquetball, croquet, or golf, swim, perhaps even chukker about a bit on these world-famous polo grounds where a recent player was Charles, Prince of Wales. The club's a collection of villages each with its own pool, and each cluster is located next door to the sport it's named after. There's a dining room and lounge too. Villas (or lodges as they call them here) are privately owned, but are available for rental at winter prices beginning at $125 to $175 for a studio or one-bedroom villa, $265 for a two-bedroom, $345 for a three-bedroom, $75 to $250 in summer. You'll need a car here, absolutely. Weekly rates save you one day's rent.

Bed and Breakfast

If you'd like to try a bed-and-breakfast establishment in the Palm Beach area contact **Bed & Breakfast of the Palm Beaches,** Eliza Hofmeister, 205 Circle West, Jupiter, FL 33458 (tel. 305/746-2545).

Boca Raton

Boca Raton Hotel and Club, on Camino Real, Boca Raton, FL 33432 (tel. 305/395-3000), is not just a hotel, it's a way of life that proves once and for all what can be done—and had—for money. Flamboyant architect Addison Mizner certainly didn't pinch any pennies back in 1925 when he built this pink palace he called the Cloisters for $1.25 million, pouring into it more money than anyone had ever spent on a 100-room hostelry. It was the pivotal point (and still is) of a booming resort city that was humbly to announce in its advertising "I am the greatest resort in the world." It is filled with Mizner's collection of treasures, including so many roof tiles from Spanish churches some feared every worshipper in Spain would be soaked.

You can get a look at the essence of 1920s boom-town Florida at the Boca Raton Hotel and Club, and get a pretty good look at boom-town 1980s Boca as well: marble pillars soar to high, high ceilings, a little statue of Pan pipes merrily away at the entrance gate, water pours from the mouth of a fanciful dolphin into trilevel pools lined with ornate ceramic tiles, candles glow and chandeliers glitter, everything seems touched with gilt, *nothing* has been overlooked—a water fountain here is no basic-gray metal stand but a stream flowing from the mouth of a somewhat perplexed brass lion.

Long hallways wide enough for a marching band are dotted with intimate little groupings of plump couches and comfortable chairs. Massive Spanish tables glow with decades of wax and daily polishing. Brass gleams, crystal glitters, candles flicker, and an ethereal golden glow filters through arched windows. You're transported into a world that doesn't concern itself much with the passage of time, enveloped in an old-world cocoon light-years from the bustle out there in the real, and oh-so-crass, world.

Mizner loved those touches of Old Spain (he's even said to have run up and down stairs in hobnailed boots to "age" them) so you'll see Spain in these beautiful big rooms, too. You'll also see all the contemporary comforts from deep chairs to modern tiled baths, big fluffy towels, and all the efficient, friendly service you'd expect at one of the nation's top resorts.

As for dining, an evening in the Cathedral is a little like dining in a ducal palace. Candles shed a delicate golden glimmer over soaring pillars and alabaster arches. Waiters in formal wear hover discreetly, buffets approach gastronomic decadence, and if you're ever looking for an exceedingly romantic spot in which to make a proposal (any proposal), this is it.

That doesn't begin to be all, of course. This dowager duchess of genteel old-world resorts has just given birth to a bouncing $20-million baby, the **Boca Raton Beach Club,** which is everything to the late 20th century that the Cloisters was to the early years. Built on its own island connected to "mother" by highway and private launch, the seven-story beach club is a study in modern magnificence: courtyards are scented by the exotic perfumes of tropical blooms and there's a quarter mile of silver sands. Spacious rooms have deep plush carpets and pale-peach decor, high-backed wicker chairs, oak doors, and even Gucci soap and guest packs designed especially for the hotel. You're treated to fluffy terrycloth robes, refrigerators stocked with cold drinks, the *Wall Street Journal* at your door each morning, chocolates on your pillow, glass elevators, nighttime shoeshines, private balconies, skylighted dining rooms filled with greenery. You don't even have to go through all that mundane front desk routine: you're greeted by name at the desk (clue: the doorman phoned up), seated, and treated to an orange juice and champagne cocktail.

Then there's a third hotel, the **Tower,** 27 stories of pink stucco with spacious and dramatic rooms plus an elegant rooftop dining room overlooking Lake Boca Raton. Finally, west of town is yet a fourth in the clan, **Boca West,** a resort haven surrounded by cool clear lakes, 27 clay tennis courts, and *four* championship golf courses that are home to international tennis and golf competitions. As a guest of the Boca Raton Hotel and Club you can use all the facilities—which total five golf courses, 49 tennis courts, every conceivable water sport, swimming pools everywhere, a cabana club at the beach, health club, bicycles, jogging track, even trap and skeet shooting.

At the stately Cloisters, rates in high season from January to May (including breakfast and dinner) are $235 double, $215 single, and parlors are $120 additional. In the Tower you'll pay $275 double (parlors at the Beach Club are $95 additional). For a corner Tower room and ocean-view Beach Club quarters the tag is a whopping $295 double. One-bedroom villas are $295. In summer, rates at the Cloister, the Tower, and the Beach Club are $75, $90, and $115 respectively, European plan, and special money-saving packages are available.

Dinners at any of the resort's beautiful dining rooms are about $25 or more per person.

Delray Beach

High on a dune you'll find **Côte d'Azure,** 2325 S. Ocean Blvd., Delray Beach, FL 33444 (tel. 305/278-2646), an attractive small motel with a variety of accommodations ranging from hotel rooms to two-bedroom oceanfront villas. The Côte d'Azure streaks back in one long wing from Route A1A to the beach, and has a pretty pool and thatched Tiki huts for shelter from the sun. Just at the end of the building is the beach, where you can walk or swim for miles along the oceanfront. Small rooms here are decorated in bright colors, and efficiencies have electric kitchens and tile baths. There are TVs and phones in the apartments too. Rates from February through mid-April range from $60 for hotel rooms, oceanfront or poolside (although there aren't many oceanfront rooms), to $70 for an efficiency and $85 to $110 for one- or two-bedroom apartments. In other months, prices drop as low as $36 to $66.

Arches, arches, and more arches set the tone at **Spanish River Resort,** 1111 E. Atlantic Ave., Delray Beach, FL 33444 (tel. 305/276-7441), where semicircular balconies are reached through arched glass doors. Across the street from the ocean, Spanish River Inn soars 11 stories and has 72 very spacious rooms decorated in tropical colors with king-size or double beds, plenty of closet space, and balconies in every apartment—three balconies in two-bedroom apartments! On the palm-strewn grounds are two pools, tennis courts, saunas, and a game room on an activities deck. Double rates are $560 a week for a studio, rising to $1295 a week for a two-bedroom executive suite in peak season, $59 to $135 a day in summer. All the beach is public in Delray, so you have miles of sand just across the street.

Camping

You can camp inexpensively in **Jonathan Dickinson State Park** (tel. 305/546-2772; see Chapter V), and here in Palm Beach, the **Vacation Inn Trav-L-Park,** at 6566 N. Military Trail, West Palm Beach, FL 33407 (tel. 305/848-6166), has an attractive country campground with a well-equipped recreation room, bike trails, snack-bar and grocery store, two large pools (one with a slide and a wading pool), lagoon, and barbecue area. Full hookups are $20 for two people.

PALM BEACH RESTAURANTS: Naturally Palm Beachites demand the best, and naturally they get it, at some of the state's better restaurants. They pay for it too, at prices that are on the steep side by Floridian standards but moderate if you're just in from Manhattan. By that I mean a few restaurants will probably present you with a bill for two in the $50 range, but you can also find a number of moderately priced restaurants as well. Here are some of Palm Beach's best, grouped by their specialties, followed by recommendations in surrounding communities.

Continental/American

Witherspoon's, 420 US Hwy. 1, North Palm Beach, in Village Square Plaza (tel. 845-6221), is a new effort of a restaurateur who's been around a long time and also operates the Galley Restaurant at Sailfish Marina on Singer Island. A pretty place of earth tones, oil paintings, fresh flowers, and cushy chairs, Witherspoon's specializes in crab fettuccine Alfredo and some other good Italian offerings, as well as quite reasonably priced, soup-to-dessert dinners for just under $10. Musical entertainment is frequent here and includes jazz and big-band sounds. Most prices are in the $10 to $15 range for dinner, but add a little extra to try some of the restaurant's hors d'oeuvres and cheeses. Hours are 11 a.m. to 2:30 p.m. for lunch weekdays, 5 to 10:30 p.m. for dinner daily, closing a little later on weekends.

Reverse chic is always in in Palm Beach, so it should come as no surprise to any of us that **Chuck and Harold's**, 207 Royal Poinciana Way, Palm Beach (tel. 659-1440), is the rage these days. You can expect to wait for a table here, for the place is almost always packed. A handsome atmosphere of Mexican tiles and beamed ceilings of hand-painted pecky cypress accounts for some of the C & H popularity, but the main attraction is homemade pizza-dough bread sprinkled with poppy seeds. Other favorites are seafood pasta pagliara and smoked salmon fettuccine. Mussels, oysters, Bahamian conch chowder, burgers, steaks, and seafood are all on the varied menu here. Prices top out at $22 for a combination of New York strip sirloin and Florida lobster tail, but generally average $10 to $15 for dinner. Try the shrimp and artichoke linguine—hearty and cheerfully unpretentious. Hours are 11 a.m. to 11:30 p.m. daily.

Take an old English pub atmosphere, throw in a little gilt and grandeur, and you've got **Doherty's**, 288 S. County Rd. (tel. 655-6200), an uncomplicated and casual restaurant where the accent's on well-prepared food at prices that are, for Palm Beach, reasonable. Dine on steaks and prime rib, bay scallops, stone crab, Maine lobster, cold crisp salads, or hearty bacon-topped hamburgers rapidly produced in an always-busy setting full of people having a good time. Entree prices are in the $9.50 to $15 range. Doherty's is open from 11:30 a.m. to 2:30 p.m. for lunch and from 5:30 to 11:30 p.m. for dinner daily. Sunday brunch is served from 9 a.m. until 3 p.m.

French

East coast Floridians are welcoming **Café L'Europe**, 150 Worth Ave. (tel. 655-4020), in the Esplanade shopping plaza, with the same enthusiasm the restaurant receives on the west coast where it holds forth elegantly in Sarasota. They've done it again here: beautiful decor, efficient service, upper-crust atmosphere, shining crystal, and outstanding cuisine with the usual French talent for blending and surprising. After a dinner here, the bottom line on the check will hover in the $20-a-person range, more if you indulge in the full line of temptations. It's open from 11:30 a.m. to 3 p.m. and 6 to 10 p.m., daily except Sunday.

A Monaco native created **Le Monegasque**, 2505 S. Ocean Blvd. (tel. 585-0071), nestled away in the corner of the Palm Beach President condominium. That native is Aldo Rinero, who has a long and impressive career behind him (Forum of the Twelve Caesars, Delmonico's, Toque Blanche) and knows exactly what he's about in his tiny world. You'll find treats like filet of pompano, chateaubriand, foie de veau Grande Bretagne, delicate veal dishes, accompanied by vegetables cooked to a T and desserts that are, well, you decide how rapturous the description. You'll pay about $15 to $22, depending on your indulgence, and the restaurant is open from 6 to 10 p.m. Tuesday through Sunday (closed June through September).

Petite Marmite, 309½ Worth Ave. (tel. 655-0550), reigns over Worth Avenue today with the same sophisticated chic it brought to this street ages ago. Petite Marmite is a gathering spot and glamor spot, the place to see and be seen, and an excellent restaurant as well. A skylight bathes the restaurant in a soft glow and lights hundreds of orchids and blooming things in a small garden. Crystal glitters and linens glow, the service is rapid, and someone important or rich (and there are lots of both in Palm Beach) may stroll through the door at any moment. Leave plenty of time to taste-read the long menus here. Crisp and brimming salads are highlights at lunch (although there are dozens of more substantial choices), and sole Véronique, tournedos, veal, mussels, or pastas are among many dinner choices in the $12 to $18 price bracket. Don't miss the dessert cart, which will send you right off to Avoirdupois Anonymous, meek but happy. Open 11:30 a.m. to 11 p.m. daily (closed on Sunday June to October).

L'Anjou, 717 Lake Ave., Lake Worth (tel. 582-7666), is another very popular French restaurant in Palm Beach County. Prices are quite reasonable here with complete dinners beginning at $12, top price about $17. Service is pleasant and charmingly French in accent and demeanor. This too is a popular restaurant and reservations are very wise, particularly in winter months. L'Anjou is open from 5 to 10 p.m. daily.

READER'S RESTAURANT SELECTION: "A really super, top-notch French restaurant in the Palm Beach area is **Café du Parc**, 612 Federal Hwy., Lake Park (tel. 845-0529). It's located opposite Kelsey Park at Park Avenue and is run by a husband and wife from the Lot Valley in southwestern France, an area known for its three-star Michelin-rated hotels and restaurants. Our meal at Café du Parc was truly outstanding, each dish prepared to perfection. The setting is an old wooden frame house, pleasantly furnished with a cozy atmosphere. Clients seemed to be 'Palm Beach regulars': Madame greeted the majority of people at the door by name and in the correct language too. Reservations are advised" (Sara Drower, Wilmette, Ill.). [*Author's Note:* Café du Parc is a lovely little French restaurant much revered by the Palm Beach set. Classical French cooking at its best is available here from 5:30 to 10 p.m. daily in winter, closed Sunday and Monday from early May to November. Entree prices are in the $12 to $17 range.]

Italian

A charming little garden patio and one of the few sidewalk cafés on this coastline would be reason enough to head for **Testa's**, at 221 Royal Poinciana Way (tel. 832-0992), but wonderful pasta and Italian concoctions and excellent steaks and seafood clinch matters. The same family has kept this pretty little place running for more than 60 years now, and is thoughtful enough to provide a children's menu so you can take the young ones along without breaking the bank. Dinners average about $10 to $14. In summer the family takes off to a northern restaurant operation, closing this Testa's from May to mid-December. It's open daily from 7 a.m. to 1 a.m.

Fettuccine Alfredo, softshell crabs, saltimbocca alla Romana, scampi—what more could there be in life? Whatever more there is, you'll find at **Nando's**, 221 Royal Palm Way (tel. 655-3031), where you dine on fine Italian creations in a brick-lined gardeny atmosphere trimmed with ornate ironwork. You're entertained in winter by strolling musicians, and anytime by soft music from the piano in the intimate candlelit lounge. Entrees here average $10 to $15, and Nando's is open from 5:30 p.m. to 1 a.m. daily.

In a subtly classic decor of vine-covered wrought iron, chandeliers, linen, and crystal, **Capriccio**, 336 Royal Poinciana Plaza (tel. 659-5955), creates continental dishes for Palm Beach audiences that are just as outstanding as those created in its former New York home where it was praised by newspaper critics. Italian touches highlight the menu, and your bill will probably average about $20 for dinner. Capriccio is an especially good choice for pre- or post-theater dinners since the Royal Poinciana Playhouse is just a few steps away. Reservations are necessary most of the time, and always in winter. It's closed on Sunday and in September; at other times Capriccio is open from 11:30 a.m. to 2:30 p.m. for lunch, from 5:30 to 10 p.m. for dinner.

A spot with the unlikely—but very well-known hereabouts—name of **This Is It Pub**, 424 24th St., West Palm Beach (tel. 832-9172), draws crowds to lunch and dinner. It has been doing so for more than 25 years now and there seems no end in sight to the popularity of this place that relies entirely on word of mouth to spread its reputation for good steaks and seafood, rack of lamb, and bouillabaisse. Northern Italian cooking is featured here, so you'll always find some delectable veal dishes among the offerings. This Is It is open from 11:30 a.m. to 11:30 p.m. daily, and prices are in the $10 to $15 range for dinner.

Seafood

A newcomer to Palm Beach is **Charley's Crab,** 456 S. Ocean Blvd. (tel. 659-1500), brother to the Sarasota operation that lures throngs of hungry seafood lovers. Naturally, the accent is on fresh-from-the-sea creatures, so each night there are specials, depending on what's just off the boat that day. Sashay up to the raw bar for iced oysters and cherrystone clams, and try the mussels or linguine with red clam sauce. There's an intimate, pubby atmosphere in this restaurant just across the street from the ocean, and the cuisine is moderately priced (in the $15 to $20 range). Charley's is open from 11 a.m. to 2:30 p.m. and 5 to 10 p.m. daily, from 10 a.m. to 2:30 p.m. for Sunday brunch.

Budget Stops

Millionaires and would-be tycoons alike whip into **Hamburger Heaven,** 314 S. County Rd. (tel. 655-5277), to dine or chow down on some of the best hamburgers in town. That's the specialty here (they grind their own beef daily), but there are plenty of other sandwich and salad choices at prices everybody likes: under $5. Open 7:30 a.m. to 9 p.m. daily, with earlier closings in summer (closed from August to September 15).

Tony Roma's, at 2215 Palm Beach Lakes Blvd., West Palm Beach (tel. 689-1703), produces barbecued ribs with a spicy sauce so excellent he's cloned his restaurant many times now to provide for throngs of hungry diners. You'll also find hamburgers on the menu, along with inexpensive steak (about $9), very inexpensive London broil (about $5), and a loaf of onion rings the likes of which you'll find only at Tony Roma's. Nothing on the menu is more than $10, and the restaurant's open from 11 a.m. to midnight Monday through Thursday, until 1 a.m. on Friday and Saturday, and 2 p.m. to midnight on Sunday.

DINING IN THE SUBURBS: the communities surrounding Palm Beach are also well supplied with fine restaurants.

Boynton Beach/Lantana

Another local favorite is **Bernard's,** 1730 N. Federal Hwy. (tel. 737-2236), one of *the* places to be seen for Sunday brunch, and indeed worth the trip from wherever you are. Bernard's is set in what once was a popular botanical garden so there are lovely views of growing things outside the windows. Inside are lovely views as well: conch chowder, coquilles topped with a bubbling cheese sauce, fresh grouper filets garnished with sauteed plantains, duckling, roast tenderloin, trayloads of desserts. It's all served on tables scattered around an old house with a massive fireplace and pretty patio cooled by paddle fans. Figure about $15 to $25 per person for dinner. The restaurant is open for lunch from 11:30 a.m. to 2 p.m. Tuesday through Friday, from 6 to 10 p.m. daily for dinner, with Sunday brunch ($11 for adults) from 10:30 a.m. to 2:30 p.m.

On Friday night you'd think everyone in three counties was packed into the **Banana Boat,** 739 E. Ocean Ave. (tel. 737-9400). There's always a crowd chattering away at the tables outside on the porch overlooking a marina or inside where low lighting glows on flocks of hungry seafood fans. Sea creatures are the specialty here, although you can find enough other selections to please everyone. The Boat's a favorite local spot for younger diners, who stay on for entertainment that lasts well into the wee hours. Prices are in the $5 to $15 range, and the Banana Boat is open at 11 a.m. daily. There's another Banana Boat farther north at 639 US Hwy 1, North Palm Beach (tel. 848-1400).

Two Georges Marina in Boynton Beach hides a place well loved by boaters who nip in here to while away an afternoon or evening chowing down on jumbo shrimp, conch fritters, fresh filets of whatever's been caught today, even freshwater catfish. Most people only know it as Two Georges Marina, but it really is the **Harbour Hut Restaurant & Raw Bar** (tel. 736-2717), and is open from 11 a.m. to 11 p.m. daily, from noon on Sunday, with later closings on weekends. Prices range from $7 to $13.

Anchor Inn, 2810 Hypoluxo Rd., Lantana (tel. 965-4794), sticks to seafood but does a very good job of it, so good that you often find local restaurant owners dining here! There are always buckets and buckets of oysters being shucked for presentation on the half shell, as oysters casino or in a special house preparation called oysters Anchor. Options for landsmen include double-thick lamb chops and thick broiled-to-order steaks. Fish is simply prepared here, but is always fresh from the sea and reasonably priced—most dinners in the $10 to $15 range. Hours at Anchor Inn are 5 to 10 p.m. daily, and you'll find the restaurant a half mile west of I-95 at Exit 45.

Stuart

Jake's, 423 S. Federal Hwy., Stuart (tel. 283-5111), has been operating for a decade or so after revamping an old building that once was condemned. A lively place with a raw bar, all kinds of seafood, steaks, and a lounge open to 2 a.m. daily, Jake's also produces lots of good quiches and salads. Prices are in a quite-reasonable $8 to $14 range for dinner, and hours are 11:30 a.m. to 2 a.m. daily, with last dinner orders taken at 10 p.m. daily (11 p.m. on weekends). On Sunday the restaurant opens at 4 p.m. and closes at 10 p.m.

Delray Beach

When I peeked in a window of **The Bridge,** 840 E. Atlantic Ave. (tel. 278-7816), one day and spotted an atmosphere straight out of Manhattan, I returned to try it out—and returned and returned and returned. A charming and savvy New Yorker opened this spot years ago in a tiny but very sophisticated dining room that could seat perhaps a dozen. Big picture windows overlooked the waterway and the decor ran to dark walls, elegantly framed French posters, and giant ferns. These days the Bridge is chic-er than ever in both decor and clientele, but has kept the same excellent menu that changes regularly as the restaurant finds seasonal goodies to place before you, contemporary, cosmopolitan, and gorgeous. You'll pay about $15 to $20 for a memorable dinner here. The Bridge is open from noon to 2:30 p.m. for lunch, from 6 to 10 p.m. for dinner (until 2 a.m. in the lounge), daily except Monday.

Every city has a landmark, and the **Patio,** at 714 E. Atlantic Ave. (tel. 276-7126), is Delray's. Nobody knows which street is where in this little village, but everyone can tell you where the Patio is. There's a good reason for that, and the good reason is a long, long history of dining, both beautiful and delectable. Back in the days when Delray was super upper crust you would have been hosted here by Prince Obolensky, who moved up to join the Palm Beach crowd in later years. The Patio got its name from its patio under the stars, and you can still dine there (the roof rolls out if it rains). Fireplaces add a cheery air in winter. The steaks are still as top-quality as they always were, the seafood fresh and outstanding, the french-fried mushrooms a must-try. Prices are in the $10 to $20 range, and hours are 11:30 a.m. to 2:30 p.m. Tuesday through Saturday, 5 to 11 p.m. for dinner daily, and noon to 3 p.m. for Sunday brunch.

There's something about this north Gold Coast area that draws Italians, and they come armed with whisks and award-winning cuisine that keeps them in business long after others have come and gone. **Vittorio's**, 25 S. US Hwy. 1 (tel. 278-5525), is one of those that's succeeded in creating a pleasant atmosphere in which the kitchen can display its many and varied culinary talents. The accent here is on northern Italian cuisine, with lots of light creamy sauces and melt-in-your-mouth pastas served in an atmosphere heavy on candlelight, antiques, and greenery. For the excellent food and matching surroundings you'll pay $10 to $20 for entrees. Vittorio's is open from 5:30 to 10 p.m. daily. Jackets are required for gentlemen.

Paoletti's, at 815 N. Federal Hwy. (tel. 272-2988), began with an enchanting restaurant in Coral Gables years ago before it moved northward to bring its award-winning Italian cuisine to Delray—to a nice little dining room, complete with intimate, low lighting and romantic, comfortable booths. Here's also that outstanding cuisine for which the restaurant was so justly famous. Fresh seafood, pasta, veal—it's all there at Paoletti's, at prices in the $10 to $20 vicinity. Hours are 5:30 to 10 p.m. daily. Closed May through October.

Just the thought of lobster Savannah, swimming in a creamy Mornay sauce and accented with delicate spices, can send me racing off for another visit to **Busch's**, 5855 N. Ocean Blvd., Ocean Ridge (tel. 732-8470). Lace curtains on the windows, a shady lounge with quiet background notes from the piano, plus the cozy look of an old house (which it is) combine to make an evening at Busch's not only gastronomically divine but atmospherically heavenly as well. After dining on the likes of she-crab soup (Thursday), broiled pompano, or red snapper fresh from the sea, you'll leave with a check in the $13 to $20 range for entrees. Hours are 5 to 10 p.m. Tuesday through Sunday.

You have to give **Arcade Tap Room**, 411 E. Atlantic Ave., Delray Beach (tel. 276-7200), credit for longevity in a state in which restaurant longevity is the exception rather than the rule. Operating here now for half a century (!), the Tap Room is the kind of place in which you will eventually see everybody around if you wait long enough. A popular meeting spot for Palm Beach County dwellers and visitors, the Tap Room features basic American cooking—prime rib, steaks, seafood (accent on seafood)—for prices in the $13 to $20 range. No doubt about it, this is an institution on the Gold Coast, and worth a look just to see who else is looking. Hours are 11 a.m. to 10 p.m. daily.

READERS' RESTAURANT SELECTIONS: "**Stonewalls**, at Delray Beach Country Club, 2200 Highland Blvd., Delray Beach (tel. 278-0311), has a very attractive country-club atmosphere, extremely friendly, warm service, a delightful salad bar, very reasonable prices, and most of all delicious food! They have another facility at **Boca Teeca Country Club**, 5801 NW Second Ave., Boca Raton (tel. 944-0400)" (Francine Sanders, Brooklyn, N.Y.).

Boca Raton

Addison Mizner, who created the glamorous Boca Raton Hotel and many elegant homes in this city, was the inspiration behind a pretty little house two top restaurateurs have turned into **La Vieille Maison**, at 770 E. Palmetto Park Rd. (tel. 391-6701). That means "the old house," but doesn't do this old house justice. Surely they should have added "belle" or "magnifique" to the name, for this 50-year-old beauty is all of that. Each of several dining rooms is decorated differently, one with a country look, another with formal high-backed chairs. Tiny tables are tucked around the tiny patio where a tree grows right through the roof, and there's a wine cellar lined with bottles. Fountains bubble, Cuban tiles add splashes of color, and flowers, flowers, and more flowers trim every flat surface. Everything's exquisite, from the crystal and fine china, to the award-winning cuisine which moves effortlessly from a pastry-trimmed pâté to escargots, pan-roasted quail in cognac, ending finally with crisp tart salads, a packed tray of cheeses and fresh fruit, double chocolate mousse, or a lemon crêpe soufflé. Prix-fixe prices here are $38 for a complete dinner, $31 if you skip the appetizer, and $22 if you forgo an entree. Seating in summer is at 6:30 or 9 p.m. (6 or 9 p.m. in winter), by reservation. Jackets for men are required in season.

Arturo's, 6750 N. Federal Hwy. (tel. 997-7373), is something of a newcomer to the area but has cut a rather wide swath here since it opened. A large and lovely restaurant with tall French windows, Arturo's specializes in Italian flavors and makes all its pasta right here. One of the specialties, spaghetti Gismondi, combines bacon drippings, Nova Scotia salmon, tomato and cream sauce with thin, thin pasta. Angel-hair pasta turns up al pesto, flavored with basil and parmesan. Mostaccioli is teamed with cognac, fettuccine with fresh tomatoes, and linguine with clam sauce. Prices are in the $12 to $20 range and hours are 5 to 10 p.m. daily.

Joe Muer's, 6450 N. Federal Hwy. (tel. 997-6688), is the Florida branch of a Detroit restaurant that settled in here about a decade ago. Muer's concentrates on seafood and does quite a creditable job, offering a wide range of seafood specialties, as well as steaks for landlubbers. This is a good place to go to try some of the more unusual Florida seafood—pompano, for instance. You'll pay $15 to $20 for dinner at Muer's, which is open from 5 to 9:30 p.m. daily in winter months (closed Monday from May to November).

Raffaello's Restaurant, 725 Palmetto Park Rd. East, Boca Raton (tel. 392-4855), is a new spot up this way. Italian flavors are favored at this colorful spot outfitted in shades of salmon and green. A small cocktail lounge presides over the entrance to this comfortable but rather formal restaurant (jackets are required for gentlemen). Out in the kitchen, talented chefs are whipping up such unusual dishes as tortellini with cauliflower and asparagus tips, a creamy-rich Italian cheese pie, eggplant rollatine stuffed with ricotta cheese and topped with a rich and spicy tomato sauce. Prices are in the $10 to $15 range for entrees, and there's a creditable wine list. Hours are 6 to 10:30 p.m. daily.

Le Bon Vivant, 171 E. Palmetto Pkwy., Boca Raton (tel. 391-4544), has been receiving kudos far and wide for its innovative cuisine. You might begin here with a salad of green beans, truffles, and goose liver, a seafood terrine with sauce verte, imported sea scallops baked in their own shells, or salmon in pastry with a chervil sauce. Then move on to filet de sole fourré bastide stuffed with crabmeat floating in both a rich lobster sauce and a piquant chablis topping. Treats like that are served in an elegant gray room and the tab runs high: $15 to $20 for entrees alone, but many people consider the fine cooking well worth the price. Hours are 11 a.m. to 2 p.m. weekdays, 6:30 to 10 p.m. daily except Sunday.

READERS' RESTAURANT SUGGESTIONS: "Another good Italian restaurant is **Roma's.** Dominic Magnano really cares about his customers and often comes out of the kitchen to find out if you're enjoying your dinner. Roma's is small and casual with prices in the $8 to $10 range. It's at 500 SE 15th Ave., Boynton Beach (tel. 737-2525). I'd also recommend **The Ark II** at 2600 Lantana Rd. in West Palm Beach for inexpensive meals, a great salad bar, and complimentary hors d'oeuvres. Prices are in the $10 to $15 range. [*Author's Note:* The Ark, which has another restaurant in Dania, near Fort Lauderdale, is open 11:30 a.m. to 2:30 p.m. for lunch, from 5 to 10 p.m. for dinner daily. The lounge is open to 5 a.m. most nights.] **The Firehouse** at 6751 N. Federal Hwy., Boca Raton (tel. 997-6006), is also a good restaurant in this area. Prices are $12 to $17 for dinner. Open 5 to 10:30 p.m. daily" (Jerry Schultz, Boynton Beach, Fla.).

"Tell your readers about **The Seafood Connection** at 6998 N. Federal Hwy., Boca

Raton (tel. 997-5562). It's got good and moderately priced seafood and is always jammed because good seafood is hard to find around here" (Roy Nickels, Delray Beach, Fla.). . . . "**Shooter's,** 2280 N. Federal Hwy., Boynton Beach (tel. 736-3550), took over what used to be La Notte's Restaurant and did a great job of renovating it. The place is gorgeous, absolutely gorgeous, and jam-packed every night. There's a big outside raw bar and windows in this two-story circular building have been replaced with sliding glass doors that open right onto views of the Intracoastal. Lots of plants inside and beautiful views. It's open from 11:30 a.m. to 2 a.m. every day" (Jerry Schultz, Boynton Beach, Fla.).

SEEING THE SIGHTS: For a dollar-by-dollar account of the city, take a tour in true Palm Beach style—in a chauffeured Rolls-Royce or a Bentley! A former television photographer, Michael Tracey, operates **Classic Motor Tours,** 1290 Manor Dr., Riviera Beach (tel. 848-4730), with a staff of guides who have researched the city's intriguing history and will show you all the notable homes, including the Flagler Museum, for $17.50 an hour, $35 for two hours (at least two people). They have done some fine research and can even show you the home of a one-time secretary who's now a millionaire (her boss started the McDonald's hamburger chain, and in the early days didn't have enough money to pay her salary so he gave her stock instead!). They'll even rent you the chauffered car for $50 an hour.

The Mansions

The palatial mansions of the rich and super-rich are Palm Beach's major sightseeing attraction. If you're touring on your own, the best way to see them is on a drive along South Ocean Boulevard, where you'll ooh and aah at the towering edifices that line the sides of this millionaire's boulevard. Don't miss 1100 S. Ocean Blvd., where you'll find a tiny brass plaque announcing the presence of **Mar al Lago,** once the home of cereal heiress Marjorie Merriweather Post, who was the mother of actress Dina Merrill. Mrs. Post was for decades a (if not *the*) grande dame of Palm Beach society, and gave her home to the nation in her will. A budget-pinched government, however, decided to return it rather than fork over the $1 million a year it takes to maintain this palace that stretches from *mar* (Atlantic Ocean) to *lago* (Lake Worth).

Farther up the boulevard behind a high wall on North County Road is the seaside villa of the Kennedy clan where that slain president spent the last weekend of his life.

And of course don't pass up a visit to the **Breakers.** In few other places in the nation, if any, is there a hotel as legendary or as spectacular in its sheer opulence as the Breakers, a behemoth that's long been dear to the hearts of those who call Palm Beach home.

If you'd like to see more of these palatial estates, stay on North County Road and continue past the sign that announces "This road terminates in 3½ miles." It does, but in those 3½ miles you'll see some of the world's richest real estate, one gasp after another. If you'd like to buy a house here, bring cash, at least $1 to $2 million—and that's just a down payment!

Henry Flagler's magnificent mansion on Whitehall Way (tel. 655-2833), is a study in the flamboyance of those *fin-de-siècle* days. You can tour both it and the railroad magnate's elegant private railroad car, each of which holds a fortune in antiques, an awesome sight in these starkly simple days. Built in 1901 for $2.5 million, the marble palace has a 110- by 40-foot marble-columned entrance that's a knockout, and rooms full of painted ceilings, gilt furniture, and period decor that reflect the lavish lifestyle Flagler and his wife adored. There's a special collection of porcelain dolls, paintings, and family treasures as well. It's open Tuesday through Saturday from 10 a.m. to 5 p.m., on Sunday from noon to 5 p.m. Admission is $3 for adults, $1 for children ages 6 to 12.

Other Sights

Bethesda-by-the-Sea Church, on South County Road just south of the Breakers, is an enchanting example of 13th-century Gothic design. Next door are the attractive formally landscaped **Cluett Memorial Gardens** (open daily 8 a.m. to 5 p.m.).

The **Society of the Four Arts,** at Four Arts Plaza just off Royal Palm Way, has a library, art museum, gardens, and an auditorium where some excellent musical and dance performances are staged. It's open from 10 a.m. to 5 p.m. daily (from 2 p.m. on Sunday) from December to April, on weekdays only the rest of the year. There's no admission charge.

See the waterside face of the city (and in Florida that's *always* lovelier than the front door) on an **Intracoastal Waterway cruise** aboard the *Island Queen,* a Mississippi paddlewheeler docked at Phil Foster Park on Singer Island, next to Blue Heron Bridge (tel. 842-0882). Cruises depart daily from 10 a.m. to 7 p.m. and cost adults $6 ($3 for children), Tuesday through Sunday.

The **Norton Gallery of Art,** 1451 S. Olive Ave. (tel. 832-5194), houses an outstanding collection of 19th- and 20th-century American and European art, and a distinguished Chinese art collection. It's open from 10 a.m. to 5 p.m. Tuesday through Saturday, from 1 to 5 p.m. on Sunday, and there's no admission charge.

If you'd like to see the stars closer than you can on a beach stroll, the **Science Museum and Planetarium,** 4801 Dreher Trail (tel. 832-1348), has planetarium productions, a computer center, a marine aquarium, an observatory, and a discovery room. It's open from 10 a.m. to 5 p.m. Tuesday through Saturday, on Sunday from 1 to 5 p.m., and Friday nights, 6:30 to 10 p.m. Adults pay $2; children, $1.

For **Lion Country Safari** take the Southern Boulevard exit off I-95, or Exit 40 from the turnpike (tel. 793-1084). You can talk with the animals—just stay in your car! Bison, lions, chimps, ostriches, antelopes, and elephants roam around in their natural habitat while you drive through the park (no convertibles). Lion Country is open from 9:30 a.m. to 4:30 p.m. daily; admission is $7.95 per person (under 3 years, free), and it's 15 miles west of West Palm Beach. You can rent a car to tour the park for $5 an hour, and you can drop Fido at a clean and free kennel while you're going through the grounds. Admission includes several rides (such as an elephant ride or a boat cruise) inside the park. But don't go on any safari here—stay in the car and gape.

For a look at the **Everglades,** drive out to **Loxahatchee Recreation Area,** Route 1, Box 642-S, Pompano Beach, FL 33060 (tel. 426-2474), at the Palm Beach entrance to the Everglades. (Get there by taking I-95 to Hillsboro Boulevard West to the end, turn right and then your first left, and drive on for six miles.) You can take airboat rides ($6.75 for adults, $3.50 for children), through the swamp accompanied by a ranger who'll explain the flora and fauna, or rent boats ($25 for five hours in a three-seater motorboat), and venture off on your own—bring a compass.

In Delray is an unusual Florida sight, the **Morikami Museum,** at 4000 Morikami Park Rd. (tel. 499-0631), depicting Japanese culture, arts, and horticulture in honor of early settlers in the area, the Yamato colony of Japanese pineapple farmers. Open daily except Monday.

SPORTS: If you've never been to a polo match, now is the time to get out there and watch them chukker. Polo's an old and exciting sport with players chasing around on horseback wielding long mallets at a tiny ball. Naturally, in this sunny city you can also find lots of golf and tennis, even some gambling sports.

Golf

The two courses at the **PGA's National Golf Club**, at 1000 Avenue of the Champions in Palm Beach Gardens, are home to major golfing tournaments each year. You can play where the top names in golf curse and cheer for $50 ($40 if you're staying at the adjacent hotel), and on a second course for $35 ($30 for hotel guests). Carts are an additional $11 per person. Call 627-1804 for tee times.

Other public courses include **North Palm Beach Country Club,** 901 US 1 in North Palm Beach (tel. 626-4343), where greens fees are $12 in summer, slightly higher in winter, and the **West Palm Beach Country Club,** 7001 Parker Ave. at Forest Hill Boulevard (tel. 582-2019), where greens fees vary from $10 to $15 year round.

Tennis

Lake Worth Racquet and Swim Club, 4090 Coconut Rd., Lake Worth (tel. 967-3900), has 15 lighted courts for $7 an hour per person, and there are six free public courts at **John Prince Park,** on Lake Worth Road just east of Converse Avenue. The **Palm Beach Recreation Department** can also guide you to other public courts near you. Call them at their leisure line (tel. 967-0109).

Fishing

Blue Heron Fishing Fleet (tel. 844-3573) will take you on fishing expeditions at 8:30 a.m. and 1:30 p.m. daily for $12 a person. They're docked at the Blue Heron Bridge near Singer Island.

A number of charter boats also operate in the area, many of them docked at Blue Heron Bridge. Rates vary widely by season, but range from $250 to $300 a day.

Sailing

Look under the Singer Causeway for **Frey's Sailing Center,** Phil Foster Park, Blue Heron Boulevard (tel. 845-7952), where you can rent boats for $15 to $30 an hour and learn how to sail them too.

Polo

Polo is the rage in Palm Beach and there are now three polo grounds just short drives from the island. Championship teams play here in winter—England's Prince Charles caused quite a stir when he showed up for a match recently—to win money and fame in this fast-paced horseback sport.

You can see the players in action at **Gulfstream Polo Field,** off the Sunshine State Parkway on Lake Worth Road (tel. 965-2057), **Palm Beach Polo and Country Club,** 13198 Forest Hill Blvd. (tel. 793-1113), and **Royal Palm Polo Club,** 6300 Clint Moore Rd., Boca Raton Beach (tel. 994-1876). Admission is $4 to $8 at any of the grounds. So posh are the crowds at this rich man's sport (it takes quite a few dollars to keep a string of polo ponies in oats) that vendors here don't hawk soft drinks, they sell champagne!

Parimutuel Sports

Greyhounds streak off after the rabbit at the **Palm Beach Kennel Club,** at Belvedere and Congress Roads (tel. 683-2222), from late October to the beginning of May with races nightly, except Wednesday and Sunday, at 8 p.m. and matinees at 12:30 p.m. on Monday, Thursday, and Saturday. Admission is 50¢ to $2.

You can *try* to watch the speeding bouncing ball at the **Palm Beach Jai-Alai Fronton,** 1415 W. 45th St. (tel. 844-2444), from early November through early April. Games are at 7:30 p.m. Tuesday through Saturday. There are matinees Wednesday and Saturday until late January, and Wednesday, Friday, and Saturday thereafter. Admission begins at $1 and ranges to about $5.

SHOPPING: In Palm Beach shopping is not just a frivolous pursuit, it's serious business, and for some a full-time job. **Worth Avenue** is the city's famed shopping street, a boulevard on which you'll find Rolls-Royces (chauffeured, of course), diamonds, fine leathers, rare blooms, and tall chocolate letters that spell out "Happy Birthday" if you can afford that many letters (perhaps "happy" will say enough).

Gucci and **Lily Pulitzer's** wildly tropical prints are here. **Saks** is here, **Courrèges** is here, and **Godiva** (I mean the chocolates, although anything is possible in Palm Beach) is here. Fabulous—and fabulously expensive—little shops are tucked away in entrancing alleys and down little "vias" where bougainvillea blooms in a riot of color and vines twine around wrought-iron balconies.

Worth Avenue isn't just a street, you see, it's an experience. And what you can't find here may not be worth having.

A new section of the avenue called the **Esplanade** is part of this posh circus of salesmanship, and Palm Beach Mall, at Palm Beach Lakes Boulevard and I-95, is the site of **Lord and Taylor's** and a host of other intriguing shops.

NIGHTLIFE: Cocktail rooms of the bigger hotels like the Colony and the Breakers are where you'll see most people hobbing and nobbing. Before or after dinner (or *for* dinner—it has quite good continental cuisine) almost everyone drops into the **Ta-Boo,** 221 Worth Ave. (tel. 655-5562), to see who's in town and to dance to nightly trio music.

The **Royal Poinciana Playhouse,** at 70 Royal Poinciana Plaza (tel. 659-3310), presents top-quality Broadway musicals and dramas in the winter season. Ticket prices vary, but you can buy a six-performance season ticket for $159.

If you join the **Palm Beach Round Table,** 319 Clementis St., West Palm Beach (memberships begin at $50; tel. 655-5266), you can attend dinner lectures by some of the history makers of our day (Nixon, for instance, was a speaker). Programs run January through April, and tickets are usually available for about $7.

Buccaneer Yacht Club on Singer Island has listening and dancing music from 7 p.m. to midnight every day but Monday.

A spot that's getting rave reviews as much for its beautiful interior design and lovely waterside setting as for its menu is **Wildflower,** 551 E. Palmetto Park Rd., Boca Raton, at the Intracoastal Waterway (tel. 391-0000). There's certainly no denying that this is an enchanting hideaway snuggled into an Intracoastal Waterway nest with decor that will knock your eyes out. A favorite gathering place for happy hour crowds, the Wildflower serves salads, crêpes, steaks, seafood. It's open from 11:30 a.m. to 2 a.m. daily, with prices about $10 to $15 for dinner, $3 to $5 for lunch. A disk jockey plays dance music nightly except Sunday.

The **Royal Palm Dinner Theater,** 303 Golf View Dr., Boca Raton (tel. 832-0262), has a regular schedule of entertainment year round. Tickets are $25 to $29 for dinner and show. There are Wednesday and Saturday matinees, and shows nightly except Monday.

Musicana Dinner Theatre, 1166 Marine Dr., West Palm Beach (tel. 428-

6018), offers lively family entertainment with three nightly musical revues performed by young professionals. Dinner's part of the deal too, and the club opens at 6 p.m., charging less than $20 for dinner and show. Closed Monday.

Top O'Spray at the SeaSpray Inn on Singer Island has regular entertainment, as does the **Ramada Inn** (Palm Lakes Boulevard at I-95), and the **Hilton Inn** on Singer Island.

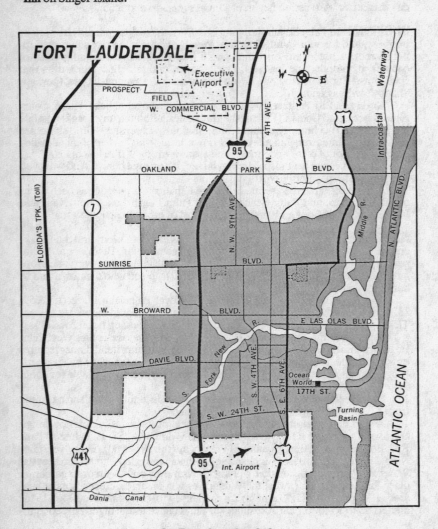

2. Fort Lauderdale

Seven miles of dazzling, glittering, golden sand fringed by swaying palms and azure ocean—this sweep of silica is Fort Lauderdale's beach, the city's pride, glory, lure, and landmark.

Certainly this sparkling strip of sand is not all there is to this sunny city by the sea, but it's what matters most to most people, and it's likely to be all the dedicated sun-seeker will see of this one-time Indian trading post, aspirant to the title "Venice of America."

While that Venice tag has perhaps just a whisper of Madison Avenue, Fort Lauderdale does indeed outpace its Italian sister in watery thoroughfares: there are now 165 miles of navigable water here. That's ten times as many canals as Venice can claim, and the number grows daily as developers dig into Florida's watery land mass, creating foundation and waterfront address in one fell scoop.

Any resemblance to Venice ends at the high-water mark, however, for Fort Lauderdale is no crumbling mass of water-stained masonry, no bastion of history. Even the fort that gave the city its name in 1838 has long since disappeared, victim to waves of sun-seekers who began their inexorable march over this land 80 years ago. Here and there you can still ferret out a touch of the city's past, but this is a town that lives strictly for today with rarely a backward glance, a place where about the only thing that's permanent is change.

In 1981 Fort Lauderdale became the nation's fastest growing city, luring the world's sun-seekers with 3000 sunny hours a year, one of the most accessible strips of sand in the state, temperatures that rarely drop below 70, and a free-wheeling, unflappable acceptance of travelers' eccentricities.

No longer small, but still retaining a firm grip on its cozy village atmosphere, Fort Lauderdale has neither the cosmopolite glitz of Miami Beach or the wealthier-than-thou sniffism of its blueblood neighbor Palm Beach. Green enough in wallet but not blue enough in blood, this city clings voraciously to a middle ground geographically, demographically, atmospherically, and spiritually. Indeed, people here have their own brand of snobbism: they look sneeringly over the wire rims of their sunglasses to dub the neon canyons of Miami Beach as *bas,* Palm Beach too *haute* to be a hot destination.

Millions of the bent-on-bronze seem to agree. They prove it by trekking here year after year for two weeks of suntan lotion and peeling noses, returning again and again to repeat as closely as possible last year's experience. The most loyal of these are college students, who appear with lemming-like regularity in hordes, gaggles, and prides, arriving by car, thumb, Jeep, and Learjet. They descend as the last March snow flurries turn to slush on northern campuses. They fry unprepared epidermis to beautiful boiled pink. They consume, in one bar in one month, 75,000 bottles of brew, and then disappear after Easter— having proven beyond question Fort Lauderdale's right to its most common sobriquet, Fort Liquordale.

Which brings us full circle in the city's history. It was sun that brought pioneers here at the turn of the century, but it was sin that kept them in the gray days of the Depression and Prohibition. Gambling, scarlet women, and booze boated in from the Bahamas by racy rumrunners first gave the city its Liquordale monicker, then kept it afloat as the nation drowned in red ink.

Pendulums will swing, however, and Fort Lauderdale left swashbuckle behind to return to a more prosaic, more predictable, central spot. Here it remains, peopled by a hardy breed, pioneers whose staunch support of capitalism is exceeded only by their successful manipulation of it.

This is the face Fort Lauderdale presents to you, a sunny, welcoming face, the cheerful countenance of a city waiting to grant you what you seek—and perhaps help you discover what that is.

USEFUL INFORMATION: For **medical emergencies,** call the Broward County Medical Association (tel. 525-1595). . . . **Dental emergency** information is available from the Broward County Dental Association (tel. 565-6319). . . .

Call 764-8040 for **legal aid.** . . . **Post office branches** are listed under U.S. Government Postal Service. . . . For fast **police and ambulance assistance,** dial 911. . . . **Foreign-currency exchange** and credit-card services are available at Landmark First National Bank, 1 Financial Plaza (tel. 765-2373). . . . **Western Union** is at 307 SW First Ave. (tel. toll free 800/257-2241, or locally 463-7281). . . . A **24-hour gas station?** Try Euro American Motors, 5751 N. Federal Hwy. (tel. 491-1713). . . . You can get one-hour and one-day cleaning at **Look-on-the-Beach Cleaners,** 3341 E. Oakland Park Blvd. (tel. 561-8412).

TOURIST INFORMATION: The friendly folks at the **Fort Lauderdale/Broward County Chamber of Commerce,** 208 SE Third Ave. (P.O. Box 14516), Fort Lauderdale, FL 33301 (tel. 305/462-6000), will fill your pockets with brochures on the city and its attractions. If you write in advance—and if you're coming here anytime between December and April you'd *better* write in advance—they'll circulate your name to area hotels and motels which will send you information on their properties.

Anytime, and particularly during the room crush from about February 15 to April 15, the **Broward County Hotel and Motel Association,** 1212 NE Fourth Ave. (tel. 305/462-0609), can help you find rooms in member hotels. A tourist directory is free.

Information on local attractions and changing exhibits is listed in the *Fort Lauderdale News/Sun Sentinel,* and the *Miami Herald,* both of which have special what's-up-this-weekend sections.

Still more information on local attractions is in free magazines, *See, Key,* or *Where,* which are available at most hotels and motels.

ORIENTATION: Fort Lauderdale's streets are laid out on a grid pattern with **Broward Boulevard** dividing the city into north and south sectors, **Andrews Avenue** sectioning it into east and west quadrants. Major east-west arteries are (from south to north): SE 17th Street Causeway, Broward, Las Olas, Sunrise, Oakland Park, and Commercial Boulevards. Bridges on each of those arteries (except Broward Boulevard) connect the mainland to the beach.

Route A1A runs north and south and is also called 17th Street Causeway, North Atlantic Boulevard, and Ocean Boulevard. With one or two exceptions, which will be noted, all recommended hotels are in the beach area, or near or on Route A1A.

Las Olas Boulevard is the city's elegant and expensive shopping street. Sunrise Boulevard has a sprawling shopping center near the beach and dozens of boutiques.

FORT LAUDERDALE'S HOTELS: Geographically Fort Lauderdale may be close to Miami, but atmospherically it's as far from it as sunshine from snow. While Miami Beach trades on glitter, Fort Lauderdale sells serenity. To this city over the years have come the rich and the famous in search of quiet elegance, young families seeking a vacation as peaceful and predictable as life back in Hometown, U.S.A., and senior citizens focusing attention on pensions.

This appeal to the less flamboyant traveler has led to a proliferation of small—sometimes downright tiny—family-run hostelries where you certainly won't be a number and can easily achieve a first-name relationship. So loyal are this city's winter visitors that many small resorts have been welcoming the same guests annually for 20 years or more. In February and March, as one hotelier puts it, "It looks a little like a family reunion around here—Bob and Rose from Ohio, the girls from Detroit, a couple from Kentucky, Ted and Rita—they've all been coming here for years."

There are, of course, a number of large hotels in the city, and several new ones on the planning boards, all of which means that despite the presence of 21,000 hotel rooms hereabouts, you can be sure nearly every one of them is filled on February 15 at the height of the winter season.

The moral of these stories is that you must—*must*—reserve early for the peak winter season (October is not too early). I won't depress you with stories of weary travelers in search of sun and fun who instead found doom and gloom because they failed to reserve a room. But it has happened.

If you want to spend time on the beach without spending half your time getting to it, location is everything. Hotels listed here were chosen for easy beach access and because they share hospitality, cleanliness, and a warm welcome for weary travelers. I've grouped them roughly by price categories, from luxury to budget hotels, based on their highest rates—which occur from mid-December to just after Easter.

The Luxury Leaders

Amid much fanfare, Marriott Corporation opened its second Fort Lauderdale hotel in 1985, a lovely oceanside resort called **Marriott Harbor Beach,** 303 Holiday Dr., Fort Lauderdale, FL 33316 (tel. 305/525-4000, or toll free 800/228-9290). As the name suggests, this hotel is right on the sand, indeed is one of the few hotels in the city at which you can step right outside the door and onto the silica.

You're greeted here by a glittering entrance, safari-outfitted doormen who reign over a huge multilevel lobby decked out in soft contemporary shades. Sleek and lovely silk flower arrangements are everywhere, and even the house phones speak of posh: they're fancy French telephones. Off to one side of the hotel is a cocktail lounge and dancing spot done up in burgundy with a lovely view out over the sand. In the other direction (but still within view of the ocean) is a tropically decorated raw bar and an intimate, candlelit formal dining room festooned with crystal chandeliers (à la carte prices in the $17 to $25 range for entrees).

Outside, a very large pool—one of the largest in the city, in fact—welcomes splashers and lap swimmers while beach cabanas lure those in search of a shady retreat from the sun.

Rooms are quite spacious here and are decorated in soft pastel shades. Many have a view of the ocean and all have loads of little extras ranging from special shampoos to bubble bath. Rates at the Marriott Harbor Beach are $145 to $200 double in the prime winter months from December through April, $85 to $125 in summer.

Marriott's Fort Lauderdale Hotel and Marina, 1881 17th St. Causeway, Fort Lauderdale, FL 33316 (tel. 305/463-4000, or toll free 800/228-9290), is a tropical waterside (but not oceanside) hotel and one of the city's newest hostelries. With 580 rooms, three restaurants, some of the spiffiest suites you'll see anywhere, it's now also one of the city's largest and one of its showiest resorts. To get a room without a view here you'd have to request a broom closet. Nestled alongside the Intracoastal Waterway with sprawling Port Everglades just across the highway, the Marriott seems to have water everywhere. Rooms on the west side overlook the Intracoastal, where sleek yachts purr in for fuel. From rooms on the east side you can watch the *Queen Elizabeth II* sweep majestically into port. From still other rooms you gaze down on a free-form swimming pool where waterfalls burble into tinkling streams shaded by palms. Marriott's multilevel lobby is dramatic: two-story windows soar over a melange of sea memorabilia from clipper ship models to copper diving helmets. Outside, wood decking forms a long wide porch overlooking a canal that wends its way along the edge of the hotel's central grounds where fountains flow and small waterfalls rush over rocks.

Choose from rooms in Marriott's central 12-story tower or in two three-story canalside wings, all decorated in red, brown, and green with plush carpets, dark-wood furniture, and lots of little touches ranging from king- and queen-size beds to stereo radios, alarm clocks, in-house movies, Neutrogena soap, and little bottles of shampoo and bath beads. Rates are $110 to $140 single or double in season, $65 to $95 single and $55 to $85 double off-season. An extra guest is $10 a day.

While you're probably not likely to opt for the $350-a-day suite, it gives you an idea how plushly this hotel is decorated: start with velvety-gray carpeting, delicate gray/blue puffy couches, a dramatic glass-topped Lucite dining table, pale-peach decor in a bedroom loft, bar, even a television in the bathroom! VIP suites have bars and fireplaces too.

There's a complimentary shuttle to the beach (about five minutes away), and golf can be arranged at a local course. There are four tennis courts and the hotel's marina operates a sightseeing boat, the 150-passenger *Good Times Too* which plies the Intracoastal on 45-minute, $3 rides. There's even a 96-foot yacht available to take you and 100 or so of your closest friends on chartered outings.

Nose to nose across the waterway is Marriott's closest competition, lush **Pier 66,** 2301 SE 17th St. Causeway, Fort Lauderdale, FL 33316 (tel. 305/524-6666, or toll free 800/327-3796). The twinkling lights of the Pier's central hotel tower have been a landmark in Lauderdale for years and mark one of the town's top gathering spots. To leave Fort Lauderdale without a sundown trip up the glass elevator to the 17th-floor glass-enclosed revolving lounge is sacrilege. Plunk yourself down in a plump swivel armchair or a long low couch in the Pier Top lounge, lean back, heave a deep sigh, and relax while a 2-h.p. motor slowly revolves the floor in a circumgyration that takes an hour to complete. Gaze blissfully out over bustling Port Everglades, elegant pastel estates, sleek yachts, golden sand, azure ocean, and some of the richest real estate you'll see anywhere in the world. Music for dancing begins at 9 p.m., but the lounge opens at 11:30 a.m. daily for lunch, noon on Sunday, with minors accompanied by adults welcome from 11 a.m. to 4 p.m. daily.

Pier 66, which poured $27 million into a 1983 renovation project, likes to call itself "grand but not grandiose," a fine line indeed at a 22-acre hotel sporting 256 rooms, two pools, tennis courts, and two restaurants, all sidled up to canals that rim three sides of the property and provide dock space for some enormous vessels.

In the central tower there are suites on each end of the corridors with rooms between decorated in soft pastel shades and featuring glass sliding doors leading to private balconies. Lanais are a private place to seek the better-than-average tan. On the Tower's ground floor is Windows on the Green and the Terrace Garden, open daily from 6:30 a.m. to 1 a.m. for casual dining with prices in the $15 to $20 range for dinner.

Rates at Pier 66 are $115 to $175 double in winter, dropping to $80 to $120 in summer. There's no charge for children under 17.

Right in the center of what the college set has dubbed "The Strip" is the **Sheraton Yankee Trader,** at 303 N. Atlantic Blvd., Fort Lauderdale, FL 33304 (tel. 305/467-1111, or toll free 800/325-3535). Now about twice its former size following the addition of an enclosed passageway connecting the original hotel to a new group of 223 rooms, the Sheraton has a total of 444 rooms, all right across Route A1A from the beach. (Sheraton's sister property, the Sheraton Yankee Clipper, is also on the beach, one-half mile south.)

At the Sheraton Yankee Trader you're greeted by a lobby filled with contemporary basketweave wicker furniture, lots of glass and chrome, and subtle lighting. From a comfortable seat on a chaise lounge at poolside you can gaze out over the splashers to the beach and ocean beyond. The Trader's recently completed 11-story tower is connected to its original building by a street-spanning glass walkway. In winter the hotel's Showplace lounge is jampacked, but anytime you'll find lots of congenial types seeking the sun.

All the modernity extends to the hotel's rooms, which are decorated in crisp brown on white geometric prints, and have wide glass windows from which you can watch the Atlantic lapping gently on miles of sand. There are two restaurants, four lounges, two pools, and tennis courts too. You'll pay $89 to $120 double daily from mid-December to May, $49 to $64 in other months.

Smack in the middle of the city's 40-acre yacht basin is the **Bahia Mar Hotel,** Fort Lauderdale, FL 33316 at Bahia Mar (tel. 305/764-2233). Twenty of the 40 acres are underwater (which makes for some impressive yacht-watching) but still leaves plenty of space for the hotel, part of which dates to the early 1950s boom days. Surrounding the spacious grounds are docks made famous by author John MacDonald's detective hero, Travis McGee, whose adventures always started on the stern of his boat as he welcomed the sunset with a cocktail. Travis may have been imaginary, but with a little judicious yacht-hopping you can spot some very good imitations around the docks here—and ogle yachts with accoutrements like helicopters and swimming pools.

A most notable feature at Bahia Mar is a long passageway that soars above Route A1A so you can walk from the beach to the hotel's second-story pool. The recently renovated accommodations are spacious, and many offer balcony views of marina or ocean. Rates are $105 to $130 in season, $75 to $95 off-season.

On the tower's second floor is the Spyglass Lounge, which sports a massive brass spyglass that provides a closeup of passing bikinis sans sand in your shoes. There's also the Seaview Restaurant, where walls of glass offer diners a view of sailing craft whizzing by on an ever-changing seascape.

A block farther north on Route A1A is the **Days Inn Lauderdale Surf Hotel,** at 440 Seabreeze Ave., Fort Lauderdale, FL 33316 (tel. 305/462-5555, or toll free 800/325-2525), a new addition to Days Inn chain of hotels. Days Inn operates other area hotels but this beachfront acquisition is their new showpiece. Rates are $115 to $125 in winter, $60 to $70 in summer.

The Upper Bracket

One of the city's least heralded hotels occupies one of the more interesting beach locations, hidden away in a posh residential district and fringed by a lagoon on one side, the Atlantic on the other. **Lago-Mar Hotel,** 1700 S. Ocean Lane, Fort Lauderdale, FL 33316 (tel. 305/523-6511), is right smack on the sand, one of only two hotels on the south end of the beach with an on-sand location. Built in 1952, this hideaway is now dwarfed by some of the city's most exclusive high-rise residences and surrounded by homes bearing Fort Lauderdale's most prestigious address, Harbor Beach. On a wall near the hotel's patio dining room, newsletters dating back ten years or more chronicle patrons from *Fortune* 500 board chairmen to a diverse collection of celluloid heroes including Eva Maria Saint, Hugh O'Brien, TV star Johnny Carson, and his sidekick Ed McMahon.

Still, you don't feel overpowered here—just gloriously uncrowded, for this is a remote area of the beach most people never see. Sit at poolside or on the long wide strip of sand and watch cruise ships steam by almost close enough to touch as they head for port just around the bend. Especially appealing to families, the resort has a playground and two pools (one just for the youngsters), four tennis courts and a practice area, a putting green and rental sailboats, a masseur, beauty salon, and boutiques. There's a patio dining room for al fresco nibbling, and outdoor snack and patio bars. Evenings, there's a buffet and dinner dance with prices averaging $30 to $40 a couple. Once a week there's a cocktail party and cookout.

Rooms come in several different configurations, ranging from hotel rooms to one-bedroom apartments with separate bedrooms to accommodate four. They're all spacious and nicely decorated, many of them in deep-blue shades with comfortable furniture and fully equipped kitchens. Rates range from $85 for hotel rooms to $230 for a two-bedroom apartment for six, including transportation from the airport, train, or cruise ship. In the summer months, rates drop about 40%.

On the north end of the beach is a strip of sand known as Galt Ocean Mile, reputedly the most expensive mile of land in the world, a piece of silica that changed hands 30 years ago for $29 million (which wouldn't buy one building there today). Now this multi-billion-dollar mile of beach is hidden from view behind a mile of towering condominiums, but you can see the sand from the **Fort Lauderdale Beach Hilton Hotel,** 4060 Galt Ocean Dr., Fort Lauderdale, FL 33316 (tel. 305/565-6611, or toll free in Florida 800/432-5141, plus toll-free numbers in every state).

Remodeled about 3 years ago, the Hilton has 226 rooms, all with balconies overlooking the ocean or city, and all decorated in contemporary muted buff tones. There are lots of little touches here, from valances with matching spreads to a rug in the lobby custom-designed to repeat the tropical print of plush couches.

Hilton has a newly remodeled lounge called Sid's, and an oceanfront restaurant, Cinnamon's, where prices are in the $10 to $20 range for dinners.

Rates are $95 to $145, single or double in season, and $70 to $90 double in summer. Additional persons are $10, and there's no charge for cribs or children sharing the room. Parking is free.

On the north end of the beach, North Atlantic Boulevard branches off to the right, continuing to run alongside the ocean while Route A1A becomes Ocean Boulevard. It sounds complicated, but what you really need to know is that at 2220 N. Atlantic Blvd., Fort Lauderdale, FL 33316 (tel. 305/565-6661), is **Ireland's Inn,** one of the city's venerable old properties and possessor of a dining room so popular you'd better be prepared to wait a little even with a reservation.

Over the years, Ireland's has absorbed several smaller hotels in the area and now has a warren of annexes. The basic structure is a seven-story tower plunked right down on the sand. Ireland's recently refurbished most of its rooms, so this hotel, which was showing its age in places, these days is looking better than ever. While plenty of things were thrown out in the renovation, what Ireland's kept was cleanliness and a special welcoming friendliness that has for years been luring back crowds of faithful followers, many of whom are now known by name from front door to back hall. Ireland's also has two annexes, one on the oceanfront across the street and the other directly on the beach.

In the main inn you can choose between hotel rooms (featuring two extra-long double beds and spreading picture windows), studio apartments (with kitchens), small suites (with sitting room, bedroom, and kitchen), or penthouse suites. Winter rates are $65 to $185 for two, for a penthouse suite; prices drop by about half in summer. There's also a three-story east lodge with balconied poolside rooms, and a garden lodge on the west side of the street. Rates there range from $60 to $80. Extra persons are charged $12. Rates drop about 50% on May 1.

Far and away Ireland's best known facility is its oceanfront dining room. Sparked by bright-rust linens, and cane and rattan chairs, the Ocean Room offers a variety of seafood from bay scallops to red snapper, shrimp, and rock lobster tails. The house specialty is country pan-fried chicken (just like mother used to make), with whipped potatoes, gravy, noodles, hot biscuits, and honey, served family style. There are veal preparations, tournedos perigourdine in Madeira sauce, plus a coupe Ireland with fresh tangerines and Mandarine Napoleon liqueur. Prices average $10 to $12 for entrees.

The Moderate Range

Fort Lauderdale owes its popularity not only to sun and sea but also to its longtime reputation as a family resort where dozens of accommodations are priced well below those of similar quality and location in other areas of the state. This city is, in two words, a Scotsman's dream.

By far the highest quality and the largest number of these moderately priced hotels and motels are located in what has become known as "The Strip," that section of sand running from posh Las Olas Boulevard on the south to Sunrise Boulevard on the north. In that mile or so of land bounded by the Intracoastal Waterway on the west and the Atlantic Ocean on the east, there are hundreds of hotel rooms that vary in quality but share one trait dear to the heart of wallet-watchers: reasonable prices.

While beachfront hotels in this area have rates in the $70 to $100 bracket, smaller properties without restaurants or bars, and located a block or two back from the ocean, are as much as 60% cheaper all year, with summer-season rates well inside the $30 to $50 moderate category.

In my book, **Bayshore Waterfront Apartments,** at 341 N. Birch Rd., Fort Lauderdale, FL 33304 (tel. 305/463-2821), is as lovely and tranquil a spot as you'll find anywhere in town. Nestled along the Intracoastal, the small hotel is not a yacht club, although there's a long dock stretching behind the property. Step through the front doorway and you're in the middle of an airy foyer leading into a tiny path that wends its way through the garden. Beyond gleams the Intracoastal, sapphire in the afternoon sun. Neatly trimmed hedges are shadowed by tall palms, there's a pool and patio overlooking the water, and a wide dock from which you may be lucky enough to catch dinner.

Rooms are spacious and beautifully decorated, many of them in Italian provincial furniture with plush wall-to-wall carpeting and floor-to-ceiling drapes in soft shades of green or gold. Small kitchens in one-bedroom apartments are completely equipped right down to wine glasses.

The Bayshore offers hotel rooms, efficiencies, and one- and two-bedroom apartments, some with balconies overlooking the Intracoastal. Winter rates range from $55 for hotel rooms to $80 for efficiencies, and $90 to $120 for apartments. Extra persons are charged $10 a day, and no children under 16 are accepted from January 15 to April 21.

As the Waterway jogs one block farther from the beach at 435 Bayshore Dr., Fort Lauderdale, FL 33304 (tel. 305/564-3261), you'll find **Casa Glamaretta,** an imposing three-story beige building. Mediterranean influences begin at its red Spanish tile roof and continue through a wide arched entrance which opens onto an airy roofed foyer. Step inside and framed before you like a postcard is a sparkling fountain spilling into a hexagonal pool bordered in tiny stalks of bamboo. Beyond is the wide expanse of blue waterway.

Running along one side of the building is a swimming pool shaded by palms, putting green, and shuffleboard court, and lounge chairs lined up along the Casa's 80-foot docks. Inside, the decor is simple but comfortable, with rooms done in citrus colors from lime to orange and gold. Hotel rooms with refrigerators are $40 double from January 15 to April; one- and two-bedroom apartments, $65 to $100. An extra guest pays $8 more. In summer, rates drop to $32 to $65.

If you're from Ohio, you can talk over the old hometown with George and Barbara Gendics, who own and operate the **Worthington,** 543 N. Birch Rd., Fort Lauderdale, FL 33304 (tel. 305/563-6819). Friendly folks who liked Ohio but love Florida, the Gendics run a small motel with several nice apartments, large enough for a family, plus some efficiencies and motel rooms. A pretty pool is the focus here, and you don't have to go far from it to pop a top: there's a big refrigerator outside for guests to keep their goodies cold. Rooms are nicely furnished in bright colors, and have color TVs and direct-dial phones. There's a complimentary continental breakfast in season. Winter rates begin at $50 for hotel rooms and range to $55 to $60 for efficiencies and one-bedroom apartments.

Next door, on the corner of Terramar Street and Birch Road, the **Sea-Chateau,** at 555 N. Birch Rd., Fort Lauderdale, FL 33304 (tel. 305/566-8331), is a two-story manse that's added some nifty inn-y touches. Now you'll find puffy comforters, ruffled pillow shams, jewel-tone carpets, lots of ruffles and ribbons, even tea services in every room. That's a bit of a departure for Fort Lauderdale motels, which tend to be more serviceable than ornamented. Burgundy trim outside is reflected in a marble-floored lobby where guests settle into high-backed wicker chairs and chatter away during the free two-hour Danish-and-coffee break that's a popular feature each winter morning. Five spacious efficiency apartments occupy the building's corners with 14 hotel rooms tucked in between. Floor-to-ceiling windows overlook a swimming pool and small central courtyard. Rooms have walk-in closets and marble bathroom floors and windowsills; efficiencies have Bahama beds (so the rooms are living rooms during the day) and compact, fully equipped kitchens. A tiny fountain tinkles in the corner of the patio and the resort's artful lighting once won it a magazine award. Rates in season are $50 for hotel rooms for two, $60 for efficiencies, dropping in summer to $25 to $30.

Those prepared to do their own laundry and maid work can save money at the **Five Coins Inn,** 4051 N. Ocean Blvd., Fort Lauderdale, FL 33308 (tel. 305/565-0541). Spacious and simply but nicely decorated rooms here are about $55 for hotel rooms, $60 for efficiencies in season. You can do your own cleaning or request it done for you at an additional cost. There are coin laundry machines in the motel, plenty of free parking under the building, a pool and spacious lobby full of plump couches and comfortable chairs, and a free coffee machine open morning to night.

Rooms with two double beds have paneled walls offset by gold coloring, and royal-blue trim in the efficiencies and studio apartments (with compact kitchens). There's a recreation room with jukebox, card tables, game machines, and refreshment facilities. In summer, rates drop to $150 a week for hotel rooms, $180 for efficiencies.

HOTELS IN SURROUNDING COMMUNITIES: Fort Lauderdale has been around a little longer than its neighbors and has built up the largest following of loyal return visitors, but several smaller towns in the area have some attractive hotels and motels in all price ranges. I've picked out a few in each city.

Pompano Beach
Sun Castle, at 1380 S. Ocean Blvd., Pompano Beach, FL 33062 (tel. 305/941-7700), is a favorite family resort clustered around a sparkling free-form pool

and wide lawns dotted with palms. The spacious rooms are decorated in lively tropical colors and have wide windows overlooking the grounds. The Sun Castle's restaurant has long been an area favorite, and has a lounge with regular entertainment. On five beautiful acres are tennis courts and a putting green. From February to April rates range from $69 to $84 double for hotel rooms, and from $89 to $96 for efficiency apartments accommodating two to four people. In other months, rates drop about 50%.

Two other motels in the area are operated by the Sun Castle: **Traders,** at 1600 S. Ocean Blvd., Pompano Beach, FL 33061 (tel. 305/941-8400), and the **Sea Castle,** at 730 N. Ocean Blvd., Pompano Beach, FL 33062 (tel. 305/941-2570). Both are on the ocean with pools and have similarly attractive rooms. Rates at those motels are about $10 to $12 lower.

Sea Garden Beach and Tennis Resort, 615 N. Ocean Blvd., Pompano Beach, FL 33062 (tel. 305/943-6200, or toll free 800/327-8920), is a lovely waterfront resort with a very popular restaurant and lounge. Many of the attractive rooms have refrigerators, and there are efficiencies and one- or two-bedroom apartments. Out in front (across Route A1A) the ocean laps at a 250-foot strip of private beach, and scattered about under the palms on six acres of manicured lawns are two pools, a putting green, and seven tennis courts. The Sea Garden's pretty dining room has tiny twinkling lights and glowing candles, lots of windows for an ocean view, and features fine home-cooking with dinners in the $7 to $10 range. The resort charges $85 to $155 from mid-December to May, $55 to $90 in other months.

Howard Johnson's and Holiday Inn both have large hotels in the area. The **Holiday Inn** is at 1350 S. Ocean Blvd., Pompano Beach, FL 33062 (tel. 305/941-7300, or toll free 800/238-8000), with grounds extending from the ocean across Route A1A to the Spanish River, and accommodations in rooms, efficiencies, and one-bedroom apartments, all beautifully redecorated. There are three tennis courts, two heated pools, and a putting green, plus a boat dock on the Spanish River. Rates are $85 to $120 from mid-December to April 16, $60 to $70 in other months.

Howard Johnson's Motor Lodge is opposite the beach at 9 N. Pompano Beach Blvd., Pompano Beach, FL 33062 (tel. 305/781-1300, or toll free 800/654-2000). It offers large rooms (a few with kitchens) and a pool. Rates are $78 to $90 from February to mid-April, $52 to $64 in other months.

Lighthouse Cove Resort, 1406 N. Ocean Blvd., Pompano Beach, FL 33062 (tel. 305/941-3410), is an oceanfront high-rise with rooms, studio efficiencies, and one-bedroom apartments, many of them overlooking the sea. There are two pools and a putting green, tennis courts to run around, and a dining room and lounge for evening activity. Two people pay rates beginning at $85 to $95 double in high season (from February to mid-April), from $45 to $60 in most other months.

A spa? Certainly. **Palm Aire,** at 2501 Palm Aire Dr., Pompano Beach, FL 33069 (tel. 305/972-3300), will house you in luxury, pummel you, cover you with avocado masks, pamper you with facials, and diet off whatever flab remains with minimally caloric dinners that actually taste good! One of the world's best known spas, Palm Aire is frequented by stars, politicians, and many of the world's most famous faces (including Elizabeth Taylor). It's the focal point of a massive development that includes a gorgeous swimming pool and all kinds of sports; they'll even see to it that you get to the beach, which is only a few miles away. Hotel rooms and one-bedroom apartments are $85 to $250. A year-round spa program is $495 a night double. From mid-December on, prices are $120 to $260 for accommodations.

Deerfield Beach

Private balconies are a special feature of some rooms at **Deerpath Apartment Motel**, 714 SE 20th Ave. (which is Route A1A), Deerfield Beach, FL 33441 (tel. 305/427-9223), an attractive resort just a few yards from the ocean. There's a soothing view out over the pool and prettily manicured lawns and grounds. Hotel rooms, efficiencies, and one-bedroom apartments, all large and cheerfully decorated in bright colors, are available at rates ranging from $280 to $395 a week in winter season, about $155 to $185 in summer months.

Berkshire Beach Club, 500 N. Ocean Blvd., Deerfield Beach, FL 33441 (tel. 305/428-1000), was once known as St. Tropez but changed its name recently when it became a time-sharing establishment. There are definite elements of St. Tropez here anyway, from the shining white building to the beach just steps away from your door. A tiny place cooled by sea breezes, Berkshire Beach Club has one- and two-bedroom apartments with tiny kitchens tucked away in corners. Since its conversion, the resort has been renovated and now features quite contemporary accommodations that are kept neat and clean. There's also a heated pool, hot tub, barbecue grill, and shuffleboard. Berkshire Beach Club charges $400 a week for a one-bedroom apartment in the spring, summer, and fall months, $800 from mid-December through Easter. Two-bedroom accommodations are $500 a week in the off-season, $900 in high season.

Hallandale/Hollywood

The king of Hallandale (and Hollywood) Beach is the **Diplomat Hotel**, at 3515 S. Ocean Dr., Hollywood Beach, FL 33022 (tel. 305/457-8111, or toll free 800/327-1212). Technically it's actually in neighboring Hallandale, and the hotel looks upon itself as an extension of Miami (which indeed it is, since it's quite close to the Dade County border). The largest hotel in the area, the massive Diplomat towers over its beach-strip neighbors, and for entertainment towers over many a Miami Beach hotel as well. Everybody who is anybody, now or ever, probably has appeared at the Diplomat, which has hosted a dizzying array of the nation's most famous stars. The hotel's elegant Celebrity Room is one of the top French dining rooms in the county (prices, $25 to $35), in the Tack Room you'll see up-and-coming stars, and in Café Cristal, the superstars. Bright new stars of comedy try out their routines at Comics' Corner in the hotel's western extension across the road, Diplomat West.

Everything's very contemporary at the Diplomat, even more so now after a fire here sparked a top-to-toe revamp in late 1984. Now the most advanced fire-detection equipment in the nation is in place at this hotel, which has updated all its rooms and public areas. Outside, a smashingly beautiful swimming pool, complete with waterfalls, swim-up bar, and towering man-made rocks, makes the beach beyond pale in significance. Across the road at Diplomat West is a golf course and still more hotel rooms.

Winter rates are $115 to $160 at the oceanside hotel, $90 to $120 at Diplomat West, and $65 to $94 at the golf club one mile west. In summer, the rates drop to $85 to $130 for the beach hotel, $65 to $95 at the extension, and $50 to $75 at the golf club.

Howard Johnson's, 2501 N. Ocean Dr., Hollywood Beach, FL 33019 (tel. 305/925-1411, or toll free 800/654-2000), has a 242-room hotel on the ocean at Taft Street that occupies a block of ocean frontage. An 11-story beauty, the hotel has all the usual comforts of this chain, plus free parking, a pool, free beach lounges, and Home Box Office television programs free. Rates are $64 to $90 in winter and $45 to $53 in summer.

The **Enchanted Isle Resort**, 1691 Surf Rd., Hollywood Beach, FL 33022 (tel. 305/925-8840), has apartments both on and across from the ocean. You'll find refrigerators and complete kitchens in the studios and apartments. There's a heated pool too. From mid-December to April, rates are $60 to $125, dropping in the summer season to $23 to $38.

FORT LAUDERDALE'S RESTAURANTS: Fort Lauderdale is said to have more restaurants per capita than any other city in the country. Certainly there's no doubt you can munch yourself into a catatonic state here in short order. So dedicated is Fort Lauderdale to elevating dining to an art form that the opening of a new restaurant here is tantamount to a presidential visit. At last count there were no fewer than six restaurant critics in this small town. In Fort Lauderdale, recommending a good dining spot isn't difficult, but narrowing the choices down to something short of a doctoral dissertation is. Here goes.

Continental/American

A beautiful new, but old, addition to Fort Lauderdale's roster of dining rooms is called **Historic Bryan Homes**, 301 SW Third Ave. (tel. 523-0177). When I saw these old stone houses moldering away alongside New River years ago, I hoped someone would work a miracle on them. Someone did—Anthony Gillette by name, a talented and creative man, joined the two small two-story homes and outfitted them in antiques, plants, brass, and etched glass to create this truly beautiful new restaurant. If you have a friend with a boat or an inclination to rent one, the most spectacular way to arrive is by water, up the river. That way the two homes, their surrounding palm trees, and dramatically lighted front lawn loom up out of the blackness like Victorian mirages. Bryan Homes has been put together by a master hand that spent quite a lot of money on both the interior and exterior of these homes that date back to the earliest days of Fort Lauderdale.

Even better, the food is top-quality. Top price, but top-quality. You dine on very good continental preparations of Florida seafood, prime beef or veal. A few southern touches crop up in dishes like oyster stew and breast of chicken Virginia. You can feast on such treats as veal cutlets Broussard stuffed with andouille sausage and roquefort cheese topped with wine sauce, perhaps pompano topped with macadamia-nut butter sauce or sweetbreads with hollandaise sauce, noisettes of lamb, smoked turkey divan, broiled seafood brochette. Orange and banana breads are served with all meals, and homemade ice creams, including praline pie, and a chocolate whipped-cream cake provide a finale. Vegetables are fresh from the produce counter and lightly cooked, sauces are creamy delights, wines are top-quality, the views are beautiful, and the service quite professional. For all that you will pay $15 to $20 for à la carte dinner entrees served with ratatouille and sliced baked potatoes. A luxurious dinner is likely to cost about $30 to $40 a person.

Bryan Homes is open for lunch from 11:30 a.m. to 3 p.m. Tuesday through Friday, and noon to 2 p.m. on Saturday and Sunday. Dinner hours are 6 to 10 p.m. Tuesday through Sunday, closing an hour later on weekends. The restaurant is closed Monday.

When Pier 66 spends money, it spends money beautifully. As you will see when you take a look at this handsomely redecorated hotel's new **Windows on the Green**, 2301 SE 17th St. Causeway (tel. 524-6666), now Fort Lauderdale's most talked-about restaurant. A strolling violinist entertains in this understated, bilevel restaurant as you dine on beautifully presented nouvelle cuisine— perhaps cold almond soup topped with toasted almonds and threads of saffron, mushrooms in puff pastry, a beaujolais sorbet, sea scallops à l'orange, and a finale of chocolate truffles. Elegant, definitely. Expensive? Very. At least $50 a person, and very likely more. You do pay for pleasure these days but it's often worth it. Windows on the Green, which gets its name from a huge, two-story-tall bank of tinted windows overlooking the hotel's tropical greenery, is open from 6:30 to 11 p.m. Monday through Saturday; closed Sunday.

Café September, 2975 N. Federal Hwy. (tel. 563-4331), has cut rather a wide swath across Fort Lauderdale in recent years, as much for its lounge and entertainment as for its merits as a fashionable dining spot. Here one is greeted by gold service plates, gleaming crystal, top-quality china and silver, lots of wood including a beamed ceiling, glass-topped tables, mirrors, and pretty garden views. Unusual unions of flavors are the tack Café September's chef has taken, so you'll dine on such combinations as tortellini with bits of salmon and scallops, fish with a basil sauce and colorful vegetable mousse, or a thick veal chop with a wine sauce, imported mushrooms, and a dollop of whipped cream. Other choices may include sauteed duck breasts with plum sauce, pheasant stuffed with pâté, a duck and chicken salad. Vegetables are fresh and lightly cooked, and desserts become showy creations that seem as sinful to look at as they are to consume. Prices are in the $17 to $25 range and rise rather rapidly as you add à la carte extras, wines, and other irresistibles. Figure a bill in the $80 to $100 region for a complete—and quite luxurious—dinner. Café September is open from 7 p.m. to 2 a.m. daily, closing an hour later on Saturday.

Le Dome of the Four Seasons occupies a 12th-floor penthouse aerie atop the Four Seasons condominium just off Las Olas Boulevard at 333 Sunset Dr. (tel. 463-3303). Flickering candles and some subtle piano music set the stage inside while you gaze out over the lights of Fort Lauderdale twinkling far below. Service is dignified and exceptionally efficient, with waiters in formal attire moving effortlessly through the intricacies of service and tableside preparation.

The main dining area is a large room sparkling with white linens, fresh flowers, and French provincial furniture; two others are somewhat smaller and more intimate, with high-backed chairs and small cozy alcoves. Tables by tall windows are coveted, so reservations here, as in most restaurants in the winter season, are vital.

Raves hereabouts go to the restaurant's crusty bread, which arrives hot and home-baked from the oven, and two house specialties, prime rib and steak Diane. Dinner prices average $12 to $15 for entrees, totaling $20 or so a person with additional courses. You can save a few dollars here by taking advantage of early dining hours from 5:15 to 6 p.m. when several courses are included in reduced entree prices. Hours are 5 to 10 p.m. daily, to 11 p.m. on Friday and Saturday.

Down Under, 3000 E. Oakland Park Blvd. (tel. 564-6984), the first of three area restaurants owned and operated by Leonce Picot and Al Kocab, has won *Travel/Holiday* awards and a four-star rating consistently for years. To say the decor is eclectic is certainly to understate, but what other way is there to describe a melange of antiques, open wood beams, wood floors, and a proliferation of plants in a prime-time setting alongside the Intracoastal Waterway?

At last count there were 63 items on the menu, but there may be more even as you read. In any case, you can spend ages just savoring the selections, ranging from oysters Muscovite topped with fresh Sevruga caviar, cold fresh mussels in mustard, or curried mayonnaise sauce, a carpetbag steak stuffed with herb-marinated oysters and sauce diable, even Idaho trout.

Open for lunch from 11:30 a.m. to 2 p.m. daily (except Saturday and Sunday), dinner from 6 to 10:30 p.m. daily, Down Under is likely to ring up a bill in the $40 to $50 range for two.

Ireland's Inn, 2220 N. Atlantic Blvd. (tel. 564-2331), has been around for ages. My friend Merry is something of a gourmet cook and, thanks to her well-traveled and well-fed husband, Bob, she's also frequently a gourmet diner reputed to have dined in 25 of the nation's 26 greatest restaurants. Nevertheless, she clucks happily at the mere thought of Ireland's country-fried chicken, a gravy-and-biscuits house specialty served family style to tables-full of equally happily clucking diners.

Ireland's cookery leans toward that kind of down-home simplicity spiced with the occasional touch of something Floridian-ly exotic like conch chowder or Florida pompano. Lamb or pork chops are on the menu, along with Virginia ham steak and veal topped with artichoke and crab. There's entertainment for dancing until the wee hours at the adjoining Edgewater Lounge (which adequately describes its view too). Entree prices, which include homemade bread, salad, potato, and entree, fall in the $10 to $15 range, with some of the more exotic specialties rising to $18 or so.

A long, long all-you-can-glurp raw bar is a favorite focus at the **Golden Spike,** 6000 N. Federal Hwy. (tel. 491-6000). Upstairs is plush, downstairs is themey, and there's a huge salad bar and matching dessert selection. In between there are good beef and seafood dishes for prices in the $12 to $19 range. It's open from 2 to 4 p.m. and 5 to 10 p.m. daily.

Yesterday's, 3001 E. Oakland Park Blvd. (tel. 561-4400), goes all out to attract the young crowd with a flashy disco and barmen in green or purple wigs. Downstairs, however, you can have a pleasant dinner overlooking the Intracoastal Waterway for $15 to $20. Try beef Oscar, lamb chops, or the coquilles St. Jacques. In summer there's an inexpensive sunset dinner, and the restaurant has menus in several languages—even braille. It's open from 11:30 a.m. to 3 p.m. for lunch on weekdays, 5 to 11 p.m. daily for dinner, later on weekends.

Barrels and packing crates hang over your head and long-gowned waitresses or safari-suited waiters deliver continental cuisine like prime rib on the bone, lobster, and heart-of-palm casserole, wonderful home-baked breads made from coconut, rum, and salt rye. That in a nutshell is **New River Storehouse,** 2175 Route 84 in the Marina Bay Club and Hotel (tel. 791-7600). You'll pay $15 to $20 or so for dinner from 6 to 11 p.m. Monday through Friday, 5 p.m. to midnight on Saturday.

Someone with more than a little imagination has capitalized on the location of **Runway 84,** 332 State Road 84 (tel. 467-8484), a mile or so from Fort Lauderdale/Hollywood International Airport. Tiny runway-ish lights glitter at the entrance. A huge red and silver recreation of an airliner cabin forms a cocktail lounge rimmed with tiny rectangular windows through which you can gaze down on the lights of New York et al. Waiters are decked out in white shirts with epaulets bearing the three gold stripes of a first officer, no less.

Plenty of seafood options are available here, including several different preparations of shrimp, plus scallops, lemon sole, a combination of scungilli diavolo and fried calamari, seafood platters, and Boston scrod. All the usual beef specialties from New York sirloin to prime rib and filet mignon are available. An Italian orientation is evident as veal and pastas occupying a prominent place on the list. Dinner prices, which range from $10 to $17, are quite reasonable when you consider that they include a substantial antipasto, a platter of steamed mussels in a red sauce, salad, spaghetti or potato, dessert, and several different kinds of breads, including an unusual marbelized brown-and-white creation. Hours are 11 a.m. to 10 p.m. daily, an hour later on Friday and Saturday, and from 4 to 10 p.m. on Sunday; the lounge is open to 2 a.m.

Harrison's on the Water, 3000 NE 32nd Ave. (tel. 566-9667), is tucked in alongside the Intracoastal Waterway just south of the Oakland Park Bridge. A very popular place, Harrison's specializes in continental cooking with lots of good steaks, prime ribs, and seafood, at dinner prices in the $12 to $17 range.

You can sit inside in attractive, intimate surroundings or outside on an open, roofed patio alongside the water. There's often entertainment in the lounge, but the best loved entertainment here comes from the huge yachts that cruise past on the Intracoastal or pull up at the dock to disgorge hungry boaters. Harrison's is open from 5 to 11 p.m. daily. Harrison's waterside location makes it a popular place, so reservations are wise.

To my way of thinking, there is almost nothing Burt Reynolds could do wrong. His newest venture, **Burt and Jack's,** 2100 Eller Dr. in Port Everglades, Dania (tel. 522-5225), confirms my suspicion. It's the occupant of a quite handsomely designed building that is a study in Mediterranean architecture: a roaring fire in several fireplaces, fringed hanging lamps, tiny shutters, a pianist playing softly, tiled floors, arches, candlelight, tables outside in an artfully lighted patio.

Burt's menu is small but significant. He's not attempting to mingle strange flavors or create bizarre combinations, but has opted instead for straightforward preparation of straightforward dishes. So you'll find double-cut prime rib of beef that nearly fills the plate, an equally thick baked veal chop topped with a creamy sauce, and for really big spenders, a $27 order of stone crab claws or a whole three-pound Maine lobster. Accompanying dinner is a large baked potato or a house specialty of hash-browns for two or an order of large and very skillfully prepared fried onion rings.

Burt and Jack's does not make for a bargain-basement evening—entrees are $12 to $17, but figure about $25 to $30 a person for dinner and drinks—but it does make for a very pleasant one in a beautiful atmosphere that could only be improved by the presence of BR himself. Hours are 4:30 to 11 p.m. daily, closing an hour later on weekends.

Frankie's, on the Intracoastal, 3333 NE 32nd Ave. (tel. 566-7853), occupies prime real estate alongside the Intracoastal Waterway just north of the Oakland Park Boulevard bridge. You may have to search a little to find Frankie's, but you won't be alone in your search. This handsomely decorated restaurant has been a favorite in Fort Lauderdale for quite a number of years now, and has a regular following of patrons who swear by the pastas, steaks, seafood, and fine continental preparations featured here. Plants, low lighting, and formal service prevail at Frankie's, which also provides a stunning view of yachts chugging by on the Intracoastal. You'll pay about $12 to $17 for entrees, and the restaurant is open from 11:30 a.m. to 3 p.m. weekdays and 6 to 11 p.m. daily. In the summer months Frankie's doesn't serve lunch and is usually closed on Sunday, but those dates vary, so if you're here in summer, give them a call.

French/Swiss

Few people can pronounce **Les Trois Mousquetaires,** 2447 E. Sunrise Blvd. (tel. 564-7513), so one of the city's finest restaurants is known around town as the Three Musketeers. A small, simply decorated spot with Trois Mousquetaires regalia on the wall, white linens and crystal on candlelit tables, this fine French restaurant is pricey but worth it. Creamy lobster bisque, cold curry soup, sirloin flamed with brandy, tournedos topped with foie gras and truffles in madeira sauce, roast chicken with artichoke hearts, crisp vegetables, flaky pastry and breads—are all part of the magic that keeps this longtime favorite on the top of gourmet lists. Your check is likely to reach $20 to $25. The restaurant is open from noon to 2:30 p.m. for lunch and from 6 to 10:30 p.m. for dinner (closed Sunday). Reservations are necessary, particularly in winter.

The look of **La Ferme,** 1601 E. Sunrise Blvd. (tel. 764-0987), is a long way from a farm, with imported porcelain chandeliers, mirrors, lace tablecloths. Except for its farm-fresh ingredients, La Ferme's connection to anything back-woodsy is minimal. Sophisticated cuisine and a clientele to match are the by-words of this small and simple restaurant on busy Federal Highway. Braised sweetbreads in a madeira sauce, delicate veal preparations, intriguing pâtés, feuilleté of Dover sole with tarragon sauce, and a distressingly tempting pastry cart are just some of the carefully concocted offerings whipped up by La Ferme's master chef Henri Terrier, whose wife you'll meet at the front door. Everything works here including the efficient staff, so you're likely to remain happy even after you've paid the bill, which will probably run about $20 to $30 per person. La Ferme is open from 5:30 to 10 p.m. Tuesday through Sunday (closed August and September).

Jean-Pierre, owner, operator, chef, and dynamo of **The Left Bank,** 214 SE Sixth Ave. (tel. 462-5376), has more energy than anyone should, and uses it to produce culinary treats that have made this one of the city's favorite restaurants. Jean-Pierre moves at 78 r.p.m. yet never seems to be rushing as he whips up delectable flaming tableside creations ranging from duckling with an amaretto apricot sauce to steak aux trois poivres with black, white, and green pepper-corns and lots of cream and brandy. In his spare time he began a mail-order pasta-gram business that has, like his restaurant, succeeded beyond his wildest dreams and was recently among the mail-order recommendations of the *New York Times.* You can meet personable Jean-Pierre at his restaurant any evening from 6 to 11 p.m., to midnight on weekends. In summer months the restaurant also serves lunch from noon to 3 p.m. Entree prices at the Left Bank, a very cozy restaurant which is indeed on the left bank of New River, are in the $15 to $17 range.

If you look closely at the last postcard you got from Switzerland, you'll see a replica of **Café de Genève,** 1519 S. Andrews Ave. (tel. 522-8928), on it some-where. Or is Café de Genève a replica of those homey little Swiss cafés? You can't be sure because this cuddly little spot with red-checked curtains and pic-tures of the snowy alpine slopes is as close as you'll get to those cool climes in flatland Florida. There's taste of the cantons here too, from the cheese fondues to creamy minced veal and mushrooms, home-brewed bean and pea soups, the Fendant or Neuchatel wine, the fresh-from-the-oven pastries, and the congenial good humor of a pleasant Swiss-efficient staff. Most prices fall in the $10 to $15 range. It's open from 11:30 a.m. to 2:30 p.m. on weekdays and from 5:30 to 10:30 p.m. daily.

Le Café de Paris, 715 E. Las Olas Blvd. (tel. 467-2900), has been a favorite in Fort Lauderdale for many years thanks to Swiss owner Louis Fermati's deft hand in the kitchen and shrewd assessment of popular taste. There's a cheery, crowded bistro atmosphere, lots of Paris posters, red and blue awnings, dining on two floors, and a generally lusty good humor that somehow keeps you going back even when you know the Gallic confusion means you'll have to wait, reser-vation or not. There's a long selection of entrees with all those favorites that keep Americans devoted to French preparations: steak au poivre, veal Cordon Bleu, onion soup, great luncheon omelets, tournedos béarnaise. A money-saving tip: Check the left corner of the menu where there's a tiny list of popular full-course dinners several dollars cheaper than you'd pay à la carte. The café is open daily from 11:30 a.m. to 2:30 p.m. for lunch, except Sunday when the res-taurant is open from 5:30 to 10 p.m., the same dinner hours it maintains daily. Expect a bill of $30 to $40 for two.

Italian
Sooner or later you'll see everyone in town at **Paesano,** 1301 E. Las Olas Blvd. (tel. 467-3266), a cheery informal spot where owner Mario Spinaci will as likely as not break into a quick aria and where you'll feel equally comfortable in

jeans or evening dress. A handsome, charming devil from Rimini, Mario delights in basic tasty foods and hearty wines, loves what he does, and infects his staff of countrymen with his own incredibly consistent good humor. The look here runs to red-and-white checks, lots of candles, wine stashed in every nook and cranny. Don't come here for elaborate atmosphere but for great rib-sticking pasta in the $8 to $12 range and some well-prepared specialties like veal Sinatra (a melange of spinach, prosciutto, and veal), tortellini in red or white sauce, fettuccine Alfredo, or snapper. Open with southern Florida's best fried mozzarella, baked clams, or spaghetti primavera, and be sure to ask Mario what's cooking today that's not on the menu. For that matter, ask Mario anything. Ask him to sing. Paesano's is open 5 to 10:30 p.m. daily. There's now a second Paesano of striking architectural design at 3850 N. Federal Hwy., Lighthouse Point (tel. 942-0006), with the same hours.

Just down the street at 609 E. Las Olas Blvd. is Il Giordino's (tel. 763-3733), a study in contemporary decor centering on rough wood paneling and smoked glass, tall plants sparkling with tiny Italian lights, candles, and crisp white linens. Very elegant.

I admit to an addiction to the restaurant's zuppa de pesce, but there are also a raft of delicately prepared veal, chicken, and seafood dishes for your perusal, and a sinfully rich beef Wellington. Prices are in the $12 to $17 range. Lunch hours are 11:30 a.m. to 3 p.m. Monday to Friday, and to 11 p.m. daily for dinner.

A couple of years ago a local educator with a flair for cooking opened a pretty little storefront restaurant called Prego, 2768 E. Oakland Park Blvd. (tel. 564-7794). It took off and is today one of the more popular Italian restaurants in this part of town. Homemade pastas, whipped up before your wondering eyes, are the specialty at Prego, which also concentrates on using fresh, natural ingredients to create Italian fare high in protein and low in calories. Pasta topped with fresh vegetables is a favorite of Prego diners, as is fettuccine topped with marsala, ricotta, and shrimp. Mmmmmm! Prego is open Monday through Saturday from 5:30 to 10 p.m., and dinner prices are in the $10 to $15 range.

Right up there at the top of the list in both prestige and price is Casa Vecchia, 209 N. Birch Rd. (tel. 463-7575), one of the trio of area restaurants owned by *Travel/Holiday* award winners Leonce Picot and Al Kocab. Newest of the duo's stable, Casa Vecchia is a beautiful old home (that's what Casa Vecchia means, by the way) once owned by a member of the Ponds Cold Cream family.

Painted a dusty rose, the rambling old house has been altered as little as possible so you can still revel in tile floors, a sweeping view of the Intracoastal Waterway and elaborate formal gardens from whence the chef plucks herbs. Inside, you can dine in rooms holding a single table for four or six or in various larger rooms scattered around the house. Every one of them is different and somehow Picot and partner have managed to take improbably eclectic elements (like a grape cluster lamp) and turn them into an integrated whole considerably greater than its parts. There are plants everywhere—one room is practically a greenhouse—and the food is northern Italian, a creamy cuisine considerably more delicate than the tomato-based offerings hailing from elsewhere in Italy.

The menu is à la carte and the food is superb and expensive. You might begin with carpaccio (paper-thin slices of raw beef with piquant mayonnaise) or breaded oysters wrapped in bacon and sauteed with chives. Move on to homemade cappelli d'angelo, feather-light "angel's hair" pasta with a light tomato cream sauce, peas, and prosciutto. Or try Idaho trout sauteed with pignoli, spezzatino di vitello al marsala, veal scaloppine layered with pancetta, sage, basil, provolone, and mozzarella.

Open daily from 6 to 10:30 p.m., Casa Vecchia is likely to present you with a bill in the $50 to $70 range for two, more if you select some of the restaurant's more exotic wine selections.

La Perla, 1818 E. Sunrise Blvd. (tel. 765-1950), is quite a diminutive restaurant, but one that has a reputation as large as its quarters are small. Pastas are made right here and the cloud-like gnocchi in gorgonzola sauce is to die for. Spinach ziti with cream, sweet peas, mushrooms, and prosciutto is another winner here. Prices are in the $10 to $15 range for dinner, and hours are 5 to 10:30 p.m. daily.

Cajun

A newcomer to Fort Lauderdale arrived a couple of years ago and has managed to keep 'em pouring in for long enough to be considered a serious contender in the ever-changing sweepstakes of Fort Lauderdale restaurants. That newcomer is **Lagniappe Cajun House,** 230 E. Las Olas Blvd. (tel. 467-7500), the first Cajun cookery in the city. Lagniappe (pronounced lan-yap and meaning "a little taste") is quite an attractive restaurant that has made clever use of a high ceiling by rimming it with a faux balcony reminiscent of the famed balconies of New Orleans.

Under that balcony, whirling paddle fans, and lots of plants, you dine on such Cajun specialties as crawfish étouffée, blackened redfish, twice-cooked duck, seafood gumbo, jambalaya. Lively spicy flavors characterize evening meals and lunches, while Saturday-morning breakfast features beignets, coffee, and a newspaper. There's often Dixieland jazz bands or a blues singer for entertainment. Prices are in the $10 to $16 range for dinner entrees, and hours are 11:30 a.m. to 3 p.m. for lunch weekdays and 6 to 11 p.m. for dinner.

Seafood

Rustic Inn, 4331 Ravenswood Rd. (tel. 584-1637), is on a back road that at the restaurant's entrance becomes a dirt road. This sort of introduces this rustic spot that looks as if it might collapse in a muddle of weathered wood and nautical junque but hasn't done so for the 20 years or more it's been holding together here beside an ocean-bound canal.

This is the place to head when you have no intention of donning anything more formal than reasonably clean jeans and a pair of sandals, which comes close to being overdressed here. That's as it should be too, for the house specialty is a big, brimming bowl of garlic-tinged steamed blue crabs, presented with a mallet, bib, and yesterday's newspaper. They are messy but worth the pounding and digging. If you don't want to bother, you'll find oysters, shrimp, scallops, lobster, stone crab, fish filets, linguine with red seafood sauce, and many other seafood treats on the menu. The finale should be a piece of the restaurant's authentic key lime pie. You'll pay $11 to $13 for most dinners, which include salad and potato too. Hours are 11:30 a.m. to 3 p.m. Tuesday through Friday and 5:30 to 10:30 p.m. daily, opening an hour earlier on Sunday.

Located a couple miles off the beach near Fort Lauderdale High School is a seafood house called the **Sea Grill** that's been around so long it's taken on whatever qualities are necessary to make it an institution. A cavernous place, the Sea Grill, at 1619 NE Fourth Ave. (tel. 763-8922), is a maze of plainly decorated alcoves, nicest of which is the lounge area. To tell you everything on the menu here would take pages, but there's Alaskan king crab, Florida and Maine lobster, shrimp, and clams prepared in several different ways. There's just about every kind of southern and northern fish, from Boston scrod to pompano, and even a couple of landlubber's specialties. Prices are in the $9 to $15 range. Be sure to try a Sea Grill specialty, rum buns. Open daily from 11:30 a.m. to 10 p.m., on Sunday from 4 p.m.

There's always a wait at **Sea Watch**, 6002 N. Ocean Blvd. (tel. 781-2200), but who cares in this rustic oceanside setting filled with plants, wicker peacock chairs, nautical memorabilia, and brass? An hour or so in the upstairs bar under the paddle fans, or outside listening to the waves roar, is super even if you *never* get to dinner downstairs. Bouillabaisse is the best thing on the menu, but the rest of the seafood fare runs a close second and the atmosphere's somehow both boisterous and subdued. It's pretty, good, and fun, the pumpernickel bread is sensational, and the prices are moderate—$10 to $18 for dinner. It's open from 11:30 a.m. to 3:30 p.m. for lunch, and 5 to 10 p.m. for dinner.

Fisherman Restaurant, 3881 N. Federal Hwy. (tel. 566-2002), is a pretty place on which the owners have spent quite a lot of money over the years. Seafood is now grilled over mesquite, the new fad in open-fire cooking, and the menu has branched out to include a large number of nonseafood items from pork chops with apples and prunes to veal in a roquefort sauce.

You dine in a comfortable and attractive dining room with banquettes lining the walls and the nautical memorabilia kept to reasonable limits. There's always a crowd here, which usually means a comparatively long wait for dinner. On the menu are such treats as snapper Pontchartrain topped with crabmeat, bouillabaisse, pompano, and grilled swordfish, all accompanied by salad and new potatoes. Your check is likely to be in the $12 to $17 range for dinner entrees. Fisherman is open from 4:30 to 10:30 p.m. daily, to 11:30 p.m. on Saturday.

By the time you've found your way to **15th Street Fisheries and Boathouse,** 1900 SE 15th St. (tel. 763-2777), you've earned the good dinner you'll find. On the Intracoastal, across the waterway from Pier 66, 15th Street Fisheries has a woodsy upstairs-downstairs dining room filled with plants, brass, and a faintly nautical look. Seafood is best here, and the beef comes in second. The desserts and ambience are top-notch, with prices about $15 to $20 for dinner, including appetizer, salad, Perrier, and dessert. To get to this pretty place, turn north off 17th Street Causeway at Cordova Road and right (toward the Intracoastal) at the first street on the right (15th). It's open from 5 to 10:30 p.m. daily for dinner upstairs, from 11:30 a.m. in the less expensive raw bar downstairs. The waterway view is terrific here.

Steaks

One of the best loved—and best attended—steakhouses in Fort Lauderdale is **Raindancer,** 3031 E. Commercial Blvd. (tel. 772-0337). Such crowds are rarely wrong, and they are quite right to favor the Raindancer, which features good steaks, chops, a really super shish kebab, and top seafood simply prepared. A maze of dining rooms upstairs and down, Raindancer also offers one of the city's most attractive lounges, a second-floor aerie outfitted in antiques, couches, even a roaring fire in the fireplace! There are special dining rooms for those who do not smoke, but I think the best seats are toward the back of this plant-bedecked dining spot where the atmosphere is coziest. In addition to all its other pluses, the Raindancer also has the very best salad bar in town, fresh pumpernickle bread, and skilled service that works like the proverbial well-oiled clock. You'll pay $10 to $18 for dinners, which include that salad bar and good baked potatoes. Raindancer is open daily from 5 to 11 p.m., closing an hour later on weekends.

Chuck's Steak House, 1207 SE 17th Street Causeway (tel. 764-3333), has been a mainstay of this neighborhood for umpteen years—and no wonder. For lack of any more fitting cliché: they have it together here. As you can see from the name, this is a steakhouse and makes no bones about it. They're not messing with sauces, offering a hundred other nonbeef choices, or playing fast and cutesy with garnishes and side dishes. If you want plain, unadorned, good steak, you come here.

Chuck's is popular for reasons other than excellent steaks at reasonable prices: it's dark, intimate, and attractive with woodsy paneled walls, some hanging plants, and simple but crisply tailored wood furnishings. An adjoining bar is a quite popular place too. Prices, which fall easily in the $10 to $15 range, include a big salad bar and baked potato or rice pilaf. Part of a chain that got its start in Connecticut and now has three restaurants in Florida, although no others in southern Florida, Chuck's is open daily from 11:30 a.m. to 2 a.m.

Eclectic

One learns fascinating things by word of mouth, and not the least fascinating of those is a new restaurant called just that: **By Word of Mouth,** 3200 NE 12th Ave. (tel. 564-3663). Here in this tiny enclave just large enough for eight tables, talented cooks are doing some downright scrumptious cooking. Imagine a tortellini salad with pink and white pasta tossed with herbs and a marinade. Or fat chicken breasts topped with a fluffy broccoli soufflé. Or even a lowly meatloaf lifted from obscurity with the addition of a creamy layer of white cheeses. Can I get your attention with the nutty flavor of dried tomatoes in vinaigrette, minty tabouli salad, chicken and tomatoes blended with capers and spices. Or lobster lasagne, ziti with prosciutto and ham, pasta bows primavera, beef tenderloin, scallops and shrimp in a sauce of tomato and fresh basil, a sausage ratatouille, an apricot-topped chicken, calamari with percatelli, a peanut-flavored Indonesian chicken? Seafood turns up seasoned with ginger or grilled with mustard sauce; ham, pork and lamb are teamed with fruit. Add to that a couple of dozen dream desserts that ought to be classified as illegal substances—a wildly destructive chocolate truffle loaf or blackout chocolate cake, for instance.

Begun as a catering operation, the restaurant was a little like some new babies: no one expected it but no one's complaining. Suffice to say, there seems to be simply no way you could be disappointed at this marvelously creative restaurant whose fame is spreading rapidly . . . by word of mouth. Entrees range in price from $10 to $15, but you'll probably spend a bit more with all these temptations. Hours are Monday through Friday from 11 a.m. to 3 p.m. for lunch, Wednesday and Thursday from 5 to 9 p.m. for dinner, to 10 p.m. on Friday and Saturday. To get there, turn north on the east side of the railroad tracks at Dixie Highway and Oakland Park Boulevard.

Budget Selections

Eating on the cheap in Fort Lauderdale is simple and super these days, no small thanks to two restaurants so popular and jam-packed that you'd better get there before 6:30 p.m. or be prepared to while away 30 to 60 minutes waiting for a table.

The first of these is **Carlos and Pepe's 17th Street Cantina,** 1302 SE 17th St. (tel. 467-7192), a spot where by 8 p.m. the crowd is belly to belly in the foyer and bar. All those people have discovered that C&P's Tex-Mex chow is worth waiting for, and the waiting is relatively painless in these serene surroundings of wood paneling, greenery, hand-woven Mexican wall hangings, and fat comfortable Spanish furniture. Tuck into one of Carlos and Pepe's giant, two-fisted margaritas, delivered with basket after basket of hot taco chips and fiery sauce, and *ole!* before you know it, it's your turn at the tortillas.

C&P's takes informality to new heights, offering you the chance to munch and crunch in jeans or vested suit. Once you've managed to claim a seat here, try my favorite, Carlos's wild tostada, a crispy, high-backed, beef-filled melange that arrives bearing every resemblance to a Viking ship in full sail. Chili Colorado is a tasty sauced beef chunks concoction, and the super-crisp Mexican pizza —a crunchy flour taco topped with meat, mushrooms, tomatoes, olives, and sauce—may ruin you forever for the mundane Italian variety. Probably the very best part of Carlos and Pepe's is the check: figure $10 to $15 for two for dinner, giant margaritas are $2.75. *Caramba!*

The second top budget spot in town is **Bobby Rubino's Place for Ribs,** 4100 N. Federal Hwy. (tel. 561-5305), which has been drawing crowds since opening day, and became so instantly popular it's now been cloned seven times locally and five times in Canada. This spot is nirvana for barbecued ribs fans. Rubino's serves 'em up with indelicate abandon, accompanied by a loaf—yes, a loaf—of onion rings. It also turns out barbecued chicken in a peppery hot sauce, and a bargain London broil for $5. The atmosphere is dark and lounge-like, and there are attractive wood-trimmed walls, a central U-shaped lounge flanked by comfortable booths, and an upstairs lounge with plump swiveling armchairs.

Ribs are now $11, chicken and ribs a bit less, and other items progressively less, so you can figure your bill for two in the $25 bracket or less. Wear your weekend cowboy gear. It's open from 11 a.m. to 2 a.m. daily, on Sunday from 1 p.m.

Southport Raw Bar and Seafood Restaurant, 1536 Cordova Rd., just off 17th Street Causeway (tel. 525-2526), has been the cult hang-out of yachtsmen and sundry other types for ages. It's not difficult to understand why. Life at Southport is as informal and comfortable as an old pair of jeans, which, incidentally, would be formal wear here. This is your basic get-down, funky spot. Their bumper sticker appears on many a car in town and reads: "Eat fish—live longer, eat oysters—love longer, eat clams—last longer."

Not for fancy-schmancy do you go here but for good simply prepared seafood and decent raw bar goodies—fat oysters carried through the restaurant in huge plastic buckets and pried apart behind one of the two big bars, cherrystone clams, spiced shrimp, conch or New England clam chowder, clam fritters. Presentation is important in some restaurants, but here refers only to slapping it on a paper plate and schlepping it down in front of you, accompanied by plastic forks, little paper cups of cocktail or tartar sauce or melted butter, a small lidded paper cup of coleslaw.

Certainly it's casual, with music blaring, beer foaming into chilled glasses, but in its own carousel style, it's fun and it's very cheap. You can have dinner and a couple of beers here for less than $15 a couple! Oysters and steamed clams are less than $5 a dozen.

Southport is nothing much to look at either: one big room with a couple of waist-high dividers down the middle, a television in one corner, one of those moving-light advertising gizmos on one wall, some nets and nautical junque scattered about, a bulletin board plastered with business cards no one will ever read. An experience, daily from 11 a.m. to 2 a.m.

Two restaurants specializing in curry offer you a choice between a tiny unimposing six-table bistro featuring Thai cuisine and a larger, more elaborate spot specializing in things Indian from vindaloo to belly dancers.

Siam Curry House is tucked away at 2010 Wilton Dr., also called NE Fourth Avenue (tel. 564-3411). Cheerful helpers here will work and work until they elicit the smile that means your dinner is just the degree of spiciness that suits your taste. Their curries are based on rich coconut milk and can be ordered from mild to super-hot. There are beef, chicken, pork, lamb, shrimp, scallop, and vegetable curries to choose from, plus such fascinating items as floating market soup with transparent noodles, or kaitumkar soup with chicken, spices, lemon grass, and coconut milk.

They make steamed dumplings, and my favorite, Ramwong chicken cooked with vegetables, spices, and peanuts. If you'd like to sample a bit of almost everything here, try the Bangkok Tonight dinner, the Royal Banquet, or the Siamese Fisherman Feast. Curries are in the $5 to $6 range, with the special dinners about $8 to $14, so your bill for two isn't likely to top $20 to $25. Siam Curry House is open from 4 to 10 p.m. for dinner, from 11 a.m. to 2 p.m. for lunch (closed Sunday).

At **Punjab,** an Indian restaurant at 1001 W. Oakland Park Blvd. (tel. 565-2522), curries come in mild, medium, hot, and extra-hot. Among the dozens of items on the menu are chicken, beef, or lamb vindaloo, chicken tandoori, and homemade Indian breads from chapati to puri and paratha. Open daily from 11 a.m. to 11 p.m. (from 5 p.m. on Sunday), and (one hour later on Friday and Saturday), Punjab offers dinner for $8 to $12 per person.

Deli fans need look no further than **Wolfie's,** 2501 E. Sunrise Blvd. (tel. 566-7476), a New York deli transplant that's pure Big Apple from unflappable major domo to matzoh-ball penicillin soup. A cavernous spot with a circular center counter flanked by wide booths and dozens of tables, this is your big basic deli, serving meals from 7 a.m. to 1 a.m. daily. There's a tiny and very dark bar on one edge of the restaurant, a small but caloric bakery on the other. In between you'll find overstuffed sandwiches, blintzes, potato pancakes, pastrami, and corned beef, plus an enormous array of sandwiches and full dinners, all of it supplemented by brimming bowls of kosher dills, coleslaw, and onion rolls to dream about, and portions huge enough to stuff Diamond Jim. Your bill will come to $5 or so for high-rise sandwiches and soup, $3 to $5 more for dinners.

Finally, if you scream for ice cream now and then, you mustn't miss **Swensen's,** 2477 E. Sunrise Blvd. (tel. 566-1847), a nifty little Victorian spot with etched glass and enough ice cream to freeze the North Pole. Heaven knows how many flavors they have here, but you can count on pumpkin and watermelon, and at least four varieties of chocolate. (Are you up to bubble gum ice cream?) Full-fledged sundae and soda concoctions are razzle-dazzle items of such dimensions a gasp is always audible here. To go into suitably euphoric descriptions of things like the Black Bart or the Earthquake (that registers a five on the Richter scale) would keep you riveted to this page, thus losing you for the rest of the book. They're your calories—get in there and spend them. Figure $3 to $7 for one of the major concoctions, $1 for fat and sassy cones. They serve sandwiches too, and are open daily from 10 a.m. to midnight, an hour later on Friday and Saturday.

Drugstores aren't usually on my list of top spots, but the **Chemist Shop,** 817 E. Las Olas Blvd. (tel. 462-6587), is. Nothing fancy here except the passing parade of boulevardiers in safari suits, but the sandwiches are huge, the salads fresh, the chili a knock-out, and their sodas and sundaes worth their weight. Open 9 a.m. to 5 p.m. Monday through Saturday.

Whatever adjective goes just beyond eclectic must be the perfect description for the odd lot that frequents **Ernie's Bar-B-Q,** at 1843 S. Federal Hwy. (tel. 523-8638). You not only can see *everything* here, you may very well see it all in one evening. Ernie himself has moved along to new challenges, but before he went he covered the walls with his own proverbial thoughts—which are about as unusual as his customers. It doesn't matter really, because what you do here is ignore it all and just pay attention to the best conch chowder in southern Florida, thick luscious Bimini bread, great barbecued pork and beef, nippy conch salads. Once a major corporation even shipped thousands of gallons of Ernie's conch chowder out to California to a giant party, and *that* is testimony! There's a raw bar upstairs and a crowd always. Prices range from about $5 to $8. Ernie's is open from 11 a.m. to 11 p.m. daily, later hours at the bar.

Pizza? Best of the rest is **Two Guys,** 701 S. Federal Hwy. (tel. 462-7140), which serves up thin crusts in its tiny enclave on South Federal Highway or delivers to you for a few dollars more. Pizzas start at $6 or so, and range upward as you add on all the goop. Open 11 a.m. to 1:30 a.m. daily (to midnight on Sunday). Two Guys also has a wide range of sandwiches, salads, and Italian dinners under $10.

DINING CHOICES IN NEARBY CITIES: Good restaurants are scattered all over the Gold Coast (chefs like warm weather too, you know!). Here are a few of the best in neighboring towns north and south.

Pompano and Deerfield

All the Bon-Saint-Come family's at work at **Le Morvan,** 677 N. Federal Hwy., Pompano (tel. 943-5980), where a two-generation team of a young couple and a set of parents greet you, seat you, and cook for you. What's more, after presenting you with pâté, perfectly cooked vegetables, creamy veal delights, steaks, seafood, salad, soup, and dessert, they don't rob you at the cash register. From pâté to cream puff, dinners are $10 to $15 or less. Le Morvan's atmosphere is cozy, its simple lighting soft and romantic, and its ambience comfortable and charming. Open for dinner daily from 5:30 to 10 p.m.

Tucked away in an unlikely spot on busy McNab Road is the **French Place,** 360 E. McNab Rd., Pompano (tel. 785-1920), where talented Jean-Pierre Bolline whips up sole meunière, boeuf bourguignon, crusty french bread, poached salmon, and mile-high pastries. He serves them up in a tiny bistro as simply decorated as any you'd see in France, and charms your socks off while he's at it. You'll be happy with the prices too, which won't top $10 to $15 for entrees. Open 11:30 a.m. to 2 p.m. weekdays, 5 to 10 p.m. daily for dinner.

It's not easy to create a nautical atmosphere that doesn't look like a demolition site, but they've managed to do nautical with taste at **Captain's Cove,** 700 S. Federal Hwy., Pompano (tel. 943-4100). Lots of boat thingamabobs, lobster traps, and such, all blended nicely together by chandeliers that cast an intimate golden glow and dark-wood touches that smooth out that theme look. On the $10 to $15 menu is more of the same, with frequent lobster offerings—a specialty here—at bargain prices. The restaurant's shore dinner runs the gamut from clam chowder to corn, steamed clams, and lobster. Open from 4 to 11 p.m. for dinner Tuesday through Sunday.

Harrison's Imperial House, 50 N. Ocean Blvd., Pompano (tel. 941-2200), looks nothing at all like a Chinese restaurant, which may be why so many conservative diners have taken to this place over the years. The Cantonese food here is quite good, and there's a huge $12 buffet guaranteed to fill. Prices are in the $10 to $15 range. Open for lunch in the winter season and from 5 to 10 p.m. daily.

They come by land and sea to dine at **Pal's Captain's Table,** at the Cove Yacht Basin, Deerfield Beach (tel. 427-4000). Watching the sea arrivals is part of the fun at this waterside restaurant plunked down beside the Intracoastal. At a table overlooking the water, you can watch huge yachts chug slowly by as you dine on sea-fresh seafood and steaks, dark onion rolls and date-nut bread, a relish tray, and perhaps key lime pie for dessert. A low-light nautical bar in front has been the scene of many a discussion, frivolous and not, for the many years Pal's has been operating here. Prices are in the $12 to $15 range, and the restaurant's open for lunch from 11:30 a.m. to 3 p.m. weekdays and for dinner from 5 to 10:30 p.m., noon to 10 p.m. on Sunday.

On the walls of the **Riverview,** 1741 E. Riverview Rd., Deerfield Beach, at the Intracoastal Waterway (tel. 428-3463), you'll see remnants of the days when this favorite waterside eatery was a gambling house. Before that it served this fishing community as a packing house, and over the years has been the site of many a frolicking evening. Things are a bit quieter at the Riverview these days, but there's still a nice hideaway atmosphere about the place, and a long menu filled with outstanding seafood and steaks. Stuffed Florida lobster and yellowtail are top of the line, and the clam chowder's a much-sold item, as are the thick cuts of prime rib and sirloin. You'll pay about $12 to $18 for dinner. The Riverview is open from 6 to 10 p.m. daily. To find the Riverview, look under the northwest side of the Intracoastal Bridge.

Cap's Place, 2765 NE 28th Court, Lighthouse Point Yacht Basin in Lighthouse Point (tel. 941-0418), is the only restaurant I know where getting there is half the fun. Here's how you do that: Head up US 1 to NE 24th Street in Lighthouse Point where you'll see a sign directing you to the Yacht Club and to Cap's. Wind around some side streets and pull up where you see Cap's sign. If there's no *African Queen* to take you across the water to Cap's, blink your headlights and shortly there will be. You chug across the waters of the Intracoastal, and there, in the middle of the waterway, is a heap of lumber—you've arrived!

Sixty years ago Cap Knight, who occasionally ran some rum into Prohibition-dry Florida, beached himself and a few barges on this islet in the stream. He tossed in a little gambling, probably a lot of proof products, and a little food, and called it Club Unique. That it is, and that it was to the likes of Winston Churchill, Jack Dempsey, Kate Smith, FDR, all of whom dropped by. Their presence still haunts these aging boards and their pictures are what little decor there is in this very rustic heap straight out of a Bogart movie. I can't think of any way they could make this place more atmospheric.

It's worth it to whip up to Cap's just for the fresh hearts of palm salad, one of the few places in the nation you can get the fresh (definitely *not* canned) variety. Besides that rare delicacy, nothing else here has fancy overtones. Just steaming spuds and a list of straight-from-the-sea foods from dolphin to sea trout, bluefish, mackerel, kingfish, sea bass, pompano, crab, shrimp, scallops, and oysters. With every dinner you get a shrimp cocktail too, and fresh bread baked right out back. Best of all, many of the prices are under $10. Don't miss the bar—if ever Bogart decides to haunt a place, this is a place he'd choose! Cap's is open from 5:30 to 10 p.m. daily, to 11 p.m. on Friday and Saturday.

The Cove, 1755 SE 3rd St., Deerfield Beach (tel. 428-1727) is a spot that manages to combine both lively and quiet, retaining the best of both. Loads of plants, cool breezes from the Intracoastal Waterway, lively entertainment, an outdoor wooden deck, candlelight, and inexpensive meals all add up to one beautifully tropical way to spend an afternoon or evening. Outside, halyards clank against masts of sleek sailboats and inside a little calypso music finishes your total immersion into Florida Tropical at its best. Menu prices top out at $15 for filet mignon, but there are plenty of choices in the $5 to $10 range. An especially good place to imbibe some kind of fruity tropical drink you'd never touch anywhere else, the Cove is open from 11 a.m. to 2 a.m. weekdays and from 8 a.m. to 2 a.m. weekends. Steel band entertainment from 4 to 11 p.m. on Sunday.

Hollywood/Dania/Hallandale

Right up there at the top of Hollywood restaurants is the **Celebrity Room** at the Diplomat Hotel, 3515 S. Ocean Dr. (tel. 457-8111). White-gloved, absolutely flawless service, top-quality cooking, a beautiful, elegant dining room, and excellent wines combine to make this restaurant simply superb. Continental cooking is the order of the day here, with excellent steaks, lots of herbs, and creamy sauces. Naturally you must be prepared to pay for perfection, so plan on a check of at least $40 a person. Dance music plays each evening and jackets are required. The Celebrity Room is open from 6 to 11 p.m. every night but Tuesday.

Wooden beams and stucco walls, ferns and fresh flowers, and most unusual of all, reasonably priced French cuisine—that's **Neptune** at 1824 Harrison Ave. (tel. 920-6773). There's a list of basic French beef and seafood dishes, but the real treasures change daily with the vagaries of the marketplace. Ask and you shall discover. Friendly, efficient service, warm comfortable surroundings, and excellent cooking focusing on seafood. For a pleasant evening you'll pay about $15 at Neptune, which is open from 5 to 11 p.m. daily.

A windowside table overlooking most everything in Hollywood is the chief allure at **Top of the Home,** 1720 Harrison St. atop the Federal Bank Building (tel. 927-1707). Continental cuisine is the fare here, with plenty of seafood and beef dishes to choose from, plus rack of lamb, stone crabs, and an intriguing cappuccino ice cream pie. Jackets are recommended. There is dancing nightly, and the restaurant, which will present you a bill in the $20 to $25 range, is open from 5 p.m. for cocktails, from 6 to 11:30 p.m. for dinner Tuesday through Sunday.

Hemmingway, at 219 N. 21st Ave., Hollywood Beach (Dixie Highway; tel. 923-0500). This popular night-and-day emporium is in Hollywood's old city hall building. It was built in the 1920s so a good-old-days atmosphere prevails: etched glass, eclectic collections of memorabilia, a tinkling piano, and later a big-band sound, plus a long, long menu of crêpes and steaks, salads and soups, burgers and barbecue, all accompanied by fresh fruit. Prices range from $7 to $19. It's open from 11 a.m. to 4 a.m. daily, from 1 p.m. on Sunday.

You'll have to drive out to the western reaches of the county to get to this little place, but when you finally arrive, you'll join dozens and dozens of others who have just accomplished the same run. Go early or be prepared to beer-and-wine-it a while in the parking lot outside. **Sea Shanty,** 3841 Griffin Rd., Ft. Lauderdale (tel. 962-1921). This place is so popular that when I first drove by, I thought the crowd outside was a wedding! Fresh, fresh seafood is what lures the masses here, and keeps them coming back despite the absolutely-no-atmosphere atmosphere. You can have snapper, yellowtail, shrimp, kingfish, and a grouper parmesan that is to faint for, plus simple breads, salads, and potatoes, with prices about $10 and service in the genre of New York deli: efficient, period. You'll love it—everybody does. Open 4:30 to 10:30 p.m. (go very early or very late).

Never on Sunday, 129 N. Federal Hwy., Dania (tel. 921-5557), is the new name on an old house owned by experienced Broward County restaurateurs, the D'Arcys. Once the proprietors of Chez Tonton, the couple are now holding forth in Dania, serving up their rich onion soup, quiches, beef Wellington, rack of lamb, and the like for prices running about $20 to $25—well worth it for the smiling welcome, the interesting location, and the outstanding cuisine. Their hours are from 5:30 to 10:30 p.m. Monday through Saturday.

For pure Spanish cooking—which means light sauces and unusual preparations of beef and seafood (with the accent on seafood)—head for **Old Spain,** at 2333 Hollywood Blvd., Hollywood (tel. 921-8485, or in Miami 944-2298). Juan Abella is a genial host who sometimes trots through the dining room with a Spanish wine bag he squirts into your mouth, compliments of the house. When you don't see him, rest assured he's out in the kitchen creating paella Valenciana, white bean soup, or that masterful seafood melange of Spain, zarzuela. Try a gypsy's arm for dessert or crêpes with vanilla sauce. You'll pay about $15 or so for dinner here. Old Spain is open from noon to 2:30 p.m. for lunch Monday through Friday, and from 6 to 10:30 p.m. for dinner every day, on Sunday from 5 to 10 p.m.

Manero's, 2600 E. Hallandale Beach Blvd., Hallandale (tel. 456-1000), has been flipping out those steaks and gorgonzola-topped salads for so long it's possible they may do this blindfolded. More than 25 years in this spot has earned the restaurant a fond place in the hearts of area beef eaters. Prices are reasonable too, with dinner in the $12 to $15 range. Manero's is open daily from 11:30 a.m. to 11 p.m.

Martha's, 6024 N. Ocean Dr., Hollywood (tel. 923-5444), is as intriguing as a $1000 bill. Tiny lights glitter in the ceiling. Pale-peach and gray tones play counterpoint to polished brass accents, glowing candles, fresh flowers. Off in a corner a handsome circular bar is draped with a trendy crowd of suburbanites, while outside, a second bar and a less formal dining area lure boaters and casual diners.

Ms. Martha, who rose to fame with a similar establishment in Key West, and who is anticipating a fair rate of return on her very impressive investment, has not produced a bargain basement here but neither is it any more expensive than most area restaurants of similarly elaborate design and decor. You'll pay $12 to $17 for entrees, which are accompanied by an attractive crystal bowl of iced crudités and potatoes or vegetables. All else is à la carte, with the tab rising along with your greed.

Unusual treats here include oysters topped with horseradish sauce and baked with three cheeses, a cold mussel soup selection called Billi-bi, and a marvelously spicy seafood gumbo not to be missed. Martha's has a masterful way with seafood too. Coconut shrimp features a piña-colada batter and orange-and-mustard sauce. A great bouillabaisse is flavored with saffron. Beef selections include prime rib with Yorkshire pudding and steaks. Veal comes in styles from saltimbocca to piccata and with a cream Calvados sauce accented with sauteed apples.

An ice-cream pie called Pontchartrain pie features sherbet and ice-cream layers topped with a chocolate sauce of such rich bittersweet goodness that a chocolate-hooked companion claimed he was going back for an order of Pontchartrain, hold the ice cream.

If you'd like to try Martha's on the cheap, trot up to the second-floor raw bar, where a selection of stone crabs, clams, oysters, and shrimp are temptingly displayed on cracked ice. Here the atmosphere is more casual: royal-blue fiberglass tabletops trimmed in wood, nauti-facts scattered artfully about, a sensational view of the waterway through a wall of windows. Some of the downstairs menu is available here too, along with steamed clams and mussels, smoked fish and oysters, peel-and-eat shrimp, and a seafood cioppino, all $5 to $8. Hours are 11:30 a.m. to 2:30 p.m. and 5 to 11 p.m. daily.

Whiskey Creek Café, Route A1A at Seafair on Dania Beach (tel. 921-4100), has much to recommend it: unusually attractive architecture and interior design, an oceanside location, some unusual menu selections, and quite good cooking. The architecture and interior design are beautifully contemporary, with wide smoked-glass windows overlooking a fountain and the beach, light woods, a striking stained-glass ceiling in shades of green, and acres of tile trim.

A long list of raw-bar and light dinners ranges from $5 to $8 in price, and includes such treats as mussels risotto, Bahamian pan fish fry featuring a whole fried fish, Maryland crabcakes, seafood St. Jacques in crêpes, scallops and mussels in a Dijon mustard vinaigrette, and oyster stew. More elaborate selections like honey-fried shrimp or prime rib top out at about $13. You will discover a decidedly Cajun bent to the cooking here: for instance, crawfish étouffée, team-ing crawfish tails with walnuts, onions, and a spicy red sauce. You will also discover the best oysters Rockefeller for miles around.

An adjoining but separate section called the **Captain's Cabin** is decked out in really lovely pink floral china, crystal, carpets, and mirrors. It is a tranquil, formal room located just far enough from the bilevel lounge and café to make it a quieter, more intimate dining spot. It's open daily from 11 a.m. to midnight, closing at 2 a.m. on weekends.

Prestidigitation has little to do with the magic you'll find at the **Magic Pan,** 800 S. Federal Hwy., Hallandale (tel. 456-4451), directly across from the entrance to Gulfstream Park. Hard work, enthusiasm, talent, and determination are what has made this tiny restaurant a kind of underground gourmet's secret hereabouts. Atmosphere is charmingly simple. To a long, squat building the Magic Pan's owners have added flower-sprigged curtains, a collection of old china and copper pots, a couple of antiques, adding up to a cozy, if simple, ambience much like many Parisian cafés.

As for the food, well . . . very, very good. Menus change daily according to what's freshest in the market, but you can usually count on steak in peppercorn sauce, fresh seafood kept light and flaky, shrimp topped in a sherry cream sauce and Swiss cheese, veal and eggplant in a marsala sauce or veal with sauteed apple slices and apple brandy, duckling in a black-currant sauce and braised peaches, brook trout pan-fried in almond oil with shrimp, mushrooms, and black olives. On Friday and Saturday rib-eye roast au jus is available. Desserts change too, but often include a towering apple pie or chocolate torrone loaf, much like a heavy chocolate mousse. Dinners include a basket of crunchy breadsticks and half a loaf of bread, buttered and run under a broiler, plus salad or soup, vegetable, and potato. Entrees range in price from $8 to $15, and the restaurant is open daily from 5 to 10 p.m., closing 30 minutes later on weekends.

Spiced Apple, 3281 Griffin Rd., Ft. Lauderdale (tel. 962-0772), is a cute little country place that really is out in what passes for country in this urban area. Here you dine on slabs of country ham, peach cobbler, corn fritters, fried chicken, and the like. Prices are quite reasonable, easily falling into the $10 to $15 range for complete dinners. Hours are 11:30 a.m. to 3 p.m. weekdays for lunch and 4 to 10 p.m. daily for dinner, closing half an hour later on weekends. On Sunday hours are 1 to 9 p.m.

Despite my best efforts, I haven't had a chance to visit **Nada's Specialty Restaurant,** at 3433 Griffin Rd., Ft. Lauderdale (tel. 981-5343). Many of those whose opinions can be trusted are regular diners there, however, and to a person they rave about the excellence of this small but significant South Broward restaurant. Owner and chef Nada whips up Yugoslavian and Hungarian treats, hearty dishes like stuffed cabbage, lamb shank, goulash, paprikash, all served with soup and salad bar. She has been doing that long enough to qualify as a permanent fixture in a community in which restaurants open and close faster than a clam shell. Nada owes her restaurant's longevity, they tell me, to good basic ingredients, wholesomely and enthusiastically prepared and attractively presented in a homey-friendly atmosphere. I'm looking forward to trying it, and am convinced you should be too. Nada's is closed Monday and Tuesday, open 5:30 to 9 p.m. other days. Prices are $7 to $12.

Napoli's, 1800 N. Federal Hwy., Hollywood (tel. 923-7250), is one of those places that are a joy to try, a tiny pack-'em-in trattoria that's filled with families and big happy groups celebrating with all the gesticulating gusto you find in Italy's best loved neighborhood restaurants. Toddlers are cuddled by the staff, tables are forever being shoved together to accommodate big family parties, and everybody's smiling.

All the best loved pasta-with-sauce selections are available for prices in the

$5 to $7 range. They serve pizza here too, with an unusual touch that's just what you would expect of this family restaurant: family pizza dinners, which include a basic tomato and cheese pizza with spaghetti, soup, and bread at $10 for two, $16 for four. Everything comes with the usual accoutrements: soup, crusty, hot garlic rolls, and salad or spaghetti. You will also find veal, chicken, shrimp, calamari, lobster, and eggplant in all the usual styles and at prices in the $6 to $10 range, plus spaghetti carbonara or carrettiera (a sauce of fresh tomatoes, garlic, olive oil, and basil), gnocchi, rigatoni bolognese, zuppa de pesce alla Napoli.

The atmosphere is simple: a tiny foyer jammed with snapshots of family and friends, some oil paintings of Italian architectural landmarks. A boisterous, bouncing, lively spot that's as much fun as it is fulfilling. Napoli's is open weekdays from noon to 10 p.m., from 3 to 11 p.m. on Saturday, and from 4 to 10 p.m. on Sunday.

Wine and thou are always an irresistible combination. Add a little singing and you've really got something. You can have all of the above and rather more at **Café del Opera,** 246 N. Federal Hwy., Dania (tel. 920-7766). Rumor has it that everyone of note in the musical world hereabouts turns up sooner or later at this new dining emporium dedicated to the glories of arias. Any night of the week you will find a pianist commanding focal and vocal attention, seated at a baby grand in the front corner of this small cheery restaurant. Cheery Tiffany-like hanging lamps cast a subtle colorful light over small wood tables. Little round stained-glass panels pay tribute to operatic heroines.

Which brings us to dinner. Café del Opera is cooking with as much simple joy as it is singing. Although the menu is rather limited—just half a dozen or so pasta selections, a few veal choices, and a couple of chicken preparations—those choices are quite marvelously prepared. Now I am not talking faint scent of woodland violets here, just simple, basic cooking accomplished with care and with what appears to be a budding talent. Fettuccine à la Enrico, for instance, is a dish so rich you could bank it. A simple veal scaloppine selection, while not showily cooked or laced with fancy herbs, is a solidly made creation of veal topped by a tangy tomato sauce adorned with mushrooms and green peppers. Among the other selections available are lasagne, linguini with clam sauce, eggplant parmigiana, green or white pasta with tomato sauce. None of the dinners tops $10; pastas are $6 to $8. Hours are 6:30 p.m. to midnight.

At **Hiro Japanese Restaurant,** 1302 S. Federal Hwy., Dania (tel. 920-7170), a kimono-clad Japanese hostess-owner has turned a real yawner of a structure into a tiny den of delicacy and good taste. At a long, polished blond-wood sushi bar, magician-cooks cut and twirl and twist and mix to create amazing little edible works of art. One room features normal tables and chairs while another is a long, narrow room designed for the Japanese customs Americans fear most: sitting near floor level. As this room comes the closest to true Japanese decor, it is perhaps not surprising that it is the loveliest room of all, with massive slabs of black marble set on a base of midnight-blue linen. Here you dine on delightfully delicate cuisine you are unlikely to understand but are likely to love. I know you will adore the prices: it's quite difficult to spend more than $8 to $10 for a complete dinner, including soup in an enameled bowl, rice, and dessert.

Among your choices are yakitori (broiled chicken on a skewer), dengaku (broiled tofu, eggplant, or shrimp), shrimp or vegetable tempura, so delicately prepared and fried you need an anchor to keep it on the table. You will never taste anything more interesting. For those less inclined to menu adventures, Hiro offers chicken, fish, and sirloin teriyaki. Oh, go ahead, you deserve an adventure. Hours are 5 to 10 p.m. daily, closing an hour later on weekends.

If you love that rib-sticking German fare, nothing could be würst than missing **Zinkler's Bavarian Village,** 1401 N. Federal Hwy., Hollywood (tel. 922-

7321), where you can gorge on schnitzel, späetzle, sauerkraut, strolling oompah-pah accordion music, and German wines. You may have to buy your liederhosen a size larger! You'll pay $8 to $12 for dinner, and the yodeling begins at 11:30 a.m. for lunch (closing at 3 p.m.), and from 4 to 11 p.m. for dinner daily (from noon on Sunday).

SEEING THE SIGHTS: With 165 miles of canals and infinite quantities of ocean, Fort Lauderdale has water sports galore, as do all the cities up and down the coastline. You'll usually find sailboat rentals right on the beach, and in larger towns like Hollywood and Fort Lauderdale shops in the beach area have all the sand requirements from suntan lotion to surfboards.

Beaches

So popular are Fort Lauderdale's beaches that they have actually been subdivided—quite informally, let me assure you. Certain people go to certain beaches, and after a few days in town you'll know exactly where to find your friends or those who may become your friends. To help you in your search, let it be known that the beach across from the Elbo Room is a collegiate hang-out in March, often a high school haven in summer. The beach across from the Marlin Beach Hotel is popular with gay sun-seekers. The beach across from the Horizon and Jolly Roger Hotels is quieter, popular with young professionals and those seeking a less raucous atmosphere; and the beach at Sunrise Boulevard is another young professionals hang-out most of the year, collegiate grounds in March. Families lean toward the beach from Sunrise north along the edges of Birch State Park.

If Fort Lauderdale's seven miles of sand are not enough for you, don't despair. There are a jillion or so other acres of silica ready and waiting for you to leave a footprint in them. Among those other beaches are:

Hallandale Beach, a condo-lined strip of sand at Hallandale Beach Boulevard.

Hollywood Beach, which runs roughly from Hollywood Beach Boulevard north to Sheridan Street. Much of the way, the sand is trimmed with a boardwalk, here called the Broadwalk, which is in turn lined by small shops and fast-food eateries.

Dania Beach, one of the region's most attractive, thanks to the absence of buildings on most of it. A new addition to the most deserted part of the beach is a long, two-story, cupola-topped, pastel building called Sea Fair which houses some attractive boutiques, a lounge, and quite an attractive restaurant called Whiskey Creek. Clambake fans can get a permit for evening clambakes on the beach, so they tell me. You'll find the beach stretching north from about Sheridan Street to Port Everglades.

John U. Lloyd State Park, a very large and jungly park with beautiful beaches, has 245 acres of parkgrounds right on the ocean, picnic tables, and a 50¢ admission charge. It's officially at 6503 N. Ocean Dr., but you'll find it by taking Dania Beach Boulevard to the ocean and taking a right turn at the stop sign there.

Lauderdale-by-the-Sea, which stretches roughly from about Commercial Boulevard south to Oakland Park Boulevard along Ocean Drive, features a fishing pier.

Pompano Beach, extending along the ocean from Atlantic Boulevard to North Ocean Boulevard, with public beaches at the end of intersecting streets. Much of Pompano Beach is hidden behind condominium buildings, which makes it comparatively deserted most of the time—good for getaway afternoons.

Deerfield Beach and Boca Raton Beach stretch north from the northern boundary of Pompano Beach and are favored by snorkelers and scuba fans. Many are backed by shady jungle growth.

Tours

Probably the city's primary attractions are its two **paddlewheelers,** the *Jungle Queen* and the *Paddlewheel Queen.*

Board one of these sparkling white antique craft and you're off down the Intracoastal Waterway for hours of oohing and ahhing at the Gold Coast's downright gorgeous canalside real estate. Waterfront dwellers here consider the water their *front* door, so the view you get of this side of these sprawling mansions is impressive indeed. Rolling lawns so perfectly manicured you could (and some residents do) golf on them, pastel mansions with ornate wide verandas soaring over pools adorned by Roman columns and statuary. One manse even has a plot of, and a lot of, land shaped like the state of Florida! Residents get right into this thing, flicking their porch lights off and on as the boat toots by, and waving merrily as you chug along in antiquated splendor.

In winter you *must* (and in summer you should) reserve a seat on evening cruises well in advance, although you can sometimes luck into a last-minute cancellation if you're on hand about 6:30 p.m. The *Jungle Queen* departs from **Bahia Mar Yacht Basin,** Route A1A, Fort Lauderdale (tel. 462-5596), on two daylight tours at 10 a.m. and 2 p.m., and a four-hour dinner cruise at 7 p.m. You get the grand tour on the way to dinner, stop at an exotic island for family-style, all-you-can-eat shrimp and chicken, then return with vaudeville entertainment. The price is $15.95 for adults or children for the evening cruise, and $4.95 for adults, and $3 for children on day cruises.

Meanwhile, if you'd like a little more formal cruise evening, board the *Paddlewheel Queen* one block south of Oakland Park Boulevard just west of Route A1A (tel. 564-7659), and sail off for a steak dinner and dancing under the stars. There are also day tours at 2 p.m. daily at $4.50 for adults, $3.50 for children. Evening cruises cost adults $21.50; children, $18.50.

To see the land side of the city, plus orange groves and Indian alligator wrestling, book a seat on the **Voyager Train,** 600 S. Seabreeze Ave. (tel. 463-0401). This group of open cars (they're covered if it rains) is pulled around town at 10 a.m., noon, and 2 and 4 p.m. daily by small white Jeeps. You'll see homes of the famous and infamous, the city's palm-lined, gaslit Las Olas Boulevard, bustling Port Everglades, Flamingo Orange Groves. There are several options (including Ocean World), and prices are $4.75 for adults, $2.25 for children.

Airboat Rides

If you'd like to see some of the mysterious Everglades swampland without driving all the way to the park in Miami, take a trip to the edge of the Glades to an area called Everglades Holiday Park. Here a guide will tuck you into a Rube Goldberg creation called an airboat and whiz you off into the swamp for a look at alligator shoes still on the hoof.

Airboats are flat-bottomed craft designed to skim over the shallow swampland with the aid of an aircraft propeller and some massive roaring engines. Certainly you'll never see one of these in Cincinnati. Besides, roaring around in one for a look at Florida's flora and fauna is just plain fun. You can also rent boats here and whiz off on your own.

Located 30 minutes west of the city at the junction of US 27 and Griffin Road (tel. 434-8111), **Everglades Holiday Park** charges $7 for adults and $3.50 for children under 12 for this look at the one-of-a-kind swamp. Rides leave every 30 minutes from 9 a.m. to 5 p.m.

Historic Sites

In the secluded area at 231 SW 2nd Street (tel. 462-4115) are the only architectural remnants of the city's past: the small but elegant old New River Inn, a verandaed hotel that's now a **Discovery Center** hands-on museum and historical center, and the King-Cromartie House, which belonged to two of the city's pioneer families.

Plunk down in a porch rocking chair at 75-year-old New River Inn, gaze out over the tranquil New River (said by the Seminoles to have sprung up overnight), listen to the breeze shush through the palms, and you are transported to long-gone days when a tourist in town was big news. The Discovery Center is a child-oriented set of nature exhibits with frequent craft classes. It's open October to June from 2 to 5 p.m. Tuesday through Friday, from 10 a.m. to 5 p.m. on Saturday, and 1 to 5 p.m. on Sunday. June through August hours are 10 a.m. to 5 p.m. Monday through Saturday, and 1 to 5 p.m. on Sunday. Admission to the museum is $2.

Next door is the **King-Cromartie House,** saved from destruction by a local social group and outfitted in furnishings of the period, right down to antique shoes and dresses in the closets and a tiny furnished dollhouse. It's open Tuesday through Friday from 2 to 5 p.m., on Saturday from 10 a.m. to 5 p.m., and on Sunday from 1 to 5 p.m. Admission is $2 per person. Guided tours, lasting 45 minutes and led by docents in period costumes, explain some of the unusual items collected there. Take a look at the flour sifter in the kitchen—who says we've progressed? At Christmas the house is a fairyland with twinkling lights and tiny wreaths hung in every window.

There are also a number of fascinating antique shops in the area. Back in the early 1900s the small two-story, veranda-trimmed house at 333 S. Federal Hwy. was Fort Lauderdale's trading post, the place Seminole Indians and pioneer Fort Lauderdale residents came to buy, sell, bargain, and trade. Evenings, trader Frank Stranahan and his new schoolmarm bride, Ivy Julia Cromartie, turned the house into the village's social center, complete with accordion music and lots of laughter. Together, Miss Ivy and Frank had cut the rock-hard wood called Dade County pine into lumber they used to build the simple but elegant home that was to become known as **Stranahan House,** the oldest remaining structure in this city.

Built in 1902, the house was a happy place but had its sorrows too: Frank lost everything in the Great Crash and committed suicide. His wife lived on for 40 years, occupying an attic room at the top of the home until she died in 1971. By that time a restaurant had been opened here, but eventually even that enterprise folded and the city's most historic building lay moldering, its hand-hewn beams slowly pulling apart, its joints loosening.

Then the Fort Lauderdale Historical Society bought the house the Stranahans had worked so hard to build and raised more than $250,000 to hire archeologists, historians, and builders to put it all back together again. When peeling paint had been scraped, brown hues sanded off a fireplace's red and white bricks, staircases replaced, and the pretty porches restored, Stranahan House was reopened.

Now it has again become one of the town's most delightful social centers, often used by local organizations for fundraising events. Stranahan House is also a museum, open to the public (tel. 524-4736 or 463-4374) on Wednesday, Friday, and Saturday from 10 a.m. to 4 p.m., and on Sunday from 1 to 4 p.m. Admission, including a tour, is $3 per person.

Romantics might wait until Friday to visit: on that night the Historical Society sponsors a Friday-night social, when you can sip a glass of wine, nibble on hors d'oeuvres, and pretend nothing has changed in eight decades. Hours for the Friday-night social are 6 to 8:30 p.m., and admission, including the tour, is $5. To find the house, take Las Olas Boulevard to the Pantry Pride store at the intersection of US 1 and turn south. You'll find the house just off a tiny circular plaza there.

Sailing Off into the Sunset
It only stands to reason that a city as serenely lovely as Fort Lauderdale (well, most of the time) should have a serenely lovely port. It does! So pretty is it, in fact, that it's worth your time to take a little reconnoiter down there. Actually, you can hardly help doing so—to get to the beach from the airport you'll pass right by the port and see some of the sleek cruise ships that anchor there.

Called **Port Everglades,** Fort Lauderdale's port features several Mediterranean-style buildings painted a pale peach. As you drive along SE 17th Street Causeway and see them on the south side of the road, you'll think you see their pretty windows, balconies, and french doors, but what you're really seeing is a trompe-l'oeil painting, a fool-the-eye façade on what was once just a rather plain old ordinary warehouse!

Port Everglades likes to call itself the "Five-Star Port," a reference to the posh ships that dock here, all of them top-quality, very plush sailing craft indeed. What do I mean? Well, for openers the *QE II* docks here frequently in winter, along with her Cunard/Norwegian American Cruises sister ships, the sleek and lovely *Vistafjord* and *Sagafjord*. Sitmar Cruises' *Fairsea* sails from Port Everglades year round on exciting trips through the Panama Canal and to a bevy of tropical Caribbean islands. Home Lines snazzy new *Atlantic* and old-worldly *Oceanic* spend the winter here, and Sun Line's *Stella Oceanis* and *Stella Maris* have been known to drop in on their way to South America.

P & O Lines, which operates a huge ship called the *Canberra,* and a smaller but still quite large craft called the *Sea Princess*—and is also owner of the "Love Boat" of Princess Lines!—begins in 1985 sailing the *Sea Princess* from here on sun-seeking winter cruises. Royal Viking Lines, which operates lovely spic-and-span Scandinavian-staffed ships, also frequently brings its *Sky* or *Sea* in here to board passengers. Clipper Cruises, which has a lovely small intracoastal cruise ship, occasionally pops in here too.

If you'd like to take a close look at the ships, you can drive into the port and watch them sail off into the sunset. If you want to get even closer, you can call any of the lines and ask if they will arrange a guest pass for you to visit the ship when it's in port. They'll be happy to do that for you.

To read more about these and all the cruise ships operating from here, and from other parts of the U.S., I'd humbly (well, not too humbly) recommend a copy of Frommer's *Dollarwise Guide to Cruises,* co-authored by Don Schultz and—guess who!

Ocean World
You can pet hijinking bottlenose "Flipper" dolphins at this attraction on the 17th Street Causeway (tel. 525-6611), gaze in wonder at the sharks as they're fed by an intrepid soul, fly high overhead in a cable car, take a boat tour, and watch fish minding their own business in a three-story-high-aquarium. Hours are 10 a.m. to 6 p.m. daily (last show is at 4:15 p.m.). Admission is $7.95 for adults; $3.95 for children 6 to 12.

SPORTS: Do 55 golf courses sound like enough to keep you busy? How about

172 public tennis courts? Fleets of fishing boats? Dozens of rental sailboats, windsurfing boards, waterboggans, even hot-air balloons? Read on.

Golf

There are 11 public courses just in Fort Lauderdale's city limits, with PGA tournament play at Inverrary, home of the annual Honda Inverrary Invitational in March. Rates vary, but public courses like the **American Golfers Club,** 3850 N. Federal Hwy. (tel. 564-8760), a 27-hole executive course near the beach, charges $10 greens fees and $1.50 for a pull cart, $10 for an electric cart. The course opens at 7:30 a.m. daily.

Tennis

Public courts in the beach area include lighted ones at **Holiday Park** (tel. 761-2304) on Sunrise Boulevard, and **George English Park** at 1101 Bayview Dr. (tel. 563-1711). Contact the city's recreation department (tel. 761-2621) for information about all sports in the city.

Boating

Try **Bahia Mar Small Boat Rentals** at Bahia Mar Yacht Basin (tel. 467-6000) or **Bill's Sunrise Rentals,** 301 Seabreeze Ave. (tel. 763-8962) for small craft, waterskiing boats, and equipment, even motorized water-going scooters called jet skis. Powerboats are $40 for the first hour, $20 for each additional hour.

Rent a **sailboat** from facilities located on the beach just south of Las Olas Boulevard and at the north end of the beach about a mile north of Sunrise Boulevard or at the Hilton Hotel on Galt Ocean Mile. Rates begin at $20 an hour. No small sailboats are rented during spring break, but large boats with a captain are available for $25 per person per hour.

Bicycling and Mopeds

Bicycles built for two, one, and the timid are available at **Florida Bicycle,** 515 W. Sunrise Blvd. (tel. 763-6974), for $18 a week, and at **Johnny's Mopeds,** 419 S. Atlantic Blvd. (tel. 763-8789), for $3 an hour, plus deposit.

Mr. Moped, Inc., at 2925 E. Las Olas Blvd. (tel. 467-3659), rents mopeds for $8 for the first hour, $3.50 for each subsequent hour. Mr. Moped and Johnny's Mopeds both have daily rental rates of $35, plus deposit.

Fishing

Try the **Dragon,** at Seabreeze Avenue behind the Holiday Inn just off Las Olas Boulevard (tel. 522-FISH) for four hours of drift fishing, including equipment, for $15. There are three trips daily, at 8:30 a.m., 1:30 p.m., and 7:30 p.m.

Charter boats at Bahia Mar will take you after the big ones. Minimum rates are generally about $60 a person, $225 for six for a half-day trip and $425 for a full day, but bargain for a better deal.

Water Sports

Scuba and Snorkeling: At 1530 Cordova Rd., **Divers Haven** (tel. 524-2112) can outfit you for less than $20 a day, but you must be certified. They're open daily from 8 a.m. to 6 p.m. About the same prices apply at **Lauderdale Diver,** 1134 SE 17th St. (tel. 467-2822).

Surfing and Swimming: The **Waterbrothers Surf Shop,** 1738 NE Fourth Ave. (tel. 525-4912), charges $10 a day for a board ($5 for students), and **BC Surf and Sport,** 2554 N. Federal Hwy. (tel. 564-0202), bills $8 a half day, $12 for 24 hours. Both are open daily from 10 a.m. to 6 p.m. and have surf reports.

You can paddle around in this city's Olympic-size public pool, the **Swim-**

ming Hall of Fame, that's the home of major national swimming and diving competitions. It costs just $2 a day, $1 for students and children, and there's a small museum on the grounds chronicling the accomplishments of famous swimmers up to and including Johnny Weissmuller, Buster Crabbe, and Esther Williams.

Texas's Six Flags has opened what it likes to call the world's largest water park in the small town of Hollywood just south of Fort Lauderdale. Called **Atlantis,** the park is located just east of I-95 at 2700 Stirling Rd. (tel. 926-1000). You won't have any trouble finding it: just look for the submarine perched on the I-95 edge of the property. Inside you'll find swooping, snaking water slides several stories high, a wave pool that splashes you with endless breakers, an outdoor roller rink, tropical trails, a waterski show, and a lake for boating. There are plenty of shady places for picnics, plus refreshment stands and some shops. Six Flags Atlantis opened its doors in May 1983 and is promising that future additions will make the park quite a fun place to spend the day. Admission is $9.95 for adults, $7.95 for children under 8. It opens at 11 a.m. daily.

There's a long and lovely strip of beach at **Hugh Taylor Birch State Park,** 3109 E. Sunrise Blvd. (tel. 564-4521), where you can also get a look at what Fort Lauderdale was like long ago when millionaire recluse Birch redeemed his eccentricity with this donation to the city. Located at Route A1A and Sunrise Boulevard, the park has access to the beach through an under-the-street tunnel, fishing in the Intracoastal, and some beautiful picnic spots under tall pines. There are canoes and paddleboats for rent, and the park is open daily from 8 a.m. to sunset. Admission is 50¢.

Water Flume Rides: Kids of all ages will love the swooping water flume rides at **Castle Park,** 1999 SW 33rd Pl. (tel. 462-8108), where you'll also find three 18-hole miniature golf courses that look like miniature Disneylands, a batting practice range, racetrack cars, 250 video games, and bumper boats. Golf costs $3.25 for adults, $2.25 for children, and the water flume's $2.50 per hour, $5 for a day of splashing. To get there from beach hotels, take the 17th Street Causeway to US 1, turn south on US 1 and then west on Route 84 (that's a right turn). Cross over I-95 and take the first left at Ravenswood Road, follow Ravenswood to the first traffic light (which is Collins Road), turn left, go over the railroad tracks and under I-95, and you'll see it. Sounds complicated, but it's not as difficult as it reads. Open from 10 a.m. to 11 p.m. daily in summer months, but there are some alterations in hours in the winter so it might be wise to call first.

Skating

Gold Coast Roller Rink, 2604 N. Federal Hwy. (tel. 523-6783), features indoor skating and will rent you skates for 50¢. Admission is $3 evenings, $2 for Saturday and Sunday matinees. Hours vary, but are generally 9 a.m. to midnight on Friday and Saturday, 1 to 5 p.m. on Sunday. On Saturday night teenagers show up, so it's not a particularly good time for younger children. Other days the rink is open for private parties or by arrangement. Give them a call to see what's happening the day you want to go.

Baseball

Baseball fans can get a look at the **New York Yankees,** who train here in spring at Yankee Stadium, 5301 NW 12th Ave. (tel. 776-1921). Tickets are $3.50 to $7.

Parimutuel Sports

Watch jai-alai players toss speeding pelotas around at 150 m.p.h. at **Dania Jai-Alai Fronton,** 301 E. Dania Beach Blvd. (tel. 945-4345 or 426-4330), which is open from late June through mid-April from 7:30 p.m. daily (7 p.m. on Saturday). Closed Sunday. In winter there are noon matinees also, and admission is $1. Summer schedules are abbreviated so it would be wise to call before setting out for the games.

There is harness racing at **Pompano Park**, on Race Track Road (tel. 972-2000), in Pompano. The track is located on West Atlantic Boulevard. You can make a lovely (and perhaps lucky) evening of it from November to April when the park has harness races nightly with seating in a multilevel dining room with huge walls of glass overlooking the track. Admission is 75¢ for the grandstand, $3 for clubhouse seats; dinner is moderately priced. Meets are daily, except Sunday, at 7:30 p.m.

For dog racing it's the **Hollywood Greyhound Dog Track,** 831 N. Federal Hwy., Hallandale (tel. 454-9400), where clubhouse admission is $1.50, 80¢ for the grandstand. It's open every night (except Sunday) and has matinees several days a week. The track is open from December 26 through about April.

FORT LAUDERDALE AFTER DARK: Back in the 1950s when the George Hamilton tan and the film *Where the Boys Are* put Fort Lauderdale on college maps and began the annual spring-break trek to the sea, the city's Elbo Room (at Las Olas Boulevard and Route A1A) acquired considerable reknown for the copious quantities of hops imbibed there. Shortly there arose competition that has now reached proportions so epidemic the city has the dubious, if unconfirmed, honor of sporting more nightspots per capita than any other city in the United States. Although there are now 3100 cases of beer consumed monthly at the Elbo Room's competitor, the Button, there are also some slightly more highbrow activities here, including an elegant playhouse (selected by Elizabeth Taylor for the opening run of her play *Little Foxes),* plus opera and symphony. Check area newspapers or *Key* or *See* magazines for up-to-the-minute reports on what's happening.

Opera, Theater, and Symphony

Fort Lauderdale has its own **symphony orchestra** (tel. 561-2997) which performs on a regular winter schedule at War Memorial Auditorium in Holiday Park on Sunrise Boulevard. Tickets vary in price, averaging about $20.

Parker Playhouse, at 707 NE 8th St. in Holiday Park (tel. 764-0700, or toll free 800/223-0120), offers top-name performers and tickets in the $25 range. Any seat in this elegant semicircular house is a good one, and the theater is a showplace, with a seating capacity of 1200 and long arc-shaped rows with plenty of room to find your seat without squashing yourself or someone else. Crystal chandeliers and champagne in the lobby from late November through April set the tone for appearances by such stars as Rex Harrison, Peter Ustinov, Shelley Winters, and Elizabeth Taylor.

There are rotating art shows in the Playhouse gallery, and opening nights (Tuesday) are a study in Cadillac limousines and diamonds. There are matinees on Wednesday, Saturday, and Sunday.

Top-name opera stars like Luciano Pavarotti show up here annually, usually in January, February, or March, to perform at **War Memorial Auditorium** in Holiday Park (tel. 566-9913). Tickets vary in price according to the star, but are usually sold out well in advance.

Far out in the western reaches of the county, the **Sunrise Musical Theater,** 5555 NW 95th Ave., Sunrise (tel. 741-8600), lures top musical entertainment that has in past years included everyone from Ol' Blue Eyes to Englebert Humperdinck, Donna Summer, comedian Don Rickles, Liza Minelli, Joel Grey, and

Santana. There's a wide range in price depending on the popularity of the star, but expect tickets to run $15 to $25 or more.

Surprisingly, a Fort Lauderdale church is one of the more prolific providers of concerts and classical music recitals. Scene of performances ranging from pianists performing Bach or Mendelssohn to choral productions by a 200-voice chancel choir or the Florida Philharmonic Orchestra is the **Coral Ridge Presbyterian Church,** 5555 N. Federal Hwy. You can call them at 491-1103 to find out what will be happening and when. Tickets rarely top $5.

Trendy Spots

Never a city to arrive late at a trend, Fort Lauderdale has quick-change nightspots—this month country and western, next month Glenn Miller. Two years ago a nightspot without a mechanical bull was bucking the tide. These days slick and woodsy decor heavy on brass and plants, loud but not label-able music, are so far "in" they're headed out the back. So don't hold me responsible if one of these chameleons has changed its hue.

As hysterically popular as **Shooter's** is these days, you practically need a shoehorn to wedge yourself in here. You'll know why this spot is so popular when you see its chic royal-blue trim and its slick woodsy-plantsy interior, not even to mention its waterside setting beside the Intracoastal Canal. You'll find drinking and dining (accent on the former), both inside and out. Very nice spot indeed. It's at 3031 NE 32 Ave. (tel. 566-2855), right between two other spots of considerable renown, **Durty Nelly's** and the **Bootlegger** (see Waterside Watering Spots).

In its last incarnation, **City Limits** at 2520 S. Miami Rd., Hollywood (but actually just on the edge of Fort Lauderdale city limits), was an urban cowboy's dream, complete with bull. This time around it is somewhere between disco and rock. Whatever it is when you get here, you can be sure it will have lots of decibels and plenty of action, particularly for the under-25 set. Telephone number to find out what's happening here is 524-7827.

My dear, my dear, you haven't heard of the **Candy Store**? Where have you been—Afghanistan? This little devil of a spot put itself and Fort Lauderdale on many a map when it started a trend lovingly known as the Wet T-Shirt Contest. Droves of network cameramen rolled in to record this important new leisure-time activity, thus keeping this place from going bust. You can see one of the competitions any Sunday when you'll have no trouble at all finding the Candy Store: just look for a huge crowd of goggle-eyed types hanging off the lamp-posts. It's in the Tradewinds Hotel at 1 N. Atlantic Blvd. (tel. 761-1888). Clue to the kind of crowd you'll find: The movie *Spring Break* was filmed here.

Penrod's chugs a double-decker bus up and down the highway as self-advertisement. It works! There's always a crowd here. If you'd like to join them you'll find Penrod's, which incidentally sponsors a ton of special events all year long, at 303 N. Atlantic Blvd. (tel. 763-1359), in the Sheraton Hotel.

The **Palace,** 2948 N. Federal Hwy. (tel. 556-0244), is a San Francisco–type saloon that's very popular at happy hour, and the crowd usually stays on well into the night. Bahamian conch chowder, conch salad, and Bimini bread lure bankers, stockbrokers, and secretaries, while the free raw bar on Wednesday and Friday lures everybody else. Hours are 11 a.m. to 2 a.m. daily.

Jazz fans can always find someone jammin' at **Café Exchange,** 729 W. Sunrise Blvd. (tel. 764-1912), which, although devoid of fancy atmosphere, is *the* southern Florida jazz center. Tickets are about $10 and performance hours and stars vary so give them a call.

If you see yourself as the cream that has risen far above such baser-instinct activities as wet T-shirt competitions, strut on over to **Park Avenue Club,** 3299

N. Federal Hwy., Pompano Beach (tel. 946-7841), where only class acts congregate. Here you'll find sleek fashion plates, male and female, mimicking whatever is avant-garde as they sip $5 scotches in surroundings that test the glitter of Versailles. Mirrors everywhere give you ample opportunity to admire your and other reflections as you sway on a black translucent dance floor, in a cascade of violet light shed down upon you by neon chandeliers.

Owners of this hottest of hot chic nightclubs in the area are said to have spent $1.5 million here, installing sleek decor and a superb sound system that even permits conversation. A circular clear-plastic cage called the Chandelier Room floats above the dance floor in a haze of white love seats, feathery flower arrangements, and, for high rollers, chilled champagne in a silver ice bucket. Waitresses are togged out in white long-tailed tuxedo jackets over waist-to-toe white stockings, and serve drinks encased in long-stemmed wine goblets. Dining is soon to be added, so they say, but in the meantime you pay a $5 cover charge on weekends only and drinks are $4 to $5. Hours are 9 p.m. to 4 a.m. daily.

What next? Not content with entertaining adults and college students (which quite often are two separate categories in this town), Fort Lauderdale now even has a nightclub for teenagers. It's called **Nepenthe Dance Club,** 3937 N. Federal Hwy. (tel. 564-8466), and it's open on Friday, Saturday, and holiday evenings from 7 p.m. to 1 a.m. Admission of $8 includes buffet, salad bar, sodas and juices. For four years Nepenthe was an adult nightclub, but when attendance sagged, the owners replaced the bar with fountain soft drinks, ice cream, and pizza, hired teen bartenders, rounded up a disc jockey, and created a teen hang-out of considerable elegance. So far the place has been packed every weekend by teens who come here to dance on a sunken floor amid lots of flash and glitter and to do what teenagers have always done: watch each other watching each other.

Ask Charlie O'Kelley, a regular attendee, about the **Parrot Lounge,** at 907 Sunrise Lane (tel. 563-1493), then lean back for an hour or two of lecture. He alone has introduced a small army of visitors to this very popular watering spot just a block off the beach at Sunrise Boulevard. There is *always* something going on at the Parrot, which makes up in decent-and-well-run what it lacks in chic decor. The Parrot has its own special atmosphere, however, characterized by such objets d'art as a marine recon patrol canoe paddle and an autographed mugshot of Sylvester Stallone (in Fort Lauderdale you were expecting photos of Buckminster Fuller?). The Parrot's an especially good choice for girls traveling without guys: they're so chivalrously friendly here they often walk lone lasses home in the wee hours.

A Very Special Event

If you're planning a December visit to Fort Lauderdale, try to schedule it so you're here for the city's annual **Winterfest** celebration, which usually occurs about the middle of December. A week of beauty pageants, marathon runs, beach dances, parades, and Christmas tree-lighting ceremonies is capped by the **Winterfest Boat Parade,** at which you'll discover one of the joys of visiting this always-warm city. While much of the rest of the nation shivers, you sit outside along the banks of a waterway, entertained by choral groups and ho-hoing Santas gliding by aboard massive yachts, lighted from gunwale to mainmast.

In Fort Lauderdale the boat parade has become the partying apex of the year, a time when anyone who lives on or near the waterway suddenly acquires many friends. Waterway dwellers take these newfound friendships in stride, however, and the parties go on . . . and on and on.

If you don't have or can't acquire a waterside-dwelling friend in time for the parade, book a seat at one of the waterside restaurants or lounges (many are detailed in the restaurants and nightlife sections), order something long and cool, then sit back and oooh and aah along with the rest as a fantasy of gleaming, light-trimmed yachts glides by in a glittering trail of light and laughter. Some lounges charge a cover for the evening, and every restaurant anywhere near the water is booked well in advance, so act accordingly. Among the spots you might consider settling are Stan's, the Bootlegger, Durty Nelly's, Shooter's, Harrison's on the Water, Frankie's, Le Dome of the Four Seasons, Riverwatch Restaurant at the Marriott 17th Street Hotel, Yesterday's, and Benihana of Tokyo.

Budget-watchers can achieve the same goal by heading off an hour or so before the parade (first boats leave Pier 66 just after dark; times are published in local newspapers) to pull up a piece of ground alongside the waterway. Some revelers add a touch of élan to these free seats by arming themselves with a fancy picnic dinner and a bottle of champagne! Likely watching spots are on or under the several bridges connecting the beach to the mainland: at 17th Street (where you can also buy tickets and sit in bleacher seats) or at Las Olas, Sunrise, Oakland Park, and Commercial Boulevards. Plan your sitting spot carefully, however, for bridges remain up until the last boat has putted through so you won't be able to leave until it's over if you're on the wrong side of the bridge.

Grand marshals of the parade are—who else?—Santa Claus and some other less famous celebrity. A recent GM was Williard the Weatherman, who broadcast his weather report from the city.

Waterside Watering Spots

Outdoors is where it's at, after all, and one of the tops in outdoor spots is the **Bootlegger,** at 3003 NE 32nd Ave. (tel. 563-4337), hard by the Intracoastal. This is your chance to try the one-arm crawl, with one arm clutching a martini, the other propelling you through the Bootlegger's private swimming pool. Hours are 11 a.m. to 2 a.m. daily, from noon on Sunday. Drink prices start at $2.25, with burgers and snacks available in the $3 to $5 bracket.

Durty Nelly's, next door at 3051 NE 32nd Ave. (tel. 564-0720), is more of the same without the pool. Drink outside in the sun or inside in the cool. Hours are 11 a.m. to 2 a.m. daily, Saturday to 3 a.m., opening at noon on Sunday. There's always a happy hour or ladies night, free hot dogs, or a two-fer going here. No cover, guitar music evenings. Drinks run $2.

Interesting Spots

September, 2975 N. Federal Hwy. (tel. 563-4331), attracts high rollers with mellow rock like Melissa Manchester and Neil Diamond, sometimes with funkier offerings. There's a specialty drink menu with lots of fog and flicker, plus a prepossessing woodsy decor, and a secluded setting amid greenery. Hours are 8 p.m. to 2 a.m. daily, to 3 a.m. on Saturday, with the restaurant open from 7 a.m. to 2 a.m. daily and a patio bar. Drinks begin at $3.25 and rise for more exotic concoctions.

Mai-Kai, 3599 N. Federal Hwy. (tel. 563-3272), has been in Fort Lauderdale more or less forever, enchanting the wide-eyed from Winnetka with its jungle setting and waggle-hipped Tahitian maidens whose 75-r.p.m. wiggling will show you why Bora-Bora is never boring-boring—lots of whing-a-ding specialty drinks here in the $3 to $5 range. Dare you try the mystery drink? Clue: Bring help, perhaps a litter. There are several rooms for dining, all of them buried in plants and high-backed wicker chairs. Dinner shows are at 7:30 and 10:30 p.m., plus a show at midnight. Drinks start at $3.50, rise to $7.95, and there's a $5.95 (in winter; $4.95 in summer) cover charge for the show. Dinners are in the $9 to $18 range.

Christopher's, at 2857 E. Oakland Park Blvd. (tel. 561-2136), attracts the three-piece-suit set at 5 p.m., a wild, weird, and sometimes wonderful variety of outfits later. Lots of woodsy-plantsy here, and some outstanding free hors d'oeuvres at happy hour. Drink prices run about $2. It's open from 11 a.m. to 2 a.m. daily, to 3 a.m. on Saturday.

One of the area's most talented architects, Don Duckham, designed **Montego Bay,** 80 Coral Center at Oakland Park Boulevard and Federal Highway (tel. 561-1333). A favorite with young, and slightly older, executive types, Mo Bay sports a multilevel setting with skylights, gigantic ferns, lots of wood, and intimate little nooks, plus backgammon boards—nice on a Saturday afternoon. Excellent complimentary hors d'oeuvres are served weekdays from 5 to 9 p.m. Drinks run $2.25 to $2.75 (two for one from 5 to 9 p.m.). Mo Bay is open from 11 a.m. to 2 a.m., to 3 a.m. on Saturday.

Lampshade wearers and other convivial types who are convinced their future lies in generating guffaws can see if they've got what it yuks at the **Comic Strip,** 1432 N. Federal Hwy. (tel. 565-8887), sister to New York's Comic Strip. Young comics throng in here for amateur night on Monday and bomb or score in about the same proportions as professionals. It's fun! Drinks are $2.95 and there's a $3.50 cover charge on Friday and Saturday ($2 Sunday through Thursday), and a two-drink minimum. Hours: 9:45 p.m. to 2 a.m., with shows at 9 and 11 p.m. on Saturday.

Discos

If you've got pink hair, you'll be perfect at **One-Up Lounge,** 3001 E. Oakland Park Blvd. (on the second floor of Yesterday's restaurant; tel. 561-4400), where live disco bands blast out sound and you're served by waiters from "The Force" in basic white jumpsuit and purple wig. Drinks are $2.25, there's no cover, and the lounge is open from 8 a.m. to 2 a.m. with live entertainment.

Xenon, 1421 E. Oakland Park Blvd. (tel. 565-5151), is hanging in there, reflective surfaces gleaming. Flash! Chrome! Mirror! Strobe! Cover charge: $5! Drinks: $3.50! Hours: 9 p.m. to 2 a.m., to 3 a.m. on Saturday. Party!

Shopping

Fort Lauderdale is also a popular shopping spot that offers everything from a street-full of trendy boutiques to several huge shopping centers that are home to the poshest names in fashion, jewelry, and home furnishings as well as several large department stores.

As far as I'm concerned, to begin from the top down here means you must start on lovely Las Olas (pronounced los OH-loss, it's Spanish for the waves) Boulevard, a street that has been luring wealthy boulevardiers to its treasures for generations. Whether or not you buy anything, window-shopping here is a delight, day or night.

Stretching from the ocean to Fort Lauderdale's rapidly-growing downtown center, Las Olas is a study in flickering gas lamps, stately royal palms, masses of colorful flowers, tiny picturesque alleyways, and winding canals. Fascinating shops tucked away in nooks and crannies offer everything from vintage lace dresses that would have pleased your great grandmother to the trendiest of nouveau duds.

Evenings, these boutiques are trimmed in jillions of tiny white lights. Many who come to the street's sleek restaurants to dine make an evening of it with after-dinner window-shopping and perhaps a libation in front of the fireplace in the lounge at the elegant old Riverside Hotel or with the blues singers at a Creole restaurant called Lagniappe.

As you will see in the restaurant section several of the city's best restaurants are located on this lovely boulevard—**Paesano's, Il Giardinos, Café de Paris, Lagniappe**—and now there's even a little British tea shop specializing in high tea and crumpets.

Among the most interesting of many interesting shops along Las Olas are: **La Belle Epoque,** a tiny antiques and vintage clothing shop one door north of the boulevard at 236 SE 10th Ter. (tel. 463-0881); **Mole Hole,** 713A E. Las Olas, an eclectic gift shop with some of everything; the **Chemist Shop,** a drugstore at 817 E. Las Olas where you can buy perfumes and upscale trinkets you can't find anywhere else; **Aamartin's Furs,** at 713 E. Las Olas, a drooling place for those who never met a mink they didn't love; **Maus and Hoffman,** at 800 E. Las Olas, purveyors of Scots plaids and tweedy things; **Polly Flinders,** at 1521 E. Las Olas, specializing in cut-rate prices on adorable smocked dresses for little girls.

There are many, many more—and I'm sure I'm soon going to hear from all the ones I've left out—including a wicker furniture shop, several antique stores, and a bevy of art galleries specializing in everything from art of American Indians to Old Masters and contemporary scuptures.

There's a couple of specialty tailor shops (**Mr. Anthony** at 234 SE 10th Ter., for instance), and even a shoe store that's so popular with winter residents the shop features a mail-in shoe repair service! Just send them your favorite floppers and they'll fix 'em up and send them back ready for another 20 years of dedicated service. It's called **Scottie's** and it's at 1102 E. Las Olas.

You bargain-hunters may luck into a couple of treasures on Las Olas at a little empire operated by the ladies of the First Presbyterian Church. These quite entrepreneurial ladies have painted several church-owned houses a bright can't-miss-it pink, named them, aptly enough, Pink House, and filled them with second-hand goodies and items made in church craft classes. You can find everything there from brand-new household appliances for $10 or so, to oil paintings, brocade gowns, books, cunning handcrocheted toy clowns and pin cushions. You'll find one **Pink House** at 1228 E. Las Olas, two others on the block behind with sidewalks connecting the three.

If you're a shopping center fan, you can do no better than massive **Galleria,** 2500 E. Sunrise Boulevard, just a few blocks from the ocean. Stores include such look-at-my-label names as **Neiman Marcus, Lord & Taylor, Jordan Marsh, Burdine's,** and **Saks.** Boutiques include the likes of **Bally, Laura Ashley, Yves St. Laurent, Brooks Brothers,** well you've got the picture. In addition to fancy jewelers, a candy store and a glittering shop filled with thousands of constantly polished crystal knicknacks including a huge horse's head that may be the perfect gift for a godfather friend, there are also many moderately priced shops and a raft of restaurants.

Smaller shopping centers are scattered throughout the county and include **Broward Mall,** way out west at 8000 W. Broward Blvd.; the newly enlarged **Pompano Fashion Square** north of Fort Lauderdale at 2001 N. Federal Hwy. in Pompano; and a cluster of discount shops in a warehouse district along NW 19th Street west of Fort Lauderdale in a small community called Lauderdale Lakes.

Antiques abound in nearby Dania, a village located just south of Fort Lauderdale's airport. So many antique sellers have set up shop there, in fact, that enthusiasts call the town's main street (US 1) **Antique Row.** Among the larger of those shops—and technically not in Dania but a mile or so north in Fort Lauderdale at 2075 S. Federal Hwy. (US1)—is **Jan's of London,** a shop specializing in brass-trimmed campaign furniture as well as antiques.

A VISIT TO THE "SWEET" LAND OF BLACK GOLD: Mile after mile of tall green stalks rustling in the breeze, in the air the sweet smell of—sugar!

Just 70 miles northwest of Fort Lauderdale is **Clewiston,** Florida's sugar capital and home of the largest sugar company in the nation. For miles around this city you'll see 300,000 acres of green cane stalks which are reaped from October to May to produce 7000 tons of cane and 1½ million pounds of raw sugar, about half the nation's total sugar consumption.

Here too is the Florida home of the U.S. Sugar Corp., which runs about everything in this sugar land and has made one lovely contribution to the area, the Clewiston Inn (more on that later).

From Fort Lauderdale, Miami, or any of the cities along the east coast as far north as Lake Worth, you can travel through fascinating central Florida's farmlands and sugar country on a roundabout trip that skirts **Lake Okeechobee,** the second-largest lake in the nation. Get there on US 27, which cuts straight through the heart of fishing, cattle, and farming country. (A word about US 27, however: It is a busy two-lane road where *very* alert driving is required.) You can also take Florida's Sunshine State Parkway north to the Lake Worth exit, turn west to just north of the exit, and go through the town of Loxahatchee. Either way you arrive at the edge of the lake upon whose existence most of southern Florida and the vast Everglades depends.

Just west of Fort Lauderdale on US 27 is **Everglades Holiday Park,** 21940 Griffin Rd. (tel. 434-8111), where you can rent boats for a trip into the Everglades or ride atop a whizzing airboat on a $7, ranger-guided tour of the Glades. Along the way you'll see some of the huge horned and hump-backed Brahma cattle Florida imported long ago from India when standard American-bred cattle perished from heat and insect pests. When the Brahma strain was bred into the cattle, the industry flourished and Florida is now among the top five cattle-producing states in the nation.

As you circle the lake on US 27, you will see not water but high levees, built following a disastrous hurricane in the 1920s which blew water out of the lake and over its banks, killing 2000 people in Moore Haven. You'll see several lovely parks where you can picnic or rent boats for a little journey out onto this shallow lake that's rarely more than 15 feet deep. You can also drive up onto the levee at marked entrances and park alongside branches of the lake for fishing or picnicking.

Generations ago, early pioneers hacked through the jungles here to discover heavy muckland below, the "black gold" in which they were able to raise prize-winning vegetables in winter. Now 30 varieties of vegetables are grown in the rich soil and shipped from here to winter tables. Huge farmsteads around Belle Glade and Pahokee welcome visitors to the packing houses, and in early April Belle Glade has a Black Gold Jubilee barbecue feast to celebrate the harvest.

To see the acres and acres of vegetables that end up on the nation's winter tables, hop a bus operated by **Lake Okeechobee Guided Tours** (tel. 305/996-2517) and set off on a three-hour look at this black gold muckland. Buses leave South Bay from December 1 to April 1 at 9 a.m. and 1:30 p.m. Monday through Friday.

If you turn north onto Route 78 at its junction with US 27, you can visit **Brighton Seminole Indian Reservation,** which 15 years ago was an isolated village with only dirt paths rarely used by Indians who lived out their lives on this reservation. They still live much as they did centuries ago, clinging closer to their ancient ways than other tribes. Technically the Seminoles are still at war with the U.S.—when Osceola was asked to sign away his tribe's lands, he answered by pinning the treaty to a table with his long knife.

Here too is **Indian Prairie,** called the flattest place on earth. Acre after acre, tens of thousands of them, stretch for miles dotted only by the occasional ranch house.

All along the sides of the great lake are small fishing camps which can arrange boats and guides for expeditions on the lake. Bass fishing is successful year round and you'll catch crappies from November to March, bream in summer months.

If you're a trivia collector, here's one more thing to look for as you tour this strange and fascinating area: **cabbage palms.** Clewiston produces most of the palms used in Florida churches on Palm Sunday, and for the *fresh* hearts of palm served in some Florida restaurants.

This here, y'all, is the heart of South Florida cracker country, and round these parts you're likely to meet a Glades cracker boy who's worth $10 million or thereabouts, but you'll never guess his net worth from the cut of his jeans— and he'll never tell you either. This is the land of the good ol' boy, who, as they say, ain't half bad!

If you decide to stay here, head straight for the soaring white pillars of the **Clewiston Inn,** on US 27, Clewiston, FL 33440 (tel. 813/983-8151). Tall arched windows match an imposing double-doored entrance crowned by a coach lamp, and in the reception area you're greeted by beamed ceilings, polished cypress paneling, and a fireplace around which wing chairs and couches are gathered in cozy clusters. Rooms here don't quite match the majesty of the lobby, but they're clean, neat, and one (no. 127) has a king-size bed. Doves coo in a quiet garden nearby. A dining room here seems to shift management and ideas fairly regularly, but you'll always find straightforward down-home cooking, and there's often a buffet and always very moderate prices in the under-$10 range for a full-course dinner. Rates at the inn are $40 double for bedroom or efficiency units. Suites and larger family rooms are $45. In summer, prices drop about $5. The Clewiston Inn's restaurant is open for all three meals and closes about 9 p.m. daily.

If you'd like to put some South in your mouth, don't miss a trip to **Old South Barbeque,** on US 27, Clewiston (tel. 813/983-9962), where you'll be greeted by life-size plaster cowboys shooting it out at the OK Corral and a white plaster horse staring down from an upper-story manger. Inside, every inch of Old South that doesn't have a table on it is packed with antique tools and Old West kitsch collections. A super-spicy sauce is the number one draw here, and you can even take a bottle of it home with you (for $1). There's also barbecued chicken and spare ribs, pork and beef sandwiches, thick shakes, and rib-sticking fare (in the $4.50 to $7 range). Open from 11 a.m. to 9 p.m. daily.

Chapter V

INDIAN RIVER COUNTRY

1. Orientation
2. Where to Stay
3. Where to Dine
4. Nightlife
5. Seeing the Sights
6. Sports

ONE HUNDRED MILES LONG and trimmed with sandy barrier islands that separate it from the Atlantic, this vast sapphire lagoon sparkles in the sunshine. Along its banks grow citrus that is the pride of Florida—Indian River tangeloes, mandarin and navel oranges, pink and white grapefruit, tangerines.

Courageous, adventurous settlers came to these lands only a century or so ago, but along the banks of this glittering river little seems to have changed in all those years. Tiny boats still bob at anchor, rustic piers jut into the river, an occasional sailboat streams by. Along the banks of the waterway you see the architecture of early Florida: Spanish tiles crown a roof, timbered houses with wide verandas glow white in the sunshine.

These are quiet communities, small towns, tranquil places where what doesn't get done today will surely be finished tomorrow . . . or soon. In this somnolent atmosphere it's not hard to imagine long-gone days when lights twinkled in simple pioneer cabins set amid hundreds of acres of the million-dollar pineapple crop that once grew here. It's easy to visualize two-masted schooners racing across these rippling waters, bringing clothing, groceries, and medicines to riverside homes, announcing their arrival with the deep bellow of a conch-shell horn.

In towns like Vero Beach, Fort Pierce, Jensen Beach, Sebastian, Jupiter, and Juno you won't find the glittering nightlife or the glamorous hotels of the rest of the Gold Coast, but you will see silvery mists rising off sapphire waters, an ocean sometimes flat and silver gray, sometimes booming and roaring, foaming and crashing on golden sand. Best of all, you'll find people whose welcome is as warm as their sunshine, whose love of this land runs deep.

Even the booming days of space mania didn't change these sand-fringed communities. Here, despite the tumultous influx of launch-watchers, you'll find little of the frenetic alteration that characterizes their southern Florida neighbors. That's to the credit of these small towns that have managed, in booming, bursting Florida, to retain the charm, the pervading peace, the lulling drowsiness that made them the desirable place you'll see today—and with any luck, tomorrow.

GETTING THERE: Eastern, Delta, Pan Am, People Express, Republic, Southern, TWA, United, and USAir fly into Palm Beach International Airport, and from there **Indian River Airport Limo Service** (tel. 305/334-5500) will take you to towns as far north as Vero Beach for prices beginning at about $15.

Greyhound and **Trailways** buses serve the area, as does **Amtrak,** which stops in West Palm Beach.

GETTING AROUND: You'll probably need a car to explore this area since public transportation is minimal or absent. Avis, Budget, Hertz, and National **rental-car companies** have offices in Stuart, Fort Pierce, and Vero Beach, and a number of other rental-car companies operate in Palm Beach.

Orange Blossom Coach Lines (tel. 305/783-0561) has service between Stuart, Fort Pierce, Vero Beach, Melbourne, Indialantic, Cocoa, and Cocoa Beach.

1. Orientation

Route A1A runs sporadically down the barrier islands from north of Vero Beach to St. Lucie, where it crosses to the mainland. It returns to the beach at Fort Pierce, to continue down wooded Hutchinson Island to Stuart where it returns once again to the mainland, running along the coastline to Jupiter where it joins US 1 to Palm Beach.

Meanwhile US 1 parallels the river, running north and south beside it from Vero Beach south.

Two enchanting side trips are on Route 707, also called the Beach Road, which meanders through mile after mile of towering Australian pines and jungley subtropical growth through some of the most exclusive real estate in Florida. It's one of the loveliest drives you'll find anywhere in the state, an avenue beneath spreading banyans. To reach a pretty beach at Hobe Sound, go straight ahead when Route 707 turns west (if you're traveling south, turn north when the road bends to the south).

You can pick up this same lovely road east of Stuart or at Fort Pierce and travel north or south on it along the banks of the Indian River past some elegant old mansions carefully restored by history lovers. Spot this road on your map by searching out the villages of Eldred, Walton, and Ancona.

INFORMATION: The **Vero Beach Chamber of Commerce** can be reached at 305/567-3491 or by writing P.O. Box 2947, Vero Beach, FL 32460. . . . The **Fort Pierce Chamber of Commerce** is at 2200 Virginia Ave., Fort Pierce, FL 33450 (tel. 305/461-2700). . . . The **Stuart-Martin County Chamber of Commerce**'s friendly people are on duty at 400 S. Federal Hwy., Stuart, FL 33494 (tel. 305/287-1088). . . . For **police or medical emergencies,** call 911. . . . If you'd like to rent one of the many condominium apartments on Hutchinson Island, contact **Condominium Agency,** 951 Colorado Ave., Stuart, FL 33494 (tel. 305/286-0055).

2. Where to Stay

You won't find hordes of glittering hotels in these small towns, but there are attractive, friendly spots with a ready welcome and lots of enthusiasm for their countryside. I've selected a few in several coastal towns.

VERO BEACH: Beachside hotels may cost a little more, but in this quiet seaside city built right on the sand they're worth the difference.

The **Driftwood Inn,** 3150 Ocean Dr., Vero Beach, FL 32960 (tel. 305/231-2800, or toll free 800/327-3152; in Florida, 800/432-3166), is hands down the most interesting resort in the city, and one of the most unusual hideaways in the state. Decades ago Waldo Sexton, a man fascinated with the sea, put together this resort that's built right over the sands. He filled it with everything nautical he could find—diving bells, buoys, driftwood, etc. Heaven forbid that anyone should ever try to take an inventory at this eclectic spot, where you can stay in rustic rooms with a hodge-podge of furniture and perhaps the most beautiful view of the sea on the east coast. To look at Driftwood Inn you'd think it was unlikely to remain standing another week, but it's been there for ages and ages, so don't take any bets on its longevity. As for its popularity, ask any Floridian on the east coast for his top three getaway places on the beach and the Driftwood is sure to be one of them. Beautifully old and equally rustic balconies on some of the oceanfront rooms are often a meeting spot for Floridians who sometimes take over the whole motel.

In recent years the inn has added some efficiencies and motel rooms in two wings that don't overlook the sea, and has revamped many of its quarters. Rooms here are worth the price, especially the front rooms with those weird and wonderful balconies overlooking the sea and a sunken wreck just offshore. The inn also has a small, pretty restaurant, Waldo's, and a pool. Rates are $73 to $95 from December to May, $62 to $86 in other months.

On Sunday, the **Holiday Inn Oceanside,** at 3384 Ocean Dr., Vero Beach, FL 32960 (tel. 305/231-2300, or toll free 800/238-8000), is the most popular place in town between 11 a.m. and 2 p.m. when visitors and residents alike pour into the oceanside Windswept Restaurant for a sumptuous Sunday brunch. Located right on the beach, the Holiday Inn has 104 spacious rooms, some with king-size beds, 12 with kitchens, plus four efficiencies, a coin laundry, heated pool, and a wading pond for the children. Rates range from $63 to $140 from February to May, slightly lower in the summer months.

A budget resort in the beach area is the **Crystal Sands Motel,** 1707 Route A1A, Vero Beach, FL 32963 (tel. 305/231-4284), where you'll find medium-size basically furnished rooms, a pool, a hot tub, and a laundry on shady grounds for rates ranging from $45 to $60, December 15 to April 15 (higher prices for efficiencies or one-bedroom apartments), $30 to $40 in other months.

FORT PIERCE: Holiday Inn Oceanside, 2600 Route A1A, Fort Pierce, FL 33450 (tel. 305/564-6000, or toll free 800/238-8000), once again manages to grab off the top beachside location. It's an attractive oceanfront hotel with a pool, wading pool, tennis court, dining room, and cocktail lounge. Rates from December to May are $74 to $84, dropping to $49 to $55 in other months.

If you know anything about sailing signal flags, you'll soon discover that the flags at the **Dockside Inn,** 1152 Seaway Dr., Fort Pierce, FL 33450 (tel. 305/461-4824), spell R-E-L-A-X. Even if you don't read the language of the sea you'll soon get the message at the Dockside, where friendly Nick and Evelyn Guardalabene run an informal, easy-going ship which is indeed dockside, with a long pier you can use for fishing or docking a boat. Fishing's the major sport around here, and signs on the Dockside's wall tell you about the kinds of fish you'll most likely catch at dockside or on local charter trips. Although not on the beach, the motel is on the waters of Fort Pierce Inlet. Two blocks away are miles of Atlantic beach sand where you can shell, snorkel, and scuba-dive. You might even find a gold doubloon as other lucky sea searchers have done here.

Lots of wood trim gives the Dockside a contemporary look, and it's a popular place for young families who relax poolside while the kids keep busy splashing or fishing. Rooms are furnished in homey basic beach, with wall-to-wall carpeting and sturdy furniture. Rates from mid-December to mid-April peak at $31 to $42 for a motel room, $33 to $44 for a studio or one-bedroom apartment. In summer, those rates are a bit lower, and even cheaper by the week.

PORT ST. LUCIE: About ten miles west of the ocean and seven miles north of Stuart in the village of Port St. Lucie you'll find another lush golfing and tennis resort, **Sandpiper Bay,** Port St. Lucie, FL 33450 (tel. 305/334-4400, or toll free 800/327-7003; in Florida, 800/432-5415). The Sandpiper occupies an attractive setting along the St. Lucie River and has everything you could ask for in a small city, let alone a resort. If you want golf, there are 45 holes of championship play. If you want tennis, you get 11 lighted tennis courts. If you want water sports, there are two pools, a marina with rental sailboats, pedal boats, and motor skiffs, fishing, and it's only a ten-minute drive from the ocean. If you want games, you get everything from Ping-Pong to basketball.

Every night there's entertainment in the resort's handsome lounges. At any time of day the restaurants will provide everything from a hamburger to a five-course dinner. You can rent a car here, practice on a driving range and putting green, bone up at golf and tennis clinics, lounge in a whirlpool. When you're finally exhausted, you can enjoy the resort's junior suites which have private dressing areas, refrigerators, and hotplates, lots of space to roam around, and a handsome contemporary decor. Two people will pay $120 to $130 a day in peak winter season, $65 to $70 a day in summer and fall.

HUTCHINSON ISLAND: A prime-time resort is sprawling **Indian River Plantation,** 385 NE Plantation Rd., Hutchinson Island, FL 33494 (tel. 305/225-3700, or toll free 800/327-4873), a magnificent condominium resort four miles north of Stuart on Route A1A. Miles of rolling golf courses line the entrance to this tranquil resort. Scattered among ponds and winding lagoons are clusters of wooded villas. Posh condominiums are tucked away among the greens. On the ocean, Plantation House Hotel's apartments welcome you with big beautiful rooms decorated in contemporary hues, balconies overlooking the sea, and big apartments that accommodate four or six. Some of the attractive rooms have king-size beds and all have big closets, comfortable chairs, and lots of extra touches designed to make you feel special. A friendly staff adds to that. There are three heated pools, charter boats, two tennis courts at the hotel and more scattered about the resort, rental boats from canoes to sailboats, fishing guides, miles and miles of deserted unspoiled beach, an 18-hole executive golf course, bicycling, and waterskiing.

When you hunger and thirst, head for the Back Porch Lounge, a woodsy spot filled with plants, or the Inlet restaurant, where you dine on excellent beef and seafood dishes in the $10 to $20 price range. For the children there are special events, games, and an activities department to plan their day.

No doubt about it, Indian River Plantation is a lovely place for those who like getaway vacations far (but not too far) from crowds. Rates for oceanfront apartments are $140 to $160 for a one-bedroom apartment, $180 to $200 for two bedrooms in peak season ($65 to $85 from May to mid-June). Tennis villas begin at $150 in peak season, $120 in other months. Weekly rates are available year round, and are *very* good bargains.

JENSEN BEACH: River's Edge, 2625 NE Indian River Dr., Jensen Beach, FL

33457 (tel. 305/334-4759), overlooks the river and has a nice rustic look; brown wood trims a two-story building. Simple but clean rooms are on lovely grounds, and there's that gorgeous strip of wide river to gaze upon in idle hours. It's one of the few motels in the area that's actually on the river's edge (not across the road from the water), and has a pool. Rates are $30 to $32 from May to December, $45 to $50 in winter.

JUPITER: **Jupiter Beach Hilton,** Indiantown Road and Route A1A, Jupiter, FL 33458 (tel. 305/746-2511, or toll free 800/821-8791; in Florida, 800/432-1420), is one of the star resorts of this star-studded Indian River coastline. These days it's more starstruck than ever, following a multi-million-dollar, top-to-toe renovation. Rooms now feature pretty cotton prints in blues, greens, corals, and yellows, handsome cornice moldings atop print curtains, and lots of typically Floridian furniture from raffia to rattan and wickers.

The Jupiter Hilton likes to say it's 20 minutes—and 20 years—from Palm Beach, and that description of this easy-going, seaside resort seems pretty accurate to me. Here you can doff the Guccis and stroll barefoot across the dunes. You can dine at the new ocean-view Sinclair's American Grill where fresh fish, seafood, and meat are prepared on wood-burning convection grills, whole fish and poultry cooked on French rôtisseries. You can sample the chef's Keys-inspired cuisine, things like conch chowder and black bean soup, fresh breads and pastries, and yummy sauces prepared with herbs grown right on the grounds.

A Barefoot Bar poolside beckons after a long day of windsurfing, sailing, or romping about the tennis courts. If you're here in late June or July you'll see marine biologists releasing baby turtles raised under the watchful eye of scientists who operate a carefully guarded hatchery here. Best of all, the Burt Reynolds Jupiter Theater (yes, *the* Burt Reynolds) is just across the street.

In winter months, double rooms at the Hilton begin at $95 on the west side of the building, rising to $105 to $185 for ocean views. From May to December, double rates fall to $65 to $110.

READER'S TIP: "In summer the **Jupiter Hilton** has some money-saving packages that include a room for two or three days plus tickets to the Burt Reynolds Jupiter Theater. When I stopped by the Hilton and asked for a price list, I discovered I could have gotten a room there—one not facing the ocean—for just a few dollars more than I paid at another hotel in the area that wasn't on the beach. Just ask for prices on rooms that don't face the beach" (Jerry Schultz, Boynton Beach, Fla.).

PORT SALERNO: If you're interested in fishing, boating, or diving, and don't mind not being right on the beach, a real find is the newly redecorated **Manatee Resort Motel,** P.O. Box K, Route A1A, Port Salerno, FL 33492 (tel. 305/283-4112). This tiny village north of Jupiter and just south of Stuart is one of those don't-shut-your-eyes-or-you'll-miss-it places. Don't miss it! New owners have refurbished this property whisker to flipper, and have done a beautiful job. Rough pine paneling adds a woodsy contemporary touch to the rooms, which have two double beds and lots of space, big closets, and tiled baths. Clean and handsome, these two-story accommodations overlook the resort's wood-decked pool rimmed by lattice fencing. Right next door is the marina, and Manatee has several cottages there too. It's a bit off the beaten track, but Manatee is every bit as attractive as its prices—rooms are $40 to $45 in winter, $25 to $32 in summer. Cottages range from $40 to $70 in winter, and all accommodations are cheaper by the week. The friendly management at this very modern and attractive spot can help you arrange boating, fishing, and diving expeditions, and if you happen to have your own boat along, dock it at the marina and stop in at the resort's small restaurant for some fresh seafood treats.

CAMPING: There are parks and campgrounds scattered throughout the area, but **Jonathan Dickinson State Park,** 14800 SE Federal Hwy., Hobe Sound, FL 33459, is the largest and prettiest, covering more than 10,280 acres of dense pine forests. Named after the courageous leader of a shipwrecked group, the park is a beautiful place that spreads out along US 1 over miles and miles of rolling dunes that give you an idea how this coastline must have looked when those first pioneers arrived. As a state park, it charges only 50¢ admission per person, $7 to $10 for campsites. It's often very crowded in summer, so camping reservations are a must. Call 305/546-2771 to book space. You can rent a cottage here too (bring your own linens), for $35 a night, $200 a week. Call 305/764-5804 for cottage reservations. There's swimming, boating, fishing, horseback riding, picnicking, and cruises on the Loxahatchee River—or rent a canoe for $5 an hour and paddle your own cruise.

Farther north, **Sebastian Inlet State Recreation Area** is on a barrier island with a lagoon, coastal hammock, and mangroves tucked away behind the beach and dunes. You can camp, picnic, swim, birdwatch, fish, scuba-dive, and surf on three miles of sandy beaches. It's about 20 miles north of Vero Beach on Route A1A.

3. Where to Dine

Floridians drive for miles to have dinner at Vero Beach's Ocean Grill, and at that city's P. V. Martin's you dine among the sea oats on a long strip of deserted beach. I've picked a few favorites in cities along this coastline and grouped them by location. Remember that the prices I've cited are for entrees, but this usually includes one or two vegetables, salad, and perhaps coffee as well.

VERO BEACH: Sea oats bend pliantly in the sea breezes and waves lap the shore around you at **P. V. Martin's,** Route A1A south of Vero Beach (tel. 465-7300 or 569-0700), an enchanting wood-trimmed restaurant sitting alone on a long, long strip of unpopulated beach. Contemporary furnishings and banks of windows overlooking the sea are softened by hanging greenery and a warm, cozy atmosphere engendered at least in part by friendly, helpful servers. From the raw bar, try snow crab claws, clams Casino, or a seafood platter. Follow that with crisp salads and excellent regional seafood concoctions or steaks and beef, for prices in the $10 to $15 range. Additional offerings are honey-wheat bread and rice pilaf. Open 5 p.m. to midnight daily.

People (and I admit to being one of them) think nothing of driving two or three hours for dinner at **Ocean Grill,** at Sexton Plaza, Route 60 at the ocean (tel. 231-5409), a dining institution on this beach for generations. Start with something cool at the bar where you gaze through a wall of windows at a sunken wreck just offshore and watch the waves roll endlessly in. Ask for a table in the back room overlooking the ocean and you'll dine in a rustic atmosphere, softened by the glow of candlelight. Try fresh seafood (coquilles St. Jacques is a top favorite here), or excellent steaks, all served with crisp salads, fresh hot breads, and a smile. Prices at Ocean Grill are in the $10 to $15 range, and the restaurant is open from noon to 2:30 p.m. and 6 to 10 p.m. Monday through Saturday; on Sunday, from 5 to 9:30 p.m.

You can't beat **Houlihan's,** 398 21st St. (tel. 569-1522), for great munchies, things like potato skins with cheddar cheese, mini nachos, zucchini sticks, and one I've yet to try called Portuguese stuffies. In summer under the cool breeze of paddle fans the restaurant gets hot on cold salad platters, a crispy cool way to beat the heat. On Saturday night the specialty is lobster tails, but you'll also find lots of quiches here, prime rib, grouper, barbecued baby back ribs for dinner, fresh fruits, vegetables, and coffee ground fresh daily. Breads, soups, and desserts are all made right here each day too. Prices are in the $10 range, and the restaurant's open from 11 a.m. to 1 a.m. daily.

A recently opened place in town is **Restaurant Forty One,** at 41 Royal Palm Blvd. (tel. 562-1141), where you'll dine under a high-beamed ceiling amid pretty paintings and a California–South Seas atmosphere with wicker touches and contemporary furnishings. There's a wide variety of salads, soups, fish, beef, and chicken to choose from, all of it with the accent on French preparation. Prices are in the $15 to $20 range. Open from noon to 2:30 p.m. for lunch Monday to Friday, for dinner nightly from 6 to 10:30 p.m.

Monti's, 1517 S. Ocean Dr. (tel. 231-6612), cooks up more than 80 entrees to feed those who never met a strand of spaghetti they didn't love. Italian flavors predominate here, but there are a few steaks and chops on the menu to tempt those who aren't pleased by baked ziti, rigatoni Bolognese, fettuccine Alfredo, veal Francese, and the like. Monti's is open from 5 to 10 p.m. daily, and prices are in the $6 to $13 range.

The Menu, 1571 S. Ocean Dr. (tel. 231-4614), is a very, very popular place in this city by the sea. With the ocean just a breath away, it figures that seafood is the specialty of the house, and you'll find many unusual selections here, including cobia and pompano. Those who don't favor finny fare will be happy here too, however: much of the menu at The Menu is devoted to New York strip steaks, pork chops, ham steak, roast leg of lamb, and chicken—all of it in a reasonable $10 to $15 price range. Hours are 5 to 10 p.m. daily.

Forty-One, 41 Royal Palm Blvd. (tel. 562-1141), is one of the most beautiful dining rooms in the region, a quiet, elegant spot of shining crystal, impeccable linens, and glowing candlelight. Prices are on the high side for Vero Beach, which has quite a number of restaurants in lower price brackets, but this restaurant's elegance and contemporary simplicity are worth every dollar. Forty-One is open from 11:30 a.m. to 2:30 p.m. and 5 to 10 p.m. daily in winter, but drops Sunday lunch in the summer months. French cuisine predominates, and although beef, chicken, and veal preparations are numerous, marvelously herbed and sauced seafood is a specialty. You'll pay $15 to $20 for entrees, which also include salad and vegetable.

Waldo's, in the Driftwood Inn, 3150 Ocean Dr. (tel. 231-2800), is another favorite hereabouts. There are, in fact, some very knowledgeable folks who swear that Waldo's has the best steaks in town at the most reasonable prices. Quite a pretty place, featuring lots of plants and plenty of the bric-a-brac that has made the Driftwood Inn famous in Florida, Waldo's serves all three meals, opening at 7:30 a.m. and closing at 10 p.m. You'll pay about $8 to $13 for good steaks and seafood, barbecued ribs, and salads.

Skip Wright's, US 1 South (tel. 562-9832), is quite a popular local steakhouse. On the menu are filet mignon, New York strip, T-bone, and Porterhouse, even a sirloin steak for two. You can team any of those with seafood as well. Prices are $13 to $15 for steaks, including salad and steak fries. Wright's is open from 5 to 10 p.m. Tuesday through Saturday, but is closed for the month of September. Wright's also sometimes closes one other day a week, so a call first is wise.

FORT PIERCE: A massive fireplace and pecky cedar paneling set the tone for the **Ocean Village Inn,** 2400 S. Ocean Dr. (tel. 461-8822), where every table has a smashing view of the ocean rolling into this quiet strip of island sand. French touches pepper the continental cuisine, for which you'll pay $10 to $15, and the restaurant is open for lunch from 11:30 a.m. to 2:30 p.m. daily (except Sunday), and from 5:30 to 10 p.m. for dinner daily. A sumptuous Sunday brunch begins at 11:30 a.m. and runs to 2:30 p.m.

Hilltop House, 4000 N. US 1 (tel. 465-2125), is perched up on what Floridians like to call a hill and features quite a lovely view over the Fort Pierce Inlet. Hilltop House wins converts with its fresh vegetables and pays such close attention to detail that they even bone their own meat. A really top spot—literally and figuratively—along this central east coast, Hilltop House charges dinner prices in the $10 to $15 range for entrees, and is open Monday through Saturday from 11 a.m. to 10 p.m., on Sunday from noon to 9 p.m.

STUART: **Benihana of Tokyo**'s familiar blue-tiled roof pops up here in Stuart at 2 Ocean Blvd. (tel. 286-0740). Plop your shoes on a rack and step into the lounge for an unshod cool one, Japanese style. Later, dine at long tables where a talented Japanese cook performs magic with shrimp and steak, and some pretty fancy fingerwork with the huge salt and pepper shakers they toss nonchalantly into the air as they cook. Benihana's been phenomenally successful in Florida (and everywhere else), so you can count on excellent Japanese preparation of foods that seem only slightly exotic to American tastes. Figure about $15 to $20 for dinner. Benihana is sizzling from 5 to 10 p.m. for dinner nightly.

HUTCHINSON ISLAND: At **Indian River Plantation** (see my hotel recommendations), 385 NE Plantation Rd. (tel. 225-3700), you dine amid lots of pretty greenery or in an elegant dining room with black-tie service. At the Porch, go casual for lunch, and feast on the chicken hawaiian, a chicken salad garnished with fresh pineapple, or sole on a roll for $5 or so. Evenings, dress up a bit and head for the Inlet, a lovely tranquil restaurant. Start with poached artichokes and work your way through oysters walterspiel, lightly battered and served with a béarnaise sauce, or shrimp stuffed with crabmeat and Monterey Jack cheese, and finish with a salad and home-baked bread. Plan on a long walk through the grounds later. Entrees are in the $12 to $17 range, and the Inlet is open from 5 to 9 p.m. daily; the Porch, from 7 a.m. to 9:30 p.m. with a Sunday brunch from 10 a.m. to 2 p.m.

READER'S RESTAURANT SELECTION—JUPITER: "**Harpoon Louie's,** 105 Route A1A, Jupiter (tel. 747-2666), is a really nice place to go for cocktails or for dinner. There's a deck that goes right out to the water and you can eat outside or inside. They specialize in seafood and steaks. Prices are about $10 to $15" (Jerry Schultz, Boynton Beach, Fla.). [*Author's Note:* Harpoon Louie's is open to 10 p.m. and has become very, very popular so you are likely to have to wait for a table at favorite dining hours and on weekends. Entrance to Harpoon Louie's is just off US 1 at the first intersection south of the bridge. The restaurant is directly across from the lighthouse on Jupiter Inlet.]

JENSEN BEACH: Look for the Tiki gods in Jensen and you'll be at **Frances Langford's Outrigger** restaurant, at 1405 NE Indian River Dr. (tel. 287-2411), where you're greeted by an elaborate Polynesian longhouse facade complete with thatched roof and ornate straw work. A tiny fountain gurgles into a small lagoon at the entrance, and multitudes of pink, red, rose, fuchsia, and yellow flowers bloom among the greenery. Inside is more of the same very showy decor, with high-backed wicker chairs, Tiki gods, and lots of South Seas touches. Set picturesquely on the riverfront, Frances Langford's is named after a famous pop singer of the 1940s who lured crowds of her friends here in days gone by. You won't be consigned to moo goo gai pan or the like. Instead you'll find a wide range of steaks and seafood prepared in ways familiar to Americans, although enough exotic specialties like shrimp with Outrigger sauce emerge from the kitchen to please more adventurous diners. Closed on Monday, the Outrigger is open from noon to 3 p.m. and 6 to 10 p.m. Tuesday through Saturday and from 1 to 9 p.m. on Sunday.

What many people don't realize is that Langford's also offers several accommodations. One-, two-, and three-bedroom villas have a kitchen and dining room area, and a screened porch. Prices range from $70 to $105 a night in winter, $40 to $65 in summer.

Foxfire Inn, 54 E. Ocean Blvd. (tel. 286-3457), has good straightforward beef and seafood dishes served in an attractive intimate atmosphere. You can start here with a Caesar salad prepared at your table, or an appetizer of fresh vegetables like broccoli, cauliflower, carrots, and asparagus with an accompanying sauce. There's always prime rib on the menu, and seafood platters with lobster, bay scallops, shrimp, crab legs, fish, and vegetables (this is one of the rare places that also serves a vegetable platter). Entree prices average about $10 to $15, with the seafood special and platter at $16. Your bill's likely to be in the $20 to $25 bracket here if you indulge. It's open from 11:30 a.m. to 2:30 p.m. and again at 6 p.m. for dinner every day but Sunday.

4. Nightlife

I did mention that this is a quiet region of the state, didn't I? Well, believe me and don't expect ring-a-ding.

Top of the line in evening entertainment is the **Burt Reynolds Jupiter Theater,** 1001 Indiantown Rd., Jupiter (tel. 305/746-5566), which presents excellent plays all year round with star performers the likes of Farah Fawcett, Sally Fields, and well, just lots of Burt's friends who traipse on down for a little R&R and put on some smashing performances while they're at it. You can count on a good time at the theater, and a good dinner (or brunch) too. Check local newspapers to see what's playing. Prices begin at $26 for Wednesday and Saturday matinees with a buffet served at 11:30 a.m., and rise to $29 for a Sunday champagne brunch at noon or Tuesday, Wednesday, and Thursday evening performances, $31 on Friday and Saturday. The theater's quite near the Jupiter Hilton Hotel.

The **Musicana Dinner Theater,** in the Sheraton Regency, 4700 Route A1A (tel. 305/231-1600) in Vero Beach, has taken the state by storm. There are now several Musicanas (one just south of Cocoa Beach and one in West Palm) featuring rollicking family entertainment provided by college music students getting in step for the big time. You'll have lots of fun here, and a good prime rib or seafood dinner and salad bar. The restaurant opens at 6 p.m. Tuesday through Saturday, and shows are 90 minutes long. Prices are $20 for dinner and the show.

For general quiet entertainment in Vero Beach, try the Holiday Inn's **Windswept Lounge,** in Village South at 2900 Ocean Dr. (tel. 569-2727)—backgammon boards and a pubby atmosphere with guitar music from 9 p.m. Monday through Saturday; or **Houlihan's,** at 398 21st St. (tel. 569-1522), is a favorite socializing spot, open Monday through Saturday to 1 a.m.

In Fort Pierce, **Teaser's Lounge** in the Holiday Inn Oceanside, 2600 Route A1A (tel. 465-6000), is a hot spot that's recently been decorated and features a split-level lounge overlooking the dance floor and bands for entertainment. It opens at 8 p.m. every day but Sunday.

Comfortable leather chairs and a rustic setting make the **Ocean Village Inn** a nice evening retreat. It's on the oceanfront at Ocean Village, 2400 S. Ocean Dr. (tel. 461-8822).

Village South, 2900 Ocean Dr. in Vero Beach (tel. 231-2727), has a pretty, old-worldly atmosphere livened up by the crowds who drop in here for happy hour sipping and stay on long after that. Happy hour here is popular because, so rumor has it, the size of the drinks increases as the price decreases.

Marvin Gardens—yes, it's a Monopoly theme—is often a madhouse, but it's particularly crazy when the lounge features its happy hour free dinner buffet loaded with roast beef, spare ribs, duck, vegetables. Crowds fill the interior of this woodsy spot first, then the overflow gets pushed out onto a huge outdoor deck. Join them at 3030 N. US 1, Vero Beach (tel. 567-3939).

Indian River Players, 633 Harvey Ogden Dr., Melbourne (tel. 723-1668), has regular performances throughout the year, as does the **Riverside Theatre**, in the Civic Arts Center, Belchland Boulevard in Vero Beach (tel. 231-6990).

Ocean Village Inn, 2400 S. Ocean Dr. (Route A1A), Hutchinson Island, attracts high-society tourists and the local upper crust, who roll in here at happy hour to enjoy sensational views over the Atlantic. Many stay on long after night has blackened the view.

5. Seeing the Sights

Cruise the Indian River and imagine yourself a pioneer struggling to raise pineapples on its shores, or prowl among Seminole artifacts in a historical museum.

Let's start with a scenic journey up the Indian and St. Lucie Rivers aboard **Hy-Line** (tel. 287-7227), which has several different cruise programs: past Stuart's waterfront and some beautiful homes, and up the St. Lucie to Lake Okeechobee. The M/V *East Chop* is in port on US 1 just north of the Roosevelt Bridge in Stuart from the end of November to mid-May. Cruises range in price from $5 for shorter journeys to $16 (including lunch) for the Lake Okeechobee sojourn. The boat's a double-decker with an open upper deck.

The **St. Lucie County Historical Museum**, at 414 Seaway Dr. in Fort Pierce (tel. 464-6635), displays Seminole Indian artifacts as part of an interesting study of the area's Indian heritage (the fort was an outpost during the Seminole Wars in the 1800s). Admission is free and it's open from 10 a.m. to 4 p.m. Wednesday through Saturday.

Sail the waters of Indian River aboard the *Vero Princess,* which goes on one-hour tours of the Indian River at 5 p.m. daily during the summer months, twice a day in the winter. It's docked at the **Vero Beach Marine Center,** 12 Royal Palm Blvd. (tel. 562-7922), from November to April, and cruises are $7.

Hutchinson Island is a thing to see all by itself. Miles and miles of untenanted jungle will give you an idea how these barrier islands looked to the pirates and pioneers who settled here.

On Hutchinson Island, at 825 NE Ocean Dr., is **Gilbert's Bar House of Refuge** (tel. 225-1875). Built in 1875, it was once a haven for shipwrecked sailors. Out of six similar dwellings that stood along this once-deserted coastline, it is the only one remaining. It is believed to have been named after a notorious pirate. It's open from 1 p.m. to 4:15 p.m. Tuesday through Sunday; closed holidays. Admission is 75¢ for adults and 25¢ for children.

One mile north, **Elliott Museum** (tel. 225-1961) houses an amazing collection of antique automobiles, including a 1953 Cunningham, a 1907 Maxwell, a Stanley Steamer, a Stutz Bearcat, a 1922 Rolls-Royce Pall Mall Phantom, and many others, plus an American collection ranging from a Seminole chickee home to a collection of shells and a group of Salem, Mass., shops brought here for display. Open 1 to 5 p.m. daily, the museum charges $1.50 for adults and 50¢ for children 6 to 13.

In June, Jensen Beach has a **"Turtle Watch" week** when you can see the giant reptiles lumber ashore, dig a hole in the sand with their huge flippers, and lay their eggs. You can watch, but don't disturb the turtles or their nests, which are guarded by the state. Later in summer you can see the baby turtles making their way to the ocean as they hatch and find their sea legs.

6. Sports

Among several golf courses in the area are the **Indian Hills Golf and Country Club,** 1607 S. 3rd St. in Fort Pierce (tel. 465-8110), and **Dodger Pines Golf Club,** 4600 26th St. in Vero Beach (tel. 569-4400). Both have 18 holes and are public or semiprivate courses. Greens fees are $8 to $10.

Tennis players will find eight courts at **Lawnwood Tennis Complex and Recreation Center,** at Virginia Avenue and 13th Street in Fort Pierce and 12 courts scattered about St. Lucie County. The Lawnwood courts (tel. 464-1777) are free days and $1 an hour at night. **Memorial Island,** on Mockingbird Drive (tel. 231-4787), has ten courts and costs $2 per hour per person.

There's jai-alai at **Fort Pierce Jai-Alai,** on Kings Highway, one mile north of Exit 56 on the Florida Turnpike (tel. 464-7500, or toll free 800/432-6147), from March to the end of September with games at 7 p.m. on Monday, Wednesday, Friday, and Saturday, plus matinees at noon on Wednesday and Saturday. Admission is from $1.

You can see the **Los Angeles Dodgers** play in Vero Beach during their winter training camp from February to April here at DodgerTown, 4001 26th St. (tel. 569-4900). Games are about $5.

This is one of the state's best **fishing** regions both in the ocean and in rivers throughout the area. Stuart, in fact, likes to call itself the "Sailfish Capital of the World." There's a four-day tournament in December during which anglers try to catch the sail-finned beauties with light tackle. To prove they really do bring in the big ones, the **Stuart Sailfish Club**'s record is a 477-pound blue marlin, among many others that didn't get away! Get information on sailfishing in the area from the club at P.O. Box 2005, Stuart, FL 33495, or call 305/286-9373.

A number of **fishing boats** are tied up at the Chamber of Commerce Dock in Stuart. Try the *Ondine* (tel. 287-1599) or the *Golden Falcon* (tel. 287-6014). In Jupiter, try **Florida Sport Fishing Service,** 825 W. Center St. (tel. 305/746-1150), for fishing reservations and information.

Charter boats charge about $400 a day, $300 a half day, for four people.

Chapter VI

ORLANDO AND CENTRAL FLORIDA

1. Orientation
2. Where to Stay
3. Where to Dine
4. Meeting the Mouse
5. Other Adventures
6. Nightlife
7. Sports
8. Shopping
9. Side Trips Around Central Florida
10. Cape Canaveral/Kennedy Space Center

WHO COULD FORGET little curly-haired Annette Funicello, black plastic mouse ears firmly in place, belting out M-I-C, K-E-Y, M-O-U-S-E?

Let me be the first to tell you that no one in Orlando forgets it. Not for a minute do they forget that Mickey is the mouse who roared his way through central Florida turning boondock to boomtown faster than you can say M-I-C-K-E-Y.

This dear little creature with the black plastic ears and the dragging tail is the mouse that brought millions here, who turned cow pasture into city and some of the meek into millionaires. "I have a little shrine in my bedroom," says one now-prosperous hotelier. "Every morning I get up, pull open the little drapes on the shrine, and kiss Mickey's feet."

Mickey is everywhere here. He's the phone on the desk of a sophisticated hotel executive, the base of many a lamp, center of nearly every T-shirt in town, icon of a city gambling its future on Mickey's black nose.

Not everyone, however, shares this slavish adoration of the black-eared figment of Walt Disney's fertile imagination. Legion is the competition for the attention (and let's face it, the dollars) of tourists who flood through the Disney gates, sometimes at the rate of 80,000 a *day*. So much competition has arisen in fact that the Orlando Chamber of Commerce, which once said you could see it all in three days, now suggests you're likely to need a week or more!

You'll certainly want to take time to see the world's heftiest ballet star, sweet Shamu. He's four tons of fun performing a graceful pirouette on his enormous tail and even planting a gentle (if somewhat damp) kiss on your waiting cheek during his daily shows at Sea World, Orlando's water wonderland. You'll want to see the hijinks and high-wire stars under the big top of Circus World, and wander along the shimmering waters of serene Cypress Gardens where the perfume of roses permeates the air. You'll want to roll across acre after acre of golden and orange citrus nestled in undulating waves of shining emerald leaves that ebb and flow across miles of silver sand dotted with gleaming sapphire lakes.

You'll need time to explore the byways and backroads in the cowboy town of Kissimmee (you pronounce it Kih-*sim*-ee). Once the "good hunting grounds" of the Calusa Indians, Kissimmee later became home to a passel of cowpunchers who roamed these sandy ranges, then rode right up to the bar to drink without dismounting. They still ride these ranges, herd hump-backed Brahma bulls, and show off their skills in one of the state's biggest rodeos.

In Orlando's suburbs you'll find enchanting villages like quaint Mount Dora. It is built on the edges of a limestone bluff and looks as much like New England as New England. You can visit a settlement where Floridians have their holiday greetings postmarked—Christmas, Florida! And don't miss the small city of Winter Park, one of the state's loveliest villages, a serene retreat so perfectly primped and painted it's called "Little Europe." It is also the home of the world's largest collection of priceless Tiffany glass. If you love horses you'll adore the horsey village of Ocala, birthplace of champions.

It's all part of central Florida, the land of grapefruit and Goofy, fast-paced fantasy and serene sandy flatlands, lush emerald forests, glowing golden blossoms, and glittering blue lakes. It's a land that loves children and the child in us all, that welcomes you with a grin, cares for you with casual sophistication, and sends even the most jaded away wide-eyed in wonderment—a magic kingdom indeed.

1. Orientation

GETTING THERE: Airlines flying into Orlando include American, Continental, Delta, Eastern, Florida Express, Frontier Horizons, New York Air, Northwest, Ozark, Pan Am, Piedmont, Republic, TWA, USAir, and United.

Greyhound and **Trailways** buses have service from all over the state and nation. Greyhound Lines stops here at 300 W. Amelia St. (tel. 843-0344); Trailways is at 30 N. Hughey Ave. (tel. 422-7107).

American International Sightseeing and a number of other tour companies have tour packages from wherever you're staying in Florida.

Amtrak has a regular schedule of train service to the area—Kissimmee is the official Walt Disney World stop. Amtrak's Auto-Train is back on track again, offering you the convenience of a car in Florida without any of the inconvenience of driving it there. Operated by Amtrak, Auto-Train begins at Lorton, Virginia, and ends at Sanford, Florida, about 23 miles from Orlando. You drive your car aboard in Lorton (which is about a four-hour drive from New York, about two from Philadelphia), and then you settle into a coach seat or bedroom and the next morning at 9:30 a.m. you roll into the station at Sanford. Cost of this simple way to avoid about 850 miles of driving is $130 per adult plus $200 for the car ($225 extra per couple for a bedroom compartment). Auto-Train leaves either Lorton or Sanford at 4:30 p.m., arriving at its destination at 9:30 a.m. the next morning. Departures from Lorton are on Monday, Wednesday, and Friday; from Sanford, on Tuesday, Thursday, and Saturday.

GETTING AROUND: Every national **rental-car agency** has offices in Orlando, and dozens of smaller rental-car companies operate here as well. National is the official Walt Disney World rental-car agency, and Alamo offers inexpensive rates throughout Florida and lets you drop the car off anywhere in the state without extra charges.

From Airport to Hotel

Airport Limousine Service (tel. 859-4667 in Orlando, 933-1808 in Kissimmee) operates airport limousine service to area hotels and has a ticket counter at the baggage claim area of the Orlando International Airport. You'll find the limousines (actually 11-passenger vans), outside the terminal building on the second floor. Prices range from about $8 to $17 for a one-way ride to hotels, depending on how far you're going. Children's fares are half price and you can save a dollar or two by buying a round-trip ticket at the airport.

Some hotels have **free shuttle service** from the airport. You can even call many of them free on telephones you'll find near the baggage claim area.

American Sightseeing Tours now operates regular **bus service** from the airport to hotels. Buses leave from both sides of the second floor of the terminal every 45 minutes around the clock. It takes about 45 minutes to get to Walt Disney World area hotels. Fares are $6 to $7 for adults, $3 to $3.50 for children, depending on where you're going. You can save about $1 on each ticket by buying a round trip.

If you'd like to arrive in style, **Prestige Limos,** 1523 Pine St. (tel. 855-0442), has a booking booth at the luggage pickup area too and will bring a Cadillac limousine around for you. Rates are about $4 higher than taxi fares and run from about $25 to $30 for most destinations. If there are enough of you traveling together, you might even save money.

For a taxi, try **Yellow Cab** (tel. 422-4455 in Orlando, 847-2222 in Kissimmee), which charges $1.20 a mile for the 15-mile trip.

Travel Around the Area

Distances are great in the sprawling central Florida flatlands, so don't expect to drop into Sea World then walk over to Disney—it's miles just from Disney's first entrance sign to the parking lot! If you're planning to sample some of the area's great dining and lively nightlife, you'd be wise to rent a car since taxi fares over the distances here can be enormous, and public transportation isn't good after park closing hours.

To get to the attractions, however, you can rely on a variety of shuttle systems and tour buses that operate in the area.

Rabbit Bus (tel. 291-2424) rolls the road from International Drive and US 192 in Kissimmee to Walt Disney World, and has trips to Sea World, Circus World, Lake Buena Vista shopping center and the Altamonte Mall. Buses pick you up at US 192 motels and campgrounds east of the Florida Turnpike or on International Drive, and take you to any of those attractions for $5 round trip, $2.50 for children. They also go to Cypress Gardens, Kennedy Space Center, and Busch Gardens for $20 to $30 including admissions, about half that for children.

In Lake Buena Vista, home of eight large hotels, **shuttle buses** operate on an every-15-minute schedule. They pick up passengers at all hotels and take them to the entrance to the Magic Kingdom and EPCOT. Buses are free to hotel guests who simply display a pass issued by their hotel. Flags painted on the sides of the buses identify where they're going. Buses operate from 8 a.m. to 2 a.m., so you can take in the nightlife at Walt Disney World and in the WDW Shopping Village.

Gray Line (tel. 422-0744) operates most of what moves on wheels in Orlando. The line's big bruisers ply constantly between attractions and area hotels. You can shuttle to Sea World or Walt Disney World for $6 round trip ($4 from hotels along US 192) for adults or children. Gray Line also operates trips to other attractions throughout central Florida (Circus World, Kennedy Space Center, Busch Gardens), for varying prices beginning at about $15. **American International Sightseeing,** Tradeport Road and Express Street (tel. 859-2250), is another tour company that has trips to, from, and around central Florida.

You can rent mopeds and bikes at **Moped Rentals,** at 6217 International Dr., across from Wet 'n Wild (tel. 351-5566), for $6.50 an hour, including insurance; bikes are $3.50 an hour. Open from 10:30 a.m. to 9 p.m.

You can even rent a motor home from **Bomar Corp.** 11251 S. Orange Blossom Trail, Orlando, FL 33830 (tel. 851-4038). Bomar rents the homes-on-wheels for prices beginning at $79 to $89 a week for a 24- to 25-foot Champion. Insurance is $7 a day and there are no mileage charges, just a $250 refundable deposit. If you're visiting Orlando in summer and want to reserve one of these rolling homes, make reservations four to six months in advance. **Holiday RV Rental,** 5001 Sand Lake Rd., Orlando, FL 32809 (tel. 305/351-3096, or toll free 800/351-8888; in Florida, 800/351-6666), has all sizes of rec vehicles for rent, for prices beginning at $59 a day.

GETTING YOUR BEARINGS: Here are a few clues to finding your way around brash and booming Orlando. The main east-west artery is **I-4,** which runs from Tampa to Daytona through Orlando. You'll notice you're often driving north-south on I-4, but just keep in mind the Tampa–Daytona orientation and you'll be all right. Exits from this huge expressway take you to Walt Disney World, Sea World, Church Street Station, downtown Orlando, International Drive, Lake Buena Vista, Altamonte Springs, and Winter Park, among others.

A toll road called the **Beeline** is a fast east-west route that intersects with I-4, crosses other major highways like Route 436, the Orange Blossom Trail, and the Florida Turnpike, and scoots eastward to Cape Canaveral. It's the quickest way to the Worlds from the airport.

A third east-wester is the **East-West Expressway,** north of the Beeline, which zips scenically across Orlando and can be reached from I-4.

From north to south the major roadways include **Route 436,** a beltline around Orlando's east side from the Beeline, past the East-West Expressway and Colonial Drive, then bending west to cross US 17/92 and some outlying suburbs. The **Orange Blossom Trail** (also called Route 441) is a north-south road with plenty of motels and restaurants—and traffic. **Orange Avenue** parallels the Orange Blossom Trail, but is farther east and goes by downtown landmarks, as does **Colonial Drive** (Route 50).

US 192 is the main east-west route past Walt Disney World, and stretches from Kissimmee, past many motels, to **US 27.**

USEFUL INFORMATION: For **police or medical emergency,** dial 911. . . . For **minor medical problems,** Family Emergency Center, 6001 Vineland Rd., one block west of Kirkman Road (tel. 351-6682) is open 9 a.m. to 9 p.m. daily and accepts MasterCard and VISA for payment. . . . For a **medical referral service,** call the Orange County Medical Society (tel. 898-3388). Some doctors listed will even make "house" calls at your hotel or motel. . . . To find out what kind of **weather** is coming, call 851-7510 in Orlando, 846-3121 in Kissimmee. . . . To find a **babysitter,** check with your hotel's Guest Services desk. . . . **Pet emer-**

gencies can be handled at Veterinary Emergency Clinic, 882 Jackson Ave., Winter Park (tel. 644-4449). . . . International House of Pancakes, 6005 International Dr. (tel. 351-0031), is near Walt Disney World on International Drive and is a **24-hour restaurant.** . . . For **emergency dental care,** call 425-1616 any time of day or night. . . . **Eckerd's Drugs,** 908 Lee Rd. (tel. 644-6908), is open 24 hours. . . . A quick cleaner is **Orchid One Hour Cleaners,** 5901 S. Orange Blossom Trail (tel. 851-0262). . . . Call **Western Union** toll free at 800/257-2241. . . . Your films can be developed overnight at **Kis Photo,** 6318 International Dr. (tel. 351-4168). . . . Get out-of-town newspapers at **Orange Avenue News,** 59 N. Orange Ave. (tel. 422-0954).

TOURIST INFORMATION: The **Orlando Area Chamber of Commerce,** 75 E. Ivanhoe Blvd., Orlando, FL 32802 (tel. 305/425-1234), will help you with everything from tourist needs to a toothache. . . . The **Kissimmee Chamber of Commerce,** 320 E. Monument Ave., Kissimmee, FL 32741 (tel. 305/847-3174), and the **Kissimmee/St. Cloud Convention and Visitor's Bureau,** on US 192 East, Kissimmee, FL 32741 (tel. 305/847-5000, or toll free 800/327-9159; in Florida, 800/432-9199), are fiercely loyal to their small town, and bureau director Gary Powell and his staff know every millimeter of it. . . . For questions about **Walt Disney World,** call the Magic Kingdom at 305/824-4321, **EPCOT** at 305/827-7414. . . . If you don't mind admitting your age, you can save a bundle of money in **Orlando's Senior Season,** from September to mid-December, when dozens of attractions and hotels offer discounts up to 50% to anyone 55 and up. The chamber of commerce can give you exact details on Senior Season.

Orlando publishes a handy **guide** called *Discover Orlando,* which includes information on attractions, hotels, and restaurants in the region. It's free and can be obtained from the Orlando Area Chamber of Commerce, P.O. Box 1234, Orlando, FL 32802 (tel. 305/425-1234).

2. Where to Stay

Hotels and motels in Orlando are clustered in several general areas: along US 192 to Kissimmee; on International Drive in an area called Florida Center; downtown; and near the airport. There are eight major resort hotels on Disney property in an area called Lake Buena Vista, and three fabulous resorts right inside the Magic Kingdom. I've divided hotels up geographically, beginning with those closest to the Kingdom, and fanning out to the airport.

IN WALT DISNEY WORLD: Closest to the park's many diversions are two hotels and a golf/villa resort located practically at the gate to Main Street, U.S.A. —the Polynesian Village, the Contemporary Hotel, and Disney Vacation Villas, all owned by Walt Disney World. Next come eight independently owned resorts on Disney property but a little farther from the Kingdom in Lake Buena Vista.

The Hotels

If you can afford it (or can't but are in the mood for a big splurge), Disney's 644-room **Polynesian Village** is a fabulous place to lei your head. Step over the thatched threshold here and you're transported to the South Seas where you stay in two-story "longhouses" set amid jungle so tropical it's a wonder there isn't a volcano around somewhere. South Seas luxury in your room translates to beautiful tropical colors, king-size beds, plush carpets, big closets, and dressing rooms. Outside are two pools with lifeguards, a sand beach, water sports, a playground, sauna, beauty and barber shops, and boutiques. For dining there's a massive buffet for under $10 (half that for children) filled with exotic treats and served in the Papeetè Bay Veranda or South Seas Dining Room where at night Polynesian reviews wiggle and flame. You can even take a moonlight cruise aboard a sidewheeler steamboat ($2.25 for adults, 75¢ for children).

When you whiz up to the **Contemporary Hotel** in the silent schuuush of the monorail and see this towering glass-and-chrome mirage, you'll think you've landed on the moon. Glass, glass, everywhere, sharp geometric patterns and miles of straight-up space are just part of the gasp-ery at this 1046-room hotel. In your room you'll find tomorrowland luxury too: two wash basins, extra-large beds, lots and lots of space, and hues as contemporary as a moon walk. Outside are two pools, a beach, health club and sauna, recreation room, a 15th-floor lounge with top entertainment, and music for dancing every night, several excellent dining rooms, huge buffet breakfast, and lunches for $5 or less.

Golf fans should putt straightaway to the **Golf Resort** or **Fairways Villas,** built right next to the greens of two 18-hole courses so you won't exhaust yourself getting from coffee cup to golf cup. There's tennis here too, plus dining, lounges, shops, a health club, and contemporary decor in very attractive, spacious accommodations. More sports? Of course: boating, waterskiing, bicycles, and a heated pool.

One of the best kept secrets at Walt Disney World—although I don't suppose *they* think of it that way—are the villas. Tucked away beside golf courses in shady stands of tall pines, the **Vacation Villas, Fairway Villas,** and **Club Lake Villas** are among the most intriguing places to stay on Disney property. All are apartment villas with kitchen facilities, big roomy places ideal for families. Everyone can spread out and the youngsters can run themselves into exhaustion in the beautiful wooded areas in which the villas are located.

Vacation Villas have cathedral ceilings and one or two bedrooms large enough to accommodate four to six people. Club Lake Villas don't have full kitchens but do have refrigerators and wet bars plus two double beds, set off slightly from a living room. Fairway Villas are handsome, woodsy two-bedroom units rimming the golf course. Six can tuck away beneath the high ceilings here.

Treehouse, anyone? Right here in the village are complete houses, each on its own large plot under the pines. Most of the living space is on the second floor, built up high among the top branches of nearby trees, hence the treehouse appellation. It's a lovely getaway spot that shares a pool with nearby Lake Buena Vista Golf and Tennis Club, where there's also a serene restaurant with prices in the $10 to $15 range. These treehouses are very quiet secluded spots far from the thundering herds and might make a good choice for families looking for a little relaxation with their sightseeing. Rates are $160 a day for up to six people.

Reservations

You can book space in any of these very busy hotels by calling 305/824-8000. You'll get the quickest response after 5 p.m., when things slow down a bit.

You can also write to any of the hotels at this address: Walt Disney World, Central Reservations Office, P.O. Box 78, Lake Buena Vista, FL 32830. For adventurous types there's a reservation desk on Main Street, U.S.A., in the Magic Kingdom, but that's a big risk since these hotels are almost always completely booked weeks in advance. Rates at the three Disney hotels are $105 to $140, year round; the Treehouse runs $160 a day.

Rates are $130 to $160 a day for Vacation Villas, $160 for a Fairway Villa, and $95 for a Club Lake Villa that can accommodate five.

One last option here: a complete house! Called **Grand Vista Suites,** these are two- and three-bedroom houses complete with maid service, daily newspapers at the door, refrigerators stocked with staples, and lovely furnishings. They will set you back $400 to $475 a day, but for a large—and prosperous—family, they are a lovely stopping spot.

Camping

You can't get much better surroundings for camping than Disney's **Fort Wilderness Resort** (tel. 305/824-8000), a 600-acre resort that is the most popular camping site in the state (translate: book ahead). A huge wooded area has room for 825 not-very-rough-its with full hookups, a grill, water, and a disposal system. If roughing it in that style is a little too rough for you, rent a Fleetwood trailer that sleeps six and is fully equipped for $105 per night. Fort Wilderness is a fun place with campfire sing-alongs and a Pioneer Hall, where you dine on barbecue and corn-on-the-cob and are entertained by can-can dancers and a foot-stompin' dinner show, at $20 for adults, $12 to $16 for children, depending on age. At two trading posts you can buy all the things somebody forgot to bring. Later watch Disney movies or go on canoe trips ($5 for adults, $4 for children) that sail you off to a marshmallow roast. There's horseback riding for $10, and full campsites are $26 to $30 a day.

AT LAKE BUENA VISTA: Exit from I-4 at Lake Buena Vista (Route 535) and you're transported to a luxurious world of manicured lawns, towering exquisite hotels, and none of the tawdry flash that characterizes some of the other sections of the city. No day-glo here, not even huge signs—just tasteful, subtle "announcements" at the front of the property. That alone gives you a clue to the luxury you will find—and pay for—here, to the tune of $100+ a night.

Walt Disney Travel Co. has dozens of tempting and money-saving packages which include accommodations at the hotels in Lake Buena Vista. Write to them at P.O. Box 22094, Lake Buena Vista, FL 32830, and they'll be happy to send you information on what they have to offer.

First hotel you'll see as you enter these beautifully landscaped grounds is the **Viscount**, P.O. Box 22205, Lake Buena Vista, FL 32830 (tel. 305/828-2424, or toll free 800/255-3050), a favorite with families and the home of that chubby charmer, dear old Sleepy Bear. Parents can tuck in the kiddies then whiz up to the Top of the Arc to relax while watching fireworks explode over the Magic Kingdom. Rooms at the Viscount are plusher than at some other of this chain's hotels, with two queen-size beds in every room, pretty decor, and all the services and extras to make for a comfortable, pampered stay. There's a pool and game room, restaurant, and lounge. Rooms are $89 to $110 year round, for up to four people.

Next comes the **Americana Dutch Resort Hotel,** 1850 Preview Blvd., Lake Buena Vista, FL 32830 (tel. 305/828-4444, or toll free 800/327-2994). Past a wall of glass is a two-story lobby where dramatic royal blue contrasts with white, and looks as scrubbed as a Dutch kitchen. Every afternoon there's a trolley-full of raw-bar treats here in the lobby and a tray-full of exotic drinks. Built beside a lake, the Dutch Resort's spacious rooms have lots of little touches like big baths, lots of fluffy towels, rocking chairs, and bedside light controls. There's an award-winning Flying Dutchman Restaurant that's an elegant place to dine on continental cuisine (in the $12 to $17 range), and the Tulip Café is open 24 hours. For entertainment there's the Hague or Nightwatch lounges. Outside you'll find tennis, racquetball, a pool, game area, playground, and a miniature golf course (with windmills, of course). Two people pay $99 to $109 a day for a room with two double beds.

Across the street, the 400-room **Hotel Royal Plaza**, 1905 Preview Blvd., Lake Buena Vista, FL 32830 (tel. 305/828-2828, or toll free 800/327-2990; in

Florida, 800/432-2920), is a study in contemporary elegance that touches on but doesn't dwell on Spanish atmosphere. Thoroughly modern rooms in a 17-story tower or in two-story wings are decorated in earthy, contemporary colors and have the best of everything: separate dressing rooms, big closets, private balconies. Amenities include four restaurants, a beauty salon, heated swimming pool, sauna, whirlpool, putting green, shuffleboard, and four lighted tennis courts you can play on for free.

Listen, if it's good enough for Bob Hope and Michael Jackson, surely. . . . Both those fellows were guests here in recent years and the resort has named two of its suites after them. Rates range from $95 to $130 for double rooms, year round. If you want to sleep where Michael or Bob slept, you'll pay $300 to $475.

At **Howard Johnson's,** P.O. Box 22204, Lake Buena Vista, FL 32830 (tel. 305/828-8888, or toll free 800/654-2000), you'll find a hotel that's been so successful it's added a new wing, and now offers 323 rooms. You'll also find all the consideration and gracious service you've come to expect from this chain that's been catering to tired travelers for many years. Like all the properties in Lake Buena Vista, Howard Johnson's is posh and plush with a cheerful, bright atrium and attractive accommodations. Rates are $95 to $115 double, year round.

Latest hotel chain to seek a piece of Mouseland is **Hilton at Disney World Village,** which recently opened a new hotel in this little conclave at 1751 Hotel Plaza Blvd., Lake Buena Vista, FL 32830 (tel. 305/827-4000, or toll free 800/445-8667).

So how did Hilton decide to face the competition of the masses of hoteliers here? Simple, electronically. Get in the elevator here, press the button for the third floor, and shortly a disembodied voice says, "Third floor, going up." This sort of state-of-the-art digital/push button/computerized electronic wizardry turns up everywhere in the hotel, from a digital telephone system that uses the touch of a single key to adjust heating or air conditioning, control the television, and call hotel service personnel, to lights that turn on and off by themselves when people enter or leave the room. Elevators are controlled by microcomputers that talk to you and guest rooms open with tamperproof magnetic cards.

Spacious hotel rooms in this ten-story building are done up in pretty contemporary pastels with attractive furnishings and big windows.

If you're traveling with the youngsters and would like to do without them for a few hours, a special Youth Hotel here offers accommodations for children 3 to 12 years old complete with video room, snackbar, and play area, with meals and scheduled recreation provided.

Complimentary transportation to both Walt Disney World parks is provided by this Disney property hotel, which also has two restaurants: American Vineyards, all dolled up in brass and featuring American regional cuisine like hickory-smoked Vermont turkey and Florida stone crabs; and a lively informal family spot called County Fair, which offers breakfast, lunch, and dinner buffets and an old-fashioned family-style dinner. Hot dogs, hamburgers, and fresh fruit are available at poolside too. There are also two tennis courts, two lounges— Rum Largo, featuring tropical drinks in a greenhouse, and John T's Plantation in the lobby—with entertainment, a swimming pool and spray pool for the youngsters, and a health club with whirlpool, steamroom, and sauna.

An 814-room hotel, Hilton at Walt Disney World charges $100, $115, $125, or $140 double for rooms, depending on their size and location in this three-wing building.

Last on this posh block is the **Buena Vista Palace,** a sister hotel (or is that brother?) to the Hotel Royal Plaza. An $85-million creation, the Buena Vista Palace, Lake Buena Vista, FL 32830, takes a little medieval flavor and whips it up with lots of contemporary to create a 27-story lakeside hotel with more than

800 rooms. You'll find a handsome Australian theme in the resort's beef-y Outback Restaurant and 80 different kinds of beer! A tall central atrium soars several stories to a stained-glass roof, and in the lobby a plush bar is decorated in glowing burgundy shades. There's an interesting architectural innovation here that may confuse you at first but will delight you later: you enter on an upper level of the hotel where a serene, unhurried atmosphere prevails because all the really busy stuff—reservations, car rentals, swimming pool, exits, and the like—is going on down at ground level. Way upstairs you can dine and imbibe in a rooftop aerie, Arthur's, where the view of EPCOT, the Magic Kingdom, and half of central Florida is awesome. Rates are $98 to $150 year round.

At all these hotels, transportation to Walt Disney World is free and some money-saving packages are available.

Hyatt Hotels hit Orlando with a bang—make that a splash—recently when the hotel opened its fabulously showy new hotel in Lake Buena Vista, just west of the Walt Disney World Hotel Village area. You'll see its stepped-pyramid building rising out of the woodlands as you whizz by on I-4. To get to the **Hyatt Regency Grand Cypress Hotel,** 1 Grand Cypress Blvd., Orlando, FL 32819 (tel. 305/239-1234, or toll free 800/228-9000), take the Route 535 (Lake Buena Vista) exit from I-4 and head west to the second traffic light, where you'll turn left (a sign directs you). Just a short distance down that road is the entrance to this hotel, which is just the first project in a massive development under way here.

First, of course, came the hotel, which is now the number one showplace in Orlando, no contest. Chief among its showy attributes is a quite incredible swimming pool featuring everything from a tall waterfall crashing into the pool to a suspension bridge swaying over it. You swim around and into rock grottoes, splash in streams and waterfalls, slide down a slippery waterslide set into rocks, and imbibe at a grotto bar. As for the hotel itself, well . . . whew! An 11-story atrium soars skyward and a fortune's worth of Oriental artworks are scattered casually about hotel and grounds. Streams trickle through the lobby and ivy streams down from high overhead.

Rooms are lovely, no question about it. In a special 11th-floor Regency Club, where rates are $195 a day, rooms are outfitted with a love seat and chair tucked into a sitting area fronted by glass doors through which the pool's dozen cascading waterfalls are visible. King-size beds are trimmed in light woods and headboards have inset fabric designed to match the bedspreads. Other rooms in the hotel are a bit smaller, but by no means small. They range in price from $120 to $160 double (about $15 less, single), and are also decorated in the most contemporary of furnishings in pale pastels, mauves, salmon, pink, light woods, handsome framed paintings. Tropical touches include wicker furniture, ceiling fans, and shutters.

When you've explored all the nooks and crannies of that spectacular swimming pool, you can sail, windsurf, canoe, or paddleboat about a 21-acre lake or sun on 1000 feet of white sand beach. Boat rentals are $8 to $10 an hour, and sailing lessons, including an hour of sailing, are $30. Bicycles are $4 an hour; tandem bikes, $6. A tennis and recreational complex offers ten tennis courts, a racquetball court, shuffleboard, and volleyball playgrounds. Tennis fees are $10 an hour, and private lessons, $30 an hour; a tennis clinic is complimentary. A children's playground keeps the youngsters busy and nature trails lure walkers and joggers.

Jack Nicklaus has added his signature to the 18-hole golf course, restricted to registered guests of the hotel and their friends. Greens fees are $40, including bag storage, club cleaning, and unlimited range use. Carts are $10 per person. A nine-hole pitch-and-putt course is free to guests, and a health club offers a weight and exercise room fitted out with shiny new equipment, a sauna, Jacuzzi, massage studio, and jogging clinics. And there's a grotto bar nearby to recuperate. A game room features video playthings for the youngsters, and there's an outdoor playground as well.

Three restaurants offer an intriguing variety of places to dine. In the Cascade restaurant, Hyatt's two-level version of a coffeeshop, a dramatic bronze mermaid keeps cool beneath a 35-foot waterfall. A pianist entertains here—at breakfast! Atop the rocks and waterfalls, a woodsy restaurant called Hemingway's pays tribute to Key West's favorite son. Prices for steaks and seafood are in the $12 to $15 range for entrees. La Coquina, Hyatt's most elegant and most expensive restaurant, is a two-story triumph overlooking the lake. Here a harpist plays as you dine on French and continental entrees in the $17 to $20 range. Figure about $70 a couple for an elegant dinner.

Cocktail lounge enthusiasts can visit Trellises, the lovely lobby bar tucked among streams and ferns; the Hurricane Bar in Hemingway's, where a strolling musician provides evening entertainment and bartenders create a combustible daiquiri called the Papa Doble; or the White Horse Saloon, a showy dancing center crowned by carousel ponies and trimmed with etched glass, brass, and an engraved tin ceiling.

Just outside the village, but still in the Lake Buena Vista area, is the **Vistana Tennis Resort,** P.O. Box 22051, Lake Buena Vista, FL 32830 (tel. 305/239-3100, or toll free 800/327-9152; in Florida, 800/432-9197), which pops up out of the pastureland like a fantasy kingdom of its own. Plunked down all by itself in the quietest of settings, on Route 535 at the Lake Buena Vista exit south, Vistana is a very comfortable tennis-oriented resort. A massive complex of gloriously contemporary apartments with two or three big bedrooms, Vistana has fully equipped kitchens, living and dining rooms, balconies or terraces, washers and dryers, and maid service. There's a pool, general store, Tiki Bar, snackshop, jogging trail, scheduled activities, and enough tennis courts for Wimbledon. Tennis is free, and the resort offers tennis instruction and clinics. Rates begin at $100 for a two-bedroom villa for six and rise to $225 for larger accommodations for as many as eight people from December to April, slightly lower in other months.

A money-saver just outside the village (but only a few hundred yards away) is **Best Western's World Inn,** on Route 535 (P.O. Box 22095), Lake Buena Vista, FL 32830 (tel. 305/876-3636, or toll free 800/327-6954; in Florida, 800/528-1234). Off by itself under a stand of rustling pines, World Inn has 245 rooms including 12 efficiencies, and refrigerators in every room. There is a coin laundry plus two pools, a large playground, and movies. Rooms are spacious and bright, with tropical colors and lots of glass. World Inn has a pretty, casual restaurant for family dining and a cocktail lounge with entertainment, plus free transportation to the Magic Kingdom, EPCOT, and Lake Buena Vista Village Shopping Center. Rates range from $58 to $77, year round.

ON US 192: Welcome to a buyer's market! Not for ten years have the prices in Orlando been so advantageous for the traveler—or so bargainable! This new budgeteer's paradise is the result of a building boom that has added more than 40,000 hotel rooms at flashpaper speed—and has 10,000 more on the drawing boards!

This stunning proliferation of hotel quarters has led to a price war, the likes of which you are not likely to find anywhere else in Florida. It's even gotten to the point that small hotel operators are bargaining down their own prices on the telephone when you call them for reservations. Some are even advertising "Make us an offer."

"If you're going to stay two or three days, come down on the second day and talk to us and we'll see if we can't do something about lowering the price," an anxious motel owner told me. And he was prepared to make a deal on a room that was only $27 a night!

Even as you read, some new Orlando hotel is planning a ribbon-cutting ceremony to celebrate its opening day. Hundreds, in fact thousands of new hotel rooms are planned or under construction, many scheduled for completion in 1985 and 1986.

To describe every one of the newcomers would take a book of its own, so suffice to say that if you drive into the area and begin looking for a spot to settle, begin looking on US 192. Small motels, and some not so small, have sprung up along this wide highway that is sometimes called the "Highway to the Worlds." Those "worlds" refer primarily to Walt Disney World, the entrance to which is reached from this highway, but also to Sea World, just a splash away, and Circus World.

Those newcomer motels, which seem to have sprung up like proverbial mushrooms, are all pretty stock material, both in ambience and in price. You'll find basic cement-block structures with clean but unprepossessing quarters: two chairs, a table, usually two double beds (usually with flowered spreads), a dresser, often a small dressing area, and a bathroom.

Owners and operators of these often family-run motels are as exotic as their motels are not: some are Chinese, many are Indian, some are Latin Americans, and of course many are Americans.

Price? About $30 to $40, year round, sometimes a few dollars less.

While they're nothing to write home about, these motels do offer a decent, if nonchic, place to put your head each evening when you weave in exhausted from a long day at one or more of Orlando's many attractions. They have the added benefit of proximity to Walt Disney World, which is not likely to be more than a 10- or 15-minute drive away.

Starting with the Orlando Hyatt Hotel, the most expensive, and working down to the money-savers, here are my choices.

After you've seen the **Hyatt Orlando Hotel,** at I-4 and US 192 East, Kissimmee, FL 32741 (tel. 305/396-1234, or toll free 800/228-9000), you may not bother with Walt Disney World. What a place this is! Every building is painted a different color (which is helpful when you're trying to find your room in this maze of 960 others). There are four swimming pools and four kiddie pools, tennis courts, a shopping mall complete with package store, game room with electronic games, and a tot lot for the toddlers. To describe the rooms here is easy: beautiful. And big, very big, decorated in subtle earthy shades with giant dressing areas and baths and all those little touches Hyatt so thoughtfully adds: French-milled soap, shampoo, shower caps, shoe shiners, even a creme rinse. In the lobby of the hotel an employee with a quirky sense of humor walks around with a puppet so convincing you jump when it reaches out to nip you, and a caricaturist sketches the real you in minutes.

For dining, there's a Big Bicycle restaurant with a changing theme that has ranged from Mexican to Italian to oom-pah-pah (prices about $10 to $12 for a huge buffet) and a fine Limey Jim's where a harpist plinks genteelly away as you dine on five- or six-course meals like steak au poivre, interrupted only by a tad of palate-clearing sherbet and ending with a half dozen or so specialty coffees laced with imported liqueurs. You'll pay $20 to $25 for this impressive repast, and to stay here you'll spend about $75 to $85 for a double room, with suites ranging from $240 to $350. (I forgot to mention that when all other amusements pale, you can take a helicopter ride aboard a whirlybird parked on the front lawn.)

The **Sheraton-Lakeside Inn,** 7711 Vine St. (US 192 West), Kissimmee, FL 32741, just west of I-4 (tel. 305/825-8250, or toll free 800/325-3535), is quite close to Disney and has 650 high-quality rooms, a seafood saloon, lounge, deli, two heated pools and two tot pools, a boat dock, paddleboats, mini-golf, tennis courts, and poolside gazebos. From February to May and June to September, two people pay $70 to $80; in other months, $60 to $70. Children under 17 stay free.

You know Florida and its superlatives. Well, how about the world's largest Days Lodge? Yes, indeed, the **Days Lodge** right here in Kissimmee, at 5820 Spacecoast Pkwy., Kissimmee, FL 32741, on US 192 east of I-4 (tel. 305/396-7900, or toll free 800/327-9126; in Florida, 800/432-9103), where every suite has 700 square feet of living space, patios or balconies, and a kitchen complete with dishwasher! There are three swimming pools, a playground, and barbecue. It is just three miles from the Kingdom. Two people pay $72 in summer ($10 more for poolside rooms), and children under 18 are free. Prices drop to $57 in other months.

Larson's Lodge/Kissimmee, 2009 W. Vine St., Kissimmee, FL 32741 (tel. 305/846-2713, or toll free 800/327-9147; in Florida, 800/432-9109), seems to attract nice people and you won't find many nicer than the friendly Larson family who own and operate this very attractive resort. There's a game room, boutique, heated pool, sundeck, and a little picket fence around the children's play area. Three-story wings house the resort's 120 pretty rooms, each with two double beds, a sitting area, and picture windows. Right next door is the Black Angus Steakhouse, where you can dine for less than $10. Most of the year a room for two is $32 and an efficiency is $55, dropping in spring and fall to $29 and $39 (children under 18 free).

Dark-wood railings add a trim touch to **Rodeway Inn Eastgate,** 5245 Spacecoast Pkwy., Kissimmee, FL 32741 (tel. 305/841-8541, or toll free 800/228-2000), a two-story motel with spacious rooms overlooking a pool and patio. In the Riviera Lounge is nightly entertainment, and the inn's dining room features an impressive buffet. There's a playground for the children and a coin laundry to keep them clean after a day on the playground. From June to September rates are $50 to $56, and in slow months drop to $30 to $35, about $10 higher from mid-December to May.

Tennis is the focal point at **Orlando Vacation Resort,** South US 27, Clermont, FL 32711 (tel. 305/656-8181, or toll free 800/874-9064). You'll find lots of lighted tennis courts plus 225 very attractive quarters with lots of space and bright colors. There's a cute little restaurant front and center with several different themes in several dining rooms. Excellent food emerges from the kitchen, with fresh bread every day and prices in the $10 range. A room for two at this vacation resort, which also supplies free shuttle rides to Walt Disney World, is $40 to $48, year round. Children under 17 are free.

Back on the east side of I-4 on US 192, the **Colonial Motor Lodge,** 1815 W. Vine St., Kissimmee, FL 32741 (tel. 305/847-6121), has 40 apartments with quite basic furnishings, but rooms clean, neat, and big enough for a family. There are two swimming pools and a game room. Motel units with two double beds go for $28 to $40, and you'll pay $54 to $60 for two-bedroom apartments. There's never any charge for children under 12.

King's Motel, 4836 W. Spacecoast Pkwy., Kissimmee, FL 32741 (tel. 305/843-3051, or toll free 800/327-9071; in Florida, 800/432-9928), is a pretty spot that shares a little lake with an adjoining motel, the Lakeview. You can swim and row around in a boat the motel will lend you, or roam among the lovely shady pine trees scattered about the grounds. Rooms have double beds with pretty velvet spreads, dark shag rugs, tiled foyers, and a pool overlooking the lake. Rates here range from $35 to $45 double in season, $29 to $39 May to December. There is no charge for children under 16.

Spot the old farm wagon sitting in the front yard and you'll have found the **Stagecoach Resort Inn,** 4311 W. Vine St., Kissimmee, FL 32741 (tel. 305/396-4213, or toll free 800/327-9155; in Florida, 800/432-9198), a rustic resort with Old West ties but nice new rooms. Set way back off the road, the inn has colorful rooms with wide picture windows overlooking the grounds where giant old trees shade a lovely pool. Next door, the inn's Overland Express Steakhouse Restaurant is more rustic yet, with antique quilts and old gowns displayed, and very inexpensive steaks in the $9 to $12 price range. Rooms at the inn are $35 to $53, year round; children under 18 stay free. If you are an AAA member or a senior citizen, they'll give you a discount.

Sunrise Motel, 801 W. Vine St., Kissimmee, FL 32741 (tel. 305/846-3224), has small, simply furnished rooms, but for the money you probably can't beat this brown-shuttered beige motel decorated inside in bright hues of blue and green. Light paneling adds a serene note and perky flowered bedspreads are nice touches. If you've got a couple of hungry young mouths to feed, there's a Burger King across the street and a McDonald's next door. Sunrise is about 15 minutes from Disney and charges $35 for two, $45 for four—"or whatever I can get" (translation: bargain a bit).

East Gate Motor Inn and Restaurant is another money-saver on US 192, 900 E. Vine St., Kissimmee, FL 32741 (tel. 305/846-4600). Its brick facade pops up in the middle of a farm, although the motel itself is just off the highway. Rooms are basic but serviceable, and there's a small pool. Rates are $24 to $34 in peak season, about $6 less in other months, and single rates are $5 to $6 less.

Embassy Motel, 4880 W. Spacecoast Pkwy., Kissimmee, FL 32741 (tel. 305/396-1144, or toll free in Florida, 800/432-0153), is a two-story spot with big glass windows across the front of every room and a small swimming pool off to one side. It's located four miles east of Walt Disney World, has color television, medium-size rooms done up in brown striped spreads, and a dressing area. Not far from the building is a small but pretty lake. Prices here are $45 in peak summer and winter months, $28 in spring and fall.

On the same lake you'll find **Lakeside Cedar Inn,** 4960 W. US 192, Kissimmee, FL 32741 (tel. 305/396-1376, or toll free 800/327-0072; in Florida, 800/432-0276). Arches add a touch of the Mediterranean to the two-story buildings here, and sparkling Lake Cecile in the back is a good place to send the kids exploring while you grab a few minutes' peace. There's a small swimming pool in the middle of the resort too. Rooms are equipped with compact stove/sink units so you can whip up the occasional lunch for yourself. Nearby, a small shopping area features plenty of souvenirs and a family-style restaurant. Rates are $29 to $45, year round.

Econolodge Main Gate East, 6051 W. US 192, Kissimmee, FL 32741 (tel. 305/396-1748, or toll free 800/446-6900), has the basic but comfortable quarters this chain has been offering for quite a number of years, in a building with just the faintest touch of Swiss chalet. They're running quite a large operation here, with a game room, laundry room, gift shop, playground, swimming pool, and shuttle service to Walt Disney World and to the airport. Rates are $35 to $47, year round, and pets are permitted.

Holiday Inn, 2145 E. US 192, Kissimmee, FL 32743 (tel. 305/846-4646, or toll free 800/465-4329), and **TraveLodge Kissimmee Flags,** 2407 W. US 192, Kissimmee, FL 32741 (tel. 305/933-2400, or toll free 800/255-3050), are both represented along this highway. Each offers clean, comfortable quarters just like those you'd find in those chains' representatives anywhere in the nation. Rates are $29 to about $35 in spring and fall, about $40 to $60 in peak summer and winter seasons at either property.

Buena Vista Motel, 5200 W. US 192, Kissimmee, FL 32741 (tel. 305/396-

2100), has an alluring spanking-clean look about its blue and white buildings. That same simple but attractive atmosphere continues inside the rooms, which are basic but well kept and serviceable. There's a pretty swimming pool here too. Rates are $35 to $45, year round.

Central Motel, 4698 W. US 192, Kissimmee, FL 32741 (tel. 305/396-2333), is yet another brand-new spot with Chinese-red doors and with a swimming pool at the rear of the building. Brick-trimmed doors welcome you to standard motel rooms with orange-and-brown floral print decor. Rates here are $27 to $35, year round.

If you like Mediterranean architecture, you'll find hints of it at **Casa Rosa Inn,** 4600 W. US 192, Kissimmee, FL 32741 (tel. 305/396-2020), painted in a delicate pink hue. Surroundings are especially attractive here: the motel's set in a small wooded area. Rates are $32 including a continental breakfast, rising in high season to $52.

Sun Motel, 5020 W. US 192, Kissimmee, FL 32741 (tel. 305/396-2673), is another of the multitude of tiny family-owned motels that have risen here in the last two years. This one is currently owned by a Chinese family who employ a bustling Chinese maid in a peaked straw hat and typical Chinese blues. Rates are $35 to $45.

To give you some more options in the busiest months, here are the names of a few of the many small places offering basic accommodations, usually a swimming pool, and best of all that proximity to Walt Disney World and all the other playgrounds here: **Chalet Motel,** 4741 W. US 192, Kissimmee, FL 32741 (tel. 305/396-1677), with prices of $34 to $66 double, year round; **Château Motel,** 4657 W. US 192, Kissimmee, FL 32741 (tel. 305/396-1033), with rates at $30 to $36 off-season, $49 to $55 in season, double; **Maple Leaf Motel,** 4647 W. US 192, Kissimmee, FL 32741 (tel. 305/396-0300), charging $22 to $40 double, year round; and **Key Motel,** 4810 W. US 192, Kissimmee, FL 32741 (tel. 305/ 396-6200), with prices of $25 to $35 double, year round.

Still more motels along US 192 that are neat, clean, and fall in the $30 to $50 price range year round are:

The Palm, 4519 W. Spacecoast Pkwy., Kissimmee, FL 32741 (tel. 305/396-0744), a pleasant new spot with stone siding, a pool, attractive rooms, and free coffee in the lobby.

Enterprise Motel, 4121 W. Vine St., Kissimmee, FL 32741 (tel. 305/933-1383), a bright, cheerful brand-new spot with queen-size beds in the rooms, HBO television service, and a swimming pool at the rear of the building (nice, less traffic noise).

Spacecoast Motel, 4125 Spacecoast Pkwy., Kissimmee, FL 32741 (tel. 305/ 933-5732), which has some rooms with whirlpools, remote-control color TVs with free Home Box Office service, and king- and queen-size beds, plus efficiencies and suites. It's 3½ miles to Walt Disney World and EPCOT Center.

Hawaiian Village Inn, 4559 W. Spacecoast Pkwy., Kissimmee, FL 32741 (tel. 305/396-1212, or toll free 800/821-9503; in Florida, 800/342-0137), has 114 rooms with two extra-long double beds in each, and some with kitchenettes. There's a swimming pool off on one side of the building, a small and simple restaurant, and a lounge with big-screen television. Package rates here can save you money too.

Radisson Inn Maingate, 7501 W. Spacecoast Pkwy. (US 192), Kissimmee, FL 32741 (tel. 305/396-1400, or toll free 800/228-9822), is an attractive choice for those who want to be close to Walt Disney World. Located just a few minutes' drive from the main gate to WDW, Radisson Inn is sleekly modern from its colorful woven wall hangings to its plant-bedecked restaurant and bar. That modernity continues in the guest rooms, which are decorated in soft pastels and come complete with lots of little extra amenities. Tucked into the middle of the several wings of this hotel is a swimming pool, and outside is a jogging trail, tennis courts, and a playground for the youngsters. A deli-style café plays to those youngsters too, and even offers take-out service. Peak-season rates are $55 to $75 double, with children under 17 free. In less popular seasons, late spring and early fall, rates drop about $10.

FLORIDA CENTER/INTERNATIONAL DRIVE: Florida Center is a name applied to a section of Orlando surrounding International Drive. It is home to many motels and fast-food chain restaurants. To get here, leave I-4 at the International Drive–Sand Lake Road exit and head east on Sand Lake Road (also known as Route 528A).

It was only to be expected that Sea World would not sit idly by and let Walt Disney World have all those hotels on its property. That's why you will now find a brand, spanking-new hotel, **Wyndham at Sea World,** 6677 Sea Harbor Dr., Orlando, FL 32821 (tel. 305/351-5555, or toll free 800/822-4200), right across the street from Sea World.

On the outside this towering new International Drive–area hotel presents a rather bland white facade sparked only by a bright-blue tile roof. But on the inside, whoooeee! Built in quadrangle style, the hotel's four wings surround an atrium bigger than a couple of football fields. Birds chatter in an atrium, fish swim in the waters surrounding a multilevel cocktail lounge, and visitors stroll past buildings designed to look like a small village. Describing this skylight-topped hotel is not an easy task. For openers, the "lobby," which is really an inner courtyard delineated by the four wings of the hotel, looks little like any lobby you've ever seen. Instead cupola-topped buildings in soft greens and blues open to reveal an aviary, an ice-cream parlor, a gazebo-like dining center, and that cocktail lounge. A couple of leaping plaster dolphins beside the entrance to the lounge keep Sea World firmly in mind, as does that aviary.

Three other restaurants reside here, one a subtly decorated, black-lacquered Oriental restaurant, another a handsome and high-priced gourmet dining room (figure $25 to $40 a person for dinner), and the third, a rather grandiose coffeeshop that becomes a steak and seafood dining room at night.

The best rooms, to my mind, are those on the north and south sides of the buildings. They have pretty French doors leading to flowerbox-trimmed balconies overlooking the magnificence of the lobby below, while the others, although just as handsomely decorated, overlook Sea World on one side, the outskirts of Orlando on the other. They have not missed anything in these rooms: remote-control TV, comfortable armchairs, lovely pastel decor, marble-clad double-sink bathrooms with a huge white clam shell full of everything from shampoo to a little bag of potpourri. Quite a place indeed! Rates at Wyndham at Sea World are $125 to $140 in season, $30 less in summer. Suites range from $270 to $1000.

The first hotel you'll see east of I-4 is the **Orlando Marriott Inn,** 8001 International Dr., Orlando, FL 32809 (tel. 305/351-2420, or toll free 800/228-9290). So sprawling is this resort you'll almost need a map to find your way around. This glamorous resort has all the amenities of a huge hotel but looks more like a posh neighborhood. Little lakes and fountains swirl about, tiny lagoons trickle under bridges, and paths lined with palms wind through clusters of two-story villas. The glamor doesn't stop outside either. Big picture windows overlook these enchanting grounds, and inside, some rooms have big puffy couches and chairs covered in subtle earthy colors, matching drapes, and deep carpets. There are oversize beds, and some units with kitchenettes in the 1079 rooms scattered over 43 acres. Naturally there's more: tennis courts, three pools with sundecks and wooded platforms for scenic sitting, a kiddie pool, game room and play area, a shopping mall, and the elegant Grove Restaurant with plush banquettes featuring a menu in the $20 price range for seafood and sizzling steaks, and nightly entertainment at a dancing spot called Illusions. If you fly into Orlando, they offer free airport transportation. In peak season, the resort charges $90 to $105 double; in months other than January to May or July to September, prices drop. Rooms with kitchens are $20 more, and children under 13 are free.

The **Hilton Inn Florida Center,** 7400 International Dr., Orlando, FL 32819 (tel. 305/351-4600, or toll free 800/327-1363; in Florida, 800/332-4600), occupies the entrance to the north end of International Drive and has a monster of a pool, covered by a roof. If you want sun, there's a second pool outside. A 400-room hostelry that includes 20 suites, the resort also features a tropical garden. Hilton Inn has spent quite a lot of money refurbishing this hotel over the years, and now it has a bright, contemporary look and a delightfully tropical feeling. There's patio dining outside under that slick roof and a woodsy inside dining room with prices in the $10 to $15 range. Lots of families find their way here since children are free at the resort. There's also complimentary airport transportation. Peak rates are $75 to $109 in winter and summer, about $30 less in less popular seasons.

The **Ramada Court of Flags Hotel,** 5715 Major Blvd., Orlando, FL 32809 (tel. 305/351-3340, or toll free 800/228-2828), sprawls over acres of ground on the west side of I-4 so it's a quick trip from here to most of the area's attractions. I can't think what you could want that you can't find here: electronic game room, a deli, two saunas, tennis courts, three swimming pools, lounges, a wading pool for children, and a handsome Glass Garden Restaurant (with continental cuisine in the $10 to $15 range). Roomy accommodations are decorated in cheery colors and have all the amenities, including private balconies. All you need to do is learn how to find your way around these 820 rooms. Two people pay $62 to $74.

One of the newest hotels you can visit in central Florida is the **Sheraton World,** at 10100 International Dr., Orlando, FL 32821 (tel. 305/352-1100, or toll free 800/325-3535), right next door to Sea World. Completed in late 1980, this 807-room hotel is thoroughly modern, from contemporary prints to arched wicker headboards and brick-floored lobby where the sun shines through a skylight onto bright banners. You can dine on favorite family fare in the Sunrise Café, sip tantalizing tropical creations in the Sunset Saloon, and for more elegant dining, Le Monde offers attentive service and continental cuisine in the $10 to $15 price bracket. The Sheraton charges $64 to $80 double, and children stay free. You couldn't be any closer to Sea World than this attractive hotel.

Right across the street from **Las Palmas Inn,** 6233 International Dr., Orlando, FL 32809 (tel. 305/351-3900, or toll free 800/327-2114), is Orlando's watery fun spot, Wet 'n' Wild, so if you're a water lover this might be a good place to settle. Las Palmas has an intriguing Spanish ambience with lots of dark wood and a red tile roof. The spacious rooms here are kept up-to-date with handsome wall coverings and subtle floral prints. You can cool off at the pool bar while the kids romp in the playground, or join them in the game room or inexpensive Palms Restaurant. Las Palmas charges $60 to $70 in the busy summer and winter months, $55 to $65 in other seasons.

You can't possibly miss **High Q,** at 5905 International Dr., Orlando, FL 32809 (tel. 305/351-2100, or toll free 800/327-1366)—just look for the tall tower with the huge Q on top. Rising out of the ground like a circular beanstalk, High Q is a 21-story landmark with views all over Orlando. Besides the 300 spacious, tastefully decorated rooms with double beds and dressing areas, there are two pools, saunas, a game room, barber and beauty salons, a lounge with entertainment, and two restaurants. At a nearby country club, High Q guests enjoy golf and tennis privileges. Rates are $38 to $46, depending on season.

Davis Brothers Motor Lodge, 6603 International Dr., Orlando, FL 32809 (tel. 305/351-2900, or toll free 800/841-9480), is part of a chain that also operates very inexpensive cafeterias, so you can sleep and eat inexpensively all in one spot. Nice rooms with plenty of space and a bright decor is a watchword of the Davises. You'll find a pool for adults and a separate shallow splashing spot for the kids. You can bring Fido here too. Meals in the cafeteria are buffet style, in the $5 range. Year-round rates for doubles are $35.95.

The **Gateway Inn,** 7050 Kirkman Rd., Orlando, FL 32819 (tel. 305/351-2000, or toll free 800/327-3808), is an attractive family resort made even more attractive by the presence of the inexpensive Sweden House Smörgåsbord where you can feed those hungry mouths for about $6.50 for adults, $3.75 for children under 11. You'll find bright floral prints in rooms that surround a big central courtyard where a gleaming pool is the center of attention. For the kids there's a playground with swings, and for everyone there's miniature golf, games, a sundry shop, and those bounteous Sweden House buffets. If a little escapism is in order, try the inn's cocktail lounge. Rates at Gateway peak at $68 double. The Gateway Inn also operates another hotel, the **Comfort Inn,** at 8421 S. Orange Blossom Trail, Orlando, FL 32809 (tel. 305/855-6060), a little farther from Walt Disney World, where the accommodations are similar and the prices $44 to $48 double. High season is $48 to $52. There's a toll-free number here too: 800/327-9742.

There's more red, white, and blue than even the flag can boast at the **1776 Inn,** 5858 International Dr., Orlando, FL 32809 (tel. 305/351-4410, or toll free 800/327-2115). In the heart of Florida Center, the 1776 sprawls around central grounds and a large pool. Paths wind through the grounds and past rooms that feature wide glass windows overlooking the trees and shrubbery. Bright tropical decor is a feature of the spacious rooms here, and outside there's a whirling ride for the kids, a shady poolside lounge for parents. Prices are $48 for poolside rooms, $44 for rooms with two double beds, $44 for rooms with king-size beds, and no charge for children under 18 sharing a room. Prices drop about $20 in spring and fall.

Are you ready for a resort with 100 electronic game machines and an 18-hole indoor miniature golf course? It's the perfect way to occupy dear little Dudley while you get in some serious sunning and swimming, and it can be yours at the **Caravan Resort Inn,** 5827 Caravan Court, Orlando, FL 32819 (from I-4, take the Route 435 North exit; tel. 305/351-3800, or toll free 800/327-2111), which bills itself as a family resort and has all the family entertainment paraphernalia to prove it. You can browse in Auntie Lil's General Store, dine in nostalgic Victoriana at Jodi's, or toss back something cool in the Choo-choo Lounge, a turn-of-the-century railroad station bar. There are big and little pools at the Caravan, and large rooms decorated in contemporary hues. Double rooms in peak seasons range from $39 to $56. Children under 17 are free.

If you'd rather swim than almost anything else, the only place in town for you is the **Radisson Inn & Justus Aquatic Center,** 8444 International Dr., Orlando, FL 32819 (tel. 305/345-0505, or toll free 800/752-0003). Designed to lure swim competitions, this new hotel has an Olympic-size swimming pool topped by a hydraulic roof that opens or closes for the weather, high diving boards, marked lanes, electronic timing equipment, underwater observation rooms, and seating for 3000 of your friends come to watch you swim. There's a complete fitness center and health club here, with simply every kind of workout equipment and class you can imagine, up to and including racquetball and handball courts. Just opened in early 1985, the Radisson cost $25 million and already is being touted as the pool to upstage Fort Lauderdale's Swimming Hall of Fame. Even swimmers must sleep, however, and here they can do that in large, lovely rooms outfitted in muted contemporary colors, often peach and gray tones. There's a restaurant and cafeteria at the hotel, which opened with introductory rates of $55 but expected to be charging $85 double, year round.

Among the moderately priced hotels on hotel-lined International Boulevard, the **Comfort Inn**, 5825 International Blvd. (at the corner of Kirkman Road), Orlando, FL 32819 (tel. 305/351-4100, or toll free 800/228-5150), is a pleasant choice. Beige stucco with Mediterranian touches to its architecture, the motel is a two-story building with small, faux balconies topped by red barrel tiles. In the center of this rather large complex is a swimming pool, and at one end of the property, Denny's Restaurant offers 24-hour service. Rooms are of medium size with two double beds, cheerful color schemes, and comfortable armchairs. Rates are $32 to $42, year round, and there's no charge for children under 17 sharing a room.

One of the larger, more elaborate **Econo Lodges,** 8738 International Dr., Orlando, FL 32819 (tel. 305/345-8195), in the country is here in Orlando. In fact it calls itself the world's largest Econo Lodge, and with 670 rooms in several four-story buildings, that's hard to dispute. Wood trim on the exterior lends the place a faintly Tudor air. Set among a stand of pines, Econo Lodge offers medium-size rooms attractively decorated with floral spreads. Few fancy amenities here, and no fancy prices: rates are $46.95, $20 more if you want a room with a whirlpool in it or a suite with a sitting room. Some efficiencies also are available for $56.95.

Quality Inn, 9000 International Dr., Orlando, FL 32819 (tel. 305/345-8585, or toll free 800/228-5151), has 340 very attractive rooms in several buildings trimmed in burgundy and tinted windows. The lobby is draped in hanging vines and leads to the pool that forms the center of this huge complex. Located practically next door to Orlando's new convention center, it makes a reasonably priced stopping spot for business travelers. Rates are $27 to $39, depending on season.

Before Walt Disney World's Magic Kingdom made its appearance here, one of Orlando's best known attractions was its many deep-blue, spring-fed lakes. These days, travelers whizzing through on major highways or racing from one man-made attraction to another rarely see those sparkling lakes, which are often hidden away on backroads.

Now, however, a new hotel has forsaken the world of glitzy lobbies and fake rocks to focus on the natural beauty of one of the region's largest lakes. Called the **Sonesta Village Hotel on Sand Lake,** 10000 Turkey Lake Rd., Orlando, FL 32819 (tel. 305/352-8051, or toll free 800/343-7170), this new resort is different in another way: it has no hotel rooms! Instead, the Sonesta Village offers two-story villas strung out in a long, winding cluster of town-house-like structures, each with its own living room, small kitchen, dining room, and bath downstairs, and large bedrooms and a second bathroom upstairs. Tall glass doors frame green lawns rolling down to the lake. Light wood and wicker furnishings are outfitted in soothing contemporary colors—rose, beige, aqua. All villas feature two double beds in each bedroom and a convertible sofa in the living room, televisions in each room.

Circling around the edge of one of the area's largest lakes, this new 97-acre resort gives visitors a closeup look at a natural spring lake that has maintained much of its wilderness character. As you sit on a private terrace overlooking green lawns that slope gently to the shore, a snowy egret stalks by in search of lunch. While it seems as far as Mars from the hustle of Orlando's other hotel enclaves, the Sonesta Village only sounds remote. Actually it is right in the middle of things, about ten minutes from Orlando International Airport and the same distance from Walt Disney World. Sea World is just across I-4, about a mile away.

Built at a cost of $100 million, the Sonesta Village has a formal restaurant, a casual café, and a lounge with entertainment. Activists can whizz off in sail or paddleboats, splash in the pool or whirlpool spas, play on lighted tennis courts, park the kids at a playground, stroll a wooden boardwalk that stretches out into the lake. Particularly convenient for families, the resort offers a daily supervised childrens' activities program and babysitting.

Rates at the resort from March to mid-December are $110 for a one-bedroom villa, $140 for a two-bedroom villa. Rates drop in May, September, and October, when the charge for a one-bedroom is $90, and $120 for a two-bedroom villa. Special rates for stays of a month or more are also offered.

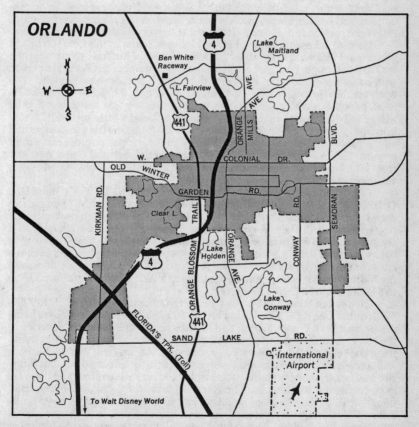

DOWNTOWN: Downtown Orlando is a pretty place that surrounds sparkling Lake Eola where a fountain shoots skyward and ducks paddle. To get there, take I-4 to the US 17/92 exit and head north to Washington Street.

At 151 E. Washington St., you'll find the **Harley Hotel,** Orlando, FL 32801 (tel. 305/841-3220, or toll free 800/321-2323), and wait till you see what Harley has done with the old Kahler Plaza Hotel! Once a dowdy downtowner, that old hotel is now a stunning, glittering place where candles glow, chandeliers sparkle, deep colors shine like jewels. Harley has wrought a miracle, and all Orlando is proud of this new addition to its hotel ranks. Hotel rooms are decorated in gentle glowing colors and modern prints, comfortable easy chairs, pretty wall prints, and shaded brass swing-out bed lamps. In the roomy baths there are shaving and cosmetic mirrors. Harley has one of the city's most entrancing restaurants: Café on the Park, where leaded glass trims bands of windows with a smashing view of Lake Eola and deep-burgundy velvet covers dark-wood armchairs and banquettes. If you get the idea I like it here, you get the idea. Rates are $69.50 to $89.50 double, all year.

Harley also owns another hotel in the area, the **Sheraton Colonial Plaza Inn,** 2801 E. Colonial Dr., Orlando, FL 32801, at the edge of downtown (tel. 305/894-2741, or toll free 800/325-3535), where there's an extra touch in four of the rooms that you'll find in few other spots in the world—a private swimming pool! In 221 other rooms you'll be sans pool, but you'll still have basic accommodations, and you can always nip downstairs and soak in a Jacuzzi. Double-room rates here run $55 to $60, and $110 for the honeymoon suite.

Howard Johnson's is, well, Howard Johnson's, and by this time you have a pretty good idea what to expect at this reliable chain. I just have to mention one in Orlando though, because here you're not just a number but a real live person with a face and personality and everything. That's because Mac Finnane, who operates this HoJo's, at 2014 Colonial Dr., Orlando, FL 32804 (tel. 305/841-8600, or toll free 800/654-2000), tries so hard to know and please you that he manages to make his resort something different. A midtown hotel about 20 minutes from Walt Disney World, Finnane's Howard Johnson's has a restaurant and all the flavors of ice cream, and charges $52 to $56 in peak summer and winter seasons, $39 to $45 at other times. Get there on the Colonial Drive West exit from I-4. Don't confuse Mac's Hideaway with the high-rise HoJo's at I-4—his is 1½ miles west of I-4.

Compared to most Orlando hotels, the **Davis Park,** 221 E. Colonial Dr., Orlando, FL 32801 (tel. 305/425-9065), is a small place with just 75 units in an enclave owners Carroll and Toni Chapin like to call "a village atmosphere in the heart of Orlando." There is a touch of village about the place too, a homey air if you will. Paneled rooms have big dressing areas, wall-to-wall carpets, and bright colors; outside, there's a pretty pool. Davis's brick-and-wood restaurant has a coziness too, and inexpensive prices. A few rooms have cooking facilities, and double rates at this hotel, about 20 minutes from Walt Disney World, are $39.50 to $44.50, about $3 cheaper for singles.

Quality Inn West, 3330 W. Colonial Dr., Orlando, FL 32801 (tel. 305/299-6710, or toll free 800/327-2016; in Florida, 800/432-8609), prides itself on being newer than Walt Disney World, and now it's newer still! Recently remodeled, the resort features attractive and spacious rooms surrounding a winding swimming pool and a lovely landscaped garden area. Rooms have two double beds and some have couches, so you can really settle in for a relaxed holiday. King-size bed fanciers will find some rooms with those big recliners too, and there are even rooms for nonsmokers. The Ranch House Restaurant, a 24-hour spot, offers meals in the $10 range or less, and the Rod and Gun Pub has a large-screen TV where weary parents can sneak off for a couple of pleasant hours away from the darlings. Two people pay $51 in peak seasons, $42 in other months.

Orlando Motor Lodge, on US 17/92 at North Mills Ave., Orlando, FL 32803, the Princeton exit from I-4 (tel. 305/896-4111), is a little off the beaten track, but when you take a look at this charming lakeside lodge I think you'll be glad it is. Bright colors trim lake-view rooms, and you can swim in the pool, breakfast in the coffeeshop, or just laze around staring at the rippling blue waters, dwelling on what a bargain you've found: rates are just $27 to $35 double in peak seasons.

AT THE AIRPORT: Orlando's fancy new jetport now welcomes international traffic. It's also far enough off the beaten path that you can usually find rooms in this area when other hotels closer to Walt Disney World are filled.

One of my favorites is the **Gold Key Inn,** 7100 S. Orange Blossom Trail, Orlando, FL 32809 (tel. 305/855-0050, or toll free 800/327-0304; in Florida, 800/432-0947), where you can tell at a glance you've found a very special place. Massive beams streak across the lobby ceiling and a brick fireplace is flanked by comfortable couches perched on floral carpets. In your room you'll find pretty floral prints, comfortable armchairs, writing tables, lots of space, reproductions of old English prints, and pretty tiled baths. Outside, landscaped tropical gardens surround a heated pool and there's a putting green and tennis courts. Shuttle buses stop here to take you to attractions. Rates year round are $66 to $88.

The Gold Key's Piccadilly Restaurant is its fame, and has won rafts of awards for its homemade soups and marvelously creamy concoctions, perfectly seared steaks, pink prime rib, excellent seafood served in an atmosphere glowing with stained-glass windows, floral prints, heavy wood beams, and a cozy country air. Gold Key's a treasure of a place, and as close as you're likely to come in Orlando to a gracious country inn.

Across the street is a **TraveLodge,** 7101 S. Orange Blossom Trail, Orlando, FL 32809 (tel. 305/851-4300, or toll free 800/255-3050), with attractive, large rooms in tropical colors and rates of $35 to $51, year round.

WINTER PARK: This dazzlingly beautiful small town is just north of Orlando. You can get there by exiting I-4 at Colonial Drive East, turning north at Mills Drive, and east again on Orange Avenue. Here in this "Little Europe" of central Florida, where everything seems to glow like precious gems, are two small hotels that to my mind are, well, pearls among pearls.

Look up as you stroll Winter Park's main avenue, Park Avenue, and you'll see red geraniums spilling from tiny window boxes and white wicker furniture sitting perkily on a small balcony. That's the **Park Plaza Hotel,** at 307 Park Ave., Winter Park, FL 32789 (tel. 305/647-1072), a glamorous little spot that's been around a long time but has recently been redecorated to a fare-thee-well and is now a fascinating study in antique decor and modern comfort. Beautiful doesn't begin to cover it. How do you explain such things as an Italian tiled foyer, brick trim, whirring paddle fans, a lobby straight (and genuinely) out of turn-of-the-century times? A big, big room I love has brass beds and a sitting room, deep plush carpets, pretty pastels, and wing chairs. And when you're feeling really dramatic you can fling open the french doors and waft onto the balcony overlooking shady Park Avenue, lean decoratively on the railing, and gaze out over this beautiful old city musing on the days when everyone used to live this way all the time. For this old-world elegance you'll pay $50 to $80 overlooking a lovely little courtyard, $60 for a view of the park, $90 to $100 for suite avec balcony. But where else can you be this dramatic for $90?

Such a charming village seems naturally to produce other beautiful things, and the **Langford Hotel,** 300 E. New England Ave., Winter Park, FL 32780 (tel. 305/644-3400), is certainly one of those. A family-owned hotel that's been around since 1955, the Langford has let no moss gather on the rolling stone of its success. Gigantic pines tower overhead, deep jungles of plants surround, and in the tropical garden there's a gurgling little waterfall that glitters at night by the light of Japanese lanterns. As for rooms, well, one has antique French chairs, a crystal chandelier, striped silk chaise, a patterned carpet, beveled mirrors, little corner bibelot shelves, and Austrian drapes at the glass entrance to a private balcony. Another is covered wall to wall in straw matting and filled with African touches like zebra-striped furniture and tall mahogany carvings. In the Empire Room, a long menu is filled with tantalizing beef and seafood dishes, and in the lounge is some of the city's top entertainment, glittering floor shows, and music for dancing. In this glamorous setting you'll pay $50 to $70 a day, year round.

IN SURROUNDING TOWNS: Roads are so good and easy to navigate in central Florida that you can easily stay outside Orlando and drive in for attraction-hopping, so I've outlined a few outlying hotels I think you'll like.

Clermont is a pretty town away in rolling citrus country, and here you'll find the **Rodeway Inn West Gate,** on US 192 and 27, Kissimmee, FL 32742 (tel. 813/424-2621), five miles west of the Walt Disney World gate, with 200 spacious and tastefully decorated rooms overlooking expansive grounds and an Olympic-size swimming pool. There's a game room and playground, lounge, and dining room with moderately priced offerings. Two people pay $43 to $58 in season, $29 to $44 in other months.

Another interesting spot is **Vacation Village,** P.O. Box 951, Clermont, FL 32711, on US 27 four miles south of Clermont (tel. 904/394-4091), a condominium resort where you can stay in a spacious loft apartment or a villa lined wall to wall with cedar paneling. Spiral staircases lead to the lofts, and there's another bedroom downstairs so eight can stay here. Outside, there's a sandy beach on Lake Louisa, barbecues for cookouts, a pool, and sports facilities for boating, tennis, bikes, horseshoes, shuffleboard, badminton, volleyball, and canoeing. It's quite a lovely woodsy place, and the rates are a real bargain too: just $48 to $60 double, or $287 to $357 a week, year round. Children under 18 stay free.

Altamonte Springs Inn, 151 N. Douglas Ave., Altamonte Springs, FL 32701, off I-4 at Route 436 (tel. 305/869-9000), is in the nearby town of Altamonte Springs but it's a bit of a distance from Disney, about a 30-minute drive. Here, however, one has the advantage of being a lulling distance from the crowds and near several top restaurants and a huge shopping mall. If you think you'd like to stay up this way, this resort is the place to settle. Recent renovations have made the attractive, spacious rooms even prettier, and for playtime there's a heated pool. The inn's restaurant, Bloomer's, is a favorite lunch and dinner spot for local residents who retreat here for some top culinary treats and some flashily prepared flambé desserts. For more casual dining, the hotel's Sprague's Restaurant fills the bill. Prices at the former are in the $10 to $15 range, lower in the latter restaurant. Rates at the inn are $53 to $63, year round.

A top budget-wise motel in the Orlando area is **Susse Chalet Motor Lodge,** I-4 and US 27 at Davenport, FL 33837 (tel. 813/424-2521, or toll free 800/258-1980), which charges just $29.70 to $37.70 for two to four people. Rooms are spartan, you understand, but have the usual amenities of phone, TV, bath, shower, swimming pool, ice machine, coin laundry, and free parking. This one's well located for Circus World and Cypress Gardens, and it's not more than 30 minutes from Walt Disney World.

Tucked away in the small town of Howey-in-the-Hills, northwest of Orlando, is the family-owned and operated **Mission Inn,** P.O. Box 441, Howey-in-the-Hills, FL 32737 (tel. 904/324-3101), a Spanish-theme inn with 100 spacious rooms and four exquisite suites with panoramic views of the countryside or an 18-hole golf course on the hotel grounds. Mission Inn has all the amenities of a big-city resort: golf course, pro shop, golf carts and lessons, tennis courts, heated pool, games, and fishing in well-stocked lakes on the inn's grounds.

Boating and waterskiing are available nearby, and the inn is about 30 miles from Walt Disney World and five miles east of the Florida Turnpike on Route 19. Limousine service from Orlando International Airport can be arranged with 48 hours' notice. Two people pay $58 to $80 in slow seasons, $96 to $106 February to May.

If you like resorts and you like golf, **Grenelefe Golf and Tennis Resort,** 3200 Route 546, Haines City, Grenelefe, FL 33844 (tel. 813/422-7511, or toll free 800/237-9459; in Florida, 800/282-7875), is an alluring alternative to Orlando hotels. Another of the state's magnificent condominium resorts, Grenelefe is snuggled away on 950 acres of emerald-green grounds shaded by towering pines and giant live oaks. Since they're condominiums, the 850 villa apartments are all individually decorated and have contemporary touches like lots of glass, flowers, wide dressing areas, big walk-in closets, kitchens with everything from built-in processing centers to zip-lock bags, high sloping ceilings, and always private balconies for a dramatic view of trees and paths (perhaps even a quail scooting home to the family). For fun there are 54 holes of golf (18 of which were rated number one in the state by a golfing magazine), four swimming pools, spa and sauna, tennis courts, plus several shining restaurants and informal lounges. If you're touring, Grenelefe is just a 30-minute drive from Orlando's doings and 15 minutes from beautiful Cypress Gardens. Two people pay $115 to $150 here in peak winter season, $75 to $110 in other months, and children under 18 are free. There's airport pickup too, for $25 a person.

Finally, if you'd like the ultimate tan, **Cypress Cove,** about 11 miles south of Kissimmee on Route 531, 4425 S. Pleasant Hill Rd., Kissimmee, FL 32741 (tel. 305/933-5870), is one of the state's largest nudist colonies. I can't say I've seen everything here, but there is a lake, tennis courts, canoes, paddleboats, a campground, restaurant, and rental units. Admission is $17 per couple, and you can rent a two-bedroom trailer for $53 to $59.

BED AND BREAKFAST: Alternative Travel, 5419 Cane Hills Circle, Orlando, FL 32819 (tel. 305/342-8986), and **Brown's Bed & Breakfast of Orlando,** 529 W. Dartmouth St., Orlando, FL 32804 (tel. 305/423-8858), operate bed-and-breakfast operations in the region.

CAMPING: You can't miss **Yogi Bear's Jellystone Park Campground**—the bear's face is on billboards all over town. There are three of these parks in the area, but the closest to Walt Disney World is a pretty, wooded 700-site campground just four miles west of the park on US 192, at 8555 W. Spacecoast Pkwy., Kissimmee, FL 32741 (tel. 305/351-4394, or toll free 800/558-2954). You'll find a lake here, a mini-golf course, boating and fishing, a grocery store, restaurant, and gift shop, not to mention all kinds of special events. Rates of $16 to $20 include water, electricity, and sewage hookup. Tent sites also are available for $13.

The second of Yogi's hangouts is a 500-site campground ten miles east of Walt Disney World at 9200 Turkey Lake Rd., just off I-4, Orlando, FL 32801 (tel. 305/351-4394, or toll free 800/558-2954). The third is about 30 miles away in Apopka on US 1, P.O. Box 2000, Apopka (tel. 305/889-3048, or toll free 800/558-2953). Rates and facilities are similar at all three campgrounds.

Port O' Call Campground, 5175 US 192, Kissimmee, FL 32741 (tel. 305/396-0110, or toll free 800/327-9120; in Florida, 800/432-0766), is a massive place with a long list of facilities ranging from fishing and shuffleboard to game room, movies, bike and paddleboat rentals, weekend entertainment, and a fancy tropical rock-bedecked swimming pool. It's about five miles east of the gates to Walt Disney World and charges $13 for two adults. There's no charge for children under 12, but additional adults pay $2. Prices include water, electricity, and the rest of those camping necessities. Tenters pay $13.

3. Where to Dine

If there's one way to describe a central Floridian, it's shrewd. These "good ol' boys" know how to turn a dollar, and do so with alacrity and aplomb. It follows naturally that when they eyed passles of excited wee ones steaming through the turnstiles of local attractions, they raced to provide for the masses.

Wee ones' taste being what it is, central Florida became hog heaven for fast-food freaks more quickly than you can say hamburger. But as the World turned desert to Disney, it spurred the creation of architecturally impressive and gastronomically top-notch restaurants designed to appeal to the fantasy-saturated cerebrums of weary parents in search of a little comic relief. Many of these are in Winter Park, which has become the gastronomic capital of central Florida. Since the offerings are many, I've divided them up by the kind of cuisine offered.

Remember that unless otherwise specified, the prices I've cited are for entrees, which usually include salad, one or two vegetables, and perhaps coffee as well.

THE TOP FUN RESTAURANT: Round a bend in Lake Buena Vista village and there rises before you like a ghostly return of another era, the **Empress Lilly** (tel. 828-3900), a fairyland of tiny white lights and a dazzling white triple-decker Mississippi riverboat. Home to no fewer than three restaurants, the *Empress* is, of course, another of Disney's sterling creations, with gleaming brass, etched glass, polished mahogany, a massive staircase between floors, Victorian furniture, lots of Dixieland entertainment, and romantic walks on decks overlooking the twinkle of the Magic Kingdom.

Seek out the glamorous **Empress Room,** site of upper-deck and upper-crust dining in Louis XIV elegance. Intimate banquettes, the charming maître d', Leon, harpist entertainment, the cozy plushness of a forest-green lounge—that's the Empress Room. Entree prices go as high as $22 to $25 for dishes like oyster-stuffed veal chops or frenched lamb chops, but average about $17 to $20, and if you splurge you're likely to spend $35 to $40 a person for a sumptuous feast. Open 6 to 9:30 p.m. daily.

Disney doesn't do things in small doses, so that (of course!) is not all. Aft, you'll find the **Steerman's Quarters,** where you dine on excellent beef concoctions in the $13 to $16 bracket in a pubby decor with wainscotting and flower-sprigged wallpaper. Don't miss the cheesecake. Open 11 a.m. to 3 p.m. and 5:30 to 10 p.m. daily.

Yes, there's still more: the **Fisherman's Deck,** where the specialty is seafood; the room, bilevel; the decor, blue velvet and gold; the ambience, dim and sophisticated; the check, $12 to $18; the hours, 11 a.m. to 3 p.m. and 5:30 to 11 p.m. daily.

And still more: the **Baton Rouge Lounge,** where banjos twang, guitarist strum, and there's a whoop-it-up good time going to 1 a.m.

AMERICAN CONTINENTAL: Park Plaza Gardens, 319 Park Ave. South, Winter Park (tel. 645-2475), has an elegant garden atmosphere with pink linen tablecloths and formal silver place settings, etched- and smoked-glass mirrors, a greenhouse alcove, and glass roof (I could go on and on). As for the menu, it includes seafood bisque, exotic shrimp in curry sauce, flounder meunière, wienerschnitzel, baked Alaska. A very tranquil atmosphere in which to contemplate your good fortune, Park Plaza Gardens is open from 11:30 a.m. to 3 p.m.

and 6 to 10 p.m. (later on weekends). You'll pay about $15 to $20 for dinner entrees at this serene setting next door to quaint Park Plaza Hotel.

The **Piccadilly Restaurant** in the Gold Key Inn, 7100 S. Orange Blossom Trail (tel. 855-0050), is one of the outstanding restaurants in Orlando, an award-winner in both cuisine and decor. A pretty pub atmosphere prevails, with pewter plates, lots of wood, a yellow glow from candles, and fresh flowers. Prices are in the $10 to $17 range for entrees like roast beef with Yorkshire pudding, rack of lamb, and poached snapper. Piccadilly is open from 6 to 10:30 p.m. daily for dinner, from 7 a.m. to 1:30 p.m. for other meals.

The **Longwood Village Inn,** at 150 E. Lake St., Longwood (tel. 422-2062). Take I-4 to the Route 434 exit, then drive east to Route 427, then north two blocks. This inn ranks among the most picturesque in Florida. Built in 1883, Longwood was once a hotel and has now been designated a national historic property. As we went to press, restoration of the property was scheduled for completion in summer 1985 by a group called Centennial Co., which is installing a new restaurant in this lovely old building. It's worth a stop just to get a look at the handsome old Florida structure.

The new place to be seen is Winter Park, which it itself the place to be seen in central Florida, is the **Pink Peacock,** 601 S. New York Ave. (tel. 628-3498). Very posh, white wine, Perrier kind of place serving hamburgers only at lunch, full dinners—steaks, chicken Wellington, seafood, veal—in the $10 to $15 range at dinner. You will be seen, by the way, surrounded by rattan furnishings and a pretty tropical atmosphere. Fitting for one of your rank, no? Hours are 7 a.m. to 3 p.m. daily, except Sunday when the restaurant is open for brunch from 11 a.m. to 3 p.m. only. Every day they reopen at 6 p.m. for dinner, which lasts until 10 p.m., closing an hour later on weekends.

They just named the place for what it is: **Two Flights Up,** at 329 Park Ave. South in Winter Park (tel. 644-9868), where you hie yourself two flights up in what was once the old Colony Theater to find understated contemporary decor, plants, wicker, wood, skylights, and flower-sprinkled tablecloths. You'll also find some mouthwatering veal specialties, good seafood, steaks, fettuccine Alfredo. Try the fudge pie, after which you'll be thankful to get some exercise climbing two flights down. Prices are in the $4 to $15 range at this casual spot that's open from 11:30 a.m. to 2 a.m. Monday through Saturday.

Limey Jim's Restaurant, in the Orlando Hyatt Hotel, at I-4 and US 192 East (tel. 846-4100), is a handsome dining room with excellent cuisine. Your check will probably be in the $20 to $25 range, but you'll dine well and atmospherically.

BASQUE: At cozy **Meson de España,** 2417 E. South St. at Bumby Avenue, in Orlando (tel. 896-9716), bright-red tablecloths are topped by napkins folded like fans, the Basque cooking is delicious, and the caldo gallego thick with sausage and beans. Clams, shrimp, and scallops are topped with a sauce green with parsley, and it's all served up steaming in a metal bowl. Prices are in the $10 to $15 range, and Meson de España is open from 5 to 10 p.m. Tuesday through Saturday.

CHINESE: Jin Ho, at 400 S. Orlando Ave., Winter Park (tel. 628-2660), became so popular that it branched out to Altamonte Springs on Maitland Avenue (tel. 339-0790). If there are two of you, try Seven Stars Around the Moon ($18.75), a melange of lobster, pork, and chicken sauteed with snowpea pods, mushrooms, baby corn, water chestnuts, bamboo shoots, and bok choy surrounded by seven butterfly shrimp. A simple, casual place with plenty of seafood and a sizzling wor bar with seafood and Chinese vegetables served over crisp rice patties, Jim Ho features prices in the $5 to $10 range for a meal. It's open from 11 a.m. to 10:30 p.m. daily, and from noon on Saturday and Sunday.

FRENCH: Genuine Tiffany windows from the McKean collection of Tiffany treasures glow at **La Belle Verrière,** 142 Park Ave. South, Winter Park (tel. 645-3377), and you will too, after a lunch or dinner in this lovely garden setting. Masses of plants and flowers play counterpoint to brick and wood, candles glow, flowers grace every table, and the menu includes vichyssoise or escargots bourguignonnes, chateaubriand, roast duck or rack of lamb, crème caramel, dusky chocolate mousse, and fresh oranges topped with honey and rum. Figure about $15 to $20 for dinner entrees, served from 6 to 10 p.m. daily (lunch from 11:30 a.m. to 2:30 p.m.).

Talented Swiss chef George Vogelbacher has earned many an award for **Le Cordon Bleu,** 537 W. Fairbanks Ave., Winter Park (tel. 645-7575). Well-deserved awards they are too, for this is a simply decorated but sophisticated restaurant famous for leisurely dining on sinful pastries and breads baked right here, filet de boeuf royale (baked in a puff pastry with capers and lemon), pompano with white wine sauce, and herbed filets. You'll pay about $15 to $20 for dinner entrees, and Le Cordon Bleu is open Monday through Friday for lunch from 11:30 a.m. to 2:30 p.m., and from 5:30 to 11 p.m. for dinner daily (except Sunday).

A very curvaceous Winter Park friend swears she keeps her perfect proportions by dining at **Maison des Crêpes,** 348 Park Ave., Winter Park (tel. 647-4469). It's simple, she says: you just down a couple of these paper-thin delicacies stuffed with incredibly rich and creamy fillings, perhaps toss off a crisp cold salad of spinach, mushrooms, and avocado, then don't eat anything else for a day or two. Heaven knows it's worked for her, and even if it's not the ultimate Scarsdale diet, it's certainly a marvelously tasty way to blimpdom. Prices at this cute café are $9 to $15. Maison des Crêpes is open from 11:30 am. to 3 p.m. Monday through Saturday and 6:30 to 10 p.m. Tuesday through Saturday; closed Sunday.

When an Orlando newspaper recently surveyed its readers on restaurants, **Maison et Jardin,** at 430 S. Wymore Rd., Altamonte Springs (tel. 862-4410), swept the boards not only as the best restaurant in the area but also as the favorite French spot, the restaurant with the best service, the most romantic, and the one with the most atmosphere! I hardly need say more (but, of course, will).

French for "home and garden," Maison et Jardin is exactly that, a gracious old home high atop a gentle slope of land and garden in a grove of tall trees. Ornate chandeliers glow, great walls of glass overlook the perfectly manicured lawns where a fountain burbles, and from the kitchen come innovative treats like wild rice bisque, mushrooms thermidor, zucchini and hearts of palm salad, veal Strasbourg, pheasant Souvaroff. On the first Sunday of the month a New Orleans jazz band plays for a brunch that on any Sunday is something to behold. Recent renovations—$100,000 worth—have made this lovely restaurant even lovelier, with more Venetian crystal chandeliers, Rosenthal china, and hand-blown crystal. Winner of numerous awards, Maison et Jardin, which is lovingly called the Mason Jar by un-Frenchified Orlando-ites, charges prices that will bring dinner to about $30 each, but it's really worth it in elegance and excellence. Hours are 6:30 to 10:30 p.m. daily except Monday and from 11 a.m. to 2 p.m. on Sunday for brunch. Jackets are required, and reservations are very, very wise.

GREEK: Epicurus was the original epicurean after all, so it's fitting that Greek

Jimmy Hansis should have named his **Epicurean Restaurant,** 7900 E. Colonial Dr. (tel. 277-2881), after that famous forebear. In a taverna atmosphere (the walls are lined with an outstanding collection of wines and a bouzouki twangs softly in the background), dine on giant Greek salads, moussaka, dolmades, kalamarakia, and pastitsio, lamb, baklava, and thick Greek coffee for dinner prices in the $10 to $15 range. Among his latest additions for adventurous diners are shark, wild boar, and alligator tail. He's open from 5 to 11 p.m., every day but Sunday.

ITALIAN: Former opera singer Joseph del Vento has found a new stage for his talents and named it after an old one, **La Scala,** 430 Lorraine Dr. at Douglas Road, Altamonte Springs (tel. 862-3257). He comes to it well prepared, with a long background not only of arias but of arte della cucina. You reap the rewards of del Vento's many years in the kitchen with such dishes as veal sauteed with peas, prosciutto, and artichokes, or red snapper with parsley, garlic, white wine, oregano, and lemon. Fresh pastas, steaks, seafood, and veal dishes round out the menu, on which prices range from about $10 to $15. La Scala is open from 11:30 a.m. to 2:30 p.m. and 5 to 11 p.m. daily except Sunday, with later closings on weekends.

Orlo Vista, just west of Orlando, is not a town one races to visit, but if you love a good Italian dinner you'll hie over there to **Gus' Villa Rosa,** 5923 Old Winter Garden Rd. (take I-4 to Route 435 and drive north; tel. 299-1950), and pounce on excellent pastas, potpourri of seafood, steak, and veal dishes that have won Gus Stamatin a place in the hearts of Orlando's Italiano worshippers. Stamatin has a long list of culinary credentials and has finally achieved every chef's dream, his own restaurant. Prices are in the $10 to $12 range. Try the shrimp Onassis with feta cheese. Villa Rosa, a casual place, is open from 11:30 a.m. to 2:30 p.m. weekdays for lunch, 4:30 to 11 p.m. for dinner, closing at 9 p.m. on Sunday.

For many, **Spinelli's,** at 1200 Pennsylvania Ave., St. Cloud (tel. 892-2435), put St. Cloud on the map. This sleepy village near Kissimmee knows it's lucky to have Spinelli's, an elegant spot with Mediterranean atmosphere that's pretty but not overpowering. Spinelli's has been winning awards for innovative cuisine and outstanding interpretations of old favorites like osso buco Milanese, and eggplant baked with a mixture of meat, cheese, and spices. Try the veal Spinelli with thyme and brandy, or chicken stuffed with crabmeat. Open from 11:30 a.m. to 2 p.m. and 5:30 to 10 p.m. weekdays, 6 to 10 p.m. on Saturday, and 5 to 9 p.m. on Sunday, Spinelli's charges about $11 to $15 for entrees and has a wide variety of continental preparations.

Villa Nova Restaurant, 839 N. Orlando Ave., Winter Park (tel. 644-2060), has been holding forth here for more than 30 years and is now run by the skilled operators of Winter Park's very successful Park Plaza Gardens. Villa Nova features northern Italian cuisine so loved by gourmets. You'll find such delicacies as carpaccio, raw beef filet in a piquant mayonnaise sauce, escargots in red wine sauce and puff pastry, mussels poached in white wine, fine steaks, fresh pastas, and a long list of veal and seafood favorites. Outstanding cooking here is complemented by one of the region's most attractive, formal dining rooms. Later, in an adjoining room there's some good entertainment too. Villa Nova's prices are in the $12 to $17 range for dinner, and hours are 11 a.m. to 2:30 p.m. weekdays, 5 to 11 p.m. daily.

MEXICAN: Colorfully dressed señoritas, a Mexican tile dining patio, ole! It's **El Torito,** at 275 W. Route 436 in Village Shoppes, Altamonte Springs (tel. 869-5061), where after a margarita or two, a quesadilla, a tostada, perhaps some camarones flores wrapped in bacon and served witth grilled pineapple and Mexican corn, and *caramba,* you're south of the border. Prices are well under $10 and the restaurant's open from 11 a.m. to 10 p.m. daily, an hour later on weekends.

SEAFOOD: A newcomer that's been getting high ratings in Orlando for both food and entertainment is **Brazil's,** 701 Orienta Ave., a block south of Route 436 on Maitland Avenue in Altamonte Springs (tel. 331-7260). A restaurant where the emphasis is on fresh seafood with creative touches, Brazil's opened recently under the tutelage of a young couple, Steve and Lynn Watts. It's decorated in batiks and has something special every day, so be sure to ask what's cooking. You'll always find shrimp San Francisco sauteed with fresh ginger, garlic, scallions, soy sauce, and dry sherry, and a crab sandwich on sourdough bread with melted cheese. Prices are in the $9 to $15 range. Brazil's is open from 11:30 a.m. to 1 a.m. Monday through Saturday.

Lots of people swear that **Gary's Duck Inn,** at 3974 S. Orange Blossom Trail (tel. 843-0270), has the best seafood in all central Florida, and Gary has plenty of awards to back up their confidence. The inn promises that if you stop here once you'll be back, and they've proven the truth of that with an operation that's been going strong since 1945. Try the french-fried jumbo shrimp here, where your check will be in the $6 to $12 range. Open 11:30 a.m. to 10 p.m. daily, later on weekends (from 5 p.m. on Saturday).

Red Lobster, 4010 W. Vine St., Kissimmee (tel. 846-3513), is a favorite in Orlando and turns out lots of what its name implies, plus other seafood and even a few landsmen dinners for moderate prices in the $10 to $15 range. It's open daily from 11 a.m. to 10 p.m., later on weekends.

STEAKS: **Freddie's Steak House,** on Route 17/92 in Fern Park (tel. 339-3265), obviously isn't adorned with a pretentious name, and inside you won't find much in the way of gilt or geegaws, but you will certainly find superlative service, thoughtful extra touches, and great steaks and seafood—so who needs more? A frequent award winner, Freddie's begins with a brimming relish tray, a crock of cheddar cheese, several good breads, and then moves on to seafood and those excellent steaks. You'll waddle out thankful for another "great American favorites" dinner for $12 to $17. Doors are open from 4:30 p.m. to 2 a.m., and there's a regular round of excellent entertainment in the lounge.

Think you can work your way through 2½ pounds of T-bone? Whip over to **La Cantina,** 4721 E. Colonial Dr. (tel. 894-4491), some Wednesday and stoke up on a monster steak plus vegetable, salad, bread, and spaghetti for $15 or so. La Cantina's been pouring out those steaks for more than 40 years now, and has recently added a pretty new dining room with fireplace, fountain, and sunken conversation pit. The beef is aged and cut right here, and in their spare time Al and Linda Seng keep the sauce on for manicotti, ravioli, and veal. Prices are in the $12 to $17 range, and the restaurant's open from 5 to 11 p.m. Tuesday through Saturday.

Charley's Steak House, 6107 S. Orange Blossom Trail (tel. 851-7130), prides itself on the care and feeding of the multitudes who never met a steak they didn't love. Aged beef is cooked over a natural wood-burning fire here using a method the restaurant says was inspired by Seminole Indian cookery. Seafood fans will find Australian lobster tails—big ones—on the menu, a fresh-catch item daily, langostinos. Charley's is also one of the few places in town you can find pork chops. A big salad bar is included with dinner entrees, which range in price from $8 to $15. Cocktails as well as beer and wine are available from 11 a.m. to 11 p.m. daily, an hour later on weekends.

At the **Orange Quarter,** 70 N. Orange Ave. (tel. 843-1747), you'll find seafood, veal, and potatoes baked in rock salt and served wih blue cheese, onions, bacon, or crabmeat, sandwiches, and crispy salads. Dinner prices at this pretty restaurant average $10 to $15. It's open from 11:30 a.m. to 1 a.m. and there's entertainment here too, plus an $8 Sunday brunch ($4.75 for children).

VEGETARIAN: **Paradise Café,** 2417 E. South St., Orlando (tel. 896-9716), has won over some diehard nonconverts to vegetarian fare. Local food critics have been singing the praises of Paradise Café, which features fish, shrimp, and scallops broiled or sauteed in parsley, white wine, and garlic, some tempura-fried and stir-fried treats with brown rice, and such unusual extras as cashew gravy, honey-baked cheesecake, and whole-wheat carrot cake. All this healthiness is delivered in a pretty atmosphere, laden with tropical plants and decorated in eye-catching turquoise and red with multicolored napery and a bar tiled in pink and black. They're quite in earnest about what they're trying to do here, so if you're at all inclined to get healthier, why not give them a chance to help you out? Lunch prices are in the $2 to $7 range, and dinner runs about $10 to $15, although some selections begin at $5. Hours are 11:30 a.m. to 3 p.m. weekdays, 5 to 10 p.m. daily, closing two hours later on weekends. You'll find the restaurant between Primrose and Bumby Streets.

LIGHT MEALS: Pecan waffles, creamy homemade ice cream, fresh oranges, grapes, apples, and cantaloupe heaped over sherbet, a gasp-able banana split, giant Black Forest layer cake—have I got your attention? You'll find all this and much more at the tiny **East India Ice Cream Co.,** 327 Park Ave. South, Winter Park (tel. 628-2305), where you tread on brick walkways and dine outside in a jungle of greenery or inside in the paddle-fanned coolness of an interior jungle. Prices for most things don't top $5, and East India Ice Cream Co. is open Monday through Thursday from 8:30 a.m. to midnight, on Friday and Saturday to 1 a.m. (from 10 a.m. to midnight on Sunday).

Jo Ann's Chili Bordello, 1710 Edgewater Dr., between Princeton and Ivanhoe Streets (tel. 425-9865), is just too good a name to resist. If you love chili, you'll adore this crazy place where the wallpaper is red flock, the carpet is red plush, and all is offset by chandeliers and fancy drapes, à la bordello style—at least I suppose it's bordello style. Waitresses dressed in French corsets and black high heels add their bit to X-rated chilis, each of which is named after a famous, er, lady. Chilis are also rated PG and R, for those who like it hot but not quite so hot. Dinners are a little more elaborate and may feature something like Hawaiian pork or stuffed chicken breasts. For dessert? Cheesecake, of course. Prices are in the $10 to $15 range for dinner, lots less for chili, and hours are 11 a.m. to 10 p.m. daily. Darling, need you ask? Never on Sunday.

BUDGET AND FAMILY SPOTS: It's not every day you get to dine in a country store, and **Mack Meiner's Country Store,** at 921 N. Mills Ave., Orlando (tel. 896-5902), is certainly that. Oilcloth and kitchen chairs, old ads and movie posters, a player piano and sheet music make this a fun spot to tie the feedbag on the family. Most prices run about $5 or less, and barbecue's a specialty, although there are also chili, soups, and heavenly hash pie. It's open from 11 a.m. to 9:15 p.m. Monday through Thursday, to 10:15 p.m. on weekends, and from noon to 9:15 p.m. on Sunday.

When you see a line outside **Ronnie's,** 2702 E. Colonial Dr. in the Colonial

Plaza Shopping Center, Orlando (tel. 894-2943), as you generally do for Sunday breakfast, you've got to figure somebody's doing something right inside. Indeed they are: a long, long menu, tables laden with bowls of kosher dills and sauerkraut, cheesecake light as a cloud and rated best in the city, pastries that are raw guilt, not to mention prices in the $5 to $10 range for most anything, less for some choices. It's open from 7 a.m. to 1 a.m. daily. You may even see jazz stars —Count Basie, Maynard Ferguson, and George Shearing (who loves matzohball soup), have been guests here.

Morrison's Cafeterias always produce creditable buffets at very creditable prices (about $5 or under). In Orlando, the cafeteria's at 7440 International Dr. (tel. 351-0050), and there are three others, one in Winter Park, one on East Route 50 in Orlando, and one in Altamonte Springs.

Duff's Smörgåsbord is another top budget choice, with gigantic buffet spreads for lunch and dinner at a grand total of $3.85 for adults, $2.45 for children! In Orlando, Duff's is at 4442 Curry Ford Rd. at Conway (tel. 277-5090), and is open from 11 a.m. to 8 p.m. daily.

TGI Friday's, at 227 Route 436 West in Altamonte Springs (tel. 869-8085), is always a good choice for inexpensive food, and with so much of it to choose from, it will take you ages just to read the several-page menu. It's a fun place with lots of weird decor and waiters who cavort about, and TGI Friday's prices are in the under $10 bracket. Hours are 11:30 a.m. to 2 a.m. daily. Very good Sunday brunch here from 10:30 a.m. to 2:30 p.m.

Holiday House, 2037 Lee Rd., Orlando (tel. 293-4930), also has restaurants in Winter Park, Mount Dora, Deland, for a total of 13 locations including another in Orlando that's closer to Disney, at 1522 Orange Ave. (tel. 425-1521). They feed you well and efficiently here in a nice atmosphere on a dinner buffet that's just $5.50, and lunch is even cheaper—$4.45. The restaurants are open from 11 a.m. to 9 p.m. daily.

The **Overland Express Steakhouse** at the Stagecoach Inn, 4311 W. Vine St., Orlando (tel. 846-4213), has dinner for under $10, lunch for under $5; and **Davis Brothers Motor Lodge,** at 6603 International Dr. (tel. 351-2900), has a fancy smörgåsbord, all you can eat for $3.50 at breakfast, under $4 for lunch, and $5 for dinner.

The **Village Inn,** 345 W. Fairbanks in Winter Park (tel. 647-7516), has good and reasonably priced food in a quiet contemporary atmosphere for $5 to $10. Choose from a long dinner list that ranges from steaks fantail shrimp, and keep in mind that prices include beverage and dessert. Open Sunday through Thursday from 6 a.m. to midnight, on Friday and Saturday from 7 a.m. to 4 a.m.

In the Midwest where they breed **Steak and Shakes** about the way they breed soybeans, some gourmets/gourmands of my acquaintance swear by the glories of this chain. Here in Florida you can find them only north of a line passing more or less from Tampa through Orlando to Daytona, a source of much grief to those of us who have gloried in Chili Mac's culinary heights. For those of you who know whereof I speak, there's a Steak and Shake at 2820 E. Colonial Dr. (tel. 896-0827), with burger prices under $2, and five others scattered around town. They're open from 10 a.m. to 11 p.m. daily, to 1 a.m. on weekends.

Fudrucker's, 160 E. Altamonte Dr. in Altamonte Springs (tel. 832-1444), is housed in a one-time automotive center gone uptown. Now a very trendy spot, Fudrucker's gets my vote for name alone. Besides that name, it also has hamburgers, sandwiches, salads, and the like for prices in the $5 to $10 range for most goodies. Hours are 11 a.m. to 11 p.m. daily, closing an hour earlier on Sunday.

If you're staying out on International Drive, you'll find **Darryl's 1883 Res-**

taurant and Tavern, 8282 International Dr. (tel. 351-1883), a pleasant place to while away a couple of hours. All weathered wood, etched glass, and the like, the restaurant has something for absolutely every tastebud ranging from pasta to salads to Mexican, burgers, steaks, sandwiches, seafood, ribs—you name it, they've got it somewhere. Prices are quite reasonable, falling easily in the $5 to $7 bracket for many menu selections, $8 to $10 for full dinners. Hours are 11 a.m. to 2 a.m. daily.

READER'S RESTAURANT SELECTION: "I would like to tell you about a superb Italian restaurant, the **Olive Gardens,** at 7653 International Dr. (tel. 351-1082). The prices are moderate (the most expensive item on the menu was $9.95). Children's portions are available at half price, and soft drink and milk refills are free. All dinners are accompanied by a basketful of delicious garlic bread sticks, a large bowl of Italian tossed salad, and your choice of vegetable. The Olive Garden was busy yet very quiet, and our waitress very attentive. They don't take reservations" (Patricia McGurk Fink, Bethel Park, Penna.)

4. Meeting the Mouse

What a magical, mystical, laughable, lovable place the cartoonist carved out of 27,000 acres of central Florida wilderness! But what a huge and exhausting place it can be too. Before we get into the delights of Disney, heed this one little warning for which you will be speechlessly grateful later: please understand that you can walk the soles off your shoes trying to see everything in this massive park, and burn your unsuspecting skin to a crisp in the Florida sunshine while you're at it. So *wear comfortable shoes and clothes, and make sure you have something to cover our skin and your eyes,* like shirts and sunglasses. No matter how cloudy or how weak the sun is, in Florida it burns—fast.

GENERAL INFORMATION: If you drive to the park, it's a good idea to get there early, say 8:30 a.m., since the crowds increase with the hour. I've been there *very* early and have yet to be first. Parking is $1, and you pay at an entrance so busy it looks like a toll booth on a major expressway.

Once you're at the entrance to the park (signs on I-4 will direct you there), follow the signs to the parking lots for either the **Magic Kingdom** or Disney's latest fascinating creation, the **Experimental Prototype Community of Tomorrow (EPCOT) Center.** From those parking lots, trams run constantly to the ticket booths at the entrance to either of the parks.

Be sure to write down or otherwise remember the name of your parking lot (in Magic Kingdom they're named for the Seven Dwarfs and other characters, and in EPCOT Center they have names like Communications, etc.) and the number of your parking line. On busy days there can be 80,000 people in the park—and that's a lot of silver station wagons!

Those trams whisk you off to the **Ticket and Transportation Center,** where you buy tickets for either or both of the parks. There's a special parking lot for handicapped visitors too, and wheelchairs can be rented for $1 a day at the stroller shop just inside the entrance to the Magic Kingdom or EPCOT Center. If you have any special problems, **Guest Relations** (tel. 824-4500) are there to help you with friendly smiles and some quick thinking. Information is also available at 824-4321.

A little general orientation here: Monday through Wednesday, strangely enough, are the busiest days at the park, and the summer months and Christmas are the busiest seasons. Restaurants are jammed between 11 a.m. and 1 p.m. so you might consider early or late lunches. (That goes for dinner too in busy seasons.)

Once you've bought your tickets (hang on, I'm coming to the prices), go directly to City Hall in the Magic Kingdom, or Earth Station in EPCOT Center and ask for a map. Look over the list of things you want to see, then plot out a more-or-less organized course through the park. You don't have to stick to it, of course, but it will help you keep from wandering aimlessly around trying to figure out where you are and what you should do next.

READER'S WALT DISNEY WORLD TIP: "During the kids' vacation from school, the park stays open to midnight. After dinner, the lines seem to diminish and from 10 p.m. to midnight you can see more than you could all day" (Sara Drower, Wilmette, Ill.).

The Magic Kingdom and EPCOT Center Prices and Hours

Now's the time you're going to have to consider how much time you are going to spend at Walt Disney World. Now that the World contains both the Magic Kingdom and EPCOT Center, there is a great deal to see. If you have only one day to spend here, you're going to have to choose between the Magic Kingdom and EPCOT Center. It is very difficult, if not impossible, to visit both in one day. In fact to make a leisurely visit to both is likely to take you about three days. Add two days to that if you'd like to spend some time at the park's sports, shopping, and special attractions (River Country and Disney Island).

Okay, here's what Disney's Magic Kingdom costs: a one-day World Pass entitling you to visit *either* the Magic Kingdom or EPCOT Center (but not both) is $18 for adults, and $15 for children (ages 3 through 11).

There are no two-day World Passes available, but a three-day passport permitting admission to both the Magic Kingdom and EPCOT Center is $45 for adults, and $37 for children 3 to 11. Finally there is a five-day World Pass for $65 and $53. It can be used anytime for a year.

Tickets may be bought with cash, travelers checks, American Express, MasterCard, VISA, or a personal check with proper identification. Credit cards can also be used at hotels, shops, and some restaurants in the parks.

You can order tickets by mail by writing to Admissions, Walt Disney World, P.O. Box 40, Lake Buena Vista, FL 32830—but allow 15 working days for processing your request.

If you leave the Magic Kingdom or EPCOT Center and plan to return the same day, have your hand stamped at the exit.

If you're staying at one of the hotels owned by Walt Disney World, you can get a few dollars off on tickets. Inquire when making your reservation.

A Little Orientation

Time for a little semantics lesson. Walt Disney World refers to the entire Disney complex which now includes the Magic Kingdom, EPCOT Center, River Country, Discovery Island, four hotel complexes, and the Walt Disney World Shopping Village and Hotel Plaza. I mention this only so you don't expect to see EPCOT Center by going to the Magic Kingdom. Those two attractions are three miles apart and each occupies acres and acres of ground!

Disney's newest creation is **EPCOT, the Experimental Prototype Community of Tomorrow,** which opened in October 1982, just ten years after the Magic Kingdom. Here in EPCOT Center, Disney takes a little more serious look at the world but still offers plenty of fun with everything from life-size dinosaurs to a 3-D movie.

EPCOT Center itself is divided into two sections separated from each other by a large lake. One side of the lake harbors the Future World exhibits provided by major corporations, and on the other side you'll find World Showcase, where nations of the world show off their cultures and products.

For a really detailed look at all the magic of Walt Disney World, read our in-depth Orlando book, *Frommer's Guide to Orlando, Disney World, & EPCOT.*

Pets, Kids, Pix

A couple more notes on protocol and when we're off. Despite the Kingdom's love for Pluto and Mickey, Dumbo and Donald, you'll have to leave Fido in the Kennel Club next door to the Transportation and Ticket Center (and pay $4 for some loving care and feeding that may spoil him for weeks). There's also a kennel at Fort Wilderness Campground, and at EPCOT Center.

Be forewarned, too, that the tiny Mickey Mouse your toddler has seen in comic books bears only surface resemblance to the park's towering Mickey, whose huge head is set on a tall strong body. This giant mouse is not always as thrilling to a two-foot person who's looking up at a monster as he is to adults. Children are often terrified at the sight of the huge cartoon characters and set up a wail that can be heard to Kansas if they are confronted too suddenly with a giant hand. So introduce little ones slowly to the World's characters so both they and you will enjoy the introduction. (If you fly Eastern to Orlando, by the way, you can take the children to a special Character Breakfast where Pluto, Mickey, Donald, and the fat bears cavort for the kids. The airline has details.)

If you'd like to take pictures in the park and don't have a camera, Kodak will lend you one. The company's booth is at the south end of Main Street, U.S.A., and you can borrow a camera free for your visit if you'll leave them a refundable $50 deposit.

There's a similar deal available at the Camera Center in EPCOT Center—it's just to your right as you face the entrance to Spaceship Earth. There's also a shop at Journey into Imagination.

Dining

As for dining at Disney, you need never fear starvation. There's food, food, and more food, from street venders to dozens of restaurants. A few outstanding ones are **King Stefan's Banquet Hall** in Cinderella Castle, the **Liberty Tree Tavern** in Liberty Square, and **Aunt Polly's** on Tom Sawyer's Island in Frontierland, where you can munch on a porch overlooking the water. Moderate prices prevail in the Kingdom, with lunch prices in the $3 to $5 range, dinner under $15 generally. You can't beat this culinary choice at Disney: frozen bananas covered in chocolate. Terrific.

For more elegant dining, Contemporary Resort Hotel's **Top of the World** (tel. 824-1000) has a Sunday brunch from 11 a.m. to 2:30 p.m. at $12.95 for adults, $6.25 to $9.95 for children, depending on age. You can have dinner here any night for $13 to $18 and stay for a razzle-dazzle Broadway show and top-name star entertainment at 6 and 9:15 p.m. Cover charge is $7.50 for adults, $3.75 for children.

At **Polynesian Village** there's a daily breakfast buffet at $5.95 for adults ($3.95 for children), and similar spreads at lunch. In the evening the hotel presents a luau buffet and fabulous Polynesian entertainment at 5 and 7:45 p.m. at $21 for adults, $12.60 to $16.80 for children, depending on age.

You must have a jacket at the Contemporary Hotel, gentlemen, and no jeans no matter whose name is on the pocket (no rules like that at the Polynesian). Reservations are required at both hotels for their evening entertainment. The Contemporary's at 824-1000; Polynesian Village, at 824-2000.

In EPCOT Center, the choices are fascinating and may be fattening as well. EPCOT's World Showcase, which features pavilions representing nine nations (soon to be 11), has full-scale and fancy restaurants "in" France, the U.K., Japan, Mexico, Italy, Germany, and Canada, plus several other "quickie" food purveyors.

So popular are these brand-new restaurants that you must make dinner reservations the minute EPCOT opens. By 9:30 a.m. most of the restaurants are fully booked. To make reservations, go straight to Earth Station when you arrive and walk over to one of the WorldKey Information Service television screens you will see lining the walls. Step right up and touch one of the screens— go on, don't be nervous—and you will see a knife and fork symbol. Touch that and you will see the smiling face of a WorldKey hostess who will help you make a reservation at the restaurant of your choice.

Which one is that? Well, *you'll* have to decide what kind of food you'd like to try, but be forewarned the most popular restaurants are **Les Chefs de France,** created by three very famous French chefs, Paul Bocuse, Roger Verge, and Gaston Lenôtre, in the French pavilion; the **Rose and Crown** in the U.K.; and **L'Originale Alfredo di Roma** in the Italy pavilion.

You'll still find crowds, however, at the **Biergarten** in the German pavilion, the **Tempura Kiku** and **Teppanyaki Dining Room** in Japan, the **Cantina de San Angel** in Mexico, **Marrakesh** in Morocco, and **Le Cellier** in Canada's pavilion. Take whatever you can get. They're all wonderful fun. Each in its own way whisks you out of Orlando and into another country effortlessly and skillfully. Prices at all the restaurants are in the $12 to $15 range for entrees, a little higher for some things in France, a little lower in Mexico. All the restaurants have some entertainment too, ranging from strolling mariachi singers in Mexico to a beret-ed combo, complete with accordion and striped shirts in France.

READER'S EPCOT TIP: "We ate in the French restaurant, and the meal definitely is worth the sprint earlier in the morning to secure the spot. These restaurants are a far better choice than the fast-food alternatives" (Sara Drower, Wilmette, Ill.).

THE MAGIC KINGDOM: Okay, map in hand and pulse pounding in anticipation, off we go for a gleeful romp in the land of mysterious haunted houses, runaway railroad cars, leering pirates, and fat, frolicking bears. . . .

Main Street, U.S.A.

There it is at the end of a two-block stretch of primped and precious Victorian village: the glittering blue-turreted magnificence of **Cinderella's Castle,** 18 stories high and topped by fluttering flags. You've arrived in Disney World!

All through the park an army of smiling workers keeps the grounds trim and shining, the flowers growing on command in just the right colors and places, and trees just high enough to produce the perfect shade. Another army keeps these grounds so spic and span you'll wonder if they're following people around with a broom. If there's one single thing you'll find remarkable about the park it's the perfect cleanliness here—from the sidewaks to the shining all-American scrubbed look of park workers.

Mainstreet, U.S.A., is turn-of-the-century America filled with penny arcades, horseless carriages, a Victorian restaurant, silent movies, and an old-fashioned ice-cream parlor. You can ride the horse-drawn trolley or the horseless carriages (all included in your tickets), and later cavort with the characters as they parade down Main Street at 3 p.m. in the **Main Street Character Parade.** On summer and holiday evenings, that parade becomes the glittering **Main Street Electrical Parade** at 9 and 11 p.m. Don't miss it!

Adventureland

Pirates of the Caribbean is the top ride here, and a favorite of both adults and children. You sail away into a mysterious grotto, then plunge into a raucous pirate raid where a drunk buccaneer lolls and leers, a mangy dog rolls his eyes, and one eye-patched devil hangs menacingly over you and is so realistic you can see the hair on his pantalooned leg! You'll soon think the **Enchanted Tiki Birds** are the real thing too. A sail through leafy lagoons aboard the **Jungle Cruise** is soothing—and fun!

Frontierland

Brass rails line the saloon, Indians raid the wooden fort, a hilarious gang of singing bears laughs it up at **Country Bear Jamboree,** and across the river, **Tom Sawyer Island** has Injun Joe's Cave, the Magnetic Mystery Mine, and a log raft ride over to Fort Sam Clemens. Don't miss the country bears (one grown man told me he's already seen them nine times and can't wait for his tenth visit!). **Big Thunder Mountain Railroad,** newest of the park's attractions, takes you on an exciting journey aboard a runaway train. It's great fun—just watch out for that last bend.

Liberty Square

Animated, life-size figures of our nation's leaders rise and talk to you in the **Hall of Presidents.** They gesture a little, and look so real you're tempted to step up and offer them a vote. It's a masterful display of wax creativity and Disney ingenuity. At the **Haunted House** you'll shriek with the rest of us cowards as the walls rise (or is it the floors that drop?) and ghosts exchange civilized chatter at a haunting dinner party. There's a delightful river cruise on a sternwheeler, and a high-stepping revue here too.

Fantasyland

Ms. White and her troop of odd little men, plus Dumbo, Mickey, and the gang perform in the **Mickey Mouse Revue,** and you can fly through the night keeping a sharp eye on the leader at **Peter Pan's Flight. Small World** is just that, a globe-circling trip accompanied by tiny singing dolls in native costumes. **Twenty Thousand Leagues Under the Sea** takes you into the depths à la Jules Verne.

Tomorrowland

Space Mountain is Disney's very own heart-stopper rollercoaster, and **Mission to Mars** is fun. Monsanto and Eastern Airlines have fascinating film exhibits. One, a CircleVision 360-degree Theater, projects a tour of America the Beautiful on a circular screen with a particularly memorable boat trip (you can see the water ahead, then turn around and see the wake behind you!).

River Country

Disney recreated the ol' swimmin' hole here just west of Pioneer Hall in **Fort Wilderness,** then added some typical Disney delights like three twisting, turning water-flume slides, rafts, and innertubes on which you ride down winding rapids and under waterfalls, ropes you swing on into the water, a pool 160 feet long, picnic areas, beach, and nature trail. Admission is $9.50 for adults, $7.25 for children 3 to 13.

Discovery Island

You can cruise across a lake to an island lined with paths that wind through colorful perfumed foliage, flowers, and trees; watch the activities of 500 birds of more than 60 species in an aviary; see rare Galapagos tortoises and bald eagles. Admission is $4 for adults, $2 for children under 13.

That's it, and believe me that's a day or three worth of fun and laughter, fantasyland at its best thanks to a talented cartoonist who shared his forest of characters and stole all our hearts.

On your way back to your car, you can keep the magic going just a few minutes more by sailing to the parking lot aboard a free ferryboat that leaves from just in front of the monorail stop and cruises you back to the ticket center, where you board a tram, tired but full of memories of a kingdom that's magic indeed.

EPCOT CENTER: Drift down from Dumbo's ear now and give a listen to the sound of the future. Here in EPCOT Center Disney has put together a look at what you can expect from tomorrow; a glance at the past to show you how far we've come just to get to *today;* and a glimpse into the ways others live in this world we all inhabit together.

All rolled together it's called **Future World,** produced by some of the nation's leading corporatons, and **World Showcase,** where nine (soon to be 11 or more) nations give you a glimpse into their "world."

In both these Worlds you'll find all kinds of special entertainment, from brass bands to huge walking "dolls" representing their countries, and a magnificent evening show on the lagoon in the center of it all. Performers from many nations also appear on a special stage in front of the U.S. pavilion.

Because EPCOT Center is so new—and so many people want to know what it's all about—we'll take a look now at this very special place in the World.

Future World

Here you will find a stirring look at how our nation gets its energy at Exxon's **World of Energy.** You'll also get an amusing, even an exciting, look at the dawn of mankind when huge dinosaurs and terrifying pterodactyls roamed the earth and skies. Don't miss this one—you can even smell the primeval, sulfurous swamps and see the steaming upheaval of the earth. It's a kick.

Kodak's **Journey into Imagination** is a strong favorite with the EPCOT crowds, and no wonder. First you go on a fanciful ride with a character named Dreamfinder, who hangs around with a little purple dragon character called Figment. With that duo you go on a chortling trip through your imagination—and goodness knows what you'll find *there!*

Here you can also see a thriller of a 3-D movie complete with lighting in a jar, a fearful witch, and a kite that persists on sitting on your eyebrow. Fun! Don't miss the creative playground of the future either, or you won't know what to do when the whole world is creating sound with light. Stop by, you'll see what I mean.

Not ones to be left far behind, General Motors' **World of Motion** takes you on a trip—what else?—through the history of man's search for mobility. AudioAnimatronics, the life-size characters who move, blink their eyes, play ukeleles, cackle, and lay eggs, are particularly good in GM's offering. There are also some futuristic automobiles, trucks, and motorcycles on display as well as GM's latest products.

At **Spaceship Earth** you explore man's age-old questions: Who are we? Where do we come from? Here too AudioAnimatronics are wonderful. They alone will show you how far we've come with our playthings.

Another big hit with the crowd is **The Land.** Presented by Kraft, The Land gives you a look into the future of food production. Here on Disney's "Land" grow cucumbers that add inches even as you watch (up to 12 inches a day!). Here in an experimental greenhouse, experts from all over the world are working together to produce plants that grow in a simulated spacecraft environment, alongside other crops so each nourishes the other, in giant rotating drums, on space-saving plastic A-frames, and in nothing but air. It's downright amazing.

You can eat some of the products produced there in the Good Turn Restaurant, a revolving dining spot which gives you a little preview of what you'll see on your ride through this land.

Horizons gives you a look at the life a family will be living in the next century: kids going on a field trip to a seaweed farm; robots, operated by voice commands, harvesting crops; and workers harvesting crystals. You travel to the future aboard a moving "spaceship."

World Showcase

Here nine nations have spread out their wares and their smiles alongside a sparkling blue lake. Each has built its pavilion around its best known architectural landmark—the Eiffel Tower, the Palace of the Doges, the Aztec pyramid.

When you step into one of these countries, you are completely immersed in the culture. Not only does each country look the way that country really looks, but all the employees come straight from their homelands and have charming accents. Ze French are veeery French, monsieur, and the Brits are veddy, veddy Brit. You'll love it.

You can get around on foot or on antique double-decker buses that stop in front of some of the countries. There can be a great deal of walking and standing because there are many things to see, so be prepared to hoof it. It's 1.2 miles around the lake, which you can also cross by boat. You'll see the boat dock at the end of the walkway that leads from Future World to the lake.

For a look at the restaurants in World Showcase, turn back a few pages.

Here's a brief look at each of the pavilions, starting with Mexico and moving clockwise around the lagoon:

Look to your left as you face the lake and you'll see a great stepped pyramid rising out of the flatlands. That's **Mexico,** and inside the pyramid you'll find candles glittering and an eerie blue glow creating a romantic mood in the midst of an adobe village. A jaguar snarls in the distance as you look over the piñatas and Mexican wedding dresses, the huarachis and guayaberas. A boat ride takes you on the River of Time through Mexcio's past and present.

Don't skip the film in the **China** pavilion—it's one of the best loved productions in EPCOT Center, and rightfully so. Projected on a 360-degree screen that wraps all around you, the film takes you to the famed Forbidden City, to the Harbin Ice Festival where ice-carving enthusiasts create bigger-than-life-size fantasies in ice, and to places in China that have never before been filmed by Westerners. It's downright spectacular! If they ever put an airline ticket machine in here, all the world will be booked on flights to China. Yes, it's that fascinating.

Africa is soon to make an appearance here complete with a typical African village and a film narrated by *Roots* author Alex Haley.

Omm-pah-pah, plenty of suds and pretzels, pretty frauleins, and some intriguing crafts are just part of the lure of the **Germany** pavilion. There's an especially amusing show here at dinner, complete with slap dancing and those incredible long Alpine horns. Fun.

An amusing street theater and an excellent restaurant are two of the lures that will bring you to **Italy** and keep you there, stuffing yourself on laughter and linguine. You'll see gondolas floating in the lagoon out front and get a chance to buy some glittering Venetian glass and soft Italian leathers.

Ben Franklin and Mark Twain take a look at U.S. history with an assist from Chief Joseph, Susan B. Anthony, and Frederick Douglass at the **American Adventure.** All this takes place in an elegant theater. This production has the distinction of being the first Disney AudioAnimatronic creation in which one of the characters actually walks—it's Benjamin Franklin, and he walks up the stairs for a visit with Thomas Jefferson.

Japan invites you to enter through a massive Torii gate. On the way you pass a dramatic pagoda trimmed with royal-blue roof tiles that glitter in the sun and tiny bells that dangle off the eaves. A priceless suit of Samurai armor is displayed here, and there are some intriguing treasures in the Mitsukoshi department store. Japan has two very good restaurants and a lovely lounge that has the best view of EPCOT in EPCOT.

Visions of veiled ladies and ghostly spooky caftans disappearing around a corner. Cladestine whispers. Humphrey Bogart in *Casablanca*. It all comes to life at EPCOT's new **Morocco** pavilion, which itself came to life in 1984 but seems, like Morocco, to have been here since the beginning of time. Here you're welcomed by a gaggle of clapping, singing, fez-topped musicians who pound on drums and strum away at stringed instruments in the shadow of a replica of the 12th-century Koutoubia Minaret.

Disney artists are a magical lot, and here they've managed to recreate the labyrinthian splendor of Morocco. A strikingly beautiful palace courtyard looks just like Spain's famed Giralda. In the small museum here you can examine some of the amazingly intricate artwork of the Moroccans. You even get a special invitation to a recreation of a Moroccan wedding, at which the bride in an elaborately embroidered wedding gown and slippers sits high atop a pile of pillows.

Artisans were brought from Morocco to build this pavilion with its intricate tilework and carved timbers. So realistic is the melange of streets, gates, and minarets they created that one workman is said to have looked down the street and pointed out the house in which he was born! Some of those artisans remained, and you can watch them here today weaving beautiful Moroccan carpets, pounding brass into trays and pitchers, tooling leather. That and many, many other kinds of treasures—sheepskins, gold-trimmed caftans, ceramics, woodwork, silver, and baskets (leather hats for about $8 are a favorite buy)—are sold in this melange of bazaar shops.

Morocco sports the newest restaurant in EPCOT—Marrakesh. A study in candlelight, ornately carved plaster, tiles, carpets, costumed waiters, and a belly dancer, Marrakesh is one of the loveliest of EPCOT's restaurants. For $12 to $15 you feast on a dinner of such Moroccan specialties as couscous (a bowl of semolina topped with vegetables, beef, lamb, and chicken) or saffron-flavored harira soup. Revel in the flavors of apricots, cinnamon, almonds, honey, prunes, delicately blended with chicken, beef, or lamb, and finish it all with glasses of hot mint tea.

If you can't get reservations under the Eiffel Tower at **France**'s Les Chefs de France Restaurant, toddle on over to the Pâtisserie, where the aroma alone is caloric. Croissants, tartin, gateaux, yum. France also has a delightful movie that skims you over the countryside and into the City of Light. Some delightful shops too—take a look at the tapestry cushion covers in the Plume et Pallette. Terrific.

Things are so British at the Rose & Crown Pub in the **United Kingdom** even the British are overwhelmed. Most people figure to hit here when exhaustion sets in so they can spend a little resting time with a cold "pint-a"—they'll even warm it up on special warmers so the beer will be the same temperature as it is in London! Tea, crumpets, and cashmeres are on sale here, and the Pearly Band, a group of Cockney singers and dancers in pearl-button-covered costumes, are a big hit.

Canada is justly proud of its *O Canada* film, another of those stirring 360-degree productions. This ones takes you to the Calgary Stampede, downhill on skis, and to the top of Toronto's most famous landmark, the C.N. Tower. You'll hear music of a lumberjack band, visit an abandoned gold-mine tunnel, and . . . whoops, watch out for the waterfall!

Here's a little known helper for you: All the treasures you buy—and you'll see dozens of things you want—can be sent out to the entrance where you can pick them up at **Package Pickup.** When you buy something, just ask the salesperson to send it over to Package Pickup, keep your receipt, and you'll find your treasures waiting for you when you leave. It beats carrying dozens of little packages with you everywhere you go.

5. Other Adventures

Not even Superman could see all there is to be seen in Orlando on a quick swing through the city, so don't expect to see this zany wonderland of life-size mouseketeers and dancing whales in a half-day visit. Walt Disney World alone takes a day (at least), and you'll probably save yourself frustration later by allowing two or three days to tour. Folks at the city's chamber of commerce advise a five-day visit to see it all without heartburn or fallen arches.

SEA WORLD: Racing right along nipping at Mickey's tail is Sea World, 7007 Sea World Dr. at the I-4 Sea World exit (tel. 351-3600), the largest marine-life theme park in the world—to see it all will take six to eight hours! Fifteen different shows are topped by star **Shamu,** the immense 4500-pound killer whale who doesn't look to me like he'd kill anything larger than a shrimp. Shamu rides his trainer lovingly around on his back, kisses pretty girls and children, and is a somewhat hefty danseuse who performs a delicate ballet, but with no toe shoes. Dolphins, sea lions, and otters cavort on command here, and there's a talented ski team that at last check were telling—on water skis—the story of the Hatfield-McCoy feud (it started over possession of a pig who was nothing at all like this hog on skis!).

Sea World has built a brand-new home—Shamu Stadium—for its precious performer and all his look-alike killer whale brothers and sisters. Eighteen of those big bruisers will be bred here and some of them will perform in this special stadium, which features 5,000,000 gallons of water and a performing pool 35 feet deep. Shamu's new home is the largest single-species research and display facility in the world, Sea World claims, and who can dispute it? Just seeing these massive creatures is worth the visit, but seeing one of them merrily racing about with a proportionately teensy human being on its back is downright mindboggling. You'll love it.

A spine-chilling attraction at this massive park is the **Shark Encounter,** which features those fearsome denizens of the deep swimming happily (I hope) around in a tank made of enormously thick clear acrylic. You ride right among *Jaws* stars aboard a "people-mover" that glides you through the tunnel while those toothy little fellows swim all around you. There are dolphins to play with, a fascinating coral reef to examine, a Caribbean tidal pool, plumed birds roaming free, a 400-foot skytower, even pearl-bearing oysters in the gift shop. Eleven theme restaurants at the park are always open when the park is, from 8:30 a.m. to 7:30 p.m., later in summer and on holidays. Admission is $13.95 for adults, $11.95 for children 3 to 12 (under 3, free). Parking and kennels are free too.

CIRCUS WORLD: If people have, on occasion, intimated you're a real clown, why not whip over to Circus World and see if it's true? You can be a clown-for-a-day there, complete with makeup and photograph, or just immerse yourself in the dramatic world of the Big Top. You can't miss Circus World's candy-stick-stripped tent at I-4 and US 27 in Haines City (tel. 813/424-2421), about ten minutes west of Walt Disney World, and you won't want to when you discover what fun they have here. Clowns, puppets, high-wire artists, snarling Bengal and Siberian tigers, a dashingly handsome ringmaster, performing elephants, and a heart-stopper called the Roaring Tiger, one of the world's fastest rollercoasters. Circus World is open from 9 a.m. to 6 p.m. daily, later in summer. Admission, which includes rides, is $12.95 for adults, $10.95 for children 5 to 11.

WET 'N' WILD: Orlando's answer to the beach is Wet 'n' Wild, at 6200 International Dr. (tel. 351-3200). Every kind of watery fun is available here, from bumper to speedboats, a surf pool where constant four-foot waves are produced by a machine. There are white-water slideways and a kamikaze slide that sends you whooshing down into a pool from a platform six stories up in the air! You can try a tiny pool with squirty games for toddlers, a Corkscrew Flume that spirals you through a figure-eight and tunnel, even a Bonzai Boggan water rollercoaster that races at 30 m.p.h. into a pool. You can picnic by the lake or stoke up at the snackbars. Admission is $10.50 for adults, $8.50 for children 3 to 12, free to others. It's open daily mid-February to November from 10 a.m. to 6 p.m.

MYSTERY FUN HOUSE: Get lost in the mirror maze, try to figure out the topsy-turvy room, walk the magic floor here in the weird Mystery Fun House, on Major Boulevard off I-4 at Route 435 North (tel. 351-3355). The price is $5.95 for adults, $4.95 for children 4 to 13. Hours are 10 a.m. to 11 p.m. daily.

REPTILE WORLD: Some people do really strange things for a living, and one of them is the person who milks the cobra and other precious vipers at Reptile World **Serpentarium,** on US 192 about four miles east of St. Cloud (tel. 892-6905). You can see that and more than 60 varieties of reptiles, from lizards to crocodiles, Tuesday through Sunday from 9 a.m. to 5:30 p.m. (venom extractions are at 11 a.m., and 2 and 5 p.m.). Admission is $3 for adults, $2 for children 6 to 17, $1 for children 3 to 5.

GATORLAND ZOO: If you know someone you'd like to feed to an alligator, you can get in a little practice with some dead meat at Gatorland Zoo, on Routes 17/92 and 441, 14501 S. Orange Blossom Trail, just north of Kissimmee (tel. 855-5496). They've recently trained those toothsome creatures to leap into the air, a feat quite uncommon for these ground-loving creatures. Have your picture taken with a boa constrictor and ride a train through all the creatures' homes from 8 a.m. to 7 p.m., later in summer. Admission is $4 for adults, $3 for children.

STAR OF SANFORD: When the fantasylands overcome you, one way to escape to something different is to sail off on the *Star of Sanford,* which cruises the waterways of the historic St. Johns River on brunch, lunch, and dinner cruises. There's entertainment on board this triple-decked ship too, but just standing up on the observation deck and watching the world float by is entertainment enough. Lunch cruises depart daily at 11 a.m., dinner trips at 7 p.m., Sunday brunch trips at 9:30 a.m., and Sunday dinner cruises at 1:30 p.m. Adult fare is $18 for lunch and brunch cruises, $25 for dinner; children 7 to 12 pay $10 at lunchtime, $15 for dinner cruises. You'll find the boat at 433 N. Palmetto Ave. in Sanford (tel. 321-2627).

XANADU: Excuse me, I must just ring Robutler for a towel so I can pop into the spa. If this is what life in the 21st century is going to be like, let us all hope we make it. At **Xanadu,** US 192 and Route 535 (tel. 396-1992), they are convinced they know just how we all will be living in days to come. It looks good to me. You can see if it looks good to you by stopping in at this Styrofoam mushroom of a house that sprouts in all fantasy, just down the road from, of all things, Medieval Times. Talk about time warps.

At Xanadu, which is certainly 21st century in materials, design, and architecture, you'll find a really intriguing look into the future of home construction. Circular rooms flow into each other. There's an indoor pool, a waterfall-spa in the master bedroom, a solar sauna, a greenhouse, sunken conversation pit, electronic hearth, projection television, a "house brain," security center, computer-voice command center, a central vacuum system, electronic exercise equipment, and best of all, a robot butler who never frosts you with a chilly "Really, madam." Make way, Jeeves.

You can't miss Xanadu—jut look for the weirdest sight on US 192 heading east from I-4. It's open daily from 10 a.m. to 10 p.m. (be there 45 minutes before closing time to make the tour), and admission is $3.75 for adults, $2.75 for children 4 to 17.

A FEW OFFBEAT ATTRACTIONS: If you still think steaks come from a steak factory, roam over to Kissimmee's weekly **cattle auction,** where you'll see real cowboys roping the main attraction of tonight's dinner. Steaks-on-the-hoof are auctioned off to cattle barons who look more like punchers than princes at this boots-and-jeans event every Wedesnday—early (say, 8 a.m.)—at the city's Livestock Market, just north of Route 17/92 and US 441 at 150 E. Donegan Avenue (tel. 847-3521). When the shouting's over (about noon), you can lunch at the Auction House while cowboys chase your dinner around outside. There's no admission charge.

Those plastic containers you use to grow green fuzzy things in your refrigerator are people too, you know. What's more they have a history, and you can find out all about it at **Tupperware's International Headquarters,** on US 441 and Route 17/92, just south of Orlando (tel. 847-3111), which maintains a museum of food containers and tells you how they're made and what to make of them. It's open from 9 a.m. to 4 p.m. Monday to Friday, free.

At Clermont, about 25 minutes west of Orlando on US 27, you can zoom to the top of **Florida Citrus Tower** (tel. 394-2145), the highest observation point in the state, and gaze out over 2000 square miles of rolling hills and sparkling emerald citrus trees laden with orange and gold fruit. It's quite a sight, and later you can visit a glassblower's workshop, a citrus packing plant, and a candy kitchen, as well as send oranges home to frozen friends. Open from 7:30 a.m. to 6 p.m., the tower charges $1.75 for adults, $1 for students 10 to 15; younger children are free.

To see a huge, working ranch, visit 40-mile-deep **Deseret Ranch,** off Route 192 about 25 miles east of St. Cloud (tel. 892-3672), owned by the Mormon church. You need to call first so they can meet you for a tour. It's free.

If you love uniforms, you shouldn't miss Friday at the **Orlando Naval Training Center,** off Corrine Drive, north of Route 50, also called Colonial Boulevard (tel. 646-4474), when the gobs graduate complete with 50-state salute, navy band, Bluejacket chorus, and drill team. Festivities begin at 9:45 a.m. and are free. Enter at General Reese Road.

Watch oranges go in one side while gum drops and other dentist's delights come out the other at the **Citrus Candy Factory,** on US 27 in Dundee (tel. 439-1698). It's between Cypress Gardens and Circus World, and open 8 a.m. to 6 p.m. daily, later in summer, and free.

See top harness horses train from 8 a.m. to noon daily except Sunday from October through April at **Ben White Raceway,** at US 441 and 1905 Lee Rd. (tel. 293-8721); free.

Orlando Science Center, Loch Haven Park, 810 Rollins St. at Route 17/92, Orlando (tel. 896-7151), amuses with an intriguing assortment of hands-on sci-

ence exhibits and a planetarium. Hours at the center are 9 a.m. to 5 p.m. weekdays (to 9 p.m. on Friday), noon to 9 p.m. on Saturday, and noon to 5 p.m. on
Sunday. Admission is $2 for adults, $1.50 for children 4 through 18. Sky shows
are at 2:30 p.m. weekdays with extra performances at 8 p.m. on Saturday and at
1 and 3:30 p.m. on Sunday. On weekends the center presents cosmic rock concerts, otherwise known as laser light shows, at 9 and 10 p.m. Admission is $2.50.

Somehow I just knew it would happen. Right. Elvis Presley (!) has joined
the fantasy world of Orlando attractions. Yessirree, step right up to the **Elvis
Presley Museum,** 5921 American Way, across from Wet 'n' Wild (tel. 345-8860).
Here lives Elvis's grand piano, Elvis's last Cadillac, Elvis's wardrobe, furniture,
paintings, Cobra race car, guitar, gun collection, karate ghi, and oh-golly-gosh,
Elvis's very own racing jumpsuit. Admission is $4 for adults, $3 for children 7 to
12. Hours are 9 a.m. to 11 p.m. daily.

Central Florida Zoological Park, US 17/92 at I-4, at Lake Monroe in Sanford (tel. 323-6471), is home to more than 200 wild and exotic animals occupying
some pretty acreage. 'Gators, crocs, lions, and tigers stare back at you here, and
the zoo also has pony rides, a children's zoo, animal-feeding demonstrations on
weekends, and an elevated nature trail through a swamp. Hours are 9 a.m. to 5
p.m. daily, and admission is $3 for adults, $1 for children under 12. Take Exit 52
from I-4 to find the zoo.

No matter how many times you see them, there's something fascinating
about a fragile shell. Some people really get into this shell fascination, and for
them the **Beal-Maltbie Shell Museum** at Rollins College, Holt Street in Winter
Park (tel. 646-2000), is something to see. They've amassed a vast collection of
shells here, including some of the rarest shells in the world. Admission is $1 for
adults, 50¢ for children under 12, and hours are 10 a.m. to 4 p.m. Monday
through Friday.

READER'S RECOMMENDATIONS: "**Walt Disney World** is flawless and the place one should
go if a person could only make one trip in a lifetime. **Sea World** is certainly worth the time
and the Shark Encounter is very impressive . . . the dolphin and stingray petting pools
are super. Everyone should avail themselves of the guided tour there or anywhere else for
that matter as they are always informative, get you behind the scenes. **Medieval Times,** a
comparatively new Orlando attraction, features dinner and a jousting tournament—I'm
enraptured with that era but I was skeptical . . . to say the least I was more than pleasantly surprised. It's a first-class production, the food is good, the show is beyond belief, I
enjoyed it so much I returned a second time and the second night felt like more than just a
guest. I felt like a friend" (Carol Brown, Las Vegas, Nev.).

6. Nightlife

Orlando's geared to families, so there's plenty of wholesome entertainment here. If you're up to your ears in ducks who quack jokes, there are a number of parent-getaway spots too, where you can find a little comic relief.
Orlando is not, however, the spot to seek razzle-dazzle nightclubs, nor is it a
place where a night on the town will cost you two days on the job.

Top of the line in Orlando entertainment is **Church Street Station** (tel. 422-
2434), the Walt Disney World of Orlando nightlife. From the moment you roll
onto downtown Orlando's Church Street and hear the first nasal notes of a
steam-driven calliope, you're in for an adventure. Here you can rise to the
heights in a hot-air balloon or get down with some funky singing, dancing, foot-
stomping entertainment.

The complex got started about ten years ago when Orlando discovered it
had a good grip on today and tomorrow, but hadn't yet begun to exploit the
past. Out it went in search of history and turned up Church Street Station, a
long-neglected railroad depot on brick-lined streets right in the center of some

of Orlando's oldest architecture. Topped by a silver cupola, the aging station became the focal point for redevelopment and Church Street Station was the crowning touch.

A rip-roarin' complex of saloons, restaurants, and entertainment, Church Street Station whizzes you back to days of banjos and bar-top can-can girls, singing waiters and silent movies, Dixieland and do-si-do. What a laugh it must have been collecting the wacky array of bric-a-brac here: huge brass chandeliers salvaged from a Boston bank, teller's cages vintage 1870 from a Pittsburgh bank, train benches from an old railroad station, cast-iron tables from an English pub, and best of all, a mahogany confessional from a French monastery as a telephone booth.

Once the dilapidated old Strand Hotel, the entertainment emporium now houses five fun centers: Rosie O'Grady's Good Time Emporium, a razzle-dazzle saloon right out of the Gay '90s (or is it the Roaring '20s?) with a belt-'em-out red-hot mama, a crooning minstrel singer, Dixieland band, can-can girls with swishing skirts and garters; Apple Annie's Courtyard, a purveyor of kebabs, fruit drinks, and bluegrass music; Lili Marlene's Aviator's Pub and Restaurant, a quieter spot with stained-glass transoms, oak paneling, a walnut fireplace once the possession of the Rothschilds, and French-flavored cuisine in the $12 to $25 range; and Church Street's token male, Phineas Phogg's Balloon Works, purveyors of burgers and boogie, a disco spot with a balloon-basket balcony from which you watch dancers cavort amid flashing strobes and puffs of fog.

Church Street Station is the number one not-to-be-missed star in Orlando's nightlife firmament. The evening cover charge is $5.95. You can even book a hot-air balloon champagne flight here for $100 a person.

Finally, if you like a rootin', tootin' good time, there's no better place to look than the Cheyenne Saloon and Opera House, newest addition to Church Street's empire. So authentic is this good-time emporium that even the appearance of Wyatt Earp wouldn't turn heads. Brass and etched glass, hand-turned wood, authentic costumes, all executed by the same skillful hands that put together the phenomenally successful Church Street Station. What are you waiting for? Get out your jeans and red bandana, your boots and silver buckle, and get on over there, podner. There's a bellying-up spot at the bar with your name on it. Everything's open from 11 a.m. to 2 a.m.

With his puckish sense of humor Shakespeare would probably have gotten a few chuckles out of the things that have been done in and with his name. There's no doubt at all that he would have enjoyed what's going on at **Shakespeare's Tavern,** 15 W. Church St. (tel. 841-4144). A recent addition to the Church Street complex of entertainment, Shakespeare's Tavern is the site of a nightly Old English banquet that begins promptly at 7:30 p.m. with a mead reception followed by a five-course dinner and scads of entertainment. While you're munching on a banquet that ranges from pâté to sherry trifle, you're entertained by a troupe of British singers, dancers, jugglers, jesters, just as you would have been at a medieval banquet. Shakespeare's has become a very popular spot so reservations are suggested. Price of dinner, show, unlimited mead (and other potables) is $24.95 for adults, $19.95 for teens 12 to 18, and $14.95 for children 3 to 11. Shakespeare's is quite an entertaining addition to the many diversions on Church Street.

These days, Orlando's seeming-boundless fascination with fantasy seems to be taking medieval form, first with a dinner-show evening lauding Shakespeare and now with a new attraction called **Medieval Times,** 4510 Vine St., Kissimmee (tel. 396-1518). Here you can, as they say, thrill to the sounds of yesteryear as knights on horseback race by defending someone's honor. Medieval tournaments, complete with jousting and good-guys/bad-guys swordplay amuses you as you dine on chicken, ribs, pastry, light potables. A family entertainment, this dinner-and-show event begins about 6:45 p.m. (the castle opens at 6 p.m.), takes about two hours, and costs $19 for adults, $17 for teens 12 to 17, and $12 for children 3 to 11.

In the Magic Kingdom, the Contemporary Hotel hosts a constant round of entertainment at its **Top of the World Restaurant,** and there's always a band for dancing. **Polynesian Village Hotel** is a fantasyland of lights and lagoons that's practically entertainment in itself, but the hotel also has Polynesian luaus every night outdoors at the Luau Cove. Island dancing and music transports you to the land of grass skirts and wiggles at $21 for adults, $16.80 for teens 12 to 17, and $12.60 for kids 3 to 11. Luaus are at 5 and 7:45 p.m., and also at 10:30 p.m. on holidays.

Empress Lilly's banjo-strumming lounge has nightly entertainment, and there's no cover or minimum. Over in the village at **Lake Buena Vista,** the lounge is one of the area's top spots for jazz, with the vibes emanating from about 8 p.m. nightly. All the hotels in Lake Buena Vista (see my hotel recommendations) also have nightly entertainment. In summer and at Christmas, when the Magic Kingdom blazes with fireworks, there's no better place to watch than from the **Top of the Lodge** at TraveLodge.

Sea World also has a **Polynesian Luau** and show in summer that's riveting fun for the whole family: fire dancers, those lovely Polynesian lasses who swivel at 75 r.p.m., and a bountiful luau buffet. It's at 7:30 p.m., and all-inclusive admission is $15.95 for adults, $5.95 for children. Call 351-3600 for reservations.

Elsewhere around town, the **Langford Hotel,** at Interlachen and East New England Avenues in Winter Park (tel. 644-3400), has outstanding entertainment and a supper club with dazzling revues. There's no cover charge and jackets are required.

Limey Jim's at the Orlando Hyatt, I-4 and US 192 (tel. 846-4100), is another good spot for entertainment, as is **Piccadilly Pub** in the Gold Key Inn, 7100 S. Orange Blossom Trail (tel. 855-0050), and **Freddie's Steak House,** Route 17/92 in Fern Park (tel. 339-3256).

In Winter Park, **Two Flights Up,** at 329 Park Ave. South (tel. 644-9868), is a favorite gathering spot, as are **Harrigan's,** 310 Park Ave. South (tel. 628-1651), and **Park Avenue Disco,** 4315 N. Orange Blossom Trail (tel. 295-3750). This latter is a monstrous two-level flash-and-flicker spot where from a balcony seat you can watch the swirling rainbows of light, rising fog, and silver snowfall. Designed for the 23-and-up set, this is the place to practice your spins and splits, from 8 p.m. Admission is $3 per person (except on Tuesday, Thursday, Friday, and Saturday, when ladies are free), and the disco's closed on Monday.

If you have a pressing desire to meet some of the kids of the Kingdom on their off-duty hours, begin your search at the **Giraffe Lounge** at the Hotel Royal Plaza in Lake Buena Vista (tel. 828-2828), where they congregate. Top-40 music is on tap daily except Sunday here.

J.J. Whispers, 904 Lee Rd., Orlando (tel. 629-4779), has become quite a hot spot in recent years. Several nightclubs under one roof, this rocking spot is unmarked, but you'll find it—just look for a million or so cars! The disco is called Shouts and is open Wednesday through Saturday. Whispers Show Room features a band for dancing Tuesday through Saturday, and several smaller rooms are for those who want to hear themselves along with the music. Hours are 7 p.m. to 2 a.m., and the cover charge is $3.

Sullivan's Trailway Lounge is one of the few stay-ers on the Orlando nightlife scene. It's been around since the early 1970s. Often jammed, Sullivan's features such stars as Mel Tillis and Moe Bandy if they're here, but most of the time it's top touring and local bands onstage at 1108 S. Orange Blossom Trail (tel. 843-2934). There's a $2 cover charge.

Townsends Fishhouse and Tavern, 35 W. Michigan St., Orlando (tel. 422-5560), has lots of woodsy-plantsy atmosphere, marble bars, and plenty of brass and copper trim. There's live entertainment here Wednesday through Saturday, a wine bar, and lots of burgers, fried vegetables, and of course, fish, in the restaurant here. There's no cover charge, and hours are 11:30 a.m. to 2 p.m. weekdays, 5:30 to 10:30 p.m. daily, much later hours in the tavern.

Theater on Park Dinner Playhouse, at 401 Park Ave. in Winter Park (tel. 645-5757), offers quite good Broadway show productions with professional performers on stage in an intimate theater. Tickets are $8.25 weekdays, $9.50 on weekends (dark on Monday).

Once Upon a Stage, 3376 Edgewater Dr., Orlando (tel. 422-3191), combines dining and theater-going with year-round productions. Dinner's at 6:30 p.m., the show at 8:30 p.m., and tickets are $14 to $16. The house is dark on Monday.

There always seems to be at least one new thing to do in Orlando and this time around it's the **Celebrity Dinner Theater,** 46 N. Orange Ave., Orlando (tel. 843-1751). A new venture opened in 1985, the theater was begun by actor and Metropolitan Opera singer Tom McKinney, who has teamed up with Florida theater developer Rick Allen, a participant in the development of the Burt Reynolds' Jupiter Theater in Jupiter.

McKinney and Allen pooled resources and talents to turn a 1921 vaudeville house in downtown Orlando into this handsome new dinner theater, which opened with Kaye Ballard playing in *Pippin*. Now seating 300 at tables outfitted in mauve and dusty rose, Celebrity Dinner Theater has matinee performances Wednesday and Saturday with doors opening at 11:30 a.m., show at 1:15 p.m., and on Sunday, when the theater opens at noon for a champagne brunch, with a show beginning at 2:30 p.m. Tuesday through Saturday doors open for evening performances at 6 p.m., with dinner at 7 and the show at 8:15 p.m. Prices are $18.50 for weekday matinees, $20.50 to $22.50 for evening performances and Sunday brunch. Gala opening-night performances on the first Friday of any new show are $27.50.

The **Central Florida Civic Theater,** 1010 Princeton St., Orlando (tel. 896-7365), has been lighting up the night with amateur and semiprofessional actors for nearly 60 years now. A community theater, the group now takes to the boards at Loch Haven Park, 1010 Princeton St., where the theater has been located for ten of its 58 years. Curtain time for each of the theater's six plays from January to June is 8 p.m. Wednesday through Saturday, with a 2 p.m. matinee on Sunday. Season ticket prices are $55, about $20 less for students under 21. Individual tickets are $9 to $10.

Orlando art and cultural activities have increased greatly in recent years. The **Orlando Symphony Orchestra** presents concerts (tel. 896-0331) in winter, and **Rollins College** (tel. 646-2233) has a concert series. Tickets are $5 to $10. And now you can attend opera performances by the **Orlando Opera Company** (tel. 896-7575) in November, January, and March.

A **Bach Festival** (tel. 646-2110) takes place in Winter Park during the last week of February.

Orlando's **Ballet Royal** (tel. 647-2717) performs several times a year, including the *Nutcracker Suite* at Christmas. Another dance group, **Dance Unlimited** (tel. 671-2155), has an annual February concert and a spring art festival at Leu Gardens, while **Dance Company of the Academy of Dance and Theatrical Arts** (tel. 645-3847) has both a senior and a children's company performing in spring and in June.

Those dance, opera, and symphonic events normally take place at the **Bob Carr Performing Arts Center,** a 2500-seat auditorium at 401 Livingston St. (tel. 843-8111). Zev Bufman, Florida's premier play producer, brings his Broadway road shows here to the Carr also.

Add to that the **Annie Russell Theatre** at Rollins College, a fascinating theater in the grand baroque style. A regular series of seven productions runs here from October through May. Learn what is when by calling them at 646-2501.

To find out everything that's happening in the arts in central Florida, pick up a copy of *Center State,* a monthly magazine with a centerfold calendar of events. It's produced by the Council of Arts and Sciences for Central Florida, and you can reach them at 629-0252. That same group runs a ticket service at 305/THE-TKTS (otherwise known as 843-8587). Yet another number for information from that council is THE-ARTS (tel. 843-2787), a recorded **Arts Hotline.**

7. Sports

If you have any time left after roaming the fascinating attractions here, use it—and some energy—on a round of sports activities.

GOLF AND TENNIS: Among the loveliest courses in Orlando are those right at Walt Disney World. There are three courses here, the **Magnolia,** the **Palm,** and a course at the **Lake Buena Vista Club.** All three started life as desert sands but have been miraculously converted into tree-lined, water-dotted, hilly areas, interesting enough to challenge golfers on the PGA Tour route which visits here each year. If you're a golfing fan, you'll find them challenging but not terrifying. All are par-72 courses up to 7000 yards. Greens fees are $35 for guests of Walt Disney World Resorts, $40 for visitors, including carts. If you really want to save money, plan your outing for the hours after 3 p.m., when a twilight rate of $19 goes into effect for all golfers, resort guests or not. Starter's telephone number is 824-3625. If you've got a young Jack Nicklaus with you, try the **Wee Links,** a course especially designed for young golfers: two feet equal a yard. The cost is $4 for golfers under 17. Adults can play here too, for $6.

Many hotels in Orlando have money-saving arrangements with golf courses, so check before you head off on your own.

Other courses in the area include: **Buenaventura Lakes Country Club,** 301 Buenaventura Blvd. (tel. 933-2582), a par-30 course with $5 to $7 greens fees and $5 to $8 cart charges; and **Cypress Creek Country Club,** 5353 Vineland Rd., Orlando (tel. 351-2187), a par-72 course that charges $16 greens fees off-season, including cart, and $25 January through April.

For tennis, the **Orlando Vacation Resort** (tel. 904/394-6171) has 17 clay and asphalt tennis courts for $2 to $5 an hour, and **Vistana Vacation Villas** (tel. 846-1200) has 16 clay courts for $5 an hour.

There are six free asphalt courts at **Oak Street Park,** Palm and Oak Streets, Orlando (tel. 847-2388), open from dawn to 10 p.m.

BOATING: Drive your own airboat through the backwaters of Kissimmee or rent canoes or electric boats from **U-Drive Airboat Rentals,** 4266 W. Vine St., Kissimmee, six miles east on US 192 (tel. 847-3672). Fees begin at $12 an hour for airboats, $3 for canoes. **Walt Disney World Village** at Lake Buena Vista has speedboats for $7.50 a half hour.

Rent a houseboat with galley, baths, and air conditioning, and tour the crystal springs of St. John's River, from **Sunshine Line** (tel. 904/736-9422). They're at Holly Bluff Marina in Deland, and the boats are $738 a week from March to October, $559 in other months.

Dee's Ski Center, Route 1, Box 595, on Lake Juliana, in Auburndale (tel. 813/688-1931 or 984-1160), has waterskiing instructions for $16 per hour or $60 per day. To get there, take Exit 21 (Route 559) from I-4, go one mile south toward Auburndale, and turn right on Lundy Road.

Ski Holidays likes to call itself the largest waterskiing instructional group in the world, and who can prove otherwise? Superlatives notwithstanding, the ski center offers a free shuttle service from all Lake Buena Vista–area hotels and from many other hotels in the area too. Skiing takes place at Lake Bryan, a clear, 350-acre spring-fed lake just minutes from the Disney hotel complex. Services range from special instructional programs for first-time skiers to hourly charters for intermediate to advanced skiers.

Rates are quite reasonable too: regardless of the number of skiers, $40 an hour, $25 a half hour, $12.50 for 15 minutes. Those prices include instructions and equipment too. They'll even teach you barefoot waterskiing here for $30 for 30 minutes, and take the kids on ski rides for $5. Parasailing is $25 a ride.

You can write to the company for a brochure at P.O. Box 22007, Lake Buena Vista, FL 32830 (tel. 305/239-4444). To get to the skiing area, take I-4 to the Lake Buena Vista exit, turn east on Route 535 toward Kissimmee (away from Walt Disney World), and about 200 yards east you'll see a sign directing you to the school and the lake.

PARIMUTUEL SPORTS: Greyhounds chase but never catch the electronic bunny at **Seminole Greyhound Park,** 2000 Seminole Blvd., Route 17/92 in Casselberry (tel. 841-3480), and **Sanford-Orlando Kennel Club,** Dog Track Road (tel. 831-1600). Seminole is open May to September; Sanford, from late December to early May; and there's racing nightly at 7:30 p.m. (except Sunday), with matinees on Monday, Wednesday, and Saturday at 1 p.m. Admission is $1.

Jai-alai is always a thriller, and you can see it at **Florida Jai-Alai Fronton,** 211 S. Route 17/92, in Fern Park (tel. 331-9191), from October through February. Admission is $1. There are noon matinees on Monday, Wednesday, and Saturday.

BASEBALL: From mid-February to early April the **Minnesota Twins** train at Orlando's Tinker Field, at the corner of Tampa Avenue and Church Street (tel. 849-6346). Tickets are $2.50 to $5. From April to September the Orlando Twins play professional baseball here. Tickets are $1.50 to $3.50.

Newest residents of Kissimmee are the **Houston Astros** baseball team, which now turns up here for spring training. A new 6000-seat stadium adjacent to the Kissimmee–St. Cloud Convention and Visitors Bureau, on US 192 and Route 441, is their playground. Contact them at 305/847-5000.

FAMILY FUN: If you'd like to get in a little mini-golf or a couple of rounds on bumper cars or go-carts, stop in at **Fun 'N Wheels Family Fun Park,** 6739 Sand Lake Rd., corner of International Drive and Sand Lake Road, Orlando (tel. 351-5651). It's open 10 a.m. to midnight, and golf is under $3 a round. Rides are $1 to $3.

Ice skating in Florida? Why not? Try it at **Orlando Ice Skating Palace,** Parkwood Shopping Plaza, 3123 W. Colonial Dr., Orlando (tel. 299-5440). Rates are $3 to $5 and the rink is open Wednesday through Sunday with skating beginning at 2:30 p.m. weekdays and 12:30 p.m., weekends. On weekdays and Sunday the rink closes at 10:30 p.m., on Saturday night it's open to 1 a.m.

8. Shopping

Orlando is a souvenir hunter's heaven, but there are now many crafts and specialty shops in the area too, plus several big shopping malls.

Lake Buena Vista has 27 lovely boutiques filled with treasures, and in downtown Orlando the **Orange Quarter,** at Orange Avenue and Washington Street, is tiny but pretty, and growing fast.

Factory outlets are popular here, and you can find **Dansk** contemporary china and teak products at 7000 International Dr.; **Fostoria Glass,** at moderate prices, at 105 W. Colonial Dr.; **Polly Flinders** hand-smocked dresses for little girls in Casselberry Square. **Second Serve,** at 1121 N. Orlando Ave., has big discounts on brand-name tennis and sportswear.

A freak-out for discount-store fanatics is **Fitz and Floyd Factory Outlet** (at the end of International Drive at Oak Ridge Road intersection, follow signs on International Drive from the Sand Lake Road exit on I-4). You'll find 70 cut-rate shops open seven days a week. They're jammed with housewares, per-fumes, gifts, entertainment items, shoes, clothes—you name it, it's all here at prices 25% to 75% below retail cost.

In Winter Park, charming **Park Avenue** is one of the state's poshest shop-ping streets, ranking right up there with Worth Avenue in Palm Beach for beau-ty and buys. At one interesting shop here, Ted Dobbs, a heraldist, will research your name, and his wife, Pat, will use her calligraphic skill to inscribe your fami-ly motto on a crest—he's worked on one for the Reagan–Davis heraldry (you do remember Ronnie and Mrs. Ronnie?), and earned an invitation to the inau-guration with it.

You say you'd rather make a deal than buy by the price tag? Then head right out to **Flea World,** a 33-acre flea market/mall in Sanford. Opened in 1982, this combination of junk and junque recently spent $2 million on an expansion program designed to create still more space for Turkish bedspreads, $3 haircuts, macramé plant hangers, antique furniture, old clothes, new clothes, and general treasure.

You'll find both indoor and outdoor marketing at this very large bargain-up-a-storm playground, which features covered and paved walkways easy for elderly and handicapped treasure hunters. You'll also find restaurants here in air-conditioned buildings, even a chimney sweep! It's open on Friday, Saturday, and Sunday from 8 a.m. to 5 p.m., and admission and parking are free. Enter-tainment too. To get there from the Kissimmee area, take I-4 to the Sanford exit (about a 40-minute drive, 20 minutes from the downtown Orlando area), turn right to Route 17/92 and south to Flea World. Or take Route 17/92 directly from downtown Kissimmee.

Loehmann's Plaza, Route 434, Altamonte Springs, has as its key tenant that now-famous fashion discount shop, Loehmann's. There are also a number of other specialty shops here, some discount, some not, all of them occupying an attractive indoor marketplace with a bit of a European-market air about it. Hours are 10 a.m. to 9 p.m. daily, closing at 6 p.m. on Saturday and Sunday and opening at noon Sunday. To get there, take the Longwood exit from I-4.

Add to that another new shopping center, **The Marketplace,** 7600 Dr. Phil-lips Blvd., just north of Sand Lake Road and west of I-4 (take Exit 29 from I-4 and turn right at the stoplight), where some creative souls have opened a pretty little woodsy shopping center with Victorian overtones. Makes an interesting, casual place to stroll as well as to shop. You'll find a pub and restaurant here, childrens' and women's fashion shops, an antiques store, and assorted other boutiques. It's open daily from 10 a.m. to 9 p.m. (tel. 351-7000).

READERS' SHOPPING TIP: "**Factory Outlet Mall** on International Drive is a bargain-hunter's paradise. Orlando Toy and Gift Outlet there was a big hit with my sons, ages two and four, who discovered the Smurfs were only $1—we had been paying $1.50" (Tricia McGunk Fink, Bethel Park, Penna.).

9. Side Trips Around Central Florida

You can have a real adventure exploring the highways and byways of central Florida, where you'll find everything from orange groves to Derby winners.

CYPRESS GARDENS AND LAKE WALES: Head south from Orlando on US 17 (or branch off I-4 onto US 27, picking up US 17 in Haines City) and stretched out before you, behind you, and on all sides are stubby green trees. Nesting in their shining emerald leaves are the bright gold and orange orbs of Florida's most important crop, none other than citrus, the state's most prolific product. Most of it's grown right here on these slopes, which produce more than 12 million boxes of fruit each year.

The Sights

Stop off for a look at one of the state's most elegant attractions, **Cypress Gardens,** west of US 27 on Route 540 at Cypress Gardens Boulevard in Winter Haven (tel. 813/324-2111), once called by *Life* magazine "a photographer's paradise." It's a stunningly beautiful cypress swamp turned into acre upon acre of exotic flowers with an antebellum town where southern belles in hooped skirts make themselves part of the scenery, a Living Forest filled with tame animals, a domed gazebo that's been the site of television shows and weddings. Wander around absorbing the hushed air of this huge tropical forest with paths that wind through ginger plants and coffee trees, ancient cypresses centuries old, and deep, hauntingly silent lagoons. But don't miss the Gardens' frequent waterskiing shows with award-winning skiers who perform precision ski tricks (like barefoot skiing and kite flying on skis) the way you and I walk to the grocery. Their grand finale is a three-tiered pyramid of skiers balanced on each others' shoulders!

Cypress Gardens has lots of restaurants and boutiques full of treasures, and for photographers there's a special section in the stands where shutter settings are marked and the skiers ski right into your picture.

Cypress Gardens has recently added another photographer's delight, the **Island in the Sky,** a revolving platform that lifts riders slowly into the sky so they can photograph these lovely gardens from the air.

If you have this one very special talent, you can try it out in March when the Gardens are the site of the Florida Watermelon Association seed-spitting contest.

Shows here include performances by a magician, alligators, and birds, plus a production called the "Critters Show" featuring regular-guy creatures like goats and ducks showing off their talents. Movie buffs should take in the Garden Cinema, where a film is shown on a giant screen.

Cypress Gardens is open from 8 a.m. to 6 p.m., with shows at 10 a.m., 2 and 4 p.m., and admission is $10.95 for adults, $7.50 for children 6 to 11 (others free).

After you've toured Cypress Gardens and **Winter Haven** (which describes what this city is for the Boston Red Sox, who train here in spring), head back to US 27 and south to **Lake Wales,** a small central Florida city built on the sloping sides of a sparkling lake fringed with citrus groves.

There are few more tranquil places in the state than stately **Bok Tower,** on US 27, Lake Wales (tel. 813/676-1408). Rising 205 feet, this Georgian Gothic tower is set in the stillness of Mountain Lake Sanctuary atop Iron Mountain, once a sacred Indian site, and the highest point in peninsular Florida. Donated to the nation by Dutch immigrant publisher Edward Bok, the 250-foot pink-

and-gray marble octagonal tower houses inside it a 53-bell carillon whose gentle notes ring out each half hour, with a 45-minute recital at 3 p.m. each day by resident carillonneur Milford Myhre. Admission to the sanctuary is free, but there's a $2 parking charge to maintain the road to it.

While you're here, don't miss **Spook Hill**, one of the state's wackiest sites— and it's absolutely free. Look for signs directing you there: it's off US 17 at North Avenue and 5th Street. Now, drive your car up to the designated spot, put it in neutral, remove your foot from the brake, and watch the car move slowly backward . . . *uphill!* Nobody's telling why it works that way, but there are lots of local yarns about an Indian chief protecting his people, a pirate, an alligator. Ask, maybe you can add another.

Here in Lake Wales, from mid-February to mid-April, you can see the **Black Hills Passion Play**, Passion Play Road, Box 71, Lake Wales, FL 33853 (tel. 813/676-1495), a dramatic recreation of the final weeks of Christ portrayed by professional actors. There are Wednesday matinees at 3 p.m. and evening performances each Tuesday, Thursday, and Saturday at 7:30 p.m. (6 p.m. on Sunday), and on Good Friday evening. Tickets are $6 to $10 (half price for children). The natural outdoor amphitheater in which it's performed is nestled in a citrus grove and is a sight worth seeing even if you don't make the play.

Two unusual sports here are hang gliding on exciting updrafts created by warm air and high elevations, and wild boar hunting which can be done all year long with written permission from the landowner on whose property you're hunting. No license is required.

Staying Over

In Lake Wales, where to stay and where to eat are one place: delightful and delicious, weird and wacky, funky, funny **Chalet Suzanne Country Inn and Restaurant**, on US 27 and 17A, four miles north of Lake Wales (tel. 813/676-6011). A whimsical spot nestled into a 70-acre orange grove, Chalet Suzanne has won prestigious dining awards galore, and its famous gourmet canned soups went to the moon with the astronauts—no wonder it's so famous. First, the dining room is a tasteful marvel of Limoges, Bavarian, German, or Italian china, no two dishes alike on a table (no two chairs are alike either). Rooms are a fascinating melange of Spanish ironwork, Moorish mosaics, Turkish treasures, and Cuban tiles. Eclectic it is, intriguing it is, and skilfully done it definitely is.

Second, this small resort falls just short of incredible. Every one of the rooms is different, each with its own name. The blue room has deep carpeting and pale-blue touches on chairs and windows. Other rooms are orchid or have brass beds, antiques like a ceramic washbowl on a stand, and one even has a bathtub made entirely of Moorish tiles. Glowing color schemes blend it all together, and there are all the modern appurtenances like color TVs, phones, and a pool.

All of this is the work of the late Bertha Hinshaw, a pillar of determination who refused to buckle in the face of an isolated outpost in Lake Wales and the Depression. Instead, she packed up her two children and tacked up signs on every byway, developed recipes that would become the rage of Florida's gastronomes, and set about creating an empire. She succeeded. Boarders came for her excellent dinners and went out to bring still more people to her door. Finally, free to indulge a passion for travel, Ms. Hinshaw visited the corners of the earth and brought back all the treasures she could find—and she was quite a finder! Her son and daughter-in-law have continued and expanded the business until now there's no place like it in Florida: peaked clock towers pop up in unexpected places, a red British telephone booth is tucked away in a corner, there's an antique store and lots of ornate wrought iron and brick, patterned tiles, and stone urns.

I can't imagine you'll see anything like it anywhere, and certainly not any-place charging room rates of just $50 to $80 double, year round. (I can't resist telling you there's a honeymoon suite where the new couple can breakfast on a little glass-enclosed terrace overlooking the dining room—but unseen to other guests—and order their breakfast delivered on a dumb waiter that sends it right up from the kitchen.)

Now to the restaurant (one of Florida's most famous), which changes its menu frequently but always has broiled grapefruit and the resort's famous ro-maine soup. Entrees might include chicken Suzanne, shrimp curry with an array of condiments, lobster Newburg, grilled lamb chops, or lump crabmeat in herb butter. Prix-fixe meals, including several courses and hot crusty potato rolls, are pegged at $17 to $25 for lunch, $33 to $39 for most dinners, with a few at $26. Children's menus are about $10, and the restaurant's open daily from 11 a.m. to 2 p.m. and 5 to 9:30 p.m. You can even arrive on a private airstrip owned and operated by the Hinshaw family.

Two other nice spots in the Winter Haven area are **Lake Ida Beach Resort Motel,** 2524 North Hwy. 17, Winter Haven, FL 33881 (tel. 813/293-0942), on the shores of a lovely lake. A cluster of cottages, efficiencies, and motel rooms on a quiet lake, the resort has a small tiled pool, laundry, beach, pier, games, barbecue, and rowboats for fishing in the lake. Rates for two from April to De-cember are $61 for a three-night stay.

In nearby Auburndale, the **Lena Motel,** at 1802 US 92, Auburndale, FL 33823 (tel. 813/967-1558), is a tiny, moderately priced place on well-maintained grounds surrounding a small pool and patio. Right on the edge of a tranquil lake, the motel has some rooms with cooking facilities. Rates are $22 to $24 a day for motel rooms, $1 to $3 more for efficiencies.

The **Coach Light Restaurant,** at 2601 Havendale Blvd. in Winter Haven (tel. 813/967-7940), has steaks, seafood, even quail at prices in the $10 to $15 range. The Coach Light is open 11 a.m. to 10 p.m. and now has a Carriage Room Lounge with entertainment.

OCALA: Mile after mile of pristine white fences and emerald grass, the gleam of a chestnut flank curried to shimmering perfection, white blaze streaking down the aristocratic nose of a proud stallion, offspring of champions—that's Ocala, center of the state's racehorse country and home of turf champions like Ken-tucky Derby winners Needles and Carry Back, and the 1978 Triple Crown champion, Affirmed.

An hour's drive from Orlando (take the Florida Turnpike to Wildwood, then north on I-75 for 15 miles) will bring you here, where equine blood lines are discussed with far more fervor than any current events, and an impending foal is likely to outrank a human baby. Grassy knolls, limestone water, and rolling hills much like Kentucky's famed blue grass help shape these champions that are bred on 150 farms in the Ocala area.

If you'd like a nose-to-nose tête-à-tête with this prize-winning equine tal-ent, stop in at **Castleton Farms,** about five miles west on Route 307, just off Route 26. This is the second-largest standard breeding farm in the world, raising foals, both trotters and pacers, for harness racing. Give the ranch a call first at 904/463-2686. The **Ocala Marion County Chamber of Commerce,** at 110 E. Sil-ver Springs Blvd., Ocala, FL 32670 (tel. 904/629-8051), also has maps outlining farm locations and the times they're open to visitors, and can tell you about visit-ing greyhound breeding farms in the area too.

Here in Ocala in 1835 an Indian agent told the Seminole tribe it would be shipped off to the West. When they refused to go, the agent cut off gun sales, infuriating Chief Osceola who helped plan an ambush in which Maj. Francis Dade and 100 of his men were massacred on Christmas Eve near Bushnell as they rode to join the battle against the Seminoles. Osceola killed the agent too, and shortly war was in the wind. Creek Indians, the Seminoles' ancestors, discovered the beauty of **Hot Springs** on the Suwanee River, about eight miles west of Trenton, centuries ago, and artifacts and fossils from those early eras can still be found here. It's also a pretty place to camp or picnic. Take Route 26 to Route 232 about four miles, and turn left on Route 344 to the 200-acre park. For camping information, call 904/463-9975 or 904/463-6422.

One mile east of Ocala on Route 40 at **Silver Springs,** you can float down cool tranquil springs in a glass-bottomed boat, watch "mermaids" frolic with the fish and even hand-feed those fish yourself, or pet a real-life Bambi. Silver Springs has been ferrying two million wide-eyed visitors around in its glass-bottomed boats each year for generations, and no matter how many times you see these crystal waters, it's fun to return. Admission is $9.75 for adults, $6.95 for children 3 to 11. The park is open from 9 a.m. to 5:30 p.m. daily. Along the banks of the Silver River, giraffes, zebra, camels, and exotic wildlife roam free. In 1978 **Wild Waters,** Route 40 at Silver Springs (tel. 904/236-2043), a water-theme park, opened. Admission to it is $6.95 for adults, $5.50 for children 3 to 11, and the park's open from 10 a.m. to 8 p.m. from late March to the fall, closing in mid-September.

Umatilla is the entrance to the **Ocala National Forest,** the world's largest stand of sand pine plus a 366,000-acre wilderness of timberland that will show you how all of Florida once looked. Route 19, called the "Backwoods Trail," is the scenic drive. You can rent canoes here at Juniper Springs Run and Alexander Springs or ride the *Rainbow Queen* paddleboat down the Oklawaha River. For camping reservations in the national park, call 904/625-3147. It's 48 miles east of Ocala.

University students are given credit for having dreamed up the sport of **tubing,** which involves floating down a stream on an innertube. Tubing down the seven-mile-long Ichtucknee Spring on huge tubes five feet in diameter has become such a popular sport that officials had to limit the number of tubers to 3000 a day! You can rent the tubes at nearby gas stations and a shuttle bus brings you back to the starting point, since floating upstream's a real talent. Call 497-2150 when you're making tubing plans.

CASSADEGA: Here's a spooky one for you. In 1875 spiritualist George Colby, with the help of three spiritual guides, founded a town and psychic center and donated 35 acres to the Spiritualist church. Today in this small village east of I-4 about 20 miles north of Orlando, you'll see small signs outside many homes announcing the presence therein of a medium. These mediums claim not to permit charlatans in their midst, and all the mediums here (and there are many) are registered by the National Spiritualist Association of Churches. Whether or not you're interested in contacting Aunt Sarah, you'll find Cassadega a lovely old Florida town where, well, who knows what might happen?

SEBRING: If there's no sound more fulfilling to you than a well-tuned engine roaring along at about 150 m.p.h., don't miss a trip to Sebring, about 86 miles south of Orlando on Route 17 just off US 98. Each March the city is mecca for machine idolizers who trek here for the **Automobile Hall of Fame Week,** highlight of which is the 12 hours of **Sebring International Grand Prix of Endurance** for sports cars. Be forewarned that there is indeed some endurance involved in attending this event, which takes place around a dusty track crowded with fans out to enjoy a day of carburetors and Coors. Every motel in the area is packed for the event too, so don't just drop in.

If you'd like to stay here in lovely surroundings, head for **Sun 'n Lake Holiday Inn and Country Club,** Sebring, FL 33870, on US 27 five miles south of Lake Placid (tel. 813/385-2561). It's a pretty place with a marina, tennis, an 18-hole golf course, lounge, and dining room. Rates are $65 to $80 for two in a one-bedroom villa, and golf packages are available. The resort's about 17 miles from Sebring near the Lake Placid Tower overlooking citrus fields.

Less expensive accommodations in the area include the 42-room **Sunset Beach Motel,** 2221 SE Lakeview Dr., on US 27 and 98 (tel. 813/385-6129), a lovely lakefront motel with a private beach. Rates are $24 to $40, year round.

Ambitious developers are hard at work trying to restore a massive old Sebring hotel called the **Kenilworth Lodge and Motor Inn,** 836 SE Lakeview Dr., Sebring, FL 33870 (tel. 813/385-0111, or toll free 800/282-4489). You can't possibly miss this huge twin-towered building driving through Sebring, and if you're looking for old-world elegance at quite low prices, you'll certainly want to look for it.

Villas and efficiencies, both of which have kitchens, are the most popular accommodations at this fabulous old hotel built in the 1920s as a sunny southern home for the super-rich. For one of those accommodations you pay $30 to $35 from December to mid-April, $10 less in summer. Rooms here are just $20 in summer, $30 in winter months, and the lodge has a small Village Restaurant open for most meals in winter, for dinner and Sunday brunch in summer. Outside there's a large swimming pool, and inside you can enjoy some lovely lake views from the hotel's lounge. Kenilworth is an hour's drive from Walt Disney World, but you'll be staying in some of the loveliest countryside in this part of the state.

ZELLWOOD: Just outside Orlando, this small city is the winter vegetable-basket of the eastern seaboard, and you can tour the miles and miles of corn, carrots, lettuce, cauliflower, and radishes, and celebrate the two-million-crate harvest at the May Sweet Corn Festival. For $7.50 you can take a guided tour of the 18,000 acres of farmland between January and April. Call 305/966-2517 for information.

GAINESVILLE: Thirty miles north of Ocala on I-75 is Gainesville, where the Gothic campus of the **University of Florida** has bred many a governor and legislator. Horticulturists who oversee Florida's massive and powerful citrus industry train here, as do veterinarians who treat the state's huge herds of cattle. For all that erudition, the university's probably best known as the chemistry department that developed famous "Gator-Ade," a drink that first hit the thirsty gullets of the university's popular football team, the fighting Gators. Look in on the university's **Florida State Museum,** which has million-year-old fossils from Florida, including a prehistoric camel. There's a walk-through exhibit of Mayan ruins, including a replica of a Mayan palace too.

Downtown, you'll see the imposing old **Hippodrome Theater,** starring a professional cast performing in an intimate 266-seat theater. It's at 25 SE Second Pl. (tel. 373-5978). Shows vary in time and price.

Just south of Gainesville is the **Marjorie Kinnan Rawlings State Historic Site.** That Pulitzer Prize–winning author lived here while she wrote *The Yearling* and two other intriguing books about Florida, *Cross Creek* and *The Big Scrub*. Her home is completely furnished just as she left it, and its isolated location beside Lake Lochloosa gives you an idea how she got the ideas for those touch-

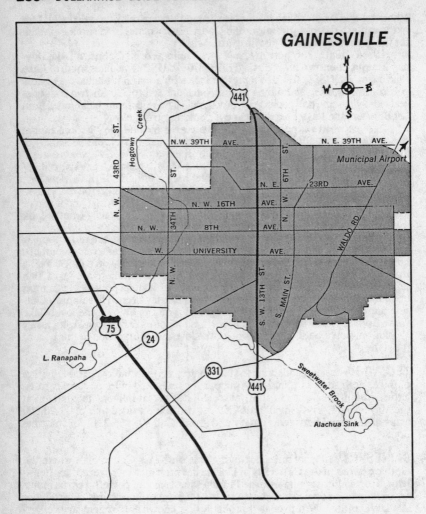

ing Florida stories. It's on Route 325, which you can reach from Route 20 East (tel. 466-3672).

At the **Yearling Cross Creek Restaurant** in Micanopy (tel. 466-3033) you will be served dinners made with recipes suggested by the author in her *Cross Creek Cookbook*. Prices are in the $10 to $15 range for dinner. The restaurant is open Tuesday through Saturday from noon to 10 p.m., on Sunday from 1 to 8:30 p.m.; closed Monday.

Staying Over

If you'd like to stay over in Gainesville, you can stay in style at the **Gainesville Hilton,** 2900 SW 13th St., Gainesville, FL 32601 (tel. 904/377-4000, or toll-free numbers in every state). There are 208 pretty rooms overlooking the

250-acre Bivens Arm Lake, an airy restaurant, and Juliana's of London Discothèque. Outside, there's a pool and barbecue area. The Hilton is quite near the university and also offers courtesy transportation to and from the airport. Year-round rates are $46 to $66 for two, depending on the view.

A moderately priced hotel is **Quality Inn University**, at 1901 SW 13th St., Gainesville, FL 32601 (tel. 904/376-2222). Here you'll find a tranquil central courtyard, a big pool, a pretty lobby with a fountain in the center, and a lounge. Some of the spacious rooms have paneling, all are decorated in bright colors with cable color TV and AM-FM stereo radios. There is complimentary coffee in the lobby. Rates are $24 to $42 double; additional guests are $4.

A good budget choice is **Motel Tabor**, 4041 SW 13th St., Gainesville, FL 32601 (tel. 904/376-4423), which has just ten small units next to a beautiful open grove of pines. Units have dressing rooms and phones, and free coffee is available every morning. Double rates are $22; extra guests are $4 each. Motel Tabor welcomes small pets too.

Two similar small motels are the **Sands**, at 2307 SW 13th St., Gainesville, FL 32601 (tel. 904/372-2045), which has a spiffy new wing with big picture windows; and the **Bambi Motel**, at 2119 SW 13th St., Gainesville, FL 32601 (tel. 904/376-2622). Rooms are small but so are the prices: $24 double. Bambi is close to the campus and has recently been refurbished.

10. Cape Canaveral/Kennedy Space Center

KENNEDY SPACE CENTER: Not so long ago a trip to the moon was as much a fantasy as anything in Disney's fanciful kingdom, but these days rockets shoot skyward with ho-hum regularity at Cape Canaveral, Florida's famed moon-shot space center. Here's where the astronauts trained for their "one small step" and where in 1980 the space shuttle first took off.

Flights continue to be launched from these pads. If you'd like to be there for one, call NASA toll free at 800/432-2153 for information on launch dates and best vantage points. A limited number of passes is issued for shuttle launches. To make reservations for a launch date, call 305/452-2121 between 8 a.m. and 4 p.m., or write NASA Visitors Services Branch, PA-VIC, John F. Kennedy Space Center Headquarters, Kennedy Space Center, FL 32899.

It's an easy day trip from Orlando to Cape Canaveral on Route 528, the Beeline, or a pretty drive along the east coast of Florida through Indian River citrus country. From Orlando, follow the signs to the **John F. Kennedy Space Center** (*not* Cape Canaveral).

At the Kennedy Space Center and NASA launch complex, begin your visit with a stop at the **Visitor Center** (tel. 867-7110) on Merritt Island, between the mainland and the cape about six miles south of Titusville. In the yard here are huge rockets and spacecraft. Inside, you can see a piece of moon rock and get a closeup look at Apollo capsules, rocket engines, and a lunar module. In the Hall of History, the space program's development is described. It's open daily from 8 a.m. to sunset, and is free.

Queue up then for the two-hour NASA escorted bus tours which leave every few minutes from the Visitor Center. The tour costs $4 for adults, $1.75 for children under 12. You can take either the Blue or the Red Tour, but the Red includes the fascinating astronaut training building. Simulators reproduce conditions of an actual space flight, and lights illuminate the craft as its components are explained by the narrator.

You'll pass the 52-story Vehicle Assembly Building and the huge transporters that carry spacecraft to the launching pads, as well as get a look at a launch pad.

Kennedy Space Center has added an **IMAX Theater,** which features a 20-minute version of the film *Hail Columbia,* depicting the launch and landing of the Space Shuttle *Columbia.* Projected on a screen five stories high and 70 feet wide, and accompanied by a sound from a six-track stereo system, it's quite an explosive production. Admission is an additional $2 for the IMAX presentation.

A CRUISE PORT: Newest resident on this spacy block is not a rocket but a cruise ship! A couple of years ago **Premier Cruise Lines** decided they saw a potential market up this way and moved in with their newly refurbished liner, the *Royale.* Now the line sails on three- and four-day cruises to Nassau and an out-island in the Bahamas. If you're headed for Walt Disney World and the thought of a few days of R&R at the beginning or end of the WDW tramp sounds wonderful to you, a travel agent can organize a package deal with hotel, transportation to the ship, and plenty of extras at quite reasonable prices.

For more on cruises from this and other ports, I'd modestly recommend another book in which I had a part, Frommer's *Dollarwise Guide to Cruises,* co-authored by another cruise enthusiast, Donald Schultz.

OTHER ATTRACTIONS: NASA did not just burn up acreage with its huge blazing rockets. Most of the thousands and thousands of acres the government owns here are unspoiled wilderness, called the **Merritt Island National Wildlife Refuge,** a haven for deer and small animals, alligators, many species of birds which remain here year round, as well as migratory waterfowl, plus many endangered species. The refuge is open from 8 a.m. to two hours before sunset daily except Christmas and launch days.

Another attraction in the Cocoa area is **Canaveral National Seashore,** which begins just east of Titusville and runs north to Turtle Mound, a total of 67,000 acres of waterfront wilderness that's home to 300 species of birds and animals, some of which are on the endangered list. Administered by the National Parks Service, the seashore is a serene place to roam among the sand dunes and listen to the breezes rustle through sea oats.

A 50-foot-high mound of seashells here was discarded six centuries ago by Indians who lived on these shores. It's called Turtle Mound, and can still be seen in the park on a nature trail that crosses the mound.

An entrance to Merritt Island National Wildlife Refuge is near here too, and you can take a self-guided tour through **Black Point Wildlife Drive,** which you enter via Route 402 just off US 1 in Titusville.

STAYING OVER: If you're staying over in the area, try the **Crossway Inn and Tennis Resort,** 3901 N. Atlantic Ave., Cocoa Beach, FL 32931 (tel. 305/783-2221), where you'll find a pool, two lighted tennis courts, and attractive rooms, some with refrigerators and some with full kitchens. It doesn't face the ocean (but is just 400 feet away from the sea) and charges $43 to $49 double from February to May and over Christmas, $39 to $45 in other months. Children under 12 stay free, and there's a game room, barbecue, and basketball court for the kids.

A moderately priced choice is **Surf Studio Beach Apartments,** 1801 S. Atlantic Ave., Cocoa Beach, FL 32931 (tel. 305/783-7100), which is right on the ocean and has just 11 units. You can select from motel rooms, efficiencies, and one-bedroom apartments for $32 to $70 in summer and $42 to $80 in winter.

Polaris Beach Resort Inn, 5600 N. Atlantic Ave., Cocoa Beach, FL 32931 (tel. 305/783-7621, or toll free 800/962-0028), is right on Cocoa Beach, which makes it perfect for surfing and swimming fans. An attractive spot stretched between the road and the ocean, the resort has free continental breakfast at the pool each morning, shuffleboard, volleyball, croquet, a video-game room, and a laundry. Efficiency apartments have microwaves and dishwashers in addition to the usual kitchen equipment. Double rates are $40 to $55, $10 more for kitchenettes, and $85 for suites from May through November. In other months, prices are $50 to $70; suites $95.

Rodeway Inn, 3655 Cheney Hwy., Titusville, FL 32780 (tel. 305/269-7110, or toll free 800/228-2000), is three miles from Kennedy Space Center and has newly remodeled rooms, either king-size or double bed, for $36 to $39, year round. Rates include a complimentary continental breakfast. There's a swimming pool at the resort and rooms for nonsmokers.

An outstanding restaurant in Cocoa—and in the state—is **Bernard's Surf**, at 2 S. Atlantic Ave. (tel. 783-2401). It may take you a while to read the menu, however—there are 40 appetizers and more than 100 entrees. Topping the weirdies list are such things as whale meat and fishballs, bear meat, fried silkworms, and chocolate-covered ants, but move right along past those to more usual kitchen treats. Here you'll find brimming platters of crab, shrimp, and super-fresh Florida seafood right off the owner's fleet. A combination of shrimp, crab, and mushrooms is a delicate dish, but then there are many good choices on the long list. Crisp, flaky breads are a specialty too. Prices are in the $12 to $20 range for dinner, and the restaurant is open from 11 a.m. to 11 p.m. daily (except Sunday, when doors open at 5 and close at 10:45 p.m.).

Poor Richards, 522 Ocean Ave., Melbourne Beach (tel. 724-0601) is one of Melbourne Beach's crowd-pleasers, thanks to a romantic atmosphere, good food, soft piano entertainment, and some very good food. A wide variety of aged steaks are the specialties at Poor Richards, but there is always plenty of local seafood on the menu too. You'll pay about $15 to $20 for dinner here. Hours at this interesting spot are 11:30 a.m. to 2 p.m. and 6 to 10 p.m., closing an hour later on weekend evenings. On Sunday, Poor Richard opens the doors from 11:30 a.m. to 3 p.m. for brunch.

Who could resist a spot with a name like **Strawberry Mansion**, 1218 E. New Haven Ave., Melbourne (tel. 724-8627)? Don't try. Strawberry Mansion has earned a spot in the heart and tummy of many a Melbourne resident and visitor, and they owe it all to an excellent kitchen that produces some of the region's best steaks and very good seafood. Best of all, the prices are as reasonable as the food is good: you'll pay about $8 to $15 for dinner here. Strawberry Mansion is open from 5 to 10 p.m. daily.

For nightlife, try **Mac's Friendly Taverns** at locations all over the area (tel. 723-3195), or the **Mouse Trap**, 5600 N. Atlantic Ave., Cocoa Beach (tel. 784-0050), where many a would-be astronaut has gone into orbit surrounded by '20s and '30s decor, antiques, and tin ceilings.

If you're in search of a surfboard up this way, call **Calema Boardsailing**, 449 W. Merritt Island Causeway, Merritt Island (tel. 453-3223). Rental rates are $10 an hour.

Fishing fans should seek out *Tradewinds V,* Port Canaveral (tel. 784-4490), which sails from 8 a.m. to 5 p.m., with night trips on weekends at 7 p.m. The fare is $30, $5 for a rod.

Chapter VII

DAYTONA

1. Orientation
2. Where to Stay
3. Where to Dine
4. Daytona After Dark
5. Seeing the Sights
6. Sports

DAYTONA HUMBLY CALLS ITSELF the "World's Most Famous Beach." There's every indication they're not far wrong. Certainly tourists have been sunning, sleeping, frolicking, and driving on these silvery sands for years. Driving? Yes, driving! As mere strips of sand these beaches have plenty of Florida competition, but as a racecourse . . . well, only in Daytona. It's been that way for nearly 100 years since Henry Flagler built his railroad and anyone who was anyone got on it and headed south.

R. E. Olds (you've heard perhaps of Oldsmobiles?) and Henry Ford, who had just started tinkering with "flivers," were among the first sun-seeking snowbirds. They wintered at the towering old Ormond Hotel, where guests settled into rockers on the long verandas and watched those new-fangled motor machines roll in and out of the garage up the street.

Something about cars arouses competitive urges. Here in Daytona those urges led Olds and Alexander Winton to the sands of Ormond Beach where they lined up cars that "rocked and popped and belched puffs of black smoke." Like modern teenagers, the two peeled off on one of the nation's first drag races, and tore straight down 23 miles of beach, nose to nose, clocking the magnificent speed of 57 miles an hour.

By 1904 a Daytona event called the Winter Speed Carnival was drawing entries from all over the world, most of them wealthy sportsmen and society financiers. Three years later Fred Marriott wrapped a mile of piano wire around the boiler of his Stanley Steamer to keep it from blowing up and raced through the timing course at a spectacular 197 m.p.h., only to crash just as spectacularly into the pounding surf. He emerged uninjured, but the accident gave rise to claims that the Stanley brothers were so upset by the spill they quit racing their cars. People still claim the Steamer's top speed is unknown because it never was tested.

Many men who were to become famous for their skill with machinery first put that skill to the test on the sands of Daytona. Glen Curtis, later to be known as the father of naval aviation for his pioneering work on flying boats and ship landing craft, once rode a motorcycle so fast here that Alexander Graham Bell asked Curtis to help him build airplanes. Daytona's favorite son, however, is all-time champion Capt. Malcolm Campbell, a millionaire English sportsman. In 1928 Campbell brought to Daytona a car powered by an aircraft engine. For days he waited for the tides to smooth out the beach, then ramrodded his flying pile of metal first to a record 206.96 m.p.h., in later years to 245 m.p.h., 253 m.p.h., 272 m.p.h., and 276 m.p.h. All that speed may not seem important, but it was—the Bluebird and Rolls-Royce engines Campbell had sped over the sands of Daytona went on to fame in a fleet of Hurricane and Spitfire fighters that beat back Hitler's Luftwaffe and halted German invasionary forces in World War II.

Worldwide depression smacked Daytona a mean blow, but the speedy sands were back in business again by the 1950s with a new beach race-course, daring drivers, and a pack of cheering fans who eventually created National Stock Car Auto Racing (NASCAR), and today's famed Daytona 500.

No longer do the racing machines take to the beaches, but *you* still can—just follow the signs and drive between the bikinis.

Beach speed is now limited to 10 m.p.h., but that certainly doesn't mean there's no racing in Daytona. Not by a long shot. Daytona's love for speed lives on. Each year in February the Daytona International Speedway is packed with race followers who come here for two weeks of trackside reverence and revelry known as speed weeks. In July the Firecracker 400 and the Paul Revere 250 are major events on racing calendars.

Once again Daytona's sands are a playground for surfers who compete here each October, for toddlers busily carting sandbuckets to the sea, and for you, the traveler, to stroll, to sun, to build castles and dreams.

1. Orientation

Daytona Beach is surrounded by water, with the Halifax River cutting right through the middle of the city and the Atlantic Ocean playing big brother on the east side. There are actually four towns on the beach: **Ormond Beach** on the north, then farther south **Daytona Beach** and **Daytona Beach Shores,** finally **New Smyrna Beach,** separated from the others by Ponce de Leon Inlet at the tip of Daytona Beach Shores. On the west side of the river is **Holly Hill** and downtown **Daytona.**

Route A1A runs along the beach from north to south and US 1 runs inland along the west side of the river. I-95 is still farther west, and I-4 joins **US 92** (also known as **Volusia Avenue**) to connect Orlando and Daytona Beach.

GETTING THERE: Eastern, Delta, and Piedmont fly into **Daytona National Airport,** and **Amtrak** disembarks passengers at nearby Deland or Palatka, about a 30-minute drive away. **Greyhound** and **Trailways** buses also serve the area.

Many people combine a visit to Orlando with a trip to Daytona—a few days at Orlando's attractions, a few days recovering on Daytona's fabulous sands. If you think you'd like to do that, you can fly into Orlando (which has much better air service than Daytona), then buzz over to the beach on the **Daytona–Orlando Transit Service (DOTS)** (tel. 904/257-5411, or toll free 800/223-1695; in Florida, 800/231-1695). If you don't have a car and don't want to rent one, that's the way to go. Fare is $14 for adults, $8 for children, one way. You can save a dollar on each ticket if you book the seven round trips.

GETTING AROUND: Orange Cab (tel. 305/252-2046) has limousine service from the airport to beach hotels, for $7 to $10.

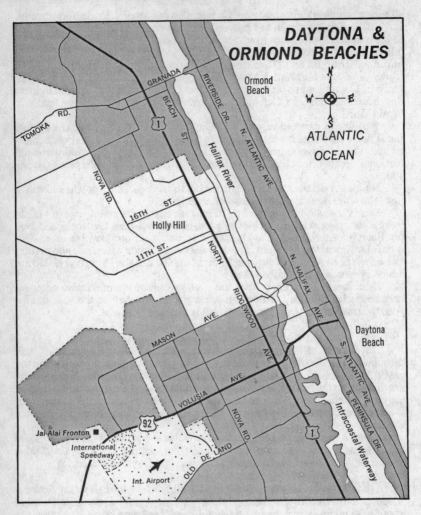

Twenty-two **rental-car companies** operate in the area, with Alamo (tel. 255-1511) leading the budget pack, and Hertz, Avis, Airport Thrifty, Ajax, National, and Dollar right behind. For a different ride around, try **Renta-Tops-Down** (tel. 673-3053), which will send you off in a convertible.

Daytona's municipal transit company, **Vo Tran** (tel. 761-7700), has regular **bus routes** from 6 a.m. to 6:30 p.m. on the beach, to the airport, and downtown at 50¢ for adults, 25¢ for children.

If you'd like to ride over to Walt Disney World or Cape Canaveral, **Gray Line Tours** (tel. 255-6506) has tours to many area attractions at varying times and prices starting at $15 to $20.

For taxi service, call **Yellow Cab** (tel. 252-5536) or **Daytona Economy Cab** (tel. 253-2522). Charges are about $1.80 for the first mile, and $1.20 for each succeeding mile.

All along the beach concessionaires rent mopeds and bicycles, or you can try **Moped Man** (tel. 788-4030) or **Bike Smith** (tel. 258-6550).

USEFUL INFORMATION: For **police or medical emergencies,** call 767-2211 in Daytona Beach Shores, 253-6701 in Daytona Beach. . . . A **24-hour drugstore** is Super X, at Mason-Nova Plaza (tel. 252-3647). . . . For food at any hour, try **Sambo's,** 100 S. Atlantic Ave., Ormond Beach (tel. 672-7764). . . . Car problems? Try **Speedway Shell,** 1392 Volusia Ave. (tel. 253-9188), which is open night and day and has wrecker service. . . . For quick **dry cleaning,** Romie's, at 1617 Ridgewood Ave. (tel. 767-4883), can help. . . . For a **doctor,** call the Volusia County Medical Association at 258-1611, and for a **dentist,** call 734-1355 or 253-2451. . . . Winn-Dixie grocery stores are open 24 hours.

TOURIST INFORMATION: The **Daytona Beach Area Chamber of Commerce,** P.O. Box 2775, Daytona Beach, FL 32015 (tel. 904/255-0981), has a cheerful staff ready to help you with information on accommodations or attractions, or to extricate you from problems. . . . The **Ormond Beach Chamber of Commerce,** P.O. Box 874, Ormond Beach, FL 32074 (tel. 904/677-3454), has all the same services.

2. Where to Stay

So frequently do prices change in Daytona that reading a rate sheet is almost like scanning a stock market report. Business (and price) heats up here when the weather does, about February through April, drops after Easter, and rises again in June through August, then drops way down in the fall. Anytime the city has a big event (like speed weeks in February, March, and July), up go the prices again, sometimes as much as $15 or $20 a day. Most hotels also hold out for three- or five-day minimum stays during those packed events. You can save on rooms here, as on every Florida beach, by giving up an ocean view.

LUXURY HOTELS: The **Daytona Hilton,** 2637 S. Atlantic Ave., Daytona Beach, FL 32018 (tel. 904/767-7350, and toll-free numbers in every state), is up there with the top runners. Hilton hotels often have unusual architecture, and they've got it here in a very contemporary hotel with a sawtoothed, multilevel exterior. There are 215 luxurious rooms and suites, with lots of special touches like wing chairs and wardrobes, ruffled bedskirts, and pretty, contemporary prints. Many of the very large rooms open onto private balconies. The Hilton has two plush restaurants, two lounges with entertainment, two pools, tennis courts, a putting green, sauna and exercise room, and a game room—and of course, all that beach. Double rates here are $54 to $104 September through December, from $54 to $130 in other months.

If you like golf resorts and don't mind not being right on the beachfront, I can't think of a more glamorous place to stay in Daytona than **Indigo Lakes Resort,** 2620 Volusia Ave., Daytona Beach, FL 32014, on US 92 at I-95 (tel. 904/258-6333, or toll free 800/874-9918). Breezes rustle through tall pines and ruffle tiny blue ponds, a flock of birds soars overhead, and nestled among shady gardens are the beautiful rooms, the likes of which you'll be hard put to match. There are 150 rooms here and a number of suites. Some king-size beds and a few efficiencies are available. All are decorated in beautiful clear colors, with contemporary furniture and attractive wallpaper. Some rooms have balconies too. On the premises are eight tennis courts and pro shops, an 18-hole PGA golf course, a putting green, a par-three course, driving range, an Olympic-size swimming pool nestled in a tropical garden, and shuffleboard. All day long the resort operates free shuttles to the beach so you won't be deprived of sand, and there's free transportation to the airport, jai-alai, the speedway, and the dog track. Major Moultrie's Cricket Club provides gourmet diners with a stunning array of fresh seafood and beef, and for family dining you can pop off to Valle's Steakhouse. Rates are $52 to $160, year round.

There's always something going on at **Aku Tiki Inn,** 2225 S. Atlantic Ave., Daytona Beach, FL 32018 (tel. 904/255-3841, or toll free 800/528-1234), where two lounges keep popping until the wee hours. To get to the resort's attractive Trader's restaurant, pass over the moon bridge near the waterfall, then dine in this exotic setting overlooking the ocean and the resort's large tiled pool. This accent on Polynesia continues outside too, where a flaring roof over the lobby looks like the prow of a Polynesian craft and a Tiki god guard stands watch. Rooms are spacious enough to hold two double beds and a couple of easy chairs, and some of them also offer cooking facilities. All 132 have private balconies overlooking the ocean. You'll also find a game room, gift shop, shuffleboard, coin laundry, pool bar, and splashing place for the youngsters here, and tours to all of Orlando's diversions can be booked right from here. Rates February through April are $60 to $80, and drop in other months to $35 to $65. Weekly and monthly rates are also offered, and children under 12 stay free.

MODERATELY PRICED HOTELS: Treasure Island, 2025 S. Atlantic Ave., Daytona Beach Shores, FL 32016 (tel. 904/255-8371, or toll free 800/874-7420), towers over the beach with 232 big rooms tucked away in a V-shaped building 11 stories tall. You'll find spacious efficiencies and suites, all with inviting balconies overlooking the ocean. Contemporary decor with a homey touch makes this a favorite spot with families, who can send the youngsters off to one of the three swimming pools or the game room, while less ambitious parents pull up a chair at the barefoot bar nearby. Double rates range from $69 to $98 in peak seasons, dropping to $39 to $63 in fall.

Turtle Inn, 3233 S. Atlantic Ave., Daytona Beach, FL 32014 (tel. 904/761-0426), has a spiffy contemporary air about it, and the cutest turtle logo you ever saw. The Turtle has just 50 spacious rooms and efficiencies, all decorated in bright colors and opening onto private balconies where you can watch the sea lapping at the sands. There's a game room for rainy days and a big pool with a glass windbreaker to keep you warm when the breezes are less than balmy. All rooms have two double beds, a private sitting area with convertible couch, and dressing rooms. In efficiencies, the kitchens are separate from the sleeping areas. To turn Turtle, you'll pay $50 to $90 in peak summer and winter months, and about $30 to $95 in other seasons.

If you're traveling with children, **Sun Viking Lodge,** at 2411 S. Atlantic Ave., Daytona Beach, FL 32018 (tel. 904/252-6252, or toll free 800/874-4469), is a place they'll love. A big hit here with the wee ones is a twisting, turning water slide that sends you splashing into a pool (and come to think of it, that sounds like fun for us so-called grownups too). At this owner-operated beach resort, there are just 40 spacious rooms, in a cozy friendly atmosphere. Tropical colors decorate rooms, and some have kitchens and will sleep six. Rooms have refrigerators too. For a double you'll pay $30 to $67 from February to September, $30 to $41 in other months.

Big picture windows gaze out over the ocean at the **Daytona Sands,** 2523 S.

Atlantic Ave., Daytona Beach, FL 32018 (tel. 904/767-2551), a small two-story motel with just 50 rooms stretched out along the ocean. You can prowl among the sea oats here (please don't pick them), roam miles of wide beaches, and relax in modest but spacious rooms cheerful with bright colors and attractive furnishings. There's a heated pool on the grounds, and some of the rooms are efficiencies. The highest rates, February through April and during special events, are $54 to $58, dropping to $22 to $44 in other months.

Three acres of beautiful grounds and a palm-fringed swimming pool greet you at **Plantation Island,** 187 S. Atlantic Ave., Ormond-by-the-Sea, FL 32074 (tel. 904/677-2331, or toll free 800/321-2432). You can stay in a low-rise, two-story building overlooking a pretty pool, or in a six-story building overlooking the ocean and a second pool. In either place you'll find wide rooms with two double beds and comfortable chairs, plus larger efficiencies and apartments. Vivid colors are popular here, complementing a long strip of beach and sky outside. The hotel is complete with dining room and lounge. Rates in February and summer are $60 to $87, with the highest price buying two-bed-room/two-bath apartments big enough for six. In shoulder seasons, prices drop to $49 to $66, and after Labor Day through mid-December they're just $28 to $36.

Daytona Inn/Broadway, Daytona Beach, FL 32014, at Broadway and South Atlantic Avenue (tel. 904/252-3626, or toll free 800/874-1822; in Florida, 800/251-1962), is a contemporary spot with a bright modern lobby, tiled floors, and a Victorian-era Broadway Street Station restaurant. Stripped alongside the beach, the inn has lots of attractive landscaping and a big sundeck overlooking the pool. A special treat for children is a small pool centered with a spouting fountain. Rooms are big and decorated in tropical colors. Rates range from $60 to $70 during February to May, and in summer, $37 to $48 in fall.

A second Daytona Inn called **Seabreeze,** Daytona Beach, FL 32014, at Seabreeze Boulevard and North Atlantic Avenue (tel. 904/252-4363), offers similar accommodations and facilities at the same price, and has some suites that sleep up to eight for $44 to $49.

You can't miss the **Maverick Motor Inn,** 485 S. Atlantic Ave., Daytona Beach, FL 32014 (tel. 904/672-3550)—just look for the white mustang pawing the air. That equine figure is right at the front door of this modern motel, and if you miss that, there's a horned bull's head painted out front. That western theme extends to the restaurant (prices, $5 to $9), and there's even a woodsy touch in the cheerful rooms of this seven-story lodge. Private balconies and lots of glass offer a nice view of the ocean, and there are some housekeeping apartments. All the rooms have refrigerators too. There's a pool for children and another for adults. Two people pay $48 to $55 from June to September, from $30 to $35 in other months.

Best Western has some very attractive motels in Florida, and the **Islander Beach Lodge,** at 1601 S. Atlantic Ave., New Smyrna Beach, FL 32069 (tel. 904/427-3452, or toll free 800/874-7420; in Florida, 800/342-5620), is one of them. You're greeted here by a South Seas island motif that continues to the resort's central pool (it's huge) where palm trees dot the grounds and a high-diving board invites you to try some fancy splashing. Rooms overlook the pool and ocean, and are wide, roomy units with lively colors and nice walled-in balconies good for sunning and relaxing. Rates range from $44 to $75, year round.

Ocean Villa Motel, 828 N. Atlantic Ave., Daytona Beach, FL 32014 (tel. 904/252-4644, or toll free 800/874-4469), is another small motel on the beach where you won't find yourself part of the masses. A two-story, 38-room motel, Ocean Villa is right on the ocean but it also has a big heated swimming pool with an aqua slide and protective windbreak. There's even a heated pool and a playground for the children. Wall-to-wall carpeting stretches across the rooms, and all have plenty of space and big picture windows. The friendly management will arrange for special golf privileges, and encourage you to grill outdoors on the resort's barbecue. Efficiencies and one-bedroom apartments are available for larger groups, and the resort charges $30 to $70 for two people in two beds ($25 to $57 for smaller accommodations) in most months, $25 to $40 in slower seasons.

If you're feeling a bit puny, you can get healthy at the **Castaways,** 2075 S. Atlantic Ave., Daytona Beach, FL 32014 (tel. 904/255-6461). This pretty, seven-story, beachside motel has just about everything you can think of at a resort: two patio pools and one for the toddlers, shuffleboard, basketball and volleyball, Ping-Pong, game rooms, shops, and a restaurant and lounge with moderate prices. A good family resort, Castaways has in-room refrigerators, full efficiencies, suites, and apartments. Rooms are nicely decorated in attractive tropical colors, and many have big balconies overlooking the sea. This is the place for country and western fans: the Barn nightclub is a 300-seat twangin' and guitar plunkin' nirvana. Two people pay $55 to $80 in top summer and winter seasons, $35 to $55 at other times.

What a swimming pool they have at **Perry's Ocean Edge!** This Quality Inn, at 2209 S. Atlantic Ave., Daytona Beach, FL 32014 (tel. 904/255-0581, or toll free 800/228-5151), has topped its competitors by enclosing its pool in a gorgeous solarium and heating it all with solar power. Three stories high, this solarium has a huge fern dangling from the heavy wood beams that support the translucent covering, and is filled with palms. Rooms have big picture windows so you can see the delighted splashing going on below. There's even a new addition: a solar-heated spa in the garden. Big, big rooms are beautifully decorated in splashy contemporary hues, and the mini-suites even have three double beds. Every morning you get complimentary homemade doughnuts and coffee. When you're looking for something to do, ask and they'll tell you about special golf privileges for guests. Double rates here (there's no family plan) are $59 to $75 in peak summer and winter months, $36 to $48 at other times. Extra guests are $6 each.

BUDGET HOTELS: Days Inn has three oceanside locations: 839 S. Atlantic Ave., Ormond-by-the-Sea, FL 32074 (tel. 904/677-6600); 1909 S. Atlantic Ave. (tel. 904/255-4492); and 3209 S. Atlantic Ave. (tel. 904/761-2050). You can reach all of them at the Days Inn toll-free number (tel. 800/325-2525). All charge $39 to $55 double, year round.

Del Aire Motel, 744 N. Atlantic Ave., Daytona Beach, FL 32014 (tel. 904/ 252-2563), is a family-style beachside resort with just 20 rooms, all kept sparklingly clean. Some of the attractive rooms are efficiencies, and all have a cozy, homey air about them, thanks to a friendly management intent on keeping a happy family of guests here. Located right on the beach, the motel has a tiled pool and lots of space to see the sun. Two people pay $40 to $55 in peak seasons, $30 to $40 in other months.

A real money-saver in the Daytona area is **Econo Travel,** at 2250 Volusia Ave., Daytona Beach, FL 32014 (tel. 904/255-3661), where the rates are $32, year round. Extra persons sharing a room are $3. These very basic accommodations are not on the beach, but they're close to the speedway, jai-alai, and dog track.

Lovely lawns slope down to a sparkling pool and wind among one-story buildings with Mediterranean touches at **Spindrift,** 3333 S. Atlantic Ave., Daytona Beach Shores, FL 32018 (tel. 904/767-3261). A tranquil spot right on the ocean, Spindrift has 14 units scattered about perfectly manicured grounds in simply furnished cottages, apartments, efficiencies, or motel rooms. You won't find lots of fancy amenities, but you will discover a serene spot for a vacation. Two people pay $19 for a room to $41 for a two-bedroom cottage September through December and $25 to $60 in summer high season.

CAMPING: **Tomoka State Park,** North Beach, also called Old Dixie Highway, at the northern border of Ormond Beach, FL 32074 (tel. 904/677-3931), is a shady spot to bed down if you're camping. Campsite rates are $7 a night for four people, $9 with electric hookup, and the park rents canoes for $3.25 an hour. Reservations are taken only by telephone—no letters—up to 60 days prior to arrival.

3. Where to Dine

Daytona has many moderately priced restaurants along the beach, and a wide selection of dining spots in the city's top resorts. I've selected some of the best in the area and grouped them roughly by price category (prices cited are for entrees, but that usually includes salad, one or two vegetables, and sometimes coffee as well).

THE TOP RESTAURANTS: At 304 Seabreeze Blvd. is the city's award-winner and most famous restaurant, **Chez Bruchez** (tel. 252-6656). From the kitchens stream veal scallops marsala, shad roe with broiled tomato, a creamy seafood casserole, delectable oysters or crab au gratin with mushrooms, all of it bearing the skillful French touches of the very talented chef, Al Bruchez, who's been in business here since 1947. Don't miss the rum cream pie. In fact, don't miss Chez Bruchez. Your dinner, including appetizer, vegetables, potato, and salad will be in the $10 to $15 range (lunch prices start at $4), and the restaurant is open from 11:30 a.m. to 2 p.m. and 5 to 9 p.m. Monday through Saturday (closed September and October).

French food fanciers usually also find their way to **La Crêpe en Haut,** 142 E. Granada Blvd. (on Route 40) in Fountain Square, next door to the Birthplace of Speed Museum (tel. 673-1999). Naturally, crêpes are the focus here, supplemented by fancy omelets, veal in several delectable preparations, sweetbreads in a flaky pastry shell, carpetbagger steaks stuffed with oysters, and tournedos Rossini. You'll pay about $15 to $17 for dinners. La Crêpe is open Tuesday through Friday for lunch from 11:30 a.m. to 2:30 p.m., and 5 to 10 p.m. Tuesday through Sunday for dinner; closed Monday.

If you like an intimate romantic atmosphere, you'll like **King's Cellar,** 1258 N. Atlantic Ave. (tel. 255-3014), where you dine in the handsome dining room of an old mansion built in the 1800s. Excellent steaks and seafood have some Italian touches, and there's always some pasta around for carbohydrate lovers. Entrees generally fall in the $10 to $15 range, although the menu begins lower, and there's a special menu for children. Open from 5 to 10 p.m. Monday through Saturday, from 5 to 9 p.m. on Sunday.

Upstairs at King's Cellar is **La Grenier** (tel. 255-7431), a beautifully decorated restaurant where you dine in an old-world atmosphere on excellent fish and beef dishes in creamy sauces, with lots of those inimitable French touches. Prices are in the $15 to $20 range, and the restaurant is open from 5 to 10 p.m. for dinner.

Klaus, 144 Ridgewood Ave. (tel. 255-7711), rocked sedate (and, frankly, not-very-gourmet) Daytona right off its culinary feet when it opened here several years ago. Once a captain of the U.S. Culinary Olympic Team, Klaus continues to just knock their socks off here with his impressive list of delicacies. Sea bass St. Augustine prepared with crab and hollandaise tops a list of treasures that include veal, seafood, lamb, and beef selections. Entrees are in the $10 to $15 range, and include a cheese and crackers board for openers, salad, popovers (oh yum), rice or potatoes, and sauteed vegetable. Mmmmmmm. Open Tuesday through Sunday from 5 to 10 p.m.; closed Monday.

MODERATE: Hanging plants and pretty paintings set the tone at **Flanigan and Company,** 3125 S. Atlantic Ave., Daytona Beach Shores (tel. 439-2801). Dine here on selections from the fresh-food buffet or settle into a table and order from an $8 to $12 menu. Flanigan's is an attractive, airy spot, with congenial help and excellent seafood and beef selections. Hours are 4:30 to 10 p.m. daily (earlier closing on Sunday).

Waitresses dress in gingham and you slip right back into days of over-the-hill-to-granny's at **Marko's Heritage Inn,** 900 S. Ridgewood Ave., on US 1 in Port Orange (tel. 767-3809). You'll see them making the bread and cinnamon rolls as you enter, then sit down to some old-fashioned food at old-fashioned prices (in the $10 range): sirloin, shrimp, crab, fresh fish, seafood chowder ladled from a tureen, and crisp salads with extravagantly rich house dressings. Shades of Mason jars and strawberry hullers! Marko's is open from 4:30 to 10 p.m. Tuesday through Saturday, with a big Sunday dinner served from 11:30 a.m. to 9 p.m.

Julian's, at 88 S. Atlantic Ave. (tel. 677-6767), is one of the city's most popular spots, and deservedly so. They produce outstanding beef and seafood dishes here, but prime rib's the specialty. Pleasant, intimate, woodsy surroundings complete the package at Julian's, where you can dine on entrees in the $10 to $12 range for full-course dinners. Open 4 to 11 p.m. daily, the restaurant also has cocktails and entertainment.

Friendly, efficient service and a cheery atmosphere are keynotes at **Kay's Coach House,** 724 Main St. (tel. 253-1944), and prime rib is one of the most ordered specialties on the long, long menu at this pleasant spot near the beach. After dinner you can slip into the cocktail lounge for a finale. Prices at Kay's run about $10 to $15 for most dinner entrees, with some as low as $5. Open 11 a.m. to 10 p.m., the restaurant is closed on Monday.

It seems miles away from the rollicking rip-roaring sands of Daytona, but it's really only a few miles to **Inlet Harbor** (tel. 767-4502), in the quiet village of Ponce de Leon Inlet, home to the area's fishing clan. Nearby is the lighthouse where you can tour around after dining in an up-on-stilts setting overlooking the waters where shrimp fishermen chug off into the sunset and pelicans swoop down on their dinner. Simple cooking and simple setting here, and plenty of seafood from oysters and scallops to crab, flounder, snapper. You can even have fish for breakfast (with grits, naturally), and at any meal you'll have to consume lots to run up a bill higher than about $12. Open from noon to 9 p.m. daily.

A newcomer that has been receiving some attention is **Steve's Venice,** 2616 S. Atlantic Ave. (tel. 761-2444). Northern Italian cooking, the most delicate and creamy of Italy's preparations, is served in a pleasant atmosphere with matching service. Prices for dinner are in the $10 to $15 range, and hours are 5 to 10 p.m. daily, an hour later on weekends.

Decidedly not a newcomer, **Riccardo's,** 610 Glenview Blvd. (tel. 253-3035), has been around for nearly 15 years now, and for a good and simple reason: good food. Fresh pastas are whipped up each day and the same can be said for crusty breads, cheesecake, and desserts. A family operation (the Segale family) keeps things humming here and even cut their own prime veal out back in the kitchen. Dinner prices are in the $10 to $15 bracket, and hours are 5 to 10 p.m.

Gene's Steak House, on US 92 (eight miles west of Route A1A; tel. 255-2059), is a beef-lover's paradise with seven kinds of steaks on the menu, all of them served in a handsome, intimate atmosphere. You'll pay about $10 to $15 for dinner here, and hours are 5 to 10 p.m. daily except Monday.

Seafood spots are everywhere of course, but top accolades go to **Red Snapper,** 2058 S. Atlantic Ave. (tel. 252-0212), which sells tons of that popular light, white fish each year for prices in the $12 to $14 range. Hours are 11 a.m. to 11 p.m. daily.

BUDGET BETS: Chart House turns out seafood like stuffed shrimp, beef-like teriyaki and kebabs, and many another goodie. It's in a nice location too, hard by the yacht harbor at 2758 Marina Point (tel. 255-9022). Entrees at this attractive spot are in the $12 to $17 range, and Chart House is open daily from 5 to 10 p.m. (an hour later on weekends).

Anchor Inn, 608 W. Dunlawton Ave., Port Orange (tel. 767-0845), is one of the area's top spots, if you can find it. Try following Route A1A from Daytona Beach to its junction with US 1, and go straight from there to the restaurant. On Dunlawton Avenue you'll find the Anchor Inn, a yellow stucco eatery standing in the shade of a massive old oak. There are no reservations taken here so you may have to wait a while, but it's worth the wait for the fresh and flaky straight-from-the-sea delicacies served. Florida lobster, shrimp, all kinds of Florida fish, wonderful scallops, and long years of training and experience have made Anchor Inn's seafood buffet (served on Friday and Saturday) a special favorite for hordes of local-ites. Open from 4:30 to 9:30 p.m. Tuesday through Saturday (from noon to 8:30 p.m. on Sunday), Anchor Inn has very moderate prices and you're likely to leave here with a check under (sometimes well under) $10. Special plates for children are offered too. If you can't find it, ask anyone around or inquire at the Port Orange Shopping Center—everyone knows where it is.

When you're looking for a light lunch or dinner, try the homemade quiches and broiled hamburgers at **Bennigan's,** 890 S. Atlantic Ave. (tel. 673-3691), part of the successful chain operation that always produces pleasant greenery-filled atmospheres and inexpensive dining. Prices are in the $5 to $10 range for most things. The restaurant's open from 11 a.m. to 1:30 a.m.

Duff's Smörgåsbord, in the Sunshine Mall, Daytona Beach Shores (tel. 788-0828), is once again the place to head for an all-you-can-eat money-saver smörgåsbord table with meats, vegetables, salads, and desserts for under $6. The atmosphere is simple but always clean and bright, and the restaurant is open from 11 a.m. to 3 p.m. and 4 to 8 p.m. daily.

Piccadilly Cafeteria, in the Volusia Mall, 1700 Volusia Ave. (tel. 258-5373), features more than 100 items every day at its long, long cafeteria line where you'll pay $5 or less for most meals. Open from 11 a.m. to 8:30 p.m.

Pizza? Try **New York Pizza,** 220 Broadway (tel. 258-5666), which creates hundreds of the New York variety for hungry customers every day from 11 a.m. to 3 a.m.

There's usually a line at the door of **Aunt Catfish's,** 1100 Ocean Shore Blvd. in Ormond Beach (tel. 441-4291), and 550 Halifax Dr., Port Orange (tel. 767-4768). No wonder: Cajun blackened fish or catfish fingerlings, baked shrimp in curry sauce with grilled bananas, crab imperial, shrimp, snapper, flounder, hushpuppies, baked beans, and grits served in a rambling, rustic spot. Aunt Catfish's offers the ultimate in casual dining on some very good and often even innovative selections, for which you'll pay about $10 or so for dinner.

Hours are 11:45 a.m. to 10 p.m. weekdays, from 4:30 p.m. on Saturday, and 9 a.m. to 9:30 p.m. on Sunday.

One would hardly expect to find a Hungarian dining spot in Daytona, which seems to have more junk-food spots per capita than any other town in Florida, but there it is—**Hungarian Village**, 424 S. Ridgewood (tel. 253-5712). Hugo and Anna Marie Tischler have been cooking up strüdel, lamb, pork, duck, goulash, and the like for ages. Devotees pour in here to dine in an attractive dining room that introduces you to that little-known land from which Anna Marie hails. Open every day but Sunday from 5 to 10 p.m., with prices from $7 to $10.

A seafood favorite is **Down the Hatch**, 4984 Front St., at Timmons Fishing Camp (tel. 761-4831) on Ponce Inlet, south of Daytona. Down the Hatch has its own fleet of ships to bring in the bacon (well, the whiting, tile fish, grouper, and snapper), and does such a sterling job of it that they offer an all-you-can-eat fish special for $6—with coleslaw and french fries! Nice setting too. Hours are noon to 10 p.m. daily, and the average dinner price is $6 to $8.

Norwood Seafood, Third Avenue (Route A1A), just off Route 44 on the beach, New Smyrna (tel. 428-4621), has been around since the 1940s and is bigger and better than ever now. Its woodsy maze of multilevels has been remodeled and expanded, and crowds are pouring into this seafood restaurant which doles out softshell crabs, seafood gumbo, and oyster stew, along with lots of other snack and finger foods. Prices are in the $5 to $12 range, and hours are 11:30 a.m. to 10 p.m. daily.

4. Daytona After Dark

The after-dark scene is pretty quiet in Daytona. There are a number of lounges and plenty of activity for the younger set, but none of the showy nightclub life available in some of the state's larger cities.

The **Plaza Hotel**, 600 N. Atlantic Ave. (tel. 255-4471), houses three different nightclubs so you can be sure there's a lively crowd there any night. Choose from 600 North, with rock-video music and two dance floors; the Plantation Club, with kinetic-light live-band shows and all the disco you can dance until the wee hours (designer jeans are better here); or 007, a bar with a big dance floor and recorded music. The cover charge varies, but it's usually about $5.

There's a show nightly at **Hawaiian Inn**, 2301 S. Atlantic Ave., Daytona Beach Shores (tel. 255-5411); but at **Aku Tiki**, 2225 S. Atlantic Ave. (tel. 255-3841), where you'd expect to see a Polynesian show, there's rock music and a cover charge.

Finky's, 640 N. Grandview (tel. 255-5059), is a cavernous revelry spot that seats a thousand merrymakers. Cover charge for DJ, bands, and special-drink nights is $3 to $8.

Big Daddy's Beachside, at 21 S. Ocean Dr. (tel. 255-8810), attracts a nightly crowd that parties until the a.m. in this five-level emporium with two bands. There's sometimes a $5 to $10 cover charge.

H. P. Cassidy's, 288 N. Nova Rd., Ormond Beach (tel. 672-4677), features a drink called the Cassidy Extravaganza, and believe me, it is—45 ounces of anything you want. Atmosphere is casual and relaxed at this hang-out for the professional crowd, who may or may not be single.

Rock 'n' roll is the scene at **P.J.'s**, 400 Broadway (tel. 258-5222), where you can get a cheap, cheap beer during happy hour to 7 p.m. and a brew for a dime in the next two hours on Friday and Saturday. P.J.'s is collegiate heaven and has lots of specials and special events for spring breakers.

Lounges in many of the hotels along the beach offer quiet listening music on weekends, and sometimes nightly in the summer months.

More? **Hole Lounge,** at 301 S. Atlantic Ave. (tel. 255-6421), and **Yum-Yum Tree,** US 1 and 7th Street in Holly Hill (tel. 253-1063), are big on '50s music, twist remembrances, and hula-hoop contests. At the city's **Ocean Pier,** Main Street at the ocean (tel. 253-1212), there are rock bands and the city's biggest dance floor, plus four bars, a real caboose, and lots of inexpensive drinks.

Just about everything in the city is open to 3 a.m.

5. Seeing the Sights

Speed, speed, and more speed are the focus of Daytona sightseeing, where the beach is a sightseeing highway.

A WORD ABOUT THE BEACH: Twenty-three miles long and 500 feet wide, Daytona's hard-packed sparkling sand is one of the tourist delights of the Sunshine State, not only for sunning but for driving. You can take your car right onto the sand at Ormond Beach and drive along the water's edge south to Ponce de Leon Inlet.

No matter how shallow the water looks, *don't drive in it* or you're likely to end up waiting for the tow truck. Just stick to the main strip where everyone else is driving, and don't go faster than 10 m.p.h. You can park anywhere on the beach, but take my chastened word for it that they did not put up those signs warning motorists off soft, unsafe areas for nothing.

On a wide boardwalk at the ocean, near the fishing pier and just north of Main Street, you'll find an **amusement park** that will delight the youngsters and maybe the not-so-youngsters too. There's a sightseeing tower and sky ride open day and night in summer months, and a bandshell in **Oceanfront Park** at the north end of the promenade. The park is open from 1 to 11:30 p.m. daily in summer, and the bandshell has concerts regularly through August 1.

At Ponce de Leon Inlet and Lighthouse you can discover some interesting facts about Florida's lighthouse system and get a look at the lighthouse (open from 1 a.m. to 8 p.m. in the summer months, shorter hours in fall and winter).

WHAT TO SEE: If you're here in the all-important **speed weeks,** beginning in January and continuing through February, you'll see cars, cars, and more cars, qualifying races, consolation races, and finally the big **Daytona 500 Grand National Winston Cup Stock Car Race** in mid-February. A **Motorcycle Classic** roars around the track during the first week of March, and the city celebrates the Fourth of July with a summer speed week and Firecracker Festival that begins at the end of June and culminates in the **Paul Revere 250** and the **Pepsi Firecracker 400.** Tickets for speedway events start at $15 and go to $65. You can get them by writing **Daytona International Speedway,** P.O. Drawer S, Daytona, FL 32015; or call 904/253-6711.

If you're not visiting here in those jam-packed, rip-roaring weeks, you might like to see where all the hoopla occurs. Bus tours of the massive racing facility go on daily from 9 a.m. to 5 p.m. at the track.

In Ormond Beach, the **Birthplace of Speed Museum,** 160 E. Granada Blvd. (tel. 672-5657), traces the history of beach races here and also houses a replica of a 1906 Stanley Steamer thought to have raced 190 m.p.h. so many years ago, and to lots of other antique cars and interesting automotive memorabilia. It's open from noon to 4 p.m. Monday through Saturday, and admission is $1 (children under 9, free).

Rumor does have a way of spreading wildly in Florida, and rumor has it that when John D. Rockefeller spent his winters in Ormond Beach, he one day heard a hotel clerk figuring someone's bill and demanded to know why his own tab was higher. "Why, Mr. Rockefeller," the clerk replied, "we thought you have so much money you wouldn't mind if we charged you more." Not only did he mind, but the next year he moved out—lock, stock, and millions. To add insult to injury (or vice versa), he built a huge home right across the street. So many windows did the house have that Rockefeller called it the **Casements,** and spent many a winter there. After he died, the beautiful old two-story home fell into disrepair, but was recently rescued by the city which now operates it as a cultural center. You can tour it daily from 9 a.m. to 5 p.m. Casements is at 25 Riverside Dr. (tel. 673-4701).

In Bunnell, 22 miles north of Daytona Beach (take Old Dixie Highway past Tomoka State Park), you can see the crumbling foundations of a great sugar plantation mansion, **Bulow Villa,** at Bulow Plantation State Historic Site. Parts of a sugar mill made of coquina rock are still standing, and there are several wheels and the plantation's old springhouse. Admission is free.

Legend has it that somewhere in Bulow Creek, a 13-mile-long stream that begins just south of Bunnell, a cache of gold is buried!

Daytona also has a **Museum of Arts and Sciences,** at 1040 Museum Blvd., off Nova Road (tel. 255-0285). Here you'll find a collection of Cuban paintings and folk art, a planetarium featuring star shows and musical laser-light shows, a library, a sculpture garden, two nature trails, and the Prehistory of Florida Wing featuring a giant ground sloth skeleton found near here. It's open Tuesday through Friday from 9 a.m. to 4 p.m., and from noon to 5 p.m. on Saturday and Sunday. Admission is $2 for adults, 50¢ for children under 12; free on Wednesday and Sunday afternoons.

6. Sports

With its very pleasant climate year round and miles of water and beach, you can always find something to keep your muscles in shape in Daytona.

GOLF AND TENNIS: All the city's 12 golf courses are within 25 minutes of the beach, and most hotels will arrange your starting times for you. Some also have special greens fees for their guests, so be sure to ask.

Daytona Beach Golf and Country Club (tel. 255-4517) is the city's largest, with 36 holes. There are par-three courses at **Holly Hill, Fair Green Golf Course,** and **New Smyrna Beach.**

Public tennis courts are at eight locations in the city, including **Seabreeze Courts,** 1101 N. Atlantic Ave. (tel. 258-9198). The city's recreation department (tel. 253-9222) can help you find the courts nearest you.

WATER SPORTS: Big rollers whiz in all along this coastline, especially in the fall, and in October each year there's a surfing competition here. If you'd like to test your balance on a board, rent one at **Daytona Beach Surf Shops,** 30 S. Atlantic Ave. (tel. 253-3366), or **Granada Surf Shop,** 394 S. Atlantic Ave., Ormond Beach (tel. 672-5415). Rates are about $10 an hour.

Rent sailboats at **Bruce's Catamaran Rentals and Rides** (tel. 788-1310), on the beach near Oceans 7 condominium in Daytona Beach Shores. Ocean rides are about $5 a half hour; rental rates vary. Open 9 a.m. to dark.

Jet skis are available at the **Halifax River** at the end of the Seabreeze Bridge (tel. 252-0972), and for motorboats try **Pelican Island Marina,** 3226 Riverview Lane (tel. 761-5884), which also has ski boats. **Atlantic Scuba Academy,** at 20 N. Atlantic Ave. (tel. 253-7558), can give you the word on diving trips.

Snow White Boats will take you out deep-sea fishing all day or on half-day trips with bait and tackle furnished. Capt. Al Kline's boats are docked at Inlet Harbor Fishing Camp (turn west off Atlantic Avenue at Inlet Harbor Road in Ponce de Leon Inlet; tel. 767-6000). The **Inlet Harbor booking office** (tel. 767-

3266) can also help you find a fishing expedition, and there are three piers in the area for inexpensive angling. Day sea trips cost about $300 for six.

Parasailing fans can take to the skies courtesy of **Power Chute,** on Halifax Drive in Port Orange. To get there follow Route A1A to Dunlawton West, then turn right on Halifax. Rides are about $20.

RUNNING: The Daytona Beach Parks and Recreation Department sponsors an Easter Beach Run each year on two four-mile courses along the hard-packed sands. Nearly 2000 runners from 8 to 80 participate.

PARIMUTUEL SPORTS: The **Daytona Beach Kennel Club,** on Route 92 just off I-4 and I-95, and next door to the Speedway (tel. 252-6484), has races every day but Sunday from early May through Labor Day week. Post time is 8 p.m., and there are matinees at 1:30 p.m. on Monday, Wednesday, and Saturday. Admission is $1.

The jai-alai season runs from February to mid-August at **Daytona Beach Jai-Alai,** on US 92 (tel. 255-0222), after which players move to nearby **Melbourne Jai-Alai** at Sarno and Wickham Roads, Melbourne (tel. 259-9800), open late August through January. Admission is $1 to $3 and the games start at 7 p.m., with matinees at noon several days a week at both frontons.

Chapter VIII

FLORIDA'S CROWN

1. Jacksonville
2. St. Augustine

NOWHERE ELSE IN FLORIDA will you be closer to the state's—and the nation's—roots than in this region called the Crown. Historically, it is indeed Florida's corona, for here the state was born. Here was thrown the pebble that stirred a ripple, then a tidal wave, of tourism that was to alter the future of Florida forever.

Miami was nothing but a swamp when Jacksonville first welcomed winter-weary visitors to its shores. And Jacksonville in turn was little more than primeval forest when its neighbor St. Augustine was born and burgeoned into a bustling colony.

Here in these cities you can find the past all Americans share, a past tied to all this hemisphere and to Europe as well. Here too you'll find a part of the state like no other. Its sands are packed hard as concrete; its lifestyle is as soft and slow as its southern drawls. Mists rise off wide rivers and pines replace palms. Giant live oaks stretch massive branches over streams once sailed by steamer passengers headed for healing—if somewhat odoriferous—sulfur springs upstream in Green Cove.

To this place came first the French, then the Spanish, then the English, then rowdy Revolutionaries called Americans. They horse-traded the territory among them for 300 years after the French started the cannons booming in Jacksonville in 1562 with a little colony of Huguenots. Today Jacksonville is a bustling, booming banking and insurance capital where only two French words are common—mortgage and champagne.

Fortunes sought here today have plenty of precedent—some of Florida's most famous fortune hunters have gravitated to the Crown. Pirates Jean Lafitte, Blackbeard, and Sir Francis Drake sacked cities that now honor those rogues with an oceanside highway known as the Buccaneer Trail. Slave trader Zephaniah Kingsley built an enormous plantation here from profits on African lives, then named as its doyenne his African princess wife. American spy John McIntosh, tired of serving a sluggish bureaucracy, tossed together a ragtag force and warred on Spain in hopes of making Florida an independent nation—and himself president.

There have been great glossy days in Jacksonville and St. Augustine, days when yards of silk rustled and frothed across the halls of great plantation houses, when champagne bubbled and money flowed. There have also been grim days, when fires burned, cannons thundered, and men died to wrest these lands from each other. Great galleons filled with yellow gold have sailed past these shores (if they could get by the wreckers), and massive sailing ships loaded with the black gold of slavery have slithered into Fernandina to unload their shackled cargo.

Waves of trouble and joy, of victors and vanquished have washed over the land leaving behind massive fortresses and tiny frame houses, gold doubloons and lacy wedding gowns, ragged fragments of the past that welcome you to a land no longer royal but always regal, a land that has bequeathed to all the nation the legacy of lineage.

GETTING THERE: American, Delta, Eastern, Ozark, Piedmont, TWA, and United fly into **Jacksonville International Airport,** as do two commuter operations, People Express and Florida Commuter Airlines. The airport is on the city's south side.

Amtrak trains stop in Jacksonville at 3570 Clifford Lane and in nearby Palatka, which is the nearest Amtrak stop for St. Augustine (about 35 miles southwest).

Trailways buses, at 410 Duval St. (tel. 354-8543), and **Greyhound,** at 10 Pearl St. (tel. 356-5521), connect the cities to the state and nation.

GETTING AROUND: Hertz and Avis **rental-car companies** are supplemented by Ajax, Econo, General, Ford, Budget, and Airport Thrifty. **Greyhound** (tel. 757-1710) is a budget leader here, with weekly rates of about $80.

Jacksonville

Airport limousines operated by **AAA Limo Service** (tel. 764-8989) can get you to downtown Jacksonville for $8, to the beaches for $20.

Jacksonville City Bus Transit system travels downtown and to the beaches. They'll be happy to give you route information at 633-7330. Bus fares are about $1, and the service runs from dawn to dusk.

Taxis are always the most expensive way to travel, but here they're a bit lower than the rest of the state with fares of $1 for the first mile and an additional $1 for subsequent miles. Call **Checker Cab** (tel. 764-2472) or **Yellow Cab** (tel. 354-5511).

St. Augustine

In downtown St. Augustine there is no public bus service. You can get around easily on **sightseeing trams** or in taxis which charge by zone. Downtown destinations are $2 to $3, beach rides about $5. **Ancient City Cab Co.** (tel. 824-8161) will also pick you up at Jacksonville Airport or elsewhere in that city for $65, one way.

1. Jacksonville

Towering skyscrapers erupt in a blaze of smoky-gray reflections. Silvery masses of metal streak across a deep-blue river. Jacksonville, antique river city, welcomer of conquerers for four centuries, once a bustling port and now Florida's banking and insurance center, is on the grow again.

Change is everywhere these days: new hotels, refurbished old hotels, and everywhere a surge of enthusiasm as this lovely old city strides toward yet another renaissance. Now the nation's largest city, with 840 incorporated square miles, Jacksonville has been growing in spurts like this for generations.

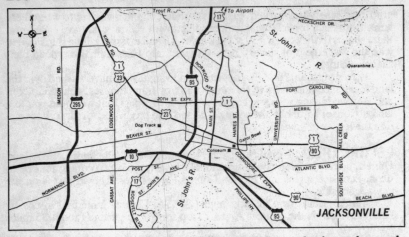

Through it all Jacksonville keeps its Old South flavor, thanks to a long and proud history that can be traced back even further than St. Augustine's to 1564 when French Huguenots settled at Fort Caroline. Spanish soldiers, intent on making the water safe for their gold galleons, made short work of the colony, however, so Jacksonville has about given up trying to win an "oldest city" place in Florida history books.

It certainly hasn't given up trying to lure tourists here, and by now it ought to know how. Jacksonville has been hosting chilled Yankees since the 1800s when steamers began bringing them from New York. Once here, they settled into Jacksonville's guest houses, or journeyed inland to spas and cool crystal springs. Long was the list of the famous who came here, including author Harriet Beecher Stowe.

You can still see the past vividly in **Mayport,** where white shrimp boats rock gently at anchor, their colorful nets swinging in the breezes, much as they have done for generations. You can see it more dramatically yet in **Fernandina Beach,** where you'll marvel at Victorian Gothic houses trimmed in lacy gingerbread and ringed by wide verandas once swept by hoop-skirted ballgowns. You can see it in the Palace Saloon, said to be the oldest watering spot in Florida, perhaps visited by pirates Jean and Pierre Lafitte, who once were lured by the action in this city President Monroe dubbed "a festering fleshpot."

As you ramble along the crumbling walls of massive Fort Clinch, roam among the gingerbread-trimmed homes, and gaze at the towering lighthouse that's been warning ships off the rocks since 1839, you'll hear the echoes of rapid-fire Spanish, clipped British tones, soft French twangs—the ghostly voices of those who fought over these strips of land for centuries, deeding it finally to the world's travelers.

Serenity and Old South drawls aren't the whole story here, however. Beneath the surface runs the fighting blood of buccaneers and pioneers who carved up this land. You'll discover that spirit in early November and late December when the entire town reverts to its rough-and-tumble roots for the traditional Florida-Georgia football clash at the Gator Bowl. Everything's high during those zany weekends, from hotel rates to most of the citizenry, who turn out in droves to cheer on the state team with the same fervor their ancestors used to remove what threatened them.

A rough-and-ready land it has always been beneath the plantations and pin-striped suits, a city of plots and pirates, a place to discover the strong roots on which this flowering peninsula blooms.

ORIENTATION: Route A1A runs from Mayport (where you take a ferry across the river for 50¢) south along Atlantic Beach, Neptune, Jacksonville, and Ponte Vedra Beaches. Part of the A1A strip is called the **Buccaneer Trail.**

In town, the Main Street bridge crosses the St. Johns into the main section of downtown Jacksonville. The city's Visitor and Convention Bureau is west of Main Street at Monroe and Pearl Streets. Hotels are on the south side of the river, off I-95 at Gulf Life Drive.

One of the most important things to know is that with its 840-mile boundary this city is *huge,* which is why you have such a difference in airport limousine fares to the city and to the beaches.

If you're staying downtown and not planning much sightseeing, you can get along with buses and taxis, but if you're planning to see the beaches and historic sights, you'll need a car—or a suitcase full of money.

USEFUL INFORMATION: For **police or medical emergencies,** call 911 or 633-4111. . . . For a **24-hour drugstore,** try Eckerd's, at 3544 University Blvd. (tel. 733-7600). . . . **Venetia Sixty Minute Cleaners** has a one-hour dry cleaning service. It's located at 5627 Roosevelt Blvd. (tel. 389-7263). . . . For **non-emergency medical needs,** call the Duval County Medical Society at 335-6561. . . . For **dental problems,** call the county dental information and referral service at 356-6642. . . . If you're a midnight muncher, head for Denny's, which has **24-hour restaurants** in the city, including one at 6 Ellis Trail (tel. 731-7437).

TOURIST INFORMATION: The **Jacksonville Chamber of Commerce** will be happy to help you out with all kinds of information. They're at 3 Independent Dr., Jacksonville, FL 32207 (tel. 904/353-0300). . . . You can also get information at the **Jacksonville Visitor and Convention Bureau,** at 240 W. Monroe St., Jacksonville, FL 32207 (tel. 904/353-9736). . . . The **Fernandina Beach Chamber of Commerce** will help you find your way around that small town. It's at 102 Centre St., Fernandina Beach, FL 32034 (tel. 904/261-3248). . . . The **Jacksonville Beaches Chamber of Commerce** is at 111 N. 3rd St., Jacksonville Beach, FL 32050 (tel. 904/249-3868).

HOTELS IN JACKSONVILLE: At this end of the state beach, hotel rooms are most expensive in summer months, although downtown hotels have year-round prices.

Downtown
Sheraton–St. Johns, Prudential Drive, Jacksonville, FL 32207 (tel. 904/ 396-5100, or toll free 800/325-3535), is the new showplace of Jacksonville. A five-story focal point for riverfront redevelopment, the Sheraton's sparkling blue roof shines as brightly as its famous neighbor, the St. Johns River. Overlooking this waterway which was the final destination for 19th-century Yankee travelers, the hotel was completed in 1980 so it's quite contemporary. Sheraton's 350 big and beautiful rooms occupy 16 scenic acres at the waterfront, many overlooking the water or lovely grounds where tiny fountains bubble and waterfalls flow. You'll find old touches here, from a wall mural in the lobby depicting life in early 19th-century Jacksonville to the very contemporary accommoda-

tions. For dining, the Admiralty Restaurant offers outstanding continental cuisine in the atmosphere of an Atlantic steamship crossing. They've created one very lovely place at Sheraton–St. Johns, with tennis courts, swimming pool, and shopping village. Rates are $75 to $97 single, $87 to $109 double, with suites from $150 to $305.

Another riverside hotel is the **Jacksonville Hilton,** at 565 S. Main St., Jacksonville, FL 32207 (tel. 904/398-3561, and toll-free numbers in every state), a 296-room hostelry with spacious newly refurbished rooms, all lined with plush carpeting and trimmed with glass doors leading to private balconies that overlook the river and the hotel's big pool. Whetby's Wharf seafood and chops dining room echoes the nautical surroundings outside, and Fanny's Row'n Club has a sporty atmosphere and lots of oars for decor. The Greenery coffeeshop offers a contemporary atmosphere with lots of what its name suggests, and a tranquil view of the river. At this Hilton, two people pay $82 to $98, year round; singles are $69 to $85.

Holiday Inn–West, 555 Stockton St., Jacksonville, FL 32207 (tel. 904/387-4661, or toll free 800/465-4329), is on the west side of town but not far—just two miles—from the city's business and financial district. Once again Holiday Inn produces bright and spacious rooms with contemporary touches, dining facilities, a pool, all the usual amenities. A double room is $46 to $59, and singles are $40 to $53.

Hotels at Jacksonville Beach

Most Jacksonville vacationers seek a quiet spot in the sunshine of Jacksonville's 30 miles of beaches. Here's a look at the selection.

Sheraton not only has a huge new hotel in the city but it also operates the **Sheraton–Jacksonville Beach,** at 11th Avenue South at the ocean, Jacksonville Beach, FL 32050 (tel. 904/249-7231, or toll free 800/325-3535), an eight-story hotel with 154 rooms and lovely little balconies overlooking the sea. Sheraton has king-size beds or two double beds in all its rooms, wall-to-wall carpeting, and breathtaking views. When you want some exercise, there are two new tennis courts and a sparkling tiled pool. Golf arrangements are available, and there are even saunas to recover from all that exercise. For dining, huge glass windows in the contemporary dining room offer a panoramic view of the Atlantic as you feast on sizzling steaks, thick slabs of prime roast beef, or seafood acquired from the pier down the way. Dinners are in the $10 to $17 range. Double rates at the Sheraton are $58 to $89, year round.

They may call it Sea Turtle Inn but there's nothing slow about the service or the effort this high-rise hotel puts out to make you happy. Located right on the beach, **Sea Turtle Inn,** at 1 Ocean Blvd., Jacksonville Beach, FL 32233 (tel. 904/249-7402, or toll free 800/831-6600), has pretty, bright rooms with lots of space and shining views of the ocean from private balconies. In the Sea Turtle Restaurant seafood is king, and on Friday you can consume copious quantities of sea treasures at a bountiful buffet. There's a pool and a game room. Rates are $60 to $80, year round.

Holiday Inn–Beaches, at 1617 N. 1st St., Jacksonville Beach, FL 32050 (tel. 904/249-9071, or toll free 800/465-4329), has 150 rooms, all of them overlooking the ocean and the resort's pool, which is right on the sand. A rooftop nightclub has a razzle-dazzle lighting system and plenty of entertainment that draws throngs of local-ites as well as visitors. Rooms are large and airy, and decorated in the tropical colors favored by this chain—they have a wall of glass, and balconies too, so you can get a tan without leaving your room. Two people pay $68 to $95, year round; rooms with king-size beds and kitchens are $105.

Eastwinds Motel, at 1505 S. 1st St., Jacksonville Beach, FL 32250 (tel. 904/

249-3858), is a cozy oceanfront motel with a pretty patio and pool. Guests gather for cookouts on the motel's grills when they're not cooking in their own small efficiencies here. Deluxe suites are also available, and the spacious rooms are decorated in bright colors. It's close to tennis and golf courses too. Highest rates are $35 to $75.

Friendship Inn Gold Coast, 731 1st St., North Jacksonville Beach, FL 32250 (tel. 904/249-5006), is indeed a friendly place with just 31 spacious rooms, all with balconies overlooking the ocean or the heated pool in the yard. Some efficiencies and apartments are also available in this cheery place trimmed in bright orange. Double rooms at the inn are $35 to $55, year round.

Jacksonville Outskirts

Sit out some morning on the big screened porches as the sun rises pink and gold on the horizon and listen to the sounds: in the distance the gentle murmur of surf, nearby a tiny bird twittering, somewhere out there the deep-throated gronk of a bullfrog, the rustle of sawgrass, the splash of a silvery fish. For me that's the very best thing about **Sawgrass,** 19 miles south of Jacksonville on Route A1A in Ponte Vedra Beach, FL 32082 (tel. 904/285-2261, or toll free 800/874-7547; in Florida, 800/432-1270), that silence, that pervading sense of peace and solitude. Which is not to say that you're going to fall into a coma at this intriguing resort that sprawls out over acres and acres of ground, with its own long strip of beach, and absolutely no neighbors. No indeed, you can play here on 63 holes of golf including a championship oceanside course that's the home of the Tournament Players Championship in March. You can lob and volley on 13 tennis courts, home of the Lipton World of Doubles, or drift in a canoe, set sail on the briny deep, drop a line in 350 acres of lake. Sawgrass's oceanside beach club has an oasis pool that's a glittering adult retreat with a poolside bar, another Olympic-size pool for the whole family, and a wading pool for the tykes. Evenings, the club becomes a flickering candlelit night scene where you can dine overlooking the sea on continental treats and great regional seafood, ending your day entertained in the Topsider Lounge, where prices are in the $15 range for dinner.

You'll stay here in a beachfront studio or a privately owned two-, three-, or four-bedroom villa, or two-story town house. All are fabulous places with spacious rooms and bright contemporary decor, big fully equipped kitchens, dining rooms, living rooms, and of course those screened porches. Rates for double accommodations at the resort from June to November are $120 to $195, lower from December to March. From March to May rates rise to $125 to $210 for units accommodating two. Prices rise as the size of the accommodations increases.

Inns are usually tiny places, but sometimes larger hostelries are so cozy they qualify for inn consideration. **Inn at Baymeadows** is *that* kind of place. Nestled into a corner of Baymeadows Golf and Country Club, this inn has 60 rooms decorated in lively contemporary colors and sporting—are you ready?—Jacuzzi whirlpools! I'd better back off a bit—not *all* rooms have those whirlpools, but some do and plans for more are in the works. Rooms here are scattered about in two-story buildings on grounds peppered with tennis courts, a swimming pool, and a lake, about as country as you can get this close to town. If you're treating yourself, book one of the ten suites, eight of which have loft bedrooms. When the developers of this Bayview section began building here a few years ago, they reserved this section of land especially to house a small inn. As owners of another inn, Inn at St. Clair in St. Clair, Michigan, they'd already learned something about the operation of such a property. That knowledge shows: complimentary newspaper, fresh orange juice, pastries and coffee served from a pewter pot every morning, golf and dining privileges at the adjoining course and country club, handsome antique prints on the wall of the small lobby, even little sewing kits in your room. In the center of things here is an attractive gazebo and all around is the sound of silence. A tranquil spot to enjoy the attractions of Jacksonville. If you're new in Jacksonville the inn's model-lovely manager, Nancy Karrer, will be happy to help you find your way around. You'll find the Inn at Baymeadows at 8050 Baymeadows Circle West, Jacksonville, FL 32216 (tel. 904/739-0739). Rates are $50 to $56 double for rooms, $66 to $82 for loft suites, and up to $175 for suites with whirlpools.

Amelia Island

It's a city. It's a world. It's bordering-on-incredible **Amelia Island Plantation,** Amelia Island, FL 32034 (tel. 904/261-6161, or toll free 800/874-6878; in Florida, 800/342-6841). How do you explain 900 acres of barely touched tidal marshland, ringed by silvery beach and turquoise waters, rustling with the sound of breezes ruffling through the pines and tugging at tall white sea oats? Glorious? Glamorous? All of that, perhaps more. Nestled around a 27-hole Pete Dye golf course, the resort's stark contemporary lines stand out like sentinels guarding this strip of coastline. At sandside is a pool nestled into a dune, and wooden walkways lead to mile after mile of sand bordered by a forest and the Atlantic. You can ride a stalwart steed through the surf here, play on 21 tennis courts, play those 27 holes of golf, loll on the beach or at poolside, dine, dance, and make merry in elegant restaurants or a disco. You can wander aimlessly on nature preserves, explore an Indian burial mound 1000 years old, bicycle, fish, and shop. For dinner, don a jacket or a cocktail dress and venture out to the Amelia Island Inn, which houses 24 spacious guest suites as well as a picturesque dining room overlooking the ocean. Dine on seafood straight from the waters in front of you at prices in the $15 to $25 range. You can choose from hotel rooms, or select a condominium villa with one, two, or three bedrooms (some even have four) overlooking the ocean, clustered about the fairways, or gazing down on a lagoon or lake. All the villa clusters have a pool (or two or three). Need I say that these are big, big apartments all individually decorated by owners with private balconies and spectacular views? Need I add that this is a very glamorous resort? I didn't think so. Rates at the resort run from $80 to $312 from June to March, from $100 to $348 from March to May.

A new inn on Amelia Island is called the **Bailey House.** That is, the inn is new but the building is not: It was built in 1895 and is a peaked-roof turreted house located downtown in an area now part of the island's restoration district. Owners Diane and Tom Hay have filled the inn with antiques, claw-footed bathtubs, paddle fans, and Victoriana, and are offering bed and breakfast (all rooms have private baths) for $55 to $85, year round. Address of the Bailey House is 28 S. 7th St., P.O. Box 805, Fernandina Beach, FL 32034 (tel. 904/261-5390).

If you consider yourself an adventurer and have an interest in historic Florida, here's a dwelling spot that is likely to fascinate you. First, a little history. Seems the Carnegie family once settled into this part of the country, operating the Palace Saloon, residing in a summer mansion, and hobnobbing with friends on Georgia's Cumberland and Jekyll Islands. A great-grandson of Andrew Carnegie has retained the family manse, called **Greyfield,** and now operates this nine-bedroom mansion as an inn. To get there, you board a supply launch which chugs over every day except Wednesday. Once there, you'll find yourself on an offshore island inhabited only by campers, day-trippers, wild horses, and a handful of Thomas Carnegie's descendants. Rooms have double or twin beds and share the inn's bathrooms (a library suite is the only room with private bath). Prices are a bit on the high side, but what is an adventure worth anyway? You pay $15 for the boat ride and $75 per person a night, including all meals, plus 20% for tax and gratuities. Where else can you dine on Carnegie china and sleep in Carnegie beds? Who knows? Perhaps some of their success will rub off! Inn operators can also fix you up with a bicycle or a horse to ride, and a naturalist can provide tours and explanations of local flora and fauna. You can contact the inn's reservations center in Fernandina Beach at the Chandlery, Centre and 2nd Streets, Fernandina Beach, FL 32034 (tel. 904/261-6408).

READER'S AMELIA ISLAND INN SUGGESTION: "Susan Caple and her husband David operate the **1735 House** (named, incidentally, for the year in which James Oglethorpe claimed Amelia Island for England). The inn has six room-suites furnished in antiques. Each unit has a private bedroom, a captain's bunk bed area, and a living room (no room televisions, however) furnished in wicker or rattan. Some have facilities for preparing snacks as well. Breakfast baskets filled with fresh fruit, juice, coffee, fresh baked goods, and the morning paper are delivered to your room each morning. Facilities for golf, tennis, swimming, fishing, and boating are nearby, and the Caples will pick you up at the Jacksonville or Fernandina Beach airports. Rates are $50 single, $60 double, and weekly family packages are available" (Hilda Inclan, Miami, Fla.). [*Author's Note:* The 1735 House, at 584 S. Fletcher (Route A1A), Amelia Island, FL 32034 (tel. 904/261-5878), has been mentioned to me by several readers for its quaint ambience and oceanside location.]

JACKSONVILLE RESTAURANTS: You'll find great seafood here and a wide range of moderately priced restaurants. Remember that the prices I've listed, unless otherwise noted, are for entrees, but that usually includes a salad, one or two vegetables, and sometimes coffee as well.

Top of the Line

Strickland's, at Mayport Ferry (tel. 246-9977), is hard by the shrimp boats docked here where the Mayport ferryboat lands each day. Naturally, the decor is nautical, but subtly mixed with comfortable contemporary touches. Seafood is the main menu item, and you can choose from huge platters brimming with shrimp, lobster, grouper, snapper, and oysters, or select just one of the many fresh fish the restaurant serves broiled or fried and delicately sauced. You pay a little more here, perhaps $15 to $20 or so for dinner, but you get a pretty, woodsy, casual setting overlooking the water, a big raw bar, a lounge, and sensational seafood. There's always a table wait, but it's worth it. Open from 5 to 11 p.m. Wednesday to Friday, from noon on Saturday and Sunday.

For a good steak and some excellent seafood in handsome surroundings, try the **1878 Steak House**, 12 N. 2nd St. in Fernandina Beach (tel. 261-4049). Sizzling sirloins and shrimp won't cost you more than $10 to $15, and you'll eat them in an old-house atmosphere—steaks upstairs, seafood down, with homemade cheesecake both places. Steaks are sold by the ounce—figure $1.50 per ounce. Open for dinner from 5 to 10 p.m. daily, except Sunday.

Strickland's also has a **Town House** restaurant, at 3510 Phillips Hwy., about three miles south of Jacksonville on US 1 (tel. 396-1682), where you can dine well on fresh seafood and perfectly done steaks in the $10 to $15 range. There's a children's menu too, and the restaurant is open for lunch from 11:30 a.m. to 2:30 p.m., for dinner from 5:30 to 10:30 p.m. Monday through Friday (dinner only on Saturday).

Le Gueridon is small in size but it looms large in local dining circles. A comparative newcomer to Jacksonville, this inconspicuous restaurant in the Costa Verde Shopping Plaza, at 2429 3rd St. (tel. 241-2426), has been getting rave reviews hereabouts since the day it moved up from St. Augustine. Now it's one of Jacksonville's top choices for special-occasion dinners and for top-quality preparations anytime. French flavors are the specialty here—try the poisson-bagatelle. Entrees are in the $14 to $20 range and the restaurant is open 6 to 10 p.m. daily, except Sunday.

Next Best

You never know what you're going to find up this way. One of the things you will find is a very simple, little restaurant—coffeeshop decor, Formica-topped tables—with one of the nation's top wine lists! Yes, indeed. **Surf Motel and Restaurant,** 3199 Fletcher Ave., Fernandina Beach (tel. 261-5711), a couple of years ago was cited by a wine magazine as having one of America's top-100 wine lists. While you're selecting from the eight-page list, you might as well look at the menu, which is just fine too. The Surf Restaurant creates some very good seafood dishes and offers landlubber treats like steaks, chicken, and pork chops. Prices are in the $10 to $15 range for dinner, but you can also stop in here for breakfast or lunch. Hours are 7 a.m. to 9:30 p.m. daily, closing 30 minutes earlier on Sunday and 30 minutes later on Saturday.

You can always count on **Victoria Station,** 7579 Arlington Expressway East on US 1A and 90A (tel. 725-3977), where you dine in the chain's railroad box-cars on prime rib and steaks. There's a big salad bar brimming with fresh vegetables and homemade salad toppings, and dinner prices top out at $11! Hours are 4:30 to 10:30 p.m. daily, an hour later on weekends (from noon to 10 p.m. on Sunday).

The Jacksonville Hilton's **Whetby's Wharf,** 565 S. Main St. (tel. 398-3561), is a fine seafood restaurant with lots of interesting nautical decor and plenty of beef choices for no-seafood types. There's a fine view of the river and city sky-line from this restaurant where you'll pay $12 to $17 for dinner. It's open from 11:30 a.m. to 2 p.m. and 5:30 to 10:30 p.m. daily.

Aged beef is a feature of the **Green Derby,** 578 Riverside Dr. (tel. 356-7691), an attractive restaurant that's been around long enough to be a big favor-ite with Jacksonville patrons. Naturally in this waterside city you'll find seafood dishes on the menu too, with prices in the $10 to $15 bracket. Hours are noon to 2:30 p.m. and 6 to 9:30 p.m., an hour later on weekends (closed Sunday).

Another outstanding place for beef is the **Tree Steak House,** 924 Arlington Rd. (tel. 725-0066), where prices are in the $10 to $12 range. It's open from 5:30 to 10:30 p.m. daily, to 9:30 p.m. on Sunday.

Budget Bets

Patti's, 7300 Beach Blvd. (tel. 725-1662), is an oft-mentioned Italian res-taurant in the Jacksonville Beach area, and it's certainly a great spot for a rib-sticking pasta freak-out that won't cost you a bundle. In fact your check will likely be less than $10—much less. It's open from 5 to 10 p.m. daily.

For gourmet Japanese cuisine it's **Ieyasu of Tokyo,** at 23 W. Duval (tel. 353-0163), where there are more bean sprouts than you ever grew in a Mason jar, and wonderfully fresh vegetables prepared by experts who serve you in the usual understated delicacy of Japanese decor. Prices are in the $10 to $15 range, and the restaurant's open from 11 a.m. to 2:30 p.m. and 5:30 to 10 p.m. Monday through Saturday, later on weekends.

Bono's Barbecue, at 4907 Beach Blvd. (tel. 392-4248), is *the* place for bar-becue, with two other locations at South Lane Avenue and Powers Avenue. Bono's is open daily from 11 a.m. to 11:30 p.m., later on weekends.

Beach Road Chicken Dinner, 4132 Atlantic Blvd. (tel. 398-7980), is the home of southern fried chicken—terrific and lots of it for $4 or less. Beach Road

Chicken opens at 5 p.m. and closes at 10:15 p.m. Tuesday through Saturday, noon to 10 p.m. on Sunday (closed Monday). Fried shrimp is a recent addition here.

Morrison's and Piccadilly Cafeteria here, as everywhere, are sure bets for very inexpensive meals. **Piccadilly Cafeteria,** at 40 Regency Square (tel. 725-5777), is open daily from 11 a.m. to 8:30 p.m. **Morrison's Cafeteria** has six restaurants in the area. The one at 3428 Beach Blvd. (tel. 398-1092), is an all-you-can-eat buffet open from 11 a.m. to 8 p.m.; the others are in the Gateway Shopping Center, Orange Park Mall, Regency Square, Independent Square, and at 4415 Roosevelt Blvd. Most meals are under $5 at these cafeterias.

NIGHTLIFE: The after-dark scene centers around this city's large hotels, including those recommended above. The Sheraton's spiffy lounge always draws crowds.

Other night action rendezvous are **Diamondhead,** at 823 Gulf Life Dr. (tel. 396-6414), a good restaurant too; **Smugglers Inn,** at 8909 Bay Meadow Rd. (tel. 737-9555), especially on Wednesday and Friday nights; **Bennigan's,** at 9245 Atlantic Blvd. (tel. 724-0991), where you party in an atmosphere of wood, greenery, and etched glass. For bluegrass, jazz, or folk music, **Applejacks,** 1402 San Marco Blvd. (tel. 398-2111; it's closed Sunday and sometimes has a $2 cover charge. Another perennial winner is **Big Daddy's,** 9278 Arlington Expressway (tel. 724-9566).

The **Alhambra Dinner Theater,** 12000 Beach Blvd. (tel. 641-1212), has year-round plays and musicals preceded by a buffet; tickets for both are $16 to $18. It's open from 6 p.m. Tuesday through Sunday.

The **Jacksonville Symphony** (tel. 354-5479) performs on the beach in outdoor concerts at the Flags Pavilion in summer and at the Civic Auditorium in Jacksonville in winter. Check local newspapers to see where they'll be and when.

Theatre Jacksonville, at 2032 San Marco Blvd. (tel. 396-4425), bills itself as "the oldest continuously producing theater in the U.S." and has 65 seasons to prove it. Ticket prices and hours vary.

WHAT TO SEE AND DO: At Green Cove Springs, 25 miles south of Jacksonville on US 17, you'll find one of Florida's first resorts, a spa where turn-of-the-century travelers "took the waters" at sulfur springs. You can enjoy those same waters today (although I'm not guaranteeing miracle rejuvenations) at **Green Cove Spring Park,** home of the mineral springs which also feed the municipal swimming pool in summer. Learn more about the spa's history at Clay County Hospital Museum in the former county courthouse at Gratio Place and Walnut Street (tel. 904/284-9644).

Amelia Island was named in 1735 by Gov. James Oglethorpe of Georgia in honor of Princess Amelia, the beautiful young sister of England's King George II. To get quickly to Amelia Island, take I-95 north to the A1A exit at Yulee, and follow A1A east to the island. For a scenic adventure, drive north on A1A through Jacksonville Beach and follow the signs to Mayport Ferry. Mayport is a colorful fishing village where you'll find car ferries (50¢ a car) that leave every half hour from 6:20 a.m. to 10 p.m. and deposit you across the St. Johns River at Fort George Island, where you continue north to Amelia Island on A1A. Amelia Island has flown eight flags and been home to the Spanish, the French, the English, and finally to combinations thereof known as Americans. **Fernan-**

dina Beach, the island's main village, can trace its history back four centuries. Roam through the 30-block historic district that's listed in the National Register of Historic Places, and stroll streets that end only because an ocean gets in the way. You'll see some intriguing old architecture (steamboat Gothic and Queen Anne) every bit as lovely (but less publicized) as Key West and Savannah. Two miles wide and 13 miles long, Amelia Island was the birthplace of the state's shrimping industry. The colorful fleet still sways at anchor in Fernandina Beach and during the early May celebration of shrimping the fishermen will welcome you on board for a close look at their craft.

Look for the men in Union soldier uniforms at **Fort Clinch** (tel. 261-4212). They'll take you through the mess hall, barracks, and supplies store, still full of uniforms and lye soap, dried beans and hardtack. To these guides the year is still 1864, so don't be surprised if they ask you if you've heard a rumor that the Yanks have burned Atlanta. Admission is 50¢ and the fort is open 9 a.m. to dusk.

In Fernandina Beach whisky still pours at the **Palace Saloon,** 115 Centre St. (tel. 261-9068), said to be the oldest bar in Florida, a 1903 creation that sports a pair of maidens holding up the ceiling.

Here too is one end of the **Buccaneer Trail,** a whimsically named section of Route A1A that winds southward to **Fort George Island.** On Fort George Island lived another of Florida's colorful characters, Zephaniah Kingsley, who built an empire in slave trading and occupied what is now the oldest standing plantation house in Florida, built in 1817. Zephaniah was either quite a liberal or rich enough to make rules, not follow them—he married a black African princess. You can still see the plantation's slave cabins made of "tabby" rock (a mixture of oyster shell, sand, and cement). They are the best preserved slave dwellings in the nation. Tours of the main house and cabins (on Route 105, follow the signs from the ferry dock; tel. 251-3122) are at 9 and 11 a.m. and 1 and 4 p.m. daily; admission is 50¢ for everyone over 6.

To see how brewmasters create the final bubbly product, visit the **Anheuser-Busch Brewery** (take I-95 north to the Busch Drive exit; tel. 751-0700), open from 9:30 a.m. to 3:30 p.m. You can sample the product in the hospitality room; both tour and product are free.

For history and architecture buffs, the **Jacksonville National Bank,** at the corner of Forsyth and Laura Streets, makes an interesting foray. Built in 1902, its beautiful marble interior has been restored to expose the original vaulted ceiling and 42-foot skylight. This was the first all-marble building in the state, and viewing is free.

Another interesting building is the **Riverside Baptist Church,** at Park and King Streets, designed by famed Florida architect Addison Mizner. It's a combination of Spanish, Byzantine, and romanesque architecture.

The **Jacksonville Zoo,** a half mile east of I-95 on Heckscher Drive (tel. 757-4462), is a popular place where the youngsters can get a close look at 700 species of animals, and see African elephants from an elevated observation deck. Open 9 a.m. to 4:45 p.m. daily, the zoo charges $2.75 for adults, $1.25 for children 4 to 12.

Jacksonville Museum of Arts and Sciences (tel. 396-7061) has a 28-foot dinosaur and other science and anthropological exhibits. It's next to another pretty sight, **Friendship Fountain,** which sprays 17,000 gallons of water a minute 120 feet into the air and is beautifully lighted at night from 6 to 10 p.m. Both are on Gulf Life Drive at South Main Street, and the museum is open from 9 a.m. to 5 p.m. weekdays (except Monday), from 11 a.m. on Saturday, and from 1 p.m. on Sunday. Adults are charged $2; children, $1.

Fort Caroline National Memorial is the site of the first clash between European powers—the French who came here in 1564, 60 years before the Pilgrims, and the Spanish. It was the first Protestant colony in the U.S., a Huguenot development. You can see a replica of the fort and some typical objects of that era at the memorial, 12713 Fort Caroline Rd. (tel. 641-7155). Open daily from 9 a.m. to 5 p.m. (free).

Two art galleries in the area are the **Jacksonville Art Museum,** at 4160 Boulevard Center Dr. (tel. 398-8336), and the **Cummer Gallery of Art,** at 829 Riverside Ave. (tel. 356-6857). The Jacksonville Art Museum has a collection of Oriental porcelain and both changing and permanent exhibits. The Gallery, surrounded by beautiful formal gardens, has 11 galleries of European and American works of art. A special feature of the museum is the 700-piece Wark Collection of early Meissen porcelain. Both are free. The Jacksonville Art Museum is open from 10 a.m. to 4 p.m. Tuesday, Wednesday, and Friday, to 10 p.m. on Thursday, and from 1 to 5 p.m. on Saturday and Sunday; closed Monday. Hours at the Cummer Gallery are 10 a.m. to 4 p.m. Tuesday through Friday, noon to 5 p.m. on Saturday, and 2 to 5 p.m. on Sunday.

Harriet Beecher Stowe, author of *Uncle Tom's Cabin,* moved to the picturesque town of **Mandarin** (Mandarin Road branches right from San Jose Boulevard heading south) after her publishing success. You can see her house and lots of other trim old homes in this lovely riverside village. The Stowe family homesite and orange grove is at 12447 Mandarin Rd. After Mrs. Stowe and her family moved in back in the late 1800s, her homesite and orange grove became such a popular tourist site she spent much of her time trying to figure out ways to shield the home from the eyes of some curious visitors who carried things just a little too far (they stole clothes from her clothesline). Mrs. Stowe wrote some observations on the life she saw around here in Florida in a book called *Palmetto Leaves.*

SPORTS: Jacksonville's 65,000-seat **Gator Bowl** (tel. 633-2900) is the scene of hilarity and horseplay during the annual Florida-Georgia game pitting the two state universities. It's usually the first weekend in November, and the postseason Gator Bowl game is the last week in December. There's soccer here too.

There's greyhound racing at **Jacksonville Kennel Club,** 1440 N. McDuff (tel. 388-2623), **Orange Park Kennel Club,** US 17 at I-295 (tel. 264-9575), and **Bayard Raceway,** 18 miles south on US 1 (tel. 268-5555), which shares dates all year round. Admission is $1.

Golf clubs welcoming visitors include the **Dunes** (tel. 641-8444), **Jacksonville Beach Golf Club** (tel. 249-8600), and **Fort George Island Golf Club** (tel. 251-3132). Fees are $8 to $10.

Jacksonville has a number of municipal **tennis courts** scattered about the city. For information on which location is nearest you, contact the city recreation department (tel. 633-2540). **Boone Park,** at 3700 Park St., has 12 courts, some lighted. You can also play golf and tennis at **Amelia Island Plantation** and **Sawgrass** (see my hotel recommendations).

From little bream to mighty tarpon, this is top **fishing** country. Charter and party boats leave Mayport and Jacksonville Beach each morning for trips on the St. Johns River and in the ocean.

Sea Horse Stables, on Fernandina Beach (tel. 261-4878), rents horses for surf canters. Prices are $15 to $20 for a five-mile ride.

PARKS: **Little Talbot Island** is a 2500-acre park surrounded by the waters of the Atlantic Ocean, Fort George River, and Nassau Sound. You can camp, picnic, swim, fish, boat, and skin- and scuba-dive here, and stroll on a long pier out over the ocean. The park's on the Buccaneer Trail just south of Amelia Island.

Mike Roess Gold Head Park (tel. 904/473-4701) is a scenic ravine about 45 miles south of Jacksonville. Take Route 21 to 16 miles south of its intersection with Route 16. Three lakes dot the park and beside a stream flowing through it are the remains of an old dam and mill. You can walk a nature trail through the ravine, camp, picnic, swim, fish, dive, and paddle a canoe or pedal a bike.

2. St. Augustine

Nowhere else in the state can you travel from century to century as easily as you can in this antique community that was 55 years old when the Pilgrims landed at Plymouth Rock. And nowhere else do you feel the small triumphs of the centuries melding so effortlessly into a 20th-century city. St. Augustine has merged past and present in shady narrow lanes dappled with sunlight, in massive old homes filled with families whose joys and sorrows are little changed from those of armored Spanish conquistadors or homespun-clad pioneers struggling to wrest survival from this demanding land.

You will, of course, also see the neon intrusions of this tourist-conscious age, but just beyond the plastic trappings of the 20th century you'll find haunting echoes of the past in a tiny two-room cottage where a simple soldier's family lived and loved under the spreading branches of a tall live oak. You'll find the past in the primped and polished magnificence of a reconstructed house where tea was served from a shining silver service in rooms of gilt and velvet. You'll find it in the foot-thick walls of the Oldest House, the awesome magnificence of the towering Castillo de San Marco, and in the touching simplicity of the red cypress schoolhouse.

Roam sleepy streets where bees buzz in small rose gardens secreted behind high courtyard walls. Gaze up at the massive walls of the Castillo de San Marco, where frightened townspeople once huddled in terror as a would-be conqueror set the city aflame. Stroll through velvety darkness and hear the echoes of cannons, of clanking 16th-century armor, clinking 19th-century champagne glasses, the echoes of the past here in the nation's first city.

SOME HISTORIC BACKGROUND: St. Augustine's hero is Ponce de Leon, once governor of Puerto Rico. He sailed here with Columbus in 1493, then returned with an expedition of his own in 1513. Legend has it that rumor of a magical spring, a fountain of youth, brought de Leon here, but there are some who suggest he searched not for youth but for another valuable—gold. Whatever his quest, he landed in Easter season, Spain's "Pascua Florida," and named the land he found La Florida, claiming it, of course, for Spain.

Two years later Capt. Gen. Pedro Menéndez de Avilés arrived to establish the first permanent European settlement in the nation. A few years earlier some French Huguenots had settled at Fort Caroline, but when the Spaniards showed up and a battle ensued, the French colony was destroyed. That battle ended near what is now Marineland, where the French soldiers who escaped from their wrecked ship were summarily dispatched by Menendez, giving name to the bay here, Matanzas, the Spanish word for slaughter.

Spain's decision to set up Menéndez de Avilés in Florida had less to do with colonization than with a desire to protect Spain's gold-filled galleons, the frequent prey of pirates who discovered a way to mine gold on the high seas. Annoyed by the Spanish roadblock on their road to fortune, pirates twice attacked St. Augustine. Those attacks spurred construction of massive Castillo de San Marco, one of the most impressive Spanish fortifications in this hemisphere.

Ever anxious to expand its empire, Britain frequently tested the strength of this massive masonry fort without success. Spain finally lost Florida, not by war but by treaty—Florida was the ransom Spain paid to England for the return of Havana in 1763.

Britain managed to hold onto the colony for 20 years. Large plantations were begun, the city became a commercial seaport, and northern Tory loyalists took refuge here. Spain, which sided with the U.S. revolutionaries in their fight against England, even planned an attack on the city during this period, a strange quirk of fate indeed.

In the diplomatic poker game that followed the Revolutionary War, Britain ceded Florida back to Spain. This time around the Spanish let everyone who had settled in the city stay, and let others join them—not a wise move. A restless rag-tag mob of Floridians strained against the Spanish, once even attacking the Castillo, until finally in 1821 Spain made the best of a bad bargain and ceded Florida to the United States. Along the way Seminole uprisings erupted and the Castillo once again held prisoners, this time the courageous Seminole warrior Osceola and his cohorts.

In the late 1800s empire-builder Henry Flagler extended his railroad to the city. Life in St. Augustine began to revolve around the fabulous resorts he built, the Ponce de Leon and Alcazar Hotels. Winter visitors streamed in from cold northern climes by steamer and train. They came to spend the entire winter here, often accompanied by servants. Spend it they did too, in lavish fashion, dancing under the stars atop the old fort, parading in carriages down Avenida Menendez, applauding concerts in lavish hotel parlors.

So popular was the city that Flagler elected to extend his empire southward and St. Augustinians today claim their city gave birth to Miami.

ORIENTATION: St. Augustine is quite a small town with a permanent population of just 15,000, so you'll find it easy to get around. If you're driving, remember that streets are narrow and parking is always a problem. The nation's oldest city is located on US 1 and Route A1A. From I-95, take exits to Route 16, Route 207, or US 1.

Avenida Menendez runs alongside the bay. Cathedral Place and King Street run through the center of town and are one-way streets, Cathedral heading west, King going east.

US 1 is also called Ponce de Leon Boulevard, and Avenida Menendez becomes San Marco Avenue as it leaves town on the north side.

To get to St. Augustine Beach, cross the Lion Bridge at Avenida Menendez and King Street and follow Route A1A to the beaches.

USEFUL INFORMATION: For **police or medical emergencies,** call 829-2226 in St. Augustine, 824-1636 on St. Augustine Beach . . . For **doctor or dentist referrals,** check with the Chamber of Commerce, which is used to handling those problems (tel. 829-5681), or go to the emergency room of Flagler Hospital, 159 Marine St. (tel. 824-8411). . . . There's a pharmacist on duty to 9 p.m. at **Eckerd's Drugstore** in the K-Mart Shopping Center (tel. 824-6167). . . . **Pantry Pride grocery store,** 1010 S. Ponce de Leon Blvd. (tel. 829-9815), is open 24 hours. . . . You can find gasoline and service help at **Assad's Gulf,** on Route 207 at I-95 (tel. 824-9244), night or day. . . . For quick cleaning, try **Star Cleaners,** 284 W. King St. (tel. 824-1577). . . . For 24-hour film processing, try **Camera Center,** 14 Avenida Menendez (tel. 829-2468).

TOURIST INFORMATION: Friendly folks at the **St. Augustine Visitor Information Center** (tel. 904/824-3334) have been taking care of lost, confused, or otherwise befuddled tourists for decades and will be happy to help you with anything from a dentist to a hotel room. They're at 10 Castillo Dr., St. Augustine, FL 32804. . . . **St. Augustine's Chamber of Commerce** can also help you with information on this fascinating city. Write to them at P.O. Drawer O, St. Augustine, FL 32804, or call them (tel. 904/829-5681). If you'd like to drop in to visit with them, they're at 75 King St. . . . Personally guided tours of the city are available from **Spanish Heritage Tours;** call them at 829-3726. If you're here in June or October you can see Grand Illumination ceremonies, when the city honors its British heritage with a full-dress British uniform torchlight parade through the city.

HOTELS: For me there's no better way to immerse yourself in the fascinating history of this very old community than to plunk yourself down in the middle of it, stroll the slumbering streets, peeking into the back lawns of centuries-old houses and peering at restoration projects still under way. Best of all, if you stay in the old city you can see it at its glowing mystical best—after the throngs of day-trippers and cursory lookers have retreated.

For my dollars there's no better way to sink instantly into this ancient atmosphere than the **Kenwood Inn,** 38 Marine St., St. Augustine, FL 32084 (tel. 904/824-2116). Two antiques buffs have turned this magnificent three-story rambling old structure into a marvel of polished wood floors, ruffled curtains, brick-lined fireplaces, brass beds, beautiful vibrant colors and delicate pastels. Built in 1865 as an inn, the Kenwood now has its second set of renovators/owners and they seem to be lavishing just as much attention on this lovely old business as did their predecessors. Here's what new owners Dick and Judy Smith had to say to me recently:

"In late 1983 we purchased the Kenwood Inn and proceeded to complete the renovation by transforming six small rooms with two shared baths into four more spacious rooms with private baths. The dining room has been completely redecorated with new ceiling and wallpaper. New curtains and slipcovers have freshened the living room where a game table now provides a spot for games and cards.

"The rooms are furnished with our collection of antiques and reproductions, each in a different period and color scheme with coordinating linens. Our guests who prefer a king-size bed may choose between the English theme of Room 2, the quiet elegance of the 'President's Room,' or 'Captain Karl's' maritime room, all with old claw-footed tubs in the bath.

"The Honeymoon Room, which overlooks the pool and courtyard, has a four-poster canopy bed, while another has an antique double canopy bed. We now have two rooms with two double beds, one on the second-floor porch with a country theme in blue and white and the other, pastel green with chintz and wicker. A choice of other themes from simple Shaker to delicate country Victorian often makes it difficult to decide."

I am really sad to say I haven't had a chance to see the amplifications by these personable new owners, but I can't wait to get up there and revel in them. I have, however, seen a couple of photographs they sent to keep me up-to-date on the changes, and I promise you, you will love what the Smiths have done here.

Every morning in the dining room you'll find complimentary coffee, freshly squeezed orange juice, and freshly baked fruit bread or pastry on the sideboard. Outside is a swimming pool, a pretty garden, and a wrap-around veranda where you can sink into the antebellum atmosphere of this quiet street.

Kenwood is Florida's newest—and one of its loveliest—contributions to the nation's roster of charming country inns, as much for the friendly welcome you'll get from the Smiths as for their considerable interior design skills. Rates at the inn, which is just a few blocks from the nation's oldest house and within walking distance of the St. George Street restoration area, are just $35 to $50, cheaper by the week year round.

Another similar old hotel is the **St. Francis Inn,** 279 St. George St., St. Augustine, FL 32084, at the corner of St. Francis Street (tel. 904/824-6068). A tiny ten-room inn, the St. Francis is tucked away behind a wrought-iron gate. A jungle of greenery and flowers surround a tiny pond, and a few steps away is a sparkling pool nestled in the last possible open area on this small property. Inside, you're greeted by Mrs. Elizabeth Davis, who oversees activities here from a desk in the hall. No fancy marble lobbies here, but just beyond the foyer is a tiny antique shop set up in what used to be a dining room (it still is, but now it's filled with artfully displayed antiques).

Each of the few rooms is different and quite modestly furnished—nothing fancy. Most are small and have the high ceilings so common to pre-air-conditioning days. You'll find glass-paned french doors, tiny balconies overlooking a small park or the front pond, an occasional fireplace, and wainscotting. One room that's especially pretty is No. 2B, where chairs are covered in a bright flowery print echoed around the room. All rooms are not as spiffy, however, and some have paddle fans for coolers, so it might be well to ask for the best they have. There aren't any phones and not all rooms have television either, but the St. Francis (just a few doors from the Oldest House) is worth in atmosphere what you might sacrifice in chain-hotel space or amenities. Rates are just $30 for a room with twin beds, $50 for doubles with a living room and convertible couch, and $45 for pretty suites.

On the north edge of town, near the information center and the fort, is **Spanish Quarter Inn,** 6 Castillo Dr., St. Augustine, FL 32084 (tel. 904/824-4457, or toll free 800/528-1234), a Best Western franchise operation and a handsome place with lots of arches and rounded Spanish decor. A small hotel, the inn has just 40 rooms, all of them bright and cozy with lots of glass to let in the sunshine. Outside there's a nice pool, and the inn always has a coffee pot going in the office for free morning eye-openers. Rates are $35 to $51 double, $32 to $49 single, all year.

Waken to the sounds of a horse-drawn carriage clopping by at **Whetstone's Bayfront Inn,** 138 Avenida Menendez, St. Augustine, FL 32084 (tel. 904/824-1681), and you'll think you've hit a time warp. Like the other hostelries along Avenida Menendez, Whetstone's is in the heart of the old section and has a pretty view of the bay tides rising and falling and boats passing under the Bridge of Lions. The large rooms are cheery, and there's a palm-fringed swimming pool in the center of the attractive grounds. Year round, two people pay $40 to $45 for a room with one or two beds. Rates drop $5 in May and September.

Monson Motor Lodge, 32 Avenida Menendez, St. Augustine, FL 32084 (tel. 904/829-2277), is another good starting point for touring the city's historic district. Just a block away (and no more than a good musket shot) from the fort, Monson has 50 bright, spacious rooms, plus a restaurant and lounge that's handy when you come back exhausted from a day of sightseeing. Monson charges $34 to $52, year round (higher on weekends), and children under 12 stay free. Most rooms have two double beds; some have king-size. Monson now has two new suites, complete with kitchen, king-size bed, and color TV, for $60 to $125 a night.

The **Monterey Motel,** 16 Avenida Menendez, St. Augustine, FL 32084 (tel. 904/824-4482), looks out over the waters of Mantanzas Bay and is only two beautiful blocks from the main St. George Street historic reconstruction area. The Monterey has one especially pretty room, just at the front of the building on the second floor, with a big window overlooking the water. The very large rooms are furnished with Spanish touches, and have phones and cable television. There's a new, large swimming pool too. Because the motel's U-shaped, many of the rooms (especially on the second floor) have a nice view of the bay. Two people pay $28 to $42, any time of year, for one of the 53 rooms here.

Besides the main hotels (Holiday Inn and Howard Johnson's each have two hotels in the area, as does Days Inn), one of the luxury hotels here is the **Ponce de Leon Lodge**, P.O. Box 98, St. Augustine, FL 32084 (tel. 904/824-2821), about three miles north of town on US 1. There are 200 spacious and attractively decorated rooms here, a restaurant, cocktail lounge, golf course, putting greens, and tennis courts. For the children there's a playground, huge cloverleaf swimming pool, and a sports clinic. Suites are also available at this lodge, which has wide lawns and very spacious grounds. Double rates are $48 to $57 all year round, about $7 less for a single.

GUIDE TO THE NUMBERED REFERENCES ON THE "HISTORIC ST. AUGUSTINE" MAP: 1. Florida School for the Deaf & Blind; 2. Fountain of Youth; 3. Mission of Nombre de Dios; 4. Authentic Old Jail; 5. Old Sugar Mill; 6. Ripley Museum; 7. Visitors Information Center; 8. Castillo De San Marcos; 9. Old World Shop; 10. The Old Drugstore and the Spanish Cemetery; 11. Museum; 12. Lighthouse Park & Fishing Pier; 13. St. Augustine Alligator Farm; 14. Cross & Sword Amphitheater; 15. Marina and Sightseeing Boat Cruise; 16. Potter's Wax Museum; 17. Old Market; 18. Government House; 19. Flagler College; 20. Trailways Bus Station; 21. Greyhound Bus Station; 22. Shrimp Boat Docks; 23. U.S. Post Office; 24. Zorayda Castle; 25. Lightner Municipal Expo.; 26. County Building; 27. Spanish Hospital; 28. Old Store Museum; 29. Art Center; 30. Historical Society Library; 31. Oldest House; 32. State Arsenal; 33. Indian Museum; 34. Llambias House; 35. St. Francis Inn; 36. City Gates; 37. Ximenes-Fatio House; 38. Old School House; 39. San Agustin Antiguo Museum Houses.

Another motel that's very convenient for sightseeing is the **Marion Motor Lodge**, 120 Avenida Menendez, St. Augustine, FL 32084 (tel. 904/829-2261). Right next door are the horse-and-buggy rides and sightseeing trains that take you on tours, and it's just a few blocks to the restoration area. A two-story building with lots of wide windows overlooking Matanzas Bay, the lodge is decorated in bright colors, and has a pool, sundeck, and all the usual amenities, like phones and cable color TV. You'll pay $32 to $40, year round, for a double room.

The **Sheraton Anastasia Inn**, Route A1A at Pope Road, St. Augustine Beach, FL 32084 (tel. 904/471-2575, or toll free 800/325-3535), is nestled alongside the sea at pretty Anastasia State Park. A two-story building with walls of glass in every room, this Sheraton is trimmed in blues as bright as the Atlantic—and bright as the sparkling blue pool in the middle of the hotel's courtyard. The airy rooms have plush wall-to-wall carpeting, lively beach colors, and two double beds, and there are a few with kitchens. A tropical restaurant has a tempting salad bar, and there's a lounge with entertainment and dancing. Two people pay $58 to $68 from mid-May to September, $76 for a kitchen, about $24 less in fall and winter.

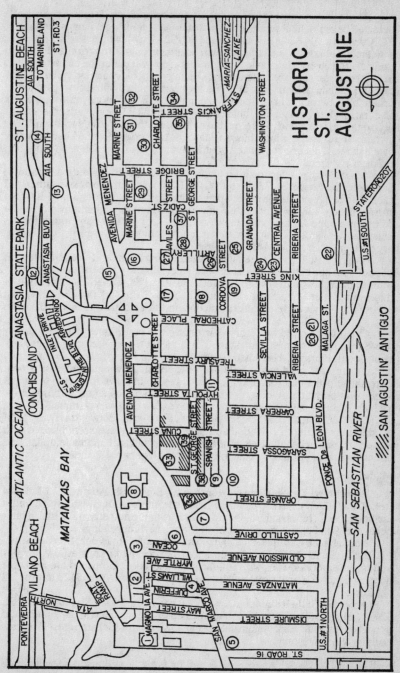

HISTORIC ST. AUGUSTINE

Another very pretty place to stay on this beautiful and sometimes almost-deserted beach is the **Ramada Inn,** on Route A1A South, St. Augustine Beach, FL 32084 (tel. 904/824-8181, or toll free 800/228-2828), which is really Spanish, with arched windows and huge wooden beams, wrought-iron trim, and a stucco exterior. Big cushy chairs in leathery colors greet you under the beamed ceiling of the reception hall, and in the resort's dining room big coach lamp chandeliers cast an intimate golden glow over tile floors and arched entranceways gated in ornate black wrought iron. See if you can get the hotel's honeymoon suite (it's all done in whites and green), but rest easy that you'll be happy with other rooms decorated in dark woods and accented with contemporary colors and prints. For a room at Ramada, which has a restaurant and poolside snackbar, a pretty beach gazebo, a game room, and entertainment, you'll pay $39 to $44; double; children stay free.

A good budget selection is **La Fiesta Motor Lodge,** 1001 Route A1A South, St. Augustine Beach, FL 32084 (tel. 904/471-2220), about five miles southeast of Lion Bridge, which also features Spanish decor and has 38 rooms on a 300-foot strip of beach. La Fiesta has three efficiencies (three-day minimum stay) and a coffeeshop open for breakfast in season, a 60-foot pool, a playground for the kids, shuffleboard, and a special bridal suite. Double rates are $55 from February to September, $35 to $45 in other months.

Okay, okay, I haven't seen this one either, but Daisy and Greg Morden are so confident about the quality of their tiny new hostelry here, they sent me pictures to prove it's all they say it is—and it seems to be. Called **Victorian House,** this new inn is at 11 Cadiz St., St. Augustine, FL 32084 (tel. 904/824-5214), not far from the city's Oldest House attraction and just a couple of blocks from the bay.

Occupying an old two-story, Victorian-style house now painted a cheery white with sky-blue trim and rimmed by a picket fence, Victorian House certainly looks adorable. Handmade quilts lie atop brass or iron beds. Gauzy, frilly curtains trim the windows, a little heart-shaped straw wreath hangs on a wall. Furnishings are antique or antique look-alikes, right down to Victorian lamps. White predominates in most rooms, giving them a bright, sunny atmosphere—and one even has a lacy, net canopy arching over a dark-wood frame.

Greg writes that "Last December, after a one-year renovation, Daisy and I opened a six-bedroom 1890 Bed and Breakfast. Our guests seem pleased with our efforts, especially Daisy's wall and floor stenciling, handmade quilts, and our collection of antiques." Rates are $25 to $40 for two.

Camping

Bryn Mawr Ocean Resorts, Route A1A South, St. Augustine, FL 32084 (tel. 904/471-3353), has 250 campsites in an oceanside campground with laundry facilities, pool, tennis, shuffleboard, game room, and recreation hall. Rates begin at $19 to $25 in summer months, lower after Labor Day.

North Beach CamResort, 2300 Coastal Hwy., North Beach, St. Augustine, FL 32084 (tel. 904/824-1806), has 80 acres from ocean to Intracoastal Waterway and heavily wooded sites with full facilities and pool. Groceries are available here, and there's a boat ramp and fishing dock. Rates are $10 to $12 a day for full hookups.

Anastasia State Recreation Area, 5 Anastasia Park Dr., St. Augustine, FL 32084 (tel. 904/471-1043), on St. Augustine Beach, also has campgrounds, and as part of the state park system charges $7 to $9 a night for campsites. Reservations by telephone only.

RESTAURANTS: St. Augustine, for all its fame, is still a small town where even the top restaurants charge low prices. (My price listings are for entrees, but these usually include salad, one or two vegetables, and perhaps coffee as well.)

Top of the Line

If you love old houses, you'll adore the **Chart House,** 46 Avenida Menendez (tel. 824-1687), a beautiful old town house built in the early days of the city. This unusual house once featured bedrooms downstairs and the parlor upstairs so you could see out over the carriages to Matanzas Bay. These days there's a very comfortable contemporary dining room upstairs outfitted with paddle fans and jewel colors. Downstairs, you enter from a side lawn into a world of glowing old wood floors and a plant-filled lounge which now features a seafood bar serving a variety of shrimp and oyster appetizers. Seafood is scintillating here, fresh from the docks, and cooked by chefs so talented they easily get my award for the city's best seafood. A grouper dinner I had here once has set the standards for me forever. So popular is this spot that you really must have a reservation on weekends and in the crowded summer months. Entree prices are in the $9 to $18 range, and the Chart House is open from 5 to 10 p.m. weekdays, later on weekends.

Another lovely old home that's become an equally lovely restaurant is **Le Pavillon,** 45 San Marco Ave. (tel. 824-6202), owned and cooked in by a gracious German-Swiss family, the Sinatsches. You can dine in this 85-year-old house on a candlelit screened front porch or inside in pretty rooms with the same romantic air about them. As for the dining, well how about wienerschnitzel, sauerbraten and spätzle, delicately smoked bratwurst, German home fries, red cabbage, hot homemade rolls or light crêpes with a long list of possible fillings? There's frequently entertainment in the evenings, and Le Pavillon is a local favorite so reservations are wise. It's open from 11:30 a.m. to 2:30 p.m. and 5 to 10 p.m. daily. No entree tops $16.

The Moderate Bracket

Antonio's, 798 Ponce de Leon Blvd. (tel. 824-0971), whips up Italian magic in the kitchen. Gnocchi, macaroni, ravioli, cannelloni, and manicotti are handmade by the Digregorio family, who use only the freshest fish, the finest baby veal, and the tenderest chicken to create scaloppine marsala, chicken parmigiana, shrimp scampi. Fettuccine Alfredo is made right here, from the fettuccine to the finished product, and the cannelloni Florentine, with veal and spinach rolled in a tender piece of homemade pasta and covered with a cream sauce, is to die for. Prices are nice too, with most entrees just $6 to $10. Hours are 4 to 9 p.m. daily (closed Wednesday from September to February).

Capt. Jack's, at 10 Marine St. (tel. 829-6846), has a nautical atmosphere from decor to menu. There really was a Captain Jack (for a change), who used to run charter boats hereabouts, but turned his talents to cookery some years back. Naturally he wasn't going to open a restaurant with a railroad theme, so today you'll see sea nostalgia around you as you dine, overlooking the city's pier on Matanzas Bay, on simply cooked seafood dishes like shrimp, the fresh catch, whole boiled shrimp in the shells. If you've had enough seafood to keep you happy for a while, try the beef-a-bob or a steak. There are children's platters too. Capt. Jack's is open Tuesday through Sunday from 11 a.m. to 9 p.m., and prices average $10 or less.

Scarlett O'Hara's, 70 Hypolita (tel. 824-6535), is one of the loveliest spots in town, and occupies a charming old renovated house at Hypolita and Cordova Streets to boot. Giant old trees and lots of plants shade O'Hara's, which is off the beaten track down a quiet side street. Inside, you can lunch on big crisp salads from the salad bar, and sandwiches and soups in the $5 range, all in an atmosphere that will transport you back to the historic days you've come here to discover. Open 11:30 a.m. to 3 p.m. for lunch, for snacks after 7 p.m., and later for entertainment.

Are you ready for Capuchin monks ministering to your culinary desires, with Gregorian chants and medieval melodies in the background? I didn't think I was either, but it's amazing how fast you can adjust to these historical throwbacks as you wander down St. Augustine's St. George Street preservation area. Drop into the **Monk's Vineyard,** 56 St. George St. (tel. 824-5888), and find out for yourself what an intriguing retreat this can be from the rigors of sightseeing. An old English look with lots of wood and pewter wine racks prevails here, and the fare runs toward excellent crêpes and quiches, salads and soups for lunch, steaks and seafood for dinner. Monk's is a most interesting hideaway and a cool shady spot with a theme miles away from conventional. Your check will be perhaps $5 for lunch, $7 to $14 for dinner, and the monks hear requests from 11 a.m. to 2:30 p.m. daily and 5:30 to 9:30 p.m. daily except Wednesday.

You can't miss the **Santa Maria Restaurant,** on the water at the city yacht pier (tel. 829-6578). Surely you can't get a much better water view than the Santa Maria's unusual pier-end location offers, and if the crowds who jam in here every night are any indication, you can't get much better seafood. Santa Maria claims it has everything in seafood, and I'm inclined to believe them: seafood platters brimming with shrimp, oysters, scallops, deviled crab, whatever fish was caught that day, broiled Florida lobsters, Alaskan king crabs, fried grouper, flounder, clams, and shrimp in all the possible presentations. A longtime landmark, the Santa Maria is open from noon to 11 p.m. every day but Thursday. Prices are in the $10 to $15 range.

Budget Bets

Sooner or later everyone in town goes to the **Chimes,** 12 Avenida Menendez (tel. 829-8141), partly because it's right in the middle of things (the fort is just across the street, the restoration district a block or so away) but mostly because owner-chef James Kalivas turns out such dependable meals from sunrise to long after sunset. He makes all the pastries at this unprepossessing but very popular restaurant, and whips out waffles for breakfast, sandwiches for lunch, and steaks for dinner. He's been at it for years and years, lots of successful years, so you can be sure you'll find a high-quality and low-priced meal here (dinners under $10; breakfasts and lunches, $2 to $3). Open 7 a.m. to 9 p.m. daily.

The **Silver Bucket Oyster Bar,** 319 Seabreeze Blvd. (tel. 258-9484), keeps busy by pouring beer by the quart and margaritas by the pitcher afternoons, then switching to loaded plates of oysters, crabs, shrimp, and all St. Augustine's super seafood in the evening. You can be sure you'll find both dinner and entertainment of one sort or another at this casual spot. Prices are in the $5 to $10 range; hours are from noon to 2 a.m. daily.

And don't miss a morning stop at the **Denoël French Pastry Shop,** at Charlotte Street and Artillery Lane (tel. 829-3974), a cozy café that sells flaky fresh-from-the-oven pastries in a pretty bistro that's also a bakery. Closed on Tuesday, the pastry shop presents its inexpensive, mouthwatering treasures from 10 a.m. to 5 p.m.

SEEING THE SIGHTS: As travel became possible for the less haughty strata of American society, St. Augustine added more and more attractions to its historic sights and today the city is filled with sometimes funky, but always fun, things to see.

Begin your visit to the city with a stop at the **Visitor Information Center,** at

10 Castillo Dr. (tel. 824-3334), where you can see an orientation movie about the city (shown twice each hour) and pick up guided-tour information and brochures to help you see it yourself. The center is open from 8 a.m. to 5:30 p.m.

A seat in a shining carriage pulled by a handsome steed is a fascinating way to clip-clop slowly through town. Call **Colee's Carriages,** 95 Riberia St. (tel. 829-2818), from 9 a.m. to 5 p.m. daily for exact times and pickup points. Tours cost $5 for adults, $2 for children 5 to 11. You'll find the carriages at the Castillo entrance, 1 Castillo Dr.

To get an idea what the city has to offer, see it all aboard **Sightseeing Trains,** at 170 San Marco Ave. (tel. 829-6545). Drivers of the trams give you a lively anecdote-spiced spiel about the city as you travel through the streets. Tickets are $5 ($2 for children ages 6 to 12) and are good for 24 hours, so you can get off and on whenever you like. Trains run every 15 to 20 minutes, and it beats trying to drive through this city of narrow one-way streets, complicated parking, and sometimes heavy traffic. Three other tours are real money-savers: they offer packages ranging from $10 to $22 for three- to eight-hour tours including all admissions.

If you're sightseeing on your own, start at the **Old City Gate,** just a short distance from the Information Center, where you'll see a replica of the original palm-log wall built in 1739 to protect the entrance to the city. A moat here was crossed by a drawbridge raised each evening, leaving nightowls outside to fend for themselves. Historic St. George Street begins here, and once was called "the street to Land Gate." The Old World Shop nearby is a stop for the sightseeing train and has tourist information and snacks.

Castillo de San Marco, 1 Castillo Dr., is the city's giant landmark, built in 1672 of coquina (pronounced koh-*keen*-a), a soft yellow stone formed from solidified masses of sand and shells. Quarried from deposits on nearby Anastasia Island, coquina (which means cockle shell in Spanish) was hauled by oxcart and floated on barges across the inlet. It took 15 years to build and so much money ($30 million) that Spain's King Philip is said to have observed dispiritedly that the fort must have been built of solid silver.

Over the years the fort has housed American Revolutionaries, Seminole leaders, Confederate and Union troops, and American deserters from the Spanish-American War. There are guided tours and firing demonstrations of historic weapons several times a day. Admission is 50¢ (free to children under 16 accompanied by adults). The fort is open from 8:30 a.m. to 5:15 p.m. daily, later in summer.

On St. George Street across from the castillo is the city's main preservation area known as **San Augustin Antiguo,** 44 St. George St. (tel. 824-6383). Here you'll get a fascinating look at an 18th-century Spanish colonial village— actually a living museum—with authentically furnished homes and intriguing craft demonstrations by a blacksmith, leather worker, ceramicist, silversmith, woodturner, printer, and baker. You'll see a wide variety of old homes dating back several centuries, and the oldest schoolhouse, where students are in their seats and the schoolmaster is up front directing lessons. A $2.50 ticket ($5 a family) admits you to most of the buildings; children 6 to 18 are only $1.25. It's open from 9 a.m. to 5 p.m. daily, closed December 25.

On this street you can also visit a **Museum of Yesterday's Toys** (tel. 829-2309), which charges $1 for adults (free for under-12s) to look at ringing-tinging toys of yesteryear inside a lovely old house. Open 9 a.m. to 7 p.m. daily.

Don't miss the **Sanchez House** on St. George either. It's been perfectly restored, with a lovely fountain in the courtyard and shining period furniture inside, right down to antique dishes on the table. It's open from 9:30 a.m. to 5 p.m. daily (except Thursday) and is free.

Over at 14 St. Francis St. is the **Oldest House** (tel. 824-1872), used as a residence since the early 1600s. Its Spanish coquina walls are a foot thick to keep the house warm in winter, cool in summer, and were built in 1702 after the British burned the town. The living room's on the second floor, a typical architectural style in the city. Maintained by the St. Augustine Historical Society, as is the adjacent museum in the Tovar House, the Oldest House is furnished with authentic antiques. Both house and museum are open from 9 a.m. to 5 p.m.; admission is $2 for adults and under 12 are free.

There's something naïvely charming about the **Oldest Store Museum,** 4 Artillery Lane (tel. 829-9729), which is packed wall to wall and ceiling to floor with antiques, from high-button shoes to red underwear and dill pickles. When you see the french-fry makers and apple peelers, the cherry pitters and biscuit makers, not to mention the 90% alcohol "medicines," you'll wonder if we've really progressed. It's open from 9 a.m. to 5 p.m. Monday through Saturday, and from noon on Sunday; admission is $2 for adults, $1 for children 6 to 12.

As a teenager I was mortified when my father raced laughing out of the **Fountain of Youth,** but in recent years I've been wondering if I shouldn't give it a try! Those magical waters old Juan Ponce de Leon was searching for are supposed to flow from the stone fountain at 155 Magnolia Ave. If you don't regress immediately, you can also visit a memorial to Ponce de Leon, a planetarium and space globe, museum, and swan pool at $3 for adults and $1.50 for children 6 to 12. It's open 9 a.m. to 4:45 p.m.

At San Marco and Old Mission Avenues, the **Mission of Nombre de Dios and Shrine of Our Lady of La Leche** is the site of the first mission in a series of religious outposts that were to culminate finally in California's famous Mission Trail. Florida's simple log missions long ago succumbed to the ravages of time, but the mission effort is honored here. Open 7 a.m. to dark daily; donations are encouraged.

Other stately old homes in the area are the **Ximenez-Fatio House,** 20 Aviles St. (tel. 829-3575), a historical guest house now maintained by the Colonial Dames of America (open free Thursday through Monday, March to September, from 11 a.m. to 4 p.m.); the **Dr. Peck House,** 143 St. George St. (tel. 829-5064), which was once the home of the Spanish treasurer, an important man who doled out the government's cash (open from 10 a.m. to 4 p.m. Monday through Friday, and admission is free); and the **Casa del Hidalgo,** at Hypolita and St. George Streets (tel. 829-6460), the Spanish National Tourist Office (open Monday through Friday from 10 a.m. to 4 p.m., free).

On King Street is a massive cluster of buildings that once was Flagler's flamboyant Ponce de Leon Hotel. Completed in 1888 after three years of construction, it remained a hotel until 1967 when it became **Flagler College.** You're welcome to wander around the grounds and look at the hotel's hexagonal dining room jutting out on the east side of the building, and peek into the main lobby where giant marble columns rise to a second-story loggia.

Flagler's other hostelry, the Alcazar Hotel, folded in the grim days of the 1930s and stayed empty until Chicago millionaire Otto C. Lightner bought it and set up his **Lightner Museum,** on Cordova Street (tel. 824-2874). You'll see a 17-shop Victorian village, Tiffany glass, Napoleon's desk, and a quilt made by Abraham Lincoln's second wife. Admission is $2 for adults, 75¢ for children 12 to 18, and free to children under 12. The museum is open from 9 a.m. to 5 p.m. daily.

Zorayda Castle, at 83 King St. (tel. 824-3097), is a bizarre sight inside and out, a to-scale replica of Spain's Alhambra complete with harem quarters. It's open from 9 a.m. to 5:30 p.m. in winter. Admission is $2 for adults and $1 for children 6 to 12.

Stare down Attila the Hun at **Potter's Wax Museum,** 1 King St. (tel. 829-9056), a surprisingly well-done museum where you can see quite lifelike figures from Marie Antoinette to the signers of the Declaration of Independence in marvelous sets. It is open from 9 a.m. to 9 p.m. daily in summer, to 5 p.m. in winter. Admission is $3.75 for adults, $2 for children 6 to 11.

Ripley's Believe It or Not Museum, at 19 San Marco Ave. (tel. 824-1606), should thrill trivia collectors. Its very existence is something Ripley probably should have included in his "Believe It or Nots." Admission is $4.25 for adults, $2.50 for children 5 to 12.

If you're here in the summer months from mid-June to mid-August, don't miss **Cross and Sword,** the state's official play, performed by a cast of 70 singers, dancers, and actors, who portray the story of St. Augustine's founding and early days. It's performed outside in the St. Augustine Amphitheater, just south of the city on Route A1A (tel. 471-1965), at 8:30 p.m. except Sunday. Tickets are $6 for adults, $4 for children under 12.

NIGHTLIFE: Long a family vacation resort, St. Augustine is a quiet place by night but you can usually find something doing in hotel lounges at the **Ramada Beach Club** (Route A1A South), the **Sheraton Anastasia Inn,** the **Ramada Inn Downtown,** and the **Monson Motor Lodge** (see my hotel recommendations).

The **Bayfront Dinner Theater,** in the Monson Motor Lodge, 32 Avenida Menendez (tel. 829-9744), has shows nightly with cocktails at 6:30, dinner at 7, and show at 8:15 p.m., for $19.95.

Dan Jan's, 36 Granada St. (tel. 829-9312), has a disco session every night and is open from 11 a.m. to 1 a.m. Another disco spot is **Mario & Chickie's,** at 180 Anastasia Blvd. (tel. 824-2952), which has dancing from 10 p.m. to 1 a.m. Thursday through Saturday.

The **White Lion,** at St. George and Cuna Streets across from the old fort (tel. 829-2388), is a favorite meeting spot, especially during its Lion's Roar happy hour, with entertainment nightly in an old English pub atmosphere. **Scarlett O'Hara's,** 70 Hypolita (tel. 824-6535), is a colorful evening meeting ground, as are **Monk's Vineyard,** 56 St. George St. (tel. 824-5888), and the **Silver Bucket Oyster Bar,** 319 Seabreeze Blvd. (tel. 258-9484).

SPORTS: Golfers should head to **Ponce de Leon Shores Golf Course,** on US 1 North (tel. 829-5314), an 18-hole course with greens fees of $20, $14 for a golf cart. There are 20 tennis courts scattered around the city, and the city's recreation department (tel. 829-8807) will be happy to tell you which location is nearest you.

A favorite **canoe trip** in the area is a four-mile run on nearby Pellicer Creek. The chamber of commerce can get you paddling.

Island Driving Range, on St. Augustine Beach across from the Fishing Pier (tel. 824-8321), has a driving range and recreation center with an 18-hole miniature golf course, baseball pitching machines, and pool tables.

Beach paddle tennis, which you play with a racquet full of holes and a dead tennis ball on the hard sand of beaches from Daytona to Jacksonville, got its start here in St. Augustine. You'll find stores for equipment around the beach.

Depth Finders Pro Dive Shop, at 21 Sanchez Ave. (tel. 824-9884), is a full-service dive shop with instructions, rentals, and dive trips.

SHOPPING: I hardly know whether to put the **Lightner Antiques Mall** among attractions or shopping spots since it's a little of both. Part of Flagler's old Alcazar Hotel, the Antiques Mall is located in what once was the hotel's huge indoor swimming pool (look at the slope of the floor). Now antiques shops and boutiques are nestled away in the pool, which was quite a showplace—from a hall-way on the second floor you could stand and watch the swimmers frolicking below, then grab a rope from rings (still in the walls), swing out over the pool, and . . . splash!

Crafts shops on **St. George Street** and at **City Gate Crafts,** at 1 St. George, have lots of intriguing handmade things from leather to silver and weavings to chocolate-chip cookies. All the craft workers in **St. Augustin Antiguo** also sell their work.

SIDE TRIPS: Take a free ferry ride across the Matanzas Inlet, just south of St. Augustine on Route A1A, to **Fort Matanzas,** built by the Spanish in 1742 to seal off the southern entrance to the Intracoastal Waterway that winds past St. Augustine's doorstep. It was here, but 200 years earlier, that Pedro Menéndez de Avilés gave the shipwrecked enemy troops from French Fort Caroline a choice: join the Spanish forces (which meant relinquishing their Huguenot Protestant religion) or die. All but about 200 died in a bloody massacre that helped limit French colonization on this continent to Canada and Louisiana. Entrance to the small fort, which is about 14 miles south of St. Augustine on A1A, is free. The 11-passenger ferry operates from 9 a.m. to 4:30 p.m. every day.

About four miles farther south on Route A1A, **Marineland of Florida** (Route 1, Box 122; tel. 471-1111) features the hijinks of dolphins and penguins. There are porpoise shows six times a day, and 11 different exhibits explaining the wonders of the sea. Marineland is Florida's oldest marine attraction; it was built in the 1930s as an underwater movie studio and is still a delightful place that's always adding something new to its fascinating bag of tricks. Admission is $6 for adults, $3.50 for children 3 to 11. It's open from 9 a.m. to 5 p.m. daily.

In Palatka, about 35 miles east of St. Augustine, you can see more than 100,000 varieties of azaleas and flowering plants lying like a blanket of rainbows across the natural ravines of **Ravine State Gardens.** Deep springs beneath the limestone created these nooks and crannies, which are open daily from 8 a.m. to sundown. Admission is free, and you'll find the gardens on Twigg Street off Moseley Avenue (tel. 328-4366).

Chapter IX

FLORIDA'S PANHANDLE

1. Pensacola
2. Fort Walton/Destin
3. Panama City/Panama City Beach
4. Tallahassee

FLORIDIANS CALL IT THEIR PANHANDLE and a glance at a map will show you why. It's as different in geography and lifestyle as the old-line Southerners who live here; and it's as anachronistic, in this chrome and plastic age, as they can keep it.

Here in northern Florida, a charming naïveté covers canny cracker wisdom. Family is important, but hospitality is a duty, an obligation, and a very great pleasure. If you extend your hand and smile here, you'll get it all back twofold.

Soft southern drawls and antebellum mansions attest to the region's long and strong affiliation with the South, and here in the northern end of the peninsula you'll find the state's sunny—and stormy—roots.

Great pine forests cover this land, and farms spread like patchwork quilts across the rolling hills. If you think you see more than the average number of churches here, you're right. This is a staunch section of the Bible Belt, and religion is serious business. Gospel sings draw thousands of listeners and participants. In a few places they're still arguing over the demerits of demon rum, to this day banned in a few "dry" counties.

Here too you'll find towns with weird and wonderful names. Some are remnants of the area's swashbuckling past and some are mysteries. There's Scratch Ankle, a bayside town once frequented by smugglers who got caught in briar thickets here and did what the name suggests. And Panacea, which is just that to landlocked Tallahasseans. And Two Egg, thought to have been named by a grocer whose first customer exchanged two eggs for a pound of flour. And Lick Skillet, whose origins nobody knows and whose chagrined residents have renamed it Lamont.

All along the coastline you'll see sand no other part of the state can claim, sand so soft it squeaks beneath your toes. Thanks to the oval shape of the grains, this strange silica cannot stick together or pack. It just floats under your toes like a bed of talcum.

Get off the superhighways here to find towns like Monticello, the state's watermelon center, a village lined end to end with antebellum plantation houses. Nearby are graves of Florida's staunchly Confederate soldiers who died in a fierce battle at Olustee—but not until they'd made Tallahassee the only southern city never captured by the Union.

Not far away at Marianna, about 60 miles northwest of Tallahassee, you can visit the state's only above-ground limestone cavern: Seminole Indians once watched from its depths as Gen. Andrew Jackson marched through to begin the attacks that would eradicate them.

Panhandle entertainment runs toward family activities—canoe outings on the region's crystal-clear rivers, reunions, and in election years political parades and fish fries. If you're here for one of the last two, you'll see a Senator Fogbottom cartoon come to life, and have more fun than a duck at a junebug social. No sleek limousines here, although you may spot the occasional Boss Hogg in white suit. As likely as not the hopeful glad-hander will be riding triumphantly down Main Street on a tractor!

Some of the most enchanting experiences you can have in Florida are here in tiny backroad towns redolent with rustic natural beauty and populated by people whose way of life is as slow-paced and satisfying as their drawls.

If a name here sounds faintly French, it probably is. France's Marquis de Lafayette, whose aid was vital to Revolutionary Americans, began a huge plantation here, struggling to prove free Frenchmen (or any free men) could serve the South as well as slaves. His experiment died with him, but the descendants of those hardy French settlers remain and continue to prove the marquis right.

In typical northern Florida style, people here remember another Frenchman, Prince Achille Murat, nephew of Napoleon and son of the King of Naples. He is famed neither for his name nor his title, but for a quirky sense of humor much like their own: the prince served his unsuspecting guests some much admired French cuisine, then told them what local products they were consuming —sheep ears, buzzard, and alligator tail!

Last (and perhaps least) is one of the oddest entertainments around, a fish fry. The main course is mullet, a fish whose popularity, to put it gently, has not yet peaked. The main attraction, however, is a chance to see these northern Floridians having a rollicking good time. Last year 80,000 of them turned up for a mess of mullet at the annual Boggy Bayou Mullet Fry.

Like Monticello's annual watermelon seed-spittin' contest and the Wausau 'Possum Festival, this land is eccentric, fun and funny, a place where you will be welcomed warmly by folks who know and love their place in the sun, and hope you will too.

GETTING THERE: Airlines serving Tallahassee, Pensacola, Panama City, and Fort Walton Beach include Delta, Eastern, Air New Orleans, Republic, TransAir Skyways, Southern Express, and PBA.

Greyhound and Trailways buses have service to Tallahassee, Pensacola, Fort Walton, and Panama City.

GETTING AROUND: Public transportation leaves much to be desired in this section of the state, and distances are great. Besides, it's fun to drive through the backroads and byways discovering much of Florida's history as you go.

You can cut quickly from east to west between Tallahassee and Pensacola on I-10, but it's far more interesting to take off on roads like US 98 (which runs along the Gulf of Mexico), US 90 (which goes through the antebellum town of Monticello), Route 65 (which cuts through the huge Apalachicola National Forest), and Route 4 (which travels through Blackwater River Park).

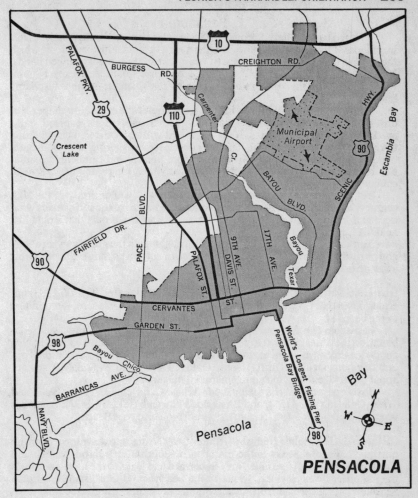

PENSACOLA

Major cities like Pensacola, Fort Walton Beach, Panama City, and of course Tallahassee, have **rental cars** available from major national operators like Hertz and Avis. Rates begin at about $20 to $25 a day with unlimited mileage.

A WORD ABOUT HOTELS: In summer, droves of sun-seekers from Georgia, Alabama, and other southern states make the quick and easy run to the Panhandle's seaside cities. This march to the sea lasts from May to Labor Day, when prices are highest and hotels are filled to the brim. You need reservations in those months. In Tallahassee, hotels are very busy when the legislature is in session (it varies but generally is between February and May), and prices rise abruptly during popular football weekends from September to December.

1. Pensacola

Pensacola is as different from its seaside sister cities in the Panhandle as it is from most of the rest of the state. It's had a long turbulent history during which the city has flown five different flags (if you count all the times it changed hands, it's welcomed 13 "conquerors"), so people recognize, guard, and respect "family" here, but offer that open-armed hospitality for which the South is justifiably famous.

There's the magic of history in Pensacola's quiet streets, where timber barons built ornate oak-trimmed mansions and Spanish dons courted dark-eyed and fair-haired señoritas. It's a magic that will transport you back in time to days of wasp-waisted blushing maids and lusty swaggering pirates, elegant dandies from New Orleans on prancing white horses, and candlelight plantation dinners served on hand-rubbed mahogany tables glittering under crystal chandeliers.

Yet just a few miles across a modern causeway you're firmly in the 20th century. Jet skis roar across gulf waters and today's peripatetic sun-seekers wander hand in hand across silvery white dunes asway in sea oats that ripple like fields of Kansas wheat.

You can capture it all in Pensacola, be caught up in the ghostly swish of ball gowns rustling down jasmine-scented streets, or catch a passing sailboat to whiz away across the waters.

GETTING AROUND: Escambia County Transit System (tel. 904/436-9383) operates buses that ply the streets on hourly schedules for a 35¢ fare, but don't go to the beaches.

Pensacola is a favorite spot for drive-in tourists from Georgia and Alabama, so the area is geared to four-wheeled travelers. **Renting a car** might be a good idea unless you plan to stay on the beach and skip exploring. National operations here include Thrifty, Avis, Dollar, Hertz, and National. Rates are about $20 to $25 a day, including unlimited mileage.

Taxis operating in the area include **Yellow Cab** (tel. 433-1143), **Black and White Cab** (tel. 432-4151), and **Blue and White Cab** (tel. 438-1497). Service is 90¢ a mile, about $13 to $15 from the airport to Pensacola Beach.

ORIENTATION: **Mobile Highway** (Route 10A/90) runs into downtown from the northwest. **Palafox Street** is the major north-south artery through town and **Garden Street** (which becomes **Navy Boulevard** and leads to the naval station) is the major east-west divider. To get to the beaches and Gulf Islands National Seashore Park, head south on Alcaniz Street or east on Garden Street to Gregory. Head west on Gregory and you'll see the Pensacola Bay Bridge (Route 30/98), which goes straight to the beach.

USEFUL INFORMATION: For **police or medical emergency,** dial 911. . . . For non-emergency help, call the **Escambia County Health Department,** 2251 N. Palafox St. (tel. 438-8571). . . . For **dental problems,** call the dental association (tel. 438-9622) or the Pensacola-Escambia Visitor Information Center (tel. 434-1234). . . . There's a **24-hour gas station** called Ecol that has several outlets in town with one convenient one at 400 E. Gregory St. (tel. 434-7776). . . . **Big B Cleaners,** at 118 E. Garden St. (tel. 433-1343), has quick dry cleaning service. . . . You can buy **groceries** around the clock at Albertson's, 5055 N. Ninth Ave. (tel. 476-7700), which also has a liquor store and pharmaceutical supplies. . . . There are **free parking spaces** just beyond Seville Quarter on Government Street so you won't have to feed the meters if you linger at the preservation district.

TOURIST INFORMATION: The **Pensacola Visitor Information Center**, 1401 E. Gregory St., Pensacola, FL 32501 (tel. 904/434-1234, or toll free 800/874-1234; in Florida, 800/343-4321), has some very nice people on duty to help you with information and maps for self-guided tours of the charming North Hill Preservation District and the naval air station. . . . The **Pensacola Chamber of Commerce** can help too; it's at 117 W. Garden St., Pensacola, FL 32501 (tel. 904/438-4081). . . . If you're looking for a condominium rental in the area, try **Metro-Merica Rentals,** at 5900 N. Ninth Ave. (tel. 904/476-8866 or 932-9369, or toll free 800/874-9245), which lists many.

WHERE TO STAY: If you'd like to be near the city's charming old Seville historic district and save money at the same time, there are several attractive hotels downtown. If you want to revel in the soft sand here, head for Pensacola Beach. Summer in this part of Florida is very, very busy from Memorial Day to Labor Day, when hotels are packed and charge their highest rates. Reservations are vital. I've arranged hotels by location. Downtown, by the way, is very quiet, so don't think you're going to face masses of traffic.

A Special Resort

Pensacola's showplace is the lovely **Perdido Bay Inn and Resort,** 1 Doug Ford Dr., Pensacola, FL 32507 (tel. 904/492-1212, or toll free 800/874-5355), a golf resort about 16 miles west of Pensacola. Five-room brick and western cedar cottages capped with shingles surround the 7133-yard, par-72 course designed to challenge the skills of long-hitting pros, with shorter tees to allow the Sunday golfer some teeway.

Every room in the cottages has its own entrance, television, and bath, and there are studio suites with a counter bar where you can gather with friends to discuss that fantastic shot on the ninth hole or the smashing serve that won you the second match on the resort's tennis courts. Some suites have cozy fireplaces and all are spacious and decorated in bright colors and darkwood furniture. A high-rise condominium-hotel on the beach is under construction.

Located quite a distance from town on the shores of shimmering Perdido Bay, the resort has a pool and two pretty restaurants featuring French preparations of local fresh seafood and beef (in the $12 to $17 range) and a lounge where you can exchange notes with other sporting guests. The Perdido Inn also has courtesy transportation and charges $76 double in peak season (from mid-February to mid-June and September through November), $66 double at other times. Two-night golf packages, including greens fees and most meals, are $130 to $144 double, year round.

Downtown Hotels

Newest star among Pensacola hotels is the brand-new **Pensacola Hilton,** 2000 E. Gregory St., Pensacola, FL 32590 (tel. 904/433-3336, and toll-free numbers in every state). Here you have the best of both worlds, the antique and the brand-new, for Hilton built its glittering new high-rise hotel right behind an antique railroad station which serves as the hotel's lobby!

Whether or not you stay here, you really ought to stop by for a look. Fat overstuffed velvet chairs and couches are perched on rose rugs edged in black. Old signs showing the way to the "Hold Luggage" counter and the ticket booth remain, as does a big old station clock, trimmed in brass, copper, and stained glass. Just off the lobby there's a lovely bar outfitted in forest green, peach, brass, and oak, and appropriately called Tickets. On the end of the "station" are the hotel's two restaurants, a cute little umbrella-clad coffeeshop and the formal 1912 Restaurant, where you can dine on veal Orloff, steak with three kinds of mushrooms, or lobster in cream and sherry, for prices in the $12 to $20 range. Hours are 11 a.m. to 2 p.m. for lunch and 6 to 10 p.m. for dinner.

Hilton's 212 rooms are furnished in soft, contemporary colors and are equipped with all the usual Hilton amenities, from special soaps to fat, fluffy towels. The hotel offers complimentary airport limousine service, and its location just across the street from the city's new civic center makes it convenient for business travelers. Rates are $55 to $75 single, $82 to $102 double, depending on the location and height of the room, and $204 for a fancy bilevel suite.

Seville Inn, 223 E. Garden St., Pensacola, FL 32501 (tel. 904/433-8331), is a moderately priced downtown hotel with a nice restaurant—the Lafitte Room, open daily from 11 a.m. to 2 p.m. and 5 to 10 p.m. with prices in the $10 to $15 range for dinner—and frequently evening entertainment as well. Seville Inn has 172 standard motel rooms, some with queen- and king-size beds, plus a heated indoor pool and an outdoor splasher. While they're not plush, they're quite clean and comfortable. Rates are low too: $25 to $41, year round, with highest rates from June to September, lowest from September to April. There's a second Seville Inn a bit out of town at 8500 Pine Forest Rd., Pensacola, FL 32506 (tel. 904/477-9150).

Lenox Inn, 710 N. Palafox St., Pensacola, FL 32501 (tel. 904/238-4922, or toll free 800/874-0710; in Florida, 800/342-0700), is one of the prettiest motels near the downtown preservation district. Crisp white shutters trim this red-brick inn built on the side of a small rolling hill. An unusually homey atmosphere welcomes you to contemporary surroundings, from curtained lobby to the quiet recesses of the small adjoining coffeeshop and downstairs lounge. Pleasant watercolors accent a striking peach and forest-green decor in the spacious rooms, and there's a shell-shaped pool to play in. Lenox will bring you here from the airport for free and likewise shuttle you to the historic district. Best of all, you don't have to go far for city information. Pensacola's information center is just across the street. You'll pay just $42 to $47 for double occupancy (some rooms offer king-size beds at slightly higher prices). Suites with a separate living room are just $52, and some rooms have a hideaway murphy bed.

It's worth going to Pensacola for no other reason than to spend a couple of beautifully tranquil days at **New World Landing,** 600 S. Palafox St., Pensacola, FL 32510 (tel. 904/432-4111), one of the loveliest tiny inns in Florida. There are just 14 rooms and two suites at this small hotel that's done up in bright shutters and surrounded by flowers, fountains, and lawns.

Inside, a cozy lobby circles around a beautiful central staircase that soars in very showy style up to rooms on the second floor. Every one of those rooms is a jewel, decorated in stylish antiques or antique styles, with high ceilings, perhaps a four-poster bed, lovely colors, wallpapers, and all the elegant accoutrements you can imagine. Four of the rooms feature antique American furniture, four focus on Spanish decor, four on French, and four on English furnishings.

An adjacent restaurant is aglitter with crystal chandeliers, glowing wood moldings, handsome furnishings, and crisp linens. One room is called the Barcelona Room, and features a semicircular wall of glass overlooking a patio garden complete with tinkling fountain. Another, the Pensacola Room, is accented with original enlarged photographs of the city, and the Marseilles Room has mirrored walls and those sparkling chandeliers. Local seafood is featured, along with a variety of continental cuisine for prices in the $10 to $15 range. Hours are 7 to 10 a.m., 11 a.m. to 2 p.m., and 6 to 9 p.m. daily, closing an hour later on weekends.

Year-round rates at the New World Landing, located just beyond the downtown bustle and very near the bay, are $68 single, $78 double, and $118 for one of two suites.

Near Pensacola's fascinating Seville preservation district, the **Sherman Motor Inn**, at 224 E. Garden St., Pensacola, FL 32501 (tel. 904/434-3201), is a nice downtown hotel, a four-story dark brick building crowned by a shingled mansard roof. Paneling adds an attractive touch to rooms decorated in jewel colors, and there's an attractive Spanish-style brick foyer and lobby area. Kids should enjoy a hallway full of electronic games. Alhambra, the hotel's dramatically decorated red and black dining room, features a wide array of grilled meats, sandwiches, and salads at prices in the $10 to $15 range for dinner, about half that for lunch.

This Pensacola inn has a massive brick facade surrounded by a raised pool where guests gather for noon-day sunning, and the leathery Don Juan Lounge is a good spot to cool off in summer. Rates for two are $48 to $52. The hotel also has a babysitting service and small gift shop.

Really thrifty travelers should seek out **Motel 6**, 5829 Pensacola Blvd., Pensacola, FL 32505 (tel. 904/477-2152). This budget-conscious motel chain has 120 small, very simple rooms, a pool, and rates of just $21.95 double.

There's also a **Days Inn**, at 6911 Pensacola Blvd., Pensacola, FL 32505 (tel. 904/477-9000, or toll free 800/325-2525). Rates are $27 to $36 for two, all year round.

Hotels on Pensacola Beach

Pensacola Beach's Holiday Inn, at 165 Fort Pickens Rd., Pensacola Beach, FL 32561 (tel. 904/932-5361, or toll free 800/465-4329), is located just outside the entrance to the national park and is on the gulf. An eight-story hotel, this Holiday Inn has 149 rooms and all the services you could ask for: courtesy airport transportation, heated pool, game room, gift shop, tennis, handball and racquetball, rental sailboats, surfing, fishing, nighttime entertainment—even a babysitting service so you'll have time to enjoy the activities. A poolside bar overlooks the gulf so sunbathers can cool off and heat up at the same time. From April to September, Holiday Inn charges $72 to $92 double, dropping November 1 to $40 to $50, and rising again in the spring.

The **Dunes**, 333 Fort Pickens Rd., Pensacola Beach, FL 32561 (tel. 904/932-9536), is a favorite spot for families, who relax together around the sparkling pool overlooking the ocean. (One little toddler I saw was really relaxed: she tossed her teeny bikini off and jumped in Godiva style, chased by somewhat less relaxed parents.) You can have a room at the Dunes from mid-May to Labor Day for $65 to $85, depending on location, with the highest prices for rooms overlooking the gulf. In winter, those rates drop on the gulf side to $42 and in spring rise to $51 to $61. There's no charge for children. Some rooms have king-size beds, and all have dressing areas and plenty of space. Check for special rates and packages.

One of my favorites is the **Sandpiper Inn**, 23 Via de Luna, Pensacola Beach, FL 32561 (tel. 904/932-2516). It's a recently remodeled, contemporary motel trimmed in pale-gray wood decking, with floor-to-ceiling picture windows. The Sandpiper has just 32 nests, some with kitchenettes, gathered around a tiny central pool. Summer rates for one double bed are $40 ($2 more on weekends), rising to $60 for more elaborate accommodations. They can even arrange villas accommodating ten people (!) for $105. Rooms here are small but immaculately maintained, with wall-to-wall carpeting and lots of contemporary touches.

Nestled in behind a dune is a 24-room motel, the **Barbary Coast Apartments & Motel,** 24 Via de Luna, Pensacola Beach, FL 32561 (tel. 904/932-2233), whose gray buildings blend so subtly into the dunes they almost look like dunes themselves. Barbary Coast has a spanking-new look, from pipe furniture to wall-to-wall carpeting, tiled foyer, and matching drapes and bedspreads in dark contemporary prints. When Hurricane Frederick swept through the area a few years ago, most of the Barbary Coast became a dune itself, covered in blowing sand, so this motel and others in the area are more contemporary thanks to the massive renovation required. All double rooms here have small kitchenettes and are located in a series of buildings usually shared with just a few other rooms. There are also small and large suites accommodating four to six people in two separate bedrooms, plus a pull-out couch. Prices range from $66 for a room with a king-size bed (without kitchen), to $76 for a double including kitchen, and from $66 to $76 for small and large suites. Rates drop about 40% in winter.

Tiki House, 16 Via de Luna, Pensacola Beach, FL 32561 (tel. 904/932-2294), is part of a group that markets itself as Gulfside Resorts and includes the Howard Johnson's and Barbary Coast among others, so if one hotel is full, you can ask if there are vacancies at others in the group. Tiki House has 86 rooms, with particularly nice ones in a wing on the ocean. Some rooms have kitchenettes, but there are restaurants nearby for those who don't want anything to do with cooking. From May to mid-September, rates are $46 to $62 double, dropping $5 to $15 in winter.

All rooms at **Five Flags Inn,** 299 Fort Pickens Rd. (P.O. Box 39), Pensacola Beach, FL 32561 (tel. 904/932-3586), overlook the gulf and swimming pool with giant picture windows. Rooms are smaller here, but prices are also smaller, ranging mid-April through September from $50 to $55 for two people in one double bed or two double beds. They'll welcome your pets at Five Flags, and there's a lovely swimming pool running alongside the dunes.

On the eastern edge of Pensacola Beach, neighboring Navarre Beach has a **Holiday Inn,** 8375 Gulf Blvd., Gulf Breeze, FL 32561, on US 98 (tel. 904/939-2321, or toll free 800/465-4329), an isolated beachside resort that once housed the cast of *Jaws II,* which was filmed hereabouts. There is a restful beach atmosphere amid the dunes and sea oats, with a tropical indoor pool and spa for entertainment, games for the kids, and tennis for exercise fans. All king-size rooms have a gulf view and there's a gift shop, two bars, a seafood restaurant, even a theater. Rates range from $75 to $100 from June to mid-September, dropping in other months to $48 to $92.

Camping

At **KOA Kampground** on the Styx River (Route 3, Box 340), Robertsdale, AL 36567 (at I-10 and Wilcox Road, halfway between Mobile and Pensacola), there's lots of watery fun amid huge man-made "rocks." You play on innertubes, water slides, and waterfalls, even motor-operated innertubes. Open year round, the Water World cuts service to weekends only in April, May, and September, and charges $8.50 per person admission, $4 after 3 p.m. At the adjoining campground, full hookups are $10 for two. Call 205/964-5998 or 205/964-6165 for reservations, which you'll need if you're planning on stopping here between May and September.

Cherokee Campground, at 5255 Gulf Breeze Pkwy., Gulf Breeze, FL 32561 (on US 98, ten miles east of Gulf Breeze; tel. 904/932-9905), is on Santa Rosa Sound and rents space in its travel park for $9 a night.

Pensacola East Safari Campground, Route 4, Box 185, Milton, FL 32570 (tel. 904/623-3936, or toll free 800/558-2954), has shady campsites, swimming pools, a gift shop, horseshoes, mini-golf, nature trails, a game room, laundry, grocery store, and gas station! Rates are $10 to $15 in summer months.

WHERE TO DINE: Restaurants are so inexpensive in the Panhandle that there's hardly any point in putting them in price categories, so I've just listed them all together. You won't find many fancy places here, just very good cooking, some of the state's best seafood, and happy places where everyone smiles and drawls out that old "y'all come back" cliché—but here they really seem to mean it. Remember that the prices I've cited are for entrees, but these usually include salad, one or two vegetables, and sometimes even coffee.

New World Landing, a lovely new inn in Florida, also has one of the city's most attractive restaurants. You'll find a description of the inn's handsome restaurants back a page or so.

One of the newer restaurants in town is **Tivoli Gardens**, 670 Scenic Hwy. (US 98A) (tel. 432-5477), a lovely, long, white clapboard restaurant trimmed in royal-blue shutters. You can look out over the goings-on in the bay here while you dine on some tempting Italian cuisine like spaghetti with a creamy clam sauce, fettuccine alla Tivoli with fresh shrimp and crabmeat, veal Bolognese baked with prosciutto and cheese, or saltimbocca stuffed with ham and cheese and sauteed in a wine sauce. Prices are in the $10 to $12 range (cheaper for pasta), and hours are 5 to 10 p.m. daily, an hour later on weekends.

Dolphins on the Bay Restaurant, US 98 in Gulf Breeze (tel. 932-6678), occupies a lovely setting beneath some trees and overlooking Pensacola Bay. Seafood seems even more wonderful here with all that water around you. Goodness knows there's plenty of it on the menu: ten different preparations of shrimp from Créole to kabob and all kinds of fish from triggerfish to amberjack, snapper, group, flounder, mullet, and even shark! Lobster, crab oysters, and scallops are on the menu as well, which also has a few beef selections for those not infatuated with seafood. Prices for complete dinners fall in the $7 to $10 range. Dolphins is open daily March through August, closed Wednesday in other months, and hours are 11 a.m. to 2 p.m. and 5 to 10 p.m.

Catfish? You want catfish? Well, there's always one in every crowd. If you're that one, try **Catfish Country**, 916 E. Gregory St. (tel. 438-9019), which features freshwater catfish—all you can eat for $9—and dinners of oysters, shrimp, flounder, snapper, and the like for $6 to $7. Sandwiches, salads, and steaks here too, at similarly low prices. Hours are 11 a.m. to 10 p.m. daily.

Rebrof's Steakhouse, 31 E. Wright St. (tel. 438-7101), is owned and operated by Harry and Karen Forber, who specialize in Iowa corn-fed beef and can cut a 24-ounce slab for trenchermen! There's a cocktail lounge and entertainment here too. Rebrof's (located two blocks west of the Hilton) is open from 5 to 10 p.m. daily except Sunday, closing an hour later on weekends. Prices are in the $10 to $17 range for dinner.

Got the midnight munchies? **Bay Window Deli**, 911 Gulf Breeze Pkwy. (tel. 932-0817), is open 24 hours and features all kinds of deli sandwiches, hoagies, salads, barbecue, cheesecake, even caviar and eggs Benedict at 2 a.m. Prices are in the $5 range for most things.

For the most budget of budget meals, try the **Elk's Dining Room**, 200 W. La Rue St., at the corner of Spring and La Rue Streets (tel. 432-5636), where the fellows of that fraternal organization prepare $1 breakfasts and $3 lunches— including entree, three vegetables, soup, salad, coffee or tea, and cornbread!— and similarly inexpensive dinners every day. It's open to the public and even has take-out service. Hours are 6 to 10 a.m., 11 a.m. to 2 p.m., and 4 to 9 p.m. daily.

You'll have to look closely for the sign that points out **Hopkins' Boarding**

House, at 900 N. Spring St. (tel. 438-3979), but once you find it you'll be enchanted. A pale-olive house with rocking chairs on the veranda, wrought-iron trim, lace curtains, and grandmotherly bric-a-brac, the Hopkins' place sits serenely under a mass of shady trees. It's a real boarding house too—one gentleman rocked slowly in the afternoon sun and allowed as how he'd lived there "gettin' on to 20 years now." Gilbert and Arkie Hopkins celebrated 40 years together in 1978 and still preside over this down-home spot. Join other diners at a long table the likes of which gave rise to that boarding-house reach your mother warned against or settle into a large round table in the parlor where you can gaze out over the lawn. Bowls heaped with cantaloupe, tomatoes fresh from nearby fields, carrot salad, and potato salad begin appearing about 11 a.m. Tuesday through Saturday, when the double doors open for lunch (closing at 2 p.m.), and at 5:15 p.m. for dinner, which continues through 7 p.m. The price is just $4.25! They're even open for heaping country breakfasts from 6:30 to 9 a.m., but there are only noon meals on Sunday (they're closed on Monday).

Menu collectors should like **Cap'n Jim's,** 905 E. Gregory St. (tel. 433-3562), where you can take a souvenir copy of the menu right with you for light reading—it looks just like a newspaper. Cap'n Jim and eight of his family work together here, the sons in the kitchen, the daughters and Mrs. Cap'n in the dining room, with smiles and efficient service.

Cap'n Jim loves water and has a constant view of it from a wall of windows overlooking Pensacola Bay. As you watch the waters of the bay roll by, dine on fresh, simply prepared seafood: fresh oysters, red snapper, fat shrimp (barbecued or atop a mound of salad). The moderate prices begin at $6 to $10 and top out at $20 for a seafood platter for two. If you've never tried home-grown freshwater catfish, now's the time. Open from 11 a.m. to 9:45 p.m. daily.

Ask most people in Pensacola for the best restaurant in town and the answer will be the **Driftwood,** at 27 W. Garden St. (tel. 433-4559). Look for the Federalist-era entrance crowned by a flying eagle on Garden Street. That's as far as the colonial motif goes, however, for inside the Driftwood's a study in modernity. Smoked mirrors are cleverly placed to create intimate alcoves and odd little corners for cozy tête-à-têtes. Tiny white lights are strung across the ceiling. There's a tranquil color scheme of Wedgwood blue and shell pink, subdued lighting, crystal, and banks of fresh flowers glowing under brass chandeliers. The Driftwood, now owned by Stephanie and William Carnley, has been operating successfully here since 1953 and has compiled an extensive menu (once lauded by *Gourmet* magazine) featuring fresh catches from this fish-rich coast. Pensacola has been known to call itself the "Red Snapper Capital of the World," so you can count on excellent snapper dishes here, as well as some house specialties like baked oysters Driftwood, delicately spiced with garlic. You can dine here on nearly any menu choice for less than $15, and cut that to $10 or so by dining à la carte. It's open from 11 a.m. to 3 p.m. and 5 to 10 p.m. Monday through Saturday.

Smörgåsbords are increasing in popularity in Florida, and so is the one at **Duff's,** 1412 W. Fairfield, in the Fairfield Shopping Plaza (tel. 433-6506). You can hardly beat it for substantial fare, low prices, and an all-you-can-eat dictum priced under $5 for lunch or dinner, even less for children. Hours are 11 a.m. to 3 p.m. and 4 to 8 p.m. daily.

At the **Marina Oyster Barn,** 505 Bayou Blvd., at the Johnson-Rooks 76 Marina (tel. 433-0511), you'll find some of the state's best shrimp tempura and freshly shucked-before-your-eyes bivalves. Your check will average $8 or less per person for sea treats at this simple rustic spot. Open daily from 11 a.m. to 9 p.m., an hour later on weekends.

You'll think you're stepping back into history when you enter **McGil-**

livray's Restaurant and Tavern, 300 S. Alcaniz St. (tel. 438-4535), and indeed that's just what you're doing. An old home on the fringes of the city's Seville Preservation District, McGillivray's has wooden floors, antique replica hat stands, bentwood chairs, lots of plants in two dining areas, and a popular long bar. Straightforward beef, ham, and lamb are served up here, along with an excellent red snapper stuffed with crabmeat or shrimp Mornay for about $9. McGillivray's honors one of the lesser known but more colorful of Floridians, trader Alexander McGillivray who slipped with the ease of an eel from side to side in the battles over this harbor, making himself a millionaire and an Indian chief in the process. It's open from 11 a.m. to 2 p.m. and 5 to 10 p.m. daily (except Monday).

Francisco Moreno built a tiny house for his daughter when she became a bride in 1879, and today you can lunch right in this minuscule honeymoon cottage at Mr. P's Wine and Sandwich Shop at 221 E. Zaragossa St. (tel. 433-0294). Daily specials of bean sprouts and shrimp tucked into pita bread, Reuben sandwiches, and the like ($3.35 to $3.95) are accompanied by a selection of domestic beer and wine. It's hard to imagine setting up housekeeping in such small quarters, but then it's also hard to imagine providing for 27 children and 127 grandchildren as did the house's builder!

If you're looking for a cool, quiet spot as you tour the Seville Preservation District, drop into Jamie's, 435 E. Zaragossa St. (tel. 438-9523). Jamie's is not only sweet with flaky pastries, it's sweet to look at: a yellow candlelit Victorian house where a tiny dining room is set with fresh flowers and crisp linens. Colonial furnishings seat perhaps 30, and classical music hums quietly in the background. Jamie's began as a bakery about four years ago and has grown into this cozy little restaurant redolent in old-world atmosphere and brimming with homemade goodies. It's open from 11:30 a.m. to 2:30 p.m. and 5:30 to 10 p.m. Tuesday through Saturday. Every day there's a cold soup and baked French onion soup with a touch of sherry. Gourmets will like the house pâté, a blend of chicken and sausage lightly touched with cognac and served with herbed toast or homemade bread. There are croissant sandwiches and a wide array of fresh crispy salads from hearts of palm to shrimp rémoulade. Lunch prices are $3 to $4.

Another cozy spot for lunch in the Seville Preservation District is E.J.'s Food Company, at 232 E. Main St. (tel. 432-5886), which occupies the first home of the Southeastern Baptist Church. E.J.'s is a cozy spot with frilly lace curtains, checked tablecloths, paintings on the wall, paddle fans, and rib-sticking lunches from pecan-chicken-salad sandwiches to barbecued pork or an oyster basket, salad bar, and chicken tempura. There's a hearty special each day, and a bounteous salad bar offering enough food to hold you for a day or two. Prices are in the $2.50 to $4 range. E.J.'s is open from 10:30 a.m. to 3 p.m. daily, and specializes in take-out orders and catering.

NIGHTLIFE: Pensacola is, shall we say, a quiet place, and that's putting it mildly. You won't find razzle-dazzle nightlife here, the city is proud to say, but that doesn't mean you have to trot off to bed at sunset.

Seville Quarter

Dixieland jazz and the Singing Swanee Man, a Flaming Hurricane drink in a souvenir glass, a wide-screen television pub, turn-of-the-century atmosphere, and a flashing, jogging disco—it's all part of *the* place to go in Pensacola for riproaring nightlife, Seville Quarter, 130 E. Government St. (tel. 433-7436), home of Rosie O'Grady's Good-Time Emporium. Built as a sister to Orlando's phenomenally successful Rosie's, the Seville Quarter is a dead ringer for that central Florida operation, from tons of brass trim to delicately etched glass and the rousing good time you can have here.

Opened in 1967, Rosie's is a labyrinth of rooms. Much of Pensacola's history has been salvaged and restored here: the building that houses Rosie's was built in 1871 as the Pensacola Cigar and Tobacco Co.; great trusses in Apple Annie's Courtyard (which features fresh-fruit drinks and bluegrass music) were retrieved from an old casino that once stood on Pensacola Beach; elaborate iron fencing and gates in the Seville Quarter's open-air courtyard were salvaged from the American National Bank of Pensacola, and bricks came from buildings throughout the city. And that's only the beginning. . . .

As for the restaurants and bars, you need a guide to lead you through the maze. Here goes:

Rosie's opens at 8 p.m. Tuesday through Sunday, and is the first door on the right after you pass through the main entrance (graced incidentally, by the impressive marquees taken from the old Saenger Theater on South Palafox Street, a few blocks away). Rosie's features rousing Dixieland jazz and the Singing Swanee Man, Nelson K. Hamilton. You sit on church pews that came from an Alabama church, or stand at a bar from an old Philadelphia hotel or near doors from an English town house.

Lili Marlene's World War I Aviator's Pub is just across from Rosie's and opens at 4 p.m. for happy hour and entertainment on the antique rosewood grand piano. There's a wide-screen TV for sports events and a back bar that came from Chicago's Blackstone Hotel.

Coppersmith's Gallery is open daily from 11:30 a.m. to 3 p.m. and 5:30 to 11 p.m. for Cajun cooking plus steaks, prime ribs, shrimp tempura, chicken Kiev, crêpes, and much more in the $8 to $15 range. The clocks here are from England, the floors from Mobile, and the cypress doors from New Orleans.

A doorway leads from Coppersmith's into **Apple Annie's Courtyard** through gates from a Liverpool town house. Apple Annie's features lovely skylighting, a fountain crowned by an eagle, and fresh-fruit drinks in souvenir glasses.

The **Palace Oyster Bar** is to your left as you enter Annie's, and features (you guessed it) oysters from 11:30 a.m., plus seafood, sandwiches, crêpes, and New Orleans Créole goodies like red beans and rice, jambalaya, and beignets.

A bricked alley entrance to the complex leads to Seville Quarter, graced by iron gates from the Old Governor's Mansion in New Orleans. Here is the entrance to **Phineas Phogg's Balloon Works** featuring nightly disco entertainment and a smoking specialty called Phogg Grog. A giant brass sailing balloon is the center of attention here, and the disco booth was once a pulpit in London.

Across the back of this maze is **Seville Quarter Courtyard,** a gaslit Victorian look-alike with open-air bar and a variety of summer entertainment from folk trios to Caribbean steel bands.

There's an evening admission charge of $3 per person from 8 p.m., but you can roam through this amazing complex free until then.

Cultural Activities

Pensacola loves a restoration, which is why the city's **Saenger Theater,** a product of the 1920s, is so popular. Now renovated into a jewel of a theater, the 60-year-old Saenger was once a vaudeville theater and is now home to many music and dance performances throughout the year. Local newspapers like the *Pelican* or the *Pensacola News-Journal* tell you what's playing when. You'll find the theater at 118 Palafox St. (tel. 438-2787).

The **Pensacola Symphony Orchestra** offers five annual concerts and other local performances at various locations, and the **Pensacola Community Con-**

certs Association brings ballet, opera, and other musical entertainment to the city.

Pensacola Museum of Art, 407 S. Jefferson St. (tel. 432-6247), is the show-case for traveling loan exhibitions and has its own collection of art and sculpture as well. Hours are 10 a.m. to 5 p.m. Tuesday through Friday, closing an hour earlier on Saturday; closed Sunday and Monday.

Pensacola Little Theater, 186 N. Palafox St. (tel. 432-2042), is the oldest continuing community theater in the Southeast and is now celebrating nearly 50 years of performances by local players. Hours and days of performances vary, so give them a call to see what's on when you're here.

University of West Florida, on US 90A (tel. 474-2403), also takes to the boards with its Repertory Theater, which presents at least three plays annually, plus seminars, lectures, and discussions presented by notable theater experts.

In 1985 Pensacola opened a brand-new **Pensacola Civic Center** to play host to a wide variety of entertainment ranging from the high-stepping Lippizaner stallions to the equally high-stepping Pointer Sisters and the rock group Kiss. You'll find the new center at 201 E. Gregory St. (tel. 433-6311). Ticket prices vary, of course, according to the popularity of the performers, but are generally in the $10 to $20 range.

Lounges and Hang-out Spots

Country entertainment is available at **Show Palace,** 9005 US 98 West (tel. 456-8991), which says it is "country and proud of it." Musicians play here Wednesday through Sunday.

The **Seville Inn,** 223 E. Garden St. (tel. 433-8331), also has frequent entertainment. A couple of lively hang-out spots are **Trader Jon's Bar,** 511 S. Palafox St. (tel. 433-9973), which calls itself the official home of the U.S. Navy Blue Angels; **Quayside Inn,** 331 S. Palafox St. (tel. 433-9752); **Pelican's Nest,** 1 W. Main St. (tel. 433-9962); and the **Red Garter Saloon,** 500 S. Palafox St. (tel. 433-9229).

Another Choice

You never can tell when you're going to get a craving for a green beer, but if you do there's always one on tap at **McGuire's Irish Pub,** 600 E. Gregory St., just west of the Bay Bridge (tel. 433-6789), a local pubby spot boasting "feasting, imbibery, and debauchery," although presumably you'll have to see to the last of those three yourself. Friendly local folks and visitors flock to McGuire's, where a moose head presides over a massive stone fireplace and Irishmen of all nationalities have donated over 15,000 autographed dollar bills and personalized mugs to the pub's collection. If you don't like crowds, forget McGuire's on Friday night when most of the Panhandle seems to be gathered here for outrageously fat sandwiches and charcoal-broiled burgers in the $3 to $5 range. Soup and stews, steaks, enormous salads, and nightly parties make this a fun favorite that has gained it acclaim in several national magazines. Open daily from 11 a.m. to 2 a.m., on Sunday from 4 p.m. to 1 a.m.

THE SIGHTS: Towering live oaks draped in ghostly Spanish moss shade the streets of this lovely old Florida city, and once were its fortune-maker. At the turn of the century a timber boom made many a millionaire in these parts, and that same timber became walls of their elaborate homes. Most of these were on rolling hills in the **North Hill Preservation District** (bounded by LaRua, Palafox, Blount, and Reus Streets), which you can tour with a map provided by the Visitor's Information Center.

Here you'll see etched glass and tall chimneys, wrap-around verandas, bay windows, turrets, shutters, and ornate gingerbread trim on typical old southern mansions that have changed hardly a whit in a century.

Pensacola and St. Augustine have a running feud over which is truly the oldest city in the nation, and Pensacola with its 16th-century foundations has an excellent claim to the title. Its shady, sleepy preservation district easily competes with St. Augustine's busier, better known (and consequently more crowded) cluster of centuries-old structures.

Perhaps it is its very naïveté that makes Pensacola's **Seville Preservation District** so charming: towering live oaks shade a small bayside park where children play, surrounded by the history their ancestors worked so hard to produce; bees buzz in gardens and there's a somnolent hush among the tiny shops and boutiques. Honeymoon cottages and sea captains' shore homes are now carefully restored, and shopkeepers will keep you spellbound with stories of the people who once worked and played, giggled and wept in these peaked-roof and pillared cottages.

Start your tour in the **Museum of West Florida History,** at Tarragona and Zaragossa Streets (open 8 a.m. to 5 p.m. Monday through Saturday; free) to learn a little about the background of buccaneers and boasters, timber lords and Spanish dons whose ancestors live here still. Then wander down Zaragossa Street past the Walton, Tivoli High, and Lavalle Houses, past Julee Cottage, and take a moment to visit the **Pensacola Historical Museum,** in Old Christ Church, the oldest church in the nation. Next door is the two-story **Dorr House,** which fronts on shady Adams Street where you can fairly see statuesque ladies with hand-span waists and feathered hats sweeping grandly down the boulevard.

There's no admission charge to the area so you can peek and peer wherever you like. In shops here you'll find colorful handmade quilts and crocheted bedspreads, hand-dipped tapers, perfumed oils, elegant kitchenware, fine old clocks, 18th-century antiques, even a Christmas cottage with a holiday tree made of driftwood hung with sand dollars.

President of the Shopkeepers of Historic Seville Square is Barbara Prince, who'll be happy to send you a map of the area with shops and historic homes sketched and named so you can find your way around. Write the shopkeepers at Seville Square Historical District, Pensacola, FL 32501, or call 904/438-6364 or 432-6717.

Edward Ball was one of northern Florida's most in-the-limelight millionaires all his long life. As trustee of the Dupont estate, he had billions under his control and was a most powerful northern Floridian. He is less well known for the funds he donated to many charitable organizations, particularly those dedicated to preserving Florida's wildlife. You can walk the **Edward Ball Nature Trail** at the University of West Florida at US 98A and University Parkway, where 2.5 miles of boardwalk honor the memory of this well-known Florida power broker. You'll find the trail on the northwest side of the campus in a wetlands area. It's open daily and is free. Hour-long guided tours are conducted weekdays by the Delta Tau Delta fraternity (tel. 474-2425).

If you're glued to the television set for space activities at Cape Canaveral, you won't want to miss a visit to the **Pensacola Naval Aviation Museum** (tel. 452-3604) at the world's largest naval air station. Now a naval air station may not sound like much of an attraction, but here in Pensacola it's as fascinating as it is important to the local economy.

Pensacola likes to call itself the cradle of naval aviation, for it was here that the first group of aviators flew in those funny-looking bales of wood and wire that were to be called airplanes. Here in Pensacola the naval air station is home to the **Naval Aviation Museum,** which displays some of those early contraptions and even has a land survival exhibit that gives you a look at a survival-skills course the swabby flyers have to survive.

To get there, take Palafox Street south to Garden Street, where the road becomes Navy Boulevard and goes straight to the naval air station. On display here is an awesome array of aircraft from Grumman Hellcats and Tigers to the Skylab command module. Let the kids try their hand at the controls of a jet trainer while you marvel at the daring of pilots who so fearlessly flew those flimsy early craft. Open from 9 a.m. to 5 p.m. daily, it's free.

Perhaps the single most fascinating part of the naval air station is the USS **Lexington,** a massive aircraft carrier that opens its doors to one and all when it's in port. Still an operating carrier, the *Lexington* is open from 9 a.m. to 3 p.m. daily on those occasions, and charges no admission for a look at the ship that is home to several thousands of sailors.

A lighthouse on the station was built in 1825 and is still operating to warn ships away from tricky coastal waters. Its beam soars across 210 miles of the Gulf of Mexico.

One final note: The naval air station is the home of those daredevil acrobatic pilots, the Blue Angels. Technically part of the Navy Flight Demonstration Team, the Angels are U.S. Navy and Marine Corps aviators who perform here frequently and make regular appearances in the skies over many American cities.

Special Events

One week a year Pensacolans drag out their history tomes and suit up as Spanish conquistadors to celebrate the five flags that have fluttered over this centuries-old village. This special week is the **Fiesta of Five Flags,** marking the settling of the city in 1559 by Don Tristan de Luna and his 1500 followers. Their arrival is recreated by local residents who go all out with fancy costumes, street fairs, celebrities, beauty queens, even a four-masted antique sailing ship that sails into port for the celebration. The fiesta's in May.

Later in the year some of the more unusual festivals take place, including a 'coon hound championship in June, a gourmet gumbo cook-out in July, a number of fishing tournaments (one for sharks), and a seafood festival in September.

Each spring the city renews its ties with the Old South when it presents its **Mardi Gras–Krewe of Lafitte Parade.** This two-week spectacular in late February and early March includes a round of parades, street dances, and jazz festivals featuring residents in spectacular Mardi Gras costumes and masks. The finale is a Mardi Gras Ball.

Other special events in the city include a massive **St. Patrick's Day** party at McGuire's Irish Pub, which sponsors kite-flying contests, a bicycle race, Irish jig competitions, and even Irish skydivers!

At **Christmas** the city celebrates in the loveliest of ways: carolers stroll the streets from Seville Square to Palafox Street past shopkeepers dressed in Victorian costumes and shops decked out in holly and red ribbons.

Pensacola's **Perdido Key,** a long sandy strip of uninhabited scrub pine island, is a favorite place for **crabbing expeditions.** I'm not talking about the kind of crabbing so loved by Lucy of the Peanuts cartoon fame. We're talking of the kind that involves crab net and bucket. Armed with those, plus a pair of ancient tennis shoes, you wade along the shoreline and scoop up those scampering crabby little fellows. Fall is the best time for blue and speckled crabs, which can be spotted just beyond the point where the waves break on the shoreline. If you assign someone else in the group to bait a hook with shrimp and toss it into the surf, you may end up with a whole seafood buffet!

For **fishing,** try the party boat *Chulamar* (tel. 932-5625), which carries up to 49 passengers and goes on private charters or moonlight cruises as well as its regular bottom-fishing cruises into the bay.

All kinds of fish live in the fresh and salt waters hereabouts, and all kinds of fishermen flock here to catch 'em. Big-game fisherman have a go at sailfish, marlin, red snapper, grouper, amberjack, and scamp.

Freshwater fans head for the Escambia and Perdido Rivers or to the lakes and streams on Eglin Air Force Base for black bass, pickerel, bream, pike, and catfish.

Surf-fishing enthusiasts do what they do most anytime, but spring, particularly April, is considered the luckiest season. Pompano, one of Florida's most highly prized delicacies can be caught in the surf along with another Florida fish called whiting.

Charter boats working in the area include the *New Florida Girl* (tel. 904/837-6422) and *Her Majesty II* (tel. 904/837-6313). Charter boats tend to move their home base now and then, so give them a call to find out where they're moored.

SPORTS: You can play golf at **Carriage Hills Golf Course,** 2355 W. Michigan (tel. 455-0366), the **Osceola Golf Club,** Osceola Heights (tel. 456-2761), and **Santa Rosa Shores Country Club,** on Pensacola Beach (tel. 456-2761). Play on 18 holes is $5 to $10. Arrangements can be made through many beach hotels.

Largest of the tennis facilities in the area is **Scott Tennis Center,** at Cordova Park (tel. 432-2939), which has 18 courts and charges $1.25 for adults, 75¢ for children, a day. The **Holiday Inn** on Pensacola Beach, 3450 Wimbledon Dr. (tel. 434-2435), has four courts, and the **Pensacola Racquet Club** (tel. 434-2435) in Pensacola has ten courts available for $2.50 a day.

Pensacourt Sports Center, 3001 Langley Ave. (tel. 478-1400), has racquetball, handball, and tennis courts, aerobics, suntanning equipment, saunas, a weight room, a restaurant, and a nursery. Weekly charges are $26.25 single, $35 for couples, and $40 for families. It's open 6 a.m. to 10 p.m. weekdays, 7 a.m. to 5 p.m. on Saturday and 9 a.m. to 5 p.m. on Sunday.

Many are the treasures rumored to be lurking beneath the seas nearby, abandoned or scuttled by pirates. You can go in search of them on diving trips operated by **Dive World,** 3090 N. Pace Blvd., in the McDonald Shopping Center (tel. 438-5485). Trips begin at about $25 to $30.

Pensacola Beach Sailing Center, Pensacola Beach Causeway, next to the Soundside Restaurant on Pensacola Beach Boulevard (tel. 932-0621), has all kinds of water sports equipment for rent, including Hobie catamarans from 14 to 18 feet, windsurfing boards, Sunfish sailboats, daysailers, and canoes. Instructions in sailing begin at $12 an hour plus the cost of the boat, which ranges from $15 to $20 an hour (depending on the size of the boat), $40 to $55 a half day, with lower long-term rates available. Windsurfing instruction is four hours long and begins at $30, with boards renting for $10 an hour, $30 a half day. Canoes are $6 an hour, $24 a day.

There is a slithery water slide, **Wild Rapids,** at 2121 Airport Blvd. (tel. 476-3334), adjacent to the shady brick campus of Pensacola Junior College. It's open daily from 10 a.m. to 10 p.m. (an hour later on weekends), in summer; winter hours and days vary. The Rapids charges $3.50 an hour.

Jet skis, those snowmobiles on waterskis, can be rented—including life jacket, instructions, and moral support—across from Howard Johnson's on Pensacola Beach for about $15 a half hour.

Surf & Sail Boardsailing, 11 Via de Luna, Pensacola Beach (tel. 932-SURF), has become the local surfboarders' headquarters. Boards are for rent for $10 an hour, $40 a day, and they'll teach you how to get them sailing for $15 for 90 minutes of instruction.

Gamblers can put a few dollars on the nose of a sleek greyhound at **Pensacola Greyhound Park,** 951 Dog Track Rd. (tel. 455-8598), on US 98 west of the city, open from May 1 to October 5. Dog races begin at 8 p.m. nightly with matinees on Friday and Saturday at 3:30 p.m. (there's no racing on Thursday or Sunday). Admission is 50¢, grandstand seating costs an additional 50¢, and clubhouse admission and seating is $1.50.

SHOPPING: Pensacola's downtown shopping district, known as Palafox Place, has had a rebirth in recent years and is now a study in lacy iron grillwork, pretty pastel storefronts, and intriguing boutiques.

The **Seville Historic District,** which stretches from Palafox to Ninth Avenue between Romana and Main Streets, has dozens and dozens and dozens of adorable little shops selling everything from country calico to Christmas ornaments, dollhouse furniture, fashions for tall girls, small girls, children, and men, antiques, toys, jewelry, kitchenware, and artwork. Many shops and restaurants are in restored 18th- or 19th-century cottages and mansions, so you can combine shopping and historic touring. Shopkeepers have even banded together to form a group called Shopkeepers of Historic Seville, and will be happy to send you a handy map and list of the shops operating in the historic district. Write to them at P.O. Box 587, Pensacola, FL 32593.

Bayou Country Store, 823 E. Jackson St. at Ninth Avenue (tel. 432-5697), is packed with countrified treasures from baskets to lamps, salt-glazed stoneware in cobalt-blue designs, quilts, hooked and braided rugs, calico lampshades, and primitive prints. They're open 10 a.m. to 5 p.m. daily except Sunday.

Quayside Thieves Market, 712 S. Palafox St. (tel. 433-9930 or 476-3677), is a cluster of quaint specialty shops and small drinking and dining spots gathered together in a beautifully restored, century-old historic brick warehouse. China, antiques, collectibles, brass, copper, linens, old books—you name it and you're likely to find it here. Beneath your feet, by the way, is 60 acres of man-made land created by ballast dumped from early sailing vessels which loaded lumber after lightening their load by dumping everything from blue stone from Italy to lava from Mount Pelee here! You'll find the market on the waterfront (take I-10 to the I-110 South exit, then go to Exit 1-C and turn right to Palafox, left on Palafox, and south to the waterfront). Market hours are 10 a.m. to 5 p.m. Wednesday through Sunday.

Cordova Mall, 5100 N. Ninth Ave. (tel. 477-7562), offers more than 70 shops in an air-conditioned mall, and **Mariner Mall,** Fairfield Drive at Mobile Highway (tel. 456-7466), features many discount shops.

In Pensacola you'll also find the headquarters of a well-known mail-order company, **J. W. Renfroe Pecan Co.,** which operates at 2400 W. Fairfield Dr. (tel. 432-2083 or 438-9405, or toll free 800/874-1929). Renfroe passes out free samples of its pecans and pecan candies from 9 a.m. to 5 p.m. Monday through Saturday.

A SAND DUNE PARK: Pensacola's greatest pride is its **Gulf Island National Seashore** (tel. 904/932-2473), a 150-mile stretch of offshore islands and keys strung between Gulfport, Mississippi, and Destin, Florida.

To get there, head to the beach across the Pensacola Bay Bridge and past Gulf Breeze, a small offshore island where you might stop to roam the **Naval Live Oaks Plantation.** Here in 1828 the live oak, the most typical tree of the Deep South, was placed under protective management to supply highly prized ship timbers. These majestic monsters, draped in spooky Spanish moss, tower here still, and you can hike through them.

There's a 35¢ toll across to the beach, then just follow the signs to Fort Pickens (you make a sharp right turn off Gulf Breeze Parkway onto Route 399) and make a right when you reach Pensacola Beach.

On your left you'll see sailboats and the occasional adventurous parasailer flying through the air (you can try it yourself for about $20).

If you take the right fork in the road, you'll be driving down a sandy strip where condominiums are springing up like fungi on a spring morning. You can stay amid the white dunes and the sea oats in a condo by contacting the Pensacola Beach Chamber of Commerce. They'll send your name to apartment owners who will write to you about their accommodations.

Here on Fort Pickens Island in Pensacola you find mile after mile of sugary white sand. At the end of this lovely deserted strip of sand is **Fort Pickens State Park** (tel. 932-5018), which charges $1 a carload entrance fee, and camping is $10 with electricity, $8 without. Six miles beyond the entrance to the park, five-sided Fort Pickens looms up like a pink mirage in a desert. Children will love prowling this giant fortification which once imprisoned the fierce and courageous Apache chief, Geronimo. Outside the fort are several batteries built in the late 1800s with rapid-fire rifles capable of hurling a 45-pound projectile more than five miles to sea in 25 seconds—not something to be facing at firing time!

Massive construction on Fort Pickens was begun in 1892 soon after Florida was ceded to the U.S. by Spain. In those days the fort protected a naval shipyard on Pensacola Bay. Geronimo was its most famous inhabitant and the tiny cell in which he huddled in winter beside a small fire, chafing under his chains, is a touching sight still. Fort Pickens never really saw much action, but these days many a shutter snaps to record the massive guns.

If you like camping, Fort Pickens is a tranquil seaside park with lots of room for roaming and a pier for fishing. There are a number of park activities including a marine museum with changing exhibits of the area's wildlife (open 9 a.m. to 5 p.m.). In summer months there are daily activities including rifle-firing demonstrations, history lessons, children's activities, and tours of the fort. Scubadiving and spearfishing are permitted, but some beaches are off-limits, and swimming is not recommended in the entrance channel to Pensacola Bay because of the strong rip current.

Fort Pickens is open daily throughout the year. Hikers can take a self-guided nature trail or join groups shepherded by rangers at noon and 4 p.m. daily in summer.

2. Fort Walton/Destin

It seems fitting somehow that this small sand-fringed city is geographically about halfway between the sleepy southern elegance of Pensacola and the frenetic fantasyland of Panama City. This is a spot neither garish nor elegant, neither expensive nor rundown cheap, a quiet miles-long strip of dunes and sugary soft sand with prices a family wallet can handle and a quiet acceptance of the impenetrability of life.

Like the foamy green sea that has washed upon these shores for millennia, people here are gentle and easy-going, full of enthusiasm for these rolling dunes and for each other. "There's something about it," one citywise but city-weary sophisticate confided. "No matter how far I go or how long I'm away, I'm always happy just to be back here where strangers don't look at you funny if you say hello to them on the street."

You can find whatever you want here, be it easy friendships or solitary walks on deserted beaches; high-rise, amenity-laden resorts or small, family-run apartments; activity-filled days or the peace of a snow-white dune where only a seagull's shriek breaks the silence.

Summer continues to be the major tourist season, and if you arrive anytime from Easter to Labor Day you'd be wise to make a reservation. Warm gulf breezes keep temperatures on a fairly even keel, although it's at least ten degrees cooler than southern Florida in winter. Prices as low as $250 to $300 a month for a posh condominium apartment are increasing the region's popularity as a winter resort.

There's a small amusement park here that doesn't begin to compare to the ringy-dingy-do of Panama City Beach. There are small but excellent restaurants where you'll find unfailingly fresh seafood and unfailingly friendly service. There are miles and miles of soft sand lapped by turquoise waters shallow enough for the children and deep enough for grownup swimmers.

It's a happy melange of entertainments in a small-village atmosphere where anyone may soon be a friend. It's a quaint rusticity, neither shabby nor contrived, where you may find *your* kind of halfway house.

GETTING AROUND: Unless you don't plan to leave the beach you might consider a **rental car,** available from Avis, Budget, Economy, Hertz, National, or Panhandle Rentals. **Avis** (tel. 769-1411) and **Hertz** (tel. 769-5181) have service desks at the airport. Rates begin at about $20 a day.

You can scoot around on a thrifty moped available from **Island Moped Rentals,** at the entrance to Aloha Village, 860 Scallop Court (tel. 243-3114). They're open from 8 a.m. to 5 p.m. daily (from 1 p.m. on Sunday). The scoot-abouts are $5 an hour.

VISITOR INFORMATION: You won't find a more enthusiastic or more knowledgeable chamber of commerce executive than Fort Walton Beach's personable Jerry Melvin, who was for ten years a state legislator and has been for a lifetime a proud Panhandle resident. His friendly **Fort Walton Beach Chamber of Commerce,** 34 Miracle Strip Pkwy. SE, Fort Walton Beach, FL 32548 (tel. 904/244-8191), will be happy to dig out information on anything and everything in the area. . . . His counterpart at the **Destin Chamber of Commerce,** US 98 East, Destin, FL 32541 (tel. 904/837-6421), will do likewise. . . . There's a **24-hour gas station** at the 7/11, 408 Mary Esther Cut-off (tel. 244-1751). . . . For late-night cravings, head for the **Donut Hole,** in Destin on US 98 East (tel. 837-8824), or **Joe & Eddie's,** 206 Florida Pl. SE in Fort Walton, both open 24 hours. . . . For groceries any time of day or night, try **Jitney Jungle Grocery,** US 98 East (tel. 837-6224), or **Delchamp's,** 904 Mary Esther Cut-off (tel. 243-5383). . . . **Super X Drugs,** in the Fort Walton Square Shopping Center (tel. 243-4013), is open 24 hours. . . . You can get color prints back in 55 minutes from **55 Minute Photo,** Fort Walton Square (tel. 244-1055).

GETTING YOUR BEARINGS: Nearly all the activity in Fort Walton Beach and Destin is centered around US 98, which travels east-west along the beaches. Most addresses on US 98 west of Fort Walton Beach have a W (for west) tacked on them. In Destin, most addresses are US 98E (for east). US 98 is also called Miracle Strip Parkway.

HOTELS: In this area, hotels are located on US 98 which runs through the beach area of Fort Walton and Destin, or on Okaloosa Island just south of the Brooks Bridge over Santa Rosa Sound. I've divided them up by city and in descending order by price.

Fort Walton

Regency Beach Resort, US 98 or Miracle Strip Parkway, Fort Walton Beach, FL 32548 (tel. 904/243-9161, or toll free 800/447-0010), is Fort Walton's top spot, and what a showplace it is! Start with a huge swimming pool in the center of which are towering rocks with waterfalls cascading over them and a grotto bar you can swim to. Move on to the rustic Buccaneer Lounge, where the bar is rigged with pirate ship sails, or to the Pelican's Roost, where you can feast on crab claws and frosty oysters on the half shell, or to Nero's Nook, where toga-clad maidens serve drinks amid Roman pillars.

Shape up after a lobster dinner at the Lobster House Restaurant with a trip to the resort's spa, complete with indoor heated pool, whirlpool, saunas, and steam and exercise rooms.

Rooms here have wall murals, dark carpets, and contemporary furnishings. There are suites with kitchenettes and separate bedrooms, some with murphy beds. Outside, 800 feet of that Panhandle sand is stripped across the front of this 450-room inn. Add tennis courts, a kiddie pool, game room, and extras like a patio snackbar and bayou country barbecues by the pool, and you have the makings of one very impressive spot. For this you naturally pay top dollar, with peak summer-season rates of $80 to $110 double, dropping to $35 to $60 from September to March.

The **Conquistador Inn,** 847 Venus Court, Fort Walton Beach, FL 32548 (tel. 904/244-6155), is an imposing six-story building hunkered down behind a tall white sand dune. Apartments have their own patios or balconies overlooking the dune, although you'll have to go up a couple of stories to see over it to the gulf. Motel rooms are available, but the apartments are especially nice here, with small kitchens separated from living rooms by an open kitchen bar. One- and two-bedroom apartments have large kitchens, plus spacious living and dining areas decorated in ocean shades. There's a pool and wooden walkways across the dunes. Rates in summer are $70 for a spacious apartment, $100 for larger quarters. Children under 6 stay free, others pay $5, and you can bring your pet for a $5-a-day charge. In winter, prices drop to $35 to $50.

For a real look at Fort Walton's carefree beachside living, zip up to the fourth floor of **Carousel Motel and Apartments,** 571 Santa Rosa Blvd., Fort Walton Beach, FL 32548 (tel. 904/243-7658), and slip into the Stowaway Lounge. Plunk down in a rattan chair, order something cool, and while away the day staring out over the rippling waters of the gulf. The Carousel is a family-oriented operation with game room, boutique, two swimming pools, shuffleboard, and beachside gazebos. There are 107 handsome, recently redecorated rooms in a cluster of buildings, many with balconies overlooking the dunes. Rooms are very large and now feature soft contemporary colors. Some have couches or kitchens and snackbars. Summer rates range from $68 for a motel room or efficiency, to $70 to $78 for one-bedroom apartments.

Sheraton Coronado Beach Resort, US 98, 1325 Miracle Strip Pkwy., Fort Walton Beach, FL 32548 (tel. 904/243-8116, or toll free 800/874-8104), is brick inside and out. The spacious bedrooms with two double beds even have an entire wall of it behind the headboards. Vibrant colors brighten all that brick, and rooms are so large that the Coronado has added couches from which you can gaze through sliding glass doors at an entrancing view of the resort's extensive gardens and the gulf beyond. The Coronado has all the extras you'd expect in a

154-room resort, from wading pool and play equipment to refrigerators in rooms, kitchenettes, game room, restaurant, and lounge. Rates in peak summer season are $75 to $100 for rooms, dropping about 30% in other months.

Tiny Holiday Terrace, at 663 Nautilus Court, Fort Walton Beach, FL 32548 (tel. 904/243-8326), is a cozy spot with just five one- or two-bedroom apartments ranging from $75 to $85 a night—and that's for up to six people. I especially like one second-story apartment with a sleek navy and yellow couch, contemporary touches, and two bedrooms, one with a sliding door separating it from the living room and a second door opening onto a private balcony overlooking the sea. The friendly management will be happy to show you their unusual antique wooden file cabinets and introduce you to their collection of parrots and finches.

You can have all that beach for less money at **Driftwood Motel and Apartments,** 683 Nautilus Court, Fort Walton Beach, FL 32548 (tel. 904/243-1716). Driftwood charges just $26 to $36 for efficiencies or one-bedroom apartments from Memorial Day to Labor Day, but requires a three-day stay on weekends and holidays during those months. Accommodations here are quite basic, but the price is low, there's a nice tiled pool to play in, and the beach is just a few steps away.

Another good value for your vacation dollar is the **Sandman Motel and Apartments,** 480 Santa Rosa Blvd., Fort Walton Beach, FL 32548 (tel. 904/243-1511), a spic-and-span spot with full kitchens and bars, tiled baths and large closets, living room, and separate bedrooms, all right on the gulf. Outside, there's a mottled brick facade, shingled mansard roof, and a sparkling pool. Best of all are the rates—just $48 to $80 for one- or two-bedroom accommodations.

If you can sacrifice beachside location, the **Greenwood Motel,** US 98E, Fort Walton Beach, FL 32548 (tel. 904/244-1141), on the Choctawhatchee Bay, makes up in tranquility and friendly management what you might miss in sand. Rates for these paneled and attractively furnished bedrooms with a homey air about them are nice too: just $34 a day double in summer for a bedroom, $42 for up to four people, and there are two-bedroom apartments for $78 a day (extra guests are $4). Some rooms have balconies overlooking a large pool, and a few even offer views of the bay. The beach is just across the highway.

Vacation and business travelers flock to **Howard Johnson's,** 314 Miracle Strip Pkwy., Fort Walton Beach, FL 32548 (tel. 904/243-6162, or toll free 800/654-2000), at least partly for its proximity to Eglin Air Force Base, but especially for its pleasant waterside (but not ocean) location. In a manicured central courtyard magnolia trees blossom in spring, and tall river oaks shade a big swimming pool. Ask for a room overlooking the courtyard, and don't miss having dinner in the hotel's Rib Room, a second-floor aerie that was a prototype for the chain's Red Coach Grilles (dinner prices are about $10 to $12). You'll pay $54 to $59 double, year round, with slightly higher rates during holidays or special events.

Destin

You aren't going to have to read far before you discover that I love the **Sandestin Beach Hilton,** US 98, Destin, FL 32541 (tel. 904/267-5000, and toll-free numbers in every state). Who wouldn't adore a hotel that brings you milk and cookies each evening? Sure enough, that's what they do here, presenting you with a little carton of milk prettily propped up in an ice bucket and accompanied by a little plate of chocolate cookies. Now I ask you!

That's not all they do, of course. They also provide you with very, very large rooms that are the most perfect rooms possible for families: in the foyer of each room, tucked neatly away along one side, are two bunk beds the youngsters are going to love. Parents granted a little privacy in the room beyond those bunks are likely to feel pretty pleased with them too. As if that's not enough, the rooms are also outfitted with big closets, a sink and dressing area outside the bathroom as well as in it, a hair dryer, shampoo, hair conditioner, lotion, even suntan oil. Am I finished raving on here? Not on your life. Set into the wall, and virtually invisible, is a refrigerator, a small hotplate adorned with a bright-blue enamel tea kettle, and a tiny stainless-steel sink.

Now downstairs in the lobby, you'll pass by a lovely multilevel dining room ($12 to $17 price range for dinner) and a swimming pool both inside and outside the building! Add to that a cute little fleet of custom-designed Jeeps for you to putt about in, a 36-hole golf course, 24 indoor and outdoor tennis courts with grass, clay, and hard-top surfaces, sauna, boutiques, game room, movie theater, open-air seafood restaurant, cocktail lounge in a Tiki hut, water-sports facilities, and even a youth program to keep the youngsters occupied. Now what else could you possibly want?

Rates at the big new hotel on the sands at Sandestin are $85 to $160 from June to September, dropping to $55 to $115 from mid-November to mid-March and rising about $15 in the hotel's intermediate season from mid-March to June and from September to mid-November.

Proof that people are discovering this long-asleep coast is the appearance of not one but two major condominium resorts: **Seascape Resort,** US 98E (P.O. Box 970), Destin, FL 32541 (tel. 904/837-9181, or toll free 800/874-8104). Seascape, seven miles east of Destin, sprawls across acres and acres of Destin dunes at Miramar Beach. When you check in they'll give you a resort map, and you'll need it to find your way around this sprawling cluster of rustic wood-sided condominiums. There's a labyrinth of roads winding around a golf course, tennis courts, pools, lakes, playgrounds. And there's a gulfside beach and a beach club where you'll find dining, dancing, and entertainment in a handsome restaurant and attractive lounge. Explaining the resort's rate structure could take several pages, but basic prices range in peak summer season from $85 to $165 for villa apartments with kitchens, living rooms, queen-size beds, and one to three bedrooms. In other seasons, prices drop about 25%.

Sandestin, on US 98E, Destin, FL 32541 (tel. 904/837-2121, or toll free 800/874-2184), is a few miles farther east and a study in modernity with striking angular lines on its 164 sloped-roof condominium villa town houses. In the center of the resort are miles of manicured golf course. Sandestin is a very posh place with all the finest accoutrements of upper-crust condominium living: beamed ceilings, split-level apartments all individually and beautifully decorated, bicycles, games of all kinds, a spa, lounges and a handsome candlelit dining room, 48 acres of lakes, tennis on honest-to-Wimbledon grass courts (the only grass ones in the state), and 18 holes of golf (two holes of which were tagged "the lawn for the Taj Mahal" by *Golf Digest*). Outside on 440 acres of grounds you can watch porpoises playing on Choctawhatchee Bay or sit on the resort's gulfside beach. Rates for a wide variety of rooms, villas, and apartments are $75 to $200 double. Children under 16 stay free, and in December rates drop a bit.

In the slightly less elevated financial brackets is a pretty place dubbed **Robroy Lodge and Marina,** on US 98E (P.O. Box 725), Destin, FL 32541 (tel. 904/837-6713). This standout resort in Destin comes complete with its own charter fishing boat. Set high over a gulf inlet (well, high for Florida), Robroy has perfectly manicured grounds with sweeps of grass and plants trimmed to a fare-thee-well. There's a small pool and a tiny rectangle of sand the resort calls its "sandbox for people who just *have* to have sand." Even the simplest rooms here are marvelously spacious, and kept trim and shining with bright sunny colors. You can stow away here in the Staterooms, the Captain's Quarters (with kitchens), or a super-spacious Admiral's Suite, with its own balcony overlooking the gulf. Prices begin at $30 for Staterooms and rise to $49 to $60 for rooms with kitchenettes, $65 to $104 for the Admiral's Suite. In winter season prices drop as low as $275 a week for kitchenette suites, $24 a day for motel rooms.

Many accommodations in the Destin area are privately owned cottages, homes, or clusters of homes rented by a central agency. Prices vary, of course, according to the quality of the properties, but any of the companies will be happy to send you information on homes or cottages that will be just right for you. Among those with whom you should check if you're interested in a private house or cottage is **Gulfside Cottages,** operated by Earl Ugedahl and Harry Walley, on US 98E, Destin, FL 32541 (tel. 904/837-2400), who have cottages with names like Skyward, Bimini, Viking, and Stilts I, for summer prices ranging from $200 to $750 a week, $200 to $500 per month in winter.

Sea Cabins, on US 98E, Destin, FL 32541 (tel. 904/837-9705), about six miles east of Destin, is a bit of a departure from the usual accommodations: they really are cabins by the sea, although these cabins are strictly uptown variety. Open for its first full season in 1980, the resort is a collection of two-bedroom patio homes next door to rustic seascape. Right on the gulf, Sea Cabins likes to point out that it's only one tank of gasoline from most southern cities. All you need is your toothbrush, for patio homes have loft walk-in closets and living rooms that convert to sleeping quarters at night. You could hardly ask for more in the kitchens: they're equipped with ice-making refrigerators, disposals, even coffee makers. What's better yet is the price: just $50 a day in peak summer season.

A Lovely New Addition

Since I last updated this book there's been a fabulous addition to what was once deserted beachfront between Destin and Panama City. **Rose Walk Cottages,** Route C-30A, Point Washington, FL 32454 (tel. 904/231-4224), is a new development in a brand-new village called Seaside, which is not an easy place to find but is worth the search. (To get there, take a very close look at a map and locate Route C-30A, which runs parallel to US 98 but right alongside the ocean from just east of Destin.)

Sooner or later you'll see Cape Cod looming up before your amazed eyes! Looking every bit like a pastel mirage, Rose Walk Cottages is actually a very carefully planned community of wood-sided, often oddly shaped little cottages painted in delicate pastels reminiscent of perhaps Bermuda or a Caribbean island. Although these are privately owned or for-sale homes-away-from-home dwellings, many of them are part of a central pool of cottages that can be rented by vacationers. My favorite is a hexagonal charmer that is really just one big room decorated with paddle fans and white wicker furniture. A teensy bedroom is tucked away behind louvered doors, as is a bath and kitchen. Adorable.

You'll also find three-story towers here, with one room on each story, and two-story cottages with lofts and some of the loveliest countrified-tropical decor in the state. Although it's quite a difficult place to describe, Seaside and its Rose Walk Cottages are quite an easy place to live with—and in. And I, for one, am certainly ready to give it a try.

Seaside was just getting under way in 1985 and will probably have construction going on for several years yet, but it's well on its way to being one of the state's most innovative—and most written-about— developments. Certainly they have done everything here to preserve the windswept-dune look of it all, to maintain ecological balance and to create a development that proves there is the occasional artist among the state's many mundane developers. Even a little shopping center is something to be seen. Instead of a blank-faced row of stores, this "mall" is a cluster of small one-room wood-sided buildings in which sellers set up the wares in and around the doorway. Seaside's developers also plan to have outdoor theater performances here in busy summer months.

In the summer months, from March to September, rates for most cottages are $120 a night or $700 a week, with two cottages available for $95 or $135 a night. Add to any rental the usual state tax (5% in Florida) and a one-time fee of $40 for cleaning. You'll also find a cute little basket full of croissants, wine, and soft drinks included in the price. From September to March rates drop to $75 a night.

If you have an interest in architecture, drive over here some day just to see what's going on. Plan to incorporate a stop at a lyrically lovely little café, fittingly called Paradise Café at Grayton Beach (tel. 231-4501). You'll find the café on Route 30A in the infinitesimal village of Grayton Beach. Skip Kirkland and Johnny Earles run the place, whipping up such delicacies as crabmeat Louisianne featuring fresh lump crabmeat sauteed with roasted almonds and Créole spices; butterflied jumbo shrimp stuffed with crabmeat, wrapped in bacon, and broiled over charcoal; tenderloin filet flanked with fat shrimp; and fish right out of the seas a block away. Prices are in the $12 to $19 range for dinner, salad, and potato, served in a tropical atmosphere outfitted in royal blue and white and adorned with plenty of plants. Check to be sure they're open before you trek on out here, however. Hours are 5 to 10 p.m. daily.

Camping
Fred Gannon State Park is on Rocky Bayou, north of Eglin Air Force Base off Route 20 (tel. 904/897-3222), and has campsites for $9 with electricity, for $7 without. There's a swimming area, fishing in Puddin' Head Lake, two nature trails, and evening presentations by park rangers.

RESTAURANTS: Back in 1931 brothers Cecil and Docie Bass turned a service station into **Staff's Restaurant,** 24 Miracle Strip Pkwy. (tel. 243-3482). Before long Model As were lined up outside (not for gasoline but for dinner!). Three generations later the Bass family is still dishing up delectables in a nautical atmosphere. Along the way this historic restaurant has housed a grocery, the first Western Union office and radio station, and has even been a hurricane shelter on occasion. Staff's staff has also played host to a host of luminaries from John Wayne to Bob Hope, Rosalyn Carter, Helen Gurley Brown, Cornelia Wallace, and Spencer Tracy, all of whom came to sample oyster stew and seafood gumbo, a creamy seafood casserole, and Staff's locally famous seafood platter. With all that history and those trend-maker drop-ins you'd expect to pay plenty, but you won't: menu prices start at just $5.50, and a brimming seafood platter for two is just $18.50. My favorite, called "shrimp in shorts," is fat gulf shrimp wrapped in bacon and deep-fried. It's open from 5 to 10 p.m. (closed Thursday).

If you like rustic, you should love the **Back Porch,** US 98E (tel. 837-2022), where the tables are wood, the floor is wood, the fare is simple seafood, and the view from this second-floor perch is terrific. There is absolutely nothing even remotely approaching atmosphere here, but perhaps that in itself is atmospheric. Suffice to say that if you ask local residents where to go for seafood, this place is sure to be mentioned. Prices may have something to do with that: they rarely top $10. Hours at the Back Porch are 11 a.m. to 11 p.m. daily.

Another new restaurant in town—well, new to me anyway—is **Louisiana Lagniappe,** Holiday Isle, in Sandpiper Cove Condominium, off Gulf Shore Drive (tel. 837-0881). A big, airy restaurant with lots of tall windows, this attractive spot specializes, fittingly enough, in those Cajun flavors. You'll find crawfish and chicken gumbos on the menu, along with trout prepared several ways (including topped with crawfish and mushrooms), and lots of local seafood treats. Lagniappe is open 5 to 10 p.m. daily and is a bit hard to find—it's in the middle of a condominium complex, but you'll be all right if you follow the signs and don't be put off by the presence of security guards at the entrance to the condominiums. They'll be happy to show you the way to the restaurant.

Leather wing chairs, plants, dim lights, and an attractive bar set the tone at **The Landing Restaurant,** 225 Miracle Strip Pkwy. (tel. 244-7134). You dine well and comfortably here at this steak and seafood haven on thick steaks, shrimp in several different preparations including a crispy shrimp tempura, snapper parmesan—all served with salad, potato, and hot breads. Prices are quite reasonable at this very large restaurant, falling easily into the $8 to $12 range. Hours at the Landing are 11 a.m. to 10 p.m. daily (except Saturday, when the restaurant is open only from 5 to 10 p.m.).

Channel House Restaurant, 104 Miracle Strip Pkwy. (tel. 243-5320), is a cute little cottagey place right on the water. Once again seafood tops the menu, but you can find a couple of landlubber's selections as well. Good cooking, and a romantic, intimate atmosphere are the chief selling points. Channel House is open from 5 to 10 p.m. daily, and won't break the bank: prices are easily in the $10 to $15 range for dinner.

You can't miss **Pandora's Steakhouse,** 1120 Santa Rosa Blvd. (tel. 244-8669)—just look for the beached yacht sitting smugly out there amid sand and parking lot in the middle of Okaloosa Island. Hop aboard for drinks in the yacht, then amble down the gangplank to the restaurant's lower level where hammered copper chandeliers glimmer on hefty wood beams. Meats are cut daily in the restaurant's kitchens and cooked over a wood-burning pit for prices in the $8 to $11 bracket, including Pandora's homemade breads. Open 5 to 11 p.m. daily.

Sand fleas aren't something you usually search out, but do seek the **Sand Flea Restaurant,** at Santa Rosa Boulevard and Siebert Street (tel. 243-2716), a woodsy, rustic spot just north of the Brooks Bridge on the west side. The Sand Flea has an oyster bar where they shuck 'em while you wait, and inexpensive seafood in the $9.25 to $12.95 range. There's entertainment nightly too, at Carney's Irish Pub. The Sand Flea is open for lunch from 11:30 a.m. to 2:30 p.m., for dinner from 5 to 10 p.m. daily.

If you like authenticity, pull up a cushion on the tatami mats at **Nikko Inn,** 310 Perry Ave. SE (tel. 244-4188). If your knees aren't up to that test, there are American-style chairs at this intimate dining room where a hostess in a kimono leads you through rooms with rafters full of Japanese lanterns, enameled trays, tiny tea bowls, and saki cups that whistle. Dine on everything from appetizers to fortune cookies and a Genghis Khan presentation made in an iron cooker that both sizzles meat and steams vegetables in meat juices. Complete dinners are in the $8 to $18 range; slightly abbreviated versions, about $10 to $12. Hours are 5 to 10 p.m. every day but Monday.

Everyone for miles around recommends **Scampi's,** US 98E, Destin (tel. 837-7686), and they're right! A two-story shingled building across from the beach, Scampi's has a long bar and lounge, dining on a mezzanine level, and more dining up on the second floor. Large as it is, it's often filled with diners who come here for a big bowl of spicy seafood gumbo or oyster chowder, a pound or so of Louisiana crawfish, a dozen or so Apalachicola oysters, or a platter of fried, grilled, or broiled seafood.

Atmosphere is casual but attractive, and prices are in the $12 to $15 range for entree, salad, potato, and french bread. Really starving gourmands can stuff themselves with a steambuck for two that includes stone crab claws, shrimp, local oysters, snowcrab, Louisiana crawfish, new potatoes, corn on the cob, salad, and french bread (about $30 for two). You can even get a local specialty called scamp (no, it's not scampi, but a fish) here occasionally. Hours are 5 to 10 p.m. daily.

Jamaica Joe's, 785 Sundial Court, Okaloosa Island (tel. 244-4137), is a typically tropical kind of place with two large dining rooms overlooking the sea. High-backed wicker chairs fill every space not occupied by plants or paddle fans, and a waterfall ripples over some rocks to provide a view for those bored with the seascapes. On the menu is a wide range of seafood from char-broiled amberjack to flounder, jumbo shrimp, grouper parmesan, and plenty of oysters (less than $3 a dozen). You can have seafood steamed, fried, broiled, or combined on gargantuan platters here for prices in the $10 to $15 bracket. Hours are 11 a.m. to 11 p.m. daily.

Destinees, on US 98 (tel. 244-4061), is another newcomer up this way, a big, sprawling restaurant with lots of glass, candlelight, and bay views. Entrees, which range in price from $10 to $14 and include lots of local seafood, juicy prime rib, and steaks, are half price from opening hour at 4:30 p.m. to 7 p.m., and those prices include soup or salad, freshly baked bread, and potato. If you'd like to sample a range of local seafood, try the First Mate's Platter, which includes shrimp, scallops, fish, oysters, and deviled crab. Destinees closes at 9:30 p.m. daily, at 10 p.m. on weekends.

Pizza? Try **BJ's Pizza Parlor,** at Mary Esther Cut-off in Fort Walton Beach (tel. 243-2052), where a 12-inch creation ranges in price from $5 to $7.

When you're in the mood for a romantic, tranquil evening (I hope that's not a contradiction in terms) in lovely, formal surroundings, try the **Beachside Café and Bar,** 958 Gulfshore Dr., Destin (tel. 837-1272). Here you can dine with candlelight and roses, starched linens and formal service on quite a wonderful menu. Try, for instance, shrimp bisque, followed by a watercress salad. Then move on to snapper with two sauces, fettuccine Alfredo with pistachios, or angel-hair pasta with shrimp, snow peas, and ginger beurre-blanc. Traditionalists have several steak options. Dinner entrees, which range in price from $10 to $15, include perfectly cooked vegetables and salad. Beachside is open daily except Monday from 6 to 10 p.m. October through March, and daily in the summer months. An adjoining bar is a quiet but popular gathering spot too.

Sooner or later everyone in Fort Walton turns up at **Perri's Ristorante,** 300 Eglin Pkwy. (tel. 862-4421), the hands-down favorite Italian restaurant in town. A columned walkway and imposing double-door entrance to the brick building add the mandatory Roman touches. Inside, arched windows and plants, tile floors, and wall murals of Italian villas keep the theme going. Chef-owner Vittorio Perri has created a full menu of Italian specialties featuring some things you don't see often enough in Florida, saltimbocca alla romana and some Bolognese preparations. Hours Tuesday through Thursday are 5 to 10 p.m., on Friday and Saturday to 10:45 p.m. Perri's prices are in a moderate $6 to $11 bracket.

For a waterside location and cozy old-house atmosphere, **The Sound,** on US 98 (tel. 243-7772), gets my vote. Snuggled in beside the tranquil waters of Santa Rosa Sound, the restaurant has handsome views of the water and an inviting, homey air that's hard to leave. Seafood is the specialty here too, and the Sound offers 18 different preparations of it, from fried soft-shell crabs to seafood St. Jacques. You can dine à la carte for about $7 to $15. Open from 11 a.m. daily, the Sound is back off the highway on the western outskirts of Fort Walton Beach.

You could spend days trying out the several restaurants at the **Regency Beach,** on US 98 (tel. 243-9161), where you can choose your atmosphere and your menu from seafood to southern cooking. (See "Hotels" for more information.)

Liollio's on the Sound, 14 Miracle Strip Pkwy. (tel. 243-5011), plays to a full house nightly as families throng here to dine on steaks and seafood with a Greek touch. Hosts John Georgiades and Paul Liollio produce a wide variety of choices, but don't miss the whole baby snapper and super-size Greek salad. Windows overlook the Intracoastal Waterway and marina, candles blaze, and the happy chatter of tucking-in diners fills the air. Your bill will probably fall somewhere between $10 and $13. It's open from 11 a.m. to 11 p.m., later on weekends (closed Sunday). There's live entertainment in the lounge.

If you're in a go-as-you-are mood, go as you are over to **Capt. Dave's at Destin Harbor,** on US 98 (tel. 837-6357). A family get-away spot, Capt. Dave's guarantees some of the freshest seafood anywhere, since the captain has only to reach his hand through the window to retrieve it from the fishing fleet that docks here. This was a favorite stopping spot for stars and crew working on the movie *Jaws II*. Prices for simply prepared seafood dishes are in the $11 to $15 bracket, and Capt. Dave's is open from 4:30 to 10 p.m. daily.

Some morning or afternoon, or anytime for that matter (and I do mean *anytime*), head over to the **Donut Hole,** 635 US 98W, Destin (tel. 837-8824), where you'll find terrific fresh-baked donuts in an atmosphere that takes rustic to new heights. Pay no attention to the "modest going on decrepit" atmosphere, for the Donut Hole turns out some yummy crullers and good coffee 24 hours a day.

One of Destin's showplaces is the revolving restaurant at the **Holiday Inn,** on US 98 (tel. 837-6181). You're guaranteed a view here. As a matter of fact, you're guaranteed *all* the views possible here as you turn ever-so-slowly high above the shimmering waters of the gulf. Tinted glass shields you from glare as you dine amid tropical rattan in shades of peach and russet. Dinner entrees are $10 to $15. Open 11 a.m. to 2 p.m. and 5 to 10 p.m. daily in summer, shorter hours in winter.

Seascape and **Sandestin** both have beautiful dining rooms overlooking those equally beautiful resorts. If you like elegant dining with surroundings to match, try these two sprawling resorts (see my hotel recommendations).

NIGHTLIFE: This area's emphasis on family vacations means you won't find many bespangled dancing girls, but you'll still have plenty to do evenings in the larger hotels, all of which have nightly or weekend entertainment, particularly in summer.

If you'd like to roam from nightspot to nightspot without traveling very far, head for the **Regency Beach Resort,** on US 98 (tel. 243-9161), where there's entertainment at Nero's Nook, Buccaneer Lounge, and the Pelican's Roost.

Both **Sandestin** and **Seascape** in Destin have entertainment in their lounges, and the Destin **Holiday Inn's** Hawaiki Lounge has music for listening.

One of the nicest nightclubs in the area is **Nightown,** at the corner of Palmetto and Azalea, just off US 98 (tel. 837-6448), which often features rock groups. If you're looking for something a little less frenetic, **Nightown's Other Bar** has easy-listening music.

At **Victor's,** 113 S. Eglin Pkwy., Fort Walton (tel. 243-1227), crowds gather for 35¢ drinks, $1 nights, and Beat-the-Clock evenings. Another favorite college crowd hang-out is **Cash Moore's Faux Pas Lounge,** 106 Santa Rosa Blvd. (tel. 244-2274), where you'll see Cash's Rolls-Royce parked outside. He operates other lounges: **Smuggler's,** at 320 John Sims Pkwy. (tel. 678-2913), and **Bachelor I** and **Cloud 9,** at 221 Miracle Strip Pkwy. (tel. 243-0833). **Barefoot**

Club, on US 98 in downtown Fort Walton Beach (tel. 243-5038), is a rock and roll club too.

For sheer hanging out on hot afternoons or lazy evenings, you can't beat a little hideaway with the enchanting name of **Hog's Breath Saloon,** 1239 Siebert St. (tel. 243-4646). It's a rustic (definitely) spot just northwest of the Brooks Bridge. The **Back Porch,** US 98 East in Destin, is similar.

If you're of a more cultural bent, Fort Walton has a ballet association, a concert group, a symphony, a community theater, and a community chorus. They all give concerts at different times of the year (but mostly in winter months) and the chamber of commerce can tell you where and when they are.

Those entranced by the sight of females in various states of undress will find that going on at the **Matador Club,** Old Eastgate Road in Valparaiso (tel. 678-1812), and **Carmicheal's Surf Side 7,** 867 N. Eglin Pkwy. at Shalimar Bridge (tel. 862-9972), but these are not places for blushers.

For oyster fans, one of the best things about the Panhandle is the abundance of cheap oysters. You'll find none cheaper than those upstairs at the **Carney's Irish Pub,** corner of Santa Rosa Boulevard and Sibert Street on Okaloosa Island (tel. 243-6512 or 243-2716). A dozen oysters is just $1.75 at happy hour from 4:30 to 7 p.m., and just $1 at lunch. Carney's is a sing-along kind of spot with a piano bar, dancing, and inexpensive food. It's open 11:30 a.m. to 2:30 p.m. and 5 p.m. until the last imbiber rolls out, every day but Sunday.

THE SIGHTS: For a look at some other creatures who love the sea, look in at **Gulfarium,** on US 98E (tel. 244-5169). Penguins strut about in their Sunday best, seals entertain, porpoises perform, and shows are continuous from 10 a.m. to 4 p.m. Admission is $6.

Bill and Yulee Lazarus, two dedicated historians, trailed the gas company as it installed lines in the area and preserved historic remains of the ancient Indians who lived here. You can see the results of their efforts at **Indian Temple Mound and Museum,** 139 Miracle Strip Pkwy. (tel. 243-6521). Exhibits in the museum (now owned by the city) depict 10,000 years of life in this Choctawhatchee Bay area. Hours are 11 a.m. to 4 p.m. Tuesday through Saturday, from 1 to 4 p.m. on Sunday. Admission is 50¢ for adults; children under 10 are free.

You'll want to take a look at **Eglin Air Force Base,** which covers more than 700 square miles of land, into which you could fit the whole state of Rhode Island. Doolittle's Tokyo Raiders trained here for their raid against Imperial Japan, and equipment that destroyed Nazi Germany's buzz-bomb launchers was created here. The Son Tay Raiders, who tried to rescue Americans from North Vietnamese prison camps, worked here too. Bus tours of the base depart at 1:30 p.m. on Tuesday and Thursday in June, July, and August from the Foster Stadium parking lot on the base. Call 244-8191 for information on the time of the tours.

One of the loveliest sights in the area is **Eden State Ornamental Gardens,** the jewel of which is a perfectly restored mansion brimming with antiques. Part of the glory of Eden is its isolation, on a tiny, almost-overgrown road (turn north of US 98E at Port Washington). Time slips away on this road, and when you see delicate white columns and verandaed elegance of Eden, it's gone completely. You're back in another era, realizing suddenly why people fought so bitter a war to keep lands and lifestyles like this intact. Admission is $1, and a guide takes you through the home and explains its furnishings and history, daily from 9 a.m. to 4 p.m. May through September (closed Wednesday and Thursday in other months). You can wander around the fabulously beautiful plantation grounds and picnic here if you like.

About an hour north of the beach is Florida's largest state forest, **Blackwa-**

ter River, where you can roam among 183,000 acres of pine, juniper, and oak, swim in spring-fed lakes and sand-bottomed streams, or hike a 20-mile trail that was once a trade route between Spanish Pensacola and the Creek Indian nation.

Near here too are six other state parks: **Florida Caverns** at Marianna, **Torreya** at Bristol, **Ochlockonee River** near Sopchoppy, **Suwanee** near Live Oak, **O'Leon** near Lake City, and **Manatee Springs** near Chiefland. You can camp in any of them for $9 a night including electricity, $7 without. A pamphlet published by the Department of Natural Resources showing locations and facilities of state parks is available by writing the department at Office of Education and Information, Room 321, Crown Building, Tallahassee (tel. 904/488-3300).

Finally, once a year Fort Walton and Destin (and most of the rest of the Panhandle) celebrate the days when a canny character named Billy Bowlegs built himself a motley crew of Indians, army deserters, and bandits, and named himself King of Florida. He played force against force with such skill that he managed to fill his own treasure chests to the brim. Billy had a certain irrefutable style, and eventually had the whole coastline quaking at the sight of his flagship. Legend has it that much of Bowlegs's loot is still buried beneath the sands of Miracle Strip. You can search for it, or just settle for a go at $500 buried with clues during the annual **Billy Bowlegs Festival,** at the end of May.

SPORTS: There's lots of sports activity in these sunny towns.

Golf and Tennis

You can play on 12 lighted courts or practice on four walls at the **Fort Walton Beach Municipal Tennis Center,** 45 W. Audrey Dr. (tel. 243-8789), where the clubhouse has lockers, showers, and a lounge area. Fees are $2 a day. Courts at **Sandestin** and **Seascape Golf and Conference Center** also are open to the public. Fees are $6 to $10 an hour. (See my hotel recommendations.)

Fort Walton Municipal Golf Course, off Lewis Turner Boulevard and Mooney Road (tel. 862-3314), is a par-72 course, has 18 holes with a pro shop, and there are no tee times or cart rentals required. Greens fees are $8 and carts are $10 for 18 holes, both cheaper after 5 p.m. in summer.

Seascape Golf and Conference Center and **Sandestin,** both on US 98 in Destin, about 12 miles from Fort Walton, have 18-hole courses, tennis courts, and pro shops. Cart rental is required at Sandestin and fees are $15; cart, $12. At Seascape, greens fees are $15; cart, $12.

You can't miss **Magic Carpet Golf,** on US 98E (tel. 243-0020), with its fantasyland of towering sphinx, Buddha, and assorted other characters, so you might as well play it. Garish as it is, it's fun, and where else can you get an hour or two of entertainment for less than $5?

There's also a tiny **amusement park,** open daily in summer with rides at about 50¢.

Sailing and Water Sports

Sail away on a charter boat from **S & S Sailing,** at Deckhands Marine (Box 2232) on US 98E (tel. 243-2022). Sloops 37 feet long take up to six persons on three-hour cruises for $120, a full day for $225. S & S also runs a sailing school charging $200 for ten hours of instruction and rents 20-foot, four-person sloops at $35 for two hours, $60 for eight hours.

Most anything you can do in the water you can do at **PBS Watersports,** behind the Magic Carpet Golf Course on US 98 (tel. 244-2933), which offers parasailing, jet skis, surf jets, and waterskiing.

The **Scuba Shop,** at 230 N. Eglin Pkwy. in Mariner Plaza (tel. 863-1341), has equipment, instruction, and trips at about $30.

Fishing

It's downright thrilling to hook a sassy kingfish or watch a sleek marlin as it streaks through the water at speeds up to 60 miles an hour, the fastest fish in the sea. Prize-winning catches are practically ho-hum around here, and Destin humbly calls itself the "luckiest fishing village in the world." Certainly comedian Bob Hope and a host of other celebrities (not to mention hundreds of everyday Joe Fishermen) agree. Hope snagged a prize-winning blue marlin one year on his first fishing trip to the city, and won the city's prize for the biggest white marlin.

Destin's annual **fishing competitions** are many, but the best are the Cobia Derby in March and April, the October Fishing Rodeo, the billfish tournaments in August and September, and the bass-fishing competition in March.

You can seek the elusive devils of the deep from Okaloosa's pride, its **Island Pier** (tel. 244-1023), where you can drop a line 1261 feet out into the gulf for $1.50, from charter boats (which charge about $200 a half day), or from party boats (which charge about $20).

Canoeing

Paddle your own canoe on cool, clear, spring-fed rivers bordered by white sandy beaches as you burble merrily along through mile after mile of hauntingly lonely northern Florida landscape. Here turtles sun themselves on river logs and white-tailed deer frisk through forests or sip at the water's edge.

Every year more and more people discover northern Florida's enchanting rivers, but there are enough to easily absorb the 75,000 who took up paddle and knapsack last year. So popular is this area with canoeists that the sleepy village of Milton likes to call itself "Canoe Capital of Florida." So diverse are the offerings of the area's rivers that everyone from beginning paddler to rapids challenger can find a river to test his mettle.

Blackwater, for instance, has deep, mysterious dark waters stained (but definitely not polluted) by the tannic acid of the cypress trees that line its banks. Crystal-clear water is the trademark of **Coldwater River,** where you can stare through the shallows at black bass finning along the bottom and drink from springs you'll see trickling down the banks. **Sweetwater-Juniper River** is the most challenging, beginning with the twisting, turning, narrow, speedy Sweetwater Creek, where logs and stumps hove out of the clear water and require a steady hand at the paddle and some experience in this sport. It's worth the effort, though, for you to drift through a tunnel of overhanging trees and finally reach the Juniper River, whose clay bluffs reach as high as 80 feet in some spots with slick slides for a slithering entrance into the waters.

Centuries ago Florida's Indian tribes roamed and splashed in these waters, and eagle-eyed searchers can sometimes find artifacts left behind by long-ago hunters or fishermen. All along the banks of these rivers you can pick wild blueberries, blackberries, and dewberries for a snack, and collect fascinating whorled pine knots and cedar driftwood that can someday grace your coffee table and remind you of warm magic days in the cool, crystal waters of northern Florida.

If you'd like to try canoeing, **Adventures Unlimited,** P.O. Box 40, Bagdad, FL 32530 (tel. 904/623-6197), operates fascinating trips that wind through some of Florida's loveliest scenery. Four adventuring Sandborn family members guide the outings to Coldwater, Blackwater, Sweetwater-Juniper, and Perdido Rivers, and can outfit you for a canoe trip for $30 per person. Adventures Unlimited also owns a campground on Coldwater River at Tomahawk Landing.

Bob's Canoes, in Milton, is operated by Vern "Bob" Plowman, whose whole family has been in the canoe business since 1971. Marie Plowman takes reservations (tel. 904/623-5457) and escorts weekend trips to Coldwater Creek. One of the Plowman daughters oversees canoeing on Sweetwater-Juniper Creeks, and a son lives and works on Coldwater Creek. It takes about six hours, and canoes are rented for $7 a person a day, with trip rates varying. There are also tubing trips down Coldwater Creek with tubes for rent for $3. Bob's has recently built new headquarters in Coldwater where you can buy supplies, and sit in comfort while you're waiting to get started on this adventure.

3. Panama City/Panama City Beach

Panama City Beach is a Coney Island look-alike that looms up out of the sand dunes. Its streets are thronged with revelers, its rollercoaster zooms and zips, carousels turn, and cotton candy is spun ingloriously onto new playsuits.

From May to September there's hardly a room to be had anywhere when southern travelers flock here to spend their time in traffic jams as long as the Panhandle, wending at turtle speed to the amusement parks. Fraternities and sororities, teenagers, and toddlers find this sheer nirvana. Adults, whose child-like inner cores have some limitations, may only find it a test of nerves.

You will find, however, lots of silky-soft Panhandle sand, and if you choose with care there are many restful resorts where the klieg lights and cotton candy of the amusement park strip will spoil neither your tranquility nor your dinner.

Be forewarned, however, that once the kids see Panama City, you will have nary a moment's peace until all the amusements here are covered, so if you've done Disney already, you might consider routing yourself through lands farther north on I-10. (Lest Panama City think I mean all this unflatteringly, let me assure you that these amusement parks can make for days of laughing fun and games, and will certainly entertain the children.)

There are many lovely strips of sand here where you can sneak away for some sailing, scuba-diving, fishing, and comic relief. Restaurants are quite good, with wonderfully fresh seafood and very low prices. But above all there is a fun and funny atmosphere that proves once again how many different kinds of fantasies there are to fulfill. Panama City has proven itself equal to all tests.

GETTING THERE: Republic, Air New Orleans, and Dolphin Airways fly into Panama City.

Amtrak has a station in Dothan, Alabama, 79 miles away.

If you're driving to the city, you can get here on **US 98,** the main east-west artery and **US 231,** the main northern access road. Routes 77 and 79 connect with **I-10.**

GETTING YOUR BEARINGS: US 98 leads into the city from west to east, but once it gets there becomes Business 98. Most motels and restaurants and attractions are on **US 98A,** which is sometimes also called Scenic 98. It runs beside the beach and parallel to Business 98, which goes to a small downtown section. Many small highways connect Business 98 and 98A. One is Route 757, which goes from the western end of 98 south to Capt. Anderson's pier and to Thomas Drive (which is an extension of US 98A). Thomas Drive is also called Route 392, and goes to St. Andrews State Park. It's not as confusing as it sounds, but remember to check addresses carefully to see if they're on US 98A or on US 98. It will also help to know that address numbers on 98A get higher as you go west.

GETTING AROUND: Twelve **rental-car companies** operate here, topped by Hertz, Avis, Dollar, and National. You can rent a **moped** for $5 an hour from **Jet Winds,** 12705 W. US 98A (tel. 234-9427), or from **Bay Pointe Marina Water**

Sports Center, in the Bay Pointe Resort (tel. 234-6911), where you can also rent bikes for $5 a day.

Beach Taxi (tel. 234-5202) operates on Panama City Beach for $1.25 a mile and officially has a $5 minimum (but unofficially, doesn't usually stick to it).

VISITOR INFORMATION: The **Bay County Motel and Restaurant Association,** 12012 W. US 98, Panama City Beach, FL 32401 (tel. 904/234-3193), is across from Miracle Strip Park and keeps a list of vacancies, so they can help you find a room in the busy season from April through the first week of September. They're open from 8 a.m. to 5 p.m. Monday through Friday. . . . The **Bay County Chamber of Commerce,** 235 W. 5th St. (P.O. Box 1850), Panama City, FL 32402 (tel. 904/234-8224), can also help. . . . The **Bay City Resort Council of 100** has plenty of information on this area too, and will be happy to send it to you; contact them at 12015 W. US 98 (Box 7943), Panama City Beach, FL 32407 (tel. 904/234-6575, or toll free 800/874-7107). . . . For **police emergency** help, call 234-2285 on Panama City Beach. . . . Insomniacs can watch all-night movies at **Isle of View Drive-In,** 514 Everitt Ave., Springfield (tel. 785-4110). . . . If you see **flags flying on the beach,** here's what they mean: a red flag warns of a dangerous undertow, a yellow flag cautions you to beware of an undertow, and a blue flag means calm seas. No flag may not mean the sea is safe, so you'd be wise to ask a lifeguard daily for a sea condition report. . . . **Local publications** that keep you up-to-date on what's happening in town include *See* magazine and the *Panama City News-Herald.*

HOTELS: You'll find one long, long row of hotels and motels stretching along the sands from the western edges of the city right down to the amusement parks and beyond. I've selected a few I found appealing and grouped them by price category, from deluxe to budget.

The Luxury Leaders

Four floors streak skyward at **Sheraton Miracle Mile,** 9450 S. Thomas Dr., Panama City Beach, FL 32407 (tel. 904/234-3484, or toll free 800/325-3535), a contemporary resort nestled on the blue-green gulf waters. Sheraton delivers here, as it does elsewhere in the state, spacious rooms decorated in a contemporary style that matches its attractive exterior architecture. A wading pool for the children is a special feature, but they didn't forget adult swimmers—there's an attractive beachside pool surrounded by tables shaded by daisy-shaped umbrellas. Sailboat lessons are free, and an 18-hole golf course is just across the street (tennis courts are nearby). Evenings, the resort's Long John Silver lounge and garden-style restaurant are popular gathering spots. From May through August rates are $78 to $104; in other months, they drop to about half that amount. Several other hotels are associated with Sheraton in a marketing group called Miracle Mile Resort, 640 rooms in all at the same number.

If you're coming toward Panama City from the east and don't mind staying about 20 miles outside the city, **El Governor Motel,** on US 98 (Box 13374), Mexico Beach, FL 32410 (tel. 904/785-8843), is a sensational find in the small enclave of Mexico Beach, and may be one of the best buys in the Panhandle. Two very contemporary two-story houses have been converted, and El Governor has furnished these with shining chrome and velvet contemporary furniture, added walls of mirrors, plants, earth colors, a small snackbar, trim modern kitchens, wallpapered baths, and huge panes of tinted glass overlooking the sea. They're downright gorgeous and rent for $85 a day in summer, $80 in other months. Other rooms here are just as beautifully decorated, with bright contemporary looks and views of the sea, and rates are $47 in summer. There's also an annex in which rooms have not as yet been refurbished, but rates are cheaper: $35 in summer, as low as $22 in the winter months.

Bay Pointe Resort, off Thomas Drive at Grand Lagoon, 100 Delwood Beach Rd., Panama City, FL 32407 (tel. 904/234-3307, or toll free 800/874-7105), is Panama City's condominium development, a sprawling complex of contemporary buildings clustered around a 27-hole championship golf course. On its own peninsula off Thomas Drive at Magnolia Beach Road, Bay Pointe wraps around the Grand Lagoon and provides you with everything you could want in a self-contained resort: an excellent and elegant dining room, yacht and country club, marina, lighted tennis courts, a practice fairway, pro shops, snack-bar, dockmaster and store, sailboats and windsurfers for rent, L-shaped swimming pool, sauna and steambath, game room for the kids, freshwater lakes, bicycle paths. Did I forget to mention rooms? Do they ever have those! Condominium villas all individually decorated, so it's like staying in a friend's home: small studio villas with a folding partition to wall off the bedroom, or two-bedroom villas for two to six, or three-bedroom villas for as many as eight vacationers. Summer rates, from mid-March through the first week of September, are $75 to $100 for a one-bedroom studio villa, $140 to $150 for two bedrooms, and $160 to $185 for three bedrooms, depending on how many people you bring along. If you stay a week there's about a 20% reduction, and in winter rates drop $20 to $30 a day.

The Moderate Range

Georgian Terrace, 14415 W. US 98A, Panama City Beach, FL 32407 (tel. 904/234-2144), has one of the loveliest pool areas in the city, a tiled beauty covered in translucent plastic and surrounded by plants and groupings of outdoor furniture. A family-owned motel, Georgian Terrace charges rates beginning at $62 for four people, $72 for six, for rooms with kitchens, mid-May to mid-September (about half that in other months). Knotty-pine paneling gives those rooms a homey, rustic look sparked by bright colors on bedspreads and drapes and there are small private sunporches off all apartments.

If you read about restaurants first, then choose a place to stay near the best ones, take a look at **Rendezvous Inn,** 17281 W. US 98A, Panama City Beach, FL 32407 (tel. 904/234-8841), just across the street from the outstanding Boar's Head Restaurant (see my dining recommendations). Tennis fans will like it here too, as the resort has installed a tennis court for racqueteers. As for the rooms, they're very special, with white rattan furniture set off by light paneling and colors. From balconies you can view all the glories of the Panhandle since all rooms front on the gulf. For this you'll pay $54 to $64 for most accommodations, $72 to $85 for larger units.

You can have a party yourself at **Fiesta,** 13623 W. US 98A, Panama City Beach, FL 32407 (tel. 904/234-2179), where you'll find striking wrought-iron trim in a sunburst pattern that plays off the pink brick exterior walls and trim black doors of this large resort. All the very neat rooms overlook the ocean through a wall of glass, and many have private balconies or terraces. Wallpaper and tropical colors spark room decor, and kitchenettes are paneled in glowing woods. Outside, palms sway over the resort's tile-trimmed pool where you can watch the sailboats skim by in the gulf. Rates range from $54 to $62 for two people in high season, $76 to $82 for larger rooms accommodating four or six.

Flamingo Dome by the Sea, 15524 W. US 98, Panama City Beach, FL 32407 (tel. 904/234-2232), stole my heart. When you pass under the blue awnings and into its glorious courtyard, you step into another world, one in which owners Reggie and Linda Lancaster have proven what a little ingenuity can do with a basic motel. The Flamingo is built in a U-shape and atop it is a translucent canopy supported by a maze of wood trusses. Underneath, a pool is snuggled amid so much greenery you'll think you've lost your way in a jungle! Palms soar to the dome and tiny walkways wend through hundreds of banana trees, palmettos, ferns, and all manner of emerald-green tropical plants. A fabulously exotic place, Flamingo has huge walls of glass, and rooms decorated in cozy woods offset by bright spreads and drapes. This is my choice of many, many, and I'd gladly pay whatever they ask. Fortunately, they're only asking $39 to $54 for hotel rooms, $39 to $90 for rooms with kitchenettes accommodating four, with additional people charged $3 each. Some rooms can accommodate up to six people. Prices drop about 30% from September to May.

Budget Choices

Another special favorite of mine in the Sunnyside Beach area is **Wave-Crest Court,** at Kiska Beach, Panama City Beach, FL 32407 (tel. 904/234-2244), where you're welcomed at a little glass-ensconced kiosk reception area. Wave-Crest is an exceptionally trim brick building and inside are accommodations equally trim. About 20 miles west of Panama City, the resort has simple furniture, bright decor, and lovely glass-enclosed porches overlooking the water. Cotton bedspreads give the rooms a nice beach-tropical look, and pine-paneled kitchens are pleasant rustic additions. For everyone the view is downright gorgeous. What's just as gorgeous are the prices: $46 to $72 in summer season only (they're closed from October to March). A two-bedroom cottage on the beach is also for rent, for rates up to $76.

For an attractive, simple place, I'd choose **Gulfside Motel,** at 22217 W. US 98A, Panama City Beach, FL 32407 (tel. 904/234-2871), built high on a dune overlooking the sea. With all that sand outside, Gulfside has opted for a distinctly beachy look, from simple uncarpeted terrazzo floors to knotty-pine paneling and basic durable furnishings. Bright colors pep things up, and the view from the pool and various spots on the grounds is devastatingly lovely. Some units are right on that beautiful strip of beach, and there are barbecue grills for simple dinners and beach umbrellas for a respite from the sun. Efficiency apartments are $49 to $52; more spacious accommodations designed for larger families or groups range from $78 to $98.

On the outer fringes of Panama City life is quieter, and here you'll find the **Sugar Sands Motel,** 20709 W. US 98A, Panama City Beach, FL 32407 (tel. 904/234-8802), where a friendly, drawling southern owner is working hard, redoing several buildings a few at a time. The newly refurbished ones are especially nice, with lots of paneling and attractive contemporary furnishings and colors, sometimes a view of the water. Right on the sands that gave this motel its name, Sugar Sands has a variety of one- and two-bedroom accommodations as well as motel rooms. Prices begin at $50 a day for motel rooms, rising to $58 to $75 for two-bedroom accommodations. There's a 60% reduction in winter, and about 20% off after Labor Day.

Camping

St. Andrews Recreation Area, at the end of Route 392 and right on the gulf, is a 1063-acre paradise of beach, dune, pine woods, and marshes. Beautiful clear waters and white beaches are irresistible, and this is an enchanting place for camping. Admission is 50¢ and camping is $7 to $9. The park is open from 8 a.m. to sundown, year round. You can contact the park at St. Andrews State Park Recreation Area, 4415 Thomas Dr., Panama City Beach, FL 32407 (tel. 904/234-2522).

Long Beach Camp Inn, 10496 W. US 98A, Panama City Beach, FL 32407 (tel. 904/234-3584), has 300 hookups right on the gulf, an Olympic-size swimming pool, camping supplies, barbecue facilities, and an attractive setting. Rates are $17 to $35 a night.

Beach Campgrounds, 11826 W. US 98, Panama City Beach, FL 32407 (tel. 904/234-3833), has rental spaces for $13 a night, and **Venture Out in America** (at 4345 Thomas Dr., Panama City Beach, FL 32407 (tel. 904/234-2247), has full hookups and camping space (no tents) at $16 for two.

Houseboating

Holiday Boat Rentals, 6400 W. US 98 (at Holiday Lodge Marina), Panama City Beach, FL 32407 (tel. 904/234-0609), has furnished houseboats available for rent for $655 a week from April through October, $425 a week in other months. Daily rates range from $120 to $190, depending on season. Holiday also rents smaller boats, ranging from 14-foot fishing boats to 24-foot pontoon craft for $19 to $50 a half day, $4 to $25 an hour. Jet skis too: $16 for 30 minutes.

RESTAURANTS: This is a relaxed and carefree beachside city where you won't find even one really formal restaurant, but there's some great seafood at some ridiculously low prices.

Captain Anderson's, on Thomas Drive at Grand Lagoon (tel. 234-2225), heads the list. This place is not just popular, it's hysterically popular. Resign yourself that there is no way to beat the lines at Captain Anderson's short of arriving at, say, noon, but face also that it's worth the wait. Definitely the hottest restaurant in the Panhandle, Captain Anderson's packs the place nightly, especially during the Memorial Day to Labor Day busy season when you may have to wait up to two hours for a chance at the captain's succulent oysters, delicate snapper, or overflowing seafood platter. Waiting isn't too tedious though if you seek air-conditioned shelter in the clipper ship look-alike lounge, or up top in the open-air deck overlooking the marina where the state's largest party fishing fleet harbors. Nautical from bow to stern, Captain Anderson's broils, bakes, fries, and stirs up a storm for 500 at a clip, but many more than that gather nightly to dine in the maze of dining rooms on fat shrimp stuffed with crabmeat, carefully tended pompano, and scampi, an unusual grouper-family fish. Dinner prices average about $10 to $15 a person, and the gangplank is down from 4 to about 11 p.m. every day but Sunday (when the captain, presumably, goes fishing). Closed December 1 to January 15.

Just across the lagoon is a restaurant complex that looms up on sedate Thomas Drive like a ghost ship. Panama City's landmark, the **Treasure Ship** is at Treasure Island Marina, 3605 Thomas Dr. (tel. 234-8881). There are no fewer than three restaurants, a couple of bars, a game room, gift shops, a disco, entertainment on open-air decks, and all of it tucked away between the gunwales of a towering landlocked inch-for-inch galleon replica. To see the Treasure Ship is not to believe it. Dining here is probably a must for the first-time Panhandle visitor if for no other reason than to ooh and ahh at the sheer stupefying size of it all.

As for the restaurants, there's a cozy little water-level Galley restaurant with pastas dishes like cappelli d'angelo and prices that begin at about $6 for pasta, peaking at $12 or so for veal. Then there's a sprawling Main Dining Room featuring seafood dishes in the $12 to $15 bracket, and finally a Wharf Snack Center with peel-and-eat shrimp and spicy gumbo for less than $5. Hours are 4 to 10 p.m. daily in the Main Dining Room, from 10 a.m. to 10 p.m. in the other restaurants. There are also two lounges on board, the Brig and the Captain's Quarters, both with entertainment to the wee hours.

It's worth a prowl around the decks, and perhaps a glass or two of something cold, as you watch the sun set over the mainsail and embark fearlessly on a voyage into the past when craft such as this docked on these shores with *real* pirates aboard. Restaurant hours vary by day and by restaurant, but all dining areas are open for dinner daily, earlier on Sunday.

A comparative newcomer to this seaside city is a waterfront dining spot called **Hamilton's,** Thomas Drive at Grand Lagoon (tel. 234-2627), where seafood, straight from the restaurant's fleet of fishing boats, is grilled over mesquite wood. Seafood is often teamed with pastas in such dishes as seafood fettuccine or seafood manicotti, but for beef lovers plenty of premium aged steaks are available. You'll pay $10 to $15 for dinner entrees at Hamilton's, which is open from 5 to 10 p.m. daily and features a Marlin Bar with more than 30 kinds of beer from around the world available.

Seahawk Restaurant, 620 Thomas Dr. (tel. 234-6795), specializes in charcoal-broiled grouper, but can also stuff you with just about any kind of fresh gulf seafood you can name. On the beef menu are strip sirloin, prime rib, and rib-eye steaks, all served with the restaurant's salad bar, fresh fruit, and soup. Prices are in the $10 to $15 range for dinner. Seahawk is open from 4 to 10 p.m. every day except Monday, and there's entertainment each night.

Harbour House, 3001-A W. 10th St. (tel. 785-9053), has a loyal following that comes here to enjoy lovely waterfront views over St. Andrew Bay and to dine on a wide selection of fresh gulf seafood, prime rib, and charcoal-broiled steaks. Each day the restaurant features a luncheon buffet laden with nine salads, five meats, and five vegetables, with a finale of soft, slurpy ice cream. Hours are 6 a.m. to 10 p.m. daily, and dinner prices are in the $10 to $15 bracket.

Yet another newcomer to the region is the **Bridge Tender,** on US 98 at the foot of Hathaway Bridge (tel. 234-2117). A handsome woodsy-plantsy restaurant, the Bridge Tender is right on the water so you can watch the fishing boats chugging by with your dinner. Steamed shellfish are a specialty of this attractive new spot, which also offers entertainment Wednesday through Sunday. Prices are in the $10 to $15 range for dinner at the Bridge Tender, which opens at 4 p.m. and keeps going until 2 a.m.

Boar's Head Restaurant and Tavern, 17290 W. US 98A (tel. 234-6628), is perhaps the most impressive restaurant in the city, and also one of the farthest out-of-town eateries. A gorgeous hunk of wood and glass with imposing entrance and fireplaces, an old English look, and a trim plant-bedecked exterior, Boar's Head serves up prime rib of beef and Yorkshire pudding that is superb! The same can be said of Boar's Head seafood dishes, from Polynesian shrimp served in a pineapple boat to luscious fried Apalachicola oysters and creamy coquilles St. Jacques. Landlubbers have plenty of beef choices here, and there's even a roast duckling in orange sauce. All are served with homemade bread and crisp salads. Prices are low for this attractive atmosphere of giant beamed ceiling and stone walls: the average check is $10 to $15. Open daily from 5 to 10 p.m. (closed Monday off-season).

The restaurant at the **Bay Pointe Resort,** on Delwood Beach Road off Thomas Drive and Magnolia (tel. 234-3307), won first place in an international food fiesta, which should give you a clue that there's some pretty sophisticated dining here. At Bay Pointe you'll dine by candlelight overlooking the Grand Lagoon on such choices as filet Wellington, steak, and scampi, or a succulent seafood platter. Average prices are in the $10 to $15 range, although a number of seafood specialties are just $5 to $8. Freshly baked pastries made right here in the restaurant's kitchens are a don't-miss item. It's open from 7 a.m. to 11 p.m.

From 11 a.m. to 11 p.m. J. Michael fills his tiny **J. Michael's Restaurant,** one mile east of the Hathaway Bridge at 5101 US 98 (tel. 785-9257), with casually dressed diners out for a feast of Créole cookery. Stained-glass windows spark the two tiny dining rooms, and a happy, friendly crowd chows down on brimming bowls of gumbo, red beans and rice, boiled shrimp, and the house special, shrimp J. Michael, a yummy tangy shrimp créole with all the trimmings. You walk out with a check that won't break banks: just $5 to $9 for dinner, lunch items from $1.50, and always a special posted on the blackboard as you enter. On a hot day pull up a spicy bowl, a frosty foamy glass, and toast J. Michael. Everyone else does! Open daily.

Budget Dining

Mexico turns up in Panama at **Loco's,** 2061 N. Cove Blvd. (that's on Route 77 across from Panama City Mall; tel. 234-4774), and at **Casa del Río,** 206 23rd St. (tel. 769-2200). You can easily walk out of either spot stuffed for less than $5, and Loco's offers free appetizers during its daily Fiesta Hour from 3 to 7 p.m. Both restaurants are open daily from 11 a.m. to 11 p.m.

Another newcomer called **The Cheese Bar,** 425 Grace Ave. (tel. 769-3892), serves crêpes, quiches, salads, pasta, and some unusual pies like strawberry pecan fluff, in a pleasant French Quarter atmosphere. Begun as a deli, the restaurant has expanded to a full restaurant that now whips up a great shrimp jambalaya, exotic black bean soup, and creamy crab Louis. Prices are quite reasonable, rarely topping $10, and hours are 11 a.m. to 9 p.m. daily, closing at 10:30 p.m. on weekends, when the restaurant also has entertainment.

Po' Folks, corner of US 98 and Balboa (tel. 784-0111), is a chain restaurant that opened a branch here to satisfy those with a taste for chittlins, grits, and very low prices. Country cookin's the fare here at Po' Folks, where prices are most often in the $5 to $7 range and children under 6 are fed free. Hours are 11 a.m. to 9 p.m. daily, closing an hour later on weekends.

Duff's Smörgåsbord, 1398 W. 15th St., in Panama Plaza (tel. 769-9479), has lunch for under $4 and dinner for under $5—and that's for all you can eat! children pay a dollar or two less, and those under 4 eat free. Hours are 11 a.m. to 9 p.m. daily.

If you've blown it all (or a lot of it) riding the whoop-de-doo at the amusement park, amble over to the **Gulf Cafeteria,** at 12628 W. US 98 (tel. 234-6457), where the day's fresh catch is always on the steam tables and there are money-saving specials for every meal. Open from 7 a.m. to 8 p.m., Gulf has a two-egg breakfast with meat, grits, and toast, and lunch in the $4 range; dinner runs about $6.

For barbecue, locals and visitors alike flock to **Minnie's Real Pit Barbecue,** under the water tower at 651 W. Hwy. 231 (tel. 769-3296), where for $5 or so you can gorge on such daily specialties as beans, garlic bread, coleslaw, tea, and chicken, or other barbecued meats. Minnie's produces a specials menu each week in local advertising, so check it out—then shovel it in at those low, low prices. There's a salad bar for vegetable fans, and regular dinners are in the $5 to $7 range. Hours are 11 a.m. to 10 p.m. daily.

THE SIGHTS: You'll find plenty to do here, from carousels to cruises.

Amusement Parks

There's hardly any way of missing Panama City Beach's amusement parks —and who would want to? They're fun, fun, and more fun! Best of all, their short season means there's plenty of time to keep the dozens of whirling, twirling, stomach-churning thrillers and the park itself neat, clean, and well oiled.

Miracle Strip Amusement Park, at 12001 W. US 98 (tel. 234-3333), is not only the main center of attention here, it's become a landmark. I guarantee that nowhere else in the state will you hear someone tell you a restaurant or hotel is just past the rollercoaster! There are dozens of rides here, from carousel to coasters and a special El Grande Cinema presentation that makes you feel as if you're soaring in planes, racing sports cars, and speeding on Everglades airboats while all you're really doing is standing still! Open from 6 to 11:30 p.m. on weekdays, 1 p.m. to midnight on Saturday and Sunday. Admission is $10.50 for adults, $7.50 for children under 11, and includes all rides.

Miracle Strip's Whata-Water Wonderworld, on US 98 (tel. 234-0368), has water bumper-car shows and zoom flumes, tube rides, and every manner of watery whoop-de-do. Admission to the amusement park is $7. Hours are 10 a.m. to 9 p.m. daily.

Other Attractions

Down in Miami they'd gasp at the sight of **Castle Dracula,** at 12390 W. US 98 (tel. 234-0125), not so much for its fearsome facade but for its location on what should be high-priced beachfront property. You'll gasp too, but your surprise will be at the realism of wax monsters who leer and chortle in their glass cages. Castle Dracula really *is* a castle, but the shows are not so scary you'll have to cope with nightmares. It's about a 20-minute walk through the attraction, which will introduce you to those shiver-delivering monsters we all know and love. Admission is $3 for adults, $1 for children 6 to 11, free for under-6s. Hours are 9 a.m. to 5 p.m., open later in summer.

This definitely isn't my sort of amusement, but there's no doubt that the **Snake-A-Torium,** at 9008 W. US 98 (tel. 234-3311), is a fascinating place to learn the easy way about snakes, alligators, and other such fearsome reptiles. Open from 8:30 a.m. to 8 p.m. in summer and from 9 to 5 p.m. after Labor Day, the Snake-A-Torium even has a snake-milking performance during which the venom used in medical treatments is extracted. Admission is $3.35 for adults, $2.30 for children 6 to 11.

Gulf World, 15412 W. US 98 (tel. 234-5271), has porpoises that shake hands and perform amazing leaps and twists, a sea lion carnival, and a scuba show, plus a shark channel featuring a static display of a great white shark. Admission is $6.75 for adults, $4.75 for children 13 to 18, and $3.75 for children 4 to 12. Gulf World is open from 10 a.m. to 8:30 p.m. daily in summer.

For a day of **sailing,** go island hopping, snorkeling, shell collecting, sunbathing, or do nothing at all aboard the *Destiny,* which leaves Bay Pointe Resort on seven-hour cruises including both bay and gulf sailing with stops on island beaches. *Destiny* (tel. 904/234-3307, or toll free 800/874-7106) departs at 8:30 a.m. daily, returning at 3:30 p.m., and costs $30 an hour. Half-day cruises are also available, and evening wine and cheese cruises depart at 5 p.m., returning at 7:30 p.m., for $12 a person.

Shell Island lies just off the coastline of Panama City and is just what its name implies, a shell hunter's dream trip. You must get there by boat, so the place to head is Capt. Anderson's Marina on Thomas Drive at Grand Lagoon (tel. 234-3435), where double-decker boats head for the island at 9 a.m. and 1 p.m. daily ($3.50 for adults, $1.75 for children). Trips are available April to September. Bay Pointe also operates a Shell Island trip at similar prices. In season, you can go out on dolphin-feeding cruises to watch these sea clowns ham it up for their chow.

NIGHTLIFE: Virtually every hotel and many, many restaurants have some kind of entertainment, most of it easy listening, vocalists or guitarists, especially in summer months when the town goes nonstop.

Restaurants with entertainment include the **Treasure Ship,** 3605 Thomas

Dr. (tel. 234-8881), which has a lounge and dancing; the **Boar's Head,** 17290 US 98A (tel. 234-6628), which has dancing and entertainment; and **Captain Anderson's,** on Thomas Drive at Grand Lagoon (tel. 234-2225).

For country music, try the **Gold Nugget Lounge,** 3901 W. US 98 (tel. 769-0497), where the top-40 twangers and live entertainment ring out nightly except Sunday. A happy hour here begins at 4 p.m.

Holiday Inn Beachside has a Crow's Nest Lounge that's a popular spot on the fifth floor, with a panoramic view over what looks like most of the world and stays open to 4 a.m. on weekends.

If you love western twang, twang, and gol dang, you're gonna love the **Ocean Opry.** You'll find zany hijinks and zealous dedication to good ole American country music and family fun. Take the kids to this one and join hundreds of other knee-slappin' funsters out for two hours of music and comdedy that begins nightly at 8:30 p.m. in the 1000-seat **Opry House,** at 8400 W. US 98 (tel. 234-5464). Running the show here is the singing Rader family, who have rounded up a cast of 11 and perform all year long. Moonshine the clown is as close as Ocean Opry gets to anything spirited, but there are sandwiches and plenty of other refreshments. All seats are reserved at $6.50 each. Ocean Opry's open every night during June, July, and August, less frequently in other months.

At **Miracle Mile Resort,** which includes **Barefoot Beach Inn** and the **Sheraton Miracle Mile Inn** (tel. 234-6551 for both), there's entertainment almost every night from about 6 p.m. to the wee hours. Other popular spots are the **Breakers East,** 1227 Beck Ave. (tel. 785-9891); **Breakers West,** 12627 W. US 98 (tel. 234-2239); the Buccaneer Lounge at the **Holiday Inn Bayside,** 211 W. Beach Drive (tel. 763-4622); and the **Holiday Lodge Lounge,** 6400 W. US 98 (tel. 234-2114).

For a romantic evening on the high seas, board **Capt. Anderson's dinner boat** (that man is everywhere!) which spends its winters in St. Petersburg Beach, its summers here. You board at the marina at 5550 N. Lagoon Dr. (tel. 234-3435) at 6:30 p.m. Monday through Saturday, dine on Delmonico steak, and dance to musical entertainment on board until the triple-decker steams back into the marina about 10 p.m. At $17.95 per person, including tip ($15.95 for children under 12), the Capt. Anderson dinner cruise operates Memorial Day through Labor Day and is a very popular outing, so make reservations, even weeks, ahead of your cruises.

At **Spinnaker II,** 8813 Thomas Dr. (tel. 234-7882), things are popping day and night. A rustic wood-sided lounge out on the dunes, the Spinnaker offers you everything from parasailing ($20 for a ten-minute ride), to a steady round of musical entertainment, food, dancing, parties, beach umbrellas, bands, steaks, plenty of spirits, a house band, and regular appearances by guest musicians. It's open from 11 a.m. to 4 a.m. daily, drinks are half price, and there's always fun to be had here.

SPORTS:

On water or on land you'll find sports here, plenty of them, from diving to divots.

Tennis and Golf

Bay Pointe Resort, off Thomas Drive at Grand Lagoon (tel. 904/234-3307), has the area's largest golf facilities, 27 holes, open from mid-March to December. Greens fees in summer are $24 for 18 holes; carts are $10. Bay Pointe also has tennis courts and charges $3 per person an hour for day or night play, $7 an hour for use of the ball machine.

Golf on two miniature 18-hole courses at **Putt-Putt Golf Course,** one mile east of Hathaway Bridge at 47 W. US 98 (tel. 769-4642). It's open from spring through fall, and charges $2 per person for 18 holes, $2.85 for 36.

The **Panama City Parks and Recreation Department** (tel. 763-6641) operates 19 tennis courts, 13 nature parks, and six community centers. The friendly folks there can give you details on these inexpensive (or free) places to play.

Racquetball/Iron Pumping

Racquetball players and fitness fans should bounce off to the **Courthouse,** on Route 390 across from the airport (tel. 769-6184), where you'll be welcomed on indoor air-conditioned courts, open daily. Rates are cheapest in the morning when courts are available for 50¢, but they're moderately priced at anytime at $3.50 an hour plus a $3 guest fee. The Courthouse has locker rooms, whirlpools, saunas, exercise rooms, and a lounge. Opening and closing hours vary from 6 to 9 a.m. and from 7 to 10:30 p.m., so check to see what's happening when you're ready to huff and puff. Fee for use of the facilities is $7 a day.

Water Sports

Bay Pointe Marina Water Sports Center, off Thomas Drive at Grand Lagoon (tel. 234-3307, ext. 4919), rents 16-foot Hobie catamarans for $20 an hour, $75 a day, and windsurfing boards for $10 an hour or $27 a day. There are snorkel trips for $10 a person, and you can rent the equipment for $8.

Hydrospace Dive Shop, 3605 Thomas Dr. (tel. 234-9463), will give you some underwater adventure on four-, six-, or eight-hour dive trips ranging from 2 to 20 miles offshore in 60 to 100 feet of water. Prices begin at $25 per person. Hydrospace will also teach you snorkeling and scuba-diving. Snorkeling classes are $30 a day; full certification scuba classes are $100.

Panama City has an active reef-building project, and there are several sunken ships including a Liberty Ship and the Grey Ghost. There are also many natural reefs and some 50 dive sites that offer fascinating looks at undersea life and rare shells.

Aquasled Waterslide, next to Surf Hut at 12608 W. US 98 (tel. 234-3430), charges $5 an hour, $8 for all day, $2 for children 5 and under with an adult.

You can rent a surfboard at **Lawrence Rentals,** 15000 US 98 (tel. 234-2432), from 6 a.m. to 10 p.m. for $3.50 an hour or $12 a day from May to September. Cheaper yet is **Surf Hut,** open 8 a.m. to 10 p.m., which charges $10 a day, $5.50 a half day. Lawrence also rents beach umbrellas for $4 a day, $18 a week.

Fishing

Here as everywhere else along the sparkling coastline, fishing is the number one sport. To find a fishing trip, head for **Capt. Anderson's Pier,** 5500 N. Lagoon Dr., Panama City, and talk to some of these skilled fishermen (it's not out of line to wheel and deal a bit over the price of a trip). To give you an idea what charges are, the *Barracuda,* run by Capt. Harry Ivy (tel. 234-9889), roars out to the sea for $160 a half day for up to six people, $320 for a full day, providing everything except your food and drinks.

Panama City Beach City Pier, 1600 feet long, is the longest pier on the Gulf Coast. You can fish from the pier, on US 98, at $2 for 24 hours, or just stroll down this long, long dock for $1.

A number of deep-sea fishing boats operate as Capt. Davis/Capt. Anderson's fleet. The fleet (tel. 234-7437; toll free in seven southern states 800/874-2415), located at Capt. Anderson's Pier, has five 85-foot fishing boats that leave at 7 a.m. and return at 5 p.m. Rates for deep-sea fishing on party boats are $14 to $40 a person.

Parimutuel Sports

Big Bend Jai-Alai Fronton is near Panama City Beach at Route 1 (Box 1251), Chattahoochee, FL 32324 (tel. 442-4111), and is open on Thursday, Friday, Saturday, and Monday nights at 7 p.m. from December through May. Matinee games are at noon on Friday and Saturday. Admission is $2 for general admission seats, $3 to $4 for box seats. To get to the fronton, take Exit 24 from I-10 and you'll find it on Route 270A.

Wager on the fleet feet of greyhounds at the **Washington County Kennel Club dog track** on Route 79 in nearby Ebro (tel. 535-4048). Open May through August, the track has racing nightly, except Sunday, at 8 p.m. and matinees at 1 p.m. on Monday, Wednesday, and Saturday. Admission is $1 and there's a lounge.

Shelling/Dolphin Feeding/Boating

Capt. Davis's Queen Fleet, Capt. Anderson's Pier, 5500 N. Lagoon Dr., will take you out to an offshore island fittingly called Shell island on a shell-gathering expedition or whiz you off to the open seas to feed the dolphins. (What I mean is, you feed the dolphins, he doesn't feed you to them.) Trips to Shell Island are from 9 to 11:45 a.m. and 1 to 3:45 p.m. March through October; dolphin-feeding safaris, from 9:30 to 10:45 a.m. and 5:30 to 6:45 p.m. daily. This fleet also operates half- or full-day deep-sea fishing expeditions and dinner/dance cruises. You can reach them at 234-3435; or toll-free in seven southern states at 800/874-2415. Shelling cruises are $4 for adults, $2 for children through 12.

SHOPPING: Olde Towne Mini Mall, 400 Grace Ave., is a cluster of shops and restaurants specializing in such countrified collectibles as wicker baskets, brass and copper kitchenware, and seashell note papers.

Field's Plaza, 12700 W. US 98A, across from the Holiday Inn on Panama City Beach, can get you togged out in typical tropical style with T-shirts, bikinis, sandals, boat shoes, and beach bag. Several shops operate here, purveying, as they put it, everything "from lotions to notions." Hours are 9 a.m. to 9 p.m. daily.

4. Tallahassee

These days one wonders why Tallahassee, which by anyone's standards is hardly more than a village, is the capital of a state in which more than half the population lives *south* of Orlando! South Florida legislators have certainly tried enough times to move the capital south, but it settled here in 1824 when Tallahassee was the midpoint between the bustling cities of St. Augustine and Pensacola, and here it has stayed, defying the forces of change.

Secretly, I think, some southern Florida legislators probably don't mind that at all, since this quiet town near the Georgia border can be a welcome relief from the crowded, busy streets of southern Florida's jam-packed tourist centers. Here in Tallahassee, life (except the legislative life) moves as slowly as the southern drawl you'll hear from its longtime residents.

History is important in this town, where many homes trace their ancestry to pre–Civil War days. Zealous efforts by preservationists have held back the let's-wreck-it forces of progress and restored many of the city's beautiful old homes and buildings. One of those, the oldest surviving building in the city, is a house called Columns. It was built by banker William Williams (who, understandably, needed a nickname, and selected "Money" as his monicker!). Today, Money's house, where he and his wife raised ten children, is the city's chamber of commerce.

There are still plenty of bankers—and others whose nicknames certainly *could* be Money—around these parts. These days, however, they're here to protect—or further—their interests at the state legislature, which turns up for two or three months each year to make laws that govern the fate of 12 million people. In the process, legislators and their followers cavort and carouse, raise money and hell, and frequently work themselves and everyone else into exhaustion. While they're here the city booms, and when they leave it slips back to the rhythmic pace it has known for centuries, seeming hardly to notice the change.

Tallahassee has had centuries to accustom itself to distractions. In the mid-1600s the Spanish marched through here and established missions along a trail similar to California's famed Mission Trail. A century later a troop of English and Indian soldiers marched in and destroyed the missions, leaving behind the name Tallahassee—it means "abandoned village."

On a walk along the city's Park Avenue you'll see houses dating back to antebellum days, and on a tour of the capital city you'll hear some fascinating tales of these lumbering old mansions. One house, so the story goes, was owned by two sisters who fell in love with the same man. He married the younger sister but the older one remained in the house, and soon the two were calling their token male "our husband." He died, perhaps predictably, at an early age, and his bedpost today adorns the front door of the home!

Calhoun Street is the setting for many of Tallahassee's oldest homes and is now a historic district where you will discover there's little new under the sun: the Bowen House was built in 1830 of New England pine that was cut, numbered, tagged, mortised, and pegged for instant construction in Tallahassee, one of the first prefab houses whose build-by-number markings can still be seen on the window shutters!

Built on rolling hillsides, Tallahassee has still another unusual feature: canopy roads where branches of towering old trees reach out across the road to touch each other and create sun-dappled tunnels. You can travel these canopy roads on the Old St. Augustine Road, which really *was* the old road to St. Augustine built on the mission trail, and other roads called the Miccousukee, Meridian, Old Bainbridge, and Centerville Roads. Here you'll discover the elegant antebellum Tallahassee that lives on, sometimes overshadowed, but never eclipsed by modernity.

GETTING AROUND: Avis and Hertz **rental-car agencies** operate here and have airport reservation offices. Other places to rent a car include American Rentals, Brogan Chevrolet-Buick, and Elkin's Ford Rent-A-Car.

Taltran is the city's **bus** company, and will be happy to give you route information if you call them at 576-5134. Fares are 30¢.

USEFUL INFORMATION: For **police or medical emergencies,** call 911. . . . For **non-emergency medical problems,** call the Capital Medical Society at 877-9018. . . . If you need a **dentist,** call the dental information service (tel. toll free 800/282-9117). . . . Interstate Texaco at Thomasville Road and I-10 has **24-hour wrecker service,** as does Capital Hills Amoco, at the corner of Magnolia and Tennessee Streets (tel. 877-6558). . . . **Jerry's Restaurants,** at 471 W. Tennessee St. (tel. 224-5104), and on US 27 North (tel. 385-1174), are open around the clock. . . . **Sullivan Drugs,** across from Tallahassee Memorial at 1330 Miccousukee Rd. (tel. 877-1166), and at Timberland Shops on the Square at 1415 Timberland (tel. 893-2171), are open to midnight every day. . . . Albertson's, at 1925 N. Monroe St. (tel. 386-7135), can supply you with **groceries at any hour.** . . . You can find out how to reach **state legislators** by looking in the center of the telephone book, where you'll find blue pages which also detail activities in the area and dole out some other useful information including seat diagrams of the Florida State University and Florida A&M University football stadiums.

TOURIST INFORMATION: Folks at the **Florida Chamber of Commerce,** 304 W. College St., Tallahassee, FL 32303 (tel. 904/222-2831), will be happy to load you down with information on every region of the state. . . . If you want to know more about just this city, call the **Tallahassee Chamber of Commerce,** 100 N. Duval St., Tallahassee, FL 32303 (tel. 904/224-8116).

ORIENTATION: Most of the things you'll want to see in Tallahassee are in a rather compact downtown area, reached on US 27 (also called Apalachee Park-

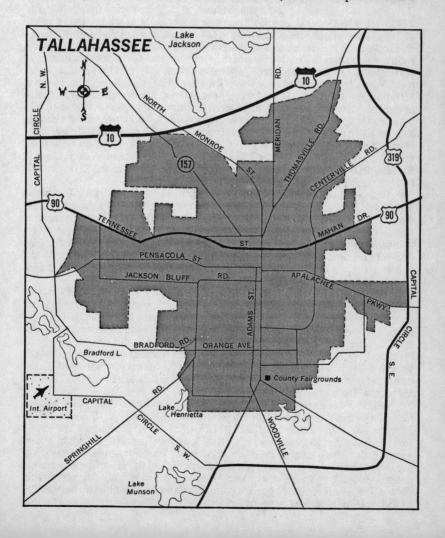

way) which will take you right to the front of the Old Capitol Building, and the new one is just a block behind it. Tennessee Street (which is also US 90) passes Florida State University. I-10 runs north of town and the best exit is US 27. If you're coming up from Apalachicola on US 98, branch off onto US 319 at Crawfordville. US 98 joins Route 61 (Monroe Street), which goes right through the middle of the city. There's metered parking in a lot on Jefferson Street just off Monroe Street.

HOTELS: In Tallahassee, hotel rates remain about the same all year long except during the big football weekends from September to December, but even then price increases aren't outrageous. During legislative sessions hotels are very busy, and unless you have a reservation *well* in advance you may find yourself staying far outside town—very far outside.

The 244-room tower at the **Hilton Hotel,** 101 S. Adams St., Tallahassee, FL 32303 (tel. 904/224-5000, or toll-free numbers in every state), is the crown jewel of Tallahassee's hotel scene. Needless to say, the place is jammed during legislative sessions as legislators and lobbyists vie for these attractive, contemporary rooms which feature two double or king-size beds and all the thoughtful extras you expect from the Hilton chain. There's swimming, free indoor parking, and if you're really going first class, a Tower Program that includes everything from a 16th-floor aerie to a *Wall Street Journal* at your door. You won't be disappointed at the Hilton, where you're likely to meet senators and mayors, cattlemen, oilmen, and maybe even the governor in Adam's dining room or Quincy's library lounge. Even the coffeeshop is a special place here, with greenery thriving in the rays under a skylight. Best of all, of course, and the reason it's often difficult to find a room here, is the Hilton's location: just a block from the state Capitol Building in the heart of downtown Tallahassee. Rates are $45 to $85 single, $57 to $105 double; children stay free.

Red Spanish ceramic roof tiles are the highlight landmark of **LaQuinta Motor Inn,** 2905 N. Monroe St., Tallahassee, FL 32303, at the Route 27 exit from I-10 (tel. 904/385-7172, or toll free 800/531-5900). Set off by itself under a stand of towering pines, LaQuinta carries its Spanish theme throughout, from Spanish leather lobby chairs to a tiny circular stucco fireplace and attractively decorated rooms with Spanish paintings, and a small central courtyard where guests gather to swim in the resort's pool. Rates at LaQuinta are $44 to $49 double, $5 less for singles, and extra persons are $5 each.

Killearn Country Club and Inn, 100 Tyrone Circle, Tallahassee, FL 32308 (tel. 904/893-2186), is not only the city's leading golf course, it's also a beautiful contemporary woodsy resort in which individually decorated rooms have original paintings by famous artists, plush furnishings, and wide balconies overlooking the wooded golf course. In the center of things is an Olympic-size pool bordered by the club's beamed-ceiling Oak View restaurant where you dine on beef Wellington, veal française, or steaks cut by ounce (for about $1.25 an ounce) at prices in the $10 to $15 range. Rates at the Killearn Inn are $65 double for rooms, $65 and up for suites.

Spacious lawns shaded by giant live oaks dripping with Spanish moss are a highlight of the **Tallahassee Motor Hotel and Dining Room,** on US 27 at 1630 N. Monroe St., Tallahassee, FL 32303 (tel. 904/224-6183). Just across the street from a small lake, the Tallahassee Motor Hotel has 92 rooms, including a new wing which offers a lovely view of the vest-pocket lake. Rooms in the new wing are larger and newer, and cost a few dollars more than the rest of the accommodations in this long single-story motel. Rooms are attractively decorated with dark-wood paneling offset by bright colors. A room for two with two beds is $30 to $36, and four can stay here for $35 to $41. There's a swimming pool on the lawns, and the motel is set well back from the highway so you won't be bothered by motor noises.

There are two Holiday Inns in Tallahassee, but you'll have no trouble discovering why the **Holiday Inn Downtown,** 316 W. Tennessee St., Tallahassee, FL 32301 (tel. 904/222-8000, or toll free 800/465-4329), is known hereabouts as the "round Holiday Inn." It is indeed round, a tower soaring 12 stories into the sky in a strategic location between the Governor's Mansion and the state Capitol Buildings. Holiday Inn's usual careful planning and thoughtful extras show up here as a Viking rooftop lounge, from every room a view over the city or countryside, and contemporary dark-wood furniture brightened by cheerful colors. Steaks and seafood are specialties in the inn's Camelot dining room, and each night there's an opulent buffet brimming with seafood and elaborate salads. You'll pay rates of $47 to $50 double, $5 less for singles (the higher price for king-size beds). Prices are sometimes higher, and reservations are necessary during football weekends in the fall.

The **Parkway Holiday Inn,** at 1302 Apalachee Pkwy., Tallahassee, FL 32301 (tel. 904/877-3141 or toll free 800/465-4329), is a mile from the downtown area on US 27, where rooms are set around open shaded lawns. Prices are $42 to $44 for a standard room, $44 to $48 for a king-size bed and larger room, and there's a pool for splashing away summer's heat.

There are lots of pretty things at the 100-room **Capitol Inn,** on US 27 at 1027 Apalachee Pkwy., Tallahassee, FL 32301 (tel. 904/877-6171), but for me the prettiest feature of all is the airy Patio Grill dining room, designed to resemble a small garden with brick floors, a white lattice-trimmed salad bar, matching wrought-iron touches, and lots of greenery rising from the floor and hanging from the ceiling. It's open from 6:30 a.m. to 10 p.m. every day but Sunday, when it closes at noon. The Capitol Inn is up high on a hill for a nice view over Tallahassee's rolling country, and there's a pretty tiled pool on the grounds. The extra-large rooms have two double beds, deep pile carpeting, color TV, and contemporary decor, with separate dressing room and bath in olive tones sparked by cheery touches of yellow. Single rooms at the Capitol Inn are $31 and doubles run $34, year round. The inn whisks you free to and from the airport or to the Capitol Building or downtown offices in its own limousine.

At the **Prince Murat Motel,** 745 N. Monroe St., Tallahassee, FL 32303 (tel. 904/224-3108), there's a lovely view of a historic mansion and its grounds. Tall pines shade the two-story Murat, where you'll find 28 bright, attractive rooms with telephones, cable television, tiled baths, and broad picture windows overlooking a sweep of lawn at a neighboring historic home, the Johnson-Carter House. Two people will pay $24 to $28 (higher during football season and special events) at Prince Murat (which, incidentally, is named for one of Napoleon's nephews, who built a plantation in the Panhandle and married a grandniece of George Washington).

One is tempted to take a look at the beautiful new **Governors Inn,** Adams Street Commons, 204 S. Adams St., Tallahassee, FL 32301 (tel. 904/681-6855, or toll free 800/342-7717), and say that it's about time a governor did something right. However, no governor had anything to do with this handsome hotel—it was the brainchild of a Florida senator's son. In a town more often characterized by hotels that could be described as utilitarian or less, this inn dreamed up by the son of Florida Sen. Lawton Chiles, is a wondrous place indeed. Created from the remains of an old livery stable, the hotel opened in the summer of 1984 and instantly became Tallahassee's most popular hostelry.

Located just a block from the old Capitol Building on a brick-lined street, Governors Inn is special from first glance to last croissant: an entrance trimmed with beveled glass and coach lamps, beams of heart-of-pine, beautiful hardwood furniture, a pine-paneled Florida Room where complimentary cocktails are served in gleaming crystal and continental breakfast appears on silver trays. There are just 41 rooms and suites, named for past governors and filled with antiques, four-posters, perhaps a black-oak writing desk or rock-maple armoire.

Suites are sumptuous and can include a whirlpool bath, loft bedroom, working fireplace. Suite or not, you're treated to evening turndown service, limousine service to destinations within five miles of the hotel, valet parking, daily newspapers delivered to your door, refrigerators, remote-control televisions, terrycloth robes, free local calls, and discount long-distance lines.

Elegant and expensively turned out, Governors Inn is without a doubt the best of the rest in Tallahassee. Rates are $80 to $97 double, $55 to $87 single, for hotel rooms. The highest rates are charged from March to June; the lowest, in July, August, and December. Convertible rooms with swing-back murphy beds are $70 to $102 double, $60 to $92 single; loft bedroom suites, $110 to $140 single, $130 to $160 double.

Bed and Breakfast

A Florida State University professor who welcomes you to his restored historic home is one of the possibilities open to you if you opt to book accommodations through **Tallahassee Bed and Breakfast,** 3023 Windy Hill Lane, Tallahassee, FL 32308 (tel. 904/385-3768 or 421-5220). Tallahassee B&B has listings for homes in town or on the coast, with rates that begin at $30.

RESTAURANTS: Thanks to the annual influx of legislators and their followers you can find some very good—and some very interesting—restaurants in the capital city.

Andrew's 2nd Act, 228 S. Adams St. (tel. 222-2759), is Tallahassee's class act, the city's number one restaurant in cuisine, decor, popularity, and status. While it's tops in quality, it's bottom in location, down in the "basement" of a nondescript building hard by the state Capitol Building. There's a small menu, but everything is elegantly prepared and you can dine on such delicacies as freshly shucked or baked oysters, deep-fried mozzarella cheese topped with créole sauce, a delicate seafood crêpe filled with crab and shrimp. Top that off with an entree from a specialty beef, chicken, veal, or seafood dish. A labyrinth of dining rooms, Andrew's 2nd Act features tiny flowered tablecloths and a French country decor peppered with antiques, enameled molds, candles, and flowers. Figure $15 to $20 each for dinner (served 6 to 10 p.m.), half that for lunch (served from 11:30 a.m. to 2 p.m. weekdays).

After Andrew scored his first success with his 2nd Act, he moved on to create three other restaurants in the same building, **Tutto Bene** (tel. 222-5592), a devastatingly good Italian restaurant where you dine amid rust and dove-gray decor in a shining contemporary atmosphere on such goodies as veal rolls stuffed with ham, parsley, mozzarella, and parmesan, and topped with a mushroom and red wine sauce. Several veal and fish preparations are supplemented with steak, chicken, and of course pastas from lasagne al forno to fettuccine with a Genovese pesto of basil, garlic, pinenuts, and parmesan. Tutto Bene's checks average $5 to $7 for pastas, $10 to $15 for other choices.

For a quick but elegant lunch in Tallahassee, head for this same building in which you'll find **Maxin's** (tel. 222-3446), occupying still another corner of this maze of dining rooms. A salad buffet is featured here from 11:30 a.m. to 2 p.m. (prices in the $5 range) Monday to Friday, and the contemporary dining room and bar open again at cocktail hour for libations and a seafood bar. Maxin's also operates a wine bar where you can experiment with new tastes by glass or bottle.

At **The Brass Rail** (tel. 222-3444), you can munch on bagels and the like in a very classy atmosphere redolent with attractive woods and brass and a Victorian look. Choose your delicacies from a cafeteria-style line of salad and sandwich makings, and dine in high-backed banquettes. You'll pay prices in the $3 to $5 range for a variety of soups, salads, sandwiches, and entrees. On Saturday and Sunday a champagne brunch is served from 10 a.m. to 3 p.m.

What do you need with a smoke-filled room when you can sneak off to your very own curtained booth for dinner? That's what they do in Tallahassee, and they've been doing it for generations since the **Silver Slipper,** at 531 Scotty Lane (tel. 386-9366), opened many legislative sessions ago. Still a favorite with legislators, the Silver Slipper was destroyed by fire several years ago and moved its operation to a new restaurant tucked away on a tiny lane just north of the Northwood Mall. There the curtained booths remain private places for those in search of a clandestine tête-à-tête (or perhaps just an escape from demanding voters). If you don't care who sees you, you can dine out in the open sections of the restaurant on a variety of steaks and seafood plus some interesting specialties like quail and bacon-wrapped shrimp. Prices begin at $7, but your check is more likely to read $12 to $15 per person for dinner on the bottom line. Open 5 to 11:30 p.m. daily.

Three Greek brothers, who operate a lovely hideaway in Panacea called Brothers Three Garden By the Sea, got their start here in Tallahassee with two very successful restaurants, **Brothers Three,** at 2696 N. Monroe St. (tel. 386-4193), and **Spartan Restaurant,** at 415 N. Monroe St. (tel. 224-9711). Both specialize in terrific seafood concoctions for which the brothers have become justifiably famous. Reasonable prices are in the $7 to $12 range. Brothers Three has two salad bars, plus prime beef in addition to seafood. A Hideaway Lounge here features nightly entertainment, and both restaurant and lounge open Monday through Saturday at 5 p.m. The restaurant closes at midnight, the lounge at 2 a.m. Spartan has an English Tudor look outside, and a comfortably intimate atmosphere with seafood, at those very moderate prices, again the specialty. It's open from 11 a.m. to 2 p.m. and 5 to 11 p.m.

Ask anyone for a good Italian restaurant in Tallahassee and they'll direct you straight to **Mom and Dad's,** 4175 Apalachee Pkwy. (tel. 877-4518), a basic red-checkered-tablecloth spot where yummy scents from the kitchen will set you salivating. Mom and Dad are the Violantes, who preside over their steaming kitchen and small restaurant with vivacity and humor, hard work, and the occasional burst of rapid Italian. Their motto is: "If you want genuine, homemade Italian food, you can fly to Italy . . . or drive to Mom and Dad's." I'd recommend the drive, and the veal and pasta offerings for which the restaurant has earned well-deserved local fame. You'll like the check too, which as likely as not will stop somewhere short of $5 to $10 a person. Hours are 5 to 11 p.m. Tuesday through Sunday.

Lucy Ho, an elegant Chinese lady, married a University of Florida professor and set out to create her own culinary world. Create she did, and today **Ms. Lucy's Bamboo Garden,** 112–116 E. Sixth Ave. (tel. 224-9099) in Governors Square Mall, and at 2814 Apalachee Pkwy. (tel. 878-3366), are among Tallahassee's most popular restaurants. Brooking no confusion of Chinese and Japanese cuisine, Bamboo Garden maintains strict lines of demarcation—Chinese at fast food Governor's Square, Japanese on Sixth Avenue and Apalachee Parkway, and never the bamboo shoots shall cross. Bamboo Garden on Apalachee Parkway is the newer of the two full-service restaurants, and you'll usually find its proprietor there overseeing that operation (or at any of the four tea houses she runs). A shrewd lady and a knowledgeable restaurateur, what ho? Bamboo Garden's dinner buffets are just $6 and the restaurant at Sixth Avenue is open

328 DOLLARWISE GUIDE TO FLORIDA

from noon to 2 p.m. weekdays and 5 to 10 p.m. (closed Sunday). The Apalachee Parkway Bamboo Garden is open daily from 11:30 a.m. to 10 p.m. and has both Chinese and Japanese food with average checks in the $5 to $10 range.

When the craving for a good steak hits, head for the **Brown Derby Restaurant,** 2415 N. Monroe St. (tel. 386-1103), a chain operation that's proud of its thick steaks at thin prices. Here in Tallahassee the restaurant's won some awards for its excellence in beef productions and super salad table and freshly baked breads. The Brown Derby's in the Tallahassee Mall and is open from 11:30 a.m. to midnight Sunday through Thursday, from 4 p.m. to 1 a.m. on Friday and Saturday. Prices are in the $8 to $10 range.

One of the more popular restaurants in town, **Julie's Place,** is located at LaQuinta Motor Inn, 2905 N. Monroe St. (tel. 386-7181). Among lots of antiques and greenery, etched glass and a tranquil atmosphere, you can dine on nachos, potato skins, crocks of onion soup, and fresh salads, a shrimp and avocado sandwich, or a number of specialties like french bread pizza or quiches, for prices in the $4 to $6 range. After 5 p.m. (and all day on Sunday) there's an array of entrees in the $7 to $9 bracket. Open daily from 7 a.m. to 11 p.m., to midnight on weekends.

On cool winter days (only your very best Tallahassee friend would ever mention the word "cold," the **Melting Pot,** 1832 N. Monroe St. (tel. 386-7440), is the perfect place for a little tête-à-tête over a bubbling fondue. But we fondue lovers go there quite happily all summer long to indulge in those steaming cheese treats, beef and seafood fondue, and a finale of chocolate fondue, for prices in the $8 to $11 range. Hours are 6 to 11 p.m. daily, closing an hour later on weekends.

A group of four restaurants on the coast not far from Tallahassee or on the way to it all advertise themselves together and offer both good food and pleasant, casual atmosphere, with prices in the $10 to $15 range for dinner. Here's who they are:

Lillian Mozelle's is on Route 319, one mile north of the village of Crawfordville (tel. 926-6019). Cooks there specialize in blackened redfish and crab cakes, which they serve from 11 a.m. to 10 p.m. daily.

St. Marks Restaurant, Route 363, St. Marks (tel. 925-6458), is a romantic, candlelit spot on the gulf. Lots of steaks make their way from kitchen to table here, abetted by plenty of fresh gulf seafood. Hours are 11 a.m. to 10 p.m. daily.

Waterfront Restaurant and Lounge, Route 370, Alligator Point, (tel. 349-9210), specializes in fresh seafood served in a casual dockside atmosphere. On weekends there's entertainment—and plenty of beach lovers who drop by after a day on the sand to see what's happening here. Hours are 11 a.m. to 9 p.m. on Wednesday, Thursday, and Sunday, to midnight on Friday and Saturday.

Fourth of the group is **Spring Creek Restaurant,** Route 365 South, Spring Creek (tel. 926-3751), another coastal restaurant designed to appeal to the beach-bound crowd. Fresh fish are featured but there are plenty of steaks on the menu too, and the finale really must be mom's world-famous chocolate-peanut-butter pie. Monday and Tuesday there's piano entertainment, and the restaurant is open daily from noon to 10 p.m.

SEEING THE SIGHTS: History is made every day here, and preserved as well in some lovely old homes and fascinating museums.

The Capitol

Certainly when you're here in a state that's had government by one country or another for more than 400 years, you'll want to take a look at the center from which the state's government operates. You can get an outline of the Florida cabinet system and state officials' responsibilities by writing the Department of Commerce, 107 Gaines St., Tallahassee, FL 32301. In the pamphlet you'll find an outline of the new Capitol Building, completed in 1978. Now you can also take a look at the state's historic old building, being restored. Florida became a state in 1845 when just 58,000 people lived in this 500-mile-long peninsula. Today almost three times that many live in Tallahassee alone, and legislators who work in this 22-story **Capitol Building** now make the laws for 12 million people, a number that's growing even as you read this—Florida is now the fastest growing state in the nation.

What you'll really want to see is one of the **legislative sessions,** which begin in April and last into June. At the west entrance to the building is a welcome station (tel. 488-6167) from which the Department of Commerce conducts guided tours from 8:30 a.m. to 4:30 p.m. daily, 11 a.m. to 4 p.m. on Saturday, Sunday, and holidays. Florida is the Sunshine State in more ways than one—it was the first state to require that all governmental meetings be open to the public—appropriately called the Sunshine Act—so feel free to attend public meetings not only here in the capital but anywhere in the state. Florida's startlingly rapid growth, its diverse ethnic groups and vested interests make this Capitol Building a volatile place most of the time—in 1981 two of the state's legislative leaders barely avoided fisticuffs over baronial rights to power!

Budding Perry Masons can watch barristers argue before the judges of the **Florida Supreme Court,** 500 block of Duval Street (tel. 488-8845). Court's in session on the first full week of each month (except August and December) from 9:30 a.m. to about noon. A pamphlet available from the security station at the entrance will help you understand some of the legalese inside.

Museums and Historic Sites

Mastodons and arrowheads, gold doubloons and cutlasses, are all part of Florida's dramatic history showcased at the **Museum of Florida History,** in the R. A. Gray Building, 500 S. Bronough (tel. 488-1484), open from 9 a.m. to 4:30 p.m. Monday through Friday, on Saturday from 10 a.m. to 4:30 p.m., and on Sunday from noon to 4:30 p.m. You can sometimes find collectors' items in the museum's gift shop, and at any time you can spend fascinating hours perusing this repository of Florida history. It's free.

Tallahassee's **Junior Museum,** at 3945 Museum Dr. (tel. 576-1636), is a 52-acre wonderland where the small fry (and parents too) can get a look at a historic world. A one-room schoolhouse is preserved here, as is an 1880s farm, complete with farm animals and demonstrations of blacksmithing, syrup making, sheep shearing, spinning, and weaving. The plantation home of Princess Murat is preserved here too. Open Tuesday through Saturday from 9 a.m. to 5 p.m. and on Sunday from 2 to 5 p.m., the museum charges $2 for adults and $1 for children. You'll find it off Route 371 near the municipal airport.

At **Lake Jackson Mounds Archeological Site** is an 81-acre excavation area where Hernando de Soto and his men spent part of the fall and winter in 1539, but the excavations here indicate this area was inhabited 1300 years before Christ.

Tours

If you're here in springtime, you can tour antebellum homes and plantations, and watch the city pay tribute to its spring flowers at **Springtime Tallahassee,** held annually April 3 to 5. There's a Parade of Governors and a series of historical and cultural events. The friendly folks at 904/224-5012 can tell you what's in store this year.

You can tour the Florida **Governor's Mansion,** at 700 N. Adams St. (tel. 488-4661), from September to May from 10 a.m. to noon on Monday, Wednesday, and Friday. It's free.

Nature on Display

Alfred B. Maclay Gardens, at 3540 Thomasville Rd. (U.S. 319; tel. 893-4232), is spread across 308 acres including 28 acres of one of the South's finest azalea and camellia collections, the prize possession and creation of philanthropist Alfred B. Maclay, whose widow gave these magnificent gardens to the state. The park is open from 8 a.m. to sundown daily; the gardens, from 9 a.m. to 5 p.m. Maclay Gardens and House Museum is open from January to April 30. Entrance fee to the park is 50¢ May through December, and $1.50 for adults and 75¢ for children to the gardens January through April.

Not far away in the town of Marianna you can visit **Florida Caverns,** 2701 Caverns Rd., limestone caverns with intriguing formations and overhead lighting that reflects on water droplets creating a rainbow of sparkling colors. You can camp, swim, hike, picnic, fish, and canoe in the park, open 8 a.m. to sunset year round. For reservations call 904/482-3632. Admission to the park is 50¢ per person, camping is $6 to $8, and cave admission is $1.50 for adults, 75¢ for children under 12.

A fascinating way to explore the inlets and byways in this magically beautiful part of the state is aboard a bicycle. A friendly fellow named Dave Pierce has taken over as owner and operator of **Suwanee Country Tours,** P.O. Box 247, White Springs, FL 32096 (tel. 904/397-2347), formerly called Suwannee River Bicycle Tours. Dave is featuring weekend tours across 58 to 75 miles of pretty countryside up here, and has added canoe tours on the Alapaha, Withlacoochee, and Suwanee Rivers to his repertoire. On either of the tours you stay overnight in small hotels or motels (a few are sleeping-out trips). Prices for a weekend trip range from $125 to $265 and include everything—canoe, food, lodging—except bicycles.

SPORTS: In a town that's about half state government and half university students, sports are more spectator than participant, although you'll find some golf and tennis, plus swimming or boating on nearby lakes.

There are few things more historical—or more hysterical—than Florida State University **football** fans, so you won't want to miss a Seminoles game if you're in town when they're playing. Everyone from doddering alumni to toddling future quarterbacks turns up for fall games when fierce competition with other Florida schools makes for many a prank. Florida A&M is known throughout the state and the nation for it's high-stepping award-winning Rattlers band, which performs here at their football games. Florida State University also has a **Flying Circus** (tel. 644-4874), which performs high-flying hijinks at a special show each May.

You can roam either campus anytime too. The **Florida State University** Visitor Information Center is at 100 S. Woodward St., just off Tennessee Street, US 90 (tel. 644-3246), and has conducted tours of the campus at 11 a.m. and at 1 and 2 p.m. Monday through Friday. **Florida A&M** has an interesting Black Archives division and a very attractive campus where visitors can get a personally guided tour from the university's public relations department (tel. 599-3414) in the main administration building. The campus is located between S. Adams Street and Wahnish Way.

The city's recreation department (tel. 222-7259) will be happy to locate tennis courts for you, but two of the best are at **Jake Gaither Community Center and Golf Course,** on Bragg Drive (tel. 576-1016). Here you can play bumper pool, basketball, and tennis on lighted courts—free—and golf on an 18-hole course open every day but Christmas. Greens fees for 18 holes are $4 ($2 for high school students and senior citizens, and for twilight golf). Call for starting times at 576-1418.

The most popular **canoeing** spots are trails on the Aucilla River (about 25 miles southwest of Tallahassee), the Ochlockonee River (30 miles north and 20 miles west), the Wacissa River (at Wacissa Springs, east of the city), and the Wakulla River (about 15 miles south of town).

Bass, bream, shellcrackers, and crappies are the fish you'll catch in nearby Lakes Talquin, Jackson, Iamonia, and Miccousukee. A *Tallahassee Area Fishing Camps and Lodges Guide* is available from the Chamber of Commerce, P.O. Box 1639, Tallahassee, FL 32303 (tel. 904/224-8116).

From May to December, you can bet on the dogs at **Jefferson County Kennel Club** in nearby Monticello, or on the skills of jai-alai players from January to June at the **Big Bend Fronton** in nearby Quincy (tel. 442-4411). Admission to the dog track is 50¢; clubhouse, $1; and box seats, $3. Post time is 8 p.m. Monday through Saturday, 2 p.m. for Saturday matinees. You can dine at the Trackside dining room too. Jai-alai admission is $1.

SIDE TRIPS: Not far from the capital are some sights worth a detour.

A Visit to an Oyster Village

For a beautiful drive through tall pines and rolling dunes, zip off on US 98 to the sleepy fishing village of **Apalachicola.** One of Florida's last frontiers, this small town is a New England–like collage of colorful fishing boats, rambling stately old homes, some dating back to the Civil War, and sleepy streets that once surged with activity when this village was a thriving cotton port.

Here in Apalachicola lived scientist John Gorrie, who invented the one single thing that put Florida on the map and Gorrie in Washington's Hall of Fame: the principles of air conditioning and ice making! A tiny state museum here (on 6th Street, one block off US 98) is manned from 9 a.m. to 5 p.m. daily and tells the story of Gorrie's determined efforts to find ways to keep his yellow fever patients cool.

When railroads usurped much of the cotton trade and the city port was blockaded during the Civil War, the town's importance as a port plummeted. It reached the heights again in the timber boom of the 1930s, but declined as the swamps were stripped of cypress. But Apalachicola has a way of bouncing back and today it's famous throughout the state for its **oyster beds,** which produce the succulent Apalachicola oysters you'll see on menus all over the state. Painstaking work it is too—gulf waters cannot be dredged, so fishermen use long-handled tongs with scissor-like scoops on the end to pluck the bivalves from the bottom. About 90% of the state's oyster production is done here, and more than half of Florida's shellfish output comes from this small town.

If you'd like to stay a while, head for **St. George Island,** a new development on an island that has welcomed pirates, Creek Indians, and European colonists over the centuries (not to mention treasure hunters: a great pirate treasure is said to have been buried here). These days you'll find 2000 acres of state parkland on the island and small privately owned beachfront cottages and apartments which you can rent from **Alice D. Collins Realty, Inc.,** Box 16, St. George Island, Eastpoint, FL 32328 (tel. 904/670-2758). Several of the cottages are built on stilts; some feature cathedral ceilings, and all are completely furnished. Prices range from a winter low of $200 per week to a summer high of $850 per week.

North of town on Route 65 at **Fort Gadsden** (it's about 25 miles) one of the most violent episodes in Florida's battle-strewn history took place. Built by the British as a recruitment center for Indians and blacks during the War of 1812, the fort was abandoned and later taken over by escaped slaves who felt they'd been left in charge by the British. Although the U.S. had no claim to the fort at that time, it felt threatened by the fort's presence and ordered it destroyed. A troop assigned to do that fired at the fort, which sheltered women and children from nearby Indian villages, and hit a powder magazine killing all but 30 of the 300 people inside. It was later named after James Gadsden, the famous negotiator of the Gadsden Purchase. The park's open from 8 a.m. to sunset year round. For information on camping facilities, call 904/670-8988.

A few miles north of Apalachicola on US 98 is the village of **Panacea,** where unexpectedly you'll find both a lovely motel and a spectacularly beautiful restaurant. It's surprising because this small town is way, way out in the middle of nothing at all except lovely forests, sparkling rivers, and beautiful beaches. How do they survive? Well, it doesn't hurt that throngs of Tallahassee legislators and government employees are just 38 miles away.

Here too is an outstanding restaurant, called **Brothers Three Garden By the Sea** in honor of its founders, George, Jimmy, and Pete Koikos, who own two equally good restaurants in Tallahassee. Open only Thursday through Sunday, Brothers Three has taken over what was once a very posh riverside home, turned the swimming pool into a fountain and the porch overlooking the river into a jungley garden. Soothing to the spirit and easy on the wallet, Brothers Three is open from 5 to 10 p.m. (from 4 to 9 p.m. on Sunday), and prices are just $7 to $10.

Another local spot, **Stone Crabber,** US 19/98, Panacea (tel. 984-5201), takes rusticity to new heights and is an absolutely wonderful place for just hangin' around. Lots of people have discovered that, so on weekends you'll usually find a crowd of Tallahassee escapees here just hangin' around. You'll also find them chowing down on fat and sassy local oysters at outrageously low prices —a dozen for about $2, a dollar more if you want them smoked in the smokehouse out back. Smoked shrimp, mullet, and amberjack are also on the blackboard menu here, for prices in the $8 to $12 range, including slaw, corn on the cob, and fresh bread. This is the kind of spot where you dump yourself into a seat, gaze out at a heron winging over the marshy waters of the bay, and let the world roll on by without you. Hours are 5 to 10 p.m. Tuesday through Thursday, and noon to 10 p.m. Friday through Sunday; closed Monday.

A Dream of Jeanie

Who can forget Stephen Foster's haunting melody about the beauties of Jeanie with the light-brown hair, or his melancholy lament for life "Way down upon the Swanee River"? Once a year Foster's considerable contribution to American music is remembered here in **White Springs** at the annual Jeanie Festival, when top female singers compete for title and scholarships at a competition that comes complete with attractive young women garbed in lacy hoop skirts of those long-gone (but never quite forgotten around here) days of the Old South.

White Springs, on US 41 about ten miles northwest of Lake City, where the festival occurs in the first week of October, is a memorial to the Pittsburgh-born composer who feted the Suwannee. Foster never actually saw this crystal river lined with moss-draped live oaks, but he discovered that its shortened form, Swanee, would just fit his melody.

The second-largest river in the state, the Suwannee begins in Georgia's Okeefenokee Swamp as an inky stream, cuts through limestone banks, and turns into a jungle-lined stream where you can cruise aboard a turn-of-the-century paddlewheeler, the *Belle of the Suwannee,* on a $1 trip that hasn't changed much since this hauntingly lovely river became a playground for Yankee tourists more than 100 years ago.

Foster's Swanee song, "Old Folks at Home," is the official state song. You can hear it played on bells of the **Carillon Tower** and see rare musical instruments in the Springer collection of bells below the tower. Boat, carillon, and collection are all at the **Stephen Foster State Folk Culture Center,** on US 41, three miles south of I-75 (tel. 904/397-2733). Admission to the park is $2 for adults, $1 for children. Fees are slightly higher during the Folk Festival in late May when the state's crafts workers and folk musicians gather here.

An Ancient Spring

About ten miles south of Tallahassee at **Wakulla Springs** (take US 319 south to Route 61 and 61 to Route 267), you can swim in a spring that's welcomed splashers for tens of thousands of years: Mastodon bones have been found in the deepest recesses of the crystal waters. At the heart of the springs more than 600,000 gallons of water a minute are filtered by limestone rock that makes the springs so clear you can't judge their depths. Along the banks of the water, you'll see sleepy alligators, shrieking bird life, and tiny forest creatures. On a glass-bottomed boat tour you can see the fish that live here and play water games with the boat's captain.

The controversial Florida financier and kingmaker Edward Ball turned the springs into a preservation area some years back and spent much of his time here over the years. In the 1930s he built a serene old Spanish-style inn, the **Wakulla Springs Hotel,** 14 miles south of Tallahassee on Route 61/267, Wakulla Springs, FL 32305 (tel. 904/224-5950), that is today one of the state's most intriguing country inns. Floors are Tennessee marble (there's even a marble checkers set). Hefty wood ceiling beams were painstakingly painted with Florida scenes and flowers by a German artist who reportedly was a court painter for Kaiser Wilhelm. You'll see rare Spanish tiles, black granite tables, decorative arches, massive doors. In the inn's high-ceilinged rooms, dark-wood furniture and a smattering of antiques are cheerfully elegant. Downstairs there's a large dining room where you can have a full dinner of home-cooked country foods for $6 to $10, and in winter sit by a huge fireplace where flames roar. Swim in the cool spring by day and at night sit beside it and listen to the murmur of forest creatures who live along these banks. If you'd like to see the springs, there are two different boat tours, each at $3.50 for adults, $1.80 for children.

Rates at Wakulla (which comes from an Indian word meaning "where the water flows upward like rays of heavenly light out of the shadow of the hill") are $32 to $60, year round.

TAMPA BAY

SOONER OR LATER someone would have laid claim to the lands on the shores of this huge bowl-shaped bay, but it was a fluke of history that got things going so soon in Tampa Bay: in 1527 Panfilo de Narvaez and four galleons, on an expedition to conquer, colonize, and find gold in Florida, were blown off course by a hurricane and landed on the Gulf Coast. De Narvaez went ashore to trade with the Indians and in their villages found a gold ornament. He thought he'd found his treasure, but here comes the second fluke: those gold pieces were really Spain's very own doubloons salvaged by the Indians from beach shipwrecks!

It was fool's gold de Narvaez sought, for the real gold on this coast was to be found centuries later in sunshine and sand. But before that could happen, the sands of this Gulf Coast were trod by many hopefuls in search of treasure. Early on, the visitors were pirates—ex-slaves Black Caesar, José Gaspar, and Jean Lafitte—but when piracy became a somewhat perilous career, fishermen began to gather on the shores. It wasn't long before bridges and causeways connected the offshore islands to the mainland cities of Tampa and St. Petersburg.

Then some modern pirates, called promoters, moved in. They found and lost some real gold here in the boom days of the 1920s after railroad magnate Henry Plant extended his tracks south and frozen northerners discovered the Suncoast. Soon they came in droves, to spend winters in Plant's fanciful Tampa hotel, his sprawling Belleview Biltmore, and later in the magnificence of the cotton-candy-pink Don CeSar.

F. Scott Fitzgerald came. Babe Ruth came. Teddy Roosevelt and his Rough Riders dropped in on their way to the Spanish-American War. Scots clansmen moved in to build a village called Dunedin, and brought with them bagpipes whose mournful wail you'll still hear here. Greek sponge fishermen arrived to dig in the oceans and dance to the twang of bouzoukis that still entertain bay dwellers.

These balmy water-locked lands have been salvation and selling point for generations. They've been a welcome sight for pirates and Union blockaders, Indians and explorers, those with giant dreams and slick schemes. Today they wait only for the sun-seeker in search of nothing more golden than sunlight and sand.

1. Orientation

GETTING THERE: So rapidly has this area been growing that the number of arrivals and departures from Tampa's sleek new airport has skyrocketed in recent years. Airlines now bring thousands of international visitors from Europe on British Airways and DER Charters, and multitudes from around this hemisphere on 25 airlines, including Air Canada, American, Eastern, Delta, Northwest Orient, Ozark, Pan Am, Piedmont, Republic, TWA, United, and USAir.

A word here about Tampa's airport, which is generally acclaimed as one of the, if not *the,* most modern airports in the nation, so much so that it is now a tourist attraction itself. If you fly in here (and even if you don't), allow an unencumbered hour or so to zip around on people movers that move passengers from plane to terminal in 60 seconds, to ride escalators through floors hung with metal sculptures on invisible strings, and to visit the penthouse revolving restaurant and lounge. Tampa's airport is so beautifully designed that it manages to seem quiet even at its busiest, and passengers can move from automobile seat to airplane seat in less than 700 steps.

On the southern end of the bay, Sarasota's small airport welcomes Delta, Eastern, Pan Am, PBA, Republic, Southern Express, and United.

Greyhound and **Trailways** buses also connect the cities to each other and to other parts of the state and nation. Miami to Tampa takes about six hours and costs $24 one way.

GETTING AROUND: For limousine service from Tampa Airport call **The Limo** (tel. 822-3333), which serves all of Pinellas County (Tampa), plus St. Petersburg and the beaches, for $9.25. **Central Florida Limo** (tel. 883-3730) charges $3.50 for rides to downtown Tampa hotels. If you'd like to arrive in style, **Bill Child's Luxury Limousine** has chauffeured Cadillacs with rates by the hour, day, or week (tel. 446-5991).

There is also limousine service, **Ambassador Limo** (tel. 355-7157), from the airport to Sarasota and Bradenton for prices beginning at $23 single, $41 for two (about $4 less to Bradenton). A two-day advance reservation is required.

Here, as everywhere else, taxis are expensive, the more so because distances are great. **Yellow Cab** (tel. 253-0121) charges $1 a mile.

Unless you plan to settle in a beach hotel and stay put right there, you'd be wise to rent a car since this is a huge area with long distances between Tampa and St. Petersburg and the Holiday Isles. All major national **car-rental companies** operate here, for prices in the $70- to $90-a-week range.

Alamo (tel. 879-4700) competes vigorously with other companies, and manages to undercut most of them, at last check offering a small car for $69 a week unlimited mileage, and no charge if you rent the car in one city and drop it off in another. The company has an office in Sarasota (tel. 355-8896) too.

A local company called **Three Dollar Car Rentals** (tel. 823-0751) has offices in St. Petersburg and branches in Clearwater and Bradenton. It offers mid-'70s cars for $3 a day plus 18¢ a mile and $4.50 a day insurance. They're all air-conditioned and power equipped. **Hire a Heep Cheap** (tel. 546-2777) in Pinellas Park has rates of $60 to $65 a week for older cars too.

To get around these sprawling metropolises in comfort and see some of the fascinating attractions, you really *need* a car. Few travelers realize that it takes half an hour or more to drive from St. Petersburg to Tampa, from Tampa to

Clearwater, from St. Petersburg to St. Petersburg Beach, and down the islands from Clearwater to Pass-a-Grille.

Unless you're content to spend your time here at or near your hotel, choose it carefully since **public transportation** operates only during daylight hours. If you are relying on local transport, the **Pinellas Suncoast Transit Authority** (tel. 530-9911) covers the county, charging 50¢ to 60¢ a ride. To get to the beaches you must connect with **Beach Airport Transport Service (BATS)** (tel. 367-3086). Folks at either of those transit companies will be able to tell you what bus to take where.

In Clearwater there's an addition to the transit system, the **Jolly Trolley,** a trolley look-alike on wheels which serves the city and the beaches for 25¢ a ride. On Treasure Island the **Dune Buggy** (tel. 360-1741) minibus prowls the island for the same prices.

Tampa has three free trolleys called the **Free Bee,** which connect downtown free parking areas with the center of the city and other city bus routes, which you can discover by calling 251-1078.

GETTING YOUR BEARINGS: If you're driving, it may help to know that Central Avenue divides **St. Petersburg** north-south, so TAPs (terraces, avenues, and places) run east-west, streets and ways run north-south.

The **Tampa** street plan is laid out in the quadrant system: Florida Avenue divides the city east and west, John F. Kennedy Boulevard and Frank Adamo Drive divide it north and south. The numbered avenues run east-west and the numbered streets run north-south.

To get from **Clearwater** to Tampa, take Route 60 (Courtney Campbell Causeway, which becomes Gulf to Bay Boulevard). Two other causeways, Howard Frankland Bridge (I-275) and Gandy Bridge (Route 92), cross Tampa Bay to St. Petersburg.

Other causeways to the beach are Belleaire (or Bay) Drive, Indian Rocks Causeway, Madeira Beach, Treasure Island, and St. Petersburg Causeways, and the Pinellas Bayway. Most are free, but one or two have small tolls.

Finally, of course, there's the famous **Sunshine Skyway** which soars majestically over Tampa Bay on its way to the Bradenton/Sarasota area.

TOURIST INFORMATION: Every one of the Holiday Isles and St. Petersburg and Tampa has its own chamber of commerce. One way to get information on St. Petersburg, St. Petersburg Beach, Indian Rocks Beach, Largo, Dunedin, Tarpon Springs, and Safety Harbor is to contact the **Pinellas Tourist Development Council,** Newport Square, Suite 109A, 2333 E. Bay Dr., Clearwater, FL 33546 (tel. 813/530-6452). Personable W. F. "Bill" Sheely is director.

At the **St. Petersburg Chamber of Commerce,** director Carol Wedge oversees a growing operation which is steadily building a large and helpful library of tourist materials. She and her staff are at 401 Third Ave. South, St. Petersburg, FL 33701 (tel. 813/821-4069).

In Tampa they'll be happy to help you if you call or write the **Tampa Chamber of Commerce** at 801 E. Kennedy Blvd., Tampa, FL 33602 (tel. 813/228-7777).

Things are changing very quickly in this rapidly growing city, so it's wise to take a look at local papers to find out what's happening when you're here. Those **newspapers** include the *Tampa Tribune,* the area's largest newspaper; the *Tampa Times,* a small afternoon daily; the *Clearwater Sun;* the award-winning *St. Petersburg Times,* one of the best newspapers of its size in the nation; and the

St. Petersburg Evening Independent. Tampa Bay magazine is a slick, professional production that keeps a sardonic eye on local trends in everything from politics to happy hours.

SPECIAL EVENTS: In February the Tampa Bay area goes slightly crazy during its annual **Gasparilla Festival.** Hundreds of otherwise staid cityfolk turn into leering pegleg pirates-for-a-day. Actually the revelry goes on for a week, but the big day is Gasparilla Day, when pinstripe suits are exchanged for pantaloons as a full-sailed, three-masted galleon stocked with this "krewe" of pretend pirates sails into St. Petersburg harbor to relive the legend of a long-ago invasion by José Gaspar.

Twice a year, in February and October, Tampa's Spanish quarter turns out in **Ybor City** to celebrate its stately, if somewhat bellicose, past with dark-eyed señoritas in lacy mantillas and swirling skirts, strolling musicians and Latin rhythms, sidewalk feasts, and illuminated parades.

In February, fat calves and porkers who have been real pigs all year are carted, pushed, and pulled to the **Florida State Fair** at Tampa's Fairgrounds, where owners vie for blue ribbons.

St. Petersburg also vies for attention in February with its **International Food Fair** fiesta, and again in March with its **Festival of the States,** which includes a marching band competition and a two-mile-long Parade of States highlighting the wonders of the other 49.

In March the mournful wail of bagpipes fills the air at Dunedin as that city's Scots community kicks off its annual **Highland Games.** Down the road a bit in Tarpon Springs, a Greek community celebrates **Greek Epiphany** in early January with street dances and a diving scramble for a luck-bringing gold cross.

Each November you can sample seafood at **John's Pass Seafood Festival,** while you enjoy fireworks, demonstrations, arts and crafts, and exhibits.

2. Tampa

In Tampa you'll see skyscrapers reaching for the clouds in shiny metallic splendor. This is a booming commercial center that's in the midst of yet another boom spiral thanks to ever-increasing air service to the city's modern airport and a Sun Belt population boom.

Tampa is a sprawling place that encompasses several colleges and universities, MacDill Air Force Base, the fascinating antique village of Ybor City, and the area's largest attraction, Busch Gardens' Dark Continent.

Long years ago a Spanish explorer dubbed Tampa the best port he had ever seen. Today the 96-year-old city is proud of its Port of Tampa, a massive complex that sprawls over miles of ground and ships out 25 million tons of phosphate a year.

You can trace some of Florida's history from Tampa's name, although there's little agreement on just exactly what it means. Prevailing theory has it that it's a corruption of an Indian word meaning a town near the bay, an area so loved by those Indians that they ran off most of the early explorers who came here from Spain in search of gold. Ponce de Leon didn't stay long, and neither did Hernando de Soto, who landed but fled when greeted by Indian arrows.

It took three centuries before change came to this wilderness. Even then you could barely call the little colony that grew up around Fort Brooke a village, let alone a city. That fort did, however, discourage some pretty unhappy Seminoles. After a couple of slumps during a Civil War blockade by Union soldiers and a yellow fever epidemic, the future arrived here in the form of railroad kingpin Henry Plant and a narrow-gauge railroad that connected Tampa to the world.

Plant and his east coast counterpart, Henry Flagler, were two rough-and-tumble types who soon were in hot competition, Plant building hotels and railroads here, Flagler moving lickety-split down east coast beaches. To go Flagler's empire one better, Plant recreated the Alhambra (at a cost of nearly $4 million) crowned by a raft of onion-shaped silver minarets topped by curving quarter moons. Intent on humbling Flagler, so the story goes, Plant sent him a telegram in 1891 inviting him to the grand opening in Tampa of what he called Florida's finest new hotel. A not-at-all-humbled Flagler shot back this succinct rejoinder: "Where's Tampa?"

Today, thanks to phosphate, Vincente Ybor's cigar factories (which moved here from Key West), the spend-iferous habits of the Rough Riders (who camped here on the way to Cuba for the Spanish-American War), the '20's land boom, shipbuilding, breweries, and finally the city's huge Busch Gardens tourist attraction, Tampa has grown into a streamlined city. No one asks "Where's Tampa?" these days.

USEFUL INFORMATION: For **police** or other **emergencies**, dial 911. . . . The **telephone area code** throughout the Tampa Bay area is 813, but some calls between Tampa and the adjoining cities are long distance, so you might check to see if there's a local number in Tampa for outlying shops and restaurants. . . . Late munchers will find **Denny's**, 1700 E. Fowler (tel. 971-9441). . . . For pharmaceutical needs, **Eckerd Drugs** stores are at various locations around the city (tel. 837-1509) and remain open 24 hours. . . . You can get quick laundry service at **Massey Cleaners**, 3209 E. Hillsborough Ave. (tel. 238-4987). . . . There's a **24-hour gas station**, Shell, at 7756 W. Hillsborough Ave. (tel. 884-9312). . . . Find the **postal station** nearest you by checking the white pages under U.S. Post Office, or call 228-2475. . . . For medical needs there's an **emergency walk-in clinic** at 2810 W. Buffalo St. (tel. 877-8450). . . . For the latest information on what's happening in **entertainment**, call 223-1111.

WHERE TO STAY: Most of Tampa's hotels are located near the airport, although some are downtown or out by Busch Gardens. I've divided them up by price. Since Tampa's a very busy commercial center you'll find that most prices vary little or not at all by season.

The Luxury Leaders

Marriott Hotel, at the airport, Tampa, FL 32600 (tel. 813/879-5151, or toll free 800/228-9290), is a showcase inside a showcase. Located right in the terminal, this super-soundproofed hotel offers you an ever-changing airscape, and inside things are just as dramatic: luxurious, spacious rooms, a special executives' sixth-floor lounge with complimentary cocktails and champagne, a lobby seafood bar, a revolving penthouse restaurant of considerable renown (and prices in the $10 to $20 range for dinner). Almost a city of its own, this hotel provides places to play (a cocktail lounge with backgammon boards, a pool, a disco), and places to dine (from a coffeeshop to a spinning rooftop restaurant), and extra-special places to sleep. Certainly one of the city's prime-time properties, Marriott charges $108 double, $98 single, all year.

Tampa Hilton, 200 Ashley Dr., Tampa, FL 33602 (tel. 813/223-2456, or toll free in Florida 800/432-5141, and toll-free numbers in every state), curves gently along the banks of the Hillsborough River within sight of the weird silver onion domes of Henry Plant's lurid but lovely old hotel, now the University of Tampa.

Soaring high over the road, the seven-story Hilton's 265 rooms have a pretty view of the meandering river as it heads for Hillsborough Bay. There's an excellent dining room called the Riverside Café and an intimate cocktail lounge with entertainment. Hilton's downtown location makes it a favorite with commercial travelers, and is a good choice for those intent on downtown shopping and dining. Year-round rates are $60 to $85 single, $70 to $95 double.

Another recent link in the chain operations is Marriott Hotels, which completed its newest Florida hotel in the summer of 1981. The **Tampa Marriott–West Shore,** 10001 N. Westshore Blvd., Tampa, FL 33607 (tel. 813/876-9611, or toll free 800/228-9290), is a 312-room, 14-story hotel on six acres of land just off I-275 about five minutes from the airport. Marriott knows plenty about building hotels, and this one has a restaurant, lounge, indoor/outdoor swimming pool, hydrotherapy pool, saunas, exercise center, game room, gift shop, and complimentary transportation to and from the airport. You'll have lots of room to spread out in the extra-large rooms, decorated in contemporary prints and furnishings. Rates are $98 to $108, year round ($85 on Friday and Saturday).

The **Bay Harbor Inn,** 7700 Courtney Campbell Causeway, Tampa, FL 33607 (tel. 813/885-2541, or toll free 800/237-7773; in Florida 800/282-0613), is as far west as you can go in Tampa. It's right at the edge of the bay, and quite near the airport as well. If you anchor in this harbor, you'll find an imposing six-story, 280-room edifice in a bayside setting complete with a crescent of beach. Just across the causeway from Clearwater, the hotel has spacious rooms with private balconies overlooking the city or bay and decorated in attractive, bright color schemes. There are tennis courts, a gift shop, heated pool, in-room movies, a playground, a lounge with plenty of entertainment, and a restaurant. You can rent sailboats too. There's also complimentary transportation from the airport. Winter rates are $80 to $95, to $190 for bay-view suites.

The **Inn on the Point,** Courtney Campbell Causeway, Tampa, FL 33607 (tel. 813/884-2000, or toll free 800/237-2555; in Florida, 800/332-6688), occupies a strip of waterfront land too. It's not on a beach, but provides a king-size pool, and there's a large public beach, shopping, and golf just minutes away on the hotel's free shuttle. Splashes of bright tropical colors make these roomy accommodations cheerful. For activity, there are tennis courts, a putting green, Ping-Pong, a game room, sauna, daily tours and parties, and a lounge and disco with nightly dancing and entertainment. Clive's Restaurant is a lovely study in pink, a tiny room that is both cozy and sophisticated. Delicacies on the menu range from crab legs with toasted almonds to steak Diane, with prices in the $12 to $20 range. Rates at the resort are $58 to $80, year round, and include a complimentary buffet breakfast and a cocktail party with open bar—every day. There's no charge for children under 17.

For the posh spa life, cart that avoirdupois over to **Safety Harbor Spa,** 105 Bayshore Dr. North, Safety Harbor, FL 33572 (tel. 813/726-1161, or toll free 800/237-0155), where you can dine and diet, be pummeled and pampered, and take it off, take it all off, with the minimum of pain and the maximum of pleasure. Safety Harbor has the works in spa facilities from mineral baths to yoga, medical exams, golf, tennis, saunas. There's a 250-room hotel here with spacious bright rooms in an older building and others in a new wing that are prettier yet. Safety Harbor's been operating from October to May now for 35 years, and charges $132 to $148 per person double, $170 to $244 single, depending on location and size of accommodations. Closed May to October.

You can tell from the address of the **Hyatt Regency,** 1 Tampa City Center, Tampa, FL 33602 (tel. 813/225-1234, or toll free 800/228-9000), just where this handsome new hotel is: right smack in the middle of town. Behind the sleek mirrored facade of the Hyatt lies a multilevel lobby filled with shops and inviting restaurants that circle a two-story waterfall. Quite a convenient spot for those attending functions at the Curtis Hixon Hall just down the street, this slick new hotel is just as good a choice for those who want to explore this old city. Slated to be right at the forefront of the downtown renaissance occurring in Tampa, the Hilton features bright contemporary furnishings in its spacious rooms, which are also equipped with all the extra amenities that have made Hyatt one of the nation's top hotel chains. A large hotel, Hyatt has 540 rooms, many of them sporting bay or river views. In the hotel's Regency Club, you're treated to complimentary breakfasts and cocktails and a special concierge staff to do your bidding. A swimming pool, two whirlpools, and a health club help you work off the calories you consume in the hotel's two restaurants. Rates are $85 to $122 double, $75 to $112 single, year round. Suites with a parlor begin at $75, with fancier one-bedroom accommodations rising from $150 to $220.

Chain operations in the area include LaQuinta Motor Inn, Holiday Inn, Howard Johnson's Motor Lodge, Sheraton, Rodeway, and Ramada Inns, all of which have toll-free numbers for rate information and fall into a moderate to expensive category.

Moderate Choices

If you'd like to stay out near Busch Gardens and spend a day or so at the attraction's Adventure Island water park, you can bunk down in any of several nice spots, least expensive of which is the **Garden View Motel**, at 2500 E. Busch Blvd., Tampa, FL 33612 (tel. 813/933-3958). Here you'll find small but tidy accommodations decorated in rose and burgundy. A small pool is tucked into the corner of the building. Double rates are just $26 to $38 a day, summer or winter.

Days Inn, 2901 E. Busch Blvd., Tampa, FL 33612 (tel. 813/933-6471, or toll free 800/325-2525), has a very large hotel here with medium-size rooms decorated in tropical colors. There's a large swimming pool and all the usual Days Inn accoutrements, including a very inexpensive restaurant with prices in the $5 to $8 range. Rates are just $36 to $42 double.

Ramada Inn, 820 E. Busch Blvd., Tampa, FL 33162 (tel. 813/933-4011, or toll free 800/228-2828), has a 268-unit hotel near Busch Gardens, with tennis courts and two pools for $52 to $60 double most of the year. **Howard Johnson's Busch Gardens,** 720 E. Fowler Ave., Tampa, FL 33162 (tel. 813/971-5150, or toll free 800/654-2000), charges $58 to $72 double.

Back in Tampa, **Tahitian Inn Motel,** 601 S. Dale Mabry Hwy., Tampa, FL 33609 (tel. 813/877-6721), is a good moderately priced inn with 79 rooms, color TV, heated pool, and a coffeeshop open 7 a.m. to 3 p.m. daily. Prices are $37 to $45 double, for the attractive medium-size rooms here.

You'll also save at the two **Expressway Inns:** at 3693 Gandy Blvd., Tampa, FL 33611 (tel. 813/837-1971), and at 3688 Gandy Blvd., Tampa, FL 33611 (tel. 813/837-1921). Both are about four miles south of I-275 on US 92. Some of the simple but attractively furnished rooms have refrigerators (for which you'll pay a few dollars extra). Both inns have a pool and color televisions. You can bring Fido, but there's a $10 charge. Rates are $34 to $40 double, all year.

Outside Town (But Worth the Drive)

Wesley Chapel is a tiny town that's not far from Tampa and not even an unreasonable distance from Orlando. I could tell you it's near Zephyrhills, site of the state's only officially sanctioned fox hunt, but suspecting that Zephyrhills is not yet a household word, let me say that Wesley Chapel is about 25 minutes from Tampa International Airport. Here you'll find one of the state's newest villa resorts, **Saddlebrook,** on Route 54, Wesley Chapel, FL 34249, one mile east of I-75 (tel. 813/973-1111, or toll free 800/237-7519). One-, two-, and three-bedroom villas at Saddlebrook are part of an $80-million condominium resort plunked down amid palms and pines 15 miles north of Tampa. All are individually and beautifully decorated, and have full kitchens, baths for every bedroom, balconies or patios, a pool and whirlpool, restaurant, and 27 holes of golf. It's a serene spot with rolling grounds laced with tiny streams and stands of pines. In peak season (from mid-September through May), the resort charges $96 to $116 for hotel rooms, $116 to $136 for one-bedroom apartments, and up to $320 for two- and three-bedroom accommodations. Summer rates range from $60 to $165. Children under 12 stay free, and the resort will arrange airport pickup for $12.50 per person if you let them know 24 hours in advance.

A Very Special Resort

Innisbrook, P.O. Drawer 1088, Tarpon Springs, FL 34286 (tel. 813/937-3124, or toll free 800/237-0157; in Florida, 800/282-9813), just north of Clearwater on US 19 North, is one of the state's loveliest golf and tennis resorts. Nowhere else will you find such glorious rolling acres of pineland or so many features designed to make anyone—golfer, tennis player, or none of the above—feel they're living in a wonderland. For openers, there are 1000 acres of grounds, left for the most part in their enchanting natural state. Chipmunks chatter high in the pines, ducks swoop around the lakes, and I'm betting there's not another resort in Florida with signs warning you to slow down for the peacocks! You'll find three magnificent golf courses here (two rated among the nation's top 50), 17 tennis courts, and a new tennis and racquetball center with indoor courts.

There are 1200 suites, all located in lodges nestled among the fairways and under the pines, their wood exteriors subtly blended into the wooded surroundings. All suites are entered from center halls and have private patios or balconies. They're individually decorated, and while all are a beautiful melange of colors and fine furniture, some are downright spectacular. They're all spacious too, and of course never far from a swimming pool since there are five on the resort. You can dine in any of three clubhouse dining rooms on huge breakfast buffets and fine continental cuisine, then spend an entertaining evening in the resort's nightclub where star-spangled revues keep things hopping all year long.

I was overawed when I first saw Innisbrook, and I think you will be too. Hotel room rates peak at $149 double from February to May; in summer larger accommodations begin with club suites at $71 and rise for two-bedroom suites to $258. In summer too, there are many money-saving package programs and prices range from $75.50 to $96 double. Golf is $20 to $24 year round, and tennis is $4 an hour, but several package plans will save you money on those fees.

Something New

April Athey, who works for the state's Department of Tourism and may just know *everything* about Florida, recently updated me on some of the country inns that have sprung up around the state. Most elaborate of those is the **Crown Hotel,** 109 N. Seminole Ave., Inverness, FL 32650 (tel. 904/344-5555), a place that had been mentioned to me by several delighted travelers. All those raves led me to the tiny village of Inverness to see for myself what all the excitement was about . . . and now I know!

What a little jewel they have here! Resurrected from the run down remains of what was once a general store, the Crown is testimony to what miracles can be wrought with $2 million. Owned by British investors who spotted the possibilities inherent in a 90-year-old building and in the growing community of Inverness, the Crown is as lacy and perky as a new Easter bonnet. There are sparkling cut-glass panels in the polished-wood doors, glowing carpets on the floors, hand-rubbed wood on the spiral staircase. In the inn's 34 rooms you'll find original wood floors polished to a fare-thee-well, shiny brass beds, ornate flounces on heavy tasseled draperies, gold bathroom fixtures, antiques and carefully chosen reproductions. Tables have polished marble tops. Doors have handsome carved moldings. Lamps have etched-glass globes and brass bases. In the lobby a 200-year-old cabinet holds an awesome collection of glittering reproductions of the British monarchy's crowns and scepters. (Ask manager Ian Young, possessor of a delightful Scots accent, to tell you what fun they had explaining those bejewelled crowns to a Customs inspector!)

Anglophiles will go all nostalgic in the Fox and Hounds Tavern, an intimate, pubby spot where steak-and-kidney pie, fish and chips, and the like are on the menu each day for under $5. For evening dining don't miss the Churchill Restaurant where sophisticated maître d'hôtel Salvatore presides over a sleek—and chic—operation. As you dine on such delicacies as lobster Evoc (Maine lobster tossed with shrimp and water chestnuts and topped with a cream sauce) or tournedos Rossini (prices in the $13 to $18 range), a pianist plays softly in the background and crystal chandeliers glitter overhead. My goodness, is tiny Inverness *ready* for all this glamor?

Outside there's a swimming pool ornamented by a lacy gazebo, and nearby are tennis courts, golfing, fishing, and boating. While you won't find bright lights and neon whoop-de-doo in Inverness, you will find a warm welcome from people who love the serenity and charm of their small village. If you want beach, the gulf is a 20-minute drive from here.

Rates at the Crown are $47.50 single, $60 double. If you have children along, the hotel can provide you with a beautiful trundle-bedded separate room for the youngsters at a special price. Inverness is about an hour's drive north of Tampa just west of the intersection of I-75 and Route 44, about 30 minutes or less to Ocala, Silver Springs, Weeki Wachee Springs, and Cedar Key. You'll find the hotel right in the middle of town just half a block off Route 44. Just look for the antique London double-decker bus parked at the front door.

WHERE TO DINE: You can dine on everything from paella to porterhouse in Tampa's outstanding restaurants. And remember that the prices I've cited are for entrees, but that usually includes salad, one or two vegetables, and sometimes coffee as well.

American/Continental

Bern's Steak House, 1208 S. Howard St. (tel. 251-2421), is without question the best known steakhouse in Florida. Real fans, of which there are many, call it the best in the nation! Certainly the menu here is a study in the great American fascination with the steer. You can buy any cut of steak—filet mignon, strip sirloin, Delmonico, T-bone, porterhouse, or chateaubriand—in any thickness and any weight you can dream up. Beef is aged five to eight weeks, cut, trimmed, and weighed to order for you, then broiled over charcoal by chefs under the watchful eye of owner/chef Bern Laxer, who is in the kitchen. To get what they want in quality, they do just about everything themselves—from grinding and roasting their own coffee beans to growing their own fresh vegetables organically on their own farm. Laxer loves and collects wines, so the wine list is just slightly smaller than a telephone book and is, he claims, "the largest variety of wines ever assembled in one restaurant anywhere in the world." Few would dispute it.

You can stake your claim on a slab of steer for prices that begin at $13.90 and go up with your capacity to eat and to pay. Many many people think elegant Bern's is worth every buffalo head it costs them, so reservations are mandatory anytime, but virtually impossible on weekends when this award-winning spot packs them in from flank to flank. Open from 5 to 11 p.m. daily.

An attractive spot in Tampa, **The Verandah,** at 5250 W. Kennedy Blvd. (tel. 876-0168), is garnering rave reviews from residents who flock here for the handsome wood and greenery atmosphere and an attractive array of menu items. On the list here you'll find very good seafood and beef dishes from $12 to $20. It's open for dinner from 6 to 11 p.m. Monday through Saturday; weekdays for lunch from 11:15 a.m. to 2:30 p.m. There's a piano bar in the lounge.

Chuck's Steakhouse, 11911 N. Dale Mabry Hwy. (tel. 962-2226), has a penchant for nature and panders to it with an aviary and aquariums scattered throughout the restaurant. With a name like that, you can figure what the specialty is, but there's also quite a selection of seafood, from shrimp teriyaki to crab, lobster tails, grouper, and swordfish. Dinner, including a copious salad bar, is in the $10 to $15 bracket. Chuck's is open 4 to 11 p.m. weekdays, an hour later on weekends, and it has also been known to be open for lunch from December through April, but that's iffy so you'd better check first if you're in search of lunch.

Cuban/Spanish

Rare is the person who is not overwhelmed at the block-long magnificence of the **Columbia,** at 21st Street and Broadway (tel. 248-4961). Florida's oldest restaurant opened in 1905 and was named by a patriotic owner, grateful for the help of "Columbia the Gem of the Ocean" in freeing his native Cuba. Caesar Gonzmart, don of the third generation of the family, now oversees this must-see spot where 11 dining rooms seat 1500 people amid Cuban tile, skylit patios, fountains, and furbelows. He also plays the violin and entertains at one of three nightly revues complete with flamenco dancers and singers. Don't fail to try the 1905 house salad—it's super in all meanings of the word. There's a four-page menu here from which I especially recommend the Spanish bean soup dotted with ham and Spanish sausage, or the chilled gazpacho resting atop a bowl of ice, picadillo Habañera prepared with capers and olives, the chicken Valenciana made with tomatoes, onions, saffron, ham, wine, and asparagus. Seafood tempters include the snapper alicante with a touch of garlic and a shrimp suprême garnish, or zarzuela de mariscos, a combination of seafoods in a light tomato sauce. Paella Valenciana is worth the 35- to 45-minute wait at this enchanting spot (try a *blue* margarita while you're waiting) where dinner entree prices average $10 to $15 (topping out with lobster dishes at $22). Open 11 a.m. to midnight daily, and to 2:30 a.m. in two jazz clubs, the Café and the Warehouse.

Don Quixote, 1536 E. Seventh Ave. (tel. 247-9454), occupies a historic site in what used to be the game room of El Centro Español in this historic city. Now it's a high-ceilinged, paddle-fanned, conscientiously maintained emporium where quantities are as large as the memories of bygone days. Even Pancho would be hard put to put away the platter-size pork chops, slabs of salted cod with a Basque touch of tomato sauce, mounds of shrimp gently glazed in wine sauce, or any of the ample treats created by the Asturian family who run Don Quixote. Prices are low with most dinners in the $4 to $10 range. The Don is open from 10:30 a.m. to 3 p.m. daily (except Sunday) and from 5:30 to 10 p.m. on Friday and Saturday. Paella for two is $24.

Sooner or later everyone in Tampa will turn up at **Café Pepe,** 2006 W. Kennedy Blvd. (tel. 253-6501), where the atmosphere is ho-hum but the Spanish food is *ole!* Huge platters of paella ($25.95 for two), luscious arroz con pollo, bacon-wrapped or garlic-spiced shrimp, picadillo brimming with olives and raisins, even coconut ice cream are all made right here. Prices are the best you'll find anywhere, ringing in at an average of $11. Dining is fun amid rapid-fire Spanish and the general clamor of al gusto dining. It's open from 11 a.m. to 11 p.m. Monday through Friday, for dinner only on Saturday, 5 to 11 p.m.

French

La Méditerranée, 5000 N. Dale Mabry Hwy. (tel. 876-6924), emphasizes its *classical* French cooking, as you will once you've visited this attractive and popular restaurant. Featured here are chef Bernard Pascal's very special interpretations of such traditional dishes as duckling à l'orange and chateaubriand béarnaise, supplemented by departures like red snapper duglère and shrimp St. Tropez. Of course there are luscious French pastries, and dinner is served nightly (except Sunday) from 5:30 to 10:30 p.m. at prices beginning about $8, averaging $10 to $15. Lunch is served weekdays from 11:30 a.m. to 2:30 p.m.

Chef Daniel Fuchs comes to Florida with some pretty impressive credentials—he once cooked at New York's Tavern on the Green, and was personal chef to France's Gen. Charles DeGaulle! Like many of the talented, he has moved south, in Tampa to create **Lafitte Restaurant,** 1601 Snow Ave. (tel. 251-4441). Here you can try some of France's best grape products at one of the state's few wine bars (50 different wines are available), and dine on such delicacies as rack of lamb, steak au poivre, filet mignon, chicken beaujolais, langouste. Entree prices, including salad and vegetables, range from $6 to $8 for lunch and from $8 to $14 for dinner. Lafitte is open from 11:30 a.m. to 2 a.m. daily. A pleasant outside patio is open when the weather's nice but the dining room is pretty and intimate too, and there's an adjoining cocktail lounge. Brunch is available from 11:30 a.m. to 3 p.m. on Saturday and Sunday.

Oriental

For Oriental cuisine in subdued surroundings, **Madame Butterfly,** 3751 W. Cypress (tel. 876-1709), gets my vote. Lovely Oriental ladies in stunning kimonos seat you on plump cushions and serve delectable Oriental dishes from several countries: Korean bulgogi and kimchi, Japanese sashimi, Thai or Chinese specialties, many of which are cooked right at your table. You'll pay $10 to $15 for dinner, and the restaurant's open from 11:30 a.m. to 11 p.m. daily (from 4 p.m. on Saturday and Sunday).

Italian

Ristorante Mama Mia, Holiday Inn–West Stadium, 4732 N. Dale Mabry Hwy. (tel. 877-6061), bills itself as the "grandest Italian restaurant ever" and gets no dispute from the thousands of patrons who pass through these doors annually. Dine on veal and shrimp dishes, Mama Mia's delicious chicken Mama Mia, fresh breads baked right in Mama's oven. Toss back free wine and free antipastos, all you can consume. A bright red and yellow painted cart is a salad bar, and so you'll feel as Italian as possible there's a Harry's American Bar! Dinners begin at $5.25, and Mama opens the doors at 5 p.m. daily, at 1 p.m. on Sunday.

Campanella's, 5051 66th St. North, in Pinellas Park (tel. 541-7541), is a small family restaurant owned and operated by Rita and Raffaele Campanella who, so the story goes, were down to their last quarter when they first opened this restaurant some years ago. Today they operate a 250-seat restaurant they built a couple of years ago. The Campanellas know their food, love it, and work hard to provide the best for diners who flock here for good, simple, rib-sticking Italian fare served in a cozy, friendly atmosphere. You'll find the traditional pastas at Campanella's, along with veal and seafood selections, all served up in copious quantities, steamy, fragrant, and altogether irresistible. Prices are reasonable too: dinner entrees are in the $10 to $15 range, less for pastas. Campanella's is open from 11 a.m. to 11:30 p.m. daily except Monday.

Seafood

In Florida someone is always out there ranking restaurants, and **Mirabella's**, at 327 N. Dale Mabry Hwy. (tel. 876-2844), frequently appears on the list of top seafood establishments. This rustic, wood-sided spot has been dishing up fresh seafood since 1952 (and catching it with its own fishing fleet since 1898). Closet sailors should adore this unabashedly nautical decor complete with trophy fish and lots of brass, not to mention offerings of oysters, clams, and good straightforward seafood preparations. Prices are in the $7 to $10 range, and Mirabella's opens Monday through Friday at 11 a.m. and closes at 10 p.m., Saturday from 4 p.m. (closed Sunday and holidays).

Just east of the International Shrine Headquarters, near the entrance to Courtney Campbell Causeway, you'll spot a hand-lettered wooden sign marking the way to **Crawdaddy's,** 2500 Rocky Point Rd. (tel. 885-7407). If there are two matching boards in this hulking mass you'll have to prove it to me. The restaurant-creation group which pulled together this amusing spot claims that in the roaring '20s Beauregard "Crawdaddy" Belvedere provided dining, entertainment, and "various distractions" for the rich who came here by yacht to, um, be distracted. You'll still find plenty of distractions at Crawdaddy's, albeit somewhat tamer than what old Beau may have devised. There's plenty to look at: long johns on the clothesline outside, hens scratching away in the pen shared with goats, the conglomeration of "antique" posters, ads, buckets, crates, sandbags, whiskey barrels, and lobster traps. You can do your looking in considerable comfort in this multilevel picture-windowed maze, from upholstered wing chairs or antique Victorian couches. Adventurous diners can try alligator ($4.95) and more conservative munchers can go for beer-batter shrimp, lobster whiskey, crunchy bass rolled in sliced almonds and corn crisps, and a variety of beef dishes in the $10 to $15 price range, including cheese or gazpacho soup, salad, baked red potatoes, and fresh breads. Open from 11 a.m. to 3 p.m. for lunch, from 5 to 11 p.m. for dinner, Crawdaddy's has entertainment nightly from 6 p.m. to 2:30 a.m., plus an electronic game room.

Budget Bets

Someday drive over to Plant City where in February you'll reel in the scent of strawberries. This strawberry capital of the world as yet has no challengers for the title. In the last days of February and the first of March, Plant City's festive **Strawberry Festival** draws crowds of red berry lovers who throng here to gorge on the massive berries on ice cream, in shortcake or topped with whipped cream, in sugar and rum, or just chomped right out in the fields.

Bobby Rubino started in Fort Lauderdale a few years back with a menu identical to that of his former employer, Tony Roma, and now has spread to cities all over the state and in Canada. It was perhaps inevitable that success should strike this spot which turns out hundreds of racks of charcoal-grilled spare ribs in a spicy sauce and just as many loaves (yes, loaves!) of deep-fried onion rings every day at moderate $10-range prices and in attractive contemporary atmospheres. **Rubino's** in Tampa is at 1902 N. Dale Mabry Hwy. (tel. 877-9112), and is open from 11 a.m. to 2 a.m. daily (except Sunday when the restaurant opens at 1 p.m.).

Victoria Stations like the one at 2903 N. Dale Mabry Hwy. (tel. 879-9800) are popping up everywhere in Florida. Boxcars and cabooses are happily welcoming diners on a trip to nowhere. Probably little better use has ever been made of old railroad cars than Victoria Station, which serves up beef and seafood for reasonable prices in the $8 to $14 vicinity, complete with brimming salad bar. All aboard begins at 11:30 a.m. (to 2 p.m. for lunch), and 5:30 p.m. daily for dinner; the last passenger is unloaded at 10 p.m.

Be advised that the **Oyster Shanty,** 7004 W. Hillsborough Ave. (tel. 886-7040), looks like what its name suggests—your basic shanty atmosphere, from newspapers over plastic tablecloths to determined diners banging merrily away on steamed crabs (all you can down), shrimp steamed in beer, steamed clams, smoked mullet, and combinations of various seafood selectons. There's chowder, smoked chicken, and lest we forget, oysters. Open 4 to 11 p.m. daily. Oyster Shanty bills will be in the $6 to $7 vicinity.

The **Morrison Cafeteria,** 717 S. Dale Mabry Hwy. (tel. 877-7119), here as everywhere offers inexpensive cafeteria dining in simple but attractive surroundings with dinners in the $5 range.

Another cafeteria chain, **Piccadilly,** has two operations in Tampa, one in West Shore Plaza, Route 60 at the junction with I-275, Exit 23 (tel. 876-6894), and one in University Square Mall, on Route 582 about a mile east of I-75 Exit 34, not far from Busch Gardens (tel. 977-0002). Both offer prices in the $5 range and are open from 11:30 a.m. to 8:30 p.m. (closed only on Christmas Day).

A Don't-Miss

It's a strawberry free-for-all at the festival, but any time of year it's worth the drive for some good down-home cookin' at **Branch Ranch,** on Thonotosassa Road in Plant City (tel. 752-1957). An offbeat spot 17 miles west of Tampa and about a mile north of the Branch-Forbes exit of I-4, Branch Ranch is on the outskirts of this picturesque farming village and is itself both picturesque and a working farm. You tie on the feed bag here for $7 to $12.50, with a relish tray, plates of preserved pickles and beets just like Grannie used to can, a basket of hot buttermilk biscuits, a jar of homemade strawberry jam. Next, out roll tin baking pans laden with summer squash, candied yams, buttered green beans cooked with country ham, chicken pot pie, entrees of chicken, beef, ham, and finally the finale—fruit cobblers, ice cream, and of course, strawberry shortcake. Branch Ranch is America's cooking heritage—all of it at once—wrapped and packaged in a barn of a building with a monstrous stone fireplace, lace curtains on the windows, and a view of passing tractors. It's open from 11:30 a.m. to 9:30 p.m. Tuesday through Sunday. Kathleen Kemp, a reader from Madeira Beach, Florida, recommends trying Branch Ranch's excellent strawberry preserves, pickled beets, and cucumber pickles.

NIGHTLIFE: Nightlife in Tampa is best in the area's large hotels, all of which have entertainment and music for dancing and listening. The Hilton and Sheraton in downtown Tampa, and the revolving restaurant and lounge at the Host International, are good places to start, but even chain operations have lounge entertainment.

One of the best shows in town is at the **Columbia Restaurant,** at 21st Street and Broadway in Ybor City (tel. 248-4961), where you'll see flamenco dancing and hear guitar music and Latin laments. It's a fun evening with entertainment that even includes the restaurant's owner and strolling mariachis from Mexico.

Cultural Activities

There's been a bit of a boom in cultural activities in Tampa in recent years, so you can now find a wide range of theater, dance, and musical presentations here.

The **Tampa Ballet,** 100 W. Kennedy Blvd. (tel. 229-8637), dances October through March. The **Florida Orchestra,** 2709 Rocky Point Dr. (tel. 887-5715), plays in the same months at various locations.

You can see theater performances put together by the **Tampa Players,** Lafayette Arcade, 444 W. Kennedy Blvd. (tel. 254-0444).

There's always something happening from symphony to rock concerts at **Ruth Eckerd Hall,** in the Richard Baumgardner Center, 1111 McMullen Booth Rd., Clearwater (tel. 725-5573), and at the **Tampa Theater,** Franklin Street Mall (tel. 223-8981). Tampa Theater is quite a show in itself. It was built in the 1920s and is decorated inside with colorful flowers, balconies, colonnades, and copies of Greek and Roman sculpture. The **Tampa Film Club** lives here.

SPORTS: You'll find lots of tennis courts, golf courses, and some parimutuel sports scattered about the city.

Golf and Tennis

There are public golf courses in the city at **Rocky Point Golf Club,** 5151 Memorial Hwy. (tel. 884-5141), and **Rogers Park Memorial Golf Course,** 7910 N. 30th St. (tel. 234-1911), plus courses at the **Hall of Fame Inn,** 2222 N. Westshore Blvd. (tel. 876-4913), and at **Babe Zaharias Golf Course,** 11412 Forest Hills Dr. (tel. 932-8932). Greens fees are about $6 to $10 at most courses; carts, about $10.

There are **tennis courts** all over town, including 11 at **Riverfront Park,** 900 North Blvd. (tel. 251-3472). Most are free or have only a nominal charge. The city's recreation department (tel. 238-6451) will be happy to locate some near you.

Water Sports

Suncoast Charters (tel. 864-3106) will take you out fishing at $20 for a half day, $35 for a full day, or on offshore trips for $25 to $40, including lunch.

For sailing, you'll find **rental boats** at Bay Harbor Inn, 7700 Courtney Campbell Causeway (tel. 885-2541), and there are usually rental sailboats on the beach at Courtney Campbell Causeway for about $22 an hour.

Professional Sports

The **Tampa Bay Buccaneers** (tel. 879-2827) play at Tampa Stadium, 4211 N. Dale Mabry Hwy. (tel. 876-8893), from August to December; admission is $5 to $20, but the team is hysterically popular and games are often a sell-out.

The **Tampa Bay Rowdies** soccer team (tel. 870-1122) kicks it around at Tampa Stadium too, from April through August; tickets are $5 to $7.

Parimutuel Sports

You can put a few dollars on the nose of a fleet-footed greyhound at the **Tampa Greyhound Dog Track,** 8300 N. Nebraska Ave., I-275 at the Bird Street exit (tel. 932-4313), open September through early January at 7:30 p.m. daily (except Sunday), with 12:45 p.m. matinees on Monday, Wednesday, and Saturday. Admission is $1; clubhouse, $2.50.

Tampa Bay Downs, on Racetrack Road (tel. 855-4401) in the town of Oldsmar (just off Route 584 east of US 19), brings out the silks in December with races through March daily (except Sunday) for a $1.50 admission ($3 for the clubhouse).

See them play jai-alai at the **Tampa Jai-Alai Fronton,** 5125 S. Dale Mabry Hwy. (tel. 441-9469), December through April daily (except Sunday). Games begin at 7 p.m., and there are noon matinees on Monday, Wednesday, and Saturday. Admission is $1.

SHOPPING: If you love Christmas no matter what time of year it is, drive over to the tiny burg of Brooksville and visit **Rogers' Christmas House,** 103 Saxon Ave. (tel. 904/796-2415), where it's always December 25 (except on December 25, when it's closed). Open 9:30 a.m. to 5 p.m. daily, the shop shimmers with Christmas lights and has multitudes of animated displays and other kinds of shops brimming with treasures only Scrooge could resist. It's 53 miles from Lakeland, at the intersection of US 98, Route 40, and US 41, about 10 miles west of I-75.

A VISIT TO YBOR CITY: It's part of Tampa, but it seems an ocean or so away. It was here, in this antique Latin Quarter, that nearly 100 years ago cigarmaker Vincente Martinez Ybor began an industry that brought this city worldwide renown—remember those famous Tampa cigars. Here too poet/patriot José Martí plotted and pled for support in the fight for Cuban independence.

Ybor lured the cigarmakers of Key West here in 1886 with offers they couldn't refuse and set them up in massive brick warehouses. They rolled tobacco into those famous small cylinders while a *lector* read them news, poetry, and literature as they worked. Millions of cigars emerged from these halls, and in 1893 Martí, who also composed the song "Guantanamera," appealed to the workers for men, money, and machetes to help free Cuba from Spanish rule. They responded with fervor. Tampa was selected as the ideal embarkation site for an expeditionary force to Cuba, the most famous of which was Teddy Roosevelt's Rough Riders. Rough they were too: according to one story a squad of them once rode their horses right into the Las Novedades Restaurant (it's now the El Goya) in a "battle" still known locally as the "Charge of the Yellow Rice Brigade."

Today the factories that housed those tobacco workers have been revamped and are home to the **Nostalgia Market,** an array of crafts and antique dealers and a small café named for Martí.

Walk the eight or so blocks of Ybor City's **Seventh Avenue** and meander through the intersecting side streets where you'll smell coffee roasting. At nearby **Navier Coffee Mill** you can buy some for $6 to $8 a pound, and find some Italian pastries to go with it at **Demmi's Italian Grocery,** a shop that's been here since the turn of the century.

In these streets you'll find 22 historical markers, plus lovely fountains and old-fashioned lamp posts. In a vest-pocket park, called Parque Amigos de José Martí, a statue of the hero memorializes the valiant Cuban effort.

Ybor City is a two-mile-square area bounded by Nebraska Avenue, 22nd Street, Columbus Drive, and East Broadway. It's filled with old grillwork and bricks, gardens and patios, and tiny cigar stores where workers still roll the smoker's delights by hand as they have for generations. Center of it all is a city block bounded by Eighth and Ninth Avenues and 13th and 14th Streets. Here is the three-story-high **cigar factory building** of massive oak and heart pine columns, brick and more bricks, and the same iron stairs on which Martí stood to appeal for help.

An adjoining building constructed in 1902 is the **Stemmery,** where tobacco stems and leaves parted company. Today it houses, fittingly enough, the Rough Riders Restaurant, where you can get an idea how things looked in those days: for celebrations, a bugle blares and out charge the boys in khaki campaign shirts and red kerchiefs looking at least a little like the motley lot of cowboys, Indians, and outlaws Roosevelt herded off to Cuba so many years ago.

You'll certainly never starve here, for this is the center of the city's **Cuban cookery** emporiums with a dozen or so fine restaurants: Gran Café Martí has guava turnovers; El Buen Gusto features Basque caldo gallego soup; Alvarez whips out black beans and roast suckling pig; Alegria has Cuban sandwiches; Don Quixote offers super-size pork chops and salted cod with tomato and onion; and La Tropicana Café is the "home of the world-famous Cuban sandwich." Here too is the elegant and eclectic Columbia Restaurant, home of the blue margarita (not to mention some outstanding cuisine which you can read more about in the section on restaurants).

Take a look at **El Pasaje Hotel** on Ninth Avenue, where Winston Churchill, Frederic Remington, and Grover Cleveland stayed, and don't miss the fascinating factories, now listed on the U.S. Register of Historic Places as much I think for their exuberant staying power as for their history.

To these streets at the turn of the century came 20,000 workers, 4000 of them employed at the Ybor factories. Cubans, Spaniards, Italians, Germans dropped roots here and set up mutual-aid societies and hospitals that are the oldest examples of cooperative social medicine in the U.S.

You can read all about it at the **Ybor City State Museum,** 1818 Ninth Ave. (tel. 247-6323), in the old Ferlita Bakery where the immigrants' success is related in colorful exhibits. It's open from 9 a.m. to 5 p.m. (closed noon to 1 p.m.) daily and charges 50¢ for everyone over 6.

Twice a year, in February and October, the city turns out to celebrate its heritage with dancing and entertainment—and of course, lots of food. In July, Ybor City honors bespectacled Teddy with a reenactment of his departure (minus the Charge of the Yellow Rice Brigade).

You can get a map for a self-guided walking tour of the city from the **Ybor Chamber of Commerce,** at 1513 Eighth Ave., Ybor City, FL 33605 (tel. 813/248-3712).

3. St. Petersburg

After years of hearing stories about aged pensioners nodding off to sleep on the city's green benches, I expected to trip over canes on Main Street here. No such thing! Certainly in winter flocks of oldsters continue to make this their warm-weather bastion, but there's a decided air of the upbeat and upwardly mobile in this rapidly growing Suncoast area. There are benches still, but sorry to say they're not painted green anymore—city fathers, belabored *ad nauseum* by the "Old Folks at Home" image, painted most of them orange some years back.

It's no wonder people of every age gravitate here, for this is one of the loveliest waterfront cities in the state. Who could fail to be enchanted on a walk or drive along the bay as you see spread out before you the glittering sapphire waters of Tampa Bay on one side and emerald-green lawns, gurgling fountains, and winding walkways on the other. Sun glints off the roof of a massive Spanish mansion. Flags fly from the masts of the pristinely maintained *Bounty* replica. You stroll on brick streets amid a pastel sparkle so magical it's no wonder snowbound snowbirds fly here to winter.

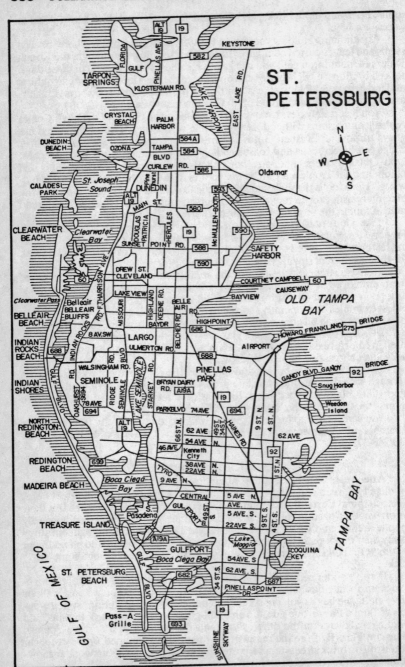

Refined and quiet as it may be on the mainland, if you cross the causeways to St. Petersburg Beach and its island neighbors, you enter a world of nonstop activity from the first morning beachcombing safari to the final shrieks of the a.m. discos.

St. Petersburg came by that old folks image when the American Medical Association reported that the city was a healthy place. St. Petersburg dragged out the green benches so the flood of elderly tourists could rest, and before long the city's "green bench" image was famous. These days city promoters are working hard to change that image, perhaps in vain since the baby boom is rapidly aging! Besides, many of St. Petersburg's sprightly senior citizens are active, alert people—so active in fact that they have a softball team here but you can't join unless you're over 70!

Old it may be, and oldsters it may have, but this is undeniably a lovely city. Stroll the two miles of shoreline past much of the city's 2000 acres of recreation area and see parks so painted, planted, and prettied you wonder if the gardeners carry rulers. Stroll among lovely old mansions renovated into even lovelier old mansions. Step back into another, more stately era, when life moved slowly and a gentleman wouldn't think of appearing in public without a tie. There's still a bit of that here in places like the Albemarle or the Soreno, where elegant old gentlemen jump to their well-shod feet and tiny silver-haired damsels flutter and blush like new brides.

It's quite a place this sunny city, a place that offers something to everyone no matter what age.

GETTING THERE: Airport limousines will bring you here from Tampa International Airport for about $10, and **Greyhound** and **Trailways** buses stop here. **Amtrak** (tel. 822-0175) also has a station here, at 3601 31st St. North, as well as in Clearwater and Tampa.

WHERE TO STAY: St. Petersburg, which incidentally was named after the city in Russia by an early Russian immigrant, has a number of small hotels and guest houses downtown that cling firmly to the old ways and want little or nothing to do with anyone under 70. They're quite frank about it, and often post signs announcing "Seniors Only." It took me a while to figure out what that meant, but after a few hotel visits I got the picture. Things are changing, but very slowly, so in the meantime I've selected a few hotels where you won't have to produce your Medicare card for proof of age. Most people by the way seem to prefer staying near the beach so you'll find many more hotel listings in the following "Holiday Isles/St. Petersburg Beach" section.

The **Holiday Inn–Bayfront Concourse Hotel,** 333 1st St. South, St. Petersburg, FL 33701 (tel. 813/896-1111), dominates the hotel scene in downtown St. Petersburg both in size and popularity. Right in the middle of the bayfront area and within easy walking distance of the city's beautiful and intriguing municipal pier, the Bayfront Concourse was in 1985 being renovated by its new owner, Holiday Inn, to offer all the amenities you'd expect from a 305-room, 15-floor hotel. Bayfront sports a pretty Greenhouse Restaurant and lounge too. The range of spacious accommodations here is large: from suites to large double rooms decorated in contemporary modes. Two people pay $70 in peak winter season, $50 from May to October. Children under 18 are free, and so is parking.

Nestled among 14 acres of tropical woodland on US 19 near the Skyway Bridge is the **Sheraton St. Petersburg Marina and Tennis Resort,** 6800 34th St. South, St. Petersburg, FL 33711 (tel. 813/867-1151, or toll free 800/325-3535). Tucked away here among hundreds of plants are two of the city's largest swimming pools, tennis courts, shuffleboard (what would St. Pete be without that?), a playground, wading pool, ice-cream parlor, and 1000 feet of private beach. The pretty, spacious rooms have glass walls and balconies so you can enjoy a constant view of the attractive gardens.

The Sheraton's tennis courts have hosted the Virginia Slims Tournaments, and the hotel's Annapolis Sailing School has polished the nautical skills of many a Sunday sailor. Parker's Landing Restaurant is a vegetable-lover's delight (with an 18-foot salad boat) and a budget-watcher's favorite, with prices in the $10 to $12 range. Later there's a not-too-frenetic disco for dancing. There's also free limousine service from the airport. You'll pay $39 to $80 double in summer, $62 to $109 in winter months.

There's something new in old St. Petersburg: the **Presidential Inn,** 100 Second Ave. South, St. Petersburg, FL 33701 (tel. 813/823-7552). Quite a lovely new addition to the city's regrettably small number of top-flight hostelries, the Presidential Inn was put together by two local entrepreneurs, Ted Wittner and Bill Bond, Jr., who took a look at the lovely new Governors Inn in Tallahassee and liked what they saw. So they set out to go the Governors one better and created the Presidential Inn, a group of 30 rooms that occupy the fifth floor of a 12-story office tower called City Center Building. Rooms overlook Tampa Bay and are fitted out with just about every accoutrement you can dream up, from remote-control televisions to telephones in the bathroom, and in eight rooms, even private whirlpools. That downtown location means these rooms are designed primarily for the traveling business person—but that doesn't mean that any traveler can't enjoy this handsome new spot. All rooms have refrigerators and one king- or two queen-size beds. At a central living room/bar area you're served complimentary continental breakfast each morning and cocktails each evening. Downstairs, a service center can arrange secretarial service, limousines, and the like. Year round, Sunday through Thursday prices are $90 to $120; on Friday and Saturday they drop to $60 to $75.

The **Princess Martha Motor Hotel,** at 4th Street and First Avenue North, St. Petersburg, FL 33701 (tel. 813/898-9751), is a venerable old name hereabouts, having catered to the famous and the not-so-famous for many years. Right in the heart of downtown St. Petersburg, the Princess Martha has a second-floor swimming pool, roof terrace, and two dining rooms. There's an air of old-world charm about the place, from wing chairs to wrought-iron trim. Wide picture windows in rooms offer views of the waterfront or picturesque Mirror Lake. The furniture has a simple but comfy hominess about it that makes it a nice change from the usual impersonality of downtown hotels. Rates are quite low, ranging in winter from $40 to $45, and in summer (from May) are $35 to $40 double.

Princess Martha, one of the most important of the hotels built during the 1920s boom, was for years queen of downtown St. Petersburg. Carl Sandburg stayed here, as did Maurice Chevalier, who called it the most European hotel in the U.S. It's not as grand as it was in those days, but it's still an attractive place, one in which you'll find it easy to imagine the booming days of yesteryear.

To stroll bayfront area streets is to take a nostalgic trip down the memory lane of old homes and hotels, sometimes combinations of both. One of those combinations that I found appealing is the **Edgepark Hotel,** 256 1st St. North, St. Petersburg, FL 33701 (tel. 813/894-9435). A long, wide veranda trimmed in the tracery of delicate wrought iron is the perfect spot to draw up one of the wicker chairs and indulge in "jest sittin'." Pots of blooms are scattered about outside, while inside is a cavernous lobby filled with wing chairs and comfortable couches. It's a bit eclectic, but it's cozy. This is a spot that caters to senior citizens but seems prepared for the occasional well-behaved soul under 70. Furnishings in the medium-size rooms are simple but clean; there's carpeting on the floors, bright bedspreads on the beds, and efficiencies have slick new kitchens. There's a television lounge downstairs and no phones or pool, but just wait until you hear the price: $140 to $200 a *month*, single, year round, 20% more for a second person!

Bed and Breakfast Inns

Ron and Danie Bernard operate **B & B Suncoast Accommodations,** 3690 Gulf Blvd., St. Petersburg Beach, FL 33706 (tel. 813/360-1753), which can lead you to area residents happy to welcome you into their homes for bed and breakfast. The Bernards list a number of houses ranging from a Victorian home to a lakeside manse for prices that range from $30 to $70 double, year round. They have access to hosts elsewhere in Florida too, including Orlando, Sarasota, Winter Park, Ramrod Key, and Delray Beach.

WHERE TO DINE: St. Petersburg is just as schizophrenic when it comes to restaurants as it is in every other way. You'll find an elegant restaurant just around the corner from a budget spot, so I've listed a few of my choices by the cuisine they serve. (Remember that the prices I've cited are for entrees, but that usually includes salad, one or two vegetables, and sometimes coffee as well.)

French

I haven't quite recovered yet from the shock of finding Peter Kersker's wondrously elegant **Peter's Place,** 208 Beach Dr. NE (tel. 822-8436), tucked in near the waterfront. In a region about equally divided between California contemporary and fishing village rustic, I didn't expect to find such subtle decor and all-around display of good taste, both culinary and decorative. But then, what else would you expect from such a Renaissance man as Kersker, who's first trade is the law but whose first love is good food and cooking. He could easily have plunked this lovely restaurant down in Manhattan, but fortunately he didn't. So now you can enjoy a menu that changes every evening, depending at least in part on what Peter thinks he might like to whip up that day: artichoke hearts and petit shrimp for starters, pâté with iced caviar, chilled dill-spiced salmon mousse, filet mignon wrapped around garlic-buttered shrimp, or something new, a couscous Maroc he discovered in his travels. Service is as smooth as the peanut butter crème pie Chantilly, as memorable as the crème de menthe Kahlúa chocolate mousse. Fixed-price five-course feasts are just $24.50 plus an 18% gratuity from $6.75 for lunch. Open for cocktails, lunch, and dinner (11:30 a.m. to 2 p.m. and 6 to 10 p.m.) Tuesday through Saturday. Reservations are wise.

rollande et pierre, at 2221 4th St. North (tel. 822-4602), has been producing outstanding French, Swiss, and American cuisine for two decades now, and shows no sign of slowing its pace. Chicken Véronique with white grapes is a good choice, as is pompano marchand de vin. You can expect a bill of about $10 to $15, and the restaurant's open from 5 to 10:30 p.m. daily (closed Sunday), and there's piano entertainment on weekends.

Italian

Bahama Bill's, 320 4th St. North (tel. 821-4931), hasn't got much to do with the Bahamas but everything to do with some rip-roaring atmosphere that may feature Bill for entertainment and always features some great Italian cooking. Stuffed clams or steak bracciole, scallops scampi, feta-topped salads, even "Mama's Ica Boxa Caka," and you just don't see that on menus anymore. You'll pay about $5 to $7 for dinner, from 5 to 10:30 p.m. (closed Sunday).

If your week isn't complete without some pasta, nip over to **Campanella's,** at 5051 65th St. in Pinellas Park (tel. 541-7541), where you can put away a trencherman's plate of homemade pasta for prices in the $8 to $12 bracket. This friendly bistro's open from 11 a.m. to 10 p.m. weekdays, to 11 p.m. on weekends.

Steaks and Seafood

People hereabouts swear by the ribs at **Spoto's,** 12999 Park Blvd., Seminole (tel. 813/393-3438), and don't mind driving out to Seminole to get them. They're known for their platter of ribs and a top-notch barbecue sauce, served in any of five dining rooms. There's entertainment and dancing nightly, and a late-night menu for insomniacs. A meal at Spoto's will set you back only about $10 or so, and the hours here are 11:30 a.m. to 3 p.m. and 5 to 11 p.m., later on weekends (but no lunch hours in summer).

For sheer tranquility of atmosphere and some rib-sticking American fare with a touch of Italian, you can't beat **Raney's Wedgwood Inn,** at 445 18th Ave. South (tel. 823-7600). It's hidden away on a side street, but once you find it you'll see lots of pretty touches: a tall fountain is at the entrance and a serene dining room with windows overlooks a stream. Best of all it's not a budget bender, with steaks topping the menu at $10 to $15. Pastas are much cheaper, there are all kinds of seafood and beef specials, and for the money you'll have to look hard to beat Raney's. It's open from 11:30 a.m. to 11 p.m. Tuesday through Sunday. Raney's also operates **The Garden,** at 217 Central Ave. in downtown St. Petersburg (tel. 896-7534), open 11 a.m. to 2 a.m. daily except Sunday.

Smoked-fish fans should head straight to **Ted Peters,** at 1350 Pasadena Ave. South (tel. 381-7931), where chefs brown split filets over red oak in Ted's smokehouse. This is strictly a shirtsleeves and T-shirts spot, where you eat on picnic tables in summer, by a fireplace in winter. German potato salad, clam chowder, rye bread, some smoked fish, and a frosty mug of root or real beer and you could face armies. It's open from noon to 7:30 p.m. Wednesday through Monday, with prices in the $5 to $7 range.

St. Petersburgers and Tampans troop off like lemmings to the **Dockside Broiler Restaurant,** in Boatyard Village near the St. Pete/Clearwater airport (tel. 536-6541), for fresh fish broiled over mesquite wood. If you're off seafood for tonight, you can try some very good barbecued pork ribs and chicken spiced by a smoker in the back room. Prices are in the $10 to $15 range, and the restaurant's open daily from 11 a.m. to 4 p.m. and 5 to 11 p.m. (from noon to 9 p.m. on Sunday).

Budget Bets

A very successful local restaurateur and chef swears by the onion rings at **Carol's Seafood and Steak House,** 7220 4th St. North (tel. 522-9907). You can also get a very reasonably priced steak and some excellent seafood, and walk out with a bill in the $7 to $10 range. Don't miss the onion rings. Open from 11 a.m. to 10 p.m. daily.

Another spot tucked in between stores just past the Pinellas Square Mall is the **Hickory Smoke House Bar-B-Que,** 6769 US 19, Pinellas Park (tel. 525-0948). This is a simple but significant spot with some of the town's best barbecued ribs, beef, and chicken, for prices like $6. It's open from 11 a.m. to 10 p.m. daily.

Side by side at 625 and 547 1st St. South, **Aunt Hattie** (tel. 822-4812) and **Uncle Ed** (tel. 898-1610) dish up wondrous delights in look-alike turn-of-the-century gingerbread, stained-glass fantasies. Aunt Hattie's fame is roast beef, chicken shortcake, and fruit salads, while Uncle Ed delivers giant roast beef sandwiches, lop-over-the-plate lasagne, nippy conch chowder, and a smashing salad bar. Both are open from 11:30 a.m. to 10 p.m. daily, and prices rarely top $10.

There are two corner **Feed Stores** in town, at 3291 64th Ave. North (tel. 525-7225) and at 553 Fourth Ave. North (tel. 821-2724), and in either one you can tie on the feed bag at prices under $5. Good salads, sandwiches, sourdough bread, and soups here from 11 a.m. to 9 p.m. daily except Sunday.

READER'S RESTAURANT SUGGESTION: "The Brown Derby restaurant chain in Sarasota, St. Pete, etc., offer excellent value, friendly service, long hours. They're very popular so it's wise to avoid peak hours" (Ann Southmayd, Newark, Del.). [*Author's Note:* Check the local *Yellow Pages* for locations of Brown Derby restaurants, which are usually open from 11 a.m. to 11 p.m. or later.]

NIGHTLIFE: This is not your top-of-the-line nightlife town, plain and simple. For nightlife you go across to the beaches. Still, there are a few things going on around town.

If big-band music and ballroom dancing are your style—or you'd like it to be—the enormous **Coliseum,** at 535 Fourth Ave. North (tel. 894-1812), is the place to head on Saturday and Wednesday nights from 9 p.m. to 1 a.m. Admission is $5.75. The **Dance World Ballroom,** 328 9th St. North (tel. 823-3312), has instruction on Friday, and on Monday you practice what they've preached from 8:30 to 10:30 p.m. Admission is $2.50 on Monday and $3 on Friday. They also fox trot up a storm at **Come Dancing Ballroom,** 5225 4th St. North (tel. 522-3898), on Tuesday at 7:30 p.m., and at the **Seminole School of Dance Arts,** 7660 Seminole Blvd., Seminole (tel. 392-3050), on Friday and Saturday with instruction beginning at 8 p.m. There's more of the same at the **Princess Martha Hotel,** 4th Street North and First Avenue (tel. 898-9751), on Thursday from 8 to 11 p.m. Admissions are $2 to $3.

For theater there's the **Showboat Dinner Theater,** 3405 Ulmerton Rd., Clearwater (tel. in Tampa: 223-2545; St. Petersburg: 576-3818), which presents Broadway productions in a plush reproduction of a Mississippi riverboat. Cocktails are at 6 p.m., buffet dinner at 7, curtain at 8:30 every night but Monday, with matinees on Wednesday and Saturday. Tickets are $21 Sunday through Thursday, $22 on Friday and Saturday; matinees are $16. A ticket includes dinner and show. Reservations required.

Country Dinner Playhouse, 7951 Gateway Mall at 9th Street North (tel. 577-5515), also brings stars to town in top-quality shows which play weeknights at 6 p.m. for an admission of $19.50, including dinner; matinees are $14.50.

Entertainment at the city's large **Bayfront Center,** 400 1st St. So. (tel. 893-3367), might be anything from the latest rock group to country musicians or Englebert Humperdinck, so check area papers or call the theater at the **Pier** to see what's going on.

The **Golden Apple Dinner Theater,** 1850 Central Ave. (tel. 821-6676), is the same theater that operates in Sarasota and produces plays here with dinner for $17.50, $13 for matinees at noon on Wednesday and Saturday.

Downtown in Williams Park along the bayfront there's a series of free concerts by the **Florida Gulf Coast Symphony Orchestra** with international guest artists, and the city has an opera company that presents performances during the year.

SPORTS: You want sports? St. Petersburg gives you sports—including ice skating and "skiing" (and I don't mean on water).

Golf

There are 31 courses in Pinellas County, 15 of them public.

One of the nation's 50 best golf courses is just three miles from **St. Petersburg** at **Mangrove Bay,** 875 62nd Ave. NE (tel. 893-7797), where you can tee up at special rates year around; carts are $14 for 18 holes (they're not required).

In Largo, the **Bardmoor Country Club,** 8000 Bardmoor Blvd. (tel. 392-1234), is the site of championship tournaments and has two public courses. Nearby **Indian Rocks Golf Course,** 12500 131st St., Largo (tel. 595-3133), has an 18-hole public course. Fees range from $8 at Indian Rocks to $45 double (including a cart) at Bardmoor.

Belleview Biltmore has a beautiful semiprivate rolling course at 1 Country Club Lane, Belleair (tel. 442-0229), and charges $20.80, including cart.

Tennis and Shuffleboard

Courts for these two popular games are scattered about the city. The recreation department (tel. 893-7441) will be happy to tell you how to find the ones closest to you.

Spectator Sports

St. Petersburg's Al Lang Stadium, near the Pier, hosts the **St. Louis Cardinals** and **New York Mets** in spring training. Tickets are $5 to $10.

Drag races at **Sunshine Speedway,** 4500 Ulmerton Rd. (tel. 577-4598), rev up every Friday from March through November. Tickets are $6 for adults (children under 12, free). On Saturday there's stock car racing at 7:30 p.m.

Indoor soccer is played at St. Pete's Bayfront Center from January through March.

You can spectate—or participate if you're *over* 50—at Pells, Gulls, and Kings oldsters' games on Monday, Wednesday, and Friday at 12:45 p.m., and on Sunday at 1:30 p.m. at **Northshore Park,** Eighth Avenue NE (tel. 896-9030). **Kids 'n Kubs** (minimum age 75!) play at Al Lang Stadium.

Sailing

Take lessons at **Coquina Key Recreation Center,** 3595 Locust St. SE (tel. 893-7738), or at **Annapolis Sailing School,** at the Sheraton St. Petersburg Marina and Tennis Resort, 6800 34th St. South (tel. 867-1151). Tuition varies.

Parimutuel Sports

From January to May, watch the greyhounds at **Derby Lane,** 10490 Gandy Blvd. (tel. 576-1361), a very pretty track and one of the nation's oldest, open daily except Sunday from 7 p.m. You can watch the races from an enclosed grandstand or on television in the plush restaurant. In fall the action moves to Tampa, and in spring and summer to Sarasota. Admission is $1.

4. The Holiday Isles

These sunny isles are every beachcomber's dream, 28 miles of soft sand and all the sun you can soak up. Their history stretches back to wild and woolly days when pirates terrorized these shores, but today the only buccaneer you'll see is a hotel.

These are the beaches for Tampa and St. Petersburg (which are not blessed with much sand of their own). So when winter tourists go home, the hometown folks move in to soak up the sun in a setting that is geographically close, but atmospherically distant.

Waters are shallow and beaches wide. There are quaint fishing villages tucked away here and there, and at the very southern tip of the islands is an artists' and writers' getaway spot with long strips of shady streets and quiet beaches. These are dazzling strips of beach that offer little of the glittering night-life of larger cities, but all the glittering days you could want.

WHERE TO STAY: Hotels and motels run the gamut on these islands from small family-owned and family-oriented resorts at inexpensive rates to towering hotels with every amenity. Looking at them is fun, and staying in them is more fun yet. I've arranged them geographically by island, going from Clearwater Beach on the north to Pass-a-Grille Beach on the southern tip of the chain, and in descending order by price.

Bed and Breakfast

Something new in the Suncoast area is a bed-and-breakfast network operated by **Suncoast Accommodations** and arranged by Bobbi Seligman, 13700 Gulf Blvd., Madeira Beach, FL 33708 (tel. 813/393-7020).

Clearwater Beach

This island didn't get its name by chance—it really does have clear water, and pretty strips of beach with the main one right in the middle of town. On it you'll find the **Adam's Mark/Caribbean Gulf Resort Hotel,** 430 S. Gulfview Blvd., Clearwater Beach, FL 33515 (tel. 813/443-5714, or toll free 800/247-5997), which is just what its name implies, a combination of Caribbean atmosphere and gulfside location. It towers 14 stories over the sand and has 206 rooms, each with a private balcony. It's definitely a luxury resort. You'll find all kinds of services here, from babysitters to pools for the kiddies and sophisticated entertainment for weary parents. Those Caribbean touches come in with a calypso galley buffet loaded with sandwiches and fresh fruit salads, a 300-seat entertainment lounge with circular bar, and a poolside Tiki bar with steel-drum band and limbo dancer. Spacious rooms open onto balconies overlooking the gulf, and those lovely vistas are reflected indoors where contemporary colors and furnishings prevail. Most rooms have two double beds but some offer king-size sleepers. Rates for two at the hotel are $63 to $95 in summer, $98 to $118 in the winter months.

The **Sheraton Sand Key,** 1160 Gulf Blvd., Clearwater Beach, FL 33515 (tel. 813/595-1611, or toll free 800/325-3535), is on a strip of beachside land all by itself just south of Clearwater Beach on Sand Key. Here you'll find an eight-story tower capped by a Sky Lounge where musical groups provide entertainment every night. A very long tiled lobby extends across the entire first floor of the building with a lobby bar, a three-tiered dining room, and boutiques. Rooms are typically Sheraton spacious and decorated in white with muted floral-print bedspreads. They have all the usual accoutrements: color TV, phone, private balcony, even washers and dryers on each floor. Outside, there's a pretty pool and thatched-roof picnic tables, a pool bar, and tennis courts. Rates at the Sheraton are $62 to $118 in winter months, $54 to $84 in summer.

The **Clearwater Beach Hotel,** at 500 Mandalay Blvd., Clearwater Beach, FL 33515 (tel. 813/441-2425), has such a small sign you hardly know it's there. And once you start exploring these exquisite emerald-green grounds covered in vivid blooms, you hardly believe it's there! Seventy modern beach- or garden-front apartments are spread over acres of grounds, and in the main reception area you're swept back to bygone days when this white wood structure housed one of the area's first inns. It still rents those small rooms in winter, but is proud now of attractively furnished and spacious accommodations with sliding glass doors and beautiful views. Room 604, with its own small porch wrapped around a corner of the building, is especially nice. Royal blue is one of the favorite colors here, and you'll find it everywhere from bedspreads in the paneled rooms to carpeting in the lobby. Guests gather in the hotel's dining room and chatter away at a cherrywood bar behind which reposes an art nouveau creation rescued from a Chicago watering hole. Amusing Victorian prints (one shows a swimming beauty captioned "Not the sea serpent but far more dangerous") line the walls, and in the oval sitting room is a delicately stenciled white piano. There are fresh roses on polished tables, shining brass chandeliers, high-backed cane chairs, and outside, a pool, tennis, and—shades of yesteryear—croquet. Winter rates are $87 to $125 until May 1, when they drop to $55.

There's a touch of the Greek at **Aegean Sands,** 421 Gulfview Blvd., Clearwater Beach, FL 33515 (tel. 813/447-3464)—actually more than a touch. From Greek lettering on the outside to the identification of rooms (Athena, Apollo) the resort carries out its Mediterranean connection. There are a variety of accommodations, from studio apartments (with a convertible couch and screened-off kitchen plus a separate bedroom) to hotel rooms and apartments. They're all quite spacious and nicely decorated with sturdy wood furnishings and bright tropical colors. Rates for a studio apartment are $88 in peak winter season, $44 to $53 in other months. Motel rooms with dressing areas and two double beds cost $58 to $64 in winter, $34 in summer; larger quarters begin at $72 in winter.

If I were staying a few weeks in Clearwater Beach, I'd seek a room at **Franzman Patio Apartments,** 15 Somerset St., Clearwater Beach, FL 33515 (tel. 813/442-1862), and then select their penthouse apartment on the second floor. Beyond a tiled kitchen is a carpeted living room with two convertible couches that open to queen-size beds. On the other side of glass doors is a roofed wooden balcony furnished with puffy lounges and a patio dining table. And beyond that is a view that goes on forever. The Franzmans, who own this quiet spot on a beach side street, are a friendly couple happy to show you around their spic-and-span little enclave, which includes 14 units in four buildings and a house. There's no pool, but you can just about dive into the gulf from your apartment. In winter, rates range from $45 to $75; in summer, $35 to $61.

If you like to watch boats gliding by, head for the **Port Vue Resort,** 101 Coronado Dr., Clearwater Beach, FL 33515 (tel. 813/446-7929), which is smack dab on Clearwater's bustling marina and just a block from the beach. Tucked into a narrow space, the Port Vue looks tiny from the street but actually is four floors of spacious rooms and efficiencies with private balconies. There's a heated pool, a boat and fishing dock, a friendly management, and a very convenient location right in the middle of shops, beach, and restaurants. The prices are nice too: motel units in winter range from $45 to $70 for rooms or efficiencies. In summer, prices drop to about $25 to $45.

Appropriately enough on-the-wing sea gulls decorate the walls at the **Sea Gull Apartment Motel,** 674 Bayway Blvd., Clearwater Beach, FL 33515 (tel. 813/446-2688), where attractive motel rooms and efficiencies have refrigerators and two double beds. There's a heated pool, laundromat, and private dock, and around the corner of a second floor, a wide balcony. In peak season, rates range from $300 to $325 a week, about 40% less in summer.

The Mediterranean roof tiles and ornate wrought-iron trim at the **New Yorker,** 332 Hamden Dr., Clearwater Beach, FL 33515 (tel. 813/446-2437), don't look much like New York, but the resort does have a touch of that city's fabled sophistication. This trim two-story cluster of apartments once won a chamber of commerce beautification award, and the interior here is just as trim as the exterior. Rooms have refrigerators and the fully equipped efficiencies have plenty of space. The New Yorker is particularly cozy at night when artful lighting reflects in the heated pool and glows in a tiny cupola atop the tiled roof. Prices here are far from New York too: just $270 to $360 a week in winter, $170 to $210 in other seasons.

Three generations of the Marsh family (the fourth was born in 1980) have owned and operated the **Shoreline View Motel,** 1941 Edgewater Dr., Clearwater Beach, FL 33515 (tel. 813/446-3390). Here you'll find tastefully decorated one- and two-bedroom apartments and efficiencies, some with balconies (many overlooking the sea). Weekly rates run from $245 to $260 for hotel rooms and efficiencies in peak season, dropping to $125 to $145 in other months.

Belleair Beach

Technically, the **Belleview Biltmore,** 25 Belleview Blvd., Belleair Bluffs, FL 33540 (tel. 813/442-6171), isn't in Holiday Isles but in an upper-crust mainland sister of this city, Belleair. Whether or not you decide to spend the money to stay there, you ought to run over for a look at this gorgeous old place that opened its carved doors in 1897. Another of Henry Plant's creations, the hotel is on 625 rolling acres which include a golf course and tennis courts. It claims to be the world's largest occupied frame structure and no one's got nerve enough to dispute the claim—there's a 2½-*acre* roof! They called this "Steamboat" architecture, and inside its glowing white facade you'll find leaded-glass ceilings, stained-glass panels, fancy wood trim, glittering boutiques, and dining and dancing every night in winter months. Rooms are as spacious as they are beautifully decorated, and as lovely as the cavernous lobby which has puffy couches and English hunt prints scattered about among tall columns. There are so many things to see and do here I could go on forever, but that would spoil the fun of seeing it for yourself. Open only from January 10 to late April, the Belleview charges $56 to $81 single, $86 to $126 double, with parlor suites at $149 to $185 double a day. Rates depend on date as well as location.

Down on Belleair Beach you'll find a strip of imposing private homes whose pastel colors are surrounded by perfectly manicured lawns and complimented by a profusion of flowers. Tucked in among them are motels you'll like as much for their elegant neighborhood as for their own amiable atmosphere.

The **Carriage House Motel,** at 3200 N. Gulf Blvd., Belleair Beach, FL 33540 (tel. 813/595-4787), is one of those, a trim contemporary building that looks as if it would attract the carriage trade. A second building was added recently so rates in the original structure are about $10 cheaper. Both buildings are decorated with handsome contemporary furniture and wall-to-wall carpeting. Maid service is weekly, with towels delivered daily, and there's a free continental breakfast every morning in winter. Rates are $60 in summer, $75 from mid-December to May in the more expensive wing.

The **Château** down the way somewhat at 2700 Gulf Blvd., Belleair Beach, FL 33540 (tel. 813/595-1397), belies its name since it's a small apartment motel overlooking the gulf. It's meticulously maintained by a real estate agent who might be able to help you find something elsewhere if the Château is booked. These small but nicely furnished apartments are decorated in woodsy orange and brown combinations; some units overlook the gulf (cheaper ones face the street). There's a small strip of beach here, and a swimming pool. Rates are $33 to $44 in summer, $44 to $55 from December to May. In off-season a little talk might bring the prices down somewhat.

Indian Rocks Beach

This quiet ribbon of beach got its name from jagged red rocks at the shoreline, but its current claim to fame is a 1041-foot fishing pier, the longest in Florida. Under it swim mackerel, kingfish, grouper, sea trout, tarpon—all just waiting for your hook.

Bob and Kay Alpaugh operate two apartment motels on this island, Alpaugh's, at 1912 Gulf Blvd., Indian Rocks Beach, FL 33535 (tel. 813/595-9421), the other a few miles away at 68 Gulf Blvd. (tel. 813/595-2589). Both occupy wide strips of beach and have homey one- and two-bedroom apartments, some fronting on the gulf, with less expensive accommodations facing the courtyards. At 1912 there are also screened cottages. At both of these trim and tidy motels rough wood exteriors fit right into the village atmosphere of the island. Neither has a pool, but there's plenty of water just steps away in the gulf. Rates are the same: $350 to $470 a week in winter, $265 to $450 in summer, and cheaper yet in fall. Cottages are $300 to $390. How's this touch? Phone calls are on the honor system!

Sea Star Apartments, 412 N. Gulf Blvd., Indian Rocks Beach, FL 33535 (tel. 813/595-3700), at $315 to $380 a week in peak season are among the more expensive accommodations on this island. Those prices are for a one-bedroom apartment on the gulf (nobody can say this coast doesn't have bargains). You'll find serviceable, comfortable furnishings that look more like home than a motel, paneled walls, dark-wood furniture, bright colors. Outside, guests gather under the palms for barbecues. Sea Star has just 16 units, some fronting on the resort's beach for rates of $167 to $261 in the off-season.

Redington Beach

Merchants moaned when they heard a new road would pass right over this area dooming them to anonymity. True capitalist spirit prevailed, however, and those moaning merchants turned disaster to delight by creating a pier and wooden walkways with a little village snuggled in between. Today it's called **John's Pass Village,** and is a favorite for tourists and locals alike, a rustic casual enclave every bit like a northern coastal fishing village (except the water's warmer). Just so you won't forget where you are, however, there's a signpost pointing the way to Greenville, Pennsylvania (1105 miles), and to Chicago (1157 miles from this sunny spot).

The **Sails Gulf Terrace Motel,** 17004 Gulf Blvd., N. Redington Beach, FL 33708 (tel. 813/391-6000), is a pristine and pretty operation centered around a sparkling swimming pool. Everything is ship-shape here, from the trim darkwood entranceways to the spacious airy rooms with crisp white bedspreads. Efficiencies and one- and two-bedroom apartments rent for $335 to $355 a week from February to May, $240 to $250 a week in other months.

Another pretty spot is **Sandalwood,** 17100 Gulf Blvd., N. Redington Beach, FL 33708 (tel. 813/397-5541), on North Redington Beach. It's a condominium motel wrapped around a pool and atrium that's beautifully lighted at night when this California-looking building sparkles. Because it's a condominium, the accommodations are especially spacious and attractive, with wall-to-wall carpeting, large closets, kitchens, tiled baths, and rates that range from $57 for efficiencies, $67 to $87 for larger accommodations, and to $125 for a penthouse with two bedrooms. In the summer months, prices drop $34 to $40, and are lower yet in fall.

A budget selection in Redington Shores is the wildly colorful **Sinbad Motel,** 17819 Gulf Blvd., Redington Shores, FL 33708 (tel. 813/391-1585). One thing for sure: you won't have any difficulty finding its hot-pink splendor. Just look for Sinbad the Sailor Man and the tile sailing ship mural on one wall. Something about Sinbad made me giggle, but not derisively; although this spot is a crazy-quilt of color, its prices are oh-so-sensible: $95 to $120 a week in summer, $120 to $180 in winter. There are lots of blooming things here, and while not directly on the ocean, it's just across the road and is on the waters of Boca Ciega Bay. There's a small dock and a friendly pelican which often perches there. Rooms are simply furnished in beach basic, but are tidy and clean, and some have a nice view of the bay.

Madeira Beach

This strip of sand was named after the pine woods *(madera)* the early explorers found here. You won't see much of that now, but there's still plenty of the sand and sea those courageous fellows loved.

Sandy Shores, 12924 Gulf Blvd., Madeira Beach, FL 33708 (tel. 813/392-1281), is an attractive five-story condominium on the beach across from John's Pass Village. All apartments here were decorated by their owners and have private balconies, some of which overlook the sea. Some are large enough to accommodate six to eight people, and for the space you're renting, rates are reasonable: $80 to $90 a day for a one- or two-bedroom apartment in winter, $55 to $65 in summer. Long visits get a discount too, and pets are welcome for a $30 charge.

If you're yawning after a wearying day at the beach, you can leap into the pool at **Tolliver's Beach Condos,** 12935 Gulf Lane, Madeira Beach, FL 33708 (tel. 813/392-8268), and let the whirlpool massage whip you back into shape. Located right at John's Pass, Tolliver's is a spot for independent types who don't mind doing their own housekeeping and are happy with simple but roomy accommodations with a pretty garden patio and sundeck on the beach. Rates are $400 to $575 per week in peak season (the highest rate buys a two-bedroom/two-bath spot for four). In other seasons, rates range between $23 and $43.

On the Boca Ciega Bay side of Gulf Boulevard, **Boca Kee Apartments,** at 14385 Bayshore Dr. North, Madeira Beach, FL 33708 (tel. 813/391-0721), snuggle together in an off-the-beaten-track location along the bayshore. Just three full-size apartments are operated by the Keenes, who have decorated them with cozy home-like touches from wicker chairs to ruffled kitchen curtains. At the moment Patt Keene is crowing over one of her latest renovations. "We had it wallpapered in a darling 'apple orchard' paper and border trim, then found a yellow and white gingham table cover which matches the ruffles on the curtains. It is pretty cute. Wish I had all the money I could spend, I would have a ball decorating our places," she says. Who can resist that kind of enthusiasm and obvious love of place? Keep at it, Patt!

Each apartment is different, but all have separate bedrooms and convertible couches so they can accommodate four, and in some you can even pack in guest number five. There's wall-to-wall carpeting, color TV, ceramic tile bath, and all of it's in a quiet residential area just off bustling Gulf Boulevard. Prices range from $720 to $795 a month for a waterfront apartment, excluding electricity, and weekly rentals are $275 to $300 in peak season. Rates drop in May to $140 to $175, and there are discounts for long stays.

A money-saver choice in Madeira is the **Stargazer,** 14048 Gulf Blvd., Madeira Beach, FL 33708 (tel. 813/393-7067), a large old house that's been partitioned off into five efficiency apartments. Karl and Bubbles Schroeder added new wood siding recently to give this gulfside Stargazer a contemporary look. A second-floor efficiency is particularly attractive, with wide picture windows overlooking the sea and sheer curtains flying in the gulf breezes. You can do your own cooking in the small kitchen area that's part of the same room. It isn't huge and it isn't fancy, but for $50 to $100 a day in high season it's a bargain. Weekly rates are cheaper, and summer prices are about $35 to $50.

Another bayside money-saver is the **Skyline Motel,** 13999 Gulf Blvd., Madeira Beach, FL 33708 (tel. 813/391-5817). Units accommodate four here, and some of the 11 efficiencies are large enough for five. They're not fancy either, but they're just $45 to $50 in peak season (from February to April), $24 to $30 in summer.

Treasure Island

If there's one marvelous story that capsulizes Florida's wacky real estate boom, it's the one about Treasure Island. It seems a promoter with low readings on his sales chart had to dream up a way to sell property on this island, so he used a little Florida ingenuity and planted a rumor that treasure was buried here. His scheme didn't get too far, but the name stuck and today it's Treasure Island, where you can indeed find something of value, but it's not likely to be Spanish doubloons.

In the center of the island, the **Bilmar Beach Resort,** 10650 Gulf Blvd., Treasure Island, FL 33740 (tel. 813/360-5531), takes the honors among the higher priced hotels. It's also one of the largest hotels in the area, although it doesn't seem so since rooms are in three separate buildings. You'll find lots to do here: miniature golf, golf privileges at a nearby course, two pools, 550 feet of beach, tennis courts just six blocks away, a Grog Shoppe pub with entertainment, a beach room where you'll hear Dixieland jazz, and Sherlock's restaurant (prices run $8 to $13); even a babysitting service so you'll have a chance to try all that fun. Most rooms have balconies and refrigerators. All are spacious and decorated in modern colors. Two people pay $40 to $74 in the winter months, $49 to $58 in summer.

A little cheaper are the **Quality Inn,** at 11500 Gulf Blvd., Treasure Island, FL 33740 (tel. 813/360-5541, or toll free 800/228-5151), and the **Ramada Inn,** at 12000 Gulf Blvd., Treasure Island, FL 33740 (tel. 813/360-7051, or toll free 800/228-2828). The Quality Inn has 54 rooms, efficiencies, and one-bedroom apartments on the gulf, plus a pool, and charges $60 to $75 in winter, $35 to $50 in summer. The **Ramada Inn** is also on the beach, and has a pool, whirlpool, playgrounds, and 98 rooms (some with refrigerators) and 23 efficiencies. Rates begin at $100 in winter, $72 to $82 in other months; efficiencies run about $10 additional. There's a dining room and lounge too.

Howard Johnson's is here as well, at 11125 Gulf Blvd., Treasure Island, FL 33706 (tel. 813/360-6971, or toll free 800/654-2000), with double rates ranging from $62 to $70 in winter, $41 to $47 in summer. HoJo's restaurant is open 24 hours with prices beginning at $4.

If you're a fishing fanatic, the **Delacado,** at 7963 Bayshore Dr., Treasure Island, FL 33706 (tel. 813/360-6362), may be nirvana: rates here cover use of fishing equipment and crab traps. Located on the bay, the Delacado will even send you pictures of some prize catches. There are just 13 units here, some with a view of the bay and some on the waterfront. They're basic but serviceable, and there's a popular fishing dock that's not a bad place for a high dive on a hot day. All rooms here have kitchens and the rates are palatable too: $230 to $280 a week, double, in peak season, $155 to $195 in other months.

On this pirate-conscious coast you'll find a resort called the **Buccaneer,** 10800 Gulf Blvd., Treasure Island, FL 33706 (tel. 813/367-1908), a cheery orange-and-white spot with ornate iron trim. Twelve of the rooms here are efficiencies; all units have color TV and daily maid service, and some have balconies overlooking the gulf. They're medium-size and colorful, and four two-room gulf apartments are big enough for four people. Naturally, a buccaneer wouldn't be far from the water, and this buccaneer is directly on the sand with a strip of beach right at the door. From February to May, double rooms are $35 to $51; efficiencies, $57 to $66. In other months, prices drop to $29 to $38 double.

A pretty, money-saving place is the **Treasure Island Motel,** 10315 Gulf

Blvd., Treasure Island, FL 33706 (tel. 813/367-3055 or 381-9714), which stretches from a swimming pool on Boca Ciega Bay to a private beach on the gulf. The Mediterranean tile roof and painted shutters give this small bayside motel a chipper look. You can paddle in the pool as yachts cruise by or, across Gulf Boulevard, stretch out on the pine-strewn lawn along 600 feet of private beach. Rooms are a somewhat eclectic conglomeration of furnishings, but they're clean, bright, and airy, and some have big picture windows overlooking the water. All have refrigerators and some queen- or king-size beds. In peak season you'll pay $42 to $58 double. In other months, rates drop to $25 to $35.

Plunk down in the living room of an apartment at the **Jefferson Motel Apartments,** 10116 Gulf Blvd., Treasure Island, FL 33706 (tel. 813/360-5826), and watch the waves lap away at the sand outside. German owners keep this spot shiny as a pfennig, from the turf-carpeted walkways outside to the spotless kitchen, baths, and dressing areas inside. The Jefferson would be my choice for a long visit if for no other reason than the pretty view and spacious, clean, and nicely furnished quarters. There are, however, extras: horseshoes, badminton, games, a handsome heated pool and patio, gas barbecue grill, and all that beach. Best of all, you pay only $50 to $65 in high season for two people, $38 to $45 in summer, with special rates for stays of four weeks or more.

St. Petersburg Beach

This is St. Petersburg's official beach, and it's the busiest of all the islands. One long strip of motels, restaurants, shops, and souvenirs, it's especially popular with families who crowd over here from St. Petersburg proper (about a half hour's drive away). King of the beach, and the city's pride, is the Don CeSar, an incredible pink hulk that almost saw the wrecker's ball but was saved in the 11th hour by some hard-working, history-conscious citizens. Let's start with a look at this eye-popper even though it's the southernmost hotel on the island.

It hits you like a giant mirage, this wacky mass of turreted pink cement shoving its massive bulk hard against the shoreline. This weird and wonderful cupcake of a building, pink as the icing at a christening, is none other than the **Don CeSar,** St. Petersburg Beach's flagship hotel at 3400 Gulf Blvd., St. Petersburg Beach, FL 33706 (tel. 813/360-1881, or toll free 800/237-8987), the city's pride and (if a bit dumbfounded) its glory. Built in 1928 by a Florida land-boom millionaire who managed to think pink in a way nobody expected, the Don CeSar for some years after the Depression had all the value of a rose-colored elephant. During the war it housed weary airmen, and later Veterans Administration employees. In 1969 when the wrecking ball was on its way, a determined group of historians managed to find a savior who poured seven million greenbacks into these ten-inch-thick walls and reopened the hotel in 1973. Now it's on the National Register of Historic Places so its bubble-gum facade will remain fanciful, farcical, and presumably here forever. But who cares what flamingo hue they chose for this landmark when inside are such beauties as Austrian crystal chandeliers, ornate trunks from Spain, antique light fixtures from Mexico, and beamed guest rooms with each beam cut to fit individually (there are no two rooms alike in size or decor). Everything that could be kept original here was, from the 13,900 panes of glass to that pink exterior, once so famous it was registered as Don CeSar Rouge. So well built is this bastion that after more than 50 years the Belgian concrete shows not one single crack in wall or floor.

Even if you don't stay here, this spot should be on your must-visit list for it is indeed a sight, from towering lobby to piano entertainment at afternoon cocktails, from grand staircase descending to Olympic-size pool to the candlelit elegance of the King Charles Restaurant—a glorious place since its halcyon days when it welcomed the likes of F. Scott Fitzgerald and Zelda, Lou Gehrig, Clarence Darrow, Dr. Walter Mayo, and Babe Ruth. If you stay, you can dip tired toes in an outdoor whirlpool bath while islanders strum soothing music, or rent a bike, go drift fishing, sail, or paddle your own canoe.

As the sun goes down in a burning glow of scarlet the mood changes, becoming elegant and dazzling, full of candlelight and canapés. Piano music tinkles delicately in the lobby bar as the last light of evening glitters on the sea beyond the glass windows of the award-winning King Charles Restaurant. Toss a few pennies into the fifth-floor fountain to ensure your return to the magic of Don CeSar. Rates are $95 to $130 in winter, with suites from $130 to $500. You'll pay $75 to $95 in summer.

Sandpiper Resort Hotel, 6000 Gulf Blvd., St. Petersburg Beach, FL 33706 (tel. 813/360-5551, or toll free 800/237-0707), is a massive Y-shaped six-story building, and its claim to fame is a swimming pool with a roof that slides open, making this the only enclosed pool in the area. That's only the beginning, however, for there's also an outside pool, tennis courts, a game room, a general store, sailboats, and a gift shop, plus a Brown Derby beef and seafood chain restaurant, a snackbar and a pub, not to mention a gorgeous wide strip of beach and four shuffleboard courts. In high season (from mid-February through mid-April), rates are $90 to $125 for double motel rooms, $125 to $275 for one- and two-bedroom suites, dropping in summer to $65 to $110.

It's sometimes hard to tell just when a dolphin is happy, but presumably those that occasionally frolic off the beach of the **Dolphin Beach Resort,** formerly Happy Dolphin Inn, 4900 Gulf Blvd., St. Petersburg Beach, FL 33706 (tel. 813/360-7011, or toll free 800/237-8916), are smiling. Guests at this 21-acre resort certainly have plenty to smile about: 174 large rooms with double beds, vanity baths, color TVs, and kitchenettes; and a restaurant and lounge, serving beef and seafood, with entertainment nightly; plus a gift shop, a package liquor store, a heated swimming pool on landscaped ground, a white sand beach, and a 24-hour shopping area nearby. Room rates here are moderate, ranging from $55 to $75 in summer (June to May) and $80 to $100 ($10 more for kitchens) in winter.

They come from miles around to dine and dance atop the **St. Petersburg Beach Hilton Inn,** at 5250 Gulf Blvd., St. Petersburg Beach, FL 33706 (tel. 813/360-1811, or toll free 800/445-8667). A favorite gathering spot for residents and visitors alike, the Top of the Hilton offers a glamorous revolving view from gulf to bay, with exotic prints in the Bali-Hi lounge, and excellent Polynesian and American delicacies in the $10 to $12 price range. This Hilton occupies its own strip of St. Petersburg Beach where you can seek solace at the poolside bar. Ride a glass elevator to the 152 spacious rooms decorated with contemporary furnishings in bright colors. An 11-story building, the inn has a coffeeshop, that Bali-Hi revolving lounge, and a disco with nightly entertainment. Rates range from $86 to $120 in winter, $72 to $101 in summer.

The **Breckenridge Resort Hotel,** 5700 Gulf Blvd., St. Petersburg Beach, FL 33706 (tel. 813/360-1833), features a beachside swimming pool and patio surrounded by a string of Roman columns. A seven-story hotel right on the gulf, the Breckenridge has bright efficiencies, some with balconies overlooking the sea plus tennis courts and a game room, and a supper club and lounge with entertainment to the wee hours. From December to May rates range from $98 to $112, depending on location, and in other months drop to $72 to $80.

If a condominium vacation appeals to you, **Isla del Sol,** at 6355 Gulf Blvd., St. Petersburg Beach, FL 33706 (tel. 813/367-3751), is an appealing spot. Located between St. Pete and St. Pete Beach on Boca Ciega Bay, Isla del Sol has one- and two-bedroom apartments, a golf course, tennis courts, the Island

House restaurant and lounge, plus card rooms and swimming rooms for each of several clusters of apartments. A large development with beautifully decorated apartments and landscaped grounds, Isla del Sol charges $525 a week double from December through April, and $385 in summer for a two-bedroom/two-bath apartment. One-bedrooms are $350 a week in winter, $280 a week in summer, and there's a one-week minimum rental.

Kick off your shoes and unwind in the shade of a thatched beach hut at the **Beachcombers Resort Hotel,** 6200 Gulf Blvd., St. Petersburg Beach, FL 33706 (tel. 813/367-1902, or toll free 800/237-1902). Stroll down paths that wind through manicured lawns bordered by palms and snuggle up to something cool at the roofed beach bar. Any beachcomber should be happy here, where spacious motel rooms and efficiencies are decorated in tropical colors, with deep pile carpeting and lots of wood paneling and trim. There's also a large heated pool, a beachwear/surf shop, and windsurfer rentals, plus all the usual amenities from phones to game room to color TV and free parking. Double rates begin at $79 in winter and $45 in summer.

El Sirata Apartment Motel, 5390 Gulf Blvd., St. Petersburg Beach, FL 33706 (tel. 813/367-2771), is a gulfside resort with a variety of accommodations including efficiencies, hotel rooms, and apartments, every one of them with a glassy view of the gulf. Splash in two swimming pools, play on the resort's shuffleboard courts, or relax in the lounge or TV room. There's a coin laundry to make that chore simple, and a restaurant for snacking. Rooms are clean and attractive, and there's a lovely strip of beach to roam. Rates are $45 to $75 from January to May, and $37 to $61 in other months.

There's such a wide variety of accommodations at the **Alden Motel/ Apartments,** 5900 Gulf Blvd., St. Petersburg Beach, FL 33706 (tel. 813/360-7081), or toll free 800/237-2530), that almost anything you want can be yours from a simple motel room to a three-bedroom/three-bath apartment for 12 people. Alden has several attractive buildings on the gulf: motel rooms and villas are in ground-level buildings with covered porches; most other apartments are in three- or four-story buildings facing the ocean or near one of the hotel's two swimming pools. There are two tennis courts and game rooms too. Rates range from $69 to $94 for efficiency suites and one-bedroom apartments (February to May), $54 to $70 in summer.

Palm Crest Resort Motel, 3848 Gulf Blvd., St. Petersburg Beach, FL 33706 (tel. 813/360-9327), offers you a chance to get some of that famous Florida sand in your shoes on their private strip of silica. Palm Crest has a shady central garden plot, and there's a large pool right at beachside. Gulf-front efficiencies are available here for $48 double in winter, and $240 a week in summer.

Two white plaster horses and a row of stately columns welcome you to **Colonial Inn,** 6300 Gulf Blvd., St. Petersburg Beach, FL 33706 (tel. 813/367-2711), where there's still another welcome surprise—a branch of the Sweden House Smörgåsbord restaurant operates here. Kiddies can splash in their own pool and romp in a special play area, while tired progenitors paddle in an Olympic-size splasher or comb the resort's 800-foot beach. Paneled walls line rooms with basic furnishings trimmed in bright tropical colors. You'll find all the amenities, right down to a Wigwam pool bar, at prices ranging from $45 to $61 in summer, $68 to $90 in winter.

Carlida Apartments and Motel, 610 69th Ave., St. Petersburg Beach, FL 33706 (tel. 813/360-7233), likes to say it's large enough to serve you, small enough to know you. If you like to be more than a number, it's certainly possible at this small apartment motel which features a pool and jungly tropical landscaping, including a tinkling dolphin fountain. Carlida is just a few steps from the beach, and offers basic accommodations including cable color TV and fully carpeted rooms. Efficiencies and apartments with simple furnishings run from $145 to $260 a week, year round.

Another bright spot on St. Petersburg Beach is **Cadillac**, at 3828 Gulf Blvd., St. Petersburg Beach, FL 33706 (tel. 813/360-1748); it's on the gulf but it also has an annex on the bay. Rooms or apartments here range from $25 to $35 in winter, about 10% lower in the summer.

Tradewinds Beach Resort Hotel, 5500 Gulf Blvd., St. Petersburg Beach, FL 33706 (tel. 813/367-6461, or toll free 800/237-0707), spreads across more than 12 acres of beachfront land and is handsomely landscaped with lots of courtyards, waterways, waterfalls, and fountains. Here you can make your way down 7½ miles of beach, paddle in indoor and outdoor swimming pools, work out in an exercise room, and sweat it out in a sauna. Créole herbs are deftly applied to seafood at the resort's Paradise Grill, while Pelican's Walk offers sandwiches and snacks. Later, cool off in the resort's lounge. As you can see, they try hard to think of your every need here, and have spacious, modern accommodations as well. Rates are $90 to $125 for motel rooms, $125 to $275 for one- and two-bedroom suites, from mid-February to mid-April. In summer, rates drop to $65 to $110.

Pass-a-Grille Beach

Robert Ripley, of "Believe It or Not" fame, called this village's beachside 8th Street "America's shortest and most beautiful main street." It is short indeed, and it's also beautiful, with palm-fringed beaches and aqua waters stretched out alongside it.

One of Florida's oldest vacation beaches, Pass-a-Grille got its odd name from early maps which showed this settlement on Long Key as Passe-aux-Grilleurs, a reference to fishermen who used this point of land to cross over the island and stopped to grill their meals. A few American garbles later, and *voilà!* Pass-a-Grille.

Whatever you call it, it's a quiet little spit of land with a wide, wide beach that's usually overlooked by beach goers, who head for the livelier strips.

At the very end of the island where gulf and bay waters mingle is the last resort, **Island's End**, 1 Pass-a-Grille Way, St. Petersburg Beach, FL 33706 (tel. 813/360-5023), which gets my vote for the most scenic spot on the Suncoast. Island's End is the creation of Enid and Ken Swanson, who retired here and have been working harder since retirement than they did before to get this cluster of cottages into the apple-pie order you'll see here. Island's End is wondrous testimony to their efforts and to their nice sense of balance between homey and serviceable. Gray weathered wood walkways wind between four small buildings which house one-bedroom and efficiency apartments, then meander past the Swansons' own wood-and-glass aerie. There are flowers everywhere, a gazebo, covered patios, and a view that goes on to . . . perhaps Mexico? I must admit I'm especially infatuated with the three-bedroom house which sports a tiny screened pool overlooking a sensational ocean view and sporting homey, comfortable furniture that's mostly new. You could say that about all the apartments here, which the Swansons are improving every day with lots of elbow grease and indomitable spirit. All the kitchens are new too, and much of the furniture is new as well, and quite contemporary. The one-bedroom villas can comfortably accommodate four and rent for $294 to $369 a week in peak season, $273 to $315 in summer, about $21 less in fall and spring. That house (easily big enough for six) is $595 a week, year round. When you work that out per person for six, it spells *bargain*. A studio unit with a hide-a-bed was just being refurbished, but I have supreme faith in their taste and am here to tell you that for $301 a week in high season, $280 in summer, it's a great buy. There are discounts for longer stays too.

In 1985 renovators were hard at work on a new guest house on Pass-a-Grille Beach. Called **Jon Jon at the Beach** (formerly known as Sea Spray), 1307 Gulf Way, St. Petersburg Beach, FL 33706 (tel. 813/360-1118), the house is being redone throughout, an owner told me, and repainted in the same bright pink and white as the Don CeSar Hotel. Not that they're trying to emulate the Don CeSar, you understand, they're just using colors typical of the '20s and '30s in which both this house and that hotel were constructed. Henceforth, Jon Jon will have 14 open, airy, tropical rooms, all with private bath, and will be seeking guests "who identify with guest houses." Owners say they will be advertising their creation "in gay publications, but we are not exclusively one way or the other." Rates will be $45 to $65, year round, including full breakfast and a free hospitality hour.

Tierra Verde

On what used to be called Cabbage Island you'll find an imposing resort called **Tierra Verde Island Resort, Yacht, and Tennis Club,** 200 Madonna Blvd., Tierra Verde, FL 33715 (tel. 813/867-8611). It's a dramatic place where you can settle in for an exhilarating visit or a loafer's holiday surrounded by the best that modern decor has to offer. Apartment accommodations here are dramatic: royal-blue carpeting with matching blue-and-white spreads, white wicker furniture, a wall of glass, deep camel carpeting, and beige and white decor. The public rooms too are dramatic; wicker furniture in vivid colors, a slick piano bar, a gorgeous circular bar of smoke-gray suede with a mirrored ceiling and dozens of tiny lights. Outside is a marina, tennis, and an Olympic-size swimming pool. Inside, a Le Club offers chic entertainment and dancing, and Land's End Restaurant flames delicious creations. Dramatic indeed for Cabbage Island, and even the prices are a bit of a surprise: $86 to $136 double from October to May, $71 to $121 in other months.

WHERE TO DINE: Some fine chefs have settled on these beaches and created restaurants recognized statewide for excellence. I've divided them up again geographically by island. The prices I've cited are for entrees.

Clearwater Beach

From the "back to the farm" fried chicken to the relish tray and home-baked gingerbread muffins, **Heilman's Beachcomber,** at 447 Mandalay Ave. (tel. 442-4144), goes after all-American diners and lures them here in droves to this beamed-ceiling, plant-bedecked dining room. Owner-host Bob Heilman is the third generation of Heilmans to see fame and fortune in the restaurant business since the family began back in Loraine, Ohio, in 1920. Works of local artists adorn the walls and a pianist offers quiet entertainment for dining on a wide selection of beef and seafood dishes, including Boston haddock flown in from Beantown. Of course, there's that famous fried chicken accompanied by fluffy whipped potatoes, relishes, fresh vegetables, biscuits, and gravy. Heilman's is open daily from 11:30 a.m. to 11 p.m., from noon on Sunday. Dinner prices are in the $10 to $15 range.

Florida restaurants either change every few years or hang on for decades—the **Pelican,** 470 Mandalay Ave. (tel. 442-3151), has managed to do both. Back in the 1930s Henry Henriquez started with a curbside fried-shrimp dispensary and hung gamely on through a 1974 fire that destroyed everything except the driftwood pelican mascot (which you'll see nesting happily on his new perch in the piano bar). The Pelican is a massive spot with red cedar beams and continues in its new avant-garde costume to lure those by now addicted to the Pelican's original stuffed shrimp mixed with lobster and crab. Grouper Grand Marnier is a good selection too, and the restaurant's bread pudding has a devoted following. Most dinner entrees are in the $7 to $20 range. The Pelican is open from 11:30 a.m. to 10 p.m. daily, from noon on Sunday.

Over on the mainland in Clearwater, the **Kapok Tree Restaurant,** at 923 McMullen-Booth Rd. (tel. 726-0504), is the Walt Disney World of restaurants— a fantasyland of lush formal gardens, classic statuary, bubbling fountains, and enough objets d'art replicas to make the Louvre blanch. This is simple food so you may not have the most memorable gourmet experience of a lifetime, but you'll certainly be visually overwhelmed. A massive porte cochère is supported by ten five-ton cast-stone caryatids. Palms soar skyward in a block-long glass arcade. A fat gold cherub clings to the neck of a swan atop an ornate fountain. It's definitely an experience. Average prices for an extremely wide variety of selections are in the $8 to $14 range. The Kapok Tree is open from noon to 10 p.m. daily.

Also over on the mainland is **Siple's Garden Seat,** 1234 Druid Rd. (tel. 442-9681), which does indeed have a garden seat just like the one grandpa and grandma sat on in their courting days. However, it's not the seat but some steady good cooking that's been packing them in here for 60 years. A picturesque spot overlooking the Intracoastal Waterway, Siple's has a long menu ranging from 'gator meat to shrimp curry with plenty of simpler cookery in between, like scallops with fettuccine or ham with pineapple sauce. A condiment tray of relishes and sweet cherries is an unusual touch here, as are the aromatic loaves of banana bread. Dinner at this award-winning spot averages $10 to $15 a person, although there are a number of items for less. Open from 11:30 a.m. to 3 p.m. and 5:30 to 9:30 p.m. daily (except August 25).

Back on the beach, **Calico Jack's,** in the Adam's Mark/Caribbean Gulf Resort Hotel, 430 S. Gulfview Blvd. (tel. 443-5714), is a popular spot for steamed clams and apple grunt served amid antiques and plants. Prices start at about $4 for dinner, and hours are 11 a.m. to 11 p.m. daily.

If you like cool, dark interiors in a straightforward steak and seafood house, **Bombay Bicycle Club,** at 2721 Gulf to Bay Blvd. at the Clearwater Mall Shopping Center (tel. 799-1841), provides exactly that. Just over the causeway from the beach, BBC draws a youthful crowd to its nightly entertainment, and attracts diners of all ages with good steaks and seafood in the $8 to $10 range. Sneak in daily for lunch, served from 11:30 a.m. to 3 p.m., or dinner, from 4 to 11 p.m. (later on weekends). Recorded music and a record spinner provide entertainment until 2 a.m. nightly.

Indian Rocks Beach

Louis La Fosse Marin and his wife, Josiane, host what can be a spectacularly good evening at **La Cave,** 1701 N. Gulf Blvd. (tel. 595-6009). La Cave occupies what looks like a tiny house with rough wood interiors and a bistro air. Skilled French cookery draws such crowds that reservations are requested. A new fish dish, the blaff, sounds interesting, but you can't go wrong sticking to specialties like coquilles St. Jacques, eggs Mornay, crêpes, or the scampi maison. It's open from 5 to 10:30 p.m. Monday through Saturday, with prices in the $5 to $11 range.

Redington Shores/Beach

If, after all the jokes about the lobster color of your skin following a day in the Florida sun, you are focused on lobster, drop into the **Lobster Pot,** 17814 Gulf Blvd. (tel. 391-8592). Dine in a quaint atmosphere on such choices as baked stuffed Florida black grouper, broiled deep-sea scallops, or banana fritters. Appetizers include homemade soups and chowders, salmon, herring, clams, oysters, and a spicy seafood crêpe. Dinners are served with fresh vegetables and salad topped with a house dressing of garlic and spices. The finale is mouthwatering apple fritters, cheesecake, or Florida banana fritters. You'll pay $12 to $17 for entrees at this very popular restaurant, open from 4:30 to 10:30 p.m. daily.

You'll need all the attentive service you get here after you've spent some time searching for **Paradise Pier** (no telephone), a teensy ramshackley spot beneath the pier at John's Pass Village. It's right up against the water under the walkways, but you have to keep a keen eye out for the sign and bend low as you enter. You can almost always find stone crab claws here, and this is the perfect rustic atmosphere to dig into those shells. Fish is straight off the boat and perfectly cooked, so go before 7 p.m. or be prepared to take a number and wait for a place in Paradise. Prices are in the $6 to $9 range, including salad, hush puppies, and french fries. It's closed on Monday and Tuesday, open other days from 5:30 to 9 p.m., on Sunday from 1 to 8 p.m.

With a name like Ted Sonnenschein you're sure to settle in Florida sooner or later (it means sunshine). Owner of the **Wine Cellar,** at 17307 Gulf Blvd. (tel. 393-3491), Sonnenschein did just that and got at least part of his credentials at the Old Swiss House in Busch Gardens. Now he prepares such favorites as choucroûte Alsacienne with weisswürst, thuringer, smoked pork and sauerkraut, and Swiss cheese soup in his own popular restaurant. You can walk out of here yodeling over the cuisine and the check, which is likely to run only about $10 to $15 a person. Closed on Monday, the Wine Cellar is open other days from 4:30 to 10 p.m., with a lounge open to 1:30 a.m.

Treasure Island

Stained-glass windows, yellow light from old lamps, rich woodwork, a brick fireplace, and cozy booths—what else could it be but the **Grogg Shoppe Restaurant,** in the Bilmar Beach Resort, 10650 Gulf Blvd. (tel. 360-5531). English hunter's pie and prime ribs with Yorkshire pudding too. Prices from $7.95. Open from 7 a.m. to 10 p.m. daily.

St. Petersburg Beach

One would hope not to emerge *el gordo* (fat) from **El Gordo's,** at 7815 Blind Pass Rd. (tel. 360-5947), but one shouldn't count on it. Tacos and tamales, refried beans, tostadas, chili rellenos, guacamole—all so inexpensive *el gordo* may be inevitable. What do I mean by inexpensive? How's a top price of $7.25 sound? Lots of "south of the border" atmosphere (just don't trip over the sleeping sombrero man) in two tiny dining rooms à la cantina. Open 11 a.m. to 10 p.m. daily, with music on Friday and Saturday from 9:30 p.m. to 1:30 a.m. in the "Upstairs" lounge.

Somewhere in all of us lurks the hermit-desire. In Silas Dent the desire not only lurked, it lived as did he on deserted Cabbage Key from whence he rowed on occasion to the mainland to pick up some beans. Old Silas is about as close as this Suncoast can come to a folk hero, so they honored him in inimitable Florida style: with a restaurant named after him. **Silas Dent's,** at 5501 Gulf Blvd. (tel. 360-6961), looks pretty much like what Silas called home too, a haphazard collection of weathered wood and some stuff lying around outside. Inside, however, things are spiffy enough to draw crowds from miles around to dine on Shell Man's Oyster Bar and very good shellfish and seafood—even alligator. Dinners are $10 to $15, and Dent's is open from 5 to 10 p.m. Sunday through Thursday, to 11 p.m. on Friday and Saturday. Entertainment nightly from 9:30 p.m.

A must-see, if not also a must-stop, spot is the **Pelican Diner** (tel. 363-9873), one of the last of those oldtime honest-to-goodness road food places, metal trailer and all, parked at 75th Street and Gulf Boulevard. An art deco delight, the Pelican serves up simple stick-to-the-ribs cuisine à la Alice's Diner for prices in the $3 to $4 range. It's open 24 hours (except noon to 7 p.m. on Monday)—"Never fear, someone's here."

The **Fishery,** 709 Gulf Way (tel. 360-1191) down Pass-a-Grille way, is a rustic little spot where a number one favorite is grouper with a creamy cheese sauce. There's a casual family atmosphere, fresh, fresh seafood goodies with plenty of greens at the salad bar and family prices in the $5 to $11 range. It's open from 11:30 a.m. to 10 p.m., later in the lounge.

NIGHTLIFE: Nearly every major hotel and many smaller ones offer evening entertainment that changes regularly all year round. Some of the best and liveliest spots in town are the mirrored **Fortune Cookie Lounge,** high atop the Hilton Inn on St. Petersburg Beach, rooftop dining and dancing at the **Holiday Inn,** a high-kicking revue at the **Beachcombers Resort,** and show groups at the **Caribbean Gulf** in Clearwater.

For easy listening there's guitar music at a restaurant called **Ten Beach Drive,** at 10 Beach Dr. (tel. 894-6398), and jazz fans should head for the **Hurricane Lounge,** Ninth Avenue and Gulf Way (tel. 360-9558) on Pass-a-Grille Beach, where there's usually some serious jamming going on.

The **Breckenridge Hotel** on St. Petersburg Beach has entertainment every night, and a Hawaiian show on Sunday at the pool deck. There's more Hawaiian entertainment and island music at **Trader Frank's** in the Tiki Gardens attraction. San Francisco's Royal Polynesians play steel guitar music of the island in the **Wikiwiki Lounge** here.

Belly Dancers? **Fifi's,** in St. Petersburg Beach's Dolphin Village, 4805 Gulf Blvd. (tel. 360-2286).

SPORTS: There isn't much room for golf courses on these islands, but you'll find plenty of tennis courts and enough water sports to keep you splashing.

Golf

Head over to the mainland where St. Petersburg has a number of fine courses, or to Clearwater where the **Clearwater Country Club,** 525 Betty Lane (tel. 443-5078), charges $11 in summer, $13 in winter, to play the club's 18-hole course. No carts are required, but if you want one they're $12 double.

Tennis

In Clearwater you can play on any of 17 courts at **McMullen Tennis Complex,** 1000 Edenville St. (tel. 462-6144), which charges $1.50 an hour days and $2 an hour nights. There are nine free courts at **Bayfront Municipal Courts,** 3 Pierce St. (tel. 462-6531).

On Treasure Island, there are 22 courts at the **Racquet Club,** and some are lighted. You can call for reservations at 360-6062.

St. Petersburg Tennis Center, 650 Tangerine Ave. South (tel. 894-4378), has 16 courts and a clubhouse open 9 a.m. to dark. In Indian Shores, **Belleview Gulf Beach and Tennis Club,** at 18400 Gulf Blvd. (tel. 595-2551), has courts.

Recreation centers for all areas are listed under government agencies in the *Yellow Pages,* and can direct you to specific sports equipment nearby. St. Petersburg's recreation department is at 893-7441.

Water Sports

If you want to go diving, call **Madeira Dive Shop** in Madeira Beach (tel. 392-8978), which has complete equipment and instructions for both beginners and professional divers with scuba instruction beginning at $95. Trips, including chowder lunch, are $30 to $35. **Hal Eglin's Holiday Water Sports** (tel. 345-3697) offers instruction in all water sports except sailing.

Windsurfing is the latest in water sports: it combines the windpower of sailing and the tipsy-doodle of a surfboard. You can try it out at **Windsurfing Florida Suncoast** at the Beachcomber Resort on St. Petersburg Beach (tel. 360-3783). On Clearwater Beach, **West Coast Water Sports**, 464 N. Gulfview Blvd. (tel. 443-1902), can also get you windsurfing. Rates for boards are $10 an hour, $50 a day. Lessons are about $50 for six hours.

Sailors can get out there and sail the briny blue with the help of **Suncoast Renta-boat**, 9450 Gulf Blvd. (tel. 360-6623) in Madeira Beach. Waterskiing, power and sailboats, plus motorcycles are for rent here. On Treasure Island, **Gulfcoast Sailboats**, 9600 W. Gulf Blvd. (tel. 367-4444), has boats too. Small boats run $15 to $20 an hour, $50 to $70 a half day. Sailboats can be rented behind the Islander Inn Hotel on St. Petersburg Beach too.

Parasailing is another wacky new water sport that uses a parachute to get you up in the air behind a powerboat. You can play at this by locating the parachuters behind the **Dolphin Resort Hotel, Holiday Inn**, or at the **Beach Bum** (tel. 367-2781) on St. Petersburg Beach. Rides are about $20.

Jet skis are waterskis that think they're motorcycles. Try them out at **O'Neill's Skyway Boat Basin** (tel. 866-6282) at the foot of the Skyway Bridge.

Fishing and Boating

If you'd like to go out on the sea but let someone else do the driving, call Capt. Memo of **Memo's Pirate Cruise** (tel. 446-2587), who is always around the Clearwater Beach Marina. He shouldn't be hard to spot: he wears an eye patch, knee pants, and assorted pirate gear. For $19.95 ($9.95 for children under 12), he'll escort you and his other passengers in oho-me-bucko style to a deserted island for shelling, sunning, and picnics complete with free wine and beer. Memo leaves daily at 10 a.m., and 2 and 5 p.m., and part of the treat is Memo himself, who has traded for pearls in Panama and cruised the Pacific.

Suncoast Sailing Center, at the Clearwater Beach Marina (tel. 581-4662), has two sailings daily, morning and afternoon, for $15 a person on a 38-foot yacht, and $20 for a ride on a 65-foot island schooner. The anchor is weighed at 10 a.m., and 2:30 and 4:30 p.m. daily.

Fishermen have lots of choices: free, a few dollars, or many dollars. If free sounds good, just look around you and you'll see **fishing piers** soaring out over the water like benedictions to Neptune. Every community has one, and the catch from these piers can be as spectacular as if you'd spent a bundle.

Izaak Walton types swear by **Big Pier 60** at Clearwater Beach (tel. 446-0060), open from 8 a.m. to midnight at $3 a day for adults, less for children under 12. **Big Indian Rocks Pier** (tel. 595-5494) at Indian Rocks Beach is open 24 hours for $2.60 a day. **Redington Long Pier** on Redington Beach (tel. 391-9398) is open night and day at $2.50 for adults, $2 for children under 12.

At **Fort Desoto** (see below in my sightseeing suggestions; tel. 866-9191) there are two free piers: Pier 2 is open 24 hours, Pier 1 from 7 a.m. to 8 p.m.

Fishing boats called party boats sail on full- and half-day expeditions for about $20 a person for an all-day trip, including tackle and bait. Among the boats operating in the area are *Daytona Cat* (tel. 391-6111) on Madeira Beach, and *Dixie, Super,* and *Gulf Queens* at Clearwater Marina (tel. 446-7666). *Flori-*

da Fisherman at **Passport Marina** in Madeira Beach (tel. 393-1947) also has overnight trips for $62.50, including berth.

For freshwater fishing, have a go at **Bass Fishing Heaven,** 8801 Seminole Blvd., which is Route 19A (tel. 392-4817), in Seminole.

5. Sarasota

Silk scarves spill over a counter, an emerald glitters on black velvet, frothy soft fabrics rustle in posh shops. Streets lined with manicured lawns are cut to the inch and along them white statues gaze benignly down. That's Sarasota, glamor girl of the west coast, western Florida's answer to Palm Beach.

It's strange to think that the man who built this opulent city filled with elegant mansions and smart shops was a circus king! But there it is: this is the city of John Ringling, granddaddy of Ringling Brothers Circus, who built a home here that cost $2 million (and that was in the 1920s), has solid-gold bathroom fixtures, and is so filled with treasures you'll think you've stepped into a European palace.

However spangled and gaudy his circus, Ringling himself was an art lover and amassed one of the nation's most outstanding collections of baroque and Renaissance art, including a large Rubens collection he bought for just $150,000! When he died, the circus king gave it all, including his fortune and his magnificent estate, to the people of Florida.

Encouraged by Ringling, many artists began to settle here. In recent years the city has been home to author John D. MacDonald (Travis McGee mystery creator), MacKinlay Kantor, *Alley Oop* creator V. T. Hamlin, Syd Solomon, and Spanish artist Julion de Diego.

It's worth a trip to this charming city just to see the repertory productions in the baroque elegance of tiny jewel-box Asolo Theater, which cost $1.5 million and was brought here piece by piece from Italy. All year long you'll find players' groups performing anywhere they can find an audience. You can tour some of the nation's best known art galleries and hear top concerts and opera in a culture-happy city that when it isn't calling itself the Palm Beach of the west coast is humbly laying claim to the title of "Cultural Capital of Florida."

GETTING THERE: Sarasota Airport welcomes Delta, Eastern, Republic, and Pan Am.

You can also get here on **Greyhound** and **Trailways** buses; **Amtrak** trains stop in St. Petersburg and Tampa.

GETTING AROUND: There are the usual dozens of **rental-car companies,** topped by Alamo and Greyhound's budget-wise fleets, with Hertz, Avis, Budget, Dollar, and Lindo's following closely behind.

Buses (tel. 922-6296 for route information) travel throughout Sarasota County from dawn to dusk for 50¢, and when all else fails you can take a taxi for which you'll pay $2 for the first mile, $1.20 for succeeding miles. Some taxi companies in the area are **Yellow Cab** (tel. 955-3341), **Airport Taxi** (tel. 365-1360), and **Blue Cab** (tel. 366-9596).

Limousines playing the area include **Airport Suncoast** (tel. 355-9645), which serves Tampa airport too. From Sarasota Airport, limo fees are $6 to $8.50; from Tampa, they're about $25.

USEFUL INFORMATION: For **medical or police emergencies,** call the Sarasota County sheriff at 366-1811 or dial 0 (zero) for operator. . . . For nonemergency **medical or dental help,** call the county's health clinic, 2200 Ringling Blvd. (tel. 365-2020). . . . **All-Night Chevron,** at 4130 S. Tamiami Trail (tel.

921-1056), can help with car repairs and gasoline 24 hours a day. . . . **Eckerd's Drugs,** 3800 S. Tamiami Trail in the Crossroads Shopping Center (tel. 955-3328), is open day and night, and the chain has three other 24-hour operations in the area. . . . **Denny's,** at 8214 S. Tamiami Trail (tel. 966-2626), is open around the clock.

TOURIST INFORMATION: You'll find some friendly faces at the **Sarasota Chamber of Commerce,** 1551 2nd St., Sarasota, FL 33577 (tel. 813/955-8187), where somebody always knows the answer to your questions. . . . **Longboat Key** has its own chamber of commerce, 510 Bay Isles Rd., Sarasota, FL 33578 (tel. 813/383-1212), as does **Siesta Key,** at 5481 Riverbluff Circle, Sarasota, FL 33578 (tel. 813/924-9696). . . . **Bradenton** also has a chamber of commerce, at 222 10th St. West, Bradenton, FL 33509 (tel. 813/748-3411). . . . Sarasota has a **Visitor Information Center** at 655 N. Tamiami Trail, Sarasota, FL 33578 (tel. 957-8177), which has lots of information on what to see and do in the area.

WHERE TO STAY: When you're looking for someplace to stay in Sarasota, you have three sandy places to look and one commercial district. If sand is what you came here for (with a little sun and ocean tossed in), then you'll want to concentrate on Lido Key, Long Key, or Siesta Key. If you're here to sightsee, you'll be a little closer to attractions if you select from some of the choices on US 41, but you'll have to sacrifice ocean frontage. Whichever area you choose, you'll find a variety of resorts, both small and moderately priced or large and beautiful with price tags to match. No matter where you are you'll never be more than 20 minutes or so from a beach. Let's start with the southernmost island, Siesta Key, and move north.

Siesta Key

Oldtimers hereabouts lament the growth that's turned the once-tropical jungle of Siesta Key into a popular beachfront getaway spot for both mainland residents and visitors. There's no doubt it's changed over the years. These days there are many condominiums on this quiet key, but it's still a lovely, jungley, offbeat spot where you'll find a number of small family-owned motels with moderate prices. There are beaches galore, from a large public beach with concession stands to tiny Turtle Beach, where you can picnic beside a lagoon in an atmosphere that's been touched just enough by human hands to make it comfortable.

To get to Siesta Key, take US 41 to Route 789, which leads you directly onto the key. You'll find it easily by following the Siesta Key signs posted on US 41.

There must be something about this island that stirs creativity for this is a favorite residence of writers and artists, including Travis McGee's creator, mystery writer John MacDonald, who fled the east coast for a hideaway here.

One of the easiest ways to locate a stopping spot on Siesta Key is to seek out **Sara-sea Circle,** a few miles from the entrance to the key. Here 11 motels have gathered their wagons into a circle around a central entertainment area with shuffleboard courts, a playground, a pool, and a beach they all share. All the motels are small properties, perfect examples of those resorts the world calls "mom and pop" operations. They're so similar in design and direction that choosing among them can be easy: just pick your favorite color.

Red is somebody's favorite color at red-trimmed and flower-bedecked **Tropical Shores,** 6717 Sara-sea Circle, Sarasota, FL 34242 (tel. 813/349-3330). Owners Manfred and Renate Kerstan are as talented with interior design as they are with landscaping—and that's talented. There are flowers everywhere

here, from bright-red geraniums to orange bachelor buttons, hanging plants on porches, greenery climbing lattices. (I even went beak-to-beak with a pair of nesting warblers so content they barely glanced up!) Tropical Shores has a cozy little annex on the right side of Sara-sea Circle as you face the sea, where small sitting rooms and picture windows offer a view of plants and curving gravel drive. Like most motels here, Tropical Shores particularly caters to week-or-longer visitors. You'll find motel rooms with queen-size beds, efficiencies, and suites as well. Prices are $295 to $390 a week in winter, $210 to $285 in summer and fall.

Sara-Sea Lodge, Sara-sea Circle, Sarasota, FL 34242 (tel. 813/349-3244), is a pretty pink-and-white motel where you'll be greeted by two fat plaster lions and a flowered central courtyard. Motel rooms are $29 to $38 in summer, peaking at $245 to $290 a week in winter. Efficiencies start at $28 a day in the summer months, lower in fall.

Another selection on Sara-sea Circle is the **Capri Motel,** 6782 Sara-sea Circle, Sarasota, FL 34242 (tel. 813/349-2626), a one-story turquoise structure with a tiny courtyard. Owners Chuck and Gay Metzel offer a smiling welcome and attractively beachside quarters on Crescent Beach. The Capri has clean, neat, and attractively decorated rooms and efficiencies beginning at $30 a day in summer, $52 in winter, and lower weekly fares.

Others on this small, perfectly manicured circle are **Captiva,** 6772 Sara-sea Circle (tel. 813/349-4131); **Gulf Sun,** 6722 Midnight Pass Rd. (tel. 813/349-2442); **Water's Edge,** 6744 Sara-sea Circle (tel. 813/349-1176); **Starlight Terrace,** 6716 Sara-sea Circle (tel. 813/349-1515); **Conclare Apartments,** 6738 Sara-sea Circle (tel. 813/349-2322), run by some very nice people who grow tomatoes under their windows; **Sea Breeze,** 6748 Sara-sea Circle (tel. 813/349-0303); and **King Neptune** (see Tropical Shores, above, for address and phone).

Back on Midnight Pass Road, the main thoroughfare on the island, seek out the **Surfrider,** at 6400B Midnight Pass Rd., Sarasota, FL 33581 (tel. 813/349-2121), where you'll find very spacious efficiency apartments with lovely screened porches where you can watch the sun setting over the gulf. Motel rooms, one- or two-bedroom apartments, and cottages are all available. In the middle is a hydrotherapy pool heated year round to 95 degrees. For those who like having a kitchen but intend doing little or nothing with it, there's a rustic little restaurant complete with vaulted, beamed ceiling, stone fireplace, and cozy candlelit ambience, not to mention a renowned rack of lamb and other treats for prices in the $8 to $15 range (open 6 to 11 p.m. daily except Monday). Winter room rates start at $68; summer, at $48.

Lido Key

Since there's no bridge over Big Sarasota Pass, you'll have to go back out the way you came and head north on US 41 and around St. Armand's Circle following the signs to Lido Key. This island is quite close to the mainland (as are all these islands, actually) so it's a good place to roost if you're planning some shopping in fabulous St. Armand's Circle. It's quite a small island, but has some high-rise resorts and, at the southern tip, a park.

Here you'll come upon the **St. Armand Inn,** 700 Ben Franklin Dr., Lido Beach, FL 33577 (tel. 813/388-2161), where each of the 116 rooms has wide picture windows overlooking the gulf so you can count waves instead of sheep. There's a bit of a colonial air here, with red brick exterior and trim white shutters. You don't have to go far from the hotel's private strip of sand for a freshwater swim—the pool is right beside the beach. Rooms are decorated in gold with dark-wood furniture, and some have kitchenettes which can become suites; some have private balconies. There's a lounge and coffeeshop, sundeck, basketball, volleyball, and shuffleboard. Rates February through April are $70 to $80 double. As usual, you pay a little more for gulf-front apartments. In summer and fall, rates are $45 to $55.

There's something musical about the name **Coquina on the Beach,** 1008 Ben Franklin Dr., Lido Beach, FL 33577 (tel. 813/388-2141), and when you see the lovely flowery landscaping and balconies you'll discover still more harmony. This is a very pretty place, with tropical bamboo and rattan furniture, floor-to-ceiling windows, spacious screened porches, and a neat, trim air about it. You can choose between bedroom apartments (with twin or double beds and convertible couches) and studio apartments (with living room/bedroom combinations), but all rooms have cooking facilities. There is a beach-front wing and one overlooking a small patio area, a private beach, a pool equipped with hydrotherapy jets, shuffleboard, and a laundromat. Mornings, a complimentary newspaper is delivered to your door. They'll even take in Fido if he's well behaved. Rates from the end of January are $85 to $95, dropping May 1 to $52 to $60, with discounts for long stays.

Three Crowns, at 1314 Ben Franklin Dr., Lido Beach, FL 33577 (tel. 813/388-2155), is a seven-story condominium tower, offering hotel rooms, efficiencies, one-, two-, and three-room apartments, and a penthouse. Every unit opens onto a gulf-view balcony. Outside are a heated pool and sundeck, and a strip of private beach. Rooms range from $30 to $79 in summer, from $45 to $97 in the winter season.

Three Crown's sister property, **Azure Tides Resort,** 1330 Ben Franklin Dr., Sarasota, FL 33577 (tel. 813/388-2101), has hotel rooms, kitchenettes, and two-room apartments with rates ranging from $51 to $67 in summer, from $65 to $75 in peak season. These motels share a restaurant, located at the Azure Tides, and a well-attended outdoor beachside lounge. Recently renovated, the restaurant is quite popular around the key for its inexpensive Sunday brunch, and dinner prices beginning at about $8.

Longboat Key

Largest of the three keys, Longboat is upper-crust Sarasota. To get there, follow the signs around St. Armand's Circle. As you leave the circle you'll pass plush Bird Key, a conclave of elegant pastel homes in the six- (approaching seven-) figure price range.

Longboat Key's a small but very involved community that has kept building to a minimum with tight restrictions, in the process creating what may be the state's most understated shopping center. So involved are people here that the tiny local newspaper prints a list of *every* call answered by the police. Imagine doing that in New York or Miami! It makes for some lively reading though, and you'll certainly discover where the week's best parties were located.

As you drive along this key, you'll find imposing condominiums blending nicely with large resorts. Tucked in between are small, modest accommodations that seem neither overwhelmed by their neighbors nor oblivious to them. There's a certain nonconformist individualism about this key that makes it both elegant and unpretentious. It's getting rare in this state to find a barrier island unspoiled by rows of high-rises, but this is one, a wonderfully tropical island that looks just the way you'd imagine an island off the coast of Florida ought to look.

A short way up the island you'll see a small rustic sign announcing the **Colony Beach and Tennis Resort,** at 1620 Gulf of Mexico Dr., Longboat Key, FL 33548 (tel. 813/383-6464, or toll free 800/237-9443; in Florida, 800/282-1138). There are many beach resorts in Florida and increasing numbers of tennis resorts, but a beach *and* tennis resort is downright sybaritic. There are 21 courts here, scattered so strategically around the property that devotees can practically tumble out of bed onto the courts. There's a tennis pro and staff, instructors, and clinic too.

Those who prefer to sit and wait can do so in considerable comfort in one-or two-bedroom apartments, each with living room, dining area, kitchenette, a private patio or balcony, even murphy beds. There are shops, a gourmet restaurant called the Beach Bistro, entertainment and dancing in the lounge, a health club, whirlpool, sauna and steambath, swimming pool and pier, and a quarter mile of white sand beach. Summer rates range from $125 to $170 double for a one-bedroom suite, $155 to $200 for a two-bedroom with cathedral ceilings and a second-floor bedroom. In winter, rates increase to $170 to $230 for a one-bedroom, $210 to $270 for two, and there is an $8 daily charge for children up to 6, $15 a day for older youngsters in winter. All kids stay free in summer.

As you head northward on the key your eye may be caught by the long orange-and-white **Diplomat Hotel,** 3155 Gulf of Mexico Dr., Longboat Key, FL 33548 (tel. 813/383-3791). An apartment resort, the Diplomat stretches out along a 500-foot strip of gulfside sand they like to call just a "sandal step away." This resort promotes its lack of restaurants, lounges, and doormen, and says that it's a spot designed for those in search of peaceful privacy. It certainly looks peaceful, with twin two-story buildings stretching from road to gulf, offering sea breezes a chance to do their cross-ventilation best. One- or two-bedroom and studio apartments are available, all with kitchens and walk-in closets, color TVs, and lovely picture windows overlooking the gulf. Prices for two range from $55 to $128 in winter, from $45 to $86 in the summer months.

If I had to choose just one place to stay on Longboat Key—and that wouldn't be easy—I couldn't resist the lure of the **Beach Castle,** 5310 Gulf of Mexico Dr., Longboat Key, FL 33548 (tel. 813/383-2639), a really lovely spot operated by the McCall family who are blessed with a flair for interior decoration. The Castle's fine location offers either gulfside or bayside views. A talented staff keeps everything sparkling, and there's a very contemporary look to the 20 apartments tucked away amid bamboo plants and fences festooned with roses. Decor runs to comfortable white rattan furniture, cool blues and greens in the spacious rooms kept neat as a pin. You can borrow the McCalls' rowboat or a canoe and float tranquilly around Sarasota Bay, then soothe newly exercised muscles in the resort's 98-degree Jacuzzi or their glittering freshwater pool. All the one- and two-bedroom apartments have screened balconies, and you can choose your view, bay or gulf. There are three rate periods here, summer, winter, and fall. Prices range from $79 to $108 double from December to May for quarters accommodating four or five. In summer, prices drop $15 to $20, and there are discounts for stays of a week or more.

If you're keeping a close watch on your wallet, **Sun 'n Sea,** at 4651 Gulf of Mexico Dr., Longboat Key, FL 33548 (tel. 813/383-5588), ought to fill the bill. Located right on the beach, Sun 'n Sea is a cluster of screened apartments, hotel rooms, efficiencies, and one- or two-bedroom cottages scattered over lawns shaded by pines and flowering shrubs. Furnishings are quite basic: duplex apartments accommodating four share a bathroom, but separate washbasins are tucked into the corner of each bedroom. There are compact kitchens, plenty of closet space, telephones, and color TV, and rooms are large. Rates are just $40 a day for a hotel room in winter, $45 for efficiencies, and $65 to $85 for cottages. Prices drop about $15 in summer and are even lower in fall.

Anna Maria Island/Bradenton

The northern and most eclectic of the three islands bordering Sarasota Bay is Anna Maria Island, where you find (from south to north) Bradenton Beach, Holmes Beach, and Anna Maria Beach.

The most scenic way to reach the island is to travel north along Longboat Key crossing Longboat Pass; but you can also come here on two causeways, Cortez Road (Route 684) and Manatee Avenue (Route 64), both of which extend to Route 401, and to its parallel highway, Route 301.

Traveling north up Longboat Key and across the path you first reach **Bradenton Beach,** a crazy-quilt spot jammed with beach cottages that line both sides of the street and tread a very narrow line between rustic and ramshackle. You'll either love this sunny, sandy strip of oceanfront, peopled by the bikini-and-sharktooth set, or you'll loathe it. It's a very busy place with lots of traffic, souvenir shops, small beer and shrimp bars, and short-order eateries.

If you opt for love and want to really absorb the atmosphere here, you can ask in any of the shops about renting private cottages in the area, or inquire at the **Anna Maria Chamber of Commerce,** 105 39th St., Holmes Beach, FL 33501 (tel. 813/778-7477), about private rentals. Or you can do this the easy way and seek out what I think are the best on the beach: Catalina Beach Resort, Via Roma, and Aquarius.

Owners Gil and Katie Pierola are Spanish and their **Catalina Beach Resort,** 1325 Gulf Dr. North, Bradenton Beach, FL 33510 (tel. 813/778-6611), reflects that heritage everywhere you turn, from its red-and-black color scheme to the ornate wood balconies and bullfight posters on the walls. Rooms are furnished with Spanish-style furniture, bedspreads are dark velvets, paintings offer views of flamenco dancers and Spanish towns. It's quite a pretty place, with medium-size rooms that are kept neat and tidy. Across the street the resort has a strip of private beach, and on the grounds there's a swimming pool, game room with bumper-pool table, a water slide, shuffleboard, laundry room, and barbecue grills. Weekly rates for two begin at $315 in winter, at $250 in summer.

Up the road a bit, **Via Roma,** at 2408 Gulf Dr. North, Bradenton Beach, FL 33510 (tel. 813/778-6691), occupies a tranquil spot along Gulf Drive and is itself a tranquil spot stretching along both sides of the beach highway. Romans loved their statues and so does Via Roma, which features a lawnful of white-washed statues including, of course, Neptune with his trident. Via Roma's beachside patio area is a departure from the usual thatched-roof chickee: it's a long, narrow gazebo supported by tall white columns. There's an attractive arched pool and formally landscaped grounds, plus a Garden annex across the road and a third building overlooking still another pool. You'll have lots of space in the rooms, and they're all decorated in attractive colors and furnishings with everything kept bright and shining. All units have kitchens now, and Via Roma features a whirlpool/hot tub as well as a heated pool. Another nice touch: A small sailboat and bicycles are available for guests. One- and two-bedroom apartments range from $90 to $140 from mid-December through April, from $55 to $110 in other months. Via Roma offers a 15% discount for a one-week rental, 20% for two weeks, and 30% for a month or more.

Aquarius Motel, 105 39th St., Holmes Beach, FL 33510 (tel. 813/778-7477), is popular with beach lovers who come here to be within steps of the shell-strewn gulf beaches. Accommodations at Aquarius include kitchens with an adjacent living room plus a separate bedroom with twin or double beds and bath. A convertible couch in the living room sleeps two more beach fans. Owners are Elsie and Herman Borstelmann, who are active in the region's chamber of commerce so they'll be able to help you find your way to the best shelling and swimming spots. Rates are $63 a day, $395 a week, from December through April; $46 a day, $289 a week, in other months.

A little farther north on Anna Maria Island is **Holmes Beach,** a serene residential area that has two lovely resorts. One of those is **Island Plantation,** at 7300 Gulf Dr., Holmes Beach, FL 33510 (tel. 813/778-1079). Tall white columns line the porch of the elegant reception area, and clusters of apartments are scattered beachside around a central courtyard. Island Plantation is a very popular place, and you'll have to reserve as far in advance as possible. Rooms have recently been refurbished and every one is different, but they all have plenty of space, bright colors, and a carefully tended look. Since there are so many kinds of accommodations available here, you would be wise to describe just what you need and ask for price quotations (month-long stays only, in winter). In winter you'll pay about $960 to $1450 a month; highest price is for a gulf-front apartment for six with three bedrooms and two baths. In summer, weekly rates of $252 to $390 are available.

Sharing the tip of Anna Maria Island is the **Blue Water Beach Club,** 6306 Gulf Dr., Holmes Beach, FL 33510 (tel. 813/778-6688), a glittering white building that arcs around a central courtyard and an extra-wide strip of beach. An English friend sometimes describes things as "neat as a bandbox," and I'd say that's the perfect description for the Blue Water Beach Club. There's a lovely bright lobby decorated in white and green, and a delightfully airy, glass-enclosed sitting-and-sipping room with white scalloped awning, hanging greenery, even a swaying birdcage. Blue Water has several different kinds of accommodations, ranging from hotel rooms to efficiencies and apartments, and they're all bright with citrus colors and sliding glass doors opening onto balconies or terraces overlooking the gulf. There's a pool shaded by banana trees in the middle of it all, and a nice friendly management. Two people pay $67 to $97, in high season, $47 to $72 after April 30, less if you're staying a week or more.

On the Mainland

Top of the line on the mainland is the **Hyatt Sarasota,** at 1001 Boulevard of the Arts, Sarasota, FL 33577 (tel. 813/366-9000), or toll free (800/228-9000), which isn't on a beach but is certainly one of the most impressive hostelries in town. It is on the waters of a marina just across from Sarasota's Van Wezel Performing Arts Hall. Here you'll find all you'd expect from this popular chain: spacious, tastefully decorated rooms, with furnishings as contemporary as the architecture. One of the city's top restaurants, Peppercorn's, is here, so you can dine in the glow of candles on an international menu that features roast duckling prepared five different ways. Down in the Boathouse you can feast in more casual surroundings in this stilt-built dining room that juts out over a lagoon. Room rates for two people are $100 to $135, year round.

Up and down Tamiami Trail you'll find large and small motels with very reasonable prices. Among the larger ones is the **Sarasota Motor Inn,** 8150 N. Tamiami Trail, Sarasota, FL 33580 (tel. 813/355-7747), which has 158 sound-proofed rooms on six acres of land crowned by a triple-arched entranceway and a flairing pagoda roof. Accommodations are spacious and nicely furnished, sparked by lively colors. Rates are $40 in winter, $28 in summer.

The **Royal Palm Motel,** 1701 N. Tamiami Trail, Sarasota, FL 33580 (tel. 813/365-1342, or toll free 800/528-1234), is also part of the Best Western chain and offers just 37 pretty rooms and efficiencies. A special feature of many rooms here are wall murals hand-painted by graduates of nearby Ringling School of Art. There's a heated pool, and the beach is just three miles away. Rates are $32 to $48 in winter, $22 to $34 in summer.

Golden Host, at 4675 N. Tamiami Trail, Sarasota, FL 33580 (tel. 813/355-5141, or toll free 800/528-1234), has beamed ceilings in some rooms, dressing areas, wood paneling, and private patios or balconies in rooms that stretch across three acres of landscaped grounds. The resort is proud of its pool, ringed by palms, and also offers shuffleboard and poolside games, and a cocktail lounge with a Hawaiian flavor. Rates in winter are $45 to $55 double; in summer, $34 to $40.

Budget watchers should head for the mansard roof of the two-story **Econolodge,** 5340 N. Tamiami Trail, Sarasota, FL 33580 (tel. 813/355-8867, or toll free 800/446-6900), where a medium-size room with double bed is just $52 to $55 for two, and extra persons are $5 each, year round. Accommodations are basic, but so is the price.

READERS' ACCOMMODATIONS SUGGESTION: "In some places in Florida there are **homes for rent** cheaper than motels or beach cottages and apartments. **Bradenton,** for instance, is loaded with all kinds of accommodations from bed and breakfast for $19 to $22 a day to homes and condominiums for as little as $800 to $1200 a month" (B. H. Sampson, Powell, Ohio). [*Author's Note:* The city's chamber of commerce can put you in touch with people who rent homes or condominium apartments, or have B&B accommodations.]

WHERE TO DINE: Sarasota has many fine restaurants with lots of atmosphere
and quite moderate prices. I've grouped them by location so you can find one easily wherever you are. (Remember that the prices I've cited are for entrees, but these usually include salad, one or two vegetables, and often coffee as well.)

Downtown and Near the Airport

A longtime favorite hereabouts is **Zinn's,** 6101 N. Tamiami Trail (tel. 355-7979), frequented as much for its serene decor as for its cuisine. A glass wall at one end of the room lets everyone have a good view of a rugged stone wall over which cascades a 14-foot waterfall. Pale peach and green is the color scheme, and you'll dine on some interesting beef and seafood dishes like planked grouper and marinated, then char-broiled prime rib. You'll pay about $7 to $13 for dinner from 5 to 10 p.m. daily (opening at 11 a.m. on Sunday for a $7.75 brunch). Closed most of September.

Peppercorn's, at the Hyatt, 1000 Boulevard of the Arts (tel. 366-9000), has a very elegant setting and excellent cuisine with prices in the $10 to $17 range. That hotel's **Boathouse** is a good place for lunch and casual evening dining, too. Both are open at 11 a.m. for lunch, and the Boathouse stays open to 1 a.m., while Peppercorn's ends lunch at 2 p.m. and has dinner from 6 to 10 p.m.

To go to Sarasota without going to **Marina Jacks,** at Marina Plaza, Island Park on the waterfront (tel. 365-4232), is some kind of sacrilege and the surest way to miss one of the finest views in town. There are lots of seafood dishes and a variety of salads from noon to 3 p.m. daily, and lots more of the same for dinner from 5 to 10 p.m. daily when prices are in the $10 to $15 range. Something new on Sarasota's waterfront is **Marina Jack II,** a double-decker paddlewheeler trimmed in oak paneling and brass, and featuring Créole and French culinary touches, plus the usual steaks and prime rib. Prices for cruise and dinner are $13 to $17, and the boat has two-hour cruises at noon and 7:30 p.m. (6 p.m. on Sunday). Don't miss Marina Jack's comfortable Deep Six Lounge, open from 9 p.m.

You can oom-pah-pah with lots of other happy wanderers at **Old Heidelberg Castle,** on US 301 at 3rd Street and North Washington Boulevard (tel. 366-3515), where you'll find lots of liederhosen, wienerschnitzel, sauerbraten, and the like. A great cavernous dining room, Old Heidelberg Castle puts together a rollicking evening for prices in the $10 to $12 bracket, with quite inexpensive libations at an early happy hour. Closed Monday.

For some of the things that have happened in this state, Florida could have invented the **Guinness Book of Records.** Certainly **Walt's Fish Market, Raw Oyster Bar, and Restaurant,** at 560 N. Washington Blvd. (tel. 365-1735), has contributed its part to that famous record: this is the site of a 1976 world-record oyster-eating event when Vernon Bass downed 684 of the little shellsters in 20.5 minutes to beat his own record of 588 in 17 minutes! Walt's has more than 40 dinners, from freshwater perch to smoked mullet, in low, low price brackets (under $10 for two). In season, Walt's packs them in from 5 p.m., so arrive early to avoid feeling like an oyster yourself. Open from 11 a.m. to 10 p.m. daily (from 4 p.m. on Sunday).

St. Armand's Key

You might have already guessed that a city peopled by artists, writers, and wealthy jet-setters is likely also to have attracted some talented restaurateurs—and you're right. Two of them are Titus Letschert and Berliner Norbert Goldner, who took this town by storm when they set up shop here a few years ago as **Café L'Europe,** 431 Harding Circle (tel. 388-4415), and this whirlwind is still going strong. Café L'Europe wins *Holiday* awards with such palate-pleasers as bay scallops Nantua, veal piccata, mignonettes aux poivres (with black, white, and green peppercorns). The decor is enchanting, with pink bricks, arches, antique Italian tile trim, potted plants, and a mouthwatering display of delicacies at the entrance. Gastronomes come from miles around to sample food and atmosphere here, so reservations are a must. Most entree prices fall in the $12 to $20 category, although your bill will probably go higher when you see all the possibilities here. Hours are 11:30 a.m. to 3 p.m. and 5:30 to 10:30 p.m. daily (6 to 10 p.m. on Sunday).

A few doors around the circle, the **Columbia Restaurant,** at 411 Harding Circle (tel. 388-3987), is the Sarasota sister of the famed Ybor City Columbia. Like its renowned relative, Columbia is classical Spanish from decor to dining, which begins at 11 a.m. and continues through 11 p.m. (from 1 p.m. on Sunday). Paella is the number one specialty, followed by an excellent zarzuela de mariscos. A new addition to this Columbia is a raw bar featuring stone crabs. Prices are in the $11 to $17 range for dinner.

Charley's Crab, 420 Harding Circle (tel. 388-3964), has taken nautical decor to tasteful new heights in dining rooms trimmed with lofty chandeliers made of delicate straw fans, white netting, and batik-looped ceiling. Try the back room for an intimate atmosphere. New offerings are displayed daily on a blackboard at the entrance and range from Canadian salmon to Boston scrod. Raw bar fans will salivate over the iced treats in the lobby. Open from 11:30 a.m. to 2 p.m. weekdays and 5 to 10 p.m. daily, later in the lounge. Prices are in the $13 to $19 range.

You're guaranteed the pastry will be delectable at **Le Rendez-vous** at the French Hearth, 303 John Ringling Blvd. (tel. 388-2313), which is first a bakery, second a tea room, and third a tiny French café. Breakfast, lunch, and dinner are served from 9:30 a.m. to 9 p.m. every day but Sunday, for prices in the $6 to $13 range. Sometimes hours change in summer.

Amid all this poshness it's nice to know there's a spot you can nip in after a long day among the Guccis. **Tail o' the Pup** is the place, on St. Armand's Circle (tel. 388-1553), which is open from 11 a.m. to 3 p.m. and 5 to 8:30 p.m. daily, later in the lounge. Dine among plants and wood on everything from a $1 hot dog to $10 steaks.

Siesta Key

You've probably seen strolling musicians, but they've got strolling magicians at **Magic Moments Restaurant,** 5831 Midnight Pass Rd. (tel. 349-9494). All the sleight-of-hand some restaurants use on tableside cookery they save here for tableside abracadabra delivered with dessert. Prestidigitational fun is the main ingredient here, supplemented by steaks and seafood served in a woodsy-plantsy atmosphere. Magic Moment's open from 5 to 10 p.m. daily, with entertainment in the Pazzazz lounge Tuesday through Sunday. Dinners run $8.95 to $16.95. Reservations requested.

Some restaurants look intriguing, and tiny **Wildflower**, at 5218 Ocean Blvd. (tel. 349-1758), is one. From its carved wooden sign to its storefront entrance, Wildflower is kind of cuddly-cute. The accent is on natural foods from wok-fried vegetables to steamed gumbo, carrot cake, veggie burgers, and carob brownies. It's open daily from 11 a.m. to 8:30 p.m., a half hour later on weekends, and costs only about $5.

If you love the "snug little cabin in the woods" atmosphere, you'll love the **Surfrider Restaurant**, 6400 Midnight Pass Rd. (tel. 349-4024), about which you'll find more in my hotel recommendations. There's a touch of the same ambience at **The Inn Between** (isn't that a great name?), which is at 431 Beach Rd. (tel. 349-7117). Here you'll find an open-hearth fireplace, a warm woody glow, and Italian accents like fettuccine Alfredo. Plenty of beef, seafood, veal, and lamb dishes are served for prices in the $9 to $15 range. It's open from 5:30 to 11 p.m. daily, and there's entertainment and dancing most nights.

After a long hard day at the beach, stop in at **Mustard's Paradise Pub**, 5023 Ocean Blvd. (tel. 349-0158), which gets my award for the best name in town. Goo some of the yellow stuff on one of Mustard's $1.10 all-beef hot dogs or sausages, roll some ketchup on the home-sliced french fries, taste a little chili Chihuahua, and *violà!* beachbum's nirvana. Open from 11 a.m. to 9:30 p.m. Monday through Friday, to 6 p.m. on Saturday. Do what the natives do on Wednesday: wear a Mustard's T-shirt and collect a 35¢ beer. Evenings, dine on prime rib or barbecued treats for $5 to $10.

Longboat Key

The **Colony Resort's Beach Bistro Restaurant**, at 1620 Gulf of Mexico Dr. (tel. 383-6464), is a lovely spot filled with rafts of fresh flowers and serving up chicken rosemary or rack of lamb Mephisto flamed in Calvados. Prices are in the $12 to $20 range for dinner, and every morning there's a trencherman's breakfast including everything from eggs Benedict to huge trays of fresh fruit.

The **Buccaneer Inn**, which along with the Colony and Far Horizons were recommended as hotels, also has an award-winning dining room whose number-one specialty is prime ribs of beef, roasted then broiled over charcoal embers. You can look out over the nearby marina as you dine under the watchful eye of life-size pirate figures. Prices are all listed in doubloons, so bring your calculators or just rely on their translations (in the $10 to $15 range). Open for all meals to 11 p.m. daily.

You can settle in for all three meals at **Shenkel's**, 3454 Gulf of Mexico Dr. (tel. 382-2500), which has plenty of breakfast choices every day, stacked sandwiches at lunch, and things like chicken pot pie and Welsh surprise at dinner. Shenkel's is closed on Monday but open every other day from 9 a.m. to 2 p.m. and 5:30 to 9 p.m.

Don't even dream of dinner without reservations at **Euphemia Haye**, 5540 Gulf of Mexico Dr. (tel. 383-3633), for this tiny storefront restaurant seats just 42 in-the-know diners. The decor is eclectic but soothing, and back in the kitchen chef/owners Raymond and D'Arcy Arpke bake their own nut bread and pastries. Steak au poivre, gambreto, cappillini, and homemade pasta with pesto sauce all pour from that same kitchen, open from 5 to 11 p.m. every day. You'll pay from $12 to $25 for dinners lauded by several major journals.

L'Auberge du Bon Vivant, 7003 Gulf of Mexico Dr. (tel. 383-2421), is an

382 DOLLARWISE GUIDE TO FLORIDA

old house converted to an attractive country French look with copper pots, beamed ceilings, old clocks, lots of plants, and crisp white napery glistening in the glow of candles. Two couples man the Auberge, Judy and Michael Zouhar (once part of Winter Park's award-winning Le Cordon Bleu) and Madeleine and Francis Hatton. Gentlemen are in the kitchen, ladies in the front, and how's this for a motto: "Love of the table is the last of the loves, but it's the consolation of all the others"? There's an impressive list of fine French offerings here for prices in the $15 range. Open from 5 to 10 p.m. (closed on Sunday).

On Anna Marie Island

Pete Reynard's, 5325 Marina Dr., Holmes Beach (tel. 778-2233), has been here since 1954 serving up good home-cooking and simple straightforward preparations of beef, seafood, baked ham, pork chops, and the like. There are three pretty dining rooms, one of which rotates so you can see the changing bayside scenery through banks of windows. You'll pay about $10 for dinner, and hours are from 11:30 a.m. to 10 p.m. daily.

Way up on the tip of the island, **Fast Eddie** started out with a little marina-side eatery and drew so many fans he's expanded to an awesome two-story wood-sided California-look monster of a building overlooking a spectacular uninterrupted view of miles of gulf and beach. It's quite an apparition among the tiny beach cottages, and its prices seem an apparition too, in this day of high, high, and higher. Four people can dine here amid paddle fans and hundreds of plants on this for-four platter: four cups of gumbo, a whole barbecued smoked mullet, a pound of fried grouper, two dozen fried shrimp, a dozen smoked oysters, four crab cakes, four mounds of french fries and four of cole slaw, plus some onion ring garnishes—for $35.95! Shades of Diamond Jim. Fast Eddie's is at 101 S. Bay Blvd. (tel. 778-2251), and is open from 11:30 a.m. to 11 p.m. daily.

A special little place on Anna Maria Island is just down the street from the island's sole "attraction," the roofless, wall-less city jail. An ice cream parlor in front at **Anthony's,** 204 Pine Ave. (tel. 778-6939), conceals a tiny tiled, greenery-strewn back room that holds perhaps 20 or so diners who trek here for very skillful cooking by Anthony who has a long chefing career. He is putting it into practice here on such delicacies as trout amandine, grouper, steaks, and king crab legs. The menu changes daily according to what's caught out in the gulf or fresh elsewhere. He's open from 11:30 a.m. to 2:30 p.m. for lunch and from 5:30 to 9:30 p.m. daily (except Monday) for dinner. Prices are in the $6 to $10 range.

READER'S RESTAURANT SUGGESTION: "You should add the **Seafood Shack,** 4110 127th St. West (just off Cortes Road), in Brandenton (tel. 794-1235)—the grouper is delicious and cheaper than other area restaurants" (Michael J. Hare, Toronto, Canada). [*Author's Note:* Hours at the Seafood Shack are 11:30 a.m. to 10 p.m. daily, closing at 9 p.m. on Sunday, and dinner prices are in the $10 to $15 range.]

Bradenton

The **Pewter Mug,** 1088 44th Ave. East (tel. 756-7577), has twice been selected by area magazine readers as one of the state's top six steakhouses. Those who love prime rib should have a go at the two-pounder here. There are some good raw-bar offerings, plus chowders and a salad bar with gorgonzola cheese dressing. The atmosphere is California contemporary, with beamed ceiling and lots of greenery. Prices are in the $7 to $15 range, and doors open at 5 p.m., close at midnight.

Plunked down on the edge of the sand just on the Bradenton side of the Manatee Avenue (Route 64) bridge is **High Seas,** at 9915 Manatee Ave. West (tel. 792-4776), a waterside emporium featuring a wide range of beef, veal, chicken, and seafood specialties. Preparations have a French flavor, and veal Oscar topped with white asparagus, crab, and béarnaise sauce is a popular favorite. Prices range from $10 to $15 at this view-full restaurant, open from 5 to 10 p.m. daily.

A historic spot serving lunch and dinner is **The Pier,** at the foot of 12th Street (tel. 748-8087), where you'll now find cathedral ceilings soaring over paddle fans and greenery. Memorial Pier, the site of this restaurant, has recently been restored so you're guaranteed not only historic atmosphere but a beautiful view across the water. Local seafood and prime rib are specialties here, but there's a wide range of other selections for dinner prices in the $10 to $18 range. Hours are 11:30 a.m. to 3 p.m. and 4:30 to 10 p.m. (from 11:30 a.m. to 9 p.m. on Sunday).

NIGHTLIFE: Sarasota bills itself as Florida's cultural capital, and for its size it does indeed present an awesome array of activities ranging from opera to theater, ballet, lectures, symphony, and jazz. So strong a cultural focus does the city have that in 1970 it hired Frank Lloyd Wright's Talesin group to create the **Center for the Performing Arts,** located on prime bayfront land. The center has since become an unmistakable Sarasota landmark—it's painted a pale lavender shade and known in these parts as the "purple people seater"!

Theater

Nowhere on this side of the Atlantic will you find a theater more enchanting—or even anything like—the jewel-box **Asolo** (pronounced Ah-so-low) **State Theater,** 5401 Bayshore Rd. (tel. 355-5137). A gold-and-white baroque gem built in 1798, the Asolo was once part of the castle of deposed Cypriot Queen Catherine Cornoro, who lived about 20 miles from Venice. This tiny theater has arcing tiers of white columns, golf-leafed and ornately festooned boxes, twinkling sconces, and it was the stage for stars such as Eleanora Duse. In its boxes were seated patrons like Englishman Robert Browning. In 1939 this horseshoe-shaped beauty was removed from the castle to make way for, of all things, a movie house, but an antique dealer with a keen eye stored the theater away for 20 years, and in 1949 Florida bought it and installed it in its own building on the Ringling grounds.

I first came here to see one play, but emerged three days later, bleary-eyed but thrilled, after indulging in an orgy of play-going provided by repertory players who perform here from mid-December through mid-August. I managed to see two matinees and three evening performances before reeling out, but came away agreeing, as you will, with those who say it is worth the price of admission just to see the theater.

Performances here are top-quality, and a number of Broadway stars strode these boards before going on to fame and fortune. Curtain time is 8:15 p.m. every night except Monday, and there are generally matinees from Tuesday through Saturday at 2 p.m. Show prices vary but tickets are about $15.

Sarasota Opera Association, Inc., 61 N. Pineapple Ave. (tel. 953-7030), presents a selection of opera and operetta productions, mostly in English, from mid-February to mid-March.

Players of Sarasota, 838 N. Tamiami Trail (tel. 365-2494), present what they like to call the "most professional nonprofessional theater in the area" at the Civic Theater, on 9th Street between Cocoanut and North Tamiami Trail (tel. 365-2494). Most of the plays are scheduled from October through May, but there are sometimes performances in other months. Tickets are $7, $3.50 for students.

September through June, and sometimes in mid-summer, you can see concerts, ballet, plays, films, lectures, and a variety of current stars performing at the **Van Wezel Performing Arts Hall,** 777 N. Tamiami Trail (tel. 953-3366). Call to see what's on when you're in town.

Siesta Key Actors' Theater, 5103 Ocean Blvd. (tel. 349-7749), and the **Florida Studio Theater,** 1241 N. Palm Ave. (tel. 366-3545), produce innovative and experimental drama on an irregular schedule. Check local newspapers or the theaters for current production schedules.

Other theater groups in the area include **Manatee Players** in Bradenton, **Spotlight Dinner Theater** at Sarasota's Best Western Motor Inn, and the **Little Theater** in Venice.

Golden Apple Dinner Theater, 25 N. Pineapple Ave. (tel. 366-5454), offers an evening out with candlelight buffet dining at 6 p.m. and curtain at 8:15 p.m. Tuesday through Sunday. Broadway plays are performed by a local cast on a "magic carpet" stage that rolls out into the center of the audience. There's a Wednesday and Saturday matinee, plus discounts for senior citizens (dark on Monday). Tickets and dinner are $19 to $20 for evening performances, $14 to $15 for matinees.

Asolo Stage Two, at the corner of 1st Street and Cocoanut, one block east of US 41 (tel. 365-0100), recently opened here with an emphasis on "intimate experience" plays in straight runs of three to four weeks each from November to May.

Lounge Entertainment

There's certainly no dearth of evening hijinks in this resort community, and the entertainment changes frequently, so even if you're here for a long stay you'll find plenty to do when the sun goes down.

In Sarasota, there is good lounge entertainment in the **Hyatt's Chaise Lounge** and the **Holiday Inn North's Moon Raker Lounge,** at the **Deep Six Lounge** at **Marina Jack's** restaurant, the **Colony Beach and Tennis Resort** lounge, and the **Buccaneer Inn** lounge. (See my hotel and restaurant listings for details.)

On Lido Beach, the **Holiday Inn** has a roof garden lounge and dining room with a nice view of the water and dinner dancing which at last check tended toward big band sounds. The **Lido Beach Inn's Pub** has long been a favorite gathering spot for residents and locals alike, and features musical sojourns through time with Sarasota entertainment fixture Tony Sacco. The **Sheraton Sandcastle** also has entertainment.

On Siesta Key, there's a piano bar at **The Inn Between,** and an orchestra on weekends at the **Magic Moments Restaurant.**

Discos

For disco and rock music and dancing, **Ruby Tuesday's,** at Tampa Bay Center Mall, 302 W. Buffalo St. (tel. 872-9270), continues to pack them in and keep them amused seven nights a week with bright lights, fogs, mirrors, and lots of flash. A second Ruby rocks at University Square Mall, Fowler Street (tel. 977-2560).

A little farther around the circle, the **Columbia Restaurant** has a Patio Lounge which, last time I was there, was packed with dancers enjoying a red-hot combination of Latin and disco beats by perspiring musicians who drum gamely on until 2 a.m. nightly except Sunday.

Playground South, 1927 Ringling Blvd. (tel. 366-3830), is an old hand at the after-dark scene and has adopted an old formula to become an instant success:

lots of music, lots of people (the place holds 900), but not lots of money to get in ($2 to $5 usually). It's open every night from 7 p.m. and features rock music.

SPORTS: Sarasota likes to call itself the birthplace of American golf, since the game was introduced here in 1885. There are now 27 courses and dozens of tennis courts scattered all around the city so you shouldn't have any trouble finding something to do.

Golf and Tennis

Longboat Key Golf Club has a 7000-yard championship course that's private, but a number of resorts on the key have arrangements for their guests to play there. Ask at your front desk.

Sarasota Golf Club (tel. 371-2431) has greens fees of $13 and carts for $14. It's about seven miles east of US 301 at 7280 Leeswynn Dr.

Foxfire Golf Club, 7200 Proctor Rd. (tel. 921-7757), is an 18-hole course charging just $8 to ride and $4 to walk after 3 p.m. Meadows Country Club, at 3101 Longmeadow (tel. 371-3000), is a par-72, 18-hole course which charges $15 including shared cart. Bent Tree Golf and Racquet Club, 4700 Bent Tree Rd. (tel. 371-8200), is home of the LPGA Bent Tree Classic and charges $10 for greens fees and $7 for a cart.

There are free public tennis courts on the beach at Siesta Key and six lighted municipal courts at the Civic Center Complex grounds just off US 41. In Bradenton, there are free lighted courts at City Courts, 17th Avenue West and Wares Creek. A call to the Sarasota recreation department will elicit some information on location of other courts (tel. 365-2200).

Water Sports

You can learn to sail at O'Leary's Sarasota Sailing School, on Island Park at the bayfront (tel. 953-7505), for $12 to $25 an hour depending on the size of the boat, and rent windsurfers for $12 an hour.

Rent a boat at Mr. CB's, 1249 Stickney Point Rd., Siesta Key (tel. 349-4400), or Cannons Marina, 6040 Gulf of Mexico Dr., Longboat Key (tel. 383-1311). Rates average about $25 to $50 a day for small craft.

Don & Mike's Boat & Ski Rental, at Marina Plaza (tel. 366-6659), offers boats and jet skis, and has waterskiing lessons for $40 an hour, jet skis for $20 an hour.

Fishing

For deep-sea fishing, drop down to Siesta Key Marina or to the Bayfront Marina near the Hyatt House about 5 p.m. or early in the morning and you'll discover everything you ever wanted to know about what they're catching and how to catch them. Charter boats take groups out fishing for about $125 for four hours in the bay, about double that for gulf trips. Party-boat fishing is fun, and you can go out for a half day for $15 to $20.

Parimutuel Sports

Sarasota Kennel Club, on old Bradenton Road between US 41 and US 301 (tel. 355-7744), sends the greyhounds after the rabbit at 8 p.m. nightly (except Sunday) from May to September, with matinees on Monday, Wednesday, and Saturday. Admission is $1. In September the action moves to nearby Tampa until January, then to St. Petersburg from January to May. The Skyline Room at the Kennel Club offers formal dining and admission.

If you like stock car racing, you can watch them race their engines from February through November at DeSoto Speedway, 14 miles east of Bradenton on Route 64. The racers line up on Friday and Saturday at 6 p.m. Adults pay $7; children under 12, $3.

Baseball

Sarasota is winter home to the **Chicago White Sox,** at Payne Park just off US 301, and there's a Kansas City Minor League Complex where minor league spring training takes place. At the Gulf Coast Rookie League, newly drafted players from seven major-league teams compete.

Bradenton is the winter home of the **Pittsburgh Pirates.** Exhibition games in February and March cost $8 to $12.

Other Sports

If you'd like to go bicycling, call the **Bicycle Center,** at 3551 Webber (tel. 924-2228) in Sarasota, which also has an outlet in Bradenton at 2610 Cortez Rd. West (tel. 756-5480). On Longboat Key, you can rent a bike from **Ed's Beach Service,** 4949 Gulf of Mexico Dr. (tel. 383-4466), and on Anna Maria Island at **George Hopps Island Cycle,** 307 Pine Ave. (tel. 778-3756). On Siesta Key, try **Mr. CB's,** 1249 Stickney Point Rd. (tel. 349-4400). Rates are $5 to $8 a day.

One last word on bicycling: Longboat Key has a 12-mile bicycle course running the length of the island, with trees for shade and a quick, cooling dip always just a few steps away.

Equestrians should head for **Myakka Valley Campground and Stable,** about 12 miles east of Sarasota off US 41 on Route 72 (tel. 924-8435), where you can trot five miles of wooded trails for $8 an hour.

Ballooning? Certainly, at **Cirrus Air Balloon,** Venice (tel. 485-8562). Call for rates.

SHOPPING: If you like shopping malls, the 70 stores at **Sarasota Square Mall,** 8201 S. Tamiami Trail, should keep you busy. Siesta Key has small and casual **Siesta Village,** 5000 Ocean Blvd., with about 100 small shops and several restaurants. On Longboat Key, there's a barely visible shopping center that's small but lovely.

On weekends, seek out bargains at the **Country Fair Flea Market** on US 301 in Palmetto, the **Roma Flea Market** at 5715 15th St. East, or the market opposite Sarasota/Bradenton Airport.

Statues from Ringling's collection ring the circle of painted, primed, and polished **St. Armand's Circle,** the area's most famous shopping district, and one so well known from coast to coast in Florida that it's almost a city in itself. There's everything here from ormolu to organdy, chocolates to cheese; you can lose weeks gazing at the treasures in these windows.

Across the bay in Sarasota, Palm Avenue is the site of **Mira Mar Plaza,** two blocks of Mediterranean architecture, wrought-iron balconies, tiny gardens, and palm-lined streets. Plunk down at the Café Prague's sidewalk tables and watch the passing parade over a lunch of wine and crêpes.

Major shopping malls in the area include **East Lake Square Mall,** East Hillsborough Avenue and 56th Street, with more than 130 stores including J.C. Penney and Montgomery Ward; **Tampa Bay Center,** at Buffalo and Himes Avenues, with 152 stores in a two-level, hi-tech design (anchor shops include Burdine's, Sears, and Montgomery Ward); **University Square Mall,** on Fowler Avenue west of the University of South Florida campus, where 125 retail stores surround J. C. Penney, Maas Brothers, Robinson's, and Sears; **Westshore Plaza,** West Kennedy and Westshore Boulevards, with more than 90 shops including Maas Brothers, J.C. Penney, and Robinson's.

In Clearwater, the **Clearwater Mall,** US 19 and Gulf-to-Bay Boulevard, has 150 stores including Ivey's Gayfers and Montgomery Ward; **Countryside Mall,** US 19 and Enterprise Road, is anchored by Penney's, Maas Brothers, Robinson's, and Sears.

Pinellas Square Mall, US 19 South in Pinellas Park, is the budget-lover's favorite, with more than 100 stores including Montgomery Ward, J. C. Penney, and Ivey's.

Tyrone Square Mall, Tyrone Boulevard at 66th Street in St. Petersburg, sports more than 200 shops, including three department stores.

SIDE TRIPS: Oscar Sherer Recreation Area, located two miles south of Osprey on US 41, offers 500 acres of tropical beauty with facilities for tent and trailer camping, picnic areas, nature trails, fishing, and docks. The park is open from 8 a.m. to sunset, and admission is 50¢ per person.

Even larger is **Myakka River State Park,** Route 1, Box 72, Sarasota, FL 33583, on Route 72 about 15 miles east of Sarasota (tel. 813/924-1027), a serene 29,000-acre wildlife sanctuary where you can rent a bike, take an hour-long guided airboat tour ($5 for adults, $3 for children under 12), or a tram tour (same prices). It's fascinating to explore these acres of Florida "prairie," and fun to picnic at tranquil wooden tables or relax under towering live oaks. There's a nature museum that will tell you what the land's all about. You can rent canoes ($5 an hour) and campsites ($6 to $8 a night), and even roomy cabins with two double beds and a fireplace ($30 a night, bring your own linens). It's lovely just to drive through the park which charges a 50¢ admission, but if you'd like to stay in one of the cabins or need specific camping information, call 813/924-1027.

6. Tours

You can sit back and leave the driving—or the sailing—to them on a number of tours operating in the area.

Gray Lines (tel. 896-2655), **Lindo's Tours** (tel. 367-3779), and **American Transportation** (tel. 526-9086) will take you to the area's attractions and also roam far afield to Walt Disney World and other attractions in central Florida. Tours begin at about $15.

St. Petersburg

In St. Petersburg, the **Junior Women's Club** operates a one-hour open-air streetcar tour (winter only) along the city's waterfront departing from the *Bounty* parking lot at the Pier at varying times. Fare is $2; for reservations, call 527-0470.

If you'd like a custom-made tour of the city, **Around the Town Custom Tours** (tel. 435-7769) will take you just where *you* want to go, with prices depending on the length of the tour.

Ah, to be that roué Erroll Flynn for a day or two. You can see just what kind of swath you'd cut on a trip aboard the *Tonga,* once the swashbuckling movie idol's own 75-foot two-masted sailing craft which sails from a yacht basin near the **Don CeSar Hotel.** For reservations, call the hotel at 360-1881 and ask for guest services, which will give you all the details on the cruises. Cruise prices are by the hour, so an afternoon or evening two-hour cruise is $10; an evening cruise (including dinner), $25.

Bradenton/Tampa

In Bradenton, the *Island Adventure* is docked at the Municipal Pier at the Pier Restaurant (tel. 223-0843 or 251-8008), and sails in air-conditioned (or open-air) comfort up the Hillsborough River and around Tampa Bay on afternoon and evening cruises on a varying schedule. Afternoon tours are $10 for adults, $5 for children. A dinner and dancing cruise is $12.50. On Sunday there's an all-day cruise that departs at 10 a.m. and returns at 4:30 p.m. with a two-hour lunch stop. The cost is $15 for adults, $8.50 for children under 12.

In summer, the cruiser moves to Tampa, where it's docked at the Mirabella Restaurant, on Ashley Street near the Hilton Hotel.

Spirit of Tampa, a 150-foot cruiser with two enclosed and one open deck, sails off on luncheon, dinner, harbor, and cocktail cruises. Luncheon cruises are at noon on Friday and are $6 per person; two-hour harbor cruises are at 10:30 a.m. on Saturday and cost $4 for adults, $2 for children under 10. Cocktail-hour cruises are also a Friday event, departing at 5:30 p.m. on a two-hour cruise that costs $2 per person. Dinner and beach outings are unscheduled, but you can call and they'll tell you when they've got another one coming up. *Spirit of Tampa* is docked at 135 S. Ashley St. in Tampa, but you can write them for information on private or group cruises at P.O. Box 1611, Tampa, FL 33601.

Holiday Isles

Over in the Holiday Isles at St. Petersburg Beach, the triple-decker *Capt. Anderson* sails from the pier at the St. Petersburg Beach Causeway, 3400 Pasadena Ave. South (tel. 360-2619), on two-hour narrated Boca Ciega Bay cruises at 1:30 p.m. Tuesday through Friday. On Saturday evenings, the craft boards at 6:30 p.m. for a romantic moonlight cruise with steak dinner and dancing on board at $16.50 for adults, $2 less for children under 12. Afternoon trips are $4.50 for adults, $2.50 for children. The *Capt. Anderson* operates from October to mid-May.

7. Seeing the Sights

There is much to see and do around Tampa Bay, ranging from a visit to the palatial mansion of a circus king to visiting with the king of the jungle. So you can see it all with as little traveling as possible, after the superstar I've grouped the attractions by location, beginning with Tampa and moving on to St. Petersburg, the Holiday Isles, and winding up in Sarasota.

BUSCH GARDENS: Would you want to miss a place where Tarzan and Jane stroll blithely by and a giraffe gives you the eye from on high? Certainly not, and hundreds of thousands of other bay area visitors agree, which is why Busch Gardens is the second most popular tourist attraction in the state (second only to Walt Disney World).

To go to central Florida without seeing **Busch Gardens** is to be forever plagued by other Florida travelers asking how you could have missed it. Indeed it is something to see, this massive jungle park built by the famous brewery. To get there, take I-275 to the Busch Boulevard exit and then just follow the signs to the park (tel. 971-8282). Address is 3000 Busch Blvd., Tampa, FL 33612.

Once you're there you can see all the hundreds of things there are in a variety of ways: on foot, on a monorail, or on a Skyride cable car that crosses the Dark Continent's Serengeti Plain and gives you a giraffe's eye view of that giraffe.

You can also toot-toot around by a train that circles a park where animals roam free, separated by moats or other natural barriers. Out there on the plain are 500 head of big game roaming freely over a 160-acre veldt. Gazelles zip off into the distance, zebras chase each other around, and elephants amble slowly about.

Turn-of-the-century Africa is the theme, from **Marrakesh** belly dancers and snake charmers to the **Congo,** where huge Bengal tigers prowl endlessly around their domain, stopping now and then to dive in for a cool swim in their pool. In **Timbuktu** the Dolphins of the Deep perform, and in **Nairobi** night creatures prowl Nocturnal Mountain. In **Stanleyville,** named after the gentleman responsible for that "Dr. Livingstone, I presume" remark, you can see Tanzanian tribesmen practicing their ancient woodcarving art.

This 300-acre park contains the largest collection of mammals, reptiles, and birds in North America—3000 in all—and enough to do to keep you busy all day: riding the state's largest log flume ride, touring the tantalizing array of craft shops, or visiting the tigers. Some, of course, think the most fun of all is tossing back a few at the Anheuser Busch brewery, where all the beer you consume is free!

Try not to lose your head on an *African Queen* boat ride up the river to a headhunters' village, or your tummy on the Python rollercoaster which does a complete 360-degree loop, and is considered one of the best rollercoasters in the nation by people who rate such things. Rest up later at the cavernous Festhaus, which comes complete with oom-pah-pah.

Busch Gardens is open daily from 9:30 a.m. to dusk (about 6 p.m. in winter, about 8 p.m. in summer). One admission of $12.50 per person (children under 3 are free) includes everything in the park except parking ($1 a car). Here, as at Walt Disney World, be sure to remember your parking lot row. Another similarity to Disney is acreage—there's lots of it, so wear comfortable clothes and shoes (especially shoes), and remember how fast the Florida sun can burn.

Next door to the gardens, you'll find **Adventure Island** (tel. 971-7978), a 13-acre water park complete with water slides and endless surf, lots of kids' games that are also fun for I'm-a-kid-again travelers. One-day admission is $9.25 a person, with children under 3 free. After 3 p.m. prices drop to $6.25 per person. It gets a little chilly for this kind of fun in winter, so the park is open only from March to October. Hours are 10 a.m. to 5 p.m. weekdays and 9:30 a.m. to 6 p.m. on Saturday and Sunday. Children under 8 must be accompanied by an adult. You can combine a visit to Busch Gardens and Adventure Island with a two-day pass for $21.95.

Florida is not yet famous for its wines, but perhaps someday it may be. In the meantime you can get a look at what Florida winegrowers are doing these days at **Wines of St. Augustine,** 1205 E. Eighth Ave., in Ybor City (tel. 273-0070). Tours of the winemaking facilities are free, but for $1 you can taste six kinds of wine, some from Florida and some from other states. Vineyards are being developed in Florida, and while they're growing the grape products are being aged in the Carolinas and Georgia. Four grape varieties grow well in Florida, says grower Edward Gogel, who has been involved in wine research for more than 30 years. What's more, he says, they will produce wines equal to or better than California's products. Gogel is also producing wine from oranges!

TAMPA: One of my favorite attractions is apparently shared by the city fathers who use the minarets of the **University of Tampa** as a logo. That's fitting too, since the Tampa Bay Hotel (now the university) put Tampa on the map as a tourist destination. Henry Plant's dream hotel, the old Tampa Bay hostelry does look a bit like something someone dreamed. Atop it are bright silver minarets and around the wide verandas is Moorish gingerbread woodwork. Tampa Bay was the grandest of grand hotels when it opened in 1891. Guests arrived in private railroad cars on a spur that ended right at the hotel's lobby! (If they came by water, they pulled the yachts up to a dock and walked an underground tunnel to the reception desk.)

The Tampa Bay Hotel cost a staggering $3 million even in those days, and today you can see it on free tours conducted on Tuesday and Thursday at 1:30

p.m. You'll see the wide verandas where Teddy Roosevelt, Babe Ruth, Clara Barton, and William Jennings Bryan once rocked, and the Music Room where long windows opened onto the veranda to accommodate overflow crowds gathered for performances by Ignace Paderewski, Anna Pavlova, and Sarah Bernhardt. There are hallways so long guests used to hire rickshaws to trot them around, and a hand-carved mahogany elevator originally powered by hydraulic force, the only one of its kind in the nation. If you're exhausted, visit the basement rathskeller, under the hotel's lobby, which was used to house Spanish-American War troops and is the place the "Cuba Libre" drink was born. A small museum on the grounds houses many of Plant's priceless art objects, and is free.

To find the university, look out for those 13 silver minarets (for the 13 months of the Mohammedan lunar year), but if you don't see them, take the Ashley Street exit from I-275 and follow Ashley toward downtown to US 60 (West Kennedy Boulevard). Turn right across the bridge and you'll see the campus guardhouse on your left.

Schlitz gives Busch a little competition in Tampa by opening its suds shop for 30-minute tours of brewery facilities at 11111 30th St. (tel. 971-7075) on weekdays from 10 a.m. to 3 p.m. When you've learned all you want to know about beer brewing, you get to the important part: a sample of the contents of those brown bottles. There's no charge for the tour or the sample.

The **Tampa Museum,** 600 Doyle Carlton Dr. (tel. 223-8130), houses a varied collection of Egyptian, Greek, and Roman antiquities, Indian artifacts, European and American paintings and sculpture, and a changing array of contemporary work. If you're traveling with children, the museum has some interesting participatory exhibits in the Lower Gallery. Guided tours are available weekdays at noon and 2 p.m. A great gift shop sells reproductions of artwork and lots of posters, books, jewelry, and toys. Hours are 10 a.m. to 6 p.m. Tuesday, Thursday, and Friday, to 9 p.m. on Wednesday, and from 9 a.m. to 5 p.m. on Saturday. On Sunday the museum is open 1 to 5 p.m.; closed Monday.

A **Museum of Science and Industry,** at 4801 E. Fowler Ave. (tel. 985-5531), has dozens of fascinating participatory science and space exhibits, and charges a $2 admission for adults, $1 for children 5 to 15. It's open 10 a.m. to 4:30 p.m. daily.

Along the Hillsborough River are 105 wooded acres devoted to **Tampa's Lowry Park,** a children's delight containing a zoo, a pet-the-deer Bambi-land, and 18 small rides (45¢ to 75¢ each). It's a pretty place at the corner of Sligh and North Boulevards (tel. 935-3121), and has concerts in a bandshell.

ST. PETERSBURG: The newest celebrity resident of St. Petersburg is Salvador Dali, who, sad to say, is not here in person but is certainly here in spirit via hundreds of his paintings on display at the **Salvador Dali Museum,** 1000 3rd St. South (tel. 823-3767). Keep a sense of humor uppermost when you visit here and you'll be rewarded with many a chuckle over Dali's whimsical paintings and sculptures, some of which make some quite amusing statements about this world of bureaucrats and bemused mankind. Don't miss the case of sculptural work which includes a replica of Dali's aphrodisiac dinner jacket, produced in 1930: his dinner jacket is composed of white female undergarments in place of a formal shirt beneath a black jacket covered with small plastic shot glasses filled with green liquid. A classic!

Dali, acclaimed as the founder of surrealistic art, lives in Spain and has never seen this St. Petersburg tribute to his work. His paintings and sculpture ended up here when A. Reynolds Morse, a Cleveland plastics millionaire, told the *Wall Street Journal* he'd give his huge collection of Dali's works to any city that would build a museum to house it. St. Petersburg jumped to accommodate him, and built a sleek new building, all gray and white inside, to house the collection.

Open from 10 a.m. to 4 p.m. Tuesday through Saturday and from 1 to 4 p.m. on Sunday, the museum now owns more than 1300 pieces of Dali's work, and displays them on a rotating basis so no matter how many times you visit you'll always be seeing something new. Surrealism, by the way, is often defined as visual expression of objects in incongruous juxtapositions, fantastic arrangements, and/or hallucinatory, dream-like settings—quite a good description of this wildly-mustachioed artist's controversial work.

It doesn't sound much like a tourist attraction, but when you see St. Petersburg's **Municipal Pier,** you'll see why it is. This streak of concrete at the foot of Second Avenue has been here so long in one form or another it's become the city's symbol, landmark, and love. First constructed in 1889 by the Orange Belt Railway, it was in those days a large, ornate bathing pavilion and a toboggan slide with a horse-drawn flatcar to carry passengers from the boat docks two miles away. It's not quite that long now after several facelifts, but there's still a jitney service to carry you down the mile of concrete. At the end of the mile you'll see an upside-down pyramid pavilion that sits in weird splendor out over the sparkling waters of the bay. Inside are gift shops, a restaurant and lounge, and an observation deck, and under it is a tiny strip of sand for bathing, but there's an admission charge—10¢!

A bridge isn't usually a tourist attraction either, but the **Skyway Bridge** soaring high over Tampa Bay is wondrous testimony to the skills of modern-day Caesars. This series of bridges and causeways stretches 14 miles across to Sarasota, four of them by bridge (50¢ toll). It's a beautiful view surrounded by water and sand.

St. Petersburg is proud of its **Museum of Fine Arts,** at 255 Beach Dr. NE (tel. 896-2667), as well as it should be since this museum not only houses an outstanding collection of 17th- to 19th-century artwork, but is an arty edifice itself, with dozens of tall columns and an arched Mediterranean courtyard. It's open daily except Monday, Christmas, and New Year's Day, from 10 a.m. to 5 p.m. (from 1 p.m. on Sunday). At 2 p.m. Thursday through Sunday there are guided tours at no charge. Admission is free, but they'd like it if you left a small donation.

If you like gardens, you can see more than 5000 varieties of plants at enchanting **Sunken Gardens,** a west coast attraction since 1903. It's at 1825 4th St. North (tel. 896-3186), and admission is $5 for adults, $3 for children 6 to 12. Doors open at 9 a.m. and close at 5:30 p.m.

MGM's Bounty, in the Vinoy Basin adjoining the Municipal Pier (tel. 896-3117), is a sight to see, its bright flags flapping merrily and its massive decks spit and polished. It's not at all difficult to imagine the epic contest between Captain Bligh and Mr. Christian when you've got narration by Charles Laughton and Clark Gable! This is a replica of the ship used to film *Mutiny on the Bounty,* and admission is $4 for adults, $2 for children 4 to 12.

St. Petersburg's Historical Museum, 335 Second Ave. (tel. 894-1052), has an amazing if somewhat eclectic array of memorabilia from the city's early days (including the original city seal, which some wag sketched with mountains in the background). A 400-year-old cypress canoe is interesting, and there's a sugar bowl used by Mr. and Mrs. Tom Thumb. It's open daily from 11 a.m. to 5 p.m. (from 1 p.m. on Sunday); admission is 75¢ for adults, 25¢ for children.

The Haas Museum Village Complex, 3511 Second Ave. South (tel. 327-

1437), is where a number of the city's old homes dating back to 1850 have been perfectly preserved and restored. It's open daily from 1 to 5 p.m. Thursday through Sunday (closed in September) and admission is $2 for adults, 50¢ for children under 12.

There's a really huge collection of old homes at fascinating **Heritage Park,** 11909 125th St. North, in Largo (tel. 462-3474). You can visit a 13-room mansion from the early years of this century, a tiny (14- by 14-foot) honeymoon cottage, and a log house that's one of the oldest buildings in the county and was the birthplace of more than 50 children (not all to the same mother, I hasten to add). It's open every day but Monday from 10 a.m. to 4 p.m. (on Sunday from 1 p.m.). The park has tours every half hour from 10 a.m. to 4 p.m., but you can look on your own anytime. It's free.

Boyd Hill Nature Trail, at 1101 Country Club Way South (tel. 893-7236), is an intriguing place at the south end of lovely Lake Maggiore. There are six different circle trails, each an easy 15-minute walk through a microcosm of Florida fauna and flora. Admission is 75¢ for adults, 35¢ for children under 17, and there's a guided tour at 11 a.m. daily. The park is open from 9 a.m. to 5 p.m. You can reach it by traveling south on 9th Street to Country Club Way South; then bear right and go three blocks.

READER'S SIGHTSEEING TIP: "My family attended a performance of the **Ringling Brothers Circus** in St. Petersburg in January. Although I didn't realize it at the time, St. Petersburg is the first stop of the annual tour of the circus, and each performance is videotaped for a national television broadcast. Those who vacation in the Tampa–St. Petersburg area may take advantage of this special opportunity" (Walt Ulbricht, Kenosha, Wis.). [*Author's Note:* Mr. Ulbricht (whose very nice comments on the *Dollarwise Guide to Florida* were most gratefully received) and others visiting the Tampa Bay area might wander south a bit to the town of Venice to visit the winter headquarters of the circus (see the information on circus visits in Chapter XI on Florida's Shell Coast), which does indeed begin its season with performances in a number of Florida cities.]

HOLIDAY ISLES: One of the more unusual stops for bird lovers is the **Suncoast Seabird Sanctuary,** at 18328 Gulf Blvd., Indian Shores (tel. 391-6211), where conservationist Ralph Heath, Jr., has set up a nonprofit organization dedicated to the rescue, repair, and recuperation of wild birds. His sanctuary's been a television star several times, and is a good spot for photography since the quarry can't just up and fly away. You can even adopt your own bird with a donation. There's no admission charge, and they're open 9 a.m. to sunset daily.

Shiver under the malevolent stare of Bluebeard and see what Cleopatra really looked like before Elizabeth Taylor at the **London Wax Museum,** 5505 Gulf Blvd., St. Petersburg Beach (tel. 360-6985). Craftsmen of Britain's famed Tussaud's Museum created these characters; everyone from Julius Caesar to Lee Harvey Oswald. It's open from 9 a.m. to 8 p.m. daily (from noon on Sunday) and costs $3 for adults, $1.50 for children 4 to 12.

Tiki Gardens, 19601 Gulf Blvd., Indian Shores (tel. 595-2567), recreates the beauty of Polynesia in 12 acres of exotic tropical blossoms, temples with peacocks, and a squawking mynah bird. There's even a Polynesian restaurant overlooking the gardens and excellent South Seas entertainment evenings. Admission is $2 for adults, $1 for children. The gardens are open daily from 9:30 a.m. to 10:30 p.m.

Perched picturesquely atop a bluff commanding a beautiful (and once useful) view of Tampa Bay is **Fort DeSoto,** a relic of Spanish-American War days complete with gun emplacements and cavernous dynamite room, neither ever used. In the shadows of this stony sentinel is an 884-acre park spread across six islands with seven miles of sparkling waterfront and three miles of silky white sand beach. You can swim and fish from piers here (free), picnic, and dress to go home in dressing rooms with showers. Toll is 65¢ and the park closes at dark.

Ponce de Leon anchored off these shores in 1513 to scrape the bottom of his barnacle-encrusted boat when Indians attacked, killing one of his men, the first white soldier to die on this continent.

SARASOTA: Man's ability to assimilate both the garishly gaudy and the gloriously grandiose is epitomized nowhere better than in the person of circus king John Ringling, who with one hand created the sequined world of the Big Top and with the other commanded the accumulation of a priceless art collection which he housed in a columned Italian Renaissance architectural creation of tranquil symmetry. It remains today one of the most beautiful museums in the world.

As if that weren't enough, Ringling went on to create **Ca' d'Zan,** at 5401 Bayshore Dr. (tel. 355-5101), a palatial bayside home for himself and his wife, Mabel. It's a multi-million-dollar Venetian Gothic palazzo (hence its name, which means House of John) combining elements of the Doges Palace in Venice and the tower at the old Madison Square Garden.

One of the ten richest men in America when he died in 1936, Ringling gave the beautiful peach art gallery and the rosy cream stucco palazzo, his 68-acre estate, his priceless art collection, and his entire fortune to the state of Florida, which now welcomes 500,000 visitors here each year and charges them only $4.50 to tour it all.

Part of what you'll see here—and even the most dedicated anti-sightseeing souls shouldn't miss this—are the **Museum of Art** styled after a 15th-century Italian villa, and featuring shiploads of columns, doorways, sculpture, and marble brought here from all the major cities of Italy. Galleries are laid out on three sides of a formal garden, and on the fourth side there's a raised bridge dominated by a bronze copy of Michelangelo's *David.* Atop the loggia is a balustrade adorned with 72 roof sculptures.

Some say that Mabel Ringling had the pretentions of grandeur that created the awesomely magnificent 30-room mansion that's 200 feet long and is capped by a 60-foot tower. Inside, carved and gilded furniture from the estates of the Astors and Goulds fills 30 rooms surrounding a 2½-story roofed court. There's a coffered ceiling of Florida pecky cypress framing an inner skylight of colored glass, priceless tapestries (some of which conceal a $50,000 Aeolian organ with 4000 pipes played both electrically and manually), and Venetian glass in every color of the rainbow. A tub in one bath is hewn from a solid block of yellow Siena marble, and there are bathroom fixtures made of gold. A bar with leaded-glass panels was once part of the Cicardi Winter Palace in St. Louis.

Convinced? There's more: a **museum of the circus** full of gilded parade wagons, calliopes, and the **Asolo Theater.** It's open from 9 a.m. to 10 p.m. (for more about the theater, see Sarasota nightlife) and it's fabulous.

It's hard to compete with Ringling, but the **Gamble Mansion,** in Ellenton on US 301 (tel. 813/722-1017), can almost do it. An antebellum mansion, the huge home is now a Confederate Museum and rightfully enough: it was here that Confederate Secretary of State Judah P. Benjamin was hidden away in an upstairs room until he could escape to freedom in England where he became a successful barrister. Scarlett and Rhett would have been right at home in this shining white-columned manse that reeks of elegant, drawling days gone by. The mansion is open from 9 a.m. to 5 p.m. daily, and admission is 50¢.

Ziegfeld Follies girls once preened here. Will Rogers performed here, and dancer Sally Rand waved her fans around here. Even Elvis Presley once took to the boards of what is now the **Sarasota Theater of the Arts.** Then hard times came to the building at 61 N. Pineapple Ave. (tel. 953-7030 or 366-8450). Built in the 1920s, the theater, once the hub of downtown Sarasota, became a derelict building, its handsome courtyard enclosed, its fanciful balconies shuttered. Then four years ago the Sarasota Opera bought the building and talked supporters into beginning a multi-million-dollar renovation of the building.

Now a crystal chandelier, rescued from the movie set of *Gone With the Wind,* glitters in the foyer and tuxedoed opera fans once again chatter at intermission. It's worth a visit just to take a look at this historic old building, even better if you're here February through April when the Sarasota Opera Association presents four operas and performances by ballet troupes and string quartets. Opera tickets are $21 to $30, slightly less if you write for a subscription. In other months the building is used by organizations which sponsor lectures and other cultural activities.

It's hard to resist a music box, and it's harder yet to resist 1400 intriguing antique music boxes ranging from calliopes to nickelodeons. Team that up with antique classic and racing cars as they have at **Bellm's Cars and Music of Yesterday,** 5500 N. Tamiami Trail (tel. 355-6228), and the child in us all demands a visit. Some of Ringling's cars are here and they're valued at $200,000. The museum is open from 8:30 a.m. to 6 p.m. Monday through Saturday, from 9:30 a.m. on Sunday. Adults are charged $4.95; children 6 to 12 years, $2.25.

Choo-choos and coquinas—how's that for a combination? They have them both at the **Lionel Train and Shell Museum,** on US 41 across from the airport (tel. 355-8184), housed in a replica of a Victorian railroad depot. Trains run automatically, although coin machines are provided so you can run them. There's even one that runs completely around the museum through 40 bridges. Hours are 9 a.m. to 5 p.m. Currently admission is $2.50 for adults, 50¢ for children under 11.

Two lovely gardens in Sarasota offer flower fans a look at jungle plants and orchids. **Jungle Gardens,** at 3701 Bayshore Rd., two blocks west of US 41 (tel. 355-5305), has flamingos in the flowers, leopards, parrots, alligators, and monkeys, plus bird and reptile shows, in a 16-acre jungle with winding trails. It's open from 9 a.m. to 5 p.m. daily and charges $4.50 for adults, $2.50 for children 6 to 16 years old.

A lesser known but equally lush tropical garden is **Marie Selby Botanical Gardens,** on US 41 at 811 S. Palm Ave. (tel. 366-5730). It's a must-see for nature lovers and serious botanists, a 16-acre site that is a research center for epiphytes and a glorious collection of orchids. An old Florida home on the grounds was built by a would-be architect, who pooled the best features he'd found in a dozen or more southern mansions to create this home. It's all there to be toured from 10 a.m. to 5 p.m. daily at $3.50 for adults, free to under-12s.

Bishop Planetarium, at 201 10th St. West, Bradenton, FL (tel. 746-STAR), opens its Cassegrainian reflecting telescope on the first and third weekends of every month at 9 p.m. for a free look at faraway glitter. There's a historical museum here too. Planetarium admission is $2 for adults, $1.25 for students, and you can buy a combination ticket ($3 for adults, $2 for children).

Thirty miles south of Sarasota and 12 miles south of Venice is **Warm Mineral Springs** (tel. 813/426-1692), where ten million gallons of mineral-laden water flow daily—four times more water than at Baden-Baden, Vichy Hot Springs, or Aix-les-Bains. It's been a watering spot for 10,000 years: bones discovered in underwater explorations of the hourglass-shaped sink hole are evidence of swimmers who paddled around here way back then. You can swim here now for $5 from 9 a.m. to 5 p.m.

7. Side Trips from Tampa Bay

Many small communities around the Tampa Bay area are tiny pockets of immigrant settlers who have kept their folklore intact for generations—in nearby Tarpon Springs, children's report cards are written in Greek!

It's fun exploring these small byways and backroads, where you'll discover shady streets and imposing city halls from the column-and-brick era, and meet some friendly people who'll welcome the opportunity to tell you about themselves and their communities.

Heading north from the Clearwater area you'll find the Scots community of Dunedin, then the Greek village of Tarpon Springs. Still farther north are the clear, cold waters of Weeki Wachee Springs and Homossassa Springs, and finally tiny Cedar Key, a community that's been far from the main road for decades.

From Sarasota you can make a fascinating sojourn to Florida's cattle country in Arcadia and see one of the state's biggest rodeos, or drive along the coastline to the villages of Venice and Englewood which were once lemon plantations and are now the state's shark's teeth and circus centers.

DUNEDIN: More than 130 years ago, two Scots created one of the first settlements on the west coast here, naming it after Scotland's Dunedin. That Scots history lives on here via the **City Bagpipe and Drum Corps** that performs at 2:30 p.m. on the first Sunday of the month and for special occasions. They wear Elliot, Dress Stewart, and Royal Stewart tartans. At the end of March each year they and the rest of the city turn out for two weeks of revelry called the **Heather and Thistle Holiday,** an event with everything from parades to Highland games and a Military Tatoo and Retreat ceremony.

At the Kirk (church) of Dunedin you can hear one of the largest pipe organs in the South on the second Thursday and Friday of each month at 8:15 p.m. from October through April, and for sports enthusiasts the city is the spring training ground for the Toronto Blue Jays.

You can spend a tranquil day here journeying by ferry to **Caladesi Island,** a 550-acre state park preserved in its natural wooded state with beautiful unspoiled beaches. Ferry trips cost $2 for adults, $1 for children, and run from 9 a.m. to 4:30 p.m. every hour, returning on the half hour. Don't miss that last one—it's a long swim!

There's another beach here too, with the romantic name of Honeymoon Beach. It's just a short drive from the city over a causeway.

A drive through this city on US 19A from Clearwater is a scenic route that takes you along the bay. Tall skinny palms march along beside you and rolling expanses of green lawns surround stately Old Florida homes. Trinity College's arches and tile roof gleam as they have since this was the Fenway Resort Hotel.

Food and Lodging

If you'd like to stay over in Dunedin (pronounced Dun-*ee*-din), you can't do better than the **Jamaica Inn,** 150 Marina Plaza, Dunedin, FL 33528 (tel. 813/733-4121), which backs up to St. Joseph's Sound and gazes out over the city's tiny marina where ferry and fishing boats are moored. Beamed ceilings, brick trim, and huge expanses of glass are architectural pluses, and bright colors give the resort a tropical look. Every room faces the water and some overlook the resort's pool from private balconies or patios.

The Jamaica Inn is also renowned in the Tampa Bay area for its fine restaurant, **Bon Appétit,** where Austrian and German chefs reign over a flower-bedecked dining room filled with silk roses and banks of blooms. Hot and cold appetizers arrive on a cart, delicate seafood, veal, and steak concoctions are outstanding, and water glasses are garnished with slivers of lemon. Prices are in the $12 to $20 range for entrees, and the restaurant is open from 8 a.m. to 10 p.m. daily, with a massive Sunday brunch from 9 a.m. to 4 p.m. Try the German pfannkuchen pancakes for breakfast here.

Rates at the inn are $35 to $59 for rooms, year round, a few dollars more for efficiencies.

TARPON SPRINGS: *Ya'sou* won't be Greek to you after a visit to the village of Tarpon Springs, a few miles north of Clearwater on US 19A. Here you leave Florida behind—for Greece! In this tiny village live the descendants of Greek sponge fishermen who settled here at the turn of the century and stayed here beside the sea they love although the sponge fishing declined in the 1930s when disease hit the sponge beds and synthetic sponges hit the markets.

Here you'll hear the staccato sounds of Greek as shopkeepers and fishermen gossip over a cup of thick black coffee or a sparkling glass of retsina. Try a friendly *Ya'sou* (hello or good-bye) yourself and win a glittering Greek smile. Gorge on honey-soaked baklava or musky dark olives piled atop a feta-laden Greek salad. Watch muscular young fishermen glide sensuously through the lazy movements of a Greek dance, or join a circle of dancers yourself as *Never on Sunday* comes to life in this sleepy seaside village.

Just strolling around this Hellenic haven is as much fun as any planned sightseeing tour. It's a photographer's paradise with strings of sturdy fat sponges drying in the sun, geegaw souvenirs, delicate hand-embroidered linens, and shrimp nets ruffling the breeze.

You can see how fishermen collect the holey little devils aboard the **St. Nicholas Boat Line** sponge boat, which leaves every 30 minutes (just listen for the barker calling out boarding times). This boat's been sailing since 1924, and has been featured in a World's Fair and several television shows. During the $2.50 trip, a diver wearing 12-pound shoes and an 18-pound suit so he can stay on the bottom jumps overboard and with a four-pronged rake spears the bounty of the deep. Next door to the boat is **Spongeorama** (tel. 937-4111), where you can visit a free museum of sponge memorabilia, including a movie ($1 for adults, 50¢ for children) that will tell you how sponge is harvested and why you shouldn't use the same sponge on your nose as you'd use on your car!

If you're really interested in the industry, look for **George Billiris,** who's usually at the boat dock. He's a flashing-eyed Greek charmer whose family has worked in the sponge trade for generations. In 1981 he tried hard—but failed—to save the town's picturesque sponge exchange warehouses from destruction. Billiris spends half his year buying and selling sponges in Europe, and will keep you spellbound with the intensity of his feelings for this unusual industry.

Stop by **St. Nicholas Greek Orthodox Cathedral,** on Pinellas Avenue, an outstanding example of glittering neobyzantine architecture and a replica of Istanbul's St. Sophia. In its cool dim interior are Grecian marble, beautiful iconography, and glowing stained glass.

If you're here in January, don't miss the city's **Greek Epiphany** celebration, when young Greeks dive into the waters of Spring Bayou for a gold cross—and 365 lucky days! In November there's an **International Glendi** (festival), when short-skirted Greek dancers perform the intricate steps of folk dances, and in April there's an art show here.

Food and Lodging

If you're staying over, a good moderately priced stop is the **Gondolier Motel,** 110 W. Tarpon Ave., Tarpon Springs, FL 33589 (tel. 813/937-6121), built on a slope overlooking the waters of Spring Bayou. Rooms are trim, wood paneled, and have all the usual requisites like color television. Outside there's a swimming pool in a tranquil setting. Rates are $33 to $39 in winter, about $6 less in summer, for rooms or efficiencies.

A mandatory stop in the village is Louis Pappamichaloupoulos' restaurant, at 10 W. Dodecanese Blvd. (tel. 937-5101), which for obvious reasons is called **Pappas'.** This family has been in the restaurant business here since 1925 when they opened tiny Riverside café. Now a new massive Pappas' welcomes even more diners through the portals and sends them out stuffed on huge Greek salads and a wide variety of seafood dishes and Greek specialties like moussaka, lamb, and pastitsio. Big windows along the water offer a picturesque view of the village's marina, and dinner prices are in the $7 to $12 range. It's open from 11 a.m. to 11 p.m. daily.

Riverhouse Restaurant and Bar, 900 N. Pinellas Ave. (tel. 937-4221), is part of a cluster of historic buildings in Plumtree Village built in 1884. Oysters from Alabama as well as Florida's own Apalachicolas are served here, along with fresh soups concocted daily, steaks, and seafood. Prices are in the $7 to $14 range, and it's open from 5 p.m. to 10 p.m. daily.

Later you'll find plenty of Tampa Bay fun-seekers at **Zorba's,** 508 W. Athens St. (tel. 937-9830), every night (except Sunday) about 9 p.m. You'll think you've slipped right into a remake of *Never on Sunday* here when Anthony Quinn look-alikes take to the floor to dance in solitary splendor saluted occasionally with a congratulatory glass of ouzo. Sometimes there's a belly dancer and there's always a singer wailing melancholy outpourings of lost love. Join a Greek circle dance where many of the laughing dancers are blonde Americans!

To get into the evening atmosphere a little more quietly, try the **Sparta** or **Athena** lounge on Dodecanese Boulevard. They're a bit more tranquil and given to evenings long on philosophical discussion.

READER'S LODGING SELECTION: "**The Livery Stable,** 100 Ring Ave., Tarpon Springs, FL 33589 (tel. 813/938-5547), charges just $21 a night for two including breakfast. Very clean, friendly hosts, and a nice beach (free) is about a ten-minute drive" (Ann Southmayd, Newark, Del.)

CEDAR KEY: An interesting day trip from the Tampa Bay area is to Cedar Key, a tiny fishing village time seems to have ignored. Once a thriving port city and a rough-and-tumble frontier town with saloons, gambling, gunfights, and general whoop-de-do, the city slumped after depletion of the area's timber fields, an 1896 fire, and a tidal wave.

Cedar Key got its name, by the way, from the dense groves of cedar trees that once grew here and provided raw material for more than 15 pencil-manufacturing companies that once lined a three-mile strip. Eberhardt (of Eberhardt-Faber fame) once owned much of this Cedar Key forest. Its trees were the, uh (I can't resist this), root of his fortune. Cedar Key trees provided softer wood that was more easily shaped around lead. What's more, pencils made from these trees were more easily sharpened and less inclined to split. See? More than you ever wanted to know about pencils.

But alas, those pencil-pushers decimated the cedar forests here and departed, leaving islanders without an industry. Undaunted, they turned their palms for a living, and I don't mean they went begging: they made palm-frond brooms that are now heirlooms in some Florida homes. But, alas, that industry too was swept away when plastic brooms were invented.

Finally, left with little but the sea around them, those indomitable Cedar Key folks managed to turn even the Gulf of Mexico to their advantage. Most are now fishermen or cater to the tourists drawn here by wonderful seafood restaurants and small, quiet seaside motels. One of those restaurants is called **Johnson's Brown Pelican,** on Docks Street (tel. 543-5428), where you can have seafood so fresh it's practically swimming. Prices are in the $5 to $12 range, and the restaurant is open daily from 7 a.m. to 10 p.m.

Another enticing restaurant is called **The Heron,** Route 24 and 2nd Street, Cedar Key (tel. 543-5666). You dine here in an old house fitted out with turn-of-the-century accoutrements. You'll find a few steak and chicken options on the menu, but the restaurant does its best work with thick clam chowders, fat clams called quahogs, scallops, oysters, sauteed shrimp, crab bisque, and all the other kinds of fresh, fresh seafood for which the island is famous among Floridians. You'll quickly feel right at home here talking to smiling workers that include the very pleasant owner/chef Janice Coupe and her husband, Dr. George Coupe, who serves on weekends as maître d'hôtel at this attractive restaurant. Prices are in the $9 to $12 range for dinner at the Heron, which is open from 11:30 a.m. to 3 p.m. Tuesday through Saturday and 6 to 9:30 p.m. on Friday and Saturday. The Heron is open weekends only in summer, from mid-May to September.

More? Sure! The **Island Hotel,** on 2nd Street (tel. 543-5111), is a rustic spot with a dining room on a screened porch, neat and pretty tables with bright linens and ferns in wine bottles. Once again seafood is the main fare, and prices fall easily in the $8 to $15 range for dinner. Hours at the Island Hotel are 6 to 10 p.m. daily, plus 7:30 a.m. to 2 p.m. for brunch on Saturday and Sunday.

To get to Cedar Key, take US 19 north to Route 24 west. You'll find the key about 80 miles north of Tampa, but the drive takes you through some very pretty country.

CRYSTAL RIVER: On the shores of Crystal River, 70 miles north of Tampa on US 19, you'll find one of the oldest and longest continually occupied Indian sites in the state. Ancient tribes who lived here are believed to have roamed as far west as the Yucatán and to have built a solar observatory. To see what they found so appealing here, hop aboard a glass-bottomed boat at Crystal River Springs or try a scuba-diving trip or canoeing expedition.

If you'd like to stay over, seek the pillared facade of the **Plantation Inn,** on West US 44 (Box 1116), King's Bay Road, Crystal River, FL 32629 (tel. 904/795-4211), an old-world resort nestled on the edge of King's Bay (take I-75 from Tampa to Route 41, and then drive north to Route 44). Surrounded by a purple profusion of azaleas in spring and scarlet poinsettias in winter, the resort has tennis courts, a golf course, and a pool. The rooms are large, with lots of closet space, separate dressing rooms, and bright tropical colors. Evenings, there's entertainment in the lounge, and there's a pretty restaurant too. This is a lovely resort out in the country, all by itself in beautiful open pine lands. Rates are $50 to $70, year round.

If you're looking for a restaurant, try the **Oyster Bar,** US 19/99 (tel. 795-2633), where oysters are prepared in countless numbers of ways, and there's other seafood as well. Prices are in the $5 range, and the restaurant's open from 11 a.m. to 5 p.m. Wednesday through Monday.

HOMOSSASSA SPRINGS: About 75 miles south of the St. Petersburg/Tampa area on US 19, huge sightseeing boats leaving from Fishbowl Drive (P.O. Box 189), Homossassa Springs (tel. 813/628-2361), take visitors down a winding tropical waterway into the heart of waters known as the **Spring of Ten Thousand Fish.** You can walk under water among thousands of finny creatures at an observatory, and watch the staffers feed the alligators and hippos at Gator Lagoon. There's a manatee rehabilitation area, where those often-injured, gentle creatures are doctored. Daily hours are 9:30 a.m. to 5:30 p.m.; admission is $6 for adults, $3.75 for children 3 to 12 (others, free).

WEEKI WACHEE SPRINGS: These **springs** are a little closer to the Tampa Bay area, at Box 97 on US 19 and Route 50 (tel. 904/596-2062). Mermaids swim around underwater and you can watch the nearly tame fish swoop and swerve with them. Admission to the springs is $7.50 for adults, $4.95 for children 3 to 12. **Buccaneer Bay,** a water park, charges $4.95 for adults, $3.95 for children.

VENICE: No place in Florida is more a circus than Venice, a small seaside village whose claim to fame is none other than the **Ringling Brothers and Barnum & Bailey Circus,** the city's most famous resident. Clowns and highwire artists, lion tamers and trained elephants aren't keen on cold weather either, so they winter here at 1401 Ringling Dr. South (tel. 484-9511 or 484-0496) and make forays into Florida towns for winter appearances.

Their arrival on Miami Beach generates pages of publicity each year as the elephants are trooped across a mainland bridge, toll and all. Ringling's been a winter fixture in Venice since 1959, and has its own arena where it rehearses two separate shows, the Red and the Blue. You can see the première of the Red and Blue Shows right here for $8.50 and $6.50 in late December and January. At any time of year you can peek at the circus trains, while they are repaired and repainted in those flaming circus colors.

Venice is a quiet waterslide town with a number of small motels lining the beach. Oddities here are fossilized sharks' teeth, which you'll find all along the shoreline. They're here because prehistoric sharks, like modern ones, shed their teeth regularly, sometimes as many as 20,000 in a ten-year period. Those on the bottom are washed up on beaches just like shells. Bones of many prehistoric creatures have been found along this 10,000-year-old coastline, and there's even said to be treasure of a somewhat less studious nature: José Gaspar's loot is rumored to be buried around here somewhere.

Food and Lodging

If you'd like to stay in the area, try Englewood, where you'll find **Chadwick Cove,** 1815 Gulf Blvd., Englewood, FL 33533 (tel. 813/474-8577). It's a new, contemporary, woodsy resort with a heated pool in an inner courtyard and attractively decorated one-bedroom apartments with lots of glass and a striking view of the sea and courtyard. Jungly landscaped grounds surround a three-story natural-wood building that blends like driftwood into its beachside locale. Two friendly Floridians, Ron and Joanne Fendt, run Chadwick Cove and will be happy to direct you to good seafood restaurants or likely fishing spots in the area, and may even have a shark's tooth for you. In summer and fall, you'll pay $350 a week; from December to May, rates are $400 to $450 a week.

For budget digs, **Days Inn,** at 2540 S. McCall Rd., Route 776 East in Englewood, FL 33533 (tel. 813/474-5544), has 48 three-room suites and 36 hotel rooms near the beach. There's a large pool for swimmers, and the usual thrifty Days Inn prices range from $45 to $61 in winter, $38 in summer and fall.

In Englewood, the **Cajun Club Restaurant,** at 750 N. Indiana Ave. (tel. 474-3383), spices things up with an array of Créole flavors in the $7 to $10 range. It's open from 4 to 9 p.m. daily (noon to closing on Sunday), with all-you-can-eat buffet for about $7 or $8.

WRANGLIN' IN ARCADIA: Tucked away about 40 miles east of Sarasota is one of Florida's last remaining cowboy towns, where you'll see gun racks on pickup trucks, cowboy hats and boots, and mile after mile of rangeland stalked by long-horned, hump-backed Brahma bulls. Here in Arcadia, things are just about the way they've always been—a couple of coffeeshops, a barbecue or two, and watermelons for sale at Carter's Fruit Stand. There's a handsome county court-house with red bricks and white columns, but visitors come here for only one reason: the **Arcadia All-Florida Championship Rodeo** in July and March. It's quite an event on a huge rodeo ground with all the bronc bustin' and calf ropin' you could want. Tickets are $7 and $8, and you can order them in advance by writing to P.O. Box 1266 in Arcadia, FL 33821, or calling 813/494-2014.

Get there from Sarasota by taking US 41 south to Route 72 west, which goes straight through town and right by the rodeo grounds. If you're staying over, the **Best Western M & M**, at 504 S. Brevard, Arcadia, FL 33821 (tel. 813/494-4884, or toll free 800/528-1234), is a simple, attractive spot where rates are $29 to $39, year round.

Chapter XI

THE SHELL COAST

1. Fort Myers
2. Naples
3. Sanibel and Captiva Islands

THIS IS THE SHELL COAST, the fantasyland of your winter dreams, a cluster of sun-kissed islands for which you yearn when bitter winds whip and temperatures fall and fall . . . and fall.

It sneaks up on you, this coastline, capturing you as it has captured the famous, and the infamous, before you. More than 2000 years before you the Calusa Indians dipped their toes into these warm waters in search of oysters and clams, conch and periwinkles, not for shells but for their contents.

Much later, fierce José Gaspar set up camp hereabouts to conduct a terrifying but financially gratifying career in plunder and pillage. Captiva Island, they say, got its name when that legendary buccaneer stored his female captives here to maintain their trading value by keeping them safe from his lecherous pirate companions. That Isla de las Captivas is, so the story goes, today's Captiva.

Florida usually has a ghost tucked away somewhere, and Gaspar's pals are said still to roam the island of Cayo Palau in Charlotte Harbor, zealously guarding a cache buried there.

Here on the Shell Coast, today's booty has little to do with gold. White sand and pearly shells are the treasures you seek here in these slow-paced villages where conversation takes precedence over change.

Scoff as you may, cynic, but when you see these miles of talcum-white sand piled with glittering gold, pink, russet, and mauve, you too will become a shell hunter, unable to resist the lure of a tiny pink cat's paw, or a rainbowed angel's wing, or a fighting conch, the giant of the deep, its wind tunnel roaring a siren's song. You too will bend, peer, and shuffle into the "Sanibel Stoop."

GETTING THERE: You can get to **Fort Myers Airport** on Delta, Eastern, Northwest, Pan Am, TWA, and United Airlines.

PBA/Naples Airlines has round-trip flights from Miami, Key West, and Tampa to **Naples Airport.**

To get from Fort Myers airport to hotels in that city, call **Yellow Cab** (tel. 332-1055). Fares to beach hotels are about $12 to $16. Around-town fares are by zone, averaging $5 to $10.

To get to Naples from the Fort Myers Airport, call **Airport Mini Bus** (tel. 263-3011), which will take you to your hotel door for about $25 for one or two people, $12 for each additional person.

Sanibel and Captiva Islands are accessible only by car or boat, and there's a $3 round-trip toll across the Sanibel bridge to the islands.

GETTING AROUND: It is virtually impossible to get around this area without a car. You can rent one from Alamo (tel. 936-3707), a leader of the budget rental pack, and 21 other **rental-car companies** including Avis, Hertz, National, Thrifty, Ajax, and Budget, all of which have offices in Fort Myers and in Naples.

On Sanibel, Hertz (tel. 472-1468) and Dollar (tel. 472-5111) can rent you a car.

I've included specific information on bus service routes in Naples and Fort Myers in those sections. Sanibel has no bus service.

1. Fort Myers

Fort Myers hardly knows what to make of it all these days. Suddenly it's booming, as twice as many planes bring twice as many travelers here, doubling the competition for a place in the sun. Just when bemused residents had grown accustomed to hearing "Fort Myers? Hmmmm. Where is that again?" in come troops of travelers and dozens of developers who know just where it is and would like a small piece of its sand to call their own.

Wherever Fort Myers is headed these days, it's traveling there fast: it's in a nip-and-tuck competition for fastest growing city in the nation. And no wonder. It's got the prime requisites of Florida travelers—a pretty beach, comfortable resorts, good restaurants, and sometimes ridiculously low prices.

One of the state's largest retirement regions, Fort Myers is taking its rapid growth easily if a bit warily. You'll see some change underway, but you won't find alteration of the city's slow-paced mañana atmosphere or its rustic beach neighborhood. Small family-owned hostelries continue to welcome travelers who have had standing reservations here for a decade or more, and in the city's restaurants decor takes a decided second place to a good platter of seafood.

There's change in the breezes here, but this is a city peopled by those whose convictions solidified long ago, so changes are gradual and gratifying. Fort Myers's favorite son, Thomas Alva Edison, who sought solace here years ago, would hardly notice the difference.

GETTING AROUND: Molly the Trolley is a different way to travel through Fort Myers. A San Francisco–look trolley on wheels, Molly has brass handrails, a silver roof, etched glass, and red oak trim, and it's the cutest thing on four wheels. She operates from 10 a.m. to 3 p.m. daily from the north end of Estero Island to Carl Johnson Park, and is free.

Lee County Transit System (tel. 939-1303) operates buses to all parts of the county, and can help you with route information. Rides are 40¢.

Taxis here, as everywhere, are expensive and charge by zone. Call them at 332-1055 for specific fares, but generally you'll pay $5 to $10, more from downtown to the beaches.

GETTING YOUR BEARINGS: Fort Myers Beach is about 15 miles south of downtown Fort Myers, which centers around US 41. McGregor Boulevard, with its rows of stately royal palms, runs alongside the Caloosahatchee River and is also called Route 867. At the Caloosahatchee River Bridge Route 867 becomes Route 80 and heads west. Route 867 heads toward Cape Coral and intersects with Route 865, the Fort Myers Beach road.

To reach the beach heading north on US 41, branch west at Bonita Springs on Route 865 to Bonita Beach where 865 turns north to Estero Island, the city's beach district. To confuse matters slightly, Route 865 is also known as Hickory Boulevard, Estero Boulevard, and San Carlos Boulevard.

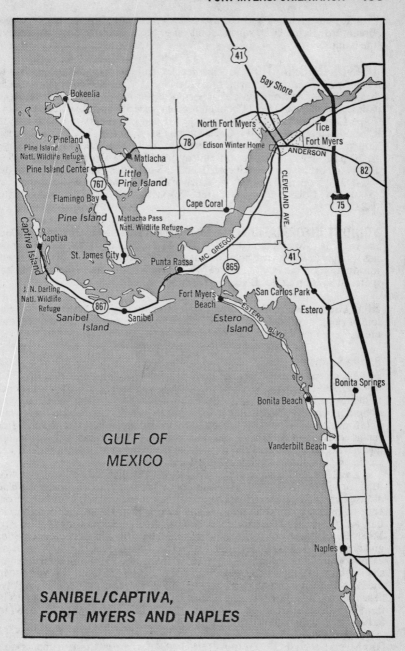

SANIBEL/CAPTIVA,
FORT MYERS AND NAPLES

To reach Sanibel and Captiva Islands from Fort Myers, take McGregor Boulevard (Route 867), which shoots off to the west across San Carlos Bay to the islands.

USEFUL INFORMATION: In **emergencies,** call the operator and explain the problem. . . . For **police help,** call 322-3456. . . . For **non-emergency medical help,** call the Lee County Medical Society at 936-1645. . . . The **Dental Health Clinic** (tel. 482-6505) has 24-hour emergency services, and there are branches in Cape Coral and Lehigh Acres too. . . . If you get hungry at odd hours, the **Clock Restaurant,** at 1414 Cape Coral Pkwy. (tel. 542-2225), is open 24 hours. . . . **Byron's Gulf Service Station,** at 2449 1st St. (tel. 334-2225), is open to 10 p.m. daily, to 8 p.m. on Sunday. . . . **Eckerd Drugs,** at 1952 College Pkwy. in Fort Myers (tel. 936-8165), and at San Carlos Plaza on the beach (tel. 481-2431), is open 24 hours. . . . **Touch of Class Cleaners** offers same-day service at 3990 College Pkwy. SW (tel. 482-5550), and 7050 Windler Rd. (tel. 482-0565).

TOURIST INFORMATION: The **Metropolitan Fort Myers Chamber of Commerce,** 2254 Edwards Dr. (Box CC), Fort Myers, FL 33902 (tel. 813/334-1133), has friendly folks who will help you out in emergencies and fill your pockets with information on the city. . . . **Fort Myers Beach** has its own chamber of commerce at 867 San Carlos Blvd., Fort Myers, FL 33931 (tel. 813/463-6451).

HOTELS: You won't find many fancy resorts in this quiet area but you'll find lots of rustic havens at very modest prices on the beach and in the downtown area.

Bonita Springs

Beach and Tennis Club, 548 Bonita Beach Rd., Bonita Springs, FL 33923 (tel. 813/992-1121, or toll free 800/526-9299), is just south of Fort Myers Beach in the tiny community of Bonita Beach. A multistoried and multibuilding condominium enclave, Beach and Tennis Club has a number of apartments available for hotel use. It has all the amenities of a condominium resort, including ten tennis courts, two pools and a third for children, and a beach just a few steps away. This resort is a bargain: from mid-December to March rates are $420 a week, and in summer months, $245 a week.

Lani Kai, 1400 Estero Blvd., Fort Myers Beach, FL 33931 (tel. 813/463-3111, or toll free 800/237-6133), pulls out all the stops on a South Seas island atmosphere from its name (which means "haven by the sea") to its beachfront entertainment, a Hu Ke Lau restaurant, Hoopi-Hapi-Ha lounge, Pupu snackbar, and Chickee Tiki sundeck bar. You can't miss this sprawling spot on Fort Myers Beach—just look for the flowers streaming up its five-story green exterior and ornamenting its colorful signs. Everywhere you look here you'll find those island touches: bright floral bedspreads, white bamboo furniture, wicker lampshades, grass mats, and Tiki gods. Lani Kai has more flowers at poolside and in the Hu Ke Lau restaurant where wood paneling floor to ceiling echoes the Polynesian theme and draws hungry hordes for French and Italian preparations in the $7 to $10 bracket. From mid-December to May, rates range from $88 to $110 a day double, falling to $55 to $75 a day in summer.

A great little hideaway is a spot called the **Beach House,** 4960 Estero Blvd., Fort Myers Beach, FL 33931 (tel. 813/463-4004), where all the apartments look more like home than a home-away-from-home. The Beach House is a rambling two-story house with a third story perched atop a brick walkway to the beach.

Every room is different, all 12 of them individually decorated in sometimes quite luxurious furniture. Apartment 1, on the third level (what the Beach House calls its penthouse), is the most expensive, and includes a living room and dining room, kitchen, two bedrooms (one with a queen-size bed), and two baths. For that one, with its fabulous view of the gulf, you'll pay $95 a day double in winter, $65 in summer. Prices drop rapidly from there, ranging from $70 double from a non-ocean-view apartment for two to $87 for an ocean-view two-bedroom on the second floor. In summer the rates begin at $38 and peak at $60 double. A nice friendly family owns Beach House, which lacks a pool but makes up for it with lots of beach and ocean.

If you dream occasionally about a little beach house, you've got it at the **Beach House Motel,** 25693 Hickory Blvd. SW, Bonita Springs, FL 33923 (tel. 813/992-2644), on Route 865 at Hickory Boulevard, a cluster of beach houses up on stilts right on the gulf sands at Bonita Beach. Simply but attractively furnished, with lots of durable fabrics in bright and sunny colors and dark-wood paneling, the accommodations come in a variety of configurations, from motel rooms and efficiencies (sleeping four "in a pinch") to large one- and two-bedroom apartments with screened porches overlooking the gulf. Anglers can fish from the bridge right behind the property, walk to the pass nearby, surf-cast in the sea, or charter boats nearby. Tiny picnic tables at beachside are roofed to match their larger cottage apartments. In this very beachy spot you'll pay prices beginning at $256 a week for hotel rooms and ranging to $278 to $340 a week for efficiencies and one-bedrooms, $535 to $596 a week for two-bedrooms from February to April. In other months, prices drop to $150 to $387.

Mainland Fort Myers

Ah, the pleasures of a nice long soak, or a nice long swim. Ah, the pleasures of doing both at the same time. Simple to arrange—just pop over to the **San Carlos Inn,** Route 22, Box 800, Fort Myers, FL 33912, on US 41, eight miles south of Fort Myers Airport (tel. 813/481-3818), a warm mineral springs resort and spa. Once featured in *McCall's* magazine, San Carlos likes to think it might be the youth-giving fountain for which Ponce de Leon was searching, so the decor here relies heavily on statues of that ill-fated conquistador. A million gallons of warm water bubble earthward from a subsurface spring every day, and the water's rich in mineral content, recommended to treat a variety of ailments from arthritis to sprains. You can have a medium-size, tastefully decorated room with Spanish decor at the inn for $32 double in summer (to about mid-December), about $25 more in winter.

Even few Floridians have explored the beauties of the meandering Caloosahatchee River, but you can get a close-up look at these blue waters at the **Tides Motel,** 2621 1st St., Route 80, Fort Myers, FL 33901 (tel. 813/334-1231). Located on one of the city's famous avenues of royal palms, the Tides has 27 modest but bright efficiencies and motel rooms with two double beds and velvet spreads, phones, and color TVs. You can dine on a free continental breakfast beside the resort's pool, or dangle your toes in the river from the edge of the motel's fishing pier. The price is right: $48.50 for two double beds, $48.50 for a king-size bed in winter months, $20 to $26.50 in summer. Efficiencies are $315 a week in winter, $145 to $175 in summer.

Let me qualify **Rock Lake Motel,** at 2930 Palm Beach Blvd., Fort Myers, FL 33901 (tel. 813/334-3242), by saying it's a *very* modest spot, but it is an enchanting little cluster of stone cottages plunked down around the edges of a tiny round lake. Flaming bougainvilleas pop brightly out between cottages whose small rooms are bright and clean, with wood floors and windows overlooking that vest-pocket lake. They're unusual and dainty, and set far back from highway noises. If you don't mind exchanging interior luxuries like phones and carpets for exterior charms, you'll like Rock Lake (they do have television and air conditioning). Certainly you'll like the prices, which are just $28 in peak season, $17 to $18 in other seasons.

Another pretty spot in Fort Myers is the **Robert E. Lee Motor Inn,** at 6611 N. US 41, Fort Myers, FL 33903 (tel. 813/997-5511, or toll free 800/528-1234), which nuzzles right up to the Caloosahatchee River. A Best Western motel rising six stories, the Robert E. Lee has won top ratings for the excellence of its accommodations, and for good reason: rooms are decorated in contemporary colors and furnishings, and have a lovely view of the river from private balconies. You can select a room with two double beds, or a suite which adds a convertible couch so six people can stay there. In winter, two people pay $47 to $52, and in summer, about $8 to $10 less. There's a lounge and pool bar here, and next door is a 24-hour restaurant, the Clock.

A Golf and Tennis (and Square Dancing) Resort

If you like wide-open acres, you'll find hundreds of them at **Lehigh Resort,** 233 E. Joel Blvd., Lehigh Acres, FL 33936 (tel. 813/369-2131 or 813/334-2500), a *way*-off-the-beaten-track hotel about 12 miles east of Fort Myers. Lehigh is in the midst of a popular retiree development and sprawls over acres and acres of grounds complete with two championship golf courses. If golf's not your game, there are tennis courts, miniature golf, volleyball, shuffleboard, bicycles, and a shady wooded nature trail.

The spacious rooms have two double beds, a bright tropical decor, and lots of glass through which you can watch swimmers splashing in the pool. For entertainment there are three lounges and four dining rooms; you'll never be far from shops, hairdressers, and the like, since they've got everything here or in the village nearby. Rates are $59 double from mid-December to mid-April, dropping in summer to $45.

One final word on Lehigh: If you enjoy watching or participating in square dancing, this resort has become a favorite do-si-do spot for many square dancing clubs.

To get there from Fort Myers, take Route 82, Route 80, or Colonial Boulevard east to the Lehigh signs. The drive takes about 20 minutes.

RESTAURANTS: You'll find some intriguing restaurants in this city, ranging from a haunted house to an elegant home.

On the Beach

Rooftop, in Casa Bonita Plaza at Hickory Boulevard in Bonita Springs (tel. 992-0033 or 597-4445), is where the third and fourth generations of the New York McCully family are holding forth after eight years. The McCullys formerly ran the Flying Fish in Montauk and the Fat Flounder in East Hampton, New York. Now Terry and son Joe keep up a regular correspondence with *Gourmet* magazine readers who seek their recipes. No wonder—few are the places you'll find a salad that includes fresh mushrooms, sliced zucchini, baby shrimp, cauliflower, and tomatoes with honey-mustard dressing, or things like onion straw appetizers, crisp light shrimp tempura, swordfish marinated in soy sauce, garlic, lemon, and herbs, then charcoal broiled, or Irish whiskey pie!

What's more, the setting for all these delicacies is lovely: deep emerald-green decor, a small waiting area with upturned kegs as tables, a bank of windows with an upper level view of surrounding waters. As for prices, you're likely to leave having dined very luxuriously on soup, that super salad, and outstanding seafood for less than $9. It's open Monday through Saturday from 11:30 a.m. to 2:30 p.m. and 4 to 10 p.m. (to 11 p.m. on Friday and Saturday). On Sunday there is a sumptuous brunch from 10:30 a.m. to 2 p.m.

Here's a short story from **Charley Brown's Restaurant,** 6225 Estero Blvd. (tel. 463-9191): "Our Gone with the Rib prime rib is so popular we run out nightly. The end." There are wood and greenery, prime rib and a salad trolley, filet mignon, top sirloin, beef kebabs, fresh bread, homemade desserts, and prices of only $8 to $14. How's that for another short story? Open 4:30 to 10 p.m. daily, to 10:30 p.m. on Friday and Saturday.

When your back's bright red and your knees are sore from shell searches, and you most certainly are *not* getting dressed up for dinner, head for **Top O' the Mast,** at 1028 Estero Blvd. (tel. 463-9424) down by the boardwalk, where you can crunch hot popovers and send that flaming sun right into the sea. Just outside the window, gulf waters offer up finny favors to pier fishermen, while inside these cool confines are broiled seafood platters, a 22-ounce cut of prime rib, fried shrimp, loaves of bread and popovers, apple butter, cheese, a relish tray—for prices in the $8 to $10 range ($18 for that big prime rib). Open daily from 11 a.m. to 11 p.m., to 2 a.m. in the lounge.

Smitty's, once known as **Ye Olde Holmes House,** 2500 Estero Blvd. (tel. 463-5519), not only sells spirits, it has them! Whenever old Sherlock shows up things go all mysterious, no less so at Smitty's (Ye Olde Holmes House), where waitresses report laughing children in the small hours and occasional weird events at other hours. But why shouldn't a poltergeist hang around? I can't think of a better spot to haunt than this excellent restaurant with its dining rooms created in a beachside home built in 1919. Many a luminary has discovered this pubby spot plunked down in the middle of Fort Myers Beach: the guest list includes Hugh Downs, authors Theodore White and Mario Puzo, baseball stars Roberto Clemente and Ted Williams, singer Perry Como, and even spooky Vincent Price. House specialties like prime rib, seafood, and beef done to carefully delineated specifications have won friends, and if there were a value-for-dollar prize they'd win: prices average about $10. Open from 4:30 to 10 p.m. daily (from noon to 9 p.m. on Sunday).

Downtown

Things are looking better than ever in downtown Fort Myers these days, and nowhere better than the **Veranda,** at Second and Broadway (tel. 332-2065), where you dine in an antebellum atmosphere inside or out in a serene garden. Brick pavements, little umbrellaed tables, a tiny pond shaded by huge tropical trees, and a first-rate southern-flavored menu make the Veranda a top choice for luxurious dining. A historic landmark hereabouts, the restaurant occupies two turn-of-the-century houses connected by a country kitchen. Special touches like freshly ground coffee beans, homemade honey molasses bread, sweet corn muffins, and southern pepper jelly complement rich desserts and continental entrees like veal française or roast duckling royale. Prices at dinner average about $15, and after dinner there's entertainment in the lounge. Hours are 5:30 to 10:30 p.m. Monday through Thursday, to 11 p.m. on Friday and Saturday; later in the lounge. Closed Sunday.

Smitty's, at 2240 W. 1st St. (tel. 334-4415), brother to the beach restaurant of the same name, has occupied a secure spot in Fort Myers dining circles for more than 20 years. The focus here is beef, supplemented by freshly baked bread and an unusual pepper salad dressing. Brandy Alexander cream pie is a favorite for dessert. Prices are in the $10 to $15 range. It's a good choice if you're dining late: there's dinner in the Wine Room from 10:30 p.m. to 1 a.m. on weekends. A popular lounge here hosts backgammon players, or you can listen to entertainment nightly (except Sundays). Smitty's restaurant is open from 11 a.m. to 10:30 p.m. Monday through Saturday, from noon to 9 p.m. on Sunday.

A top-notch budget choice in town is a little restaurant tucked away in the **Farmers Market,** at 2736 Edison Ave. (tel. 334-1687). Produce right off the vine comes to the market for distribution to the tables of the restaurant, where it's accorded some down-home southern cookin' touches. There's little (going on no) atmosphere here, just lots of fresh vegetables and good cooks to whip them into shape, along with some other goodies like baking powder biscuits and corn bread. You'll pay low, low prices too, in the $3 to $5 range. The restaurant is open from 6 a.m. to 9 p.m. daily.

Latest recipient of a Florida magazine readers' award in Fort Myers is regional favorite **The Shallows,** on College Parkway at 5833 Winkler Rd. (tel. 481-4644), a spot opened in 1979. Shallows went on to win still another award, naming it one of the top 14 eateries in Florida. When you see the brimming salad bar, the breadbasket girl's load of cranberry, banana, and orange nut breads, then try some of the seafood on the menu, you'll see why. You can dine here in this tasteful restaurant from 4:30 to 10:30 p.m. Monday through Saturday, to 9:30 p.m. on Sunday, for prices in the $10 to $15 range.

Two other budget goodies in the area are the ever-reliable **Morrison's Cafeteria,** 3057 Cleveland Ave. (tel. 334-3227), and **Duff's Smörgåsbord,** which has two restaurants in the area, one in North Fort Myers at 870 Pine Island Rd. (tel. 997-9322), and the other at Gulf Points Square on the road to Sanibel (tel. 481-4478). You can find inexpensive meals and a casual atmosphere at these two, where dinner prices rarely top $5. Both are open from 11 a.m. to 8 p.m. daily, but Duff's takes an hour off between 3 and 4 p.m.

In Punta Gorda

About 25 miles north of Fort Myers, the town of Punta Gorda has a name that sounds glamorous if you don't know what it means: Fat Point. If you think Fort Myers is a quiet retirement village, you haven't met Punta Gorda, which until recently took quiet to new heights. These days, however, the general boom is reaching even this little fishing village, set on a point where the Peace River joins the gulf. The most recent addition to the community is a nifty new shopping and dining area called **Fishermen's Village,** in which you'll find two attractive restaurants: **Earl Nightingale's Village Point Dining,** at 1200 W. Retta Esplanade (tel. 637-1177), and the more casual **Village Oyster Bar** (tel. 637-1212). To get to the village, turn west off US 41 on the south side of the Peace River bridge.

Earl Nightingale, you may recall, is a well-known lecturer based in Fort Lauderdale. In the restaurant to which he's lent his name, you'll find elegant dining in a two-level dining room, both levels overlooking a bank of windows through which you can watch the waters of the Peace River snaking toward the gulf. Crisp linens, candlelight, flowers, formally dressed waiters, and an elegant atmosphere prevail here, where the menu focuses on outstanding French seafood preparations and some beef and veal entrees. Could they interest you in smoked salmon garnished with cream cheese and capers, or crab and scallop cardinale topped with a sherry-laced cream sauce? You'll pay about $10 to $15 for entrees in this very pretty dining room, more if you indulge in extras. Open from 11:30 a.m. to 3 p.m. daily for lunch, from 4 to 9:30 p.m. for dinner (when jackets are requested). The lounge is open from 11:30 a.m. to 11 p.m.

The Oyster Bar is a simple, casual place that delivers up those freshly shucked bivalves plus a wide range of seafood in a woodsy-plantsy atmosphere that goes well with the rustic shrimp-boat ambience of the dock area. Prices are under $15, and the bar's open from 11 a.m. to 9:30 p.m. daily, later on weekends.

NIGHTLIFE: Fort Myers does not have a population given to rip-roaring nightlife, but you can enjoy some quiet entertainment and dancing in hotels and restaurants.

The **Cape Coral Golf and Racquet Club,** at 4003 Palm Tree Blvd. (tel. 542-3191) in Cape Coral, has a dance band from 7:30 p.m. to about midnight Wednesday through Sunday, and two attractive dining rooms frequented by residents of the Gulf-American Corp. development.

Five nights a week (Tuesday through Saturday) the **Rooftop Restaurant** in Bonita Springs (see my restaurant recommendation) has entertainment in its Locker Lounge. **Jarrod's** in the Ramada Inn, 2220 W. 1st St., Fort Myers (tel. 332-1141), has dancing and entertainment in its lounge overlooking the river daily (except Sunday) to 2 a.m.

There's something for just about everyone at **ABC Liquor Lounges,** 4150 S. Cleveland Ave., Fort Myers (tel. 936-1526), and 590 Tamiami Trail NE in Charlotte Harbor (tel. 995-7958). ABC lounges feature country, rock, and dance music, computerized light shows, an "earthquake" sound system, and a revolving bar with fountain. On Sunday and Monday, drinks are 50¢; on Tuesday, 75¢; other nights, there are specials and two-for-one offerings.

At **Hu Ke Lau** lounge in the Lani Kai Resort (see my hotel recommendation) a pianist provides evening entertainment from 8 p.m. Monday through Saturday, and a steel band performs on Sunday from 1 to 6 p.m.

Drinks Saloon operates three pubby spots in the city, at 3980 College Pkwy., 1000 Estero Blvd., and Hancock Bridge Parkway at Marinatown in North Fort Myers. Entertainment and special events like sock hops and clambakes are held every night at these spots.

SPORTS: You won't have any difficulty finding a place to play in Fort Myers, which has 13 golf courses and tennis courts scattered about the city, plus all the water sports you'd expect in an oceanside city.

Golf and Tennis

Cape Coral Golf and Racquet Club, at 4003 Palm Tree Blvd., Cape Coral (tel. 542-3191), has 18 holes open to the public and plenty of courts for tennis players. **Lehigh Country Club,** in Lehigh Acres, 225 E. Joel Blvd. (tel. 369-2121), has two courses, one a 6710-yard, par-71 championship course, and more tennis courts.

On the beach, **Bay Beach Golf Club,** at 7401 Estero Blvd. (tel. 463-2064), is open to the public seven days a week from 7:30 a.m. to dusk. In summer, rates are $8 for 18 holes, carts are $9, and fees are slightly higher in winter. Most area clubs are in the same price range.

Estero Island Racquet Club, 120 Lenell Rd. (tel. 463-4473), is a beachside tennis spot.

Water Sports

Rent Sunfish, sailboats, catamarans, swim tubes, kayaks, paddleboats, speedboats, waterskis, bicycles, and beach umbrellas from **Happy Sailboat Rental,** 1010 Estero Blvd. (tel. 463-3351), behind the Sandpebble Shop on the beach. Sailboat prices start at $9 an hour, bicycles at $4, and speedboats at $20 an hour.

Deep-sea fishing expeditions and charter boats leave from **Gulf Star Marina** on Fort Myers Beach (tel. 463-2224), from **City Marina** in downtown Fort

Myers, or **Snug Harbor,** under the bridge at Fort Myers Beach. **Ford's Fleet** (tel. 334-2348) charges $22 a day per person for four hours of fishing in the area.

Parimutuel Sports

Follow the perils of the electronic lure at **Naples–Fort Myers Kennel Club,** on US 41 in Bonita Springs (tel. 334-6555), which opens the second week in December and closes the third week in April, with races five or six nights a week and matinees on Wednesday, Friday, and Saturday. Admission is $1.50 for the clubhouse, 50¢ for general admission, and the track opens at 6:30 p.m. for night races, at 11:30 a.m. for matinees.

THE SIGHTS: Sightseeing in this part of the country is a little different since several companies offer cruises up nearby rivers into the interior of the state. Rivers in the area are deep blue and very calm, so you're in for a scenic, comfortable trip.

Tours

Caloosahatchee River cruises are available from October through April on the *Teresa Ann,* in the **Fort Myers City Yacht Basin** (tel. 337-1938), and include luncheon, brunch, or sunset-dinner cruises on varying days and times with prices beginning at $12.50 for adults, $4 for children.

Showboat Everglades Jungle Cruises chug up the calm waters of the Caloosahatchee from Fort Myers City Yacht Basin (tel. 334-7474) from December through April on any of five different cruises on three double-decker boats which also range as far as Sanibel Island, Lake Okeechobee, and the Gulf of Mexico. Cruises vary in length and price, from $7 to $139.

Sights

Thomas Alva Edison, who shed a little light on all our lives, is quite a luminary in Fort Myers. Edison moved down in 1885, attracted by the weather, and wintered here regularly for more than 40 years. He built a 14-acre estate, and indulged his love for gardening by importing hundreds of blossoms. You can see his rambling old home where the carbon filament bulbs he created in 1910 still burn 12 hours a day, not one of them replaced! Many of the inventor's creations are displayed here too, from wax recordings to talking machines. **Edison's house** is open from 9 a.m. to 4 p.m. Monday through Saturday, from 12:30 to 4 p.m. on Sunday. His home is at 2350 McGregor Blvd. (tel. 334-3614) on US 41; admission is $3 for adults, $1 for children.

Waltzing Waters, 18101 US 41 SE, Fort Myers (tel. 481-2533), between Naples and Fort Myers, is a fantasyland of lighted fountains rising and falling, swaying and swirling to music. Here now for 20 years, Waltzing Waters has indoor and outdoor shows it likes to call "liquid fireworks," and that's not far off the mark. Light set to music makes a fascinating display. Waltzing Waters also operates Rainbow Golf, a putting course in a tropical setting, and a gift shop stacked with international treasures. Hours are 9 a.m. to 9 p.m. daily, with shows every hour. Admission is $2.50 for show or golf, $3.50 for evening shows, which include both indoor and outdoor performances.

The **Lee County Junior Museum and Planetarium,** on Ortiz Avenue Extension just off the Colonial Boulevard Extension (tel. 332-2206), is a 100-acre nature center with an aviary for injured birds. There are tours on weekends. Admission is free and the museum is open from 9 a.m. to 4 p.m. daily, from 11 a.m. on Sunday.

2. Naples

When you drive down Naples's main street, Fifth Avenue, you're driving down what was once a runway for aviator Charles Lindbergh, who zipped in here for vacations on nearby Sanibel Island. Lindbergh could still find a runway here, but he certainly wouldn't recognize this small town which has grown—and is growing—as rapidly as Jack's famous beanstalk.

Naples is summer home to many Miamians and winter home to an impressive list of *Fortune* 500 types who come here to revel in its quiet, refined atmosphere, and laze in condominiums and homes whose values are fast approaching the seven-figure mark. Here you'll find some of the state's trimmest streets, and a seven-mile beach fiercely protected by strict zoning laws. Shops line the city's small downtown area and are so primped and polished you wonder if someone doesn't stroll by each morning with a bucket of whitewash. Inside these shining emporiums are an Arab's ransom in glowing jewels, designer clothes, dark chocolates, and tweed jackets perfect for cool nights in Petoskey, Michigan, where half the town spends its summers. You can find elegant treasures of all varieties on these streets (once I even saw a huge chess set, each giant piece a jungle animal!) and some attractive restaurants.

Naples is a quiet spot where nightlife ends about 10 p.m. but tranquility goes on forever. It's a place to go to meditate on serene beaches, wander among small boutiques, a place to pause a while and consider where you're going . . . and why.

GETTING AROUND: Taxi rates are $1.65 for the first mile, 90¢ for each additional mile. For taxi service, call **Yellow Cab** (tel. 262-1312) or **Maxi Taxi** (tel. 262-2828).

Dolly the Trolley clangs and dings around town 13 times a day from 9:30 a.m. to 5 p.m., but Dolly's a snowbird too—she only operates from December 1 to April 20, at a fare of 25¢. Call 262-4209 for exact route information.

ORIENTATION: The **Tamiami Trail** (US 41) is the way most people come to Naples, but once the highway arrives here it becomes **Fifth Avenue** until it leaves town, when it once again is called the Tamiami Trail (which was for many years the only link between Tampa and Miami).

Several blocks around 3rd Street South are known as **Olde Naples,** and are lined with beautiful and intriguing shops that stretch from about Broad Avenue South to 14th Avenue South.

Gulf Shore Boulevard runs alongside the gulf in Naples and in nearby Vanderbilt Beach, but you must return from Gulf Shores to US 41 and head north for a few miles before swinging west to Gulf Shore again at Vanderbilt Beach.

VISITOR INFORMATION: For any kind of **emergency,** dial 911. . . . The **Naples Chamber of Commerce** has workers who will be happy to answer your questions or help you out with problems. They're at 1700 N. Tamiami Trail, Naples, FL 33941 (tel. 813/262-6141). . . . Harvey's, in the Gulf Gate Shopping Center at 2638 Tamiami Trail (tel. 774-4737), offers **one-hour dry cleaning** service. . . . Castel Service Center, at 1999 Route 951 (tel. 455-1100), has **24-hour wrecker service** and diesel fuel. . . . **Clock Restaurant,** 660 9th St. North (tel. 261-6724), is open 24 hours.

HOTELS: Naples doesn't have many hotels, but those it does have are attractive and comfortable. I've divided them geographically so you can decide where you'd like to stay: in the downtown/Tamiami Trail area, nearby Vanderbilt Beach, or at a sprawling resort on nearby Marco Island.

Downtown/Tamiami Trail

Naples Beach Hotel and Golf Club, 851 Gulf Shore Blvd. North, Naples, FL 33940 (tel. 813/261-2222), is the showplace of Naples, a serene resort set down beside the gulf and lavished with beds of tiny yellow blossoms, hedges of hibiscus, swaying palms, and acres of green lawns. The new and spacious rooms are decorated in pale-peach contemporary prints and blonde wicker furniture that echoes the resort's beachside atmosphere. You'll find large tiled baths in pastel colors, big roomy closets, plush wall-to-wall carpets, and wide balconies overlooking vast expanses of emerald-green grass dotted with tiny waterfalls and crowned by an enormous pool. Wandering farther afield you come upon the resort's championship PGA golf course, where a very young Jack Nicklaus broke his first 40. For tennis fans there are Har-tru courts, and five miles of silvery beach for beach fanatics. The Everglades Dining Room is a study in pale green and shell pink, with huge wall murals of Florida bird and Indian life. It's a place to dine by candlelight on mangrove snapper plus straightforward steaks and roasts in the $12 to $15 range (open 6 to 9 p.m.). Off by itself is the hotel's Brassie's Dining Room and Lounge, where you'll enjoy entertainment that has made this spot a late-night playground of Naples.

Owned by the Watkins family since 1946, the Naples Beach Hotel has a number of package plans, especially in summer, that can save you money. Rates in winter (from mid-December to May) are $130 to $165 double, with suites and efficiencies higher. In other months, rates drop to $50 to $90. If you'd like to have meals here, they'll provide breakfast and dinner for $23 to $28 per person.

Tides Motor Inn, 1801 Gulfshore Blvd. North, Naples, FL 33940 (tel. 813/262-6196), is a quiet, elegant spot with its own strip of private snow-white sand. The spacious rooms have screened balconies overlooking a central courtyard where a terrace stretches down to beachside. Palms and shrubbery are scattered artfully around the property and give this handsome resort a soothing look. Rooms echo those pretty gardens, with lots of yellow and green touches and tropical rattan furniture. In winter, two people pay $63 to $94, up to $140 for larger quarters. In the summer months (beginning about May), rates drop to $38 to $43 for hotel rooms, $53 to $75 for efficiencies or for one-bedroom apartments.

Soothe away your worries in a hot tub at the **Buccaneer Inn,** 2329 9th St. North (US 41), Naples, FL 33940 (tel. 813/261-1148). Set in a shady spot near the resort's pool, the hot tub is a good spot to warm up on cool winter days or soak sedately in summer. Several two-story buildings overlook attractive lawns and two pools, so you can be sure you'll have a nice view from these spacious rooms decorated in greens and golds. All rooms have hotplates and refrigerators, so snacks are a snap. The Buccaneer has a popular restaurant where pirate flags carry out the resort's skull-and-crossbones theme. Local boats supply the Buccaneer with fresh seafood, and chefs prepare it with skill for prices in the $9 to $12 range. The Buccaneer's restaurant is open daily from 4 to 11 p.m., and the Pirate's Den Lounge features oldtime sing-alongs and silent movies to midnight six days a week (closed on Sunday). Two people pay $59 to $79 from December through mid-April for poolside rooms or suites with sitting rooms, dressing areas, and refrigerators. In summer, prices begin at $39 to $59 double.

The **Beachcomber Motel,** at Fifth Avenue and 3rd Street South, 290 Fifth Ave. South, Naples, FL 33940 (tel. 813/262-8112), is an attractive downtown motel two blocks from the gulf with screened porches where you can enjoy the tranquil atmosphere and sleek look of this small resort. It's quite near many of the town's excellent restaurants and well-stocked shops. Spacious and tastefully decorated one-bedroom apartments, efficiencies, and combinations are available, plus some larger quarters including a three-bedroom villa. Rates for two in peak season begin at $55 to $65 for motel rooms and efficiencies, $75 for most larger accommodations. In other months, prices begin at $31 and range to $43.

If you want to see a striking example of Florida's favorite color scheme—citrus colors—take a look at **Stoney's Citrus Inn,** 2630 N. Tamiami Trail, Naples, FL 33940 (tel. 813/261-3870). Stoney's is a nickname for the family that owns this resort and also owns a nearby orange grove, and this may be why they so love the color of citrus. They also love tourists, and will invite you out to the groves when the fruit's ripe so you can pick your own oranges right off the trees! Back at the inn, there are lime-green and lemon-yellow doors, bright-yellow headboards, lime-green bedspreads, even citrus colors out by the swimming pool. Stoney's is a favorite family spot you can't miss as you drive north on US 41. Two people pay just $45 to $50 in the winter months (beginning in mid-January) and $30 to $35 double in summer (beginning about mid-May).

The **Fairways Motel,** at 103 Palm River Blvd., one mile east of US 41 on Route 846, Naples, FL 33942 (tel. 813/597-8181), is a money-saving hideaway in a golfing community called Palm River Estates, just north of downtown Naples. You couldn't find any place quieter than the Fairways, which is set down in the middle of a residential area. A friendly German family runs things here, and keeps the spacious rooms spic and span. Rooms have two double beds, dressing area, and wide closets, and are decorated in golds and blues. They have sliding glass doors that open onto a tranquil central courtyard in the center of which is a sparkling pool. Prices in high season (from mid-December through mid-April) are $40 to $45 double a day, $350 a week for an efficiency. In summer, you can hardly beat the prices anywhere in the area: just $25 to $35. Weekly summer rates are $160 to $275. There's no charge for children under 12 either.

Downtown in the shady streets of Naples you'll find the **Flamingo Apartments,** 383 Sixth Ave., Naples, FL 33940 (tel. 813/261-7017). Tucked away on a serene side street, the Flamingo is a small place, just two single-story buildings facing each other across a flowery courtyard and pool where pink hibiscus bloom. The only motel room here is completely paneled, with a queen-size bed, wood wardrobe, and bright rust tones. Apartments at this interesting small resort are unusually spacious, with a wide kitchen, living room, dining room, and separate bedroom, and five have beamed cathedral ceilings. For this apartment and others like it (they sleep five) you'll pay rates as attractive as the apartments: just $55 to $70 for studio or one- or two-bedroom apartments from mid-December to mid-April, $47 for the motel room. In summer, rates begin at $25 to $40.

READER'S MOTEL SELECTION: "**Naples Motor Lodge,** 250 9th St., Naples, FL 33940 (tel. 813-262-1414), is spacious and exceptionally clean. It has a convenient location and is a friendly place" (Kathleen Kemp, Madeira Beach, Fla.).

Vanderbilt Beach

Every room seems to have a dazzling view at **La Playa Beach and Racquet Inn,** on Vanderbilt Beach, 9891 Gulfshore Dr., Naples, FL 33940 (tel. 813/597-3123), but then what else would you expect in a motor inn that overlooks a waterway in one direction, the gulf in another, and has its own palm-shaded pool at the front door? Gauguin is a favorite artist here, and the unusually spacious rooms are decorated in Gauguin blues or the golds with which that artist was so enamored. A wall of glass opens onto a private balcony overlooking the gulf or

Vanderbilt Lagoon across the way. Downstairs at beach level is Café La Playa, where you can dine while viewing the gulf waters in a small intimate restaurant gleaming with candles and serving up shrimp tempura or lobster sauteed with peppers, onions, mushrooms, and wine, for prices in the $10 to $15 range. Sweeping in a long arc across a quiet strip of beautiful Vanderbilt Beach, La Playa is Vanderbilt's premier resort with pool and tennis courts. From mid-January to mid-April you'll pay $78 to $120 for hotel rocms, from $95 to $110 for efficiencies, depending on the room's location and dates you select. One- and two-bedroom town-house suites range from $184 to $250 in high season. In summer, prices drop to $45 to $124.

Beamed ceilings and paneled walls are a highlight of the spacious rooms at the **Vanderbilt Beach Motel,** 9225 Gulf Shore Dr. North, Naples, FL 33963 (tel. 813/597-3144), which stretches between the gulf and a deep-blue lagoon. The motel rooms, efficiencies, apartments, and suites have bright floral fabrics that contrast with dark-wood touches. From every unit there's a view of glittering gulf waters and the carefully tended lawns that surround the resort's pear-shaped pool. Tennis players have been allotted a place to work off steam, and there's a private boat ramp, pier, and dock. In summer (from May to mid-December) rates begin at $37 for motel rooms (including a complimentary continental breakfast), and range from $39 to $56 for efficiencies and apartments. Rates are about double that in winter.

Marco Island

A few miles south of Naples off US 41 at Route 951 is Marco Island. A University of Miami professor once dubbed Marco "Florida's Last Frontier." He termed it that just minutes before developers discovered it, and today Marco is a frontier no longer, its lonely isolation and touching loveliness fallen before the pace of progress in the form of hundreds of condominiums in every size, shape, and color. You can find out how to rent one of those by calling or writing the **Marco Island Chamber of Commerce** at P.O. Box 913, Marco Island, FL 33937 (tel. 813/394-7549).

In the midst of this mass of development is **Marriott's Marco Island Resort,** 400 South Collier Blvd., Marco Island, FL 33937 (tel. 813/394-2511, or toll free 800/228-9290). This Marriott is a showplace in anybody's terms, built high over the waters with two-story windows rising from the sand capped by yet a third story of glass. Lovely vistas of garden and sea stretch out before you as you stand on the balcony of very spacious rooms decorated in deep blues and yellows. It is luxurious here, with contemporary furniture, lots of closet space, handsome wall coverings, and little extras from slick magazines to keep you up-to-date on local activities to heaps of towels and separate dressing areas.

Rates are $165 in season and range as high as $330 (for suites). A beach-level wing of villas with living rooms and kitchens begins at $145 in season. In summer, those rates drop to $75 to $95 for rooms in the main hotel, $150 to $215 for one- and two-bedroom lanais or suites. There's even a two-bedroom penthouse apartment that rents for $375 a day in *summer!*

Marriott Marco Island lies beside three miles of white sand and has a fleet of Sunfish and catamarans for rent, 15 tennis courts, two pools, a par-three golf course, and a sports center for everything from volleyball to mopeds. There are six restaurants and lounges, ranging from a coffeeshop to the Gulfside restaurant. Prices in the main dining room, where tableside cookery is a favorite, average $12 to $17.

Another lovely choice on Marco Island is **The Pavilion,** 1170 Edington Pl., Old Marco Village, P.O. Box 847, Marco Island, FL 33937 (tel. 813/394-3345). Here you can choose among 29 one- and two-bedroom apartments, each with private patio or balcony and handsome French provincial furnishings. Guests gather around this two-story resort's swimming pool and revel in views of the bay. Rates for a one-bedroom apartment are $70 from May to December, $90 in other months; $100 in summer and $120 in winter months for a two-bedroom apartment for four. Monthly rates also are available and save you a bit of money.

To experience "my" Marco the way it used to be many years ago have lunch or dinner at the **1883 Marco Island Inn.** Occupying a very old island home, this handsome restaurant has three dining rooms bathed in the ruby-red glow of shining glassware. Overhead, crystal chandeliers glitter, and beneath them a well-trained staff serves good basic cooking, often with Austrian or German touches, things like wienerschnitzel, jaeger Madagascar. Prices are in a quite reasonable $10 to $20 range for dinner. You'll find Marco Island Inn at 100 Palm St. (tel. 394-3131), and it's open daily from 5:30 to 10 p.m. (but closed for a month from about mid-August to mid-September).

A similar place, although a bit more rustic perhaps, is the **Marco Lodge,** a restaurant occupying quarters built in 1869—and for Florida that is very old indeed. These weathered gray walls have seen both little and much over the years, and today enclose quite an attractive restaurant featuring good steaks and seafood in the $10 to $15 price range for dinner. Hours are 6 to 10 p.m. for dinner daily except Monday, closing an hour later on weekends. You'll find the restaurant at 1 Papaya St. in Goodland (tel. 394-3302), a tiny settlement just down the road from the main activity on Marco. Anyone can direct you there, and road signs also point the way. Marco Lodge is also open from 11 a.m. to 4 p.m. on Sunday for lunch.

Snook Inn, 1215 Bald Eagle Dr., Marco Island, FL 33937 (tel. 813/394-3313), is about on the opposite end of the scale from the fancy Marco Island Marriott, but it occupies quite an enviable waterside spot. Guests gather around an outdoor bar overlooking the water and dine in a rustic restaurant here in this serene setting. Accommodations are similarly simple, but kept clean and neat. There are just 13 rooms at this inn, many with small kitchens, and all the rooms were revamped in 1985 with new carpeting, drapes, and paneling added. Rates are $35 to $60, year round, with highest rates in winter, of course.

You can get to Marco by air on **Marco Island Airways** (tel. 305/442-1556, or toll free 800/282-3805), which flies here on a regular schedule from Tampa and Miami. The resort provides complimentary transportation from the airport.

RESTAURANTS: Miamians have long come to Naples to escape the hectic city life, then returned here later. A high-rolling crowd gets the good food it seeks at moderate prices and in quite expansive atmospheres. Dining seems to get better and better in this small town, which keeps adding new restaurants to its roster. This is such a small town that you can just roll in, park your car, and stroll through town looking at restaurants as you go. Remember that the prices I've cited are for entrees, but that these usually include salad, one or two vegetables, and sometimes coffee as well.

French

Set high over a canal bordered by a fascinating condominium complex that's a Venice look-alike, the **Shore Club,** at 4050 Gulf Shore Blvd. North (tel. 261-4050), never lacks for scenery. When you tire of those incredible clusters of salmon, white, gray, and green villas spread out along the waterway, look around at long expanses of emerald-green rugs sparked by white rattan furniture and glittering paned windows. A handsome maître d' presides expertly over a crew of friendly workers who specialize in tableside cookery, including new productions—eight just added to an already impressive menu ranging from steak tartare to tournedos with brandy and garnished by artichoke bottoms filled with peas, mushrooms stuffed with pâté. Almond and coconut shrimp is an irresistible crunchy delicacy too. For the view, excellent service, and outstanding cuisine, you'll pay prices in the $15 range for entrees, about $3 to $5 for appetizers and desserts. It's open from 5:30 to 10 p.m. Tuesday through Saturday, from 10:30 a.m. to 2 p.m. on Sunday.

A glorious newcomer, well, two glorious newcomers, to Naples are the **Chef's Garden** and **Truffles,** the former occupying the downstairs quarters at 1300 3rd St. South (tel. 262-5500), and Truffles bustling merrily upstairs. Downstairs, a garden atmosphere prevails, with tables running alongside a wall of glass through which a tiny garden is visible. The bright contemporary design in deep, glowing shades of green and royal blue makes this a handsome spot to dine on spinach salads, cucumber soup, crêpes, or a jellied poached salmon at lunch, or rack of lamb or filet of beef Wellington at dinner. Upstairs, you'll be starved by the time you reach a table: to get there you have to pass a glass case containing shimmering pâtés, delicate sliced salmon, and golden cheeses. Shading the windows here are yards and yards of dramatic salmon-pink fabric echoed in peach accents on rattan chairs. In this striking decor you dine on cassoulets or steak-and-kidney pie, caper-rimmed steak tartare, elegant sandwiches of avocado, muenster, tomato, and bean sprouts on honey-wheat bread, heaping salads with Greek or Italian flavors, watercress crunchy with almonds, or unusual cold fish plates including curried mussels, marinated herring, shrimp, or scallops. Top prices here run about $9, but most items are in the $5 to $7 range. Truffles is open Monday through Saturday from 11 a.m. to 1 a.m., on Sunday from 4:30 to 10:30 p.m. You'll pay about $10 to $15 for dinner at the Chef's Garden, which is open from 11 a.m. to 2:30 p.m. for lunch, from 6 to 10 p.m. for dinner Tuesday through Saturday.

Italian

Farino's, at 4000 N. Tamiami Trail (tel. 262-2883), isn't much on showy decor and in fact isn't much—just one of the best Italian kitchens on the state's west coast. The friendly Farino family reigns over the simplest of award-winning dining rooms with a couple of wine racks and some wood paneling for atmosphere in this storefront eatery. But who needs fancy furbelows when from the herb-scented kitchen pour out more than 50 classical Italian dishes including zuppa di vongole, pastas, hot and cold antipasti, milk-fed veal, chicken, and seafood treats in the $10 to $15 range? Open from 5 p.m. daily. Farino's is often jammed, so reservations are a wise move.

Note: In honor of her mother, who started it all, proprietress Valerie Farino Stiles is slowly changing the restaurant's name to Gilda's Casa Italiana, so you might look for that name too.

Steaks and Seafood

St. George and the Dragon are still battling it out at the restaurant of that name, at 936 Fifth Ave. (tel. 262-6546), where you dine in an atmosphere that's more pub than medieval, with dim lighting and some nautical touches under a vaulted ceiling. The fare is solid beef and seafood dishes (in the $10 to $15 range), an incredible conch chowder, and key lime pie. St. George packs them in, but a wait at the well-stocked bar can be a pleasant interlude, especially on weekends. Hours are 11:30 a.m. to 11:30 p.m. Monday through Saturday.

Ristorante Marker 4 (formerly Pate's), 1193 Eighth St. South at the end of 9th Street beside the Cove Inn (tel. 262-4953), is another top dining room in this small town. Located right at the water's edge with fascinating views of shrimpboats chugging in and out of the harbor, Marker 4 is a high-ceilinged study in heavy wood beams and walls of glass through which the setting sun glitters and gleams off crystal and crisp linens. Seafoods, beef, chicken, and veal in continental preparations are featured. Dinner averages about $10 to $15, and is served from 5 to 11 p.m. Monday through Saturday, noon to 9 p.m. on Sunday.

The Dock at Crayton Cove, 899 12th St. South (tel. 261-9940), is just what its name implies, a dockside restaurant plunked down beside the City Docks. Which means, of course, that there's always an interesting view of yachts and fishing boats coming and going, and some good seafood (including shark) served up in a rustic atmosphere—you read the day's menu on the blackboard. Prices are in the $10 to $15 range, and the friendly help in sailor outfits are on hand from 11:30 a.m. to 11 p.m. (from 1 to 10 p.m. on Sunday) to make your dining shipshape.

You'd be hard pressed to find a pubbier spot than **Pate's Piccadilly Pub,** at 625 Fifth Ave. South (tel. 262-7521), outside Piccadilly itself. Dark wood from floor to (and including) ceiling, lots of fascinating pub signs, brass chandeliers and wall sconces, and low lighting give this restaurant that glowing golden atmosphere so familiar in British pubs. Piccadilly Pub has been winning awards for its culinary talents for years now, and is one of the most popular spots in Naples. A "Hot Brown," a slice of baked turkey topped with cheddar cheese sauce and browned, is the pub's bestseller, and oysters Rockefeller touched with Pernod and topped in béarnaise are worth the wait you may find here in winter. Steak and seafood dishes are on the moderately priced menu which features lunch in the $4 to $6 range, dinner from $10 to $15. Open from 11:30 a.m. to 3:30 p.m. Monday through Saturday and 5:30 to 10 p.m. daily, Piccadilly Pub has five dining areas and a suitable dim lounge, but the front room where sunbeams glitter through paned windows is the favorite.

Budget Bets

Tin City probably ought to be listed under what to see and do since it is certainly plenty of both. An old tin warehouse with tin roof and sides, Tin City was recently converted to a fascinating shopping center in which you'll find everything from ice-cream shops to fresh doughnuts, antiques to bikinis. Here there are two restaurants well loved by local diners: **Riverwalk Ale House** (tel. 263-2734), which features lots of inexpensive seafood in the $8 to $10 bracket; and **The Eatery** (tel. 261-3477), which specializes in ribs and barbecued chow in the same range, although both have less expensive fare also. Both also have lots of wood and greenery, with the Riverwalk leaning to nautical bric-a-brac. You can eat outside on tables overlooking the wharf or inside among the oars and nets. Look up in the Eatery and you'll see an antique sleigh dangling from the ceiling; stroll through this woodsy antique atmosphere for a look at painted antique iron horses.

Tin City's just off US 41 south of Naples at the intersection of 12th Street and Sixth Avenue South. The Riverwalk is open from 11:30 a.m. to 1 a.m. Monday to Saturday (from 1 p.m. on Sunday); the Eatery's hours are the same daily, from noon on Sunday.

READER'S "TIN CITY" TIP: "Most unusual item I found at Naples 'Tin City' was canned key lime pie filling stocked in the butcher shop. It's canned pureed key limes, perfect flavor and texture and I've never seen it anywhere else. It's about $2 for an 18-ounce can" (Kathleen Kemp, Madeira Beach, Fla.).

READER'S RESTAURANT SUGGESTION: "Paddlewheel Restaurant, 990 Tamiami Trail (tel. 262-1700), looks like a huge paddlewheel steamer and has a Gay '90s decor that is worth seeing. Good food is moderately priced and plentiful" (Kathleen Kemp, Madeira Beach, Fla.).

SPORTS: There are plenty of places to play in this seaside city.

Golf and Tennis: Golf fans can play at the **Naples Beach Hotel and Golf Club,** 851 Gulf Shore Blvd. North (tel. 261-2222), a par-72 course where greens fees are $12; carts, $16. Tennis courts at the hotel are $4 an hour and there are public courts at **Cambier Park** (tel. 262-5115) in downtown Naples. The **Riviera Golf Club,** on Route 864, just east of US 41 South (tel. 744-1081), and **Golden Gate Inn and Country Club,** at 4100 Golden Gate Pkwy. on Route 951 (tel. 813/455-1010), also have 18-hole courses open to the public. Greens fees are in the $10 range.

Diving: You can rent equipment at **Sealandia Scuba Center,** 625 8th St. South (tel. 261-3357), where they can show you how to use it and arrange tours and diving trips offshore.

Fishing and Shelling: A most unusual craft with two carved heads astern and a thatched roof atop, *Tiki Islander,* of **Tiki Islander Tours,** 1200 Fifth Ave. South (tel. 262-7577), goes on half-day fishing, shelling, and sightseeing sojourns at 9 a.m. and 2 p.m. daily for $14 to $18 for adults, $8 to $12 for children under 12. The *Tiki* is docked at Old Marine Market Place behind Tin City just off US 41. Another shelling/fishing boat is the *Queen,* docked at the Naples Boat Haven Marina next to the second bridge on the South Tamiami Trail (tel. 774-3149). Trips leave for shelling or fishing at 9 a.m. every day except Saturday, when the craft goes out for fishing only. Prices are $10 for adults, $6 for children.

Sailing: You can rent sailboats at the **Naples Beach Hotel and Golf Club** for $20 to $25 an hour; it even has a few kayaks for those with excellent balance. Call the hotel at 261-2222, extension 2352.

SEEING THE SIGHTS: You can get a wonderful look at some strange and beautiful flora and fauna at two large preservation areas here.

You are of course at the tip of the Everglades, and just 17 miles from Naples is **Big Cypress Swamp,** last refuge of the Seminoles after land-hungry white men captured their leader Osceola (under a flag of truce) and forced many of the tribe to emigrate to what is now Oklahoma. Some of the Seminoles fled into this swamp to hide, and remain here today, still able to predict hurricanes and cold winters from the activities of swamp creatures. Big Cypress joins the massive Everglades at **Collier-Seminole Park,** 6423 acres of nature trails, camping and picnic sites, fishing, and boating facilities. It's a favorite spot for canoeing through a 13-mile loop trail at the Blackwater River and Royal Palm Hammock Creek inside the park. To get there, follow the Tamiami Trail (US 41) 16 miles east. Call 657-3771 for camping information.

At **Corkscrew Swamp** you'll see the nation's largest remaining stand of virgin bald cypress and walk beneath some of the oldest trees in North America. Located about 16 miles east of Naples, the 11,000-acre park is named after a crooked creek that flows through it. From a rustic mile of boardwalk you look down on huge ferns, and up at rare orchids. Look carefully at the "logs"—one of them may be an alligator! Admission is $3 for adults, $1 for students under 12, and the park (on Route 846) is open from 9 a.m. to 5 p.m. daily.

NIGHTLIFE: Brassie's, at the Naples Beach Hotel, 851 Gulf Shore Blvd. North (tel. 261-2222), is one of the top nightspots in the area, and features entertainment and dancing on weekends. The hotel's **Gulf Terrace Lounge** is popular for dancing too.

The **Naples Dinner Theater,** 1025 Piper Blvd. North (tel. 597-6031), is a stunning three-tiered candlelit room where you select from a buffet table that seems to extend for miles. After dinner a stage floats into view and talented performers present classic and current plays and musicals that range from *Mr. Roberts* to *Showboat* and *Carousel*. The Naples Dinner Theater has an elegant rococo atmosphere heavy with gilt mirrors and fountains, and a ticket to an evening of dining and theater is just $18.65 to $24.95. Jackets are required and the buffets are at 5:30 p.m., curtain at 8:15 p.m. Tuesday through Saturday, with matinees at 11 a.m. on Thursday, Saturday, and Sunday.

The **Eatery** and **Riverwalk** both have entertainment. They're in **Tin City,** off US 41 at 12th Street and Sixth Avenue South (see my restaurant recommendations).

SPECIAL EVENTS: Naples whoops it up twice a year at **swamp buggy races** held on the last Sunday of February and October. Begun in 1949 to signal the start of the hunting season, this event is mud wrestling on wheels as the crazy cars with the giant wheels plunge off through mud four to six feet deep to see whose machine is king pig. They even crown a Mud Duchess. It's fun—if you stand way back. Call 813/774-2701 for information about the race, which is often shown on a national television show.

3. Sanibel and Captiva Islands

Cockles, conchs, and calico scallops. Tiger's eyes, ladies' ear, and kitten's paw. Sand dollars and angel wings. These are the stuff dreams are made of on Sanibel, one of the world's three top shelling beaches, and perhaps the only place in the world famous for a posture—the Sanibel Stoop, the stooped-over gait of the shell hunter!

Sanibel and Captiva are a Gauguin paradise, two islets bathed in a golden glow, fringed in powder-soft silver sands, green with misty tunnels of Australian pines. They're exotica, splashed with scarlet, lemon, and fuschia blossoms peeking from behind giant banyans and huge green sea grape leaves, flashing bright in the scarlet flight of a roseate spoonbill or the dazzle of a white heron.

Almost everyone who has seen them has been captured by the sultry tropical beauty of these islands. Include among those Anne Morrow Lindbergh, who saw reflections of her past in the shells she found here and recorded those images in *Gift from the Sea,* artist Robert Rauschenburg, journalist Roger Mudd, author Edna St. Vincent Millay, editorial cartoonist "Ding" Darling.

If you join them, you'll find yourself slipping into a lazy mañana mode, a sun-baked tropical serenity. Finally one day you'll pick up one small shell, then another and another, tuck them into a pocket and take them away where their pearly glory will forever remind you of sun-drenched days and sea-lulled nights, of breezes whispering through the pines, and a pervasive peace as eternal as a shell.

GETTING THERE: You can get to the islands by car from Fort Myers on Route 867. If you're coming from the south from Naples toward Fort Myers on US 41, you'll see a small sign about four miles south of the city pointing west to Sanibel. It's easy to miss the sign, so keep a sharp eye out as you near Fort Myers. There's a $3 round-trip toll to the islands, but if you're planning several crossings you can save money with a $10, 20-trip ticket book.

GETTING AROUND: The **Sanibel Taxi Cab Co.** (tel. 472-4160 or 472-4169) operates 24 hours a day on Sanibel, and can arrange airport transportation from

Fort Myers for $18 to $22. Taxi rates on the island are $1.80 for the first mile, $1.20 for each additional mile.

Island Moped, at 1470 Periwinkle Way (tel. 472-5248), rents mopeds for $6 an hour or $25 a day, bikes for $1.50 an hour, $8 a day. They're open from 9 a.m. to 5:30 p.m. daily.

USEFUL INFORMATION: The **Sanibel/Captiva Chamber of Commerce** is at the entrance to the island on Causeway Road (address and telephone below), and can give you reams of information on everything about these islands. It's open from 10 a.m. to 9 p.m. Monday through Saturday and from 10 a.m. to 5 p.m. on Sunday. You can use the telephone there free to find a room on the island. . . . For **emergencies,** dial 472-1414. . . . For **medical problems,** Dr. Louis Wegryn can be reached 24 hours a day at 472-4131. . . . **Island Garage** (tel. 472-4318) has 24-hour wrecker service and is open 8 a.m. to 5 p.m. Monday through Saturday for repairs. . . . **Bailey's General Store,** in the Island Shopping Center (tel. 472-1516), is open from 8 a.m. to 7 p.m. weekdays, an hour later on weekends, and until 6 p.m. on Sunday. They have groceries, beach hats, and such, and fishing supplies, and can get your film developed. . . . The **Sanibel Grog Shop** is also in the Island Shopping Center and has liquors, beer, and wine. . . . If you need **quick cleaning service,** call Prathers (tel. 472-2442). . . . There's overnight film processing at **Island Apothecary,** Palm Ridge and Tarpon Bay Roads (tel. 472-1519), where you can also find prescription service to 5:30 p.m. daily or in an emergency by calling pharmacist **Leonard Kensler** at 472-2768. . . . **Western Union** (tel. 472-1516) is in Bailey's General Store too. . . . The postal **ZIP Code** for the islands is 33957.

HOTELS: You can be certain you'll find something to suit you on Sanibel/Captiva, where accommodations range from simple rustic beach cottages to slick chain motels, one of the state's loveliest resorts, and hundreds of privately owned condominium apartments. If you're interested in condominiums, the **Sanibel/Captiva Chamber of Commerce** office, Causeway Road, Sanibel, FL 33957, at the entrance to Sanibel (tel. 813/472-1080), has a wallboard listing names and numbers of individual renters. Many realtors in the area also deal in vacation condominium rentals. Try **Executive Services, Inc.,** 455 Periwinkle Way, Sanibel, FL 33957 (tel. 813/472-4195), which has apartments in many island buildings, or **Priscilla Murphy Realty,** 9067 Causeway Rd., Sanibel, FL 33957 (tel. 813/472-4113 or 472-4114), which has several offices on both Captiva and Sanibel.

The Luxury Leaders

Among the island's multitudes of condominium resorts, serene **Pointe Santo de Sanibel,** on Gulf Drive at Tarpon Bay Road, Sanibel, FL 33957 (tel. 813/463-1141, or toll free 800/237-5141), is a magically quiet place far from the frenetic activity that characterizes some of the island's other accommodations. Situated on the southernmost point of Sanibel, Pointe Santo is kept immaculate and sparkling by management and owners who soon know everyone by name and seem really to care about the caliber of the resort they oversee. You can lie beside a sparkling pool overlooking the beach, wander over a footbridge to a heated Jacuzzi, or while away the hours in a wood-beamed clubhouse where a glass floor lets you follow the antics of fish swimming in the lagoon below. You can whack a few around on the tennis courts, or search for the perfect shell on miles of silver white beach. Select from one-, two-, or three-bedroom elaborately decorated villas, or go whole hog in penthouse apartments with private rooftop sundecks (one of these is valued at more than a quarter of a million dollars!), for prices ranging from $128 to $278 a day in peak winter season, from $68 to $158 in the summer months.

Dear old Clarence Chadwick, the man who made a fortune with his "Checkwriter" and then blew it all in an attempt to make another fortune in copra and key limes, simply wouldn't believe what's now gracing his groves. You'll have just a little trouble believing it too when you see the 330-acre **South Seas Plantation Resort and Yacht Harbour,** Captiva Island, FL 33924 (tel. 813/ 472-5111, or toll free 800/237-3102; in Florida, 800/282-3402). This multi-million-dollar wonder sprang up on Captiva Island a few years ago and captured the imagination (and the wallets) of many a south Floridian. If there's something they can't provide, I have yet to discover it: there are 20 tennis courts presided over by a touring pro, 1977 Wimbledon Champ Virginia Wade, 16 (count 'em) swimming pools, a nine-hole oceanside golf course, a marina, two miles of private beach, a rustic Capt'n Al's Pub at harborside, and award-winning Chadwick's Restaurant where the Friday night $19.95 seafood buffet is bounteous and the $10.95 Sunday brunch could easily carry you into Tuesday.

All that and I haven't even started on where you'll stay: you can choose among seaside apartments, hundreds of them, snuggled in clusters, each around its own pool; villa efficiencies; and one-, two-, and three-bedroom cottages right on the beach, raised high over the sand on stilts. If you aren't interested in anything remotely related to a kitchen, there are rooms in the pillared Plantation House with luxuries like double vanities. From mid-December to May, one or two people in hotel rooms pay $110 a day; in summer, $70. Resort Villa efficiencies with living room, dining room, and sleeping area in one large room are $120 in winter, $80 in summer. The one- and two-bedroom villa suites with separate living and sleeping areas are $130 to $180 a day in winter (depending on the number of bedrooms), $80 to $115 in summer. Equally attractive gulf cottages have three bedrooms with a loft, private porches, washers and dryers, private pool and tennis court in the cluster of connecting cottages on the beach, and range from $295 for one to four persons, to $320 for up to six persons in high season, $195 to $220 in summer. Beach homes with two, three, or four bedrooms and two or three baths, plus all the amenities of cottages including lofts, pool, and tennis court, are $300 to $360 in winter, $200 to $250 for a four-bedroom accommodating eight in summer. There's a seven-night minimum. A fishing-village motif predominates at Bayside Villas, which can operate as hotel rooms or one- or two-bedroom apartments for prices ranging from $85 to $240 in winter, $100 to $145 in summer. There are also two-bedroom/two-bath cottages, duplex or quadruplex at $265 to $285 a day in winter, $150 to $170 in summer. Beach villas begin at $180 in winter, $120 in summer, and tennis villas with a rooftop sundeck run from $145 in winter, $85 in summer.

Ranging over 330 acres, South Sea Plantation has retained much of its plantation atmosphere, so you can stroll through mile after mile of wooded pine and mangrove island that hasn't changed much in many centuries, and is home to hundreds of varieties of colorful birds (occasionally you may even hear the deep-throated gronk of a bull alligator). For about $250 you can learn to sail here at a branch of the prolific Offshore Sailing School, or you can let someone else do the sailing on a trip aboard the 65-foot cruiser *Silver Lady* at prices which vary from $9 to $16 (tel. 472-5111). For dining, Chadwick's is a charmingly eclectic melange of multilevel seating areas. One has an intriguing attic look, one's a gardeny gazebo trimmed in white lattice and furnished in wicker, another displays the cheery warmth of a library area furnished in high-back leathery wing chairs. Dine here on filet mignon béarnaise or roast prime rib, shrimp in a delicate beer batter laced with sherry, or sea scallops simmered in garlic butter and white wine. Figure your check in the $15 to $20 range per person. Finally, at

King's Crown you'll dine in a former warehouse/commissary that once served plantation workers. Under the original wood beams and a massive fireplace enhanced by crystal and deep carpeting, you'll dine on raw beef dijonnais accompanied by aromatic herb and mustard sauce, cold cream of avocado soup, salads of artichokes or avocado touched with truffles, followed by soft-shell crabs sauteed with green peppercorns, fresh fish topped with coconut sauce, rack of spring lamb, roast pigeon with lime, poached lobster topped with a sauce laced with sorrel. Finish with flaming coffees and key lime pies from Chadwick's trees, which still grow here. Expect to pay in the $60-a-couple range for your splurge.

The Moderate Range

'Tween Waters Inn, on Captiva Island, FL 33924 (tel. 813/472-5161), could hardly be more aptly named—it's snuggled in between the gulf and the waters of the Pine Island Sound, and at a narrow point on this tiny island that's snuggly indeed. Here you'll discover a helter-skelter scattering of cottages where you can settle into a super-casual, uninhibited, lazy beachcombing life. Everything's simple, from the basic white painted furniture, uncarpeted terrazzo floors (so you don't have to concern yourself with tracking sand around), bright bedspreads with matching drapes, and even the occasional cottage with a fireplace. Don't expect anything more luxurious than maid service at this inn. It's simplicity itself, but what could be nicer than sand between your toes and days that drift by as casually carefree as the waves that lap upon the sands outside your door? Captiva's only road runs between this casual resort and the sea, but you're only steps away from the inn's private strip of beach shaded by giant sea grape trees, palms, and lacy Australian pines. A frequent guest here years ago was J. N. "Ding" Darling, a famed New York editorial cartoonist who retired to the island and created a wildlife refuge nearby that still bears his name. Motel room rates for two are $50 to $70 in summer and $65 to $100 in winter; cottage efficiencies begin at $60 in summer and $75 in winter.

There's nary a blade of grass at the **Island Inn,** at the corner of West Gulf Drive and Island Inn Road, 3111 West Gulf Dr., Sanibel Island, FL 33957 (tel. 813/472-1561), just acres of sand dotted with palms and shrubbery. With all that sand around it's almost like sleeping right on the beach. Fortunately, you won't have to pull up a piece of sand since the Island Inn lures you with exceptionally attractive rooms with wildly colorful drapes and bedspreads and with unusual scalloped valances. Beyond those drapes are spacious balconies where you can have your morning coffee (and orange juice, of course) beneath the shade of sea grape trees. The Island Inn is a cluster of lodges, each with its own identifying name. One of them, Kimball Lodge, houses a spacious lounge complete with fireplace, library, a second-floor sundeck, bridge tables, and (naturally) a view of the gulf. Sharkey Lodge has large efficiency units with two double beds and Bahama beds; Matthews Lodge features rooms with twin beds, refrigerators, and screened balconies. Several cottages on the grounds will accommodate up to eight people, and there are smaller ones for two or four. The friendly management keeps things spiffy and adds some unusual touches like an intriguing carved totem pole. In the winter months the inn's dining room serves all meals, two of which are included in resort rates, which range from $85 for a double room without balcony to $116 for a kitchen unit or cottage. Summer rates (beginning May 1 to mid-November) are $41 to $65 for rooms or cottages with or without kitchens.

A small stone boy staring pensively out over his domain sets the tone at **Song of the Sea,** 863 E. Gulf Dr., Sanibel Island, FL 33957 (tel. 813/472-2220), a gracious resort that likes to call itself an old-world inn. There is indeed something of the old world in this tranquil spot with rambling grounds. Mediterranean red brick curved roof tiles lend a classic touch of old-world charm to three simple white two-story buildings set amid palms and grassy walkways. Inside, wingback chairs and oak whisper of a French country home. Despite its genteel touches, Song of the Sea is a casual, informal spot where you can soak in a modern Jacuzzi, paddle about an unusually shaped pool, roam the small well-kept grounds, or settle into a chaise and let your worries ebb with the tides. A meticulous merger of old world and new, Song of the Sea has successfully blended gentility with beachside comfort. You can choose between one-bedroom apartments in a building overlooking the beach or efficiencies in the resort's wo other structures overlooking the pool. From mid-December to May, efficiencies with two double beds covered in quilted spreads or one-bedroom apartments are $98 to $118. In other months, prices drop to $58 to $72.

Pale-green cottages blend perfectly into 25 acres of manicured lawns at the **Colony,** one mile from the Causeway on East Gulf Drive, Sanibel Island, FL 33957 (tel. 813/472-5151). Cottages are scattered far apart, so they're very private hideaways indeed. If you prefer neighbors, there are two-story buildings housing sunny motel rooms decorated in a cheery green-and-orange decor and lots of windows overlooking the lawns. This seaside cluster of accommodations is back on one of the less frequented areas of the island, so you get a real feeling of getaway island living here. Still, you're not deprived of the accoutrements of civilization: there's a heated freshwater pool, cable color TV, picnic tables and grills for cookouts, rental bicycles, and best of all, 1000 feet of shell-strewn beachfront. On a rapidly crowding island, the Colony is an unusually large property offering lots of uncluttered space with tiny walkways winding through the lawns, palms, and beautifully landscaped grounds. Motel rooms with two double beds are $70 mid-December to May, and one-, two-, and three-bedroom apartments and cottages range from $70 to $80. In summer, prices are $10 less on each. A handy map the resort will send you shows the location of cottages and rooms so you can pick the view you like best.

If the Sanibel Stoop gets to you before you've found the perfect shell, the managers of the **Gallery Motel,** 541 E. Gulf Dr., Sanibel Island, FL 33957 (tel. 813/472-1400), have collected some beauties you can buy. That's not reason enough to stay, but it's one of the many thoughtful extras you'll find at this tropical enclave located right on the sand at the quieter, less frenetic southeastern tip of Sanibel. Just a short walk away is the historic Sanibel lighthouse and the fishing pier on San Carlos Bay. You can choose from motel rooms, efficiencies, cottages, and apartments at the Gallery, but I'm partial to the cottages, which face a central courtyard. They're especially spacious, decorated in off-white rattan furniture cushioned in bright yellow. In the living room it's fun to gather a few kindred souls at the high-stooled bar evenings and move onto small raised porches for a view of dramatic sunsets. You can't miss the Gallery as you drive along East Gulf Drive—it's painted a delicate shade of cocoa trimmed with darker shades of the same color on railings and shutters. In high season (from mid-December to mid-April), motel rooms are $58 to $68, efficiencies run $66 to $79, and cottages and apartments are $86. At other times you'll pay just $44 to $58 for motel rooms, $62 for cottages, even less after Labor Day.

Sanibel's gorgeous sand is king at most motels on the island, but at the **Jolly Roger Motel,** 3201 W. Gulf Dr., Sanibel Island, FL 33957 (tel. 813/472-1700), rooms overlook a tranquil shady strip of lawn and garden that stretches along the side of this neat and trim property. Which is not to say, of course, that the resort is without sand—it's located right on the beach. The Jolly Roger gets my vote for one of the most tranquil resorts on Sanibel for its cool, collected look and decor, and its spacious rooms set at an angle to make the most of triangular screened balconies overlooking the lawns, pool, and gulf beyond. Beachside there is a freshwater pool set up over the beach and surrounded by umbrellaed picnic tables plus a tennis court and barbecue. Some rooms have kitchens, and families can arrange for two- and three-room suites. In the winter season (beginning the middle of December), prices start at $59 to $79 for motel units, $84 to $94 for efficiencies, changing on May 1 to $60 to $65. Larger accommodations begin at $129 in winter, $104 in summer.

At the **Beachview Cottage,** 3306 W. Gulf Dr., Sanibel Island, FL 33957 (tel. 813/472-1202), you'll find cute rustic beach cottages with screened porches shaded by waving palms and rustling sea grape trees. On the beach there's a sundeck and Tiki hut; inside, cottages have fully equipped kitchens, cable TV, and simple durable furnishings much loved by families. The friendly management's around to advise on shelling, fishing, and dining at Beachview, where from mid-December to mid-April you'll pay $55 to $60 for studio efficiencies, to $85 for a large deluxe one-bedroom gulfside cottage, and about $18 more for a two-bedroom duplex accommodating four. In other months, rates range from $40 to $80.

Budget Bets

If you'd like to enjoy all the fun and serenity of Sanibel Beach without paying beach prices, just on the Fort Myers side of the bridge to Sanibel is the best budget find you'll discover anywhere in the vicinity. Overlooking Shell Point, a retirement village, you'll find the **Shell Point Village Guest House,** Shell Point Boulevard, Fort Myers, FL 33908 (tel. 813/466-1111), built high on a rise above a huge Y-shaped swimming pool, marina, and the Caloosahatchee River. Although it's called a guest house (probably because it was designed primarily to house guests of the village's residents), this is no clapboard house run by a den mother. Rather, it's a modern, two-story, 39-room motel with picture windows and contemporary decor the equal of any chain-motel operation. Rooms are unusually spacious with a wall of glass overlooking the community, and feature dark-blue decor or contemporary off-white spreads with blue and rust stripes. You'll pay just $49 double from December to May, $32 to October 1, slightly higher between October and December. There's no charge for children, but other additional guests are $5 each. If you're a senior citizen, there's a 10% discount. Meals in the glass-enclosed crystal room overlooking the village are about $7 to $10. Shell Point's guest house is 12 miles southwest of Fort Myers, two miles north of Route 867 on Shell Point Boulevard, a road that heads north about two miles just east of the Sanibel bridge.

A budget-saver motel on Sanibel Island is **Kona Kai,** at 1539 Periwinkle Way, Sanibel Island, FL 33957 (tel. 813/472-1001), a lush jungly spot festooned with flowers and shaded by tall palms. Bright-pink hibiscus peek out from behind hedges and leafy bushes. Kona Kai is not on the beach and has very basic furnishings, to which the owners, LeNita and Leon Matheny, have added ceiling fans and new carpeting. In the meantime you'll find comfortable, reasonably spacious rooms, spic and span, with lots of wood paneling and a very attractive and alluring pool set amid so much greenery it's almost like swimming in a Polynesian lagoon. Summer rates at this 12-unit South Pacific–theme beauty are $24.30 double daily, $37.38 for efficiencies, rising to $47.66 a day for motel rooms, $10 more for efficiencies in other months.

RESTAURANTS: With so many people crammed into islands as small as Sanibel and Captiva you may have to wait a while to get into the islands' restaurants in the winter season (or for that matter, in summer). It's worth the wait, however, for there are some talented cooks on the island. Because distances are so small here, I've divided the area's restaurants up by cuisine, beginning with what's almost always the most expensive, French. The prices I've listed, by the way, are for entrees unless otherwise noted.

French

Jean-Paul Cavanie brought a little bit of Paris with him when he opened **Jean-Paul's French Corner,** 708 Tarpon Bay Rd. (tel. 472-1493), near the Sanibel post office, some years back. A teensy bistro filled with fascinating bibelots (take a look at the ornate birdcage on the bar), the French Corner has a cozy, homey air about it (it doesn't hurt that Edith Piaf is warbling in the background). There are fresh flowers on the candlelit tables and perfumes emanating from the kitchens. Jean-Paul has a good cook, to put it mildly, who whips up a storm of escargots, filet mignon au poivre vert, and duck with fruit sauces. Fortunately prices here are nothing like Paris, topping out at perhaps $15 to $30 a person for full soup to super mousse. He's open for dinner from 6 to 10 p.m. (closed on Sunday and in some summer months).

Since 1957, **Nutmeg House,** at 2761 Gulf Dr. (tel. 472-1141), has occupied a small plot of green grass and flowers on Gulf Drive, so they must be doing something right. Dine in a tropical garden atmosphere on an excellent veal Armagnac or snapper Florentine en croûte. An unusual specialty here is seafood chowder en croûte, and Nutmeg's fresh chicken and avocado salad is a very special event. Expect to pay $15 to $18 for dinner, $2 to $5 more if you indulge in appetizers, soups, or special salads, which are very tempting. The Nutmeg House is open from 5:30 to 9:30 p.m. every day but Monday.

Italian

Letizia's, 3313 Gulf Dr. West (tel. 472-2177), doesn't look like much from the front, but once you've searched out the side entrance off a tiny alleyway and been greeted by a smiling host, you'll know you've found something special. Paneled wall to ceiling, the restaurant has a warm yellow glow and a melange of knickknacks strung about the tiny rooms tucked away in what was once a small house. From the kitchen come smells so mouthwateringly good that even a lackluster appetite will soon revive to enjoy a selection from the tantalizing array of Italian delicacies: red snapper en pappillote (cooked and served in a paper bag opened at your table so you can sniff the herbs within), bracivolini (steak stuffed with sweet Italian sausage), hearty pastas. Letizia's has even thought up a way to please those of us who take forever to decide: there are dinners for two featuring combinations of several entrees, priced at $26 to $34, and for an additional $13.95 Letizia tosses in a bottle of wine, soup, desserts, and coffee for two. Other entrees here average $10 to $15; pastas, about $8. It's open from 5:30 to 9:30 p.m. every day.

Steaks and Seafood

For a long time I thought **Timbers Restaurant and Fish Market,** at 975 Rabbit Rd. (tel. 472-3128), was a fancy condominium sales office. When I discovered it was really an excellent steak and seafood restaurant, well, such are the joys of discovering Sanibel. At Timbers everything's fresh, fresh, and fresher, from the seafood that comes straight out of the gulf to the excellent beef, to the vegetables and salads and breads baked here. For openers, try oysters or shrimp by the half or three-quarter dozen. Scampi or sirloin is a good choice. You'll pay $10 to $12 for dinner at the Timbers, which is open daily from 4:30 to 10 p.m. from Christmas Day through Easter Sunday. Stop in at Twigs lounge for postprandial sipping.

There's a Tudory look about the **Coconut Grove,** at the corner of Tarpon Bay Road and Periwinkle Way (tel. 472-1366), with diamond-paned glass, lots of wood and plants scattered about, and a varied menu ranging from seafood to steaks and chops in the $8 to $12 range. For children there's a special menu, and for light eaters, a salad plate. The house specialty is baked stuffed jumbo shrimp with a hint of garlic; another good choice is shrimp de jonghe. Don't miss the restaurant's prize-winning shell collection on the way out. Hours are 11 a.m. to 10 p.m. daily, although schedules vary some in the summer.

On Captiva, **'Tween Waters Inn** (tel. 472-5161) has two attractive dining rooms decorated with amusing sketches by cartoonist "Ding" Darling who was a favorite guest of this resort. He used to team up with manager Maggie White in pranks aimed at livening things up a bit: the duo once carefully created panther tracks in the sand opposite the inn and waited for the uproar to begin. 'Tween Waters hasn't changed much since those days, and still has a cozy little front dining room with ruffly curtains and a view across the road to the waters of the gulf. Dinners at 'Tween Waters are straightforward preparations of steaks cut to order in the inn's kitchens, shrimp, crab, scallops, and whatever unsuspecting fish was caught that day. Prices are in the $12 to $15 range for dinner, and food service is available from 7 a.m. to midnight daily. On Wednesday there's a $15.95 seafood buffet; Saturday is prime rib night; a brunch on Sunday.

It isn't possible to resist a restaurant with a name like **Mucky Duck,** Andy Rosse Lane SW, Captiva Island (tel. 813/472-3434). Once you get there and join the other Mucky lovers, the Duck will capture you once and for all time. In a rustic atmosphere jammed with other diners chowing down on very good seafood, you're greeted by someone who recites whatever is on the fabulously good seafood menu that night, but it's a bit difficult to keep your attention riveted on this presentation because somewhere on this person (in an earlobe, perhaps?) is a tiny red light. Of decor there is little to be said; of ambience, probably less; of great seafood at great prices (in the $8 to $13 range), volumes. Sooner or later everyone but absolutely everyone goes here, so if you don't trust *me,* trust the *world.* Mucky Duck is open daily (except Sunday) from noon to 2:30 p.m. and from 6 to 9:30 p.m. Don't leave without a Mucky Duck T-shirt for someone, and consider buying one of those teensy, pinhead red lights, which operate on a hearing aid battery (lots of laughs at board meetings).

It would be difficult to find a crazier place than the **Bubble Room,** Captiva Road, Captiva (tel. 472-5558), where servers are dressed in Boy and Girl Scout uniforms. Add to that a ramshackle three-story building built around a towering palm tree, a huge plastic Mickey Mouse at the entrance, Goofy marionettes and statues of Laurel and Hardy, and bubbles, bubbles, and more bubbles: bubbles in the stained-glass windows, those bubbling Christmas ornaments, delicate glass bubbles. They're a little more serious about the food, but not much: each entree bears some kind of Hollywood tag, like Henny Young-One (a chicken breast) and Eddie Fisherman (a grouper).

The food is quite interesting here, ranging from a big glass bubble-full of bouillabaisse to bread baked with roquefort cheese and oregano, salads of romaine, mushrooms, cucumber, pimiento, and red cabbage with buttermilk or Caesar dressing. Steaks and seafood are the mainstays, and are served with herbed rice, twice-baked potatoes, and several vegetables. Desserts vary daily and are as imaginative as the prime ribs Weismuller are huge: fudge-nut brownie pie, cappuccino cheesecake, several kinds of chocolate cake. You'll pay about $15 to $20 for dinner entrees here. Bubble's effervesces from 5 to 10 p.m. daily.

McT's Shrimphouse and Tavern, 1523 Periwinkle Way (tel. 472-3161), calls itself an "honest" place to eat on Sanibel Island, and lots of people agree. An attractive gardeny look inside is pleasant but unprepossessing, and loads of hungry islanders line up every night for simple fish preparations. McT's "McDeal" is a $7 agreement to cook whatever you provide and toss in the trimmings, or let them do the fishing and treat yourself to all the steamed shrimp or crabs you can consume. McT's has lots of oysters and shrimp, fish and chips, even a "Mc-Jawger and Chips" combo of battered and deep-fried shark. Finish off with a Sanibel mud pie and figure dinner at $8 to $10 (a few dollars more if you succumb to that pie). Open 5 to 10 p.m. daily, McT's is equally well known for its adjoining tavern where throngs gather nightly for jukebox music and lively entertainment until 2 a.m. daily.

Budget Bets

An old post office has been converted fittingly enough into the **Olde Post Office Deli,** 632 Tarpon Bay Rd. (tel. 472-6222), where you can feast on fat sandwiches, bagels, sundaes, shakes, and french-bread pizza. If someday you decide you're going to sit on the beach and never move, not once the entire day, rest easy—you won't starve: the deli will fix you a beach box packed with meats, cheeses, salads, and pickles for $10 or so, if you'll just explain your determination. Believe me, they've heard that one before. Open 11 a.m. to 9 p.m. daily.

You have this incredibly gorgeous cottage at the pearly beach, sapphire gulf waters sparkle wildly outside your windows, and somebody suggests a lovely little candlelight dinner on the terrace. Do you panic? No, you pop over to **Tarpon Bay Seafood,** in the Tarpon Bay Marina (tel. 472-3196), and order up a platter of lobster stuffed with crabmeat, some clams and mussels, a shrimp croquette or two. Slip it all neatly wrapped into a handy little take-away bag, toss in a few cups of clam chowder, pay the person less than $20, and whip back to that breathlessly lovely terrace. *Voilà!* Ingenuity triumphs over sloth. Tarpon Bay is open from 10 a.m. to 7 p.m., bless them.

SPORTS: Shelling is the islands' major sport, but there are also some places to pursue some more common activities.

Golf and Tennis

Golfers can putt around an 18-hole course at the **Dunes Golf and Tennis Club,** where there are also six tennis courts for racquet fans. These facilities are open only to guests of motels and condominiums on the island, however. To find the courts and course, turn off Periwinkle Way at Bailey Road and left off Bailey at the Dunes sign. Call 472-2535 for lessons or golf starting times, 472-3522 for tennis court times or lessons.

Boating and Canoeing

The **Boat House,** at the Sanibel Marina on North Yachtsman Drive (Box 271; tel. 472-2531), rents powerboats beginning at $40 a half day, $70 a day, and has sailboats available. You can take a complete course in sailing at the **Offshore Racing School** which operates at South Seas Plantation on Captiva (see my hotel recommendations).

Mark "Bird" Westall (tel. 472-5218) will set off with you on three-hour expeditions to parts of Sanibel and Buck Key that few people have ever seen. One trip goes through Ding Darling National Wildlife Refuge where there are more than 250 species of birds; another trip goes to Buck Key, inhabited once by Indians and later by pirates. Contact Westall between 1 and 10 p.m. to plan trips, which vary in price.

Shelling

You'll soon be hooked, like everyone else who visits here, on a sport known as shelling. There are two types of shelling on the island, gulf shelling and bay shelling. Along the Gulf of Mexico shells are deposited along the shoreline by what is known as "floor sweeping," a combination of tide and wind that cleans the bottom of empty shells and deposits them on beaches. Shelling is especially productive after strong northwest winds and storms which deposit even more shells on the beach. City shelling restrictions—and a respect for maintenance of this unusual environment—prohibit collecting more than two live shells per species. You know a shell is live if you see the inhabitant close its trapdoor (called an operculum). If you see the tiny closed "door" over the open section of the shell, or see the creature itself, or aren't sure, leave it behind. Egg cases look like long paper leis, and should be left behind if they are not hatched and open.

For Sanibel shuffling, wear sneakers to protect your feet from broken shells and stingrays that sometimes bury themselves in the shallow sandy waters where you will be shuffling along; they'll race away and won't hurt you.

The best shelling occurs just after the peak of high tide, and every motel on the island has tide tables that will tell you just when that is. December, January, and February are the top months for shelling, but winds in March and in the fall months often turn up some beauties.

If there's a living creature in your shell or you don't know for sure that there isn't, heed this warning: boil it out or your nose will know you didn't. Most motels on the island have tiny stoves and old pots for shell boiling. Immersing shells in a bleach and water solution kills the fishy odor and won't affect the colors. To make them really shine, add a light coat of baby oil.

A number of enterprising shell collectors have set themselves up as guides and will show you their favorite hunting grounds. The chamber of commerce can supply you with a pamphlet called *Things to Do on Sanibel and Captiva,* which provides names and numbers of seven island shell guides.

Fishing

You can arrange fishing expeditions at any of the island's five marinas on Sanibel, including **Blind Pass** (tel. 472-1020), **Sanibel** (tel. 472-2723), and **Tarpon Bay** (tel. 472-1323); and on Captiva at **'Tween Waters** (tel. 472-5161), **Twin Palms** (tel. 472-1727), and **South Seas Plantation** (tel. 472-5111).

Parks

Ding Darling National Wildlife Refuge, on Sanibel Island (tel. 472-1100), welcomed a million visitors last year to four miles of woodland. Alligators, otters, and manatees call this 4800-acre preserve home, and giant sea turtles nest along its shores. A schedule of walking tours is available at the lighthouse on the island, and canoeists can rent a canoe at the trail entrance at Tarpon Bay. Admission to the refuge is free and it's open daily from 7:30 a.m. to 4 p.m.

SHOPPING: There are shops packed from the bay to the gulf, so don't think you're on some desert island. **Elsie Malone,** at 2422 Periwinkle Way, Sanibel Island (tel. 472-1121), is called the queen of shells, and has bought and sold shells worth several thousand dollars in her lifetime of collecting. Another shell spot is **She Sells Sea Shells,** at 1938 Periwinkle Way (tel. 472-3991).

If you could use a pair of cool drawstring beach pants, you'll find them at the **Brown Bag,** in the Periwinkle Place Shopping Center (tel. 472-7171). The **Olde House Shoppe** has an intriguing atmosphere where you shop for women's clothing, especially lovely cottons, in an old house.

Finally, **Three Crafty Ladies,** 1445 Periwinkle Way (tel. 472-2893), are just that.

ISLAND HOPPING: You can see some intriguing backcountry villages by traveling to some of the nearby islands, which are home to fishermen, and in one case to a fabulous historic resort.

Pine Island

Just north of Sanibel/Captiva is Pine Island, a barely populated conclave of infinitesimal fishing villages where people take laid-back literally. Builders have made few forays onto the island, and it remains a spot for just ambling along sandy lanes, sitting on a deserted pier, fishing, or watching the rippling sea through the windows of the ramshackle Crab Shack Restaurant, where owner Frank Passante welcomes you to the three-house village of Bookelia with a repast of boiled shrimp and a frosty grog or two.

To get there, head north on US 41 out of Fort Myers three miles to Route 78. Turn left, heading west, for 15 miles. You'll pass the village of Matlacha (pronounced Mat-la-*shay),* and go over a little causeway where Route 78 deadends; turn north to Bookelia or south to Pine Island's southern village of St. James City. (You can find a fisherman or a boat for a chug over to Useppa, a millionaire's retreat reachable only by plane or boat.)

At **Passante's Crab Shack,** you'll have a nice view of miles of ocean and some good home-cooking for prices under $10. If you're not there when hunger strikes, you can head for the long raw bar at the **Matlacha Oyster House,** on Pine Island Road or Route 78 (tel. 283-0520), where you can work your way down 40 feet of bar claimed to be the longest in the South. It's brimming with oysters from everywhere oysters call home—Apalachicola, Chesapeake, Long Island, Alabama. Stuffed examples of what you'll eat here adorn the walls of a ship-shape restaurant that features a wide array of taste-teasing temptations. It's open from 5 to 9 p.m. Monday through Thursday, to 10 p.m. on Friday and Saturday, and from noon to 8:30 on Sunday, with prices in the $10 to $15 range or less.

Useppa Island

Now get this one! You pull up alongside a marina, inquire at the only lighted building around, and a friendly soul suggests you stop across the street for a drink while someone takes your luggage to the boat.

To the *what?* Hey, they mean just what they say. This brand-new resort is on an island and the only way you'll get there is by boat! Fortunately they provide the boat, and once you settle into a beautifully decorated apartment equipped with absolutely everything you could possibly need, surrounded by an incredibly quiet strip of sand, you'll agree that this is certainly one of the most seductively luxurious resorts in the state.

Just getting under way in 1985, **Island Harbor Resort,** 7092 Placida Rd., Cape Haze, FL 33946 (tel. 813/697-4800), is slated to be quite a substantial development of low-rise condominium apartment buildings and private homes before they're finished. No one could ask for a more tranquil place to settle than this small island just off the coast of a tiny village called Cape Haze. Getting there is quite an adventure, particularly if you arrive after dark, relax over dinner at Garfield's (more on that later) while someone delivers your luggage, then set off on the five-minute putt across the dark gulf waters guided by a couple of mysterious lights twinkling through the shoreside jungles.

Home here is a one- or two-bedroom apartment with a fully equipped laundry and kitchen, a small bar, dining room, large living room, wide expanses of glass that take full advantage of the ocean views, even a small screened porch overlooking the sea. All are decorated in handsome jewel tones, perhaps navy blue offset by light-wood furnishings and shades of peach. Rates at this unusual resort are $75 to $95 for a mainland apartment, $150 double for a two-bedroom gulf-front apartment, and $180 to $195 for four people sharing a two- or three-bedroom oceanfront apartment. In summer, beginning April 15, those rates drop to $55 to $75 on the mainland, $90 for a two-bedroom oceanfront island apartment, and $110 to $120 for four people sharing a two- or three-bedroom gulf-front island apartment.

By day, you awake to the sound of waves lapping at a shell-strewn beach. Shallow gulf waters beckon to swimmers, breezes rustle through the pines, a little bus scoots around to pick you up for the boat trip to the mainland for shopping, exploring, or for lunch or dinner at Garfield's.

One of the best things to happen to this coastline in many a year is **Garfield's**, a shining white clapboard restaurant plunked down in the middle of a small marina. Wood floors, candlelight, an attractive wood-and-brass bar, and handsome copper and brass panels featuring a montage of "found" objects gathered along these shores, make this a tranquil haven to while away some time as you wait for your ship to come in.

On the menu at Garfield's, 7090 Placida Rd., in the village of Cape Haze (tel. 697-2686), are such treats as baked clams topped with bacon, garlic, shallots, and seasoned bread crumbs; sauteed or broiled grouper; or gulf shrimp sauteed in provincial herbs, garlic, and white wine, or wrapped in bacon and marinated in a tangy barbecue sauce. Steaks, veal, and poultry also turn up on the menu, which has quite reasonable prices in the $11 to $14 range. Hours at Garfield's are 11:30 a.m. to 11 p.m. daily except Monday.

Boca Grande

A millionaire's fortune does help one to discover wondrously beautiful hideaways. That's exactly what happened at two offshore west coast islands, Useppa and Boca Grande.

In the 1920s moneyed men like John Jacob Astor, Barron Collier (whose name this county now bears), Henry du Pont, and J. Pierpont Morgan happened upon the fishing haven of Boca Grande, where in spring the rich and the not-so-rich rub gunwales in pursuit of the mighty tarpon, silver king of the seas. Here they built magnificent little winter mansions that tower over the sand in awesome isolated elegance. Today's moneymakers have joined them, creating a little enclave of luxurious homes-away-from-home on the tip of this tropical island.

You can join them for a while by journeying to the stately magnificence of the **Gasparilla Inn**, on North Palm, Boca Grande, FL 33921 (tel. 813/964-2201), an aging grande dame, beautifully maintained, of pale limey-yellow exterior, elegant white pillars, etched glass, wood floors, sweeping verandas, and posh cottages. Today the Gasparilla Inn is almost a village in itself, albeit a small one: it has an 18-hole golf course, tennis courts, a beach club, pool, even a regulation croquet court! Meals are served in very refined style in a lofty-ceilinged dining room, and the hotel also operates a more casual seafood restaurant called the Pink Elephant, a two-story dining room a short stroll down the street. There's a grocery here, a drugstore where you can buy the Sunday *New York Times* (although it may not get there by Sunday), bike rentals, and those plush and elegant old-worldly cottages on the inn's stately grounds. To get to this quite exclusive resort—the guest list reportedly is closely screened, and once included J. P. Morgan—take US 41 north to about four miles past Port Charlotte, then turn west on Route 771, which goes to the island.

Open only from mid-December to July, the Gasparilla Inn and Cottages includes three meals in its rates, which are $94 to $120 for a single room in the hotel, $91 to $109 per person for a double room with lanai. The hotel can also arrange connecting rooms for $81 to $136 per person, and adjoining private parlors for $39 to $54. Add to those prices a $7.50 charge which covers dining room and housekeeper tips. The Gasparilla Inn also welcomes fishing fans to its "tarpon season," which runs from mid-April to the end of June. During that time rates are $80 single, $64 per person double, and include breakfast and dinner. Waitresses in the inn's handsome restaurant will prepare a box lunch for an additional charge. All this is assuming you pass the scrutiny of the front desk.

Elsewhere on the island you can get into the lazy feel of the place with lunch or dinner at **Bogart's,** Fourth and Park Avenues (tel. 964-0806), a casual, wood-lined enclave adorned with photographs of Bogie and his famous films. Open for lunch and dinner, the two-story restaurant features Maltese grouper (get it?) topped with an orange hollandaise sauce, veal piccata Lorre with lemon and caper sauce, and shrimp Bacall or Casablanca with mango chutney, along with some less exotic treats like beef Wellington, scallops, a seafood potpourri, and bouillabaisse for dinner prices that range from $10 to $15, including salad, potato, and vegetable. At lunch, prices are in the $5 to $7 range or less. Bogart's is open from 11 a.m. to 3 p.m. and 6 to 10 p.m. daily.

Whether or not you stay at Gasparilla Inn, Boca Grande's worth a trip for its street names alone: where else but on a Florida islet would you find boulevards called Dam-If-I-Care, Dam-If-I-Know, and of course, Dam-If-I-Will?

NOW, SAVE MONEY ON ALL YOUR TRAVELS!
Join Arthur Frommer's $25-A-Day Travel Club

Saving money while traveling is never a simple matter, which is why, over 23 years ago, the **$25-A-Day Travel Club** was formed. Actually, the idea came from readers of the Arthur Frommer Publications who felt that such an organization could bring financial benefits, continuing travel information, and a sense of community to economy-minded travelers all over the world.

In keeping with the money-saving concept, the annual membership fee is low—$18 (U.S. residents) or $20 (Canadian, Mexican, and foreign residents)—and is immediately exceeded by the value of your benefits which include:

(1) The latest edition of any TWO of the books listed on the following page.

(2) An annual subscription to an 8-page quarterly newspaper *The Wonderful World of Budget Travel* which keeps you up-to-date on fastbreaking developments in low-cost travel in all parts of the world—bringing you the kind of information you'd have to pay over $25 a year to obtain elsewhere. This consumer-conscious publication also includes the following columns:

Hospitality Exchange—members all over the world who are willing to provide hospitality to other members as they pass through their home cities.

Share-a-Trip—requests from members for travel companions who can share costs and help avoid the burdensome single supplement.

Readers Ask . . . Readers Reply—travel questions from members to which other members reply with authentic firsthand information.

(3) A copy of *Arthur Frommer's Guide to New York*.

(4) Your personal membership card which entitles you to purchase through the Club all Arthur Frommer Publications for a third to a half off their regular retail prices during the term of your membership.

So why not join this hardy band of international budgeteers NOW and participate in its exchange of information and hospitality? Simply send $18 (U.S. residents) or $20 U.S. (Canadian, Mexican, and other foreign residents) along with your name and address to: $25-A-Day Travel Club, Inc., 1230 Avenue of the Americas, New York, NY 10020. Remember to specify which *two* of the books in section (1) above you wish to receive in your initial package of members' benefits. Or tear out this page, check off any two books on the opposite side and send it to us with your membership fee.